The Routledge Guide to British Political Archives

This major new reference work provides an authoritative and wide-ranging guide to the many archives now becoming available for British political history since 1945. Compiled by a leading historian in association with the LSE Library, this comprehensive, easy-to-use and indispensable guide is an invaluable resource for researchers of modern British history.

Covering key aspects of British history since the end of World War II, and providing a fascinating insight into the nature and concerns of the post-war era, this guide provides details of over two thousand non-governmental archives, including information on the history and scope of the archive, a survey of records available and notes on location and accessibility. Divided into two sections, the guide includes information on those organisations, institutions and societies that have made a significant impact on political and public life since 1945, as well as documenting the personal papers of over one thousand influential and important individuals. The first section of the book covers a remarkable range of statesmen, writers, campaigners, diplomats and generals whose papers are essential to an understanding of post-war Britain. The second section provides compact entries on a range of organisations, including the major political parties and national organisations, such as the TUC. It also includes information on a range of pressure groups, past and present, concerned with an array of social, religious, political and welfare matters.

A resource that will become a key research tool, packed with information that is unavailable elsewhere, *The Routledge Guide to British Political Archives* is an invaluable guide for the modern historian.

Chris Cook is former Head of the Modern Archives Unit at the London School of Economics. Editor of the best-selling *Pears Cyclopaedia* for over thirty years, he is also author of *The Routledge Companion to European History since 1763*, *The Routledge Companion to World History since 1914* and *The Routledge Companion to Britain in the 19th Century*. He is currently compiling a major companion volume on European archives since the end of World War II.

The Routledge Guide to British Political Archives

Sources since 1945

Chris Cook

in association with the LSE Library

Routledge
Taylor & Francis Group

LONDON AND NEW YORK

First published 2006
by Routledge

Published 2014 by Routledge

2 Park Square, Milton Park, Abingdon, Oxfordshire OX14 4RN

Simultaneously published in the USA and Canada by Routledge

711 Third Avenue, New York, NY 10017

First issued in paperback 2014

Routledge is an imprint of the Taylor & Francis Group, an informa business

© 2006 Chris Cook and the LSE Library

Typeset in Palatino by
Keystroke, Jacaranda Lodge, Wolverhampton

British Library Cataloguing in Publication Data
A catalogue record for this book is available from the British Library

Library of Congress Cataloging in Publication Data
A catalog record for this book has been requested

ISBN 978–0–415–32740–4 (hbk)
ISBN 978–1–138–87829–7 (pbk)

Contents

Acknowledgements

This book could not have been compiled without the help and support of Jean Sykes, Librarian at the London School of Economics Library. A special debt is also due to the staff of the archives department there, in particular to Sue Donnelly and her deputy, Anna Towlson. Thanks are also due to the many other staff there who provided secretarial and computing help so generously.

It would be impossible to thank by name all those persons in the archive world without whose help this volume either would not have appeared or would have looked very different. I am, however, especially indebted to the very many archivists who spent much time and effort in responding to numerous enquiries.

I have relied heavily on suggestions, advice and information supplied by academic colleagues and friends, both at the London School of Economics and elsewhere. On a personal level, I must particularly thank Richard Storey, Harry Harmer, James Robinson and John Stevenson.

Finally, the appearance of this volume owes much to the encouragement and practical support of Victoria Peters at Routledge. I must record my grateful thanks to her.

Chris Cook
London School of Economics

Introduction

This volume is the successor to the two-volume *Longman Guide to Sources in Contemporary British History* which appeared in the 1990s.[1] Although much has changed in the past decade, its debt to my co-authors on the earlier volumes (David Waller, Jane Leonard and Peter Leese) remains high.

This new volume describes the archives (and careers) of more than 1500 individuals involved in British politics and public life after 1945 as well as the archives of numerous organisations, societies and pressure groups in the same period.

This volume has concentrated on describing those papers known to have been deposited, or where custodians of papers still in private hands have indicated their willingness to try to facilitate the needs of researchers.

The period covered by the survey starts in 1945 with the ending of the Second World War and the advent of the Attlee Government, the first-ever majority Labour government in Britain. These two events constitute a major watershed in modern British political history and thus provide a natural starting point for this volume. The volume has no final cut-off date – hence it records the existence of very recent papers even though it is very rare for collections less than fifteen or twenty years old to be currently available for research. Many of the individuals included were active in politics before 1945. Others are still active. To discuss only material relating to their post-1945 careers would be misleading, and a brief account of pre-1945 records has therefore been given where appropriate. Researchers are reminded that fuller details of the pre-1945 material can frequently be found in the *Sources in British Political History, 1900–51* series (cited in this volume as *Sources*).[2]

The entries in this guide are, in general, arranged alphabetically, under the last known name of the individual concerned. Each entry has attempted to give brief career details followed by a description of the records which survive and notes on their location and availability. Most organisations are cited under their most recent name.

More detailed unpublished lists of archives both in repositories and libraries and in the custody of their originators may often be found in the National Register of Archives (NRA), now based at the National Archives in Kew. Where an NRA list is known to exist for a collection of papers described in this volume it is indicated by its NRA number. In many cases, however, researchers will want to access lists and guides electronically. Table 1 provides details of some electronic pathways. A list of useful archive websites is given on p. 448.

Any guide of this type, with its restrictions on space, can only hint at the richness of some of the specialist archive centres around the country. Table 2 below gives a quick-fire guide for some obvious first starting points.

---

[1] *The Longman Guide to Sources in Contemporary British History: Vol. I: Organisations and Societies*, by Chris Cook and David Waller (Longman, 1994); *Vol. II: Individuals*, by Chris Cook, Jane Leonard and Peter Leese (Longman, 1994).

[2] *Sources in British Political History, 1900–51* (5 vols), compiled by Chris Cook *et al.*, (Macmillan, 1975–78). A supplementary sixth volume was published in 1985.

Table 1 Key electronic pathways

National Register of Archives

http://www.nra.nationalarchives.gov.uk/nra/default.htm

Contains information on the nature and location of manuscripts and historical records that relate to British history. The National Archives website also includes links to other archival databases (some of which are listed below), as well as information resources to aid with research into particular subjects and listings of record repositories.

AIM25

http://www.aim25.ac.uk/index.stm

AIM25 (archives in London and the M25 area) is a major project funded by the Research Support Libraries Programme to provide networked access to descriptions of the archives of more than fifty higher education institutions and royal colleges and societies of medicine and science based in London.

Archives Hub

http://www.archiveshub.ac.uk

A national gateway to collection-level descriptions of archives held by UK universities and colleges.

Access to Archives (A2A)

http://www.a2a.org.uk

Contains catalogues describing archives cared for and made available by various organisations (national and local government, universities, private) across England. The majority of these catalogues have been selected, often by regional or subject-based archivists, to reflect a particular theme.

Genesis

http://www.genesis.ac.uk

Initiative to identify and develop access to women's history sources in the British Isles. Access to information on women's history is through:

- a web-accessible database of collection descriptions from archives, libraries and museums around the British Isles
- the Guide to Sources – a comprehensive list of national and international websites relating to women's history sources.

CASBAH

http://www.casbah.ac.uk

Initiative to identify research resources relating to Caribbean Studies and the history of Black and Asian peoples in the UK, including a database containing information from a UK-wide sample of relevant archive, printed and audio-visual resources held in academic, public and special libraries and repositories.

Table 2 Key starting points

Trade Unions	Modern Records Centre, University of Warwick
Labour Party/Communist Party	Labour History Archive and Study Centre, John Rylands University of Manchester Library
Imperial/Commonwealth	BLCAS (The Bodleian Library of Commonwealth and African Studies), Oxford
	School of Oriental and African Studies, University of London.
Women's studies	The Women's Library, London Metropolitan University
Gay history	The Hall-Carpenter Archives, LSE Library
Military commanders	Liddell Hart Centre for Military Archives, King's College London
	Imperial War Museum
Conservative Party	Bodleian Library, Oxford
Medical history	Contemporary Medical Archives Centre, Wellcome Institute, London

Researchers should be aware that the names of archive centres and record repositories frequently change. In recent years, the Fawcett Library has become the Women's Library, the National Museum of Labour History has become the Labour History Archive and Study Centre. The list is a long one. In the case of the Public Record Office (now the National Archives) and also Rhodes House Library (now the Bodleian Library of Commonwealth and African Studies) the older, more familiar names have been retained in this volume. Similarly many of the private organisations given here frequently change address. Current addresses should be found from the appropriate website.

Inevitably, as new collections are deposited and additions are made to archives described in this volume, the information given here will gradually change. A supplement of known changes to this volume will be kept at the LSE Library. For further information (or if you can add to the database) please contact:

Archives Division
Library, LSE
10 Portugal Street
WC2A 2HD
Tel: +44 (0)20 7955 7223
Fax: +44 (0)20 7955 7454
E-mail: document@lse.ac.uk
http://www.lse.ac.uk/library/archive

Part I

A Guide to the Archives of Selected Individuals

A

ABBOTT, DIANE JULIE (1953–) MP (Lab) Hackney North and Stoke Newington after 1987.

Her extensive constituency papers (dating back to 1987), together with other political papers are in Hackney Archives Department. They are not yet accessible.

ABEL SMITH, BRIAN (1926–96) Professor of Social Administration, London School of Economics, 1965–73. Expert on public policy. Adviser to the World Health Organisation, the Social Affairs Division of the United Nations, International Labour Organisation, etc. His numerous books included *Introduction to Health Policy, Planning and Financing*.

The papers are in the LSE Library. They cover the period 1966–89 and include extensive correspondence with other academics, organisations and Government bodies regarding health policy and other areas of social administration. The collection also contains material relating to the Sainsbury Committee on the Pharmaceutical Industry, the Hunter Committee on Medical Administration, and the Fisher Committee on the Abuse of Public Service. Research material used by Abel Smith, concerning pensions, hospitals and social security is also available.

ABSE, LEO (1917–) MP (Lab) Pontypool, 1958–83; Torfaen, 1983–87.

The correspondence and papers (c. 600 files) are held at the Welsh Political Archive, National Library of Wales. The collection reflects his long parliamentary career and special interest in a variety of issues including divorce reform, homosexual rights, abortion reform and Welsh affairs. The permission of the donor is required for access to the collection. See NRA 41666.

ACHESON, SIR ERNEST DONALD (1926–) Chief Medical Officer, Department of Health and Social Security, 1983–91.

His diaries for the period 1984–91 are in Churchill College, Cambridge.

ACLAND, SIR RICHARD THOMAS DYKE (1908–90) MP (Lib, later Common Wealth) Barnstaple, 1935–45; (Lab) Gravesend, 1947–55.

Sir Richard Acland deposited the majority of his surviving correspondence, diaries and papers at Sussex University Library. A list is available (NRA 19484). The collection relates mostly to his activities in Common Wealth during World War II and includes correspondence, a typescript diary, letters, election addresses and a small collection of press-cuttings on Common Wealth.

ADAM, GORDON JOHNSTON (1934–) MEP (Lab) Northumbria since 1979. There are 43 files of papers, 1980–95, in the EUI, Florence. A further collection of papers covering the period 1977–99 has been deposited with the Tyne and Wear Archive Service. There are files of reports, speeches and working papers. Enquiries regarding access should be directed to the Archivist.

ADAM, GENERAL SIR RONALD FORBES (1885–1982) Military career until 1946. Chairman and Director-General, British Council, 1946–54. Member, Executive Board, United Nations Educational, Scientific and Cultural Organisation (UNESCO), 1950–54 (Chairman, 1952–54).

The Liddell Hart Centre for Military Archives, King's College, London holds his papers, 1916–61. These include diaries, letters, and memoranda. His years as Adjutant-General of the Army (1941–46) are particularly well documented. The collection also includes a narrative on various aspects of administrative work undertaken during World War II (NRA 23081).

ADDIS, SIR JOHN MANSFIELD (1914–83)
Diplomat. Junior Private Secretary to Attlee, 1945–47.
Ambassador to the Philippines, 1963–69; China,
1970–74.

His papers, including correspondence and
diaries, 1925–82, have been deposited in the School
of Oriental and African Studies (ref. PP/MS 25). A
list is available (NRA 33451).

**ADDISON, 1ST VISCOUNT Christopher
Addison (1896–1951)** MP (Lib) Hoxton, Jan.
1910–22; (Lab) Swindon 1929–31; 1934–35. Various
ministerial posts, 1914–21; 1929–31. Secretary of
State for Dominion Affairs, 1945–47; for Common-
wealth Relations, 1947. Lord Privy Seal, 1947–51.
Paymaster-General, 1948–49. Lord President of the
Council, 1951.

The papers of Lord Addison at the Bodleian
Library, Oxford (ref. Addison Papers), together with
letters of condolence on his death (ref. MS Eng
lett d 332), and the diaries of Lady Addison at the
British Library (ref. Reserved MS 109 1–3) are fully
described in *British Cabinet Ministers, 1900–51*.
Most of Lord Addison's papers relate to his pre-1945
career. However, the very full diaries of Lady
Addison (1938–58) provide an alternative source.

AGNEW, PATRICK (fl. 1930s–50s) Ulster trade
unionist and politician. Stormont MP (NILP) South
Armagh, 1938–44.

His papers and correspondence, 1933–59, have
been placed in the Public Record Office of Northern
Ireland (ref. D1676/3/1–14). The collection includes
two personal diaries, 1955–56; correspondence as
a trade unionist and county councillor in Armagh
1929–59; and two minute books of the Armagh
branch of the Northern Ireland Labour Party, 1933
and 1946–47.

**ALANBROOKE, 1ST VISCOUNT Field Marshal
Sir Alan Francis Brooke (1883–1963)** Military
career, 1902–46. Served in World Wars I and II.
Commanded 2nd Army Corps, France, 1939–40;
Home Forces, 1940–41. Chief of the Imperial General
Staff, 1941–46.

Sixty-four boxes of diaries and papers, 1883–1963,
are held at the Liddell Hart Centre, King's College,
London. A list is available (NRA 23116). The post-

war section of the collection includes his diaries
(until 1946); Chief of the Imperial General Staff
papers, 1941–46; correspondence with senior officers, 1941–47; and notes for his memoirs. The collection also documents the non-military aspects of his
career, including his years as Chancellor of Queen's
University, Belfast, 1949–63. The material gathered
by his biographers is included in the collection. It
consists of correspondence and interviews with
colleagues and friends in which his contemporary
and posthumous reputations are discussed.

ALBU, AUSTEN (1903–94) MP (Lab), Edmonton,
1948–Feb. 1974. Minister of State, Department of
Economic Affairs, 1965–67.

The papers have been deposited in BLCAS
(Rhodes House), Oxford and also the LSE Library.
The LSE Library papers include his constituency
correspondence. The colonial papers are in BLCAS.

**ALEXANDER OF HILLSBOROUGH, 1ST EARL
Albert Victor Alexander (1885–1965)** MP (Lab and
Co-op) Sheffield, Hillsborough, 1922–31; 1935–50.
First Lord of the Admiralty, 1929–31; 1940–May 1945;
Aug. 1945–46. Minister without Portfolio, Oct.–Dec.
1946. Minister of Defence, 1946–50. Chancellor of the
Duchy of Lancaster, 1950–51.

The correspondence and papers are deposited
in Churchill College, Cambridge. A list is available
(NRA 12665). The papers of his agent, Alderman
Dr Albert Ballard, are in Sheffield City Library (NRA
17108). Both collections are described in *British
Cabinet Ministers, 1900–51*.

**ALEXANDER OF TUNIS, 1ST EARL Field-
Marshal Sir Harold Rupert Leofric George
Alexander (1891–1969)** Senior military commander,
World War II; Supreme Allied Commander,
Mediterranean Theatre, 1944–45. Governor-General,
Canada, 1946–52. Minister of Defence, 1952–54.

Some Alexander papers are located at the Public
Record Office and consist of official and semi-official
letters, 1941–45 (ref. CAB, 214/1–69). A list is available (NRA 28825). Accounts of various campaigns,
1942–48, are also held in the National Archives of
Canada. Some wartime correspondence is available
in the Alanbrooke papers at the Liddell Hart Centre,
King's College, London.

ALEXANDER, MAJOR-GENERAL HENRY TEMPLER (1911–77) Military career; battalion commander in World War II. Commanded 1st Cameronians (Scottish Rifles), 1954–55; 26th Gurkha Brigade 1955–57. Chief of Defence Staff, Ghana, 1960–61.

Reports and correspondence relating to Ghana, Congo and Nigeria, 1960–70, have been deposited at the Liddell Hart Centre, King's College, London. These papers are currently closed.

ALEXANDER, STANLEY WALKER (1895–1980) Private Secretary to Lord Beaverbrook. Financial Editor of the *Daily Express, Sunday Express* and *Evening Standard*. President, Free Trade League. Treasurer of the Anti-Dear Food Campaign and opponent of the Common Market.

A small collection is held at the LSE Library (ref. COLL MISC 565). This includes various circulars from the early 1970s related to the Free Trade League and the Anti-Dear Food Campaign.

ALEXANDER-SINCLAIR, JOHN (1906–88) UN official and human rights campaigner Served as Vice-Chairman, UNICEF, etc. Founder and Chairman, Human Rights Trust, 1969. Chairman, British League for Animal Rights.

Some papers have been placed in the UN Career Records Project Archive, Queen Elizabeth House, Oxford. A list is available (NRA 39527).

ALLAUN, FRANK (1913–2002) MP (Lab) Salford East, 1955–83.

A substantial collection of papers (*c.* 40 boxes) has been deposited at the Working Class Movement Library, Salford. These cover the whole of his career including work as a journalist, as a member of the Labour Party National Executive Committee (1967–83) and as its Chairman, 1978–79. The files are in chronological order from 1944, and include letters, articles, Parliamentary Private Bills, reports, pages from Hansard, etc. Mr Allaun retained two tapes of interviews and speeches together with copies of his own books and pamphlets, and numerous photographs.

ALLEN OF HURTWOOD, LADY Marjory Allen (Née Gill) (1897–1976) Campaigner for children's rights and pioneer of nursery education. Vice-President, Institute of Landscape Architects, 1939–46. Chairman, Nursery Schools Association of Great Britain, 1942–48; President, 1948–51. Founder-President, World Organisation for Early Childhood Education. Chairman, United Nations Children's Fund (Child Welfare in Europe and Middle East), 1950–51.

The papers are available at the Modern Records Centre, University of Warwick (ref. MSS 121). The material relating to nursery education (mainly during the 1940s) includes speech notes, copies of the Nursery Schools Association newsletter, correspondence and files on the Curtis Committee, the Children Act 1948, and the World Organisation for Early Childhood Education. There is also material on the Lollard Adventure Playground Association (1954–60), including minutes, correspondence and a newsletter.

ALLEN, (WILLIAM) MAURICE (1908–88) Executive Director, Bank of England, 1964–70. Previously, Assistant Director of Research, International Monetary Fund, 1947–49; Adviser, Bank of England, 1950–64.

There are 30 files of papers, covering the period 1950–70, in the Bank of England archive.

ALPORT, BARON Cuthbert James McCall Alport (1912–98) Director, Conservative Political Centre, 1945–50. MP (Con) Colchester, 1950–61. Assistant Postmaster-General, 1955–57. Parliamentary Under-Secretary, Commonwealth Relations, 1957–59. High Commissioner, Federation of Rhodesia and Nyasaland, 1961–63.

The main collection of papers is in the Albert Sloman Library, University of Essex. Papers on local affairs are in Essex Record Office at Colchester. The main collection includes papers as Special Representative to Rhodesia.

ALTON, BARON, David Patrick Alton (1951–) MP (Lib 1979–88; Lib Dem after 1988) Edge Hill, 1979–83; Mossley Hill 1983–97. Liverpool City Councillor, 1972–80; Deputy Leader and Housing Chairman, 1978.

The papers are to be deposited in Liverpool. They include constituency correspondence and parliamentary papers from 1979 onwards; files on his membership of the Donaldson Commission which investigated the political situation in Northern Ireland (1984–87); papers relating to the Environment Select Committee (1981–85); to his period as Liberal Chief Whip during the Liberal/SDP Alliance (1985–87); and 20,000 letters relating to his Private Members' Bill on abortion legislation (1987). There is also some correspondence, press-cuttings and ephemera from his period on Liverpool City Council (1969–80).

AMERY, BARON Julian Amery (1919–97) MP (Con) Preston North, 1950–66; Brighton Pavilion, 1969–92. Under-Secretary of State for War, 1957–58; Colonies, 1958–60; Secretary of State for Air, 1960–62. Minister of Aviation, 1962–64; Public Buildings and Works, 1970; Housing and Construction, 1970–72; Foreign and Commonwealth Affairs, 1972–74.

The archives have been acquired by Churchill College, Cambridge (ref. AMEJ). The collection (*c.* 500 boxes, covering the period 1945–97) includes all his political papers, plus published and unpublished literary works, photographs and diaries. The papers were given to the nation in lieu of tax.

AMIGO, PETER EMMANUEL (1864–1949) Roman Catholic Bishop of Southwark, 1904–49.

The papers are deposited in the Southwark Diocesan Archives. A list is available (NRA 27760). The collection includes diaries, appointment books and routine diocesan correspondence. There are also files relating to the many issues with which he was involved during his long ministry, including Irish independence, the Spanish Civil War and the position of Catholic chaplains within the British Forces during World Wars I and II.

AMMON, 1ST BARON Charles George Ammon (1875–1960) MP (Lab) Camberwell North, 1922–31, 1935–44. Government Chief Whip, House of Lords, 1945–49.

Lord Ammon's papers have been deposited at the Brynmor Jones Library, University of Hull. A list is available (NRA 27799). The collection includes correspondence from throughout his career; an incomplete set of diaries (1920s–50s); drafts for an autobiography; press-cuttings up to the 1950s;

election literature; details of trips to Africa, Canada and China; papers relating to the National Dock Labour Board; and copies of articles and lectures. Southwark Central Reference Library holds additional diaries (1938–39 and 1947) and scrapbooks containing press-cuttings and photographs.

AMORY, VISCOUNT Derick Heathcoat Amory (1899–1981) MP (Con) Tiverton, 1945–60. Various Cabinet appointments, culminating as Chancellor of the Exchequer, 1958–60.

No collection of papers appears to have survived. The National Archives has some relevant material from the Ministry of Education (ED 136/694–898) and Ministry of Agriculture and Fisheries (MAF 236/13–23). Papers relating to Budgets are in T 171.

ANDREWES, ADMIRAL SIR WILLIAM (GERRARD) (1899–1974) Naval career. Chief Staff Officer (CSO) to Commander-in-Chief, Portsmouth, 1944; CSO to Vice-Admiral, Pacific, 1944–45. Commanded British and Commonwealth Naval Forces in Korean War, 1950, and United Nations 'Task Force 95', 1951, Deputy Supreme Allied Commander, Atlantic, 1952–53.

Sir William's correspondence and papers are available on microfilm at the Imperial War Museum. They include a diary kept intermittently between 1925 and 1932; records relating to 'Operation Overlord', 1944; and reports on British Commonwealth naval operations in Korea (1950–51). A list is available (NRA 28528).

ANDREWS, PHILIP WALTER SAWFORD (1914–71) Economist. Leading expert on restrictive practices.

An extensive collection of papers, 1930s–70s, has been acquired by the LSE Library. The collection includes the papers of the Oxford Economic Research Group (1930s); material relating to a history of the UK steel industry and to the International Nitrogen Cartel; extensive papers on his involvement with the restrictive practices court; and empirical research on the economy of the firm. Also included are the papers of his colleague, Professor Elizabeth Brunner. Parts of the collection may be viewed by arrangement with the Archivist.

ANDREWS, SIR (WILLIAM) LINTON (1886–1972)
Journalist. Chairman of the Press Council, 1955–59.
Editor, *Leeds Mercury*, 1923–39; *Yorkshire Post*,
1939–60.

Papers and correspondence covering the period
1950–65 are deposited in the Brotherton Library,
Leeds University. A list is available (NRA 19812).
The collection is arranged in five sections. The first
consists of files on the Press Council's discussions
with the medical profession, 1955–66, on the release
of medical information to the press. The second
section concerns the Press Council's investigation
of the conduct of the British press after the Munich
air crash in 1958. The remaining three sections
contain miscellaneous material.

ANGER, NICK (NICHOLAS RICHARD) (1949–)
MP (Lab) Pembroke, 1992–97, Carmarthenshire
West and Pembrokeshire South after 1997.

His constituency papers and other material are
in the Welsh Political Archive, National Library of
Wales.

**ANNAN, BARON Noel Gilroy Annan (1916–
2000)** Academic. Lecturer in Politics, King's
College, Cambridge, 1948–66; Provost, University
College, London, 1966–78; Vice-Chancellor, University of London, 1978–81. Chairman, Enquiry
on the Disturbances at Essex University, 1974;
Committee on the Future of Broadcasting, 1974–77.

The papers are in the Modern Archive Centre,
King's College, Cambridge. They include files of correspondence with numerous academic colleagues,
politicians and scientists. These correspondents
include Sir Isaiah Berlin, Sir Maurice Bowra,
Nigel Clive, John Fay, Alastair Forbes, John Grigg,
Lord Kahn, Dorothea Krook, Arthur Marshall,
Sheldon Rotblatt, Lord Rothschild (3rd), Sir Steven
Runciman, G.H.W. Rylands, John Sparrow, Lord
Dacre, Lord Vaizey, and L.P. Wilkinson. There are
also documents relating to his published work, and
to the Report on the Disturbances at Essex University
in 1974, the British Control Commission in Germany
and the Report of the Committee on the Future
of Broadcasting.

**APPLETON, RIGHT REVEREND GEORGE
(1902–93)** Director of Public Relations in Government of Burma, 1943–46. Anglican bishop. Archbishop of Jerusalem and Metropolitan, 1969–74.

The papers have been placed in the Hartley
Library, University of Southampton (ref. Ms 243).
Covering the period *c.* 1929–92 they relate not only to
Jerusalem but to work in Burma.

ARCHER, LORD Jeffrey Howard Archer (1940–)
MP (Con) Louth, Dec. 1969–Sept. 1974. Vice-
Chairman, Conservative Party, 1985–86. Popular
novelist.

Lord Archer states that his papers will eventually
be deposited at the Bodleian Library, Oxford.

**ARCHER OF SANDWELL, BARON Peter
Kingsley Archer (1926–)** MP (Lab) Rowley Regis
and Tipton, 1966–74; Warley West, 1974–92.

Lord Archer states that he has retained some case
files, correspondence and diaries. These are to be
deposited in an appropriate record office.

**ARDEN-CLARKE, SIR CHARLES NOBLE (1898–
1962)** Governor, Sarawak, 1946–49; Gold Coast,
1949–57. Governor-General, Ghana, March–May
1957.

A collection of papers has been deposited at
Rhodes House Library, Oxford. Special conditions of
access apply to the collection, and readers should
contact the librarian at Rhodes House in the first
instance. Rhodes House also holds some notes on
the development of local government in Sarawak,
1945 (ref. MSS Ind Ocn s 223). These are not subject
to any restrictions.

**ARMSTRONG OF SANDERSTEAD, BARON Sir
William Armstrong (1915–80)** Civil Servant. Joint
Permanent Secretary to the Treasury, 1962–68; Head
of the Home Civil Service, 1968–74.

Private Office papers concerning his time as Head
of the Home Civil Service are held at the Public
Record Office (ref. BA/6). The papers of Clement
Attlee, deposited in the Bodleian Library, Oxford,
include correspondence, 1943–51.

**ARMSTRONG, CAPTAIN MICHAEL HENRY
(1924–82)** Unionist Politician, Northern Ireland.
OUP Convention member for Armagh, Northern

Ireland Assembly, 1975–76. OUP security spokesman and honorary secretary, Ulster Unionist Council.

The Armstrong family papers are deposited in the Public Record Office of Northern Ireland and include papers relating to his political career and membership of such public bodies as Armagh County Council, the Ulster Farmers' Union Council and the Ulster Folk Museum (ref. D3727 and D3727 add). Certain sections of the collection, relating to his political activities, are closed (ref. D3727/G–J).

ARNOT, ROBIN PAGE (1890–1986) Communist. Historian of the labour movement. General Secretary, Labour Research Department.

An extensive collection of papers has been deposited in the Brynmor Jones Library, University of Hull (ref. DAR). A list is available (NRA 34112). The collection includes correspondence (1917–74); writings and lectures (1931–74); general files (1916–74); and one file on his experiences as a conscientious objector (1917–18). There is extensive correspondence with Angela Tuckett, Rajani Palme Dutt, Clemens and Violet Duff, Margaret Cole, D.N. and Mollie Pritt and Maurice Dobb.

ARROWSMITH, SIR EDWIN PORTER (1909–92) Colonial Service. Resident Commissioner, Basutoland, 1952–56. Governor, Falkland Islands, 1956–64.

Seven boxes of his papers, 1932–65, including correspondence, reports and memoranda, are deposited in Rhodes House Library, Oxford (ref. MSS Brit Emp s 411). A list is available.

ARROWSMITH, PAT (1930–) Pacifist campaigner and socialist.

The papers have remained in her possession and provision will be made for their eventual deposit. An interview concerning her career has been recorded by the Department of Sound Records at the Imperial War Museum.

ARTHUR, SIR OSWALD RAYNOR (1905–73) Colonial Service. Governor, Falkland Islands, 1954–56.

His letters home, 1954–56, are deposited in Rhodes House Library, Oxford (ref. MSS Atlan s 11).

ASHBURNER, MICHAEL (1942–) Cambridge University geneticist and anti-nuclear campaigner.

There are 35 boxes of papers at Churchill College, Cambridge (ref. ASHB). Much of the material consists of files from the early 1960s on the Campaign for Nuclear Disarmament, the Committee of 100 and other non-violent disarmament and anti-nuclear pressure groups with which he was involved.

ASHBY, DAME MARGERY IRENE CORBETT (1882–1981) Feminist and Liberal. Secretary to the National Union of Women's Suffrage Societies. Liberal Parliamentary candidate, 1918–44. Hon. President, International Alliance of Women; British Commonwealth League.

An extensive set of correspondence and papers has been acquired by the Women's Library, London Metropolitan University. The family papers include correspondence, various diaries (1930–79), address books and sections of autobiography. National issues are dealt with in detail, although much of this concerns the pre-World War II period. International issues relating to disarmament and peace conferences are included, as are various photographs, press-cuttings and some unsorted papers. A list is available (NRA 31808).

ASHDOWN, LORD Jeremy John Durham Ashdown (1941–) MP (Lib, then Lib Dem) Yeovil 1983–2001. Leader of the Liberal Democrats, 1988–99. High Representative in Bosnia, 2002–05.

Paddy Ashdown's papers have placed in the LSE Library (ref. M1789). The 17 large boxes relate to his leadership of the party and cover the period 1980s–90s. The LSE Library also has his diary. Constituency papers (closed until 2024) are in Somerset Archive and Record Service, Taunton (see NRA 43089).

ASHMORE, BRIAN (fl. 1945–97) Liberal Party activist. PPC for Carlisle, 1964.

Eleven boxes of papers are in the LSE Library. The papers comprise correspondence, leaflets, material from Penrith and Borders Liberal Association and Carlisle Liberal Association, along with material from the Liberal Party Organisation and Liberal Candidates Association. There are two boxes of pamphlets.

ASKINS, JACK (fl. 1950s) Trade unionist. Joint

Secretary of the British Campaign for Peace in Vietnam.

The Modern Records Centre, University of Warwick, has acquired the papers (ref. MSS 189). A list is available (NRA 22696). Section 1 relates to his work as a union activist, and especially the organisation of the Manchester Corporation busmen 1954–56, including copies of *Busman's Clarion*, 1954–55 (ref. MSS 189/B). A second, larger group of papers concentrates on Askins' part in the anti-Vietnam War movement (ref. MSS 189/V). Further papers are to be found in the Working Class Library, Salford.

ASQUITH OF YARNBURY, BARONESS Lady (Helen) Violet Bonham Carter (1887–1969) Liberal politician, writer and broadcaster. President of the Women's Liberal Federation, 1923–25 and 1939–45. President, Liberal Party Organisation, 1945–47. President, Royal Institute of International Affairs, 1964–69.

The Bonham Carter family papers, including those of Violet Bonham Carter, have been placed in the Bodleian Library, Oxford.

ASTOR OF HEVER, 1ST BARON John Jacob Astor (1886–1971) MP (Con) Dover, 1922–45. Chief Proprietor of *The Times*, 1922–66.

Such personal papers of Lord Astor as have been retained are in the care of the family. Enquiries should be directed to the current Lord Astor of Hever. Two boxes of Astor's papers, one of which includes appointment diaries, 1944–62, are retained in the archive of *The Times*. Reference should be made to the 1991 biography by J.D. Haeger.

ATCHERLEY, AIR MARSHAL SIR RICHARD (1904–70) Royal Air Force career. Squadron and Group Commander during World War II; Commander, Central Fighter Establishment, 1944. Commanding-in-Chief, Pakistan Air Force, 1949–51. Head of RAF Staff, British Joint Services Mission, Washington, 1953–55. Air Officer Commander-in-Chief, Flying Training Command, 1955–59.

The papers, 1923–67, are in the Royal Air Force Museum, Hendon (ref. AC 73/6). They include logbooks, 1923–40; a large collection of photographs, 1948–57, recording official functions and visits such as that to the Royal Pakistan Air Force College, 1950; and scrapbooks kept by his wife concerning his career and that of his father, Major-General Sir Llewellyn Atcherley.

ATTLEE, 1ST EARL Clement Richard Attlee (1883–1967) MP (Lab) Limehouse, 1922–50; Walthamstow West, 1950–55. Parliamentary Secretary for War, 1924. Chancellor of the Duchy of Lancaster, 1930–31. Postmaster-General, 1931. Lord Privy Seal, 1940–42. Secretary of State, Dominion Affairs, 1942–43. Deputy Prime Minister, 1942–45. Prime Minister, 1945–51.

The Bodleian Library, Oxford, holds a large collection of correspondence and papers covering the period 1924–57. A list is available (NRA 27633). The collection comprises miscellaneous correspondence, 1945–51; official Labour Party correspondence, 1939–44; correspondence with Labour Party members, 1945–50; Labour Party Committee Papers; a large selection of speeches, 1945–51; and papers on the 1950 and 1951 general elections. The Public Record Office holds official correspondence and papers for 1939–45 (ref. CAB 118). A list is available (NRA 32908). Churchill College, Cambridge holds two files of papers (listed in NRA 12661). These include a draft of the memoir *As it Happened* (1955); notes from diaries on his local government and parliamentary careers; and correspondence with Churchill, Lady Megan Lloyd-George and others.

AUCHINLECK, FIELD MARSHAL SIR CLAUDE (1884–1981) Indian Army officer. Served in World Wars I and II. General Officer Commanding-in-Chief, Northern Norway, 1940; Southern Command, 1940; Commander-in-Chief, India, 1941, 1943–47; Middle East, 1941–42. War Member, Viceroy's Executive Council, 1943–46. Supreme Commander in India and Pakistan, 1947.

A large collection of papers is deposited in the John Rylands Library, University of Manchester. A list is available (NRA 25966). Most of the papers relate to his World War II commands and to post-war South Asia. Principal correspondents include Lord Alanbrooke, L.S. Amery, W.S. Churchill, Sir John Dill, the Marquess of Linlithgow, Sir N.M. Ritchie, Field Marshal Smuts and Field Marshal Lord Wavell. The National Army Museum holds the papers of

W.R.P. Ridgeway, his private secretary. These contain material relating to Narvik (1940) and India (1941–47).

AVEBURY, 4TH BARON Eric Reginald Lubbock (1928–) MP (Lib) Orpington, 1962–70.

His constituency papers, including case and subject files covering the period 1962–70, as well as later papers for the years 1970–99, have been placed in the Brynmor Jones Library, University of Hull.

AVES, DAME GERALDINE (1898–1986) Chief Welfare Officer, Ministry of Health, 1941–62.

The Women's Library holds 19 boxes of papers covering her entire career (ref. 7/GMA). The deposit includes Ministry of Health papers and correspondence, 1941–60s and additional papers dating from the 1950s and 1960s. There are also Ministry of Health papers and correspondence (private and official) with Robin Huw Jones from 1953; private correspondence with Evangeline de Saint-Albin; and domestic and financial papers from 1940. In addition, there are private letters; speech notes; various United Nations papers including material on the Wegimont Seminar (1955) and UNRRA, 1945–47. The post-retirement papers consist of material on voluntary organisations and some correspondence.

AVON, 1ST EARL Sir (Robert) Anthony Eden (1897–1977) Prime Minister, 1955–57. MP (Con) Warwick and Leamington, 1923–57. Secretary of State for Foreign Affairs, 1935–38, 1940–45, 1951–55; Dominion Affairs 1939–40; for War, 1940.

The collected papers and correspondence are held at Birmingham University Library. A list is available (NRA 28779). The papers cover his parliamentary career as MP for Warwick and Leamington, as minister in various governments, and as Prime Minister, as well as his private life (a number of these files are withdrawn from circulation until a later date). There are extensive Foreign Office papers from the war period; public, political and private correspondence; constituency papers and documents; diaries, speeches and press-cuttings.

The Public Record Office holds copies of the Private Office papers for his time as Secretary of State for Foreign Affairs (ref. FO 954). A list is available (NRA 23627 Foreign Office). Additional material is available in PRO series FO 851. Reference should also be made to the official biography by Sir Robert Rhodes James.

AWBERY, STANLEY STEPHEN (1888–1969) MP (Lab) Bristol Central, 1946–64.

A collection of papers, 1899–1969, has been deposited with Glamorgan Archives Service (ref. D/D Aw). A list is available (NRA 26546). The material includes appointment diaries, 1908–68, Bristol Labour Party and Independent Labour Party election addresses and ephemera, 1945–59, and files relating to his parliamentary career. These include correspondence with Ernest Bevin, Arthur Deakin, Stafford Cripps, and Dom Mintoff; documents relating to the Campaign for Moral Re-armament (1958) and to the *Ambatielos* (Greek prisoners) affair (1963); and records of visits to Malaysia, East Germany and Algeria. There are also various articles by Awbery on both labour and local history, and a collection of photographs. Correspondence on colonial issues, 1949–55, can be found in the Fabian Colonial Bureau papers at Rhodes House, Oxford (NRA 16153).

B

BADER, ERNEST (1890–1982) Campaigner for industrial democracy.

An extensive collection of papers and correspondence has been retained by Scott Bader Commonwealth Ltd. A list is available (NRA 27758). It documents his involvement with the peace movement, the Industrial Commonwealth movement, Intermediate Technology and training in developing countries as well as his views on religion and philosophy, including travels to Africa and India. Requests for access should be made to the Commonwealth Secretary, Scott Bader Commonwealth Ltd., Wollaston Hall, Wollaston, Wellingborough, Northants NN9 7RL.

BAGOT, COMMANDER ARTHUR GUY DENIS (1896–1981) Naval career. Attached to the Naval Control Service, Ceylon, 1943–46; Palk Strait Oil Transhipment Scheme, 1945–46; observer, Greek Elections, 1946. On staff of Control Commission Germany, 1947–49. Commanded *LST Reginald Kerr* and *LST Charles McLeod* during Korean War, 1951–54.

A large collection of papers covering his career, 1913–54, has been deposited in the Imperial War Museum. A box list is available at the Museum.

BAILLY, VICE-ADMIRAL SIR LOUIS EDWARD STEWART HOLLAND LE (1915–) Naval career. Naval attaché, Washington. Director General of Intelligence, Ministry of Defence, 1972–75.

The papers (20 boxes) have been placed in Churchill College, Cambridge. A list is available (NRA 44039). The collection is not yet open.

BAIN, SIR GEORGE SAYERS (1939–) Industrial relations analyst. Professor of Industrial Relations, University of Warwick, 1979–89. Director of the London Business School, etc.

Many of the papers, including his research notes on the 'Union Growth' project, have been placed in the Modern Records Centre, University of Warwick. Access requires prior permission from the depositor.

BAKER, FIELD MARSHAL SIR GEOFFREY HARDING (1912–80) Military commander. Director of Operations and Chief of Staff to the Governor of Cyprus, November 1955–57. Chief of Staff, Supreme Headquarters, Allied Powers, Europe, 1961–63. Vice-Chief of the General Staff, 1963–66; Chief of the General Staff, 1968–71.

His typescript report on the Cyprus Emergency, 1958, is in Rhodes House Library, Oxford (ref. MSS Medit s 28). According to information supplied to the Liddell Hart Centre, King's College, London, there are no other papers.

BAKER, JOHN RANDAL (1900–84) Scientist. Reader in Cytology, Oxford University, 1955–67.

Sixty-three boxes of correspondence and papers, 1928–80, have recently been deposited in the Bodleian Library, Oxford (ref. MSS Eng misc b 239–44, c 907–21, d 1308–13, e 1478–1513). They include extensive material on birth control; various societies for the prevention of cruelty to animals; the Race Relations Board (1974); the Institute of Jewish Affairs; and the press and publishing.

BAKER, COLONEL JOHN SLADE (d. 1966) Military service. *The Sunday Times* correspondent.

A collection of papers (*c.* 1948–65) is held at the Middle East Centre, St Antony's College, Oxford. Included are Palestine press-cuttings for 1948; notes for lectures; interviews with King Hussein; and diaries (1952–65) covering service for *The Sunday Times* in the Middle East.

BALFOUR, HONOR (fl. 1940s–70s) Liberal Party activist and radical campaigner.

The papers, covering the 1940s to the 1970s,

together with papers of Radical Action, 1941–48, have been placed in the Bodleian Library, Oxford.

BALFOUR, SIR JOHN (1894–1983) Diplomat. Minister, Washington, 1945–48. Ambassador to Argentine Republic, 1948–51; Spain, 1951–54.

Sir John's memoirs, *Not Too Correct An Aureole*, were published posthumously in 1984. A draft of the memoirs had previously been deposited in the Foreign and Commonwealth Office Library, together with a copy of a short essay entitled 'Encounters with the Windsors'. The Imperial War Museum has his letters as a civilian internee in Germany, 1914–18.

BALLANTRAE, BARON Brigadier Sir Bernard Edward Fergusson (1911–80) Military career. Served in Palestine, 1937, and World War II. Director of Combined Operations (Military), 1945–46. Assistant Inspector-General, Palestine Police, 1946–47. On intelligence staff, Supreme Headquarters Allied Powers Europe, 1951–53. Governor-General, New Zealand, 1962–67.

A collection of papers has been deposited in the National Library of Scotland. The material relates particularly to his time in the Middle East and in New Zealand. A list is available (NRA 43297). Other papers have remained in his family's possession.

BALOGH OF HAMPSTEAD, LORD (1905–85) Economist. Fellow of Balliol College, Oxford. Reader in Economics, University of Oxford, 1973–76. Economic Adviser to the Cabinet, 1964–67. Minister of State, Department of Energy, 1974–75.

It is understood the papers have been placed in Balliol College, Oxford.

BARBER, BARON Anthony Perrinott Lysberg Barber (1920–) Conservative politician, Chancellor of the Exchequer, 1970–74.

Lord Barber has stated that he kept no relevant political papers. Material from his time as party chairman is in the Conservative Party Archive in the Bodleian Library, Oxford. Some Budget papers are in the National Archives (ref. T171).

BARBOUR, NEVILL (1895–1974) Arab specialist. Writer and broadcaster. Expert on North Africa.

There are papers in St Antony's College Middle East Centre, Oxford. A list is available (NRA 41055). The material is mainly articles and broadcasts.

BARCLAY, CAPTAIN A.C. (fl. 1940s) Royal Artillery officer. Commanded military escort on the *Runnymede Park*, one of a convoy of ships containing Jewish immigrants who were refused permission to land at Haifa by the Royal Navy and returned to Hamburg, 1947.

One box of papers has been deposited in the Hartley Library, University of Southampton (ref. MS 87). The material includes a report on the Jewish immigrants on board the *President Warfield*, a list of those on the *Runnymede Park* and Captain Barclay's journal of the convoy.

BARKER, COLIN (1939–) Leading member of the International Socialist Group (Oxford and later Manchester), from 1962; on editorial board of *International Socialism*.

A substantial collection of papers has been deposited in the Modern Records Centre, University of Warwick (ref. MSS 152). They include files on the shipbuilding industry, local government and housing during the 1960s and 1970s. There is considerable correspondence with individual members over the same period as well as some financial and administrative records of *International Socialism*, 1964–67; and ISG committee minutes, national circulars, internal bulletins, branch and conference reports and papers 1964–73. There are also issues of various British and international radical journals. Prior permission is required from Mr Barker to use the unpublished material.

BARKER, GENERAL SIR EVELYN HUGH (1894–1983) Served in World Wars I and II. Commanded VIII Corps, 1944–46; British Troops in Palestine and Transjordan, 1946; General Officer Commanding-in-Chief, Eastern Command, 1947–50.

Papers relating to British operations in Northern France, 1944–45, are held by the Imperial War Museum. The only post-war papers that have been located are three 1946 letters in the papers of General J.C. D'Arcy at the Middle East Centre, St Antony's College, Oxford. The Liddle Collection, Leeds University, holds some World War I material.

BARKER, SIR WILLIAM (1909–92) Diplomat. Minister, Moscow, 1960–63, Assistant Under-Secretary of State, Foreign Office, 1965–66. Ambassador to Czechoslovakia, 1966–68.

Two boxes of papers on the Soviet Union, Czechoslovakia and the Cold War, 1964–85, are in Churchill College, Cambridge. A list is available (NRA 43707).

BARLOW, SIR JOHN (DENMAN) (1898–1986) MP (Nat Lib) Eddisbury, 1945–50; (Con) Middleton and Prestwich, 1951–66.

His political and constituency papers, 1957–68, are in Bury Archive Service, Bury.

BARNARD, VICE-ADMIRAL SIR GEOFFREY (1902–74) Naval career. Deputy Chief of Staff to Naval Commander-in-Chief, North Africa, 1942, and to C-in-C, Mediterranean, 1942–43. Chief Staff Officer to Flag Officer (Air), 1946–47. Director, Royal Navy Tactical School, 1948–49. Squadron commander, Royal Indian Navy, 1950–51. Assistant Chief of Naval Staff (Warfare), 1952–53. Deputy Chief of Naval Staff, 1953–54. On British Joint Services Mission, Washington, 1954–56.

A collection of correspondence and papers is available at the Imperial War Museum. The post-war material includes appointment diaries, 1945–51 and some Royal Indian Navy policy, training and development files, 1950–53.

BARNES, ALFRED (1887–1975) MP (Lab Co-op) East Ham South, 1922–31 and 1935–55. Minister of Transport, 1945–51.

Hazlehurst found that no papers were kept. Ministry of Transport Private Office papers are available at the Public Record Office (ref. MT 62/125–129). These include some policy papers on shipping, shipbuilding and road haulage.

BARNES, ERNEST WILLIAM (1874–1953) Anglican clergyman. Bishop of Birmingham, 1924–53.

The papers have been placed in Birmingham University Library. A list is available (NRA 26562). The collection includes correspondence, papers and engagement diaries, 1888–1953.

BARNES, LEONARD JOHN (1895–1977) Writer, philosopher and poet. Critic of British colonial policy. Author of *Caliban in Africa* (1930), *The Duty of Empire* (1935), *Empire or Democracy* (1939), etc. Secretary of the Delegacy of Social Training, Oxford University, 1947–62.

The School of Oriental and African Studies, University of London, holds his correspondence and papers, 1932–77 (ref. PP MS 9). The collection includes articles and other publications, notebooks and working papers, and papers relating to his African visits and writings (mainly 1960s). The collection also contains some correspondence with Colin Knight-Adams (1965–71), and the correspondence and diaries of Dr L.N. Tackson (1960–71). Further correspondence is available at Rhodes House Library, Oxford, in the papers of Rita Hinden (ref. MSS Brit Emp s 365), and F.S. Livie-Noble (ref. MSS Afr s 1427).

BARNES, MICHAEL CECIL JOHN (1932–) MP (Lab) Brentford and Chiswick, 1966–Feb. 1974.

He has retained some papers including material on the policy of the British Government during the Nigerian Civil War, 1967–70; Britain's entry into the EEC and the activities of Labour 'pro-marketeers'; and the formation of the SDP, 1981–83. Enquiries regarding access should be directed to Mr Barnes.

BARNES, SIR WILLIAM (LETHBRIDGE) GORELL (1909–87) Civil servant. War Cabinet Official, 1939–45; Treasury, 1945–46; Colonial Office, 1948–63. Personal Assistant to the Prime Minister, 1946–48. Deputy Under-Secretary, Colonial Office, 1959–63.

Sir William's papers have been deposited in Churchill College, Cambridge (ref. BARN). These cover a number of important aspects of his work as Personal Assistant to Clement Attlee while Lord President of the Council during World War II, and as Prime Minister after the war. Also included is material on Colonial and Common Market affairs, both as Assistant (later Deputy) Under-Secretary of State at the Colonial Office, and later through the Conservative Commonwealth and Overseas Council. With some exceptions, the collection is open to researchers. Access to the Conservative Commonwealth and Overseas Council papers requires the permission of the Chairman of the Conservative Party. Applications should be made in the first instance to Churchill College, Cambridge. A list is available (NRA 32587).

BARNETSON, MAJOR-GENERAL JAMES CRAW (1907–84) Royal Army Medical Corps officer. Director of Medical Services, BAOR, Dec. 1964–66; Deputy Director-General, Army Medical Services, 1961–64.

One file of articles relating to Army medicine, 1945–60, is held at the Liddell Hart Centre for Military Archives, King's College, London. This includes an account of the surrender of German medical services, 1945, and the treatment of radiation injuries, 1958.

BARNETT, CORRELLI (DOUGLAS) (1927–) Military historian.

The papers will be deposited at Churchill College, Cambridge.

BARR, SAMUEL (fl. 1960s–70s) Trade unionist. Convenor, Upper Clyde Shipbuilding Yard.

The papers have been placed in the University of Glasgow (ref. DC140). A list is available (NRA 34748). The collection includes papers, minutes and correspondence on trade union matters, 1969–78; health and safety at work legislation, 1973–79; socialist and trade union publications, 1978–79; the running of the Upper Clyde Shipbuilding Yard, 1969–75; and trade union activities at the Charles Connell Shipyard, 1957–65.

BARRACLOUGH, BRIGADIER SIR JOHN (ASHWORTH) (1894–1981) Military career. Served in World Wars I and II. Regional Commander, North Rhine Province, 1945–46; Deputy Regional Commander, North Rhine-Westphalia, 1946–50.

His diary and papers, 1941–50, are at the Imperial War Museum and are a useful source for the post-war military administration of Germany. The collection includes a file of correspondence, 1955–64, and reports on the dismissal of Konrad Adenauer as Mayor of Berlin in October 1945. A photocopy of his diary has been deposited in the Modern Records Centre, University of Warwick (ref. MSS. 021/35 33).

BARRETT, EDWIN CYRIL GEDDES (1909–86) Malayan Civil Service, 1931–57. President, Municipal Council, Kuala Lumpur, 1951. British Adviser, Kedah, Federation of Malaya, 1953–57. Malay lecturer, School of Oriental and African Studies, London University, 1957–71.

Rhodes House Library, Oxford, has the diary he kept as secretary to a 1946 parliamentary delegation which investigated whether Sarawak sought cession to the British Crown (ref. MSS Pac s 89). No other papers have been located.

BARRY, SIR GERALD REID (1899–1968) Journalist and Public Servant. Editor, *Saturday Review*. Founder and Editor of *Week-end Review*. Later a Director of the *New Statesman*. Editor, *News Chronicle*, 1936–47. Director-General, Festival of Britain, 1947–52. Co-founder, Political and Economic Planning (PEP). Education Adviser, Granada Television.

Sir Gerald Barry's papers are deposited at the LSE Library (ref. M 1377). A list is available (NRA 29735). The post-war sections of the collection include drafts of an incomplete autobiography and articles, broadcasts, speeches and addresses (1930s–50s). There are typescript *News Chronicle* articles on Greece, France, Israel, and the USA, 1944–57, and articles on America written for the *New Statesman*, 1947. The files on the Festival of Britain contain diaries, correspondence, speeches, minutes of meetings, commentaries, records relating to the Design Centre and 'Post Festival' media and critical assessments, 1952–58. His later career and interests are documented in files on the Society of Authors and its Censorship Reform Committee; the future of the Crystal Palace area; and the demise of the *News Chronicle*. Much of his correspondence was destroyed after his death.

BARTLETT, (CHARLES) VERNON (OLDFIELD) (1894–1983) Broadcaster and journalist. MP (Ind Prog) Bridgwater, 1938–50.

The papers, formerly at Sussex University Library, have now been transferred to Reading University Library. The collection consists of scripts of broadcast talks starting in the late 1920s and continuing intermittently until after World War II. The first series of talks covers international affairs, particularly the rise of Nazism; the second provides an 'unofficial' picture of domestic life in Britain during the war. The British Library has purchased some of his correspondence, including letters from prominent politicians.

BATTERSHILL, SIR WILLIAM DENIS (1869–1959) Colonial administrator. Various diplomatic postings in Jamaica, Cyprus and Palestine, 1929–41. Assistant Under-Secretary and Deputy Under-Secretary, Colonial Office, 1942–45. Governor and Commander-in-Chief, Tanganyika Territory, 1945–49.

An important collection of papers (14 boxes), covering the period 1908–60, has been deposited at Rhodes House Library, Oxford (ref. Brit Emp s 467). A list is available (NRA 26072). The papers, diaries and correspondence deal mainly with his time as Governor of Tanganyika.

BATTLEY, JOHN ROSE (1880–1952) MP (Lab) Clapham, 1945–50.

There are papers in Lambeth Archives Department (ref. 2002/24).

BEATTIE, JOHN (1886–1960) MP (Irish Lab) West Belfast, 1943–50; 1951–55.

The correspondence and papers, covering the period 1927–58 have been placed in the Public Record Office of Northern Ireland (ref. D2784). The papers (c. 300 documents) relate mainly to his involvement with the Irish Labour Party during the period 1940–55. There are papers on his career in parliamentary and party politics, including speeches, pamphlets and administrative records; papers on his service as an alderman (1944–57); Belfast City Council conference reports and agenda; Irish Labour Party newsheets (Dublin); and educational papers on his work as Secretary and Organiser of the Irish National Teachers Organisation.

BEAVER, SIR HUGH EYRE CAMPBELL (1890–1967) Industrialist. Managing Director, Arthur Guinness Son and Co. Ltd., 1946–60. Director-General and Controller-General, Ministry of Works, 1940–45. Director, Development Corporation, 1951–60. President, Confederation of British Industry, 1957–60.

A collection of papers, 1900–66, is held at the LSE Library. A list is available (NRA 19938). In addition to a large personal correspondence (1929–66), there are lectures and speeches, press-cuttings, published reports, notebooks and memoranda, and autobiographical notes and diaries. Of particular interest is his correspondence relating to the British Army in India. There is extensive correspondence relating to his business career and to his period in the Ministry of Works. Other files relate to his presidency of the CBI and to his contacts with various educational institutions. His correspondents include Lord Reith and Sir Winston Churchill.

Other records concerning his presidency of the FBI (1957–59) are held at the University of Warwick Modern Records Centre (ref. MSS 200/F/3/P 17) (NRA 23238).

BEAVERBROOK, BARON Sir William Maxwell Aitken (1879–1964) Politician and newspaper proprietor. MP (Con) Ashton-under-Lyne, Dec. 1910–16. Minister of Information, 1918–19. Minister of Aircraft Production, 1940–41; Supply, 1941–42; War Production, Feb. 1942; Lord Privy Seal, 1943–45.

The papers are held at the House of Lords Record Office. A list is available (NRA 19284). Much of the collection relates to his life and career before 1945. Among the later material there is family, political and business correspondence; and numerous letter files on politicians, journalists, writers, poets and artists. The post-war history of the newspapers he owned (the *Daily Express* and the *Evening Standard*) is well documented. Additionally, there are engagement diaries, private account books, extensive press-cuttings, and files relating to his published work including reviews.

BECKETT, JOHN WILLIAM WARBURTON (1894–1964) MP (Lab) Gateshead, 1924–29; Peckham, 1929–31.

Miscellaneous papers have been placed in Sheffield University Library (ref. MS 238).

BEDDINGTON-BEHRENS, SIR EDWARD (1897–1968) Founder member of European Movement. Chairman, European Industrial Conference, 1958; Political and Economic Conference of the Seven, 1960. President, European Atlantic Group.

It is understood that some papers have survived with the family.

BEGG, ADMIRAL OF THE FLEET SIR VARYL (CARGILL) (1908–95) Naval career, 1926–68. Served in World War II, 1939–45; *HMS Warspite*, 1940–43. Vice-Chief of the Naval Staff, 1961–63. Chief of the Naval Staff and First Sea Lord, 1966–68. Governor of Gibraltar, 1969–73.

Enquiries should be directed to the Imperial War Museum.

BEHRENS, SIR LEONARD (1890–1978) Liberal Party activist. President, Liberal Party Organisation, 1955–57; Chairman, Liberal Party Executive, 1959–61. Vice-President, United Nations Association. Manchester businessman.

The papers and correspondence covering the period 1916–76 are held at John Rylands Library, University of Manchester. A list is available (NRA 25962). The collection comprises correspondence, diaries, and files on the Liberal Party (1949–74). Correspondents include Jo Grimond, Norman Angell, Sir Basil Liddell Hart, Eleanor Rathbone and Ivan Smith.

BEITH, ALAN JAMES (1943–) MP (Lib, then Lib Dem), Berwick-upon-Tweed since 1973.

Mr Beith states that he has retained his papers and will make provision for their eventual deposit.

BELGION, (HAROLD) MONTGOMERY (1892–1973) Author and biographer. Served Royal Engineers during World War II. Pre-war journalist.

Some 46 boxes of papers are deposited in Churchill College, Cambridge. A list is available (NRA 23854). The collection includes files on war crimes and the Nuremburg trials; political movements and related journalism; and photographs and personal letters. His correspondence on war crimes issues with Lord Hankey (1949–61) is also held at Churchill College (NRA 31396). Letters sent to the *Manchester Guardian* (1951–54) are held at the John Rylands Library, University of Manchester (NRA 18162).

BELL, SIR GAWAIN WESTRAY (1909–95) Colonial Service. Sudan Political Service, 1931–37. Seconded to Palestine, 1938–40. Lieutenant-Colonel, Arab Legion, 1942–45. Governor, Northern Nigeria, 1957–62. Secretary-General, South Pacific Commission, 1966–70.

Some letters and papers were promised to Rhodes House Library, where tapes and transcripts of an interview regarding the Sudan and Northern Nigeria, 1931–62, are already held (ref. MSS Afr s 2001; these are subject to restricted access). Much of the material covers his career to 1944, especially his time with the Arab Legion. Other papers relate to Nigeria and the Sudan. He also retained some photograph albums.

Copies of orders to Arab Legion officers (1940–43) are in the Imperial War Museum. The originals were given by Bell to the Jordanian National Memorial Museum.

The Sudan Archive at Durham University has a collection of diaries, correspondence and papers, 1927–64. A list is available (NRA 34328).

BELL, GEORGE KENNEDY ALLEN (1883–1958) Bishop of Chichester, 1929–58.

There are currently over 320 volumes of correspondence, letters and papers relating to Bishop Bell's various activities at the Lambeth Palace Library. These include 61 volumes of German Papers, 1925–57, dealing especially with peace movements and contacts in the German resistance. Four volumes, 1919–55, concern peace campaigns and the National Peace Council; while another 20 volumes contain material relating to the German Church struggle as well as correspondence and papers on refugees, 1933–49. There are letters with and concerning Dietrich Bonhoeffer and with Martin Niemoller, as well as correspondence with a number of German pastors. Other material relates to post-war Germany and de-Nazification, resistance movements, war criminals, and evangelical church meetings. The collection also includes material on trade unions and unemployment (1945–58); political developments in Africa (1940–57); the Baltic states (1940–48); Cyprus (1954–58); Hungary (1945–88); South Africa (1949–57); Suez (1956–57); and Yugoslavia, 1942–45. A list is available (NRA 36514).

BELOE, ROBERT (1905–84) Anglican administrator. Secretary to Archbishop of Canterbury, 1959–69. Liaison Officer between Anglican Communion and

World Council of Churches, 1969–71. Member, Mauritius Electoral Boundary Commission, 1957. Member of various educational boards.

Some miscellaneous papers are held at Lambeth Palace Library (ref. MSS 3256–62). The papers of Lord Monckton, in the Department of Western Manuscripts, Bodleian Library, Oxford, include correspondence, 1962–64.

BENENSON, PETER (1921–2005) Founder, Amnesty International, 1961.

An oral history on the conception and foundation of Amnesty International by Professor Andrew Blaine, including a major contribution from Mr Benenson, is held in the archives of the International Secretariat, together with a collection of papers related to the establishment and early progress of the movement.

Mr Benenson retained other records from the early years of Amnesty including extensive correspondence. He also had papers from his period as an Alderman of Bethnal Green, 1948–52 and as Labour Parliamentary Candidate, 1950–59; papers on the British Section of the International Commission of Jurists ('Justice'); and papers relating to various groups assisting coeliacs.

BENN, ANTHONY (NEIL WEDGWOOD) (1925–) MP (Lab) Bristol South East, Nov. 1950–60; Aug. 1963–83; Chesterfield, Mar. 1984–2001. Postmaster-General, 1964–66; Minister of Technology, 1966–70; Industry Secretary and Minister for Posts and Telecommunications, 1974–75; Energy Secretary, 1975–79. Labour Party National Executive Committee member, 1959–60, and 1962–93.

Mr Benn currently retains a wide-ranging and comprehensive collection of political papers which document his own career as well as developments within the Labour Party and Labour movement since 1945. The main categories are: private political diaries, with associated notes and documents (kept since 1950); ministerial papers; speeches, articles, broadcasts and press-cuttings (since 1946); files on the peerage campaign; and personal papers. Since 1963 the diaries have been recorded on tape and substantially edited sections of some have been published. The archive also includes some cabinet and departmental files and Labour Party National

Executive Committee minutes. There are also files on specific crises including Suez, the IMF (1976), the Zircon spy satellite (1987) and the Gulf War (1991). The tapes recording his successful campaign for the renunciation of his peerage are held at St Antony's College, Oxford.

Requests for access to the collection should be directed to Mr Benn. Eventually, the papers are to be deposited in the British Library.

BENNETT OF EDGBASTON, 1ST BARON Sir Peter Frederick Blaker Bennett (1880–1957) MP (Con) Edgbaston, 1940–53. Parliamentary Secretary, Ministry of Labour, 1951–52.

Some papers, 1930–57, have been deposited at the University of Birmingham Library. A list is available (NRA 42277).

BENNETT, NICHOLAS JEROME (1949–) MP (Con) Pembroke, 1987–92. Parliamentary Under-Secretary, Welsh Office, 1990–92.

In 1992 Mr Bennett deposited his political papers with the Welsh Political Archive at the National Library of Wales. The papers are closed. A list is available (NRA 38944).

BENSON, SIR ARTHUR EDWARD TREVOR (1907–87) Colonial administrator. Administrative Secretary, Uganda, 1946–49. Chief Secretary, Central African Council, 1949–51; Nigeria, 1951–54. Governor, Northern Rhodesia, 1954–59.

Some papers have been deposited in Rhodes House Library, Oxford (ref. MSS Afr s 1400).

BENSON, MAJOR-GENERAL EDWARD RIOU (1903–85) Deputy Director, Military Government (British Element), Berlin, 1948–50. Chief of Staff, General Headquarters, Middle East Land Forces, 1954–57.

Copies of papers relating to his career are deposited in the Liddell Hart Centre, King's College, London. They consist of minutes taken at a meeting of Deputy Commandants Allied Forces, Berlin, May 1948; a file on British Military Government, Berlin, 1948–50; and a transcript account *Suez: The Seven Day War* by A.J. Barker.

BENSON, MARY (1919–2000) Civil rights campaigner, South Africa. Founder, Africa Bureau,

London, 1952; Secretary, 1957. Secretary to the Treason Trials Defence Fund, Johannesburg. Expelled from South Africa, 1966.

The Institute of Commonwealth Studies, University of London, holds a collection of unpublished material and press-cuttings. A list is available (NRA 28846). Data on political prisoners and conditions in South African prisons are included in this collection. The correspondence, press-cuttings, photographs and other working papers, which she gathered for her biography of Tshekedi Khama, 1949–82, are among the Africa Bureau's collection in Rhodes House Library, Oxford (ref. MSS Afr s 1908).

BERKELEY, HUMPHRY JOHN (1926–94) MP (Con) Lancaster, 1959–66.

Mr Berkeley retained certain files relating to two pieces of legislation with which he was closely involved. These were the second reading of the Sexual Offences Act 1966 (which legalised homosexuality between male consenting adults), and the 1965 Act which abolished the death penalty for murder.

BERLIN, SIR ISAIAH (1909–97) Philosopher. Served during World War II on staff of Ministry of Information in New York, Washington DC and Moscow, 1941–46. President of Wolfson College, Oxford, 1966–75 and of the British Academy, 1974–78.

The papers have been catalogued by Dr Henry Hardy of Wolfson College, Oxford, and are now in the Bodleian Library.

BERNAL, JOHN DESMOND (1901–71) Physicist, writer on science and society and Marxist publicist. Fellow of the Royal Society. Professor of Physics, Birkbeck College, University of London, 1937–63; Professor of Crystallography, 1963–68. Lenin Peace Prize, 1963; Foreign Member, Academy of Sciences, USSR, 1958. Author of *The Social Function of Science* (1939), *Marx and Science* (1952) and *Science in History* (1954).

Cambridge University Library holds some 56 boxes of correspondence and papers (ref. Add MS 8287). These contain his own research papers and writings as well as files on government policy and funding for science during the 1950s; Labour Party policy on science and education (including corre-

spondence with Gaitskell (1959) and Crossman (1963–64)); atomic bombs and nuclear warfare: disarmament; population issues; the peace movement (especially the World Peace Council and the 1949 Warsaw World Peace Conference); the Korean War (1950–51); UNESCO, 1945–62; and various cultural and intellectual groups (including the Fabian Society (1945–62) and the British-Soviet Society (1946–67)). There is a large correspondence series arranged by country. His notes on attitudes to science, the history of science, Marxism, and existentialism form part of the collection. The remainder of the material consists of personal diaries, correspondence, and notes and other papers from his work at Birkbeck College (1938–69).

Birkbeck College, London has some additional papers which include scientific, political and philosophical writings. These will eventually be merged with the Cambridge collection.

The LSE Library holds a series of papers documenting his involvement with the World Peace Council and other pacifist organisations, 1950–65, and also some papers collected by his wife on the history of the Peace Councils Movement (ref. M 537). A list is available (NRA 30247).

BERRY, PETER SAIN LEY (fl. 1980s) Liberal, then SDP, activist. Founder member of SDP. PPC for Swansea West, 1983; Pontypridd, 1987 and Pembroke, 1992.

A miscellany of papers has been acquired by the Welsh Political Archive, National Library of Wales. The papers relate to parliamentary, European and local elections and to the administration of the SDP and the Alliance Committee for Wales. There is also material concerning the Lloyd George Society, 1985–93, and the Welsh Centre for International Affairs, 1986–91.

BEST, KEITH (LANDER) (1949–) MP (Con) Ynys Mon, 1979–87.

Mr Best has deposited 271 files of parliamentary correspondence and papers with the Welsh Political Archive at the National Library of Wales. A list is available (NRA 30281). Files 1–83 hold correspondence and subject files on a wide range of subjects. Files 84–271 contain constituency correspondence. All the files are subject to a 25-year embargo.

BETTS, TRISTRAM (1908–83) Famine relief and resettlement worker, 1950s onwards.

There are papers in the Refugee Studies Programme Documentation Centre, Queen Elizabeth House, Oxford. The Centre also holds the papers of the international refugee lawyer Paul Weis (1907–92) and papers of the Refugee Health Collection (formerly in the London School of Hygiene and Tropical Medicine).

BEVAN, ANEURIN (1897–1960) MP (Lab), Ebbw Vale, 1929–60. Minister of Health, Aug. 1945 to Jan. 1951; Labour and National Service, Jan.–Apr. 1951.

Michael Foot, who used the papers for his biography of Bevan, stated that they would be deposited at the Open University Library, Walton Hall, Milton Keynes. Some correspondence with his agent and the Ebbw Vale Constituency Labour Party Secretary, Ron Evans, 1954–58, is at the National Library of Wales. This collection also includes various speeches and correspondence relating to his constituency. A list is available (NRA 31259).

BEVERIDGE, 1ST BARON Sir William Henry Beveridge (1879–1963) Director of Labour Exchanges, 1909–16. Assistant General Secretary, Ministry of Munitions, 1915–16. Second Secretary, later Permanent Secretary, Ministry of Food, 1916–19. Director, London School of Economics, 1919–37. Master, University College, Oxford, 1937–45. MP (Lib) Berwick-on-Tweed, 1944–45. Chairman, Interdepartmental Committee on Social Insurance and Allied Services, 1941–42.

An extensive collection of papers covering his life and career, 1886–1963, is held at the LSE Library. A list is available (NRA 25115). The collection includes a large correspondence together with various family and personal papers, including diaries. The main categories are: unemployment and labour exchanges, World War I, universities, politics, reports, published works, and visits abroad. Each group of papers includes correspondence, related papers, reports and memoranda. The collection also includes a large number of press-cuttings, pamphlets and offprints.

The post-1945 papers document his work in the Lords and the Liberal Party organisation, as well as his other wide interests including health services, old age, demography and new towns (Peterlee and Newton Aycliffe Development Corporations). There are also various papers on world government and peace aims, including his involvement with international organisations such as the UN, Federal Union and the Parliamentary Association for World Government. There is extensive documentation on both his own 'Beveridge Report' and on several other bodies on which he served, including the Broadcasting Committee of 1949–50.

BEVIN, ERNEST (1884–1951) MP (Lab) Wandsworth Central, 1940–50; Woolwich East, 1950–51. Minister of Labour and National Service, 1940–45. Secretary of State for Foreign Affairs, 1945–50. Lord Privy Seal, 1951.

Churchill College, Cambridge holds 78 boxes of correspondence and papers dating mainly from 1940 to 1945 (ref. BEVN). A list is available (NRA 19698). The papers include memoranda, drafts and notes relating to his ministerial work, with additional material on the Labour Party and the general election of 1945; political correspondence; speech notes, manuscripts, mimeographed conference minutes and press conference reports and related press-cuttings; files on official visits including programmes, correspondence, speeches and pamphlets; general correspondence; and writings by and about Bevin. The Modern Records Centre, University of Warwick, holds additional correspondence and papers as part of the archives of the Transport and General Workers Union (ref. MSS 126/EB). A list is available (NRA 24096). These relate to his activities as General Secretary of the TGWU during the inter-war period, including subject files; material on trade union organisations; official committees and commissions; and non-official bodies. The Private Office papers for the period 1945–51 are deposited at the Public Record Office, Kew (ref. FO 800). A list is available (NRA 23627). These extensive files cover a wide range of topics divided according to region and country, and including papers on Palestine, Commonwealth and Colonial Territories, the United Nations, Industrial Affairs, and War Criminals.

BIGGS-DAVIDSON, SIR JOHN ALEC (1918–88) MP (Con) Chigwell, 1955-Feb. 1974; Epping Forest, Feb. 1974–88.

A collection of papers, covering the period 1943–88, is held at the House of Lords Record Office (ref. Hist Coll 101). The collection is currently closed to researchers. The Bodleian Library, Oxford, holds 54 albums and 5 boxes of press-cuttings covering his career from 1955 to 1986.

BILLINGTON-GREIG, TERESA (1877–1964) Campaigner for women's rights. Activist in organisations such as the Women's Social and Political Union, Women for Westminster, and the Women's Freedom League.

The 32 boxes of papers held at the Women's Library cover her life and career up to the early 1960s (ref. 7/TBG). The collection includes papers on many of the organisations with which she was involved, such as Women for Westminster (1942–49); the Married Women's Association; and the British Federation of Business and Professional Women (1960–61). There are notes, leaflets and pamphlets and press-cuttings on the Commonwealth, the Third World, and notes collected for a biography of Mrs Charlotte Despard. The subject files cover women's suffrage; feminist and other societies; post-suffrage activities and campaigns; the status of women; marriage and divorce; sex and prostitution; relations between the sexes; equal pay; women workers; children; education; war and peace; and the consumer. There are also autobiographical notes, photographs and press-cuttings. The papers of Fiona Billington-Greig (d. 1996) are also housed here.

BIRD, JEAN LENNOX (1912–57) First female member of the Royal Air Force.

The papers are lodged in the Royal Air Force Museum, Hendon, and consist of flying logbooks, 1930–35; instruction notes and teaching manuals, 1953; papers relating to her duties, 1953–55; and articles relating to her time in the Hong Kong Flying School, 1934–50 and in the RAF, 1948–57 (ref. AC73/10).

BIRKBECK, MAJOR-GENERAL THEODORE HENRY (1911–76) Military career. Served in the King's African Rifles, World War II. Commanded 3rd Battalion, Parachute Regiment, Palestine, 1947–48; 70th Infantry Brigade (King's African Rifles), Kenya, 1955–58. Deputy Military Secretary, War Office, 1958–60. Director, Territorial Army Cadets, War Office, 1962–66.

Papers relating to his service with the King's African Rifles, 1935–58, are deposited in the Imperial War Museum. They include material from his period commanding 70th Infantry Brigade during the operations against the Mau Mau in Kenya, 1955–58. (ref. 83/21/1). The Liddell Hart Centre, King's College, London, has reported that material relating to his Territorial Army command, c. 1960–66, is held at the Border Regiment Museum, Carlisle.

BISHOP, MAJOR-GENERAL SIR (WILLIAM HENRY) ALEXANDER (1897–1984) Served in World Wars I and II. On staff of Control Commission Germany post-war, 1945–46, and North Rhine-Westphalia Regional Commissioner, 1948–50. Deputy British High Commissioner, Calcutta, 1957–62. British High Commissioner, Cyprus, 1964–65.

A large collection of papers covering his service with CCG and as a regional administrator in post-war Germany, 1945–50, has been placed in the Imperial War Museum. It is an extremely important source for the history of the Allied Military Administration of Germany and of social and economic reconstruction there. Copies of his unpublished 1971 memoir, *Look Back With Pleasure, 1914–65*, are held at the Liddell Hart Centre, London, and Rhodes House Library, Oxford.

BLACKBURNE, SIR KENNETH WILLIAM (1907–80) Colonial administrator. Director of Information Service, Colonial Office, 1947–50. Governor, Leeward Islands, 1950–56. Captain-General and Governor-in-Chief, Jamaica, 1957–62; Governor-General, 1962. Author of *Development and Welfare in the Gambia* (1954).

Twenty-five boxes of correspondence, diaries, speeches, and administrative reports have been deposited at Rhodes House Library, Oxford (ref. MSS Brit Emp s 460). A list is available (NRA 26249). The records cover the whole of his career (1929–63), including service in Nigeria, Palestine, Colonial Office, Gambia, Barbados, Leeward Islands, and a number of papers on his governorship of Jamaica. The collection includes notes on development issues and welfare in the West Indies; Colonial Office Information Services; the tour of East Africa and development plans for the Gambia; and the appointment diaries of Lady Blackburne. There are also drafts of *Lasting Legacy*, and miscellaneous printed material. A large amount of material relates to the Governorship of Jamaica, including a collection of press-cuttings.

BLACKER, CARLOS PATON (1895–1975) Secretary, Eugenics Society.

Twenty-three boxes of his papers are in the Contemporary Medical Archives Centre.

BLACKETT, LORD Patrick Maynard Stuart Blackett (1897–1974) Nuclear physicist. Fellow of the Royal Society. Government Adviser. Professor of Physics, University of Manchester, 1937–53. Professor of Physics, Imperial College of Science and Technology, 1953–65. Chairman, Research Grants Committee, 1956–60. Scientific Adviser, Ministry of Technology. President, British Society for the Advancement of Science, 1957–58. President of the Royal Society, 1965–70.

An extensive collection of papers arranged in eight sections has been deposited at the Library of the Royal Society. A list is available (NRA 22627). Section A contains 106 boxes of personal papers. Sections B and C relate to his work as a nuclear physicist. Section D records his wartime activities and work on government committees, 1936–73, including files on bombing policy, 1941–46, the anti-U-boat campaign, the Chiefs of Staff Sub-committee on future weapons and its successors, the Advisory Committee on Atomic Energy and various other committees. Section E documents his political activities and includes 10 files on the Gaitskell Group and 12 on miscellaneous socialist and Labour Party activities, 1956–64, including his membership of the Fabian Society Science Group and the Labour Party Science and Industry Sub-committee. There are 13 on his work on the Advisory Council on Technology and as Scientific Adviser to the Ministry of Technology, 1963–72. Eight files consist of testimonies to various Labour Party and official committees such as the PLP Science Group, 1960–62 and the Fulton Committee on the Civil Service, 1966–67. There are two folders of press-cuttings and printed matter on Labour's science policy in the 1964 General Election. Section F contains 85 files of science-related notes and working papers, lectures, broadcasts, publications and correspondence. Section G consists of 126 files dealing with his overseas activities relating to science, defence and economic development. Section H has 157 files of lectures, broadcasts, and publications, 1934–73.

BLANCH OF BISHOPTHORPE, BARON Stuart Yarworth Blanch (1918–94) Anglican clergyman. Archbishop of York, 1974–83; Bishop of Liverpool, 1966–74. Warden of Rochester Theological College, 1960–66.

His literary correspondence and other papers have been placed in York Minster Library.

BLAND, SIR GEORGE NEVILE MALTBY (1886–1972) Diplomat. Ambassador to The Netherlands, 1938–48. Special Representative of Secretary of State for Foreign Affairs, 1960–70.

Twelve boxes of his papers have been placed in Churchill College, Cambridge (NRA 43512).

BLOOD, SIR HILARY RUDOLPH ROBERT (1893–1967) Governor, Gambia, 1942–47; Barbados, 1947–49; Mauritius, 1949–54. Constitutional Commissioner, British Honduras, 1959; Zanzibar, 1960. Chairman, Constitutional Commission on Malta, 1960.

Seven boxes of articles, correspondence and reports are deposited in Rhodes House Library, Oxford (ref. MSS Brit Emp s 408). A list is available (NRA 17878).

BLUNDELL, SIR MICHAEL (1907–93) British settler and politician in Kenya. Member of Legislative Council, Rift Valley Constituency, 1948–62. Minister on Emergency War Council, Kenya, 1954; Minister of Agriculture, 1955–59 and 1961–62. Leader of New Kenya Group, 1959–63.

The papers are deposited at Rhodes House Library, Oxford (ref. MSS Afr s 746). A list is available (NRA 22652). The papers cover the period 1948–76 and include 7 files on the Kenya Constitutional Conferences of 1960 and 1962 (Boxes 25–27); 10 files on political and economic affairs in Kenya 1948–72 (Boxes 28–29); and 29 files of press-cuttings 1954–62 (Boxes 30–33).

BLUNKETT, DAVID (1947–) MP (Lab) Sheffield Brightside since 1987. Member, Sheffield City Council, 1970–88; Leader, South Yorkshire County Council, 1980–87. Served in Blair Cabinets.

Some of his papers have been placed at intervals in Sheffield City Library. These relate to his time as Leader of the Sheffield City Council; as a member of the Labour Party National Executive Committee; as an MP and Front Bench Spokesman on Local Government (1988–92) etc. Access to the collection requires the permission of Mr Blunkett.

BLUNT, SIR ANTHONY (1907–83) Art expert. Professor of the History of Art, University of London, and Director, Courtauld Institute of Art, 1947–74. Surveyor of the Queen's Pictures, 1952–72. Exposed as a Soviet spy in 1979.

A memoir compiled by him has, it is understood, been lodged in the British Library. It will not be published until 2013.

BOLT, REAR-ADMIRAL ARTHUR SEYMOUR (1907–94) Served in World War II. Captain, *HMS Theseus*, Korea, 1949–51. Director, Naval Air Warfare, Admiralty, 1951–53. Chief of Staff to Flag Officer Air (Home), 1954–56. Deputy Controller of Military Aircraft, Ministry of Supply, 1957–60.

Admiral Bolt informed the Liddell Hart Centre, King's College, London, that he had retained certain papers. They include a night order book for *HMS Theseus* during the Korean War. These papers may be deposited in the Liddell Hart Centre. The papers of Captain Stephen Roskill, deposited in Churchill College, Cambridge, include some correspondence.

BOOTH, HARTLEY (1946–) MP (Con) Finchley, 1992–97. Special Adviser to Prime Minister, 1984–88.

Some political material, including research papers, constituency correspondence, etc., is in London Metropolitan Archives. A list is available (NRA 41326).

BOOTHBY, BARON Sir Robert John Graham Boothby (1900–86) MP (Con) Aberdeenshire East, 1924–58. Parliamentary Secretary, Ministry of Food, 1940–41. British delegate to Consultative Assembly of the Council of Europe, 1949–57.

A substantial collection of papers has remained in family possession and is fully described in the biography *Bob Boothby* (1991) by Robert Rhodes James. They include correspondence and press-cuttings covering his entire career in both Houses of Parliament including personal and political controversies such as his divorce and the Czech assets affair of 1941. Among his correspondents are Churchill, Beaverbrook, Oswald and Diana Mosley and Harold Nicolson. An extensive correspondence with Lady Dorothy Macmillan was destroyed. The collection includes several appointment diaries and a 1949 journal.

BOOTHROYD OF SANDWELL, BARONESS Betty Boothroyd (1929–) MP (Lab) West Bromwich, 1973–74, West Bromwich West 1974–2002. Speaker of the House of Commons, 1992–2000.

The papers have been placed in the Open University.

BOTTINI, REGINALD NORMAN (1916–99) Trade unionist. General Secretary, National Union of Agricultural and Allied Workers, 1970–78. Member, TUC General Council, 1970–78.

His papers are in the Rural History Centre, University of Reading.

BOTTOMLEY, BARON Arthur George Bottomley (1907–95) MP (Lab) Chatham, 1945–50; Rochester and Chatham, 1950–59; Middlesbrough East, 1962–74; Middlesbrough, 1974–83. Parliamentary Under-Secretary of State for the Dominions, 1946–47; Secretary for Overseas Trade, Board of Trade, 1947–51; Secretary of State for Commonwealth Affairs, 1964–66; Minister of Overseas Development, 1966–67.

There are papers mainly relating to Commonwealth affairs in the LSE Library. The collection covers the years 1944–83 and includes correspondence, notes for speeches, correspondence and letters from the public, records of official visits, pamphlets, press-cuttings and photographs. The subject files cover the 1946 Parliamentary Delegation to India; visits to Burma and the Panglong Conference (1947); UDI and the Rhodesian problem (1965–80s); the Common Market; race relations; Kenya, Ghana and Ethiopia; Hong Kong, and Cyprus. A memoir of Burma, covering *c.* 1945–47, is held at the India Office Library (NRA 25125).

BOTTOMLEY, AIR CHIEF MARSHAL SIR NORMAN HOWARD (1891–1970) Served in

World Wars I and II. Assistant Chief of Air Staff (Operations), 1942–43; Deputy Chief of Air Staff, 1941, 1943–45; Air Officer Commanding-in-Chief, Bomber Command, 1945–47. Inspector-General, Royal Air Force, 1947–48.

The Royal Air Force Museum, Hendon, has a series of records, including subject files, speeches and publications, covering the period 1915–61 (refs AC 71/2 and AC 71/8). Most of the material relates to the RAF in the immediate post-war years. This includes several reports by the British Bombing Survey Unit on the effects of strategic bombing on German towns (1947) and copies of the official reports on Hiroshima and Nagasaki; extensive files and draft, interim and final reports of the RAF Manpower Economy Committee and related reports on National Servicemen in the RAF, 1947–49; papers on biological warfare, 1949–50; Staff College lectures on strategic airpower; and printed papers on military management and staff training, 1946–47.

BOURNE, SIR FREDERICK CHALMERS (1891–1977) Indian Civil Service from 1920. Governor, Central Provinces and Bihar, 1946–47; East Bengal, 1947–50.

Some correspondence and press-cuttings covering the period 1933–71 have been deposited in the India Office Library (ref. MSS Eur E 364). The collection also includes a travel journal.

BOWEN, (EVAN) RODERIC (1913–2001) MP (Lib) Cardiganshire, 1945–66.

His constituency correspondence, covering the period 1953–61, can be found with the records of Cardiganshire Liberal Association in the National Library of Wales. A list is available (NRA 30554). The correspondence and papers are a useful source for party branch organisation and election campaigns in a rural constituency. The collection includes material on the Liberal Party of Wales (later the Welsh Liberal Party).

BOWER, LIEUTENANT-GENERAL SIR ROGER HERBERT (1903–90) Military commander. Served in World War II, 1939–45. Commanded Hamburg District, 1948–49. Director, Land/Air Warfare (and from 1951 also Director of Military Training), War Office, 1950–52. Chief of Staff, Allied Forces Northern Europe, 1955–56. General Officer Commanding and Director of Operations, Malaya, 1956–57. Commander-in-Chief, Middle East Land Forces, 1958–60.

A collection of papers is deposited in the Imperial War Museum. The collection is composed of official briefs and reports, with statistics, maps and similar related information, on operations in Holland, Norway, Palestine and Malaya, in which Bower was involved.

BOWLBY, (EDWARD) JOHN (MOSTYN) (1907–90) Consultant Psychiatrist, Tavistock Clinic, London, 1946–72; Hon. Consultant, 1972–90. Mental Health Consultant, World Health Organisation, from 1950.

The papers are deposited in the Wellcome Contemporary Medical Archives Centre, London. Enquiries regarding the collection should be directed to the Archivist.

BOWRA, SIR (CECIL) MAURICE (1898–1971) Scholar and critic. Fellow of Wadham College, 1922–38; Warden of Wadham College, 1938–70; Vice-Chancellor, University of Oxford, 1951–54; President of the British Academy, 1958–62.

Sir Maurice Bowra appears to have destroyed his papers at regular intervals. However, a box of personal papers and a few letters from prominent persons have survived in the Library at Wadham College. The College is also endeavouring to establish a list of papers in other collections and to obtain, where possible, copies. All enquiries should be directed to the Keeper of the Archives, Wadham College, Oxford.

BOYD OF MERTON, 1ST VISCOUNT Alan Tindal Lennox-Boyd (1904–83) MP (Con) Mid-Bedfordshire, 1931–60. Minister of State, Colonial Affairs, 1951–52; Minister of Transport and Civil Aviation, 1952–54; Secretary of State for the Colonies, 1954–59.

The papers (350 box files) have been deposited at the Bodleian Library, Oxford. The Public Record Office holds his Private Office papers (ref. AVIA 9). Viscount Boyd made extensive tape recordings relating to his career, and these are retained at St Antony's College, Oxford.

BOYD, ANDREW (1921–) Northern Irish trade unionist and academic. Author of *Holy War in Belfast* (1987) and *The Rise of the Irish Trade Unions* (1972).

Mr Boyd has deposited his papers in the Modern Archives Department, University College, Dublin (ref. P37). They include material from his period as a trade union organiser in Belfast (1950s) and as the Trades Union Congress's education officer for Northern Ireland, 1964–71. The bulk of the collection consists of reports, articles and his lecture and research notes.

BOYD, THOMAS WILLIAM (1903–91) Northern Ireland Labour Party MP.

His political papers have been placed in the Public Record Office of Northern Ireland (ref. D/4276).

BOYD-CARPENTER, BARON John Archibald Boyd-Carpenter (1908–98) MP (Con) Kingston-on-Thames, 1945–72. Numerous Ministerial appointments including Minister of Pensions and National Insurance 1955–62 and Chief Secretary to the Treasury and Paymaster-General 1962–64.

Lord Boyd-Carpenter promised his papers to the Bodleian Library, Oxford.

BOYD ORR, 1ST BARON John Boyd Orr (1880–1971) Nutritionist and scientist. Professor of Agriculture, University of Aberdeen, 1942–45. Director-General, United Nations Food and Agricultural Organisation, 1945–48. MP (Ind) Scottish Universities, 1945–46. Awarded Nobel Peace Prize, 1949.

The surviving papers have been given to the National Library of Scotland. A list is available (NRA 29231). Very little incoming correspondence has survived and the bulk of the papers consists of typescripts of talks and articles. The surviving letters include *c.* 200 from various correspondents (1948–64), drafts of outgoing letters (1950–51) and letters of condolence to his widow. There is also a manuscript volume containing mostly economic and political notes and quotations (1956–67); a bound volume of newspaper cuttings from his 1947 visit to South America; and miscellaneous press-cuttings (1947–58).

BOYLE, BARON Sir Edward Charles Gurney Boyle (1923–81) MP (Con) Birmingham, Hands-worth, 1950–70. Parliamentary Secretary, Ministry of Supply 1954–55; Economic Secretary, Treasury, 1955–56; Parliamentary Secretary, Ministry of Education, 1957–59; Financial Secretary, Treasury, 1959–62; Minister of Education 1962–64. Opposition Spokesman on Education and Science 1964–69. Vice-Chancellor, Leeds University, 1970–81.

The correspondence and papers (1940–81) have been deposited at the Brotherton Library, University of Leeds. A list is available (NRA 30282). The collection covers a wide range of personal and political subjects. These include family and domestic papers, 1945–81; diaries, 1964–80; general and personal correspondence, 1940–81; constituency and West Midlands political papers and non-political papers on Conservative Party organisation and policy 1947–76; parliamentary and ministerial papers, 1950–70; House of Lords papers; miscellaneous political papers; Leeds University material; speeches, publications and general subject files, as well as a catalogue of correspondence and papers. A taped interview with Anthony Seldon, recorded in 1980, is held at the LSE Library.

BOYLE, MARSHAL OF THE ROYAL AIR FORCE SIR DERMOT ALEXANDER (1904–93) Royal Air Force career, 1924–59. Director-General of Personnel, Air Ministry, 1948–49. Director-General of Manning, Air Ministry, 1949–51. Air Officer Commanding-in-Chief, Fighter Command, 1953–55. Chief of Air Staff, 1956–59.

The Royal Air Force Museum, Hendon, has some unsorted papers (ref. AC74/19). The Air Historical Branch of the Ministry of Defence has recorded an interview mainly concerning his cadet training at Cranwell, but which also covers the later phases of his career. Access to the recording and transcript are at the discretion of the Head of the Air Historical Branch.

BOYLE, KEVIN (fl. 1960s–90s) Civil rights campaigner in Northern Ireland during 1960s. Founder of People's Democracy, 1968.

Some papers concerning the Northern Ireland Civil Rights Association and People's Democracy have been deposited in the Public Record Office of Northern Ireland.

BRACKEN OF CHRISTCHURCH, 1ST VIS-COUNT Brendan Rendall Bracken (1901–58) MP (Con) Paddington North, 1929–45; Bournemouth, 1945–50; Bournemouth East, 1950–51. Minister of Information, 1941–45. First Lord of Admiralty, 1945.

One box of papers is held at Churchill College, Cambridge (ref. BBKN) (NRA 23365). The papers consist of source material for Andrew Boyle's biography together with xerox copies of letters to Lord Beaverbrook from the House of Lords Record Office.

BRADDOCK, ELIZABETH (BESSIE) MARGARET (1899–1970) MP (Lab) Liverpool Exchange, 1945–70.

The only surviving papers are held in Liverpool City Record Office together with those of her husband, John Braddock, a local politician (ref. Acc 2335).

BRADFORD, ROY HAMILTON (1921–98) Northern Ireland politician. Served as Unionist MP (various constituencies). Chief Whip, 1968–69. Minister for the Environment, 1973–75 (Northern Ireland Executive).

Political, professional and business papers are in the Public Record Office of Northern Ireland (ref. D/4211).

BRADWELL, 1ST BARON Thomas Edward Neil Driberg (1905–76) MP (Ind 1942–45 and Lab 1945–55) Maldon; Barking, 1959–74.

The papers are held in the Library of Christ Church, Oxford.

BRAINE OF WHEATLEY, LORD Bernard (Richard) Braine (1914–2000) MP (Con) Billericay, 1950–55; South-East Essex, 1955–83; Castle Point, 1983–92.

Seven boxes of correspondence and papers, 1947–93, have been deposited in the House of Lords Record Office (ref. Acc 4011). In addition, papers relating to Canvey Island, the redistribution of parliamentary seats etc. are in Essex Record Office (Southend Branch). (ref. S3014).

BRAMALL, SIR (ERNEST) ASHLEY (b. 1916) MP (Lab) Bexley, 1946–50. Member (Lab), Greater London Council, Tower Hamlets, 1964–73; Bethnal Green and Bow, 1973–86. Chairman, Greater London Council, 1982–83; Inner London Education Authority, 1965–67 and 1984–86; Leader, Inner London Education Authority, 1970–81.

Sir Ashley stated that he had retained some dozen box files of documents relating to his period as Leader of the Inner London Education Authority (1970–81), and up to 1986 when he ceased to be a member. Provision will be made for their eventual deposit.

BRAND, 1ST BARON Robert Henry Brand (1878–1963) Banker and public servant. Treasury Representative in Washington, 1944–46; Chairman, British Supply Council in North America, 1942 and 1945–46; United Kingdom Delegate, Bretton Woods and Savannah Conferences.

Some 147 box files of correspondence and papers have been deposited at the Bodleian Library, Oxford. They fully document his career as an international financier, as well as his role (during World War I) in the Ministry of Munitions, interwar economics and Liberal Party politics. His World War II service with British Food and Supply Missions to South and North America is also covered as is the part he played in post-war reconstruction. The collection is uncatalogued but a card index to the contents can be consulted in the library.

BRAUNTHAL, JULIUS (1891–1972) Austrian socialist resident in the UK from 1937. Editor of *Tribune* from 1937 and *International Socialist Forum*, 1938–48; Secretary of the Committee of the International Socialist Conferences, 1949–51; Secretary of the Socialist International, 1951–56. Author of the *History of the International* (3 vols, 1961–71).

A collection of papers is held at the International Institute of Social History, Amsterdam. This includes general correspondence with Austrian, British and other socialists such as Rafail Abramovic, Friedrich Adler and Karl Kautsky, 1891–1972; material issued by Braunthal as Secretary of the Socialist International, 1951–56, and some relating to *International Socialist Forum*. There are copies of radio talks for the BBC, 1939–43 and 1948–49, and manuscripts of published and unpublished books, articles, lectures and speeches, together with related reviews and correspondence. Topics include political affairs and socialism in Austria, Germany, Israel and Asia. Additional material consists of notes, documents and a manuscript on Victor and Friedrich Adler, together with miscellaneous documents, press-cuttings and printed matter.

BRAY, DR JEREMY WILLIAM (1930–2002) MP (Lab) Middlesbrough West, 1962–70; Motherwell & Wishaw, Oct. 1974–83; Motherwell South after 1983. Parliamentary Secretary, Ministry of Power, 1966–67; Ministry of Technology, 1967–69.

His political and economic papers (over 300 boxes) have been placed in Churchill College, Cambridge (ref. BRAY). The papers relate to Parliamentary Committees on nationalised industries, science and technology, and other political and economic issues 1952–84. The collection is closed to researchers for an indefinite period and the list (NRA 28332) is confidential.

BRENNAN, MARY (fl. 1980s) Campaigner for peace, Christian CND, etc.

There are papers in the Modern Records Centre, Warwick University (ref. MSS 181). The collection relates to work for peace movements, 1982–94. They include papers and photographs relating to the Campaign for Nuclear Disarmament (Christian CND, CND in the Midlands), international peace demonstrations (for example in Russia), non-violent direct action, the health effects of Chernobyl and nuclear disasters (including the atomic bombs at Hiroshima and Nagasaki), 1990–93.

BRETT, SIR CHARLES EDWARD BAINBRIDGE (1928–) Northern Ireland solicitor and politician. Chairman, Northern Ireland Labour Party, 1962. Served numerous public bodies.

Papers relating to the Northern Ireland Labour Party and Housing Executive, 1962–92 are in the Public Record Office of Northern Ireland (ref. D/4200).

BRIDGES, 1ST BARON Sir Edward Bridges (1892–1969) Civil servant. Secretary to the Cabinet, 1938–46. Permanent Secretary, Treasury, 1945–56.

There are several files of Cabinet Office papers and correspondence at the Public Record Office (ref. CAB 127/259–281, 326–337) (NRA 32409). These cover India, Pakistan, commercial and colonial policy, notes on the dissolution of the wartime cabinet and the 'caretaker' government. Lord Bridges' family have stated that he left no diaries or other papers relating to his public life.

BRIMELOW, BARON Thomas Brimelow (1915–95) Diplomat. Post-war postings included Moscow, Havana and Ankara. Counsellor, Washington, 1960–63; Minister, British Embassy, Moscow, 1963–66; Ambassador to Poland, 1966–69; Deputy Under-Secretary, FCO, 1969–73; PUS and Head of the Diplomatic Service, 1973–75. MEP, 1977–78.

A typescript interview is held at Churchill College, Cambridge (ref. BIMO). This covers his time in the Russia Section of the Foreign Office, 1945–47. Enquiries regarding access should be directed to the Archivist.

BRIND, ADMIRAL SIR (ERIC JAMES) PATRICK (1892–1963) Naval commander. Served in World Wars I and II. President of Royal Naval College, Greenwich, 1946–48. Commander-in-Chief, Allied Forces, Northern Europe, 1951–53.

A few papers, 1919–58, are deposited in the Liddell Hart Centre, King's College, London. They mostly relate to the *Amethyst* incident, 1949, and also include copies of lectures concerning the development of sea power and the role of NATO.

BRITTAIN, VERA MARY (1893–1970) Feminist, pacifist and writer. President, Society of Women Writers and Journalists; Married Women's Association. Vice-President, Women's International League for Peace and Freedom; National Peace Council.

The correspondence and literary papers are deposited with those of her husband in the Library of McMaster University, Hamilton, Ontario. They include the original manuscript and typescript versions of almost all her published work as well as a substantial body of unpublished material. There are journals and diaries, 1911–68, lectures, notes and an extensive series of scrapbooks and press-cutting files.

In addition to an extensive correspondence (spanning half a century) with her husband, there are approximately 25,000 letters from writers, politicians, publishers, readers and friends. The majority of these have carbon copies of replies. Her correspondents include Leo Amery, Harold Macmillan, Alex Comfort, Nevill Coghill, Hugh Gaitskell, Winifred Holtby, Julian Huxley, C.E.M. Joad, Kingsley Martin, Vanessa Redgrave, Bertrand Russell, Eleanor Roosevelt, Beatrice Webb, Virginia Woolf and Ellen Wilkinson. There are also letters to her daughter, Baroness Williams, with some 450 press-cuttings.

Some notebooks detailing her participation in the World Pacifist Conference in India, 1949–50, are in the Bodleian Library, Oxford (ref. Eng hist d 343, e 304, f 24).

Some collected material for a biography is in Somerville College Library Oxford (NRA 43953).

BRITTAN, SIR SAMUEL (1933–) Economist. Principal Economic Commentator, since 1966, and Assistant Editor, after 1978, of the *Financial Times*.

Sir Samuel states that his working papers will eventually be placed in the LSE Library, which already holds a diary covering his time as adviser to the Department of Economic Affairs, 1964–66.

BROCK, REAR ADMIRAL PATRICK WILLET (1902–88) Naval career. Served in World War II. Director, Operations Division, 1951–53. Flag Officer, Middle East, 1954–56.

According to the Liddell Hart Centre, King's College, London, the papers have remained in family possession in Canada. They are to be placed in an appropriate repository, either in the UK or in Canada, in due course.

BROCKLEBANK, JACK (d. 1990) Trade unionist. Leader of the Agricultural Workers' Union.

His trade union and other papers, covering the period 1940s–80s, have been placed in the Brynmor Jones Library, University of Hull.

BROCKWAY, BARON Archibald Fenner Brockway (1888–1988) Pacifist and Labour politician. MP (Lab) Leyton East, 1929–31; Eton and Slough, 1950–64.

Churchill College, Cambridge, holds 68 boxes of post-war papers (ref. FEBR). A list is now available

(NRA 44348). Other relevant material can be found in the Labour Party Archive at the Labour History Archive and Study Centre in Manchester (ref. LP/ JLP/32/1–9). The Department of Sound Recordings, Imperial War Museum, holds two interviews relating to conscientious objectors during World Wars I and II (ref. 436/4 and 4826/2).

BRODETSKY, SELIG (1889–1954) Mathematician and Zionist leader. Professor of Applied Mathematics, Leeds University, 1924–48. President, Hebrew University of Jerusalem, 1949–51. Executive Member, World Zionist Organisation; Jewish Agency for Palestine. Hon. President, Zionist Federation of Great Britain. President, Board of Deputies of British Jews, 1940–49.

Many of the relevant papers can be found in the Hartley Library, University of Southampton, including material on his involvement with the Board of Deputies and Zionism, 1939–53. A list is available (NRA 23208). The Board of Deputies Archive, now deposited in the London Metropolitan Archives, also contains a number of subject and correspondence files from his time as president, 1940–49 (NRA 19919). The Central Zionist Archives holds additional papers on the Hebrew University (ref. A82).

BRODIE, SIR ISRAEL (1895–1975) Jewish leader. Chief Rabbi, 1948–65.

A group of papers has been placed in the Hartley Library, University of Southampton (ref. MS 206). The papers are almost entirely for the 1950s onwards, with the exception of a volume of newspaper cuttings, 1948–49, and a small quantity of correspondence and papers ranging from 1923–73.

BROOK, CASPAR (1920–83) Director, Family Planning Association, 1968–74; David Owen Centre for Population Growth Studies, 1974–83.

The papers (29 boxes) have been placed in the Wellcome Contemporary Medical Archives Centre, London. The material includes correspondence, speeches, memoranda and printed matter on various aspects of his career. There are annotated copies of minutes from Family Planning Association meetings and publications of the Planned Parenthood Association and related international organisations.

The Contemporary Medical Archives Centre also holds records deposited by the David Owen Centre.

BROOKE OF CUMNOR, BARON Henry Brooke (1903–84) MP (Con) Lewisham West, 1937–45; Hampstead, 1950–66. Financial Secretary to the Treasury, 1954–57; Minister of Housing and Local Government, and Minister for Welsh Affairs, 1957–61; Chief Secretary to the Treasury and Paymaster-General, 1961–62; Home Secretary, 1962–64.

No papers have so far been deposited. An interview recorded in 1980 is held at the LSE Library, which also holds the papers of Lord Finsberg, his successor as MP for Hampstead. Lord Finsberg's papers include some election ephemera and other items relating to Lord Brooke.

BROOKE, SIR CHARLES ANTHONY JOHNSON (fl. 1934–50) Rajah of Sarawak.

His correspondence and papers, 1934–50, have been placed in Rhodes House Library.

BROOKEBOROUGH, 1ST VISCOUNT Sir Basil Stanlake Brooke (1888–1973) Prime Minister, Northern Ireland, 1943–63. Minister of Agriculture, Northern Ireland, 1933–41. Minister of Commerce, 1941–45 (jointly with Premiership). Stormont MP (UU), Lisnaskea, 1929–68.

The Brookeborough papers are in the Public Record Office of Northern Ireland (ref. D3004). A list is available (NRA 41208). They include diaries, 1940–63; correspondence, 1910–73; a memoir covering his early life to 1918; photographs; and indexed volumes of press-cuttings. The diaries and correspondence are largely subject to a fifty-year closure rule from the file termination date. The remainder of the collection consists of family and estate papers; correspondence and other papers belonging to his wife and to his son; and a series of recorded interviews, 1955–73. The collection was extensively used in Brian Barton's biography of his early career, *Brookeborough: The Making of a Prime Minister* (1988). A later volume is in preparation. The papers of Sir Wilfred Spender (also in the Public Record Office of Northern Ireland) and of Lord Beaverbrook (in the House of Lords Record Office) contain relevant material.

BROOKEBOROUGH, 2ND VISCOUNT Captain John Brooke (1922–87) Stormont MP (UU), Lisnaskea, 1968–72, and Conservative peer, House of Lords, 1973–87. Stormont Government Chief Whip, 1971–72. Represented North Down in Northern Ireland Assembly, 1973–74, and Northern Ireland Constitutional Convention, 1975–76.

The Brookeborough family papers, which are held in the Public Record Office of Northern Ireland, include his *Draft History of the Parliament of Northern Ireland* and other political papers, *c.* 1965–80 (refs D3004/C/15). The same collection includes photographs and press-cuttings relating to his earlier service as ADC to Wavell in India, 1946, his period in Tibet at the end of World War II (ref. D3004/E/11 and D3004/G/11); and taped interviews with him regarding the political situation in Northern Ireland, 1972–73, (ref. TP10).

BROOKES, BEATA (1931–) MEP (Con) North Wales, 1979–89.

A large deposit of papers has been received by the Welsh Political Archive, National Library of Wales. Many of the files are concerned with county and district councils and the activities of local Conservative Associations. Other papers deal with the logistics of the 1979 Euro-election campaign, and the impact of the Strasbourg Parliament on the North Wales constituency. Miss Brookes' strong interest in the problems of the mentally handicapped is also reflected in the papers, as is her concern for the problems facing the North Wales farming community.

BROTMAN, ADOLPH (1896–1970) Secretary, Board of Deputies, 1934–66.

The Board of Deputies Archive, recently deposited in the London Metropolitan Archives, includes his subject files, correspondence and other papers as Secretary (ref. B5/2; B5/3/1–10 and B5/4/1–18). The subject files include material on the Council of Continental Zionists, the Federation of Zionist Youth, the Jewish Agency, etc. Relevant material can also be found in the papers of the Foreign Affairs Committee (ref. C11), the Palestine Committee (ref. C14), and various special files (ref. E1).

BROWN OF MACHRIHANISH, LORD Wilfred Banks Duncan Brown (1908–85) Industrialist. Minister of State, Board of Trade, 1965–70.

The papers have been placed in Churchill College, Cambridge. A list is available (NRA 44319).

BROWN, SIR ERNEST HENRY PHELPS (1906–94) Economist. Professor of the Economics of Labour, London School of Economics, 1947–68. President, Royal Economic Society, 1970–72.

The papers are in the LSE Library (ref. M0921). Sir Henry deposited 14 boxes of papers on wages and prices during his lifetime; his widow Lady Phelps Brown deposited a further 10 metres of papers relating to research and public work in 1995.

BROWN, HUGH DUNBAR (1919–) MP (Lab) Glasgow Provan, 1964–87. Parliamentary Under-Secretary of State, Scottish Office, 1974–79.

Mr Brown deposited his papers (*c.* 20 boxes) at the Strathclyde Regional Archives in 1992. The collection consists mainly of files on constituency matters. There are also some papers relating chiefly to parliamentary bills on subjects such as Scottish local government, housing and the Community Charge.

BROWN, LESLIE WILFRID (1912–99) Anglican bishop. Bishop of Uganda, 1953–65. Archbishop of Uganda, Rwanda and Burundi, 1961–65. Subsequently Bishop of St Edmundsbury and Ipswich, 1966–78.

His correspondence, diaries and papers covering the period 1935–92 have been placed in Lambeth Palace Library (ref. MSS 3779–3827).

BROXBOURNE, BARON Sir Derek Colclough Walker-Smith (1910–92) MP (Con) Hertford, 1945–55; Hertfordshire East, 1955–83. Various ministerial posts, including Minister of Health, 1957–60.

A small collection of Lord Broxbourne's papers is in the possession of his son, Sir Jonah Walker-Smith Bt. The collection, which is open, includes a draft memoir.

BRUCE, DAVID KIRKPATRICK ESTE (1898–1977) American Ambassador to the United Kingdom, 1961–69.

A collection of papers is held at the Virginia Historical Society, Richmond, Virginia (NRA 32583). The papers cover his entire career and include diplomatic diaries (1949–74) which detail the stormy relations between Britain and America during the 1960s. Access to the diaries requires written permission from Mrs Bruce. All enquiries should be directed to the Archivist.

BRUCE LOCKHART, SIR ROBERT HAMILTON (1887–1970) Diplomat and intelligence agent. Head of Special Mission, Russia, 1918. Commercial Secretary, Czechoslovakia, 1919–22. Political Intelligence Department, Foreign Office, 1939–40. Representative to Provisional Czechoslovak Government, London, 1940–41; Deputy Under-Secretary, Foreign Office, and Director-General, Political Warfare Executive, 1941–45. Journalist and author post-war.

The House of Lords Record Office holds his diaries and journals, 1915–65. The papers of Lord Beaverbrook, held in the same repository, include correspondence with him, 1928–64. Other letters and papers have remained in the family's possession. The papers of Lord Avon, at Birmingham University Library, include post-war correspondence, 1957–68, as do the private papers of Sir Percy Loraine, 1945–48, which are in the Public Record Office (ref. FO 1011/282). Reference should also be made to the papers of Sir Robert's brother, General Sir Rob Lockhart, which are now deposited with the National Army Museum.

BRUNDRETT, SIR FREDERICK (1894–1974) Scientist and civil servant. Scientific Adviser, Ministry of Defence. Chairman, Defence Research Policy Committee, 1954–59.

Two boxes of papers and lectures are held in Churchill College, Cambridge. A list is available (NRA 23365). They are concerned mainly with science and defence issues, 1951–72.

BRUSH, LIEUTENANT-COLONEL EDWARD J.A.H. (PETER) (1901–84) Military career to 1946. Ulster Unionist activist, 1969–82. Organiser of loyalist paramilitary group, Down Orange Welfare, 1973. On Ulster Workers Council co-ordinating committee for 1974 anti-power-sharing strike.

Member (OUP) for South Down in Northern Ireland Convention, 1975–76.

A typescript memoir of his military career, 1921–45, and his later involvement in Northern Irish politics, 1969–82, is deposited in the Imperial War Museum (ref. 85/8/1). It includes an account of his role in the 1974 general strike, the Stormont Convention of 1974–75, and his recollections of Edward Heath, Airey Neave and Sir Norman Stronge.

BRYANT, SIR ARTHUR WYNNE MORGAN (1899–1985) Freelance writer, lecturer, political commentator and popular historian.

The Liddell Hart Centre, King's College, London, acquired 241 boxes of papers in 1990. The collection includes the original manuscripts of his works and the papers of his father, Sir Francis Morgan Bryant (1859–1938), a Buckingham Palace official. Some of his military correspondence, including letters from Field Marshals Lord Alanbrooke and Viscount Montgomery, 1946–70, is deposited in the Imperial War Museum. Further correspondence, 1955–63, can be found in the papers of Lord Woolton at the Bodleian Library, Oxford.

BUCHER, GENERAL SIR ROY (1895–1980) Military career. General Officer Commanding, Bengal and Assam, 1946; Eastern Command, 1946–47. Chief of Staff, India, 1947. Commander-in-Chief, Army of India, 1948–49.

A substantial collection of correspondence and papers has been deposited at the National Army Museum (ref. 7901–87). A list is available (NRA 23387). His career in the Indian Army and (from 1945–49) the Army of India, and his post-retirement activities until 1977 are fully documented. The material includes correspondence (1948–72), maps, operational orders and reports (on *inter alia* the Calcutta Disturbances of August 1946 and the situation in Hyderabad, March–September 1948, and in Kashmir, 1947–48). His correspondents include Attlee (1949–50), Nehru (1949–64), Philip Noel-Baker MP (1949–65), Lord Slim (1949–58) and Sardar Patel, Nehru's deputy (1949–70). The post-retirement papers include material on Bucher's work for the British Legion, 1968–77.

Copies of papers concerning his time as Commander-in-Chief of the Indian Army are in the Mountbatten Archives and the Nehru Memorial Library, New Delhi, India.

BUIST, JOHN STEWART (1904–82) Journalist. Foreign Editor, *The Times*.

Nine volumes of his diaries, 1959–63, have been placed in the British Library.

BULLARD, SIR EDWARD CRISP (1907–81) Geophysicist. Government adviser on science policy.

There are 117 boxes of papers in Churchill College, Cambridge (ref. BLRD). A list is available (NRA 28785). The material includes personal and research papers and correspondence and records of the various committees and bodies on which he served.

BURHOP, ERIC HENRY STONELEY (1911–80) Professor of Physics, University College, London, 1960–78. President, World Federation of Scientific Workers. Foreign Member, Academy of Sciences, German Democratic Republic. Lenin Peace Prize, 1972.

His papers, concerning the Cold War and the Pugwash Conferences, have been placed in University College, London (ref. MS Add 385). A list is available (NRA 36166).

BURN, DUNCAN LYALL (1902–88) Economist and consultant. Leader writer and Industrial Correspondent of *The Times*, 1946–62. Historian of the steel industry. Served Executive Committee, National Institute of Social and Economic Research.

Some papers, including material on steel nationalisation and nuclear power are in the LSE Library.

BURNS, SIR ALAN CUTHBERT (1887–1980) Colonial Service. Governor, British Honduras, 1934–40; Gold Coast, 1941–47; acting Governor, Nigeria, 1942. Permanent UK Representative, United Nations Trusteeship Council, 1947–56.

No papers concerning his career in the Colonial Service have been located. The Department of Sound Records at the Imperial War Museum holds an interview and transcript from the BBC series, *Tales from the Dark Continent* (ref. 4708/3B). His diary of World War I service in the Cameroons, 1914–15, is in Rhodes House Library, Oxford.

BURROUGH, ADMIRAL SIR HAROLD MARTIN
(1888–1977) Naval career; served in World War II, with commands at Gibraltar, Mediterranean Approaches, etc. Assistant Chief of Naval Staff, 1939–40. Allied Naval Commander-in-Chief, Expeditionary Force, 1945. British Naval Commander-in-Chief, Germany, 1945–46. Commander-in-Chief, The Nore, 1946–48.

A microfilm of papers, 1916–46, is available at the Imperial War Museum. The pre-war section includes material on Royal Navy relief work during the Spanish Civil War. The bulk of the collection concerns wartime convoys and the surrender and occupation of Germany after World War II. Copies of speeches and unpublished articles are also held by the Museum.

BURT, SIR CYRIL LODOWIC (1883–1971)
Psychologist. Advocate of intelligence testing. Pre-war educational psychologist to the London County Council. Professor of Education, University of London, 1924–31; Psychology, University College London, 1931–50. Editor, *British Journal of Statistical Psychology*.

An extensive collection of papers was deposited in Liverpool University Archive by his biographer, Emeritus Professor L.S. Hearnshaw between 1977 and 1981 (ref. D191). A list is available (NRA 29444). The material includes reports, 1948–68, case studies, 1949–51, and research notes, 1958–71 (ref. D191/20–26). There are also notes and drafts for lectures, articles and books. In 1985 Professor Hearnshaw deposited an additional four boxes of correspondence, newspaper cuttings and notes gathered while writing the biography (ref. D336).

BURTON OF COVENTRY, BARONESS Elaine
Frances Burton (1904–91) MP (Lab) Coventry South, 1950–59.

Extensive files of correspondence with constituents, with members of the local Labour Party and with other Coventry MPs are held in the Coventry Borough Labour Party Archive at the Modern Records Centre, Warwick University. There are also various documents related to her parliamentary work and to the many campaigns with which she was involved (ref. MSS 11 and MSS 168).

BUTLER OF SAFFRON WALDEN, BARON
Richard Austen Butler (1902–82) Statesman. MP (Con) Saffron Walden, 1926–65. PUS, India Office, 1932–37. Parliamentary Secretary, Ministry of Labour, 1937–38. PUS, Foreign Office, 1938–41. President of the Board (later Minister) of Education, 1941–45. Minister of Labour, 1945. Chancellor of the Exchequer, 1951–55. Lord Privy Seal, 1955–59. Home Secretary, 1957–62. First Secretary of State and Deputy Prime Minister, 1962–63. Foreign Secretary, 1963–64.

An extensive collection of correspondence and papers was deposited at the Wren Library, Trinity College, Cambridge, on his retirement as Master of the College in 1978. A list is available (NRA 32443). The papers comprise personal correspondence and papers, 1916–76; family and genealogical papers, 1778–1956; official papers and correspondence, 1904–68; Conservative Party files, 1935–64; speeches, articles and press-cuttings, 1926–79; photographs, 1868–1964; and obituary notices, 1981. A later deposit in 1996 included some 1922 Committee papers, 1955–61. Certain papers including some constituency material are subject to restricted access. A transcript interview is held at the LSE Library, whilst there are Private Office papers in the series FO1109 at the National Archives.

BUTLER, SIR ADAM (COURTAULD) (1913–)
MP (Con) Bosworth, 1970–87. PPS to Minister of State for Foreign Affairs, 1971–72; Minister of Agriculture, Fisheries and Food, 1972–74; PPS to Leader of the Opposition, 1975–79. Minister of State, Department of Environment, 1979–81; Northern Ireland Office, 1981–84; Defence Procurement, 1984–85.

Sir Adam has retained papers relating to his political career and is prepared to consider requests for access from academic researchers.

BUTLER, BASIL CHRISTOPHER (1902–86)
Roman Catholic Auxiliary Bishop of Westminster, 1966–86. Abbot of Downside, 1946–66. Abbot President of English Benedictine Congregation, 1961–67. Theologian and ecumenist. Delegate to Vatican II, 1963.

His papers are deposited in the Westminster Diocesan Archives and include extensive correspondence. The collection is subject to a thirty-year closure rule. Earlier files relating to Vatican II are held at Downside.

BUTLER, DAVID EDGEWORTH (1924–)

Political scientist. Leading exponent of psephology. Author (or co-author) of Nuffield General Election Studies since 1951. Fellow of Nuffield College, Oxford.

David Butler states that he has retained an extensive collection of papers. They are mainly notes of interviews held (from the early 1960s onwards) with almost every type of British politician. They will ultimately be deposited in Nuffield College Library. Some restrictions on access will apply while those interviewed are alive.

BUTLER, HERBERT WILLIAM (1897–1971) MP

(Lab) Hackney South, 1945–55; Hackney Central, 1955–70.

A small collection of correspondence and pamphlets (c. eight files) is held at the London Metropolitan Archives. It includes some constituency records for 1960–68 and some earlier material covering his time as a borough councillor and his relations with the Hackney Labour Party. It is understood that he destroyed much of his correspondence.

BUTLER, SIR NEVILLE MONTAGUE (1893–1973)

Diplomat. Head of North American Department, Foreign Office, 1941–44; Assistant Under-Secretary, 1944–47. Ambassador, Brazil, 1947–51; Netherlands, 1952–54.

The Private Office papers at the Public Record Office (ref. FO 800) contain various files relating mainly to nuclear weapons and the development of atomic energy, 1947–54. The series documents the acquisition of raw materials, especially from the Belgian Congo, the implications of nuclear weapons for international relations and includes correspondence between various government leaders and papers on the development of various related advisory bodies. A list is available (NRA 23627).

BUZZARD, REAR-ADMIRAL SIR ANTHONY WASS (1902–72) Director of Naval Intelligence, 1951–54.

A large collection of papers, not at present available, has been deposited in Churchill College, Cambridge. The collection (64 boxes) includes conference papers on deterrents and disarmament (1960s); lectures; correspondence; material on the World Council of Churches; files on the Middle East and South Africa; and one file of his early naval papers.

BUZZARD, G.G. (fl. 1940s) Diplomat. Second Secretary, British Embassy, Moscow, 1946–48.

The Imperial War Museum holds three files of correspondence and cuttings from his posting in the Soviet Union, 1946–48 (ref. 87/43/1). Two files contain items from the Soviet press while the third records his domestic situation in Moscow and his removal from the posting following allegations of blackmarketeering.

C

CACCIA, BARON Sir Harold Anthony Caccia (1905–90) Diplomatic career, 1929–65. High Commissioner (and from 1951, Ambassador) Austria, 1950–54. Ambassador, United States, 1956–61. Permanent Under-Secretary, Foreign Office, 1962–65. Head of Diplomatic Service, 1964–65.

A previous survey was informed that there were no papers. The papers of Lord Avon at Birmingham University Library include correspondence, 1957–76 (ref. AP23/14).

CADOGAN, SIR ALEXANDER GEORGE MONTAGU (1884–1968) Diplomat. PUS, Foreign Office, 1938–46. Permanent Representative, United Nations, 1946–50. Government Director of Suez Canal Company, 1951–57. Chairman of the BBC, 1952–57.

The papers of Sir Alexander Cadogan (20 boxes) are deposited at Churchill College, Cambridge (ref. ACAD). A list is available (NRA 21965). There is a diary for each year from 1933 to 1967, together with scrapbooks, family and general correspondence, official papers, speeches and articles, and autobiographical drafts. The majority of the private correspondence dates from the time of his retirement. Also included are papers on the Suez Canal. Special conditions of access apply.

CAINE, SIR SYDNEY (1902–90) Assistant Under-Secretary, Colonial Office, 1944–47; Deputy Under-Secretary, 1947–48. Third Secretary, Treasury, 1948. Head of UK Treasury and Supply Delegation, Washington, 1949–51. Director, London School of Economics, 1957–67.

Sir Sydney's papers were acquired by the LSE Library in 1991. The collection mainly relates to the early history of the London School of Economics and the student unrest of 1968. There are also two diaries, 1942 and 1943; copies of articles by Janet Beveridge; and a photograph album of the West Indian Sugar Commission.

CAIRNCROSS, SIR ALEC (1911–98) Professor of Applied Economics, Glasgow University, 1951–61. Economic Adviser to the Government, 1961–64. Head of Government Economic Service, 1964–69.

The correspondence and papers for the period 1946–82 are deposited in the Glasgow University Archives (ref. DC106). A list is available (NRA 30897 and NRA(S) 2949). The material includes papers and notes on the Channel Tunnel Committee, 1980–81; correspondence and reports relating to the Radcliffe Committee on the working of the Monetary System, 1958–59; and reports on textile machinery. There are some additional more recently deposited papers (ref. ACC 1934, 1968). His Treasury diary, 1964–69 has been published.

CALDWELL, THOMAS (1921–) Stormont MP (Ind U) Belfast Willowfield, 1969–71.

Mr Caldwell has retained a collection of papers which chiefly consist of correspondence, notes and press-cuttings concerning his mediation role in 1973, as the first Northern Irish politician to hold talks with the Provisional IRA. His correspondents during this period included Harold Wilson, Reginald Maudling, William Whitelaw, Edward Heath and several journalists. Another file details his meetings with Cardinal Conway. The remainder of the collection consists of texts of Stormont speeches, press statements, election ephemera and papers relating to his long service with the Territorial Army in Northern Ireland. He will make provision for the deposit of his papers in due course.

CALLAGHAN, BARON Leonard James Callaghan (1912–2005) Statesman. MP (Lab) South Cardiff, 1945–50; South-East Cardiff, 1950–83; Cardiff South and Penarth, 1983–87. Home Secretary, 1967–70. Foreign Secretary 1974–76. Prime Minister, 1976–79.

The Callaghan papers have been brought together in the Bodleian Library, Oxford. They were deposited there after the completion of the biography by Kenneth Morgan. There are 56 boxes of papers from what was formerly two separate collections. Researchers should access the detailed Bodleian electronic catalogue.

CAMBELL, BEATRIX (1947–) Journalist, socialist and feminist.

Ms Cambell holds some papers on the development of the women's movement during the 1970s. She has also retained her working notes on *Wigan Pier Revisited* (1984) and *Iron Ladies* (1987) and the transcripts of the judicial enquiry and other material on the Cleveland child abuse case (1989).

CAMERON, BARON Marshal of the Royal Air Force Sir Neil Cameron (1920–85) Served in World War II, 1939–45. Assistant Chief of Defence Staff (Policy), 1968–70. Senior Air Staff Officer, Air Support Command, 1970–72. Air Member for Personnel, Ministry of Defence, 1974–76. Chief of the Air Staff, 1976–77. Chief of the Defence Staff, 1977–79.

Some papers have been given to the Royal Air Force Museum (ref. M10, 153). They include material on religion and on the armed forces. There are also items from his wartime service including a flying logbook for USSR operations, 1939–44. His posthumous autobiography, *In the Midst of Things*, was published in 1986, and was based on these papers and other records at the Public Record Office.

CAMPBELL, DONALD ALPHONSUS (1894–1963) Roman Catholic Archbishop of Glasgow, 1945–63; Bishop of Argyll and the Isles, 1939–45.

A collection of correspondence and papers is held at the Glasgow Archdiocesan Archive.

CAMPBELL, IAN AND THALIA (fl. 1980s) Activists in the Peace Movement and in Labour and trade union politics.

An extensive collection of papers has been deposited at the Welsh Political Archive, National Library of Wales. The collection includes correspondence, papers and leaflets on the work of Thalia Campbell as a founding member of the Greenham Common Peace Camp (1981–88). There are papers on CND and on various 'Peace Marches' from Cardiff to Greenham Common, to the Camp at RAF Brawdy, Dyfed and to several other women's peace camps. Other files concern Ian Campbell's unsuccessful Labour candidacy in the Clwyd North West constituency in the 1983 General Election and in the 1984 European Election. A substantial collection of photographs of protest meetings and marches has been deposited.

CAMPBELL-JOHNSON, ALAN (1913–98) Public Relations consultant after 1953. Political Secretary to Sir Archibald Sinclair, Parliamentary Liberal Party Leader, 1937–40. Served in World War II. Liberal candidate, 1945 and 1950 general elections. Press Attaché to Lord Mountbatten, India, 1947–48. Author of several political biographies.

Mr Campbell-Johnson's papers from his wartime service in the South East Asia Command and with Lord Mountbatten in India have been placed in the Hartley Library at the University of Southampton. They include the original of his 1947–48 diary (later published as *Mission with Mountbatten*). He also retained material concerning his period with Sir Archibald Sinclair including notes, articles, speeches and a diary, 1936–39. The bulk of his papers relate to his post-war career in public relations.

CAMPION, 1ST BARON Gilbert Francis Montriou Campion (1882–1958) Clerk of the House of Commons, 1937–48; Clerk of the Consultative Assembly, Council of Europe, 1949. Editor of *May's Parliamentary Practice* (14th and 15th editions).

There are twenty boxes of papers covering the period 1906–58 in the House of Lords Record Office (ref. Hist Coll 259). The contents include parliamentary diaries, a diary and papers recording an official tour of Commonwealth Parliaments, 1948–49, and also files relating to his period at the Council of Europe. There are copies of articles and lectures, also various notes and drafts relating to publications, and some papers on the Inter-Parliamentary Union and the History of Parliament Trust.

CANNON, SIR LESLIE (1920–70) Trade union leader. General President of the Electrical Trades Union from 1963. Member of the Trades Union Congress General Council from 1965; and of the Industrial Corporation from 1966.

A collection of correspondence and papers (largely concerning the early 1960s campaign against the Communist leadership of the Electrical, Electronic, Telecommunications and Plumbing Union) can be found at the Modern Records Centre, Warwick University (ref. MSS 137). A list is available (NRA 29717).

CARADON, 1ST BARON Sir Hugh Mackintosh Foot (1907–90) Diplomat. Colonial Secretary, Cyprus, 1943–45; Jamaica, 1945–47. Chief Secretary, Nigeria, 1947–51. Governor, Jamaica, 1951–57; Cyprus, 1957–60. Ambassador, United Nations, 1961–62. Minister of State for Foreign and Commonwealth Affairs and UK Permanent Representative, United Nations, 1964–70.

A recorded interview and transcript covering his career are held at Rhodes House Library, Oxford. His memoirs, *A Start in Freedom*, appeared in 1964. No other papers have been located.

CAROE, SIR OLAF KIRKPATRICK (1892–1981) Indian Civil Service and Indian Political Service career, 1920–47. Foreign Secretary, Government of India. Governor, North-West Frontier Province, 1946–47.

Two separate collections of papers have been placed in the India Office Library. The first consists of 12 boxes of correspondence and papers, 1946–81, among them items relating to his Governorship of the North West Frontier Province, 1946–47 (ref. MSS Eur F 203). A list is available (NRA 27558). The collection also includes material relating to his literary and retirement activities (among them his involvement in Tibetan affairs following the Chinese invasion and the flight of the Dalai Lama from Tibet). There is also some official correspondence with the British Government regarding Sikkim. The second deposit consists of his autobiographical narratives (ref. MSS Eur C 273). Additional correspondence, 1959–63, is available in the papers of Sir Robert Reid (also at the India Office Library).

CARR OF HADLEY, BARON (Leonard) Robert Carr (1916–) MP (Con) Mitcham, 1950–Feb. 1974; Carshalton, Feb. 1974–76. Parliamentary Secretary, Ministry of Labour and National Service, 1955–58, Secretary for Technical Co-operation, 1963–64.

Employment Secretary, 1970–72. Lord President of the Council and Leader of the House of Commons, 1972. Home Secretary, 1972–74.

Lord Carr states that he has not kept his papers systematically, but has retained some material which has now been deposited at the Bodleian Library, Oxford. The collection refers principally to his membership of the Shadow Cabinet (1967–70) and the various policy studies set up by Edward Heath after he became Leader of the Party in 1965. The papers especially document Lord Carr's work as Shadow Minister for Labour, his chairmanship of the study group responsible for drafting what eventually became the 1970 Industrial Relations Bill and Sir Edward Heath's efforts to establish closer contact and better understanding between businessmen and politicians. There are also copies of speech notes and articles, together with a certain amount of personal correspondence. In addition, Lord Carr retained the transcripts of two interviews conducted by Anthony Seldon as part of the Oral Archives Project. Transcripts of these interviews are also held at the LSE Library and applications for access should be made to the Archivist.

CARR-SAUNDERS, SIR ALEXANDER (1886–1966) Social scientist and academic. Director, London School of Economics, 1937–56. Member of the Commission on Higher Education in the Colonies, 1943–45; and Chairman of its Statistical Committee. Chairman of the Commission for Higher Education for Africans in Central Africa in 1943.

No significant collection of papers has yet been found. However, the LSE Library holds some of his LSE administrative files in addition to material on his research activities and public service. In addition, his son, Dr Edmund Carr-Saunders, has donated letters of congratulation on his father's appointment as Director of the London School of Economics and his engagement diaries, 1945–65.

CARRON, BARON Sir William John Carron (1901–69) Trade union leader. President, Amalgamated Engineering Union 1956–67. Chairman, British Productivity Council, 1959–68. A Director of the Bank of England from 1963.

A substantial collection of papers (some 47 boxes) was deposited at Churchill College, Cambridge, in

1970 (ref. CARN). A list is available (NRA 26807). The main categories include: the Amalgamated Engineering Union and Industrial Relations; offices, societies, honours; correspondence; diaries; lectures, articles, reports; press-cuttings; photographs; personal material; books and pamphlets. The largest part of the collection relates to his period as President of the Amalgamated Engineering Union. In addition, there are transcripts of speeches and writings by Carron and others on industrial harmony and productivity. The growth of the communist faction within the AEU is also reflected in the papers as is his work for other commercial and educational bodies (including his chairmanship of the All Party Group for the Chemical Industry and as a Governor of the Ditchley Foundation).

CARTER, RAYMOND JOHN (1935–) MP (Lab) Birmingham Northfield, 1970–79.

Mr Carter has retained some papers including files on British Leyland and on the 1976 Congenital Disabilities (Civil Liability) Act. These are to be deposited in the LSE Library.

CARTER, SIR RICHARD HENRY ARCHIBALD (1887–1958) Civil servant. Pre-war career in the India Office. Permanent Secretary, Admiralty, 1936–40. Chairman, Board of Customs and Excise, 1942–47. Permanent Under-Secretary, India Office, 1947. Joint PUS, Commonwealth Relations, 1948. Chairman, Monopolies and Restrictive Practices Commission, 1949–53.

Some papers are held at the India Office Library (ref. MSS Eur C.200). A list is available (NRA 27459). These are mainly notes on the powers of the Secretary of State for India and the Council of India. In addition, there are files relating to the future of India, Burma, Kashmir and Pakistan.

CARTLEDGE, SIR BRYAN (GEORGE) (1931–) Diplomat, 1960–88. Head of East European and Soviet Department, Foreign and Commonwealth Office, 1983–84. Private Secretary to Prime Minister (Overseas Affairs), 1977–79. Ambassador, Hungary, 1980–83; Soviet Union, 1985–88.

Sir Bryan informed the LSE in 1992 that he did not keep a diary during his career and that he did not retain any classified material. The papers of Lord Avon at Birmingham University include Sir Bryan's letters to him, 1958–69.

CARVER, BARON Field Marshal (Richard) Michael (Power) Carver (1915–2001) Army officer and military historian. Tank Commander during World War II. Staff Officer, Supreme Headquarters, Allied Powers, Europe, 1952. Deputy Chief of Staff, East Africa, 1954; Chief of Staff, East Africa, 1955. Director of Plans, War Office, 1958–59. Commanded Joint Truce Force, Cyprus, and Deputy Commander, United Nations Forces in Cyprus, 1964. Director, Army Staff Duties, Ministry of Defence, 1964–66. Commanded Far East Land Forces, 1966–67. Commander-in-Chief, Far East, 1967–69. Chief of the General Staff, 1971–73. Chief of the Defence Staff, 1973–78. Designated British Resident Commissioner in Rhodesia, 1977–78.

The Imperial War Museum has some papers, 1939–2002, including material on his United Nations command in Cyprus. Certain sections are closed. The Museum's Department of Sound Records holds an interview concerning his role in Rhodesia, September 1977 (ref. 6919/1). Copies of several unpublished lectures on his peacekeeping role during the 1960s have been given to the United Nations project at the Bodleian Library, Oxford.

CASEY, BARON Sir Richard Gardiner Casey (1890–1970) Australian diplomat and politician. Minister of State Resident, Middle East, and member of War Cabinet, 1942–43. Governor, Bengal, 1944–46. Federal President, Liberal Party of Australia, 1947–49. Cabinet Minister, 1950–60; Minister for External Affairs, 1951–60. Resigned from Government and Parliament, 1960. Governor-General, Australia, 1965–69.

Copies of Lord Casey's diaries as Governor of Bengal, 1944–46, are deposited in the India Office Library (ref. Photo Eur 48).

For the present location of the main collection of papers, which include diaries kept over many years, correspondence, bound volumes of his public statements, and volumes of press-cuttings, see *British Cabinet Ministers, 1900–51*. During his lifetime, these were not generally available for research, but several books based on them were published including his *Personal Experience 1939–46* (1962) and *Australian*

Foreign Minister, The Diaries of R. G. Casey 1951–60 (edited by T. B. Millar, 1972).

CASTLE OF BLACKBURN, BARONESS Barbara Anne Castle (1910–2002) MP (Lab) Blackburn, 1945–50; Blackburn East, 1950–55; Blackburn, 1955–79. MEP (Lab) Greater Manchester North, 1979–84; Greater Manchester West, 1984–89.

The papers have been deposited at the Bodleian Library, Oxford. Lady Castle's diaries, 1964–76, have been published in two volumes. The original typescripts of her diaries are in the J.B. Priestley Library, University of Bradford.

CATHERWOOD, SIR HENRY FREDERICK ROSS (1925–) Conservative MEP. Vice-President, European Parliament.

His papers relating to Europe were deposited in Churchill College, Cambridge, in 1995. The papers (19 boxes) concern particularly economic, political and monetary union, CAP, GATT, Northern Ireland and relations with Eastern Europe. A list is available (NRA 43998). His constituency papers are in Cambridgeshire County Record Office (ref. R94/50). They are closed for 30 years from the date of creation.

CATLIN, SIR GEORGE EDWARD GORDON (1896–1979) Political scientist. Provost, Mar Ivanios College, South India, 1951. Bronman Professor of Political Science, McGill University, 1956–60. Joint founder, American and British Commonwealth Association.

A very large collection of papers concerning Sir George Catlin and his wife, Vera Brittain (q.v.), is housed in the Library of McMaster University, Hamilton, Ontario. The collection includes an extensive 50-year correspondence with his wife, as well as Catlin's correspondence with various British and American literary, political and other public figures. There are also lecture notes, book manuscripts and biographical material.

CATLING, SIR RICHARD CHARLES (1912–) Colonial police officer; Palestine, 1935–48; Federation of Malaya, 1948–54; Commissioner of Police, Kenya 1954–63; Inspector-General of Police, Kenya, 1963–64.

A collection of papers mainly relating to Palestine is held at the Rhodes House Library, Oxford (ref. MSS Medit s 20). The material includes intelligence briefings on illegal Jewish organisations; notes and memoranda on prominent individuals; notes on Jewish-Arab co-operation, 1909–41; and situation reports for 1947. The Department of Sound Records at the Imperial War Museum holds an interview covering his entire career (ref. 10392/9).

CATTERMOLE, JIM (fl. 1940s–70s) East Midlands and London Labour Party Regional Organiser.

Material relating to his time as a Labour Party Regional Organiser has been deposited at the Modern Records Centre, University of Warwick (ref. MSS 9). There are files on the organisation of election campaigns in the East Midlands during the 1950s; constituency boundary reviews, and party organisation from the mid-1960s to early 1970s. His reports to the Labour Party National Agent, 1940s–70s, are of particular interest.

CATTO, 1ST BARON Thomas Sivewright Catto (1879–1959) Governor, Bank of England, 1944–49.

Three files of his papers can be found in the archives of the Bank of England (ref. G18). A list is available (NRA 33132).

CAZALET, VICE-ADMIRAL SIR PETER GRENVILLE LYON (1899–1982) Naval career, 1918–56. Served in World War II. Deputy Director of Plans, 1946–47. Chief of Staff to Flag Officer, Central Europe, 1950–52; and to Allied Commander-in-Chief Mediterranean, 1953–55. Flag Officer Commanding Reserve Fleet, 1955–56.

His papers and correspondence (1940–57) are deposited at the Imperial War Museum. A list is available (NRA 28532). The material for the post-war period includes situation reports from Shanghai, 1948–49, and on the Yangtse Incident of 1949; files on NATO issues, 1951–55, and on the Nevada atom bomb tests, 1955; and letters from Lord Mountbatten, 1950–56.

CHAIN, SIR ERNST (BORIS) (1906–79) Professor of Biochemistry, Imperial College, University of London, 1961–73. Émigré from Nazi Germany. Winner of Nobel Prize.

Some papers are at the Contemporary Medical Archives Centre, the Wellcome Institute. There is material on Jewish refugees and the National Council for Soviet Jewry.

CHALFONT, BARON Alun Arthur Gwynne Jones (1919–) Journalist and politician. Military career, 1940–61. Defence Correspondent, *The Times*, 1961–64. Minister of State, Foreign and Commonwealth Office, 1964–70. Foreign Editor, *New Statesman*, 1970–71.

The papers have been placed in the Bodleian Library, Oxford. Enquiries regarding access should be directed to the Archivist.

CHAMBERLAIN, GEORGE DIGBY (1898–1994) Colonial civil servant. Colonial Secretary, The Gambia, 1943–47; Acting Governor, 1943–44. Chief Secretary, Western Pacific High Commission, 1947–52.

Rhodes House Library, Oxford acquired his papers as Chief Secretary of the Western Pacific High Commission in 1968.

CHANDOS, 1ST VISCOUNT Oliver Lyttelton (1893–1972) MP (Con) Aldershot, 1940–54. President of the Board of Trade, 1940–41 and 1945. Minister of State, 1941–42. Minister of State Resident in the Middle East, 1942. Minister of Production, 1942–45. Secretary of State for the Colonies, 1951–54.

His family's papers and correspondence (1906–72) are deposited at Churchill College, Cambridge (ref. Lyttleton Papers). A list is available (NRA 19700). With the exception of his World War I letters, they contain little on his own career. His Private Office papers as Colonial Secretary are in the Public Record Office (ref. CO 967/239–276). A list is available (NRA 28778).

CHANNON, SIR HENRY (1897–1958) MP (Con) Southend-on-Sea, 1935–50; Southend-on-Sea West, 1950–58.

The diaries he kept between 1934 and 1952 have been published as *Chips: The Diaries of Sir Henry Channon*, edited by Robert Rhodes James (1967). Additional diaries covering the period 1954–58 were discovered in 1991. All the originals remain with the trustees of the estate.

CHAPMAN, GUY PATTERSON (1899–1972) Historian and author. Professor of Modern History, Leeds University, 1945–53.

The manuscript of his work, *A Passionate Prodigality*, is in Churchill College, Cambridge, together with other material including items concerning his wife, Storm Jameson, and letters from Sir Basil Liddell Hart. The papers of Monty Belgion, also at Churchill College, include some correspondence while the Liddell Hart papers in the Liddell Hart Centre, King's College, London, contain extensive correspondence. Some literary correspondence from the 1920s is in Washington University Library, St Louis, Missouri. Material concerning his service in World War I is deposited in the Brotherton Library, Leeds University.

CHAPPLE, BARON Francis Joseph Chapple (1921–) General Secretary, Electrical, Electronic, Telecommunications and Plumbing Union, 1966–84.

Lord Chapple states that his papers are currently unavailable. They are to be deposited eventually at the LSE Library.

CHASTON, N. (fl. 1970s) Advocate of British withdrawal from Northern Ireland. Organiser of the 'Bring Back the Boys from Ulster' campaign, 1973–74.

The Imperial War Museum holds 15 files and two scrapbooks of letters concerning the above campaign. Correspondents include Michael Heseltine, Lord Mason, Lord Prior, and Peter Shore.

CHATAWAY, CHRISTOPHER JOHN (1931–) MP (Con) Lewisham North, 1959–66; Chichester, May 1969–Sept. 1974. Minister of Posts and Telecommunications, 1970–72; Minister for Industrial Development, Department of Trade and Industry, 1972–74.

Mr Chataway states that he has retained his papers and will make provision for their eventual deposit.

CHELWOOD, BARON Sir Tufton Victor Hamilton Beamish (1917–89) MP (Con) Lewes, 1945–Feb. 1974.

The papers are deposited at the East Sussex Record Office and at Churchill College, Cambridge. A list is available (NRA 28523). The East Sussex Record

Office holds his Lewes parliamentary constituency papers and general political files, including papers on his role as observer in the 1980 Zimbabwe General Election and various publications and speeches. Churchill College, Cambridge, holds a political diary, some correspondence and notes for an auto-biography. Copies of some of the papers held at Churchill College are also available in the East Sussex Record Office.

CHERWELL, 1ST VISCOUNT Frederick Alexander Lindemann (1886–1957) Personal Assistant to the Prime Minister, 1940–42. Paymaster-General, 1942–45 and 1951–53.

An extensive collection of papers has been deposited at Nuffield College, Oxford. A list is available (NRA 16447). Among the papers are seven boxes of minutes for the Prime Minister, and a large collection of personal and social correspondence. There are also subject files which cover a variety of topics including military and scientific questions; politics and the Conservative Party; refugees; atomic power; post-war research; reconstruction and reparations. Cabinet Office papers are held at the Public Record Office (ref. CAB 127/194–203). A list is available (NRA 32409). These papers deal mainly with technical warfare matters, and were also prepared by Cherwell during his time as special adviser to the Prime Minister. One section deals with advice on the currency crisis of 1952.

CHESHAM, LADY MARION (1903–78) Political activist in Capricorn Africa Society. Member of Tanganyika Legislative Council from 1958 and sub-sequently member of National Assembly, Tanzania until 1972. Intermediary between Julius Nyerere's TANU nationalist party and government officials during 1960s negotiations.

The Centre for Southern African Studies, University of York, has a collection of papers. Box I contains correspondence with, among others, officials of the Capricorn Africa Society and its suc-cessor, the Tanganyikan National Society; with Julius Nyerere, 1961–65; and members of the Legislative Council. Box II includes material on the Legislative Council; correspondence and documents on the 1964 army mutiny; diaries and notebooks from 1958–63. Box III includes press-cuttings, photographs and

Nyerere's notebook on British history. Box IV contains further correspondence and miscellaneous materials.

CHESHIRE, GROUP CAPTAIN (GEOFFREY) LEONARD (1917–92) Royal Air Force career until 1946. Won VC during World War II; member of British Joint Staff Mission, Washington, 1945; official British observer at dropping of atomic bomb on Nagasaki, 1945. Founder of Cheshire Foundation Homes for the Sick.

The Imperial War Museum holds a collection of papers including flying logbooks and accounts of and articles about Hiroshima and Nagasaki. The Museum's Department of Sound Records holds a 1945 British Forces Broadcast Service interview regarding his role at Nagasaki (ref. 6984/E/B).

CHESHIRE, AIR CHIEF MARSHAL SIR WALTER (GRAEMES) (1907–78) Royal Air Force career. Air Officer Commanding, French Indo-China, 1945–46; Gibraltar, 1950–52; Malta, 1959–61. Air Member for Personnel, Ministry of Defence, 1964–65.

His memoir of the Allied Disarmament Mission in Saigon in 1945, entitled *The Gremlin Task Force*, was acquired by Churchill College, Cambridge, in April 1979.

CHESTER, SIR (DANIEL) NORMAN (1907–86) Political economist. Warden of Nuffield College, 1954–78; Fellow, 1945–54. Served in Economic Section, War Cabinet Secretariat, 1942–45.

His working papers and manuscripts were left to the Library of Nuffield College, Oxford.

CHEVINS, HUGH (1898–1975) Journalist. On staff of the *Daily Telegraph* from 1934, first as news editor and later as industrial and labour correspondent.

Seven boxes of correspondence and press-cuttings on industrial and labour related issues, mainly after World War II, are held at the LSE Library. A list is available (NRA 25120).

CHICHESTER-CLARK, SIR ROBERT (ROBIN) (1928–) MP (UU) Londonderry, 1955–Feb. 1974. Chief Opposition Spokesman on Northern Ireland, 1964–70. Minister of State, Department of Employment, 1972–74.

Sir Robin has retained some papers. They are unsorted at present but he intends to make provision for them in due course.

CHILDS, HUBERT (1905–83) Colonial Service. Chief Commissioner, Sierra Leone, 1949–59. Administrator, Southern Cameroons plebiscite, 1960–61. Observer, Malta referendum, 1964.

Rhodes House Library, Oxford, holds a series of journals, reports and papers covering his career in West Africa (ref. MSS Afr s1861).

CHORLEY, 1ST BARON Robert Samuel Theodore Chorley (1895–1986) Sir Ernest Cassel Professor of Commercial and Industrial Law, University of London, 1930–46. Lord in Waiting, 1946–50.

The LSE Library holds a small collection of papers (ref. Coll Misc 299). A list is available (NRA 28876). These contain largely printed material on governmental committees of which he was a member. Some additional papers on his membership of the Parliamentary Delegation to India (1946) can be found at the Centre for South Asian Studies, Cambridge.

CHRISTIE, J. STUART (1946–) Anarchist, activist and writer.

A few papers are held at the International Institute of Social History, Amsterdam. The collection is mostly photocopies and press-cuttings together with some correspondence and documents. There are subject files on his trial and imprisonment for an attempted attack on Franco, 1964–67, and the arrest in Germany of Brenda Earl Christie in 1970. Additional papers concern the trial and imprisonment of anarchists in Spain, Italy, etc., 1961–74; photocopies of documents related to John Olday and a manuscript of his *Spartacus 1918–74 and Insurgent Anarchism*. There are also typescripts of *The Christie File* and *The Floodgates of Anarchy* (written with Albert Melzner).

CHRISTISON, GENERAL SIR ALEXANDER FRANK PHILIP (1893–1993) Military career. Served in World War II. Commander-in-Chief, Allied Land Forces, South-East Asia, 1945; Allied Commander, Dutch East Indies, 1945–46.

Typescript copies of his memoirs, written in 1980, are held by the Imperial War Museum and Churchill College, Cambridge.

CHURCHILL, SIR WINSTON LEONARD SPENCER (1874–1965) MP (Con) Oldham, 1900–04; (Lib) 1904–06; (Lib) Manchester North-West, 1906–08; Dundee, 1908–22; (Con) Epping, 1924–45; Woodford, 1945–64. President, Board of Trade, 1908–10; Home Secretary, 1910–11; First Lord of the Admiralty, 1911–15 and 1939–40; Chancellor of the Duchy of Lancaster, 1915; Minister of Munitions, 1917–19; Secretary of State for War and Air, 1919–21; Colonies, 1921–22; Chancellor of the Exchequer, 1924–29; Minister of Defence, 1940–45; Prime Minister, 1940–45 and 1951–55.

The papers are currently held at Churchill College, Cambridge, to where all enquiries concerning access should be addressed. The Chartwell papers (*c.* 2,000 boxes), covering the period 1874–1945, were opened in late 1992 (NRA 20556). The Churchill papers covering the period 1945–65 (*c.* 1,000 boxes) were opened shortly thereafter. It is planned to put all the papers on the Internet. His Private Office papers as Prime Minister are in the Public Record Office (ref. PREM).

CHURCHILL, WINSTON SPENCER (1940–) MP (Con) Stretford, 1970–83; Daveyhulme, 1983–97.

Mr Churchill has retained his papers.

CHUTER-EDE, BARON James Chuter Ede (1882–1965) MP (Lab) Mitcham, Mar.-Nov. 1923; South Shields, 1929–31 and 1935–64. Parliamentary Secretary, Ministry of Education, 1940–45. Home Secretary, 1945–51.

Correspondence and papers are held at the Surrey Record Office, Kingston. A list is available (NRA 20267). Included in the collection are constituency papers; material relating to his work with the National Union of Teachers and Surrey County Council; and diaries for the period 1946–49. Some Private Office papers relating to education are held at the Public Record Office (ref. ED 136). The British Library holds 14 volumes of diaries and a few related papers. The BBC Written Archives Centre has a collection of press-cuttings, interviews, letters, and the transcript of an interview given in 1960. Epsom

Borough Library holds Chuter-Ede's library, as well as various literary papers, photographs, and newspaper cuttings.

CILCENNIN, 1ST VISCOUNT James Prudon Lewes Thomas (1903–60) MP (Con) Hereford, 1931–55; Junior Lord of the Treasury, 1940–43; Financial Secretary to the Admiralty, 1943–45; First Lord of the Admiralty, 1951–56.

Some correspondence and papers are held at the Dyfed Record Office (Carmarthen) (ref. ACC 5605). A list is available (NRA 24422). The material consists mainly of correspondence with Bobbety Cranborne on the internal rifts within the Conservative Party, 1945–51, its attempts to generate greater public support, and the factional struggle to oust Churchill from the leadership. There are also letters from Earl Mountbatten and Prince Philip, when Cilcennin was First Lord of the Admiralty.

CITRINE, 1ST BARON Walter McLennan Citrine (1887–1983) Trade union leader. Assistant Secretary, Trades Union Congress, 1924–25; General Secretary, 1926–46. President, International Federation of Trades Unions, 1928–45. Chairman, Central Electricity Authority, 1947–57.

Certain papers are in the LSE Library. A list is available (NRA 21464). The collection contains diaries and diary notes, 1924–57; correspondence and papers, including visits to Germany in 1946; papers on the Industrial Relations Bill, 1970; and files on contemporaries such as Lord Beaverbrook, Ernest Bevin and Winston Churchill.

CLAGUE, SIR JOHN (1882–1958) Indian and Burmese Civil Service. Adviser to the Secretary of State for India, 1942–48.

Some correspondence, diaries and papers, 1898–1947, are in the India Office Library (ref. MSS Eur E 252). A list is available (NRA 30188). The material includes several reports on post-war reconstruction in Burma and constitutional developments prior to independence. The correspondence includes some letters to his wife describing in detail the work of the Boundary Commission.

CLARK, BARON Kenneth Mckenzie Clark (1903–83) Art historian. Director of the National Gallery, 1934–45. Slade Professor of Fine Art, Oxford, 1946–50. Numerous public offices, including Chairman of the Arts Council of Great Britain, 1953–60 and Chairman, Independent Television Authority (ITA), 1954–57.

The papers and correspondence have been placed in Tate Britain, London (NRA 32463). The collection includes correspondence, diaries and other papers covering the period 1925–81.

CLARK, ALAN KENNETH MCKENZIE (1928–99) MP (Con) Sutton, Feb. 1974–92. Under-Secretary of State, Department of Employment, 1983–86; Minister for Trade, 1986–89; Minister of State, Ministry of Defence, 1989–92.

Mr Clark retained extensive papers. They include detailed diaries (published in 1993); constituency case files; and material on the Falklands War, the EC Presidency and recent defence policy including the 'Options for Change' review of 1991. The papers are currently with his widow.

CLARK, SIR GEORGE ANTHONY (1914–91) Northern Ireland politician. Senator, Northern Ireland Parliament, 1951–69. President, Ulster Unionist Council, 1980.

His political papers are in the Public Record Office of Northern Ireland (ref. D/4234).

CLARK, SIR THOMAS FIFE (1907–85) Public Relations and Principal Press Officer, Ministry of Health, 1939–49. Controller of Home Publicity at the Central Office of Information, 1949–52; Adviser on Government Public Relations and Adviser on Public Relations to Sir Winston Churchill and Sir Anthony Eden, 1952–55; Director-General, Central Office of Information, 1954–71.

A collection of papers is held at Churchill College, Cambridge (ref. FICA). A list is available (NRA 31390). The collection covers his early career as a parliamentary correspondent, including information papers on enemy propaganda and overseas broadcasts during World War II, but there are also papers related to the Central Office of Information and insights into the daily running of the department. Relatively little has survived on his work for Churchill and Eden. However, there are some taped reminiscences on Churchill (poor sound quality), as well as press-cuttings, personal papers and photographs.

CLARK, WILLIAM DONALDSON (1916–85) President, International Institute for Environment and Development, 1980–85. Press Attaché, British Embassy, Washington, 1945–46. Diplomatic correspondent of the *Observer*, 1950–56. Public Relations Adviser to Anthony Eden, 1955–56. Third World correspondent for BBC and the *Observer*, 1957. Director, Overseas Development Institute, 1960–68. Director, then Vice-President, World Bank, 1968–80.

A large collection of papers has been deposited in the Bodleian Library, Oxford. A list is available (NRA 36204). The collection is a valuable source for the history of the *Observer*, broadcasting, post-war British politics and Third World development. The material comprises diaries, notebooks, correspondence files, texts of broadcasts and speeches, notes and papers used in his publications, press-cuttings and photographs. One of the most important components of the collection is the original of the diary which he kept from September 1955 to November 1956. This records his resignation from Anthony Eden's staff in protest at the handling of the Suez crisis. The letters sent to Clark after Suez, which were used in a volume of memoirs *From Three Worlds*, published posthumously, are not part of the collection, and cannot now be located. Most of the collection is open except the post-1970 material which is at present restricted. These sections include files on his close association with Robert MacNamara at the World Bank, 1968–80, and on the Social Democratic Party, 1982–84.

CLARKE, ALEXANDER (fl. 1940s–50s) Journalist and civil servant, Northern Ireland. On staff of *Belfast Telegraph* and *Belfast Newsletter* until World War II; on editorial staff of Northern Ireland House of Commons Debates, 1943–47; assistant clerk, Stormont, 1948–52. On retirement worked as publicity officer to the Ulster Unionist Council.

About 250 files and volumes of papers are held in the Public Record Office of Northern Ireland (ref. D2519). They include background biographical notes on Northern Irish MPs for both the Stormont and Westminster parliaments; files on the Ulster Unionist

Council and its membership, 1903–47; notebooks, cuttings and returns relating to elections in Ulster, 1918–35; and material on the Irish Boundary question, 1920–24.

CLARKE, SIR (HENRY) ASHLEY (1903–94) Diplomat, 1925–62; Ambassador to Italy, 1953–62. Governor of the BBC, 1962–67.

Sir Ashley informed the LSE Library in 1992 that he had retained his papers. He did not keep a diary. The papers of Lord Avon in Birmingham University Library include correspondence, 1957–62 (ref. AP23/21).

CLARKE, KENNETH (HARRY) (1940–) MP (Con) Rushcliffe since 1970. Under-Secretary of State for Transport, 1979–82; Minister of State, Department of Health and Social Security, 1982–85; Paymaster-General and Minister for Employment, 1985–87; Chancellor of Duchy of Lancaster and Minister for Trade and Industry, 1987–88; Secretary of State for Health, 1988–90; Education and Science, 1990–92; Home Secretary, 1992–93; Chancellor of the Exchequer, 1993–97.

Mr Clarke states that he has kept a considerable quantity of papers throughout most of his parliamentary career. His papers are being transferred to the Bodleian Library, Oxford, at regular intervals. Access to the material will not be permitted during his lifetime.

CLARKE, SIR RALPH STEPHENSON (1892–1970) MP (Con) East Grinstead, 1936–55.

The Imperial War Museum holds his World War II diaries, kept between 1941 and 1945. These cover his command of the 12th Light Anti-Aircraft Regiment RA, with which he served in the Middle East and Mediterranean theatres of war. The diaries for the last year of the war include useful comments about the major parliamentary debates which he attended and the background to and conduct of the 1945 election. Other papers concerning his demobilisation from the army in 1944, together with some press-cuttings and notes on a visit to Russia have remained in family possession. His parliamentary correspondence and files have apparently not survived.

CLARKE, SIR RICHARD (1910–75) Civil servant. Permanent Secretary, Ministry of Technology, 1966–70.

Some 40 boxes of papers are deposited in Churchill College, Cambridge (ref. CLRK). They include departmental files, 1966–69; speeches, lectures and published writings; and some personal correspondence and press-cuttings. Enquiries regarding access should be directed to the Archivist.

CLAUSEN, HUGH (1888–1972) Naval armaments engineer. Chief Technical Adviser to Naval Ordnance Department of the Admiralty from 1936.

Clausen's technical papers, lectures and other material, are in Churchill College, Cambridge. A list is available (NRA 18561). The collection consists of technical papers, 1938–62; articles, 1940–60; lectures, 1947–70; miscellaneous material, including press-cuttings and correspondence with Sir Roy Harrod; personal papers, including naval service records, 1914–18, and official papers about this service; his history of Branch 5 of the Electrical Engineering Department of the Admiralty; and Captain Stephen Roskill's correspondence on Clausen.

CLAUSON, SIR GERALD LESLIE MAKINS (1891–1974) Colonial Service, 1919–51; Assistant Under-Secretary, 1940–51.

His family returned all his official papers to the Foreign and Commonwealth Office (Commonwealth Relations Office) except for World War II diaries kept in a form of Turkish shorthand which have remained with his son. His World War I diary, some notebooks and wartime letters are in the Imperial War Museum. His Chinese philology papers are deposited in the School of Oriental and African Studies in the University of London. The papers of Sydney Moody, in Rhodes House Library, Oxford, include some correspondence, 1942–46, regarding Palestine.

CLEDWYN OF PENRHOS, BARON Cledwyn Hughes (1916–2001) MP (Lab) Anglesey 1951–79. Leader of the Opposition, House of Lords, 1982–92. Opposition spokesman on Housing and Local Government 1959–64; Minister of State for Commonwealth Relations 1964–66; Welsh Secretary, 1966–68; Minister of Agriculture, Fisheries and Food 1968–70. Chairman, Parliamentary Labour Party, 1974–79.

Some papers, covering the period c. 1945–82, have been placed in the Library of the University College of North Wales at Bangor. Further records are in the Welsh Political Archive, National Library of Wales. These include files accumulated as Secretary of State for Wales, 1966–68, and as Minister of Agriculture, 1968–70, as well as his 1970–78 diary. This contains his notes on the resignation of Harold Wilson as Prime Minister in 1976 and the election of James Callaghan as his successor. As PLP Chairman, Cledwyn was in charge of organising this election. A list is available (NRA 37128).

CLEGG, SIR 'ALEC' (ALEXANDER BRADSHAW) (1909–86) Chief Education Officer, West Riding County Council, 1945–74.

A collection of West Riding Education Authority committee papers (73 boxes) is held at the Brotherton Library, Leeds University (ref. MS 731). The papers cover 1902–74 but mostly relate to the post-1945 period.

CLEGG, HUGH ARMSTRONG (1920–95) Professor of Industrial Relations, University of Warwick, 1967–79. Member, Royal Commission on Trades Unions and Employers' Associations, 1965–68; Committee of Inquiry into Port Transport Industry, 1964–65; Committee of Inquiry into Seamen's Dispute, 1966–67; National Board for Prices and Incomes, 1966–67; Committee of Inquiry into Local Authorities Manual Workers' Pay Dispute, 1970.

The Modern Records Centre, University of Warwick, holds extensive documentation from Professor Clegg's membership of various commissions and courts of inquiry and from his chairmanship of the Standing Commission on Pay Comparability. The deposits also include arbitration files; professional correspondence for 1966 only; and miscellaneous original material, especially relating to industrial relations in the boot and shoe industry, mainly pre-1914 (ref MSS 35 and 54).

CLEMENT, JOHN HANDEL (1920–) Civil servant, Welsh Office, 1946–81; Under-Secretary, 1976–81.

A collection of papers is held at the National Library of Wales. This includes memoranda on

Welsh social and economic difficulties during the 1940s and 1950s. There is also material relating to the Welsh Reconstruction Advisory Council (1942–45) and the Council of Wales (1949–58).

CLIFF, TONY (1917–2000) Trotskyist. Member, Revolutionary Communist Party. Founded Socialist Review Group, which became International Socialism Tendency in 1962. Founder and leader of Socialist Workers Party.

Some papers have been placed in the Modern Records Centre, University of Warwick (ref. MSS 459). The papers include notes for books, personalia, and a collection of his publications.

CLIFFORD, ESMOND HUMPHREY MILLER (1895–1970) Served in World War I. Senior British Commissioner, British Somaliland–Ethiopia Boundary Commission, 1931–36. Chief Engineer, China Command, 1940–41; Prisoner of War, 1941–45. British Commissioner, Kenya-Ethiopia Boundary Commission, 1950–57.

There are seven boxes of papers, photographs and printed material in the Liddell Hart Centre, King's College, London. They include material on the Boundary Commission which consists of diaries, 1951–55; correspondence, 1950–60 (including letters exchanged with the Ethiopian Government, 1956–60); and the Commission's reports.

CLIFFORD, SIR (GEOFFREY) MILES (1897–1986) Military and Colonial Service. Governor of the Falkland Islands, 1946–54.

Ten boxes of papers, 1930–78, are held at BLCAS (Rhodes House Library), Oxford (ref. MSS Brit Emp s 517). These include his papers as Governor of the Falkland Islands, 1946–54, and as Chairman of the United Nigeria Group (Biafran war), and other records relating to Nigeria. There are also tape recordings and the transcript of an interview. A set of additional papers on the Falkland Islands Dependencies Survey and polar regions is held at the Scott Polar Research Institute, Cambridge.

CLISSOLD, STEPHEN (1913–82) Public servant and writer. On staff of British Council in Yugoslavia during the 1930s and member of British Military Mission during World War II. Post-war career with

British Council and Foreign Office (researcher on Latin-American affairs).

His correspondence and papers, 1940–82, have been placed in the Bodleian Library, Oxford, and are a useful source for Anglo-Yugoslav and Anglo-Hispanic relations (ref. MSS Eng c 2683–92, c 2695).

CLUTTERBUCK, MAJOR-GENERAL RICHARD LEWIS (1917–98) Army career. Colonel Commandant, Royal Engineers, 1972–77. Expert on terrorism. Reader in Politics, University of Exeter, 1972–83. Author of numerous works on guerrilla warfare, etc.

Two boxes (11 files) of his papers on international terrorism, 1971–95, are in Churchill College, Cambridge (ref. CLBK)(NRA 43181).

CLWYD, ANN (1937–) MP (Lab) Cynon Valley since May 1984; MEP, Mid and West Wales, 1979–84.

Her constituency papers, 1979–86, have been placed in the Glamorgan Record Office (ref. D/D MP2).

COATES, KENNETH SIDNEY (1930–) MEP (Lab., then Ind. Lab.) Nottingham (then Nottinghamshire North and Chesterfield) 1989–99. Member, Bertrand Russell Peace Foundation, Institute of Workers Control, etc.

His political papers have been placed in Nottingham University Library (ref. ACC 1685).

COCKCROFT, SIR JOHN DOUGLAS (1897–1967) Scientist and academic. Fellow of the Royal Society. Chief Superintendent, Air Defence, Research and Development Establishment, Ministry of Supply, 1941–44. Director, Atomic Energy Division, National Research Council of Canada, 1944–46. Director, Atomic Energy Research Establishment, Harwell, 1946–58. Chairman, Defence Research Policy Committee, and Scientific Adviser, Ministry of Defence, 1952–54. Master of Churchill College, Cambridge, 1959–67. President, Manchester College of Science and Technology, 1961–67. Holder (with Ernest Walton) of the Nobel Prize for Physics, 1951.

Churchill College, Cambridge, has a substantial collection of papers (ref. CKFT). A list is available (NRA 14614). Many of the papers date from his AERE years. The collection includes lecture notes, lectures, articles and speeches; the papers and correspondence of the Kapitza Club, an informal gathering of Cavendish physicists, which met until 1958; and notes on research trips abroad (including papers on the Ghana Academy of Sciences) from 1931 onwards. There are also internal Churchill College administrative files. Similar records are available for his Manchester post.

Wider issues covered in the collection include science education and policy, the place of science in the Commonwealth, nuclear deterrence, disarmament and the work of the Pugwash Conferences. The collection also documents his membership of the Liberal Party (the Presidency of which he was once offered), including his correspondence with various East Anglian Liberal Associations.

COCKFIELD, LORD Francis Arthur Cockfield (1916–) Conservative politician. Secretary of State for Trade, 1982–83. Chancellor of the Duchy of Lancaster, 1983–84. European Commissioner. Vice-President, European Commission, 1985–88.

The papers have been promised to the European University Institute, Florence, which already holds a transcript of an interview concerning his time in Brussels.

COGGAN, LORD Archbishop (Frederick) Donald Coggan (1909–) Anglican clergyman. Bishop of Bradford, 1956–61; Archbishop of York, 1961–74; Archbishop of Canterbury, 1974–80.

The Borthwick Institute, York, has some papers, mainly relating to his years in York (ref. BP1/COG). These include sermons, addresses and writings; correspondence and personal papers, 1944–74; House of Lords papers; and also various photographs and press-cuttings.

Further papers are in the Church of England Record Centre. A list is available (NRA 31970). They include files from his time in Bradford and material on 'Anglican-Methodist Conversations'.

COGHILL, SIR (MARMADUKE NEVILL) PATRICK SOMERVILLE, 6TH BT (1896–1981) Military career. Served in Middle East during World Wars I and II. Colonel, Arab Legion, 1952–56.

The papers are deposited in two repositories. The Middle East Centre, St Antony's College, Oxford, has

copies of his unpublished autobiography, *Before I Forget*; a diary and notes, 1941–45; and two volumes of *Middle East Wartime Jottings*. The Imperial War Museum has copies of the two diaries, *Before I Forget*, and *The War Diary of Lt. Col. Sir Patrick Coghill, Bt, RA, August 1941–July 1945*.

COHEN OF BIRKENHEAD, LORD Henry Cohen (1900–77) Physician.

Some papers are in the Department of Special Collections and Archives, University of Liverpool (ref. D200). A list is available (NRA 40734).

COHEN, SIR ANDREW BENJAMIN (1909–68) Colonial Service. Assistant Under-Secretary, Colonial Office. Governor, Uganda, 1952–57. UK Representative, United Nations Trusteeship Council, 1957–61. Permanent Secretary, Ministry of Overseas Development, 1964–68.

No papers have been located. However, relevant material can be found in the papers of several of his colleagues and associates. Sir Keith Hancock's papers at the Institute of Commonwealth Studies, London University, include some correspondence, 1954–56 (NRA 21997), as do those of W. Jackson, Imperial College, London, for the 1962–66 period (NRA 18379). The papers of Margery Perham and E.B. Worthington at Rhodes House Library, Oxford, include post-war correspondence, and the same library also holds recollections of Cohen in Uganda, 1952–54, by his private secretary, Owen Griffith (ref. MSS Afr s 2027).

COLBY, SIR GEOFFREY FRANCIS TAYLOR (1901–58) Colonial Service, 1925–56. Administrative Secretary, Nigeria, 1945. Governor, Nyasaland, 1948–56.

One box of papers, 1948–56, has been deposited in Rhodes House Library, Oxford. A list is available (NRA 39153).

COLBY, REGINALD (d. 1969) Freelance journalist, 1919–39 and 1947–68. On staff of Political Intelligence Department, Foreign Office, during World War II; served in the Mediterranean, 1943–45; Berlin, 1945–46. Founder member of the Anglo-Malagasy Society.

A large collection of papers, 1919–68, is held by the Imperial War Museum. A list is available (NRA

28535). It includes correspondence, reports, journals, typescript articles and autobiographical accounts, press-cuttings and transcripts of his broadcasts. The papers detail his role as wartime propagandist in Madagascar (1943) and Berlin (1945–46), and his career as a journalist and broadcaster in Austria and Germany both before and after World War II.

COLE, GEORGE DOUGLAS HOWARD (1889–1959) Socialist writer and lecturer. Chairman, Fabian Society, 1939–46 and 1948–50; President from 1952. Chichele Professor of Social and Political Theory, Oxford, 1944–57. Research Fellow, Nuffield College, 1957–59.

Nuffield College, Oxford, holds an extensive collection of papers (NRA 39325). For the post-war period, there are files on the Fabian Society; the London County Council Education Committee (1940s); the Buscott conferences of the early 1950s; UNESCO (1950s); and the International Society for Socialist Study, 1955–57. The collection also contains some incomplete diaries, 1925–55, as well as his research and lecture notes and drafts of various published and unpublished work. The research papers include some trade union records that he collected. Nuffield College also holds the papers of his wife and biographer, the journalist Dame Margaret Cole (NRA 39324). Additional correspondence and literary papers are in Ruskin College, Oxford (ref. MSS 33).

The International Institute of Social History, Amsterdam, holds some further papers including personal correspondence, 1954–57; correspondence on the World Socialist Movement, 1955–57; and various typescripts of books and articles. The Braunthal Collection at the Institute also has some correspondence.

COLEMAN, DONALD RICHARD (1925–) MP (Lab) Neath after 1964. Served in junior ministerial posts. Delegate to Council of Europe and WEU, 1968–73.

There are some papers, covering the period 1964–91, in the Welsh Political Archive, National Library of Wales. These mainly relate to his work for the Council of Europe, Westminster affairs and Labour Party matters. Other papers, 1964–96, are in West Glamorgan Archive Service, Swansea.

COLLICK, PERCY HENRY (1897–1984) MP (Lab) Birkenhead West, 1945–50; Birkenhead, 1950–64. Joint Parliamentary Secretary, Ministry of Agriculture, 1945–47. Assistant General Secretary, Associated Society of Locomotive Engineers and Firemen, 1940–57.

A small collection of papers has been deposited at the LSE Library (ref. COLL MISC 765). The papers include correspondence, photographs and personal papers, 1945–47. His pamphlet collection has been given to the International Institute of Social History in Amsterdam.

COLLINS, LEWIS JOHN (1905–82) Anglican clergyman and anti-nuclear campaigner. Canon of St Paul's Cathedral, 1948–81. President, International Defence and Aid Fund from 1964. Leading CND member.

His papers have been placed in Lambeth Palace Library (ref. MSS 3287–3319). The collection includes articles, correspondence, sermons and addresses. There are papers on the Oxford Committee for Promoting Friendship and Understanding in Europe (1948–49), Christian Action (1951–62), including the Association for World Peace, War on Want, as well as material on South Africa and racial discrimination (1954–68).

COLQUHOUN, MAUREEN MORFYDD (1928–) MP (Lab) Northampton North, 1974–79.

The papers have been promised to the LSE Library.

COLVILLE, SIR JOHN (1915–87) Diplomat. Assistant Private Secretary to Neville Chamberlain, 1939–40. Private Secretary to Winston Churchill, 1940–41 and 1943–45. First Secretary, British Embassy, Lisbon, 1949–51. PPS to the Prime Minister, 1951–55.

His papers covering the period 1939–87 have been placed in Churchill College, Cambridge. A list is available (NRA 32585). Of particular importance are his wartime diaries and the notebook of the 1953 Bermuda Conference. An edited version of these diaries was published as *The Fringes of Power: Downing Street Diaries 1939–55* (1985). In 1989, his widow deposited additional papers (including speeches and writings) in Churchill College.

CONESFORD, 1ST BARON Henry George Strauss (1892–1974) MP (Con) Norwich, 1935–45; Combined English Universities, 1946–50; Norwich South, 1950–55.

The papers have remained in family possession.

CONWAY, CARDINAL WILLIAM (1913–77) Roman Catholic Archbishop of Armagh and Primate of All Ireland, 1963–77; Auxiliary Bishop of Armagh, 1958–63.

A collection of uncatalogued papers is deposited in the Archdiocesan Archives in Armagh. The material is not yet open to researchers.

COOK, DAVID SOMERVILLE (1944–) Deputy leader, Alliance Party, Northern Ireland, 1980–84; member for South Belfast in Northern Ireland Assembly, 1982–86. Lord Mayor of Belfast, 1978–79.

The Linen Hall Library, Belfast, holds a collection of Mr Cook's papers. They include material relating to his time on Belfast City Council and constituency papers for the Northern Ireland Assembly. Prior permission to consult the collection is required from the Linen Hall Library.

COOKE, SIR ROBERT GORDON (1930–87) MP (Con) Bristol West, 1957–79. Special Adviser on the Palace of Westminster to the Secretary of State for the Environment, 1979–87.

A collection of papers was placed in the House of Lords Record Office in 1988 (ref. Hist Coll 343). The collection contains some miscellaneous papers for the period 1970–87, relating to the restoration of the Palace of Westminster. There are also some political papers which are closed.

COOMBS, DEREK MICHAEL (1937–) Political journalist. MP (Con) Birmingham Yardley, 1970–Feb. 1974.

Some papers have been deposited in the Modern Records Centre, University of Warwick (ref. MSS 132). These consist of constituency correspondence and a series of subject files on a wide range of topics, including Bangladesh, Uganda, Ireland, the Common Market, immigration and local government reform.

COOPER, MAJOR DEREK (fl. 1980s) Humanitarian worker. Founder, Medical Aid for Palestinians,

1982. Founding member, Council for the Advancement of Arab-British Understanding.

There are papers in the Refugee Studies Documentation Centre, University of Oxford. A list is available (NRA 42611). The collection covers refugee issues, the Council for the Advancement of Arab-British Understanding, his involvement in numerous pressure groups, etc. The collection includes papers of his wife, Mrs Pamela Cooper.

COOPER, SIR FRANK (1922–2002) Civil servant. Assistant Under-Secretary of State, Air Ministry, 1962–64; Ministry of Defence, 1964–68. Deputy Under-Secretary of State, Ministry of Defence, 1968–70. Deputy Secretary, Civil Service Department, 1970–73. PUS, Northern Ireland Office, 1973–76; Ministry of Defence, 1976–82.

Several boxes of texts and notes for speeches and articles, mainly on UK defence procurement and contributions to seminars on defence issues, 1955–96, are deposited in the Liddell Hart Centre, King's College, London. There is also material on Northern Ireland.

COOPER, BRIGADIER HENRY (1916–85) Member of British Military Mission to Bulgaria, 1944–47.

The Liddell Hart Centre, King's College, London, holds a copy of a typescript account, *The British Military Mission to Bulgaria, 1944–47.*

CORBETT, MARTIN (d. 1996) Labour councillor and gay activist. Mayor of Islington.

One box of papers was given to the LSE Library in November 1996 by his executors, Robert Cook and John Jackson. There is material on Gay Pride Week, 1981–83, the campaign for legislation on gay and lesbian rights and minutes, etc., of the Organisation for Lesbian and Gay Action.

CORFIELD, SIR CONRAD LAURENCE (1893–1980) Indian Civil Service, 1920–47. Political Adviser to the Viceroy as Crown Representative, 1945–47.

Three boxes of correspondence and papers, 1939–72, have been deposited in the India Office Library (ref. MSS Eur D 850). They include memoirs, articles, semi-official correspondence and other papers. An interview recorded for the BBC series 'Plain Tales from the Raj' is held in the Imperial War Museum's Department of Sound Records.

CORFIELD, SIR FREDERICK (VERNON) (1915–2005) MP (Con) South Gloucester, 1955–Feb. 1974. Minister of State, Board of Trade, June–Oct. 1970; Minister of Aviation Supply, 1970–71; Minister for Aerospace, Department of Trade and Industry, 1971–72.

His political papers, 1960–80, have been placed in Churchill College, Cambridge (ref. CFLD). The three boxes include his correspondence with the Prime Minister, 1970–72, on issues affecting the British aviation industry, including the collapse of Rolls Royce and the Bristol-Siddeley contracts controversy. He had also retained files on Concorde, the European Community and his Private Member's Bill on compensation for the compulsory acquisition of land. A list is available (NRA 43997).

CORKEY, ROBERT (1881–1966) Northern Irish politician and clergyman. Stormont MP (UU) Queen's University, Belfast, 1929–43. Minister for Education, Northern Ireland, 1943–44. Stormont Senator, 1943–66. Moderator of the Presbyterian Church in Ireland, 1945–46.

Professor Corkey's papers have recently been deposited in the Public Record Office of Northern Ireland (ref. D3883). They include incomplete diaries, 1914–66. Of particular interest are those kept during the 1929 General Election and his first months as an MP; as Education Minister in the wartime Stormont Government; and of visits to congregations while Moderator, 1945–46. The collection also includes publications, articles and book reviews.

CORMACK, SIR PATRICK THOMAS (1939–) MP (Con) Cannock, 1970–74; Staffordshire South-West, 1974–83; Staffordshire South after 1983.

His political papers, including constituency correspondence, have been deposited at intervals in the Brynmor Jones Library, University of Hull.

CORTAZZI, SIR (HENRY ARTHUR) HUGH (1924–) Diplomat. Deputy Under-Secretary of State, Foreign and Commonwealth Office, 1975–80. Ambassador to Japan, 1980–84.

Sir Hugh has informed the LSE that he has kept no diary or papers relating to his diplomatic service. The only materials which he has retained are the research notes on Japan which he has amassed since his retirement and copies of his articles and other publications.

COTTON, SIR JOHN RICHARD (1909–) Indian Political Service, 1934–47; Deputy Secretary, Political Department, 1946–47. Diplomat, 1947–69. First Secretary, Karachi, 1947–48. Ambassador to Congo Republic (Zaire) and Burundi, 1965–69.

A memoir of his career to 1948 is deposited in the India Office Library (ref. Eur F 226).

COULSON, CHARLES ALFRED (1910–74) Scientist and humanitarian. Fellow of Royal Society. Professor of Theoretical Physics, King's College, London, 1947–52. Professor of Mathematics, Oxford University, 1952–74. Member of the Central Committee, World Council of Churches, from 1962. Vice-President, Methodist Conference, 1959.

The papers were catalogued by the Contemporary Scientific Archives Centre and have been placed in the Bodleian Library, Oxford. A list is available (NRA 21828). The collection consists of 171 boxes of diaries, correspondence, lectures, publication and research papers as well as files on the non-scientific issues and movements with which he identified. These include conscientious objection during World War II; the Aldermaston March Committee, 1958; Amnesty International; CND; the British Council of Churches, 1955–69; the National Campaign for the Abolition of Capital Punishment, 1961–69; the National Council for Civil Liberties, 1962–68; the Society for Anglo-Chinese Understanding, 1965–68; the British Council for Peace in Vietnam, 1965; the Medical Aid Committee for Vietnam, 1965; Czechoslovakia, 1957–58; and Labour Party politics and community groups in Oxford. The collection is subject to restricted access.

COURTNEY, DAME KATHLEEN D'OLIER (1878–1974) International peace campaigner. Vice-Chairman, League of Nations Union, 1939. Deputy Chairman, United Nations Association; Joint President, 1949–51.

Papers covering the whole of her career (mainly pre-war) are deposited at the Women's Library. A list is available (NRA 29386). There are files on international cooperation and the United Nations Association and copies of speeches and articles. Her correspondents include Gilbert Murray and Maude Royden.

COUSINS, FRANK (1904–86) Trade union leader. MP (Lab) Nuneaton 1965–66. Minister of Technology, 1964–66. General Secretary, Transport and General Workers' Union, 1956–64; and from 1966–69. Chairman, Community Relations Board, 1966–68.

A large deposit of papers has been made in the Modern Records Centre, University of Warwick (ref. MSS 282), by John Cousins (son). There are papers relating to his work as General Secretary of the TGWU, including material on busworkers, dockers and incomes policy; as well as his work while Minister of Technology and as an MP. The collection also includes personal and family correspondence and papers concerning his service on public bodies such as ACAS, the Central Training Council, the Community Relations Commission, Joint Port Trade Development Authority, National Economic Development Committee and National Freight Corporation. Enquiries concerning access should be directed to the Archivist.

COWEN, H.E. (fl. 1970s–80s) Legal adviser, Campaign for Homosexual Equality.

There are papers relating to Law Reform and the Campaign for Homosexual Equality, 1971–91, in the Hall-Carpenter Archives, LSE Library.

COWLEY, LIEUTENANT-GENERAL SIR JOHN GUISE (1905–93) Military career, 1925–62. Served in World War II in the Middle East, Italy and North West Europe. Master-General of the Ordnance, War Office, 1960–62.

Churchill College, Cambridge, has acquired his papers for the period 1930–80 (ref. CWLY). A list is available (NRA 23365). They include a memoir of the Suez operation of 1956, when Cowley was Vice Quartermaster General at the War Office; correspondence and press-cuttings relating to a controversial 1959 lecture on nuclear deterrence; and

four tape cassettes of reminiscences on his life and career.

COX, SIR CHRISTOPHER (WILLIAM MACHELL) (1899–1982) Educational adviser to the Colonial Secretary, 1940–61, and to the Minister for Overseas Development, 1964–70. Fellow of New College, Oxford, 1926–70.

His papers, 1924–70, have been deposited at the Public Record Office (ref. CO 1045). His academic correspondence and files covering his career prior to 1940 are held in New College, Oxford. Other pre-war items are deposited in the Sudan Archive, Durham University. A list is available (NRA 40616).

COX, IDRIS (1899–1989) Communist Party activist in South Wales.

The correspondence, lectures, speeches and political writings, c. 1950–85, together with an unpublished biography, are in the National Library of Wales.

CRAIG, KEVIN AND CRAIG, PAT Peace activists.

There are papers in the Peace Archive, University of Bradford, which also holds papers of such organisations as the Medical Association for the Prevention of War and collections of papers on, for example, the Scott Inquiry.

CRAIGEN, JAMES BROWN (1938–) MP (Lab and Co-op) Glasgow Maryhill, Feb. 1974–87.

The papers have been deposited in the National Library of Scotland (ref. Acc 10476). The collection consists mainly of printed pamphlets, annual reports, conference proceedings and correspondence (1960–91). These relate to the Labour Party in Scotland and the Scottish Labour Group; Scottish devolution (1968–84); the Co-operative Party and the Co-operative Wholesale Society (1960–91); the Housing Corporation of Scotland, Scottish homes and various housing associations (mainly 1980s); and Scottish rating reform, and the introduction of the Community Charge (mainly 1980s). There are also brief histories of labour politics in various Scottish cities (1970s and 1980s). An earlier deposit contains miscellaneous material on his opposition to the flotation of the Trustees Savings Bank and other material on the history of the Scottish Trades Union Congress (ref. Acc 10361).

Additional papers related to his Maryhill constituency are at the Mitchell Library, Glasgow.

CRAMPTON, PETER DUNCAN (1932–) MEP (Lab) Humberside, 1989–99. Chairman, European CND.

His political papers, 1989–99, have been placed in the Brynmor Jones Library, University of Hull.

CRATHORNE, BARON Sir Thomas Lionel Dugdale (1897–1977) MP (Con) Richmond, Yorks, 1929–59. Junior Lord of the Treasury, 1937–42; Minister of Agriculture and Fisheries, 1951–54.

According to Hazlehurst, *British Cabinet Ministers, 1900–51* (q.v.), the papers remain with the family and consist of more than 50 boxes of correspondence, speeches and diaries.

CRICK, ALAN JOHN PITTS (1913–95) Public servant. Counsellor, Washington, 1963–65. Assistant Secretary, Cabinet Office, 1965–68. Director of Economic Intelligence, Ministry of Defence, 1970–73.

There are papers in the Liddell Hart Centre for Military Archives, King's College, London.

CRIPPS, SIR (RICHARD) STAFFORD (1889–1952) MP (Lab) Bristol East, 1931–50; Bristol South-East, Feb.–Oct. 1950. Solicitor-General, 1930–31; Ambassador, Soviet Union, 1940–42; Lord Privy Seal and Leader of the House of Commons, 1942; Minister, Aircraft Production, 1942–45. President, Board of Trade, 1945–47; Minister, Economic Affairs, 1947; Chancellor of the Exchequer, 1947–50.

The papers, formerly in Nuffield College and also with Sir Maurice Shock, have now been placed in the Bodleian Library, Oxford. The former Nuffield College papers consist of a large number of subject files and speech files, *c.* 1930–50. Researchers should access the collection via the Bodleian website.

CROHAM, LORD Douglas Albert Vivian Allen (1917–) Civil servant, 1939–77. Permanent Secretary, Treasury, 1968–74. Head of Civil Service, 1974–77.

Lord Croham states that he has retained no papers which complement official records. He may at some stage write his memoirs. The LSE Library holds an interview concerning his career.

CRONIN, JOHN DESMOND (1916–86) MP (Lab) Loughborough, 1955–79.

There are a very few items relating to his parliamentary work in Leicestershire Record Office, deposited in 2003 (ref. DE6338). Enquiries concerning scope and access should be directed to the archivist.

CROOKENDEN, LIEUTENANT GENERAL SIR NAPIER (1915–2002) Military career. Served in World War II. On staff of Director of Operations, Malaya, 1952–54. Director, Land/Air Warfare, Ministry of Defence (Army Dept), 1964–66. Commandant, Royal Military College of Science, Shrivenham, 1967–69. General Officer Commanding, Western Command, 1969–72.

Some papers have been deposited in the Liddell Hart Centre, King's College, London.

CROOKSHANK, VISCOUNT Harry Frederick Comfort Crookshank (1893–1961) MP (Con) Gainsborough, 1924–56. Financial Secretary to the Treasury 1939–43. Postmaster-General 1943–45. Minister of Health 1951–52. Lord Privy Seal 1952–55. Leader of the House of Commons 1951–55.

A collection of diaries (1934–61), notes for speeches and press-cuttings (1931–52) is held at the Bodleian Library, Oxford (ref. MSS Eng Hist b 223, b 596–605, d 359–61). Additional press-cuttings are in the Lincolnshire Record Office.

CROSLAND, (CHARLES) ANTHONY RAVEN (1918–77) MP (Lab) Gloucestershire South, 1950–51; Grimsby 1959–77. Minister of State, Economic Affairs, 1964–65. Secretary of State for Education and Science, 1965–67. President of the Board of Trade, 1967–69. Environment Secretary, 1974–76. Foreign Secretary, 1976–77.

An extensive collection of personal and political papers was deposited in the LSE Library in 1984 by his widow. The political material includes party, constituency and ministerial files for the period 1950–77; correspondence with family and various political figures, 1927–76; copies of various articles, speeches and broadcasts, press-cuttings; and notes and notebooks, 1940–80. There are also a number of printed articles and speeches in the collection. Nine further boxes of material were acquired in 1998 (ref. M 1889). The LSE Library also has Susan Crosland's journals (after 1964) and miscellaneous scrapbooks.

CROSS, SIR RONALD HIBBERT (1896–1968) MP (Con) Rossendale, 1931–45; Ormskirk, 1950–51. Parliamentary Secretary, Board of Trade, 1938–39. Minister of Economic Warfare, 1939–40. Minister of Shipping, 1940–41. UK High Commissioner, Australia, 1941–45. Chairman, Public Accounts Committee, 1950–51. Governor, Tasmania, 1951–58.

The Imperial War Museum holds a microfilmed collection of correspondence and speeches mainly concerning his World War II appointments (ref. PP/MCR/164). A list is available (NRA 28536). The material includes some post-war correspondence on the Australian Food Parcels for Britain Scheme, 1947–50. The papers of Paul Emrys-Evans at the British Library include correspondence, 1935–55 (ref. Add MSS 58235–58273). Further wartime correspondence can be found in the papers of Sir Harry Batterbee which are in Rhodes House Library, Oxford (NRA 26608).

CROSSMAN, RICHARD HOWARD STAFFORD (1907–74) MP (Lab) Coventry East, 1945–Feb. 1974. Minister of Housing and Local Government, 1964–66. Lord President of the Council and Leader of the House of Commons, 1966–68. Secretary of State for Social Services, 1968–70. Editor, *New Statesman*, 1970–72.

The full transcripts of the diaries which he kept as a cabinet minister (published in three volumes, 1975–77) are deposited in the Modern Records Centre, Warwick University. A list is available (NRA 19144). The Crossman Archive holds extensive additional material including political, constituency and personal correspondence and papers, a few diaries, broadcast transcripts and press-cuttings; several files of political correspondence with Gaitskell, Bevan and others (1956–74); letters selected by Crossman as significant, including correspondence with W.H. Auden, Naomi Mitchison, Rebecca West, Hugh Gaitskell, Sam Watson and Thomas Balogh; and complementary personal material from Mrs Anne Crossman. There are also letters to his parents and an extensive correspondence with his second wife, Zita. His literary output is represented in the files of his literary agent, Helga Green. The papers were used in the preparation of *Crossman: The Pursuit of Power* (1990) by Anthony Howard, who subsequently deposited some of his research notes with the collection. A list is available (NRA 40315). Some papers of Tam Dalyell (PPS to Crossman) are also in the collection (these were used in Dalyell's biography of Crossman).

Some further papers and correspondence on the Anglo-American Committee on Palestine (1946–47) are held at St Antony's College, Oxford (NRA 20811). The collection includes letters, drafts and press-cuttings on the Anglo-American Committee, the United Nations Special Committee on Palestine during 1946–47, and the subsequent recognition of Israel. There are also letters to Zita Crossman on the trip to Palestine, including a visit to Chaim Weizmann.

CROSSMAN, ROBERT (d. 1997) Labour politician and gay activist. Mayor of Islington.

Three boxes of papers, covering the period 1970–90, concerning local government matters, the Labour Party and his term as Mayor of Islington are in the LSE Library (ref M 1861). The deposit, part of the Hall-Carpenter Archive, is not yet open.

CROWE, SIR COLIN TRADESCANT (1913–89) Diplomat. Chargé d'Affaires, Cairo, 1959–61. Deputy UK Representative to the United Nations, 1961–63. Ambassador, Saudi Arabia, 1963–64. High Commissioner, Canada, 1968–70. UK Permanent Representative to United Nations, 1970–73.

An account of the restoration of relations between Britain and Egypt after the Suez episode (1957–61) is held at the Middle East Centre, St Antony's College, Oxford.

CROWTHER, BARON Sir Geoffrey Crowther (1907–72) Economist and journalist. Editor, *The Economist*, 1938–56. Served at the Ministry of Supply and Information, and as Deputy Head of Joint War Production Staff, Ministry of Production, during World War II. Chairman, Central Advisory Council for Education (England), 1956–60; Committee of

Consumer Credit, 1968–71. Chairman, Royal Commission on the Constitution, 1968–72.

Lord Crowther's papers are understood to have remained in his family's possession.

CROWTHER, (JOSEPH) STANLEY (1925–) MP (Lab) Rotherham, 1976–92.

Mr Crowther states that he has retained extensive files on a variety of subjects.

CROWTHER-HUNT, BARON Norman Crowther Hunt (1920–87) Fellow and Lecturer in Politics, Exeter College, Oxford, 1952–82; Member, Fulton Committee on the Civil Service, 1966–68; Commission on the Constitution, 1969–73.

The papers have been placed in the Bodleian Library, Oxford. Enquiries regarding access should be directed to the Archivist.

CUDLIPP, LORD Hugh Cudlipp (1913–98) Newspaper magnate. Publisher, Mirror Group Newspaper, after 1984. Chairman, International Publishing Corporation.

His personal papers were donated to Cardiff University's School of Journalism, Media and Cultural Studies in 2002. The collection includes over 3000 letters, 40 reports and 550 cuttings.

CUNNINGHAM, GENERAL SIR ALAN GORDON (1887–1983) Military commander. Served in World Wars I and II; General Officer Commanding, 8th Army, 1943–44; Eastern Command, 1944–45. High Commissioner and Commander-in-Chief Palestine, 1945–48.

The main collection of papers, 1918–76, is held in the National Army Museum (ref. 8303–104). A list is available (NRA 30032). The material largely covers his wartime commands. His Palestine papers are deposited in the Middle East Centre, St Antony's College, Oxford. A list is available (NRA 20811).

CUNNINGHAM, SIR GEORGE (1888–1963) Governor, North-West Frontier Province, 1937–46 and 1947–48.

Papers and correspondence are deposited in the India Office Library. A list is available (NRA 27456). The collection consists of papers, letters, notes and reports, mainly concerning the North-West Frontier Province and Waziristan (1937–48).

CUNNINGHAM, PATRICK (1878–1960) MP (Independent Nationalist), Fermanagh & Tyrone, 1935–50. Abstentionist until 1945.

The papers of Anthony Mulvey in the Public Record Office of Northern Ireland include a file of correspondence with Cunningham during the period when both represented this double-membered constituency, 1935–50 (ref. D1862).

CUNNINGHAM, SIR (SAMUEL) KNOX (1909–76) MP (UU), South Antrim, 1955–70. PPS to Harold Macmillan as Prime Minister, 1959–63. On Ulster Unionist Council, 1943–76.

Sir Knox Cunningham left no heirs, and the present location of his unpublished memoir of Macmillan, *One-Man Dog*, is unknown. His letters to Norman Laird, a Stormont Unionist MP, form part of the Laird collection in the Public Record Office of Northern Ireland (ref. D2669).

CUSHNAHAN, JOHN (1948–) Irish politician. Alliance Party official and elected representative, Northern Ireland, 1974–87. Alliance Party leader, 1984–87. Member, North Down, Northern Ireland Assembly, 1982–86. MEP (Fine Gael), Munster constituency, Republic of Ireland since 1989.

Mr Cushnahan informed the LSE Library in 1992 that he has retained his papers.

D

D'ALTON, CARDINAL JOHN (1882–1963)
Roman Catholic Archbishop of Armagh and Primate
of All Ireland, 1946–63; Bishop of Meath, 1943–46.

Papers for the 1946–63 period are in the Archdiocesan Archives, Armagh. They are catalogued
and open to researchers.

**D'ARCY, LIEUTENANT-GENERAL JOHN
CONYERS (1894–1966)** Military career. Served in
World Wars I and II. Commanded 9th Armoured
Division, 1942–44. General Officer Commanding,
Palestine, 1944–46.

General D'Arcy's son has a collection of letters,
including some relating to service in Palestine. The
Middle East Centre, St Antony's College, Oxford, has
copies of the Palestine letters.

**DACRE OF GLANTON, LORD Hugh Trevor-
Roper (1914–2003)** Historian. Regius Professor of
Modern History, Oxford University, 1957–80. Master
of Peterhouse, Cambridge University, 1980–87.

Lord Dacre retained extensive papers.

DALE, SIR HENRY HALLETT (1875–1968)
Physician. Member of the Scientific Advisory
Committee to the War Cabinet, 1940–47; Chairman,
1942–47; Advisory Committee on Atomic Energy,
1945–57.

The Public Record Office holds a collection of
correspondence and papers related to Sir Henry
Dale's work on the Scientific Advisory Committee,
1940–48 (ref. CAB 127/213–238). A list is available
(NRA 32409). His scientific papers, mainly pre-
war, can be found at the Royal Society, and at the
Wellcome Contemporary Medical Archives Centre.

DALLEY, FREDERICK WILLIAM (1885–1962)
Trade unionist. Member of Labour Party Advisory
Committee to Secretary of State for the Colonies.
Vice-President, National Peace Council.

A collection of papers has been deposited at the
Brynmor Jones Library, University of Hull (ref.
DDA). A list is available (NRA 34116). The collection
is divided into correspondence and files on trade
union and political activities. The former includes
the papers of the National Guild League, National
Guild Council, and the Workers Central League.
The latter includes material on Trinidad, 1927–52;
British Guiana, 1947–54; Nigeria, 1946–60; West
Africa, 1950–53; trade unionism (especially the
World Federation of Trades Unions), 1945–50; and
articles and notes for lectures and miscellaneous
papers.

**DALRYMPLE-CHAMPNEYS, SIR WELDON
(1892–1980)** Served Ministry of Health. Deputy
Chief Medical Officer of Health, 1940–56.

His correspondence and papers are in the Contemporary Medical Archives Centre, Wellcome
Institute (ref. GC/139). A list is available (NRA
36147).

**DALTON, BARON (1887–1962) (Edward) Hugh
(John Neale) Dalton** Statesman. MP (Lab)
Peckham, 1924–29. Bishop Auckland, 1929–31; 1935–
59. PUS, Foreign Affairs, 1929–31. Minister of
Economic Warfare, 1940–42. President of the Board
of Trade, 1942–45. Chancellor of the Exchequer,
1945–47. Chancellor of the Duchy of Lancaster,
1948–50. Minister of Town and Country Planning,
1950–51; Local Government and Planning, 1951.

The Dalton papers were deposited at the LSE
Library between 1962 and 1966. A list is available
(NRA 16530). The collection includes diaries, 1916–
60, and an extensive set of papers for the period
1929–60. Section A (1929–40) of the papers contains
Foreign Office, economic, Labour Party and defence
material as well as correspondence and speeches.
Section B (1940–45) consists of political papers and
correspondence as well as general correspondence.

Section C (1945–60) has political papers and correspondence, letters of congratulation and also letters from Ruth Dalton. These include all the papers relating to Dalton's Chancellorship, some material on the Labour Party, and miscellaneous records relating to the Council of Europe. Section D contains various items such as writings, undated papers and photographs. The final part of the collection has press-cuttings and various pieces of printed journalism by Dalton.

Additional Private Office papers for the period 1940–52 are held at the Public Record Office (ref. CAB 127/204–212, 217/211–212) (NRA 32409). These relate mainly to his role as Minister of Economic Warfare and his responsibility for the Special Operations Executive. There are also papers dating from his brief period in opposition in 1951, and comments on his memoirs by the Secretary of the Cabinet.

DALY, CARDINAL CAHAL BRENDAN (1917–)

Roman Catholic Archbishop of Armagh and Primate of All Ireland 1990–96. Bishop of Down and Connor, 1982–90; Ardagh and Clonmacnoise, 1967–82. Reader in Scholastic Philosophy, Queen's University, Belfast, 1962–67.

Cardinal Daly states that his lectures, addresses, sermons and papers are deposited with the Archdiocesan Archives at Ara Coeli, Armagh. They are subject to a thirty-year closure rule but the lectures, addresses and sermons are open to researchers. His files concerning his role as Pertitus (or theological consultant) at Vatican II are bequeathed to Queen's University, Belfast.

DALY, LAWRENCE (1924–)

Trade union leader and peace activist. General Secretary, National Union of Mineworkers, 1968–84.

Some correspondence and papers have been deposited in the Modern Records Centre, University of Warwick (ref. MSS 302). A list is available (NRA 32741). They document Communist Party activities in Fife (1944–56), the post-1956 Fife Socialist League and the emergence of the New Left (1957–63). His correspondents include Sir Kenneth Alexander, V.L. Allen, Jane Buchan, Norman Buchan, Ken Coates, Peggy Duff, Peter Fryer, John Gollan, Hamish Henderson, John Rex, John Saville, E.P. Thompson

and William Wolfe. There are also NUM correspondence files and papers, 1946–74; correspondence concerning CND and the Scottish Plebiscite Appeal Fund 1944–79; minute books of the Fife Socialist League 1957–60; and files on the West Fife parliamentary election of 1959. The remainder of the collection includes material on national fuel policy, 1961–72; Bertrand Russell's International War Crimes Tribunal on the Vietnam War, 1966–68; his visits to the USSR, 1945–46 and 1976; diaries, notebooks and autobiographical notes, 1942–77; and press-cuttings and ephemera, 1940s–80s.

DANIEL, SIR GORONWY HOPKIN (1914–)

Civil servant. Chief Statistician, Ministry of Fuel and Power, 1947–55; Under-Secretary, Coal Division, 1955–62; General Division, 1962–64; PUS, Welsh Office, 1964–69. Chairman, Welsh Fourth Channel Authority, 1981–86; Member, Welsh Language Council.

Sir Goronwy states that he has retained some unpublished reports, letters and memoranda connected with the Ministry of Fuel and Power, 1950–64; local government in Wales and the case for a Welsh Assembly; the Welsh language and the establishment of the Welsh Fourth Channel Authority; the investiture of Prince Charles; and the Bank of Wales.

DANSON, ERNEST DENNY LOGIE (1880–1946)

Anglican clergyman. Bishop of Edinburgh, 1939–46; Primate of the Scottish Episcopalian Church, 1943–46.

His collected diaries (36 vols) and scrapbooks (2 vols) are held at the Scottish Record Office (ref. CH 12/33). A logbook as Bishop of Edinburgh and papers on a survey of the Anglican Communion can be found at the National Library of Scotland (ref. Dep 172). A list is available (NRA 27988).

DARLING OF HILLSBOROUGH, BARON

George Darling (1905–85) MP (Lab and Co-op) Sheffield Hillsborough, 1950–Feb. 1974. Minister of State at the Board of Trade, 1964–68. President of the Trading Standards Administration. Vice-President, Council of Europe Assembly, 1970. Industrial Correspondent, BBC, 1945–49.

His correspondence and papers, 1944–85, are held at Sheffield City Library (ref. LD 2404–2420). A list is available (NRA 29943). The collection includes personal letters, 1944–83, and files on various issues such as consumer protection and waste disposal.

DARLING, ERNEST WILLIAM (1905–) Leading member, Communist Party of Great Britain.

The papers are held by the Hoover Institution on War, Revolution and Peace, Stanford University, California. They include writings, correspondence, memoranda, reports, leaflets and cuttings, 1920–60, relating to the communist movement, political conditions, labour and housing in Great Britain.

The Modern Records Centre, University of Warwick, has duplicates of this material.

DARLING, GENERAL SIR KENNETH THOMAS (1909–98) Military career, 1929–69. Served in World War II: North West Europe, 1944–45; Java, 1946. General Officer Commanding, Cyprus District and Director of Operations, 1958–60. Commander-in-Chief, Allied Forces, Northern Europe, 1967–69.

His military papers covering 1930–63 have been placed in the Imperial War Museum. These include material on Indonesia (1946) and Cyprus (1958–60).

DARLING, SIR MALCOLM LYALL (1880–1969) Indian Civil Service, 1904–40. Indian Editor, BBC, 1940–44. Chairman, Horace Plunkett Foundation, 1947–58.

The Cambridge South Asian Archive has a collection of papers, 1887–1960 relating to rural conditions in India; periodical articles written from 1921 to 1959, reprints and reviews; notes and drafts of published works; notes on a mission to Yugoslavia, 1951 and on land reform and cooperation in Egypt and Italy, 1955; and also correspondence.

DARLINGTON, CYRIL DEAN (1903–81) Sherardian Professor of Botany, University of Oxford, 1953–71.

About 250 boxes of correspondence and papers are held in the Bodleian Library, Oxford (ref. MSS Darlington b 1–3, c 1–118, d 1–24, e 1–21, f 1–36, g 1–45). A list is available (NRA 27939). The collection includes research papers and correspondence with other scientists, drafts of publications and lectures and broadcasts. There are some files on the position

of German scientists under the Third Reich and the Control Commission for Germany, 1948–49. Other files concern post-war university administrative reforms in Britain.

DAVID, WAYNE (1957–) MEP (Lab) South Wales, 1989–94; South Wales Central, 1994–99. Leader, European Parliamentary Labour Group. MP, Caerphilly after 2001.

Some papers, for the period 1987–94, have been placed in the Welsh Political Archive, National Library of Wales. Many of these papers relate to the environment and to European issues. There are files concerning the constituencies of south Wales, 1987, and the reborn Parliament for Wales Campaign of 1993–94.

DAVIDSON, AIR VICE-MARSHAL SIR ALEXANDER PAUL (1894–1971) Royal Air Force career. Served in Bomber Command and in the Middle East during World War II. On post-hostilities planning staff, Air Ministry and Deputy Chief of Air Division, Control Commission Germany, 1946; Chief of Combined Service Division, Control Commission Germany, 1947. Director-General, Air Ministry, 1947–51.

Some uncatalogued papers, 1916–54, are in the Royal Air Force Museum, Hendon (ref. AC 71/25).

DAVIDSON, BASIL (1914–) Historian of Africa. Author. Vice-President, Anti-Apartheid Movement.

A collection of papers has been deposited in the Library of the School of Oriental and African Studies, University of London. The papers include extensive documentation on the struggle for independence in Portuguese Africa.

DAVIDSON, MAJOR-GENERAL FRANCIS HENRY NORMAN (1892–1973) Director, Military Intelligence, War Office, 1940–44. British Army Staff, Washington, 1944–46. Colonel Commandant, Intelligence Corps, 1952–60.

There are papers in the Liddell Hart Centre for Military Archives, King's College, London. A detailed on-line catalogue is available.

DAVIES, (EDWARD) CLEMENT (1884–1962) MP (Lib) Montgomeryshire, 1929–62. Leader, Liberal Party, 1945–56.

A large collection of papers is held at the National Library of Wales. A four-volume catalogue is available (NRA 31414). This extensive collection includes material on his political career, 1929–62; the Liberal Party, 1928–62; Welsh Affairs; constituency matters; the peace movement; foreign affairs; home affairs; domestic political issues; press-cuttings, speeches and correspondence. A futher deposit of papers (after his widow's initial deposit in 1967) was made by his sole surviving son in 1977. These are also catalogued.

DAVIES, ERNEST ALBERT JOHN (1902–91) MP (Lab) Enfield, 1945–50; Enfield East, 1950–59. Parliamentary Private Secretary to the Minister of State, Foreign Office, 1946–50. Parliamentary Under-Secretary, Foreign Office, 1950–51.

The papers were deposited at the LSE Library in 1990 (ref. M1674). There are five boxes of papers detailing his involvement with various United Nations delegations (1945–51) and the Four Power Talks of 1951 in Paris. There are also a variety of subject files on European nations, the Middle and Far East, and an unpublished autobiography. Three boxes of additional papers were deposited in 1991, mainly texts of broadcasts, articles and press-cuttings from the 1930s–80s (ref. M1726).

DAVIES, ITHEL (1894–1989) Barrister and political activist.

A collection of correspondence and papers, 1942–83, including his election address as Welsh Republican candidate for Ogmore in 1950, is held at the National Library of Wales.

DAVIES, ROBERT (1918–67) MP (Lab) Cambridge, 1966–67.

His papers (c. 50 files) were donated to Cambridge University Library by Mrs Kathleen Davies in 1974 (ref. Add MS 7999). There are subject files on planning; housing, rating, public health and education; and committee work, as well as annotated printed material.

DAVIES, RON (1946–) Welsh Labour politician. Various ministerial posts. Secretary of State for Wales, etc.

Enquiries should be directed to the Welsh Political Archive, National Library of Wales, which has his constituency correspondence and papers, 1983–94.

DAVIES, RUPERT ERIC (1909–94) Methodist and ecumenical leader. Served World Methodist Council, Anglican-Methodist Unity Commission, 1965–68, etc.

There are papers in the Methodist Archives and Research Centre, University of Manchester. A list is available (NRA 39364). The collection includes correspondence, diaries and papers, 1969–94.

DAVIES, STEPHEN OWEN (1886–1972) MP (Lab) Merthyr Tydfil, 1934–70; (Ind Lab) 1970–72.

Some papers are held at University College Library, Swansea. A list is available (NRA 14694). The collection includes correspondence, notebooks, personal documents and other material relating to his trade union and political career. Some additional papers can be found at the Glamorgan Record Office.

DAVIS, ADMIRAL SIR WILLIAM WELLCLOSE (1901–87) Naval career. Served in World War II. Director of Under-Water Weapons, 1945–46. Naval Secretary, Admiralty, 1950–52. Vice-Chief of Naval Staff, 1954–57. Commander-in-Chief Home Fleet and Eastern Atlantic (NATO), 1958–60.

A copy of his eight-volume manuscript auto-biography, *My Life*, was presented to Churchill College, Cambridge, in 1976. A list is available (NRA 23365). This covers all aspects of his life and miltary career in detail, and the later sections include his views on international political events.

DAVISON, MADGE (d. 1990) Civil-rights activist, Northern Ireland.

Four boxes of papers relating to the Northern Ireland Civil Rights Association (NICRA), 1971–76, are held in the Northern Ireland Political Collection at the Linen Hall Library, Belfast. The bulk of the collection relates to the introduction of internment without trial in August 1971 and includes NICRA press and policy statements, correspondence, questionnaires, branch reports and statements made by internees, and surveys of the economic position of their families. There is also correspondence with international civil rights organisations and peace groups.

DAVY, BRIGADIER GEORGE MARK OSWALD (1898–1983) Military career. Member of military missions to France and Belgium, 1939–40. Commanded Armoured Brigades, Western Desert, 1941; Land Forces, Adriatic, 1944–45. War Office Representative with the Polish Forces, 1945–47.

The Liddell Hart Centre, King's College, London, holds two boxes of papers, 1939–82. They include sections from an unpublished memoir of his career until 1945.

DAWSON, AIR CHIEF MARSHAL SIR WALTER LLOYD (1902–94) Royal Air Force career. Served in World War II. Air Officer Commanding, Levant, 1946–48. Assistant Chief of Air Staff (Policy), 1952–53. Deputy Chief of Staff (Plans and Operations), Supreme Headquarters, Allied Powers, Europe (SHAPE), 1953–56. Inspector-General, RAF, 1956–57. Air Member, Supply and Organisation, 1958–60.

Sir Walter had informed previous surveys that he has kept no papers apart from photographs. The Air Historical Branch of the Ministry of Defence holds an interview chiefly concerning his cadet training at RAF Cranwell, but which also covers aspects of his later career, including his SHAPE appointment. Access is at the discretion of the head of the Air Historical Branch.

DAY, GROUP CAPTAIN HARRY MELVILLE ARBUTHNOT (b. 1898) Royal Air Force career. Served in World War II. Stationed in Germany postwar.

An interesting collection of papers is held at the Royal Air Force Museum, Hendon (ref. AC72/31). Material concerning his service career includes logbooks, 1926–50, and photographs of the Berlin airlift. Much of the collection concerns post-war service reunions including those of the Concentration Camp Association. There are several files on Anglo-German compensation claims for Nazi victims, 1963–68. The remainder of the collection consists of notes and correspondence from the 1960s relating to his published work.

DAY, SIR ROBIN (1923–2000) Prominent broadcaster and political interviewer. Liberal candidate, Hereford, 1959.

His correspondence and press cuttings have been acquired by the Bodleian Library, Oxford.

DEAKIN, PHYLLIS (fl. 1940s) Journalist. War correspondent, Paris, 1945.

There are some papers in the Women's Library (formerly the Fawcett Library).

DEAN, SIR MAURICE JOSEPH (1906–78) Civil servant. Deputy Secretary, Control Commission for Germany and Austria, 1946; Foreign Office (German Section), 1947–48; Ministry of Defence, 1948–52. Second Secretary, Board of Trade, 1952–55; Air Ministry, 1955–63. Joint PUS, Department of Education and Science, Ministry of Technology, 1964–66.

Twelve boxes of correspondence and papers covering his career, 1928–79, are held at the Liddell Hart Centre, King's College, London. These include his 1970s' lectures on management, education and the Civil Service.

DEANE, JIMMY (1921–) Trotskyist. Co-founder of the Revolutionary Socialist League in 1955. Activist within the Workers' International League, Revolutionary Communist Party, *Parti Communiste Internationaliste* and others.

The papers (104 boxes) have been deposited in the Modern Records Centre, University of Warwick (ref. MSS 325). The collection (several thousand letters) traces the development of Trotskyism in Britain, *c.* 1940–65, through the various movements and parties of which he was a member. Among the papers are correspondence, agendas and minutes, resolutions, reports, statements and declarations, discussion material, perspectives, Revolutionary Communist Party Conference documents, constitutions and standing orders, addresses, speeches and lectures, printed material including cuttings leaflets and books. A list is available (NRA 35299).

DE BLANK, JOOST (1908–68) Churchman and Archbishop of Cape Town. Assistant General Secretary, Student Christian Movement, 1946–48. Suffragan Bishop of Stepney, 1952–57. Archbishop of Cape Town, 1957–63. Canon of Westminster,

1964–68. Assistant Bishop, Diocese of Southwark, 1966–68. Chairman, Greater London Conciliatory Committee, 1966–68.

The Centre for South African Studies, York University, has 14 boxes of diaries, correspondence and papers covering his career as Bishop of Stepney, Archbishop of Cape Town, and Canon of Westminster, 1941–67. A list is available (NRA 24316). The collection also contains various sermons, conference papers, notes for lectures, and diaries of visits, as well as a typescript of *The Return of the Sacred* and of the autobiography *Six Years Hard*. An additional 22 boxes are held in the Archives of the Church of the Province of South Africa, University of Witwatersrand, Johannesburg. A list is available (NRA 20321). These relate to his time as Archbishop of Cape Town, including lectures, sermons and correspondence with particular reference to the Emergency of 1960. There is also an unpublished typescript biography, *My Brother Joost: A Personal Memoir of Joost de Blank*, by Bartha de Blank.

DE COURCY, KENNETH HUGH (1909–99) Writer and publicist. Host and socialite. Confidant of Cabinet Ministers. Forger and fraudster.

It is understood that de Courcy left a large collection of his private papers to Stanford University, California.

DE COURCY IRELAND, JOHN (1917–) Irish socialist, journalist and maritime historian.

The papers are held in the Modern Archives Department, University College, Dublin (ref. P29 and P29a). They include post-war correspondence relating to the Irish Labour Party, 1942–74, on the Northern Ireland Labour Party, and on trade unions in Ireland. There is also material on the Irish CND movement. His personal correspondence includes letters exchanged with Stanley Cooper-Foster, 1944–66, regarding politics and the arts in Northern Ireland.

DE FREITAS, SIR GEOFFREY STANLEY (1913–82) MP (Lab) Nottingham Central, 1945–50; Lincoln, 1950–61; Kettering, 1964–79. Parliamentary Under-Secretary, Air, 1946–50; Home Office, 1950–51. High Commissioner, Ghana, 1961–63; Kenya, 1963–64. Chair, Labour Committee for Europe, 1965–72.

There are 62 boxes of papers covering the period 1927–82, in the Bodleian Library, Oxford. The collection includes material on general elections, 1945–74; the Suez crisis; British relations with Ghana (1957, 1962–63), Kenya (1961–64); and Europe, 1950s–70s. There are also various diaries, a draft autobiography, photographs and press-cuttings.

DE LA WARR, 9TH EARL Herbrand Edward Dundonald Brassey Sackville (1900–76) Conservative politician.

A small collection of his papers was deposited in East Sussex Record Office in 1989 (ref. A 5411). The papers include the transcript of a diary as a member of the British delegation to Ethiopia 1944; and political papers and speeches 1936–55.

DE L'ISLE, 1ST VISCOUNT William Philip Sidney, 6th Baron De L'Isle and Dudley (1909–90) MP (Con) Chelsea, 1944–45. Parliamentary Secretary, Ministry of Pensions, 1945. Secretary of State for Air, 1951–53. Governor-General, Australia, 1961–65.

A collection of papers relating to his time as Secretary of State for Air, 1951–55, which had earlier been given to the Royal Air Force Museum, Hendon, was returned to Lord De L'Isle in 1989. The collection is closed. The Royal Air Force Museum did not retain copies of the documents which included his minutes to the Prime Minister, 1951–55; election speeches, 1955; and files relating to the Conservative Party and to the Commonwealth Parliamentary Association.

DELL, EDMUND (1921–99) MP (Lab) Birkenhead, 1964–79. Minister of State, Board of Trade, 1968–69; Department of Employment and Productivity, 1969–70. Paymaster-General, 1974–76. Trade Secretary, 1976–78. Founder-Chairman of Channel Four Television Company, 1980–87.

The papers have been deposited at the Bodleian Library, Oxford. The collection includes a taped diary (partly transcribed) covering his time at the Treasury as Paymaster-General. There are also subject files including material on the European 'Committee of Three Wise Men' (1978–79), the Channel Four Television Company and various working parties which he chaired; appointment diaries; drafts of articles and books; and a series of letters received for almost sixty years from his brother Sidney Dell (a senior United Nations official, see below) and other family members. Many of these records are held on computer disks.

DELL, SIDNEY (1918–90) Economist. Head, New York Office, United Nations Conference on Trade and Development (UNCTAD). Brother of Edmund Dell, MP.

His papers have been placed in the Bodleian Library, Oxford (ref. MSS Eng c 5798–5889 etc.). A list is available (NRA 39524).

DENNING, BARON Alfred Thompson Denning (1899–1999) Judge of the High Court of Justice, 1944; a Lord Justice of Appeal, 1948–57; a Lord of Appeal in Ordinary, 1957–62; Master of the Rolls, 1962–82.

The collected personal and family papers have been placed in Hampshire Record Office (ref. 202M86). A list is available (NRA 38113). In addition, his papers concerning the Conference on the Future of Law in Africa are in Rhodes House Library, Oxford (ref. MSS Afr s 1193).

DENNING, VICE-ADMIRAL SIR NORMAN (1904–79) Served in Naval Intelligence, World War II. Director of Naval Intelligence, 1960–64. Deputy Chief of the Defence Staff (Intelligence), 1964–65. Secretary of the Defence, Press and Broadcasting Committee, 1967–72.

A collection of papers has been acquired by the National Maritime Museum (ref. MS 84/192). Reference should also be made to the papers of his brothers, Lord Denning and Lieutenant-General Sir Reginald Denning, which are deposited in the Hampshire Record Office. The papers of Lord Denning are subject to special terms of access.

DENNING, LIEUTENANT-GENERAL SIR REGINALD (FRANCIS STEWART) (1894–1990) Military career. Principal Administrative Officer to Lord Mountbatten as Supreme Allied Commander, South-East Asia, 1944–46. General Officer Commanding, Northern Ireland, 1949–52.

His correspondence and papers, 1922–86, have been deposited in the Hampshire Record Office (ref. 93M88). A list is available (NRA 31865). Reference

should also be made to the papers of his brother, Lord Denning, which are held in the same repository.

DEUTSCHER, ISAAC (1907–67) Polish-born Communist. Expelled after an active career in the Communist Party of Poland. Member of the editorial staff on *The Economist* (1942–49) and the *Observer* (1942–47). Participant in the Washington-Berkeley-New York 'teach-ins' on the Vietnam War, 1965–66. Member of the Tribunal concerned with International War Crimes, 1966–67. Historian, whose most famous writings include *Stalin: A Political Biography* (1949), *The Unfinished Revolution: Russia 1917–67* (1967), and a three-volume biography of Leon Trotsky.

The papers were acquired in 1977 by the International Institute of Social History, Amsterdam, from his widow, Mrs Tamara Deutscher in London. The collection contains a comprehensive correspondence with many political friends, left-wing historians and scholars, including Heinrich Brandler, E.H. Carr, Pierre Frank, Daniel Guerin, Bertrand Russell and Natalya Sedova-Trotsky. In addition, there are copies of various lectures and broadcasts; files on the International War Crimes Tribunal (1967); and press-cuttings and articles dating from 1944 onwards. There are also numerous manuscripts of Deutscher's works.

DEVLIN, BARON Patrick Arthur Devlin (1905–92) Legal career. Justice of the High Court, 1948–60. Lord of Appeal in Ordinary, 1961–64. Chairman of the Press Council, 1964–69.

Some papers relating to the Nyasaland Inquiry Commission which he chaired in 1959 have been deposited in Rhodes House Library, Oxford. They include submissions, memoranda and draft reports. Prior permission is required in order to consult these papers. The papers of Monty Belgion at Churchill College, Cambridge, include some correspondence.

DEVLIN, PATRICK JOSEPH (1925–) Northern Irish politician and trade unionist. Chairman, Northern Ireland Labour Party, 1967–68. Founder-member, SDLP, 1970. Stormont MP, Belfast Falls Division, 1969–72. Minister of Health and Social Services, Northern Ireland Executive, 1974. Northern Irish District Secretary, Irish Transport and General Workers Union, 1976–85.

It is understood that the papers have remained in his possession and may be deposited in an appropriate archive in due course.

DIAMOND, HARRY (fl. 1930s–60s) Irish Labour Party activist, Northern Ireland.

A small series of papers relating to the Irish Labour Party (ILP) and various smaller socialist and republican groupings in Northern Ireland, 1930–64, is deposited in the Public Record Office of Northern Ireland (ref. D2474). The collection includes a minute book for the Falls and Central Belfast branches of the ILP, 1951–53; miscellaneous issues of left-wing and republican publications and pamphlets; and ephemera from the 1945, 1953 and 1964 elections.

DICKENS, JAMES MCCULLOCH YORK (1931–) MP (Lab) West Lewisham, 1966–70.

Mr Dickens has retained about a dozen files of constituency correspondence, papers written for the Tribune Group (1966–70) and copies of various articles and reviews from the same period.

DICKSON, ALEXANDER GRAEME (1914–94) Charity worker. Founder of Voluntary Service Overseas (VSO) and Community Service Volunteers (CSV).

The papers are held by Community Service Volunteers, but they have been listed (NRA 40389). The collection relates primarily to his work for CSV in the period 1962–94.

DICKSON, REAR-ADMIRAL ROBERT KIRK (1898–1952) Naval career. Deputy Director of Plans, Naval Staff, 1943–44. Chief of Naval Information, 1944–46. Commanded aircraft carrier *HMS Theseus*, 1946–48. Head of British Naval Mission to Greece, 1949–51.

A collection of family correspondence and other papers, 1904–52, has been acquired by the National Library of Scotland (ref. MSS 13501–588). His correspondence and diaries cover his service in both world wars as well as social and diplomatic life in Athens, 1949–51. A set of autobiographical notes is in the Scottish United Services Museum.

DICKSON, AIR MARSHAL SIR WILLIAM (FORSTER) (1898–1987) Royal Air Force career.

Served in World War II in Fighter Command, Tactical Air Force and Desert Air Force. Vice-Chief of Air Staff, 1946–48. Commander-in-Chief Middle East Air Force, 1948–50. Chief of the Air Staff, 1953–56. Chairman, Chiefs of Staff Committee, 1956–59, Chief of Defence Staff, 1958–59.

The correspondence and papers were deposited by his widow at Churchill College, Cambridge, in 1988 (ref. DCKN). A list is available (NRA 32586). The collection covers his service as Chief of Air Staff, Chairman of the Chiefs of Staff Committee, and Chief of Defence Staff. The papers include official and private correspondence, papers on tours, and briefings and notes on lectures.

The Air Historical Branch of the Ministry of Defence holds the transcripts of two very full interviews covering his entire career (including his comments on Suez). Access is at the discretion of the Head of the Air Historical Branch.

DICK-READ, GRANTLY (1890–1959) Pioneer in natural childbirth.

A collection of correspondence and papers for the period 1910–57 is held at the Contemporary Medical Archives Centre, Wellcome Institute (ref. PP/GDR). A list is available (NRA 29599). The collection includes extensive correspondence with mothers and with organisations on natural childbirth. Additional material includes medical papers, articles, press-cuttings, the manuscript of *No Time for Fear* (1955) and a copy of the film *Childbirth Without Fear*. There are also some personal and biographical papers.

DILHORNE, LORD (1905–80) Conservative politician. Solicitor-General, 1951–54. Attorney General, 1954–62. Lord Chancellor, 1962–64.

Researchers have been informed by the 2nd Lord Dilhorne (son) that his father destroyed all of his papers before his death.

DIMOLINE, MAJOR-GENERAL WILLIAM ALFRED (1897–1965) Military career. Served in World Wars I and II. General Officer Commanding, East Africa, 1946–48. UK representative on United Nations Military Staff Committee, 1951–53.

There are 23 boxes of papers (1914–62) in the Liddell Hart Centre, King's College, London. A list is available (NRA 11384). The collection documents his wartime postings in Burma, India and Africa, and his work in East Africa immediately after the War. The collection is an important source for the waning of British colonial rule in Central and East Africa. His later work as Chairman of the Army Cadet Force Association (1954–60), and as Secretary to the British Section of the Inter-Parliamentary Union (1959–62) is also covered. The collection also includes maps and a large number of photographs and press-cuttings.

DIVERS, BRIGADIER SYDNEY THOMAS (1896–1979)
Civil servant. Army officer during World War II. Controller, Ministry of Pensions and National Insurance, 1946–54. Under-Secretary, Ministry of Supply, 1956; Admiralty, 1957–59. United Nations Adviser, Burma, 1954–55; Nepal, 1959–62, Asia and Far East, 1962–64; Iraq, 1965–66; Trinidad, 1967; and Saudi Arabia, 1971.

The Brigadier's papers, 1945–79, are deposited in the Liddell Hart Centre, King's College, London. With the exception of a few retrospective articles on World War II, they largely concern his civil service career. The collection includes his manuscript reflections on the lessons of the war and the state of post-war Britain entitled *A Wanderer Returns*; correspondence relating to his various appointments; and miscellaneous personal correspondence, 1948–79, including letters from various Allied Commanders such as General Mark Clark.

DIXON, SIR CHARLES WILLIAM (1888–1976)
Assistant Under-Secretary of State, Commonwealth Relations Office, 1940–48; Adviser, Commonwealth Relations Office, 1948–67.

A memoir of his life and career has been placed in Dundee University Library (ref. MS 15/137).

DIXON, SIR PIERSON (JOHN) (1904–65)
Diplomat. Principal Private Secretary to Foreign Secretary, 1943–48. Ambassador to Czechoslovakia, 1948–50. Deputy Under-Secretary of State, Foreign Office, 1950–54. UK Permanent Representative to UN, 1954–60. Ambassador to France, 1960–64.

His papers, covering the period 1944–65, have been placed in the Special Collections Department, University of Birmingham.

DOBB, MAURICE HERBERT (1900–76)
Cambridge University economist. Published extensively on the Soviet economy.

The papers have been given to the Wren Library, Trinity College, Cambridge. The collection includes correspondence, lectures and articles covering the period *c.* 1919–76.

DOBRSKI, LIEUTENANT-COLONEL J.A. (fl. 1940s) (known as MAJOR DOLBEY)
Served with Special Operations Executive (SOE) in Italy, Greece and the Balkans during World War II.

The Liddell Hart Centre, King's College, London, holds four boxes of papers chiefly relating to his SOE career. The post-war section of the collection includes some 1947 reports on SOE activities in Greece and the Aegean; an account of his interview in 1949 with René Pleven, the new French Defence Minister, regarding French politics and foreign and defence policies; and papers on the French textile industry, 1949–50.

DODDS-PARKER, SIR (ARTHUR) DOUGLAS (1909–)
MP (Con) Banbury, 1945–59; Cheltenham, 1964–Oct. 1974. Joint Parliamentary Under-Secretary, Foreign Affairs, 1953–54, 1955–57; Commonwealth Relations, 1954–55.

Sir Douglas retained approximately 12 boxes of papers which have now been deposited in Magdalen College, Oxford. A list is available (NRA 41250). These are essentially of a personal nature but also include material on his wartime operations with Special Operations Executive and files dating from his leaving office in 1957. There is material on Europe.

DOLL, PROFESSOR SIR (WILLIAM) RICHARD (SHABOE) (1912–2005)
Regius Professor of Medicine, Oxford University, 1969–79. On Royal Commission on Environmental Pollution, 1973–79, and the Standing Commission on Energy and the Environment, 1978–81. Chairman, Adverse Reaction Sub-committee, Committee on Safety of Medicines, 1970–77; UK Co-ordinating Committee on Cancer Research, 1972–77.

A collection of papers is held at the Wellcome Contemporary Medical Archives Centre, London. Enquiries regarding access should be directed to the Archivist. There is material on anti-smoking, etc.

DONALDSON, ARTHUR W. (fl. 1946–72) Scottish Nationalist. Chairman of the Scottish National Party, 1960–69. Journalist. Editor, *Scots Independent*.

His papers, covering the period 1930–83, are held in the National Library of Scotland (refs Acc 6038 and Acc 11908). The collection includes minutes, reports and correspondence on the Scottish National Party (10 boxes, 1924–72), and miscellaneous nationalist pamphlets and printed matter (17 boxes). There are also 14 volumes of press-cuttings.

DONNELLY, DESMOND LOUIS (1920–74) MP (Lab and from 1968, Ind) Pembroke, 1950–70. Political columnist, *Daily Herald*, 1960–63. Chief political correspondent, *News of the World*, 1968–70. Founder of the Democratic Party, 1969.

A substantial collection of papers has been deposited at the National Library of Wales. A list is available (NRA 41723). This includes a large number of correspondence files on specific subjects, including parliamentary elections in Pembrokeshire, 1949–70; Cyprus, 1958–60; Donnelly's expulsion from the Labour Party, 1968; steel nationalisation, 1964–65; and the administration of the Democratic Party, 1969–70. The 17 files of general correspondence include letters exchanged with British and international statesmen during the period 1950–74, among them Sir Anthony Eden (1956–72), Dean Acheson (1960–71) and Sir Roy Welensky (1967–74). There are two files of diary notes, February 1963 – October 1967, and part of a draft autobiography. There are also extensive files of press-cuttings, 1940–74, speeches, articles, addresses and reports. Requests for access should be addressed to the Librarian.

DONOUGHUE, BARON Bernard Donoughue (1934–) Economist. Lecturer, London School of Economics, 1963–74. Senior policy adviser to the Prime Minister, 1974–79. Assistant Editor, *The Times*, 1981–82.

The papers are promised to the LSE Library.

DORMAND, LORD John Donkin Dormand (1919–2002) MP (Lab) Easington, 1970–87. Government Whip, 1974–79.

His political papers and correspondence, 1950–99, have been placed in Durham County Record Office (ref. D/DOR).

DOUGLAS OF BARLOCH, 1ST BARON Sir Francis Campbell Ross Douglas (1889–1980) MP (Lab) Battersea North, 1940–46. Governor, Malta, 1946–49.

A collection of correspondence and papers has been deposited at the LSE Library. A list is available (NRA 33418). There are various personal and professional papers; correspondence with politicians, public servants and others, including Hugh Dalton, Lord Wootton and Lord Hailsham, as well as various photographs and press-cuttings.

DOUGLAS OF KIRTLESIDE, 1ST BARON Marshal of the Royal Air Force William Sholto Douglas (1893–1969) Served in World Wars I and II. Air Officer Commanding-in-Chief, British Air Forces of Occupation, Germany, 1945–46. Commander-in-Chief and Military Governor, British Zone of Germany, 1946–47. Chairman of British European Airways (BEA), 1949–64.

An extensive set of papers covering the period between 1915 and 1966 is held at the Imperial War Museum. A list is available (NRA 28539). The papers relate to various military operations during World War II; Coastal Command problems, 1948–49; and his BEA years. There are also notes, drafts and correspondence relating to his published works, especially *Years of Combat* (1963); House of Lords speeches; miscellaneous correspondence; photographs; and newspaper cuttings.

DOUGLAS-HAMILTON, LORD JAMES ALEXANDER (1942–) MP (Con) Edinburgh West since October 1974.

His papers for the period 1968–83 are held at the National Library of Scotland. A list is available (NRA 29126). The collection includes correspondence and papers on political subjects (1974–76) and research material related to his various publications, especially *Motive for a Mission: The Story Behind Hess's Flight to Britain* (1971). Access requires the permission of Lord Douglas-Hamilton.

DOUGLAS-HOME, CHARLES COSPATRICK (1937–85) Journalist. Aide-de-Camp to Sir Evelyn Baring as Governor of Kenya, 1958–59. Joined *The Times*, 1965; Defence Correspondent, 1965–70; Features Editor, 1970–73; Home Editor, 1973–78;

Foreign Editor, 1978–81; Deputy Editor, 1981–82; Editor, 1982–85.

There are nine boxes of correspondence and papers, 1966–85, deposited at the Liddell Hart Centre, King's College, London. The collection relates chiefly to his travels as a journalist and editor for *The Times*, and to his book *Evelyn Baring: The Last Proconsul* (1978). It is presumed that papers relating to his editorship of *The Times* remain with the News International Archives.

DOVE, MAJOR-GENERAL ARTHUR JOHN HADFIELD (1902–85) Military career. Pre-war service in Palestine. Served in World War II. Deputy Director of Military Operations, 1944–47. War Office Representative, Council of Foreign Ministers and at Peace Conference, 1946–47. Deputy Adjutant-General, British Army of the Rhine, 1948–50. Brigadier, General Staff, Middle East Land Forces, 1951–53.

According to information supplied to the Liddell Hart Centre, King's College, London, a collection of unsorted papers remains in the family's possession. General Dove had previously stated that his papers included a memoir of his Palestine service.

DOW, SIR HUGH (1886–1978) Indian Civil Service, 1909–47. Governor of Sind, 1941–46; and Bihar 1946–47. British Consul General, Jerusalem, 1948–51. Chairman of the Royal Commission on East Africa, 1952–54.

Five boxes of correspondence and papers are deposited in the India Office Library (ref. MSS Eur E 372). A list is available (NRA 30616). The collection includes semi-official correspondence with the Viceroy, 1941–47; correspondence, reports and rough journals while in Jerusalem; various printed articles and books; and a collection of photographs.

DRUMALBYN, BARON Niall Malcolm Stewart Macpherson (1908–87) National Liberal and Conservative MP. Leading National Liberal.

Some papers have survived with his daughter, but apparently very little relates to the National Liberal Party or his time at Westminster.

DRUMMOND-WOLFF, HENRY (1899–1982) Promoter of the Commonwealth. Vice-Chairman of the Empire Economic Union, 1949; President, 1952.

A collection of papers and correspondence is held at the Brotherton Library, Leeds University (ref. 709). A list is available (NRA 27395). The collection includes extensive correspondence files and autobiographical notes. These cover various visits to Berlin during the 1930s; publications, memoranda and documents related to his Anti-Common Market campaign; and papers on the Commonwealth and international affairs.

DUNBAR, CHARLES (1900–92) Expert and writer on road haulage and transport.

The papers have been placed in the Modern Records Centre, University of Warwick (ref. MSS 347). A list is available. The bulk of the deposit comprises minutes and correspondence, 1937–42, of the National Conference of Express Carriers, which Dunbar was instrumental in setting up in 1937 as the National Conference of Parcels Carriers. There are also files relating to other aspects of road haulage organisation, including the Road & Rail Central Conference and the Liaison Committee of the ARO, CMUA, etc.

DUNBAR, MAJOR-GENERAL CHARLES WHISH (1919–81) Military career. Served in World War II. Post-war active service, Palestine, Cyprus, Suez, Jordan and Aden. Director of Infantry, Ministry of Defence, 1970–73.

Two boxes of papers, 1944–70, are held at the Liddell Hart Centre, King's College, London. Much of the material concerns the Cyprus emergency.

DUNCAN-SANDYS, BARON Duncan Edwin Sandys (1908–87) MP (Con) Norwood, 1935–45; Streatham, 1950–Feb. 1974. Financial Secretary, War Office, 1941–43. Parliamentary Secretary, Ministry of Supply, 1942–44. Minister of Works, 1944–45; Supply, 1951–54; Housing and Local Government, 1954–57; Defence, 1957–59; Aviation, 1959–60. Commonwealth Relations Secretary, 1960–64, and also Colonies Secretary, 1962–64.

Over 300 boxes of papers were deposited at Churchill College, Cambridge, by Lord Duncan-Sandys in 1976 (NRA 18561). They constitute a full record of his parliamentary career and include papers, reports and correspondence from his various ministries; constituency files; subject files; speeches and official publications; newspaper cuttings; and personal papers and photographs. There are also files on his role in the foundation of the European Movement in 1947 and in other organisations and conferences (including the World Security Trust, the Hague Congress, May 1948 and the Strasburg Bureau, 1949–50). There are also records of the campaign to restore capital punishment which he initiated in 1968. The collection is now open. Some Private Office Papers are available at the Public Record Office (ref. AVIA 11).

DUNNETT, SIR ALASTAIR MACTAVISH (1908–98) Editor, *Daily Record*, 1946–55; *The Scotsman*, 1956–72; Chief Press Officer, Secretary of State for Scotland, 1940–46. Chairman, *The Scotsman* Publications Ltd; Director, Scottish Television Ltd, 1975–79; Thomson Petroleum Ltd after 1979.

His correspondence and papers for the period *c*. 1955–86 have been placed in the National Library of Scotland (ref. Acc 9179). Of particular interest are the files relating to Thomson Petroleum's interests in North Sea oil. The material includes minutes and correspondence with industrialists such as Dr Armand Hammer and John Paul Getty.

DURBIN, EVAN FRANK MOTTRAM (1906–48) MP (Lab) Edmonton, 1945–48. Senior Lecturer in Economics, London School of Economics. On economic staff of the War Cabinet Secretariat, 1940–42.

Personal Assistant to the Deputy Prime Minister, 1942–45. Parliamentary Secretary, Ministry of Works, 1947–48.

The papers were deposited at the LSE Library by Mrs Marjorie Durbin in 1987. A list is available (NRA 20574). The collection consists of 14 boxes of correspondence, manuscript and typescript drafts, diaries and lecture notes. Much of the material relates to his career in the 1930s and early 1940s. Among the correspondence are political, election and semi-official letters from his later career, including letters from Attlee, Herbert Morrison, John Parker, E.D. Simon and Carr Saunders.

DUTT, (RAJANI) PALME (1896–1974) Communist politician, author and philosopher. On Executive Committee of Communist Party, 1922–65.

A substantial collection of correspondence and papers (*c*. 100 volumes) is held in the archives of the former Communist Party of Great Britain, now deposited in the Labour History Archive and Study Centre, Manchester. There are additional papers at the British Library, including six volumes of his column 'Notes of the Month', published in *Labour Weekly*, 1921–73; 26 volumes of typescript letters and articles, 1922–70; typescript memoranda and reports, 1934–50, mainly relating to policy matters within the Communist Party of Great Britain; eight volumes of press-cuttings, 1921–73; and letters and pamphlets.

E

EADE, CHARLES STANLEY (1903–64) Journalist, newspaper editor and public relations adviser. Editor, *Sunday Dispatch*, 1938–57.

Two boxes of papers, including correspondence with and a diary relating to Winston Churchill, 1938–54, are in Churchill College, Cambridge (ref. EADE). A list is available (NRA 43161).

EAMES, ROBERT HENRY ALEXANDER (ROBIN) (1937–) Anglican clergyman. Archbishop of Armagh and Primate of All Ireland after 1986. Bishop of Down and Dromore, 1980–86; Derry and Raphoe, 1975–80.

Dr Eames states that some papers, including copies of published articles, are deposited with the Church of Ireland Representative Church Body Library in Dublin.

EASTWOOD, CHRISTOPHER GILBERT (1905–83) Colonial Office service. Principal Assistant Secretary, Cabinet Office, 1945–47. Assistant Under-Secretary, Colonial Office, 1947–66. Commissioner of Crown Lands, 1952–54.

Six boxes of papers chiefly relating to Africa, the West Indies and Aden are in Rhodes House Library, Oxford (ref. MSS Brit Emp s 509). The collection comprises diaries, reports, memoranda, letters and photographs.

EATON, VICE-ADMIRAL SIR JOHN WILSON MUSGRAVE (1902–81) Naval career; served in World War II. Director of Royal Naval Staff College, 1949–51. Commander-in-Chief, America and West Indies, 1955–56. Deputy Supreme Allied Commander, Atlantic, 1955–57.

There are three boxes of papers, covering the period 1951–70, in the Liddell Hart Centre, King's College, London.

ECCLES, 1ST VISCOUNT Sir David McAdam Eccles (1904–99) MP (Con) Chippenham, 1943–62. Minister of Works, 1951–54; Education, 1954–57 and 1959–62; President of the Board of Trade, 1957–59. Paymaster-General (with responsibility for the Arts), 1970–73.

Lord Eccles stated that he had retained possession of his papers and had made provision to bequeath them to his son. Some constituency papers are in Wiltshire Record Office.

EDELMAN, MAURICE (1911–75) MP (Lab) Coventry West, 1945–50; Coventry North, 1950–Feb 1974; Coventry North-West, Feb. 1974–75. Novelist.

A collection of correspondence and papers is held at the Modern Records Centre, University of Warwick (ref. MSS 125). A list is available (NRA 19144). The main subject files and correspondence files cover constituency matters, including local industry and employment. There are also files on general elections from 1964 to 1974; parliament; public bodies; newspaper cuttings; and engagement diaries, 1958–75.

EDELSTEN, ADMIRAL SIR JOHN HEREWARD (1891–1966) Naval career. Served in World Wars I and II. Vice-Chief of Naval Staff, 1947–49. Commander-in-Chief, Mediterranean Station, 1950–52; Portsmouth, 1952–54. Allied Commander-in-Chief, Channel Command, 1952–54.

The papers which are deposited in Churchill College, Cambridge, include letters (1936–51) and speeches (1947–55).

EDMONDS, CECIL JOHN (1889–1979) Diplomat. Served Iraq as Adviser to Ministry of the Interior, 1935–45. Consul General. UK Permanent Delegate to International Refugee Organisation.

Some papers are in the Middle East Centre, St Antony's College, Oxford. A list is available (NRA 41061). Much of the material is pre-war, but there are files of post-1945 correspondence.

EDMUND-DAVIES, BARON Herbert Edmund Davies (1906–92) Judge of the High Court of Justice, Queen's Bench Division, 1958–66; a Lord Justice of Appeal, 1966–74; a Lord of Appeal in Ordinary, 1974–81. Chairman of various committees of enquiry; member of the Royal Commission on Penal Reform, 1964–66.

A large collection of papers has been deposited at the National Library of Wales. A list is available (NRA 26130 NLW misc). The papers reflect his career as a barrister, High Court judge and Lord of Appeal in Ordinary. The collection includes material relating to the trial of the 'great train robbers' in 1964; and his Chairmanship of the Tribunal of Enquiry into the Aberfan Disaster, 1966–67. There are also extensive files of correspondence, speech notes and legal papers. These include general legal papers (e.g. counsel's opinions) (1947–56), judge's notebooks (1976–85), speeches and lecture notes (1927–86), correspondence (1967–87) and various subject files.

EDWARDS, HUW THOMAS (1892–1970) Welsh trade unionist and politician.

A collection of papers has been deposited at the National Library of Wales. It includes correspondence, 1929–70, relating to the Council of Wales, the Welsh Tourist Board, the Welsh Gas Board, Welsh Economic Council and the Transport and General Workers' Union. There are printed reports, articles and press-cuttings, 1932–67. The material on the re-organisation of local government in Wales and on Welsh language and culture is of particular interest. A list is available (NRA 42410).

EDWARDS, ADMIRAL SIR RALPH ALAN BEVAN (1901–63) Naval service from 1914; served in World Wars I and II. Assistant Chief of Naval Staff, 1948–50. Third Sea Lord and Controller of the Navy, 1953–56. Commander-in-Chief, Mediterranean Station, and Allied Forces, Mediterranean, 1957.

The collection of papers deposited at Churchill College, Cambridge, includes 77 diaries kept between 1938 and 1950, and reports, naval messages and miscellaneous items, 1938–55. A list is available (NRA 14619).

EDWARDS, ROBERT (BOB) (1906–90) MP (Lab) Bilston, 1955–87. General Secretary, Chemical Workers' Union, 1947–71.

Some 60 files of papers, 1935–87, have been given to the Labour History Archive and Study Centre, Manchester. A list is available (NRA 35300). They include material on his service in the Spanish Civil War, his membership of the Labour Party and the Independent Labour Party. There are also files on various trade unions, the chemical industry and foreign policy.

The Imperial War Museum's Department of Sound Records holds an interview concerning the Spanish Civil War, his stance as a conscientious objector during World War II and trade union activities in Germany in 1946 (ref. 4669/4).

EGERTON, SIR ALFRED (1886–1959) Expert on energy. Member, Scientific Advisory Committee, War Cabinet; Chairman, Scientific Advisory Committee, Ministry of Fuel and Power, 1948–53; Secretary, Royal Society, 1938–48.

The Imperial College of Science and Technology holds a collection of papers for the period 1908–59. A further set of personal papers and correspondence has been placed by his widow in the Royal Society.

EINZIG, PAUL (1897–1973) Journalist and economist. Political correspondent, *Financial Times*, 1945–56. London correspondent of the *Commercial and Financial Chronicle*, New York, from 1945.

There are 132 files of correspondence and papers, 1925–68, in Churchill College, Cambridge. A list is available (NRA 19699). They include working notes and drafts for articles and books and a considerable quantity of material relating to Brendan Bracken.

ELIS-THOMAS, LORD Daffyd Ellis Thomas (1946–) MP (Plaid Cymru), Merioneth, Feb. 1974–83: Merionydd Nant Conwy, 1983–92. President, Plaid Cymru, 1983–91.

Some 725 files of papers have been deposited with the Welsh Political Archive at the National Library of Wales. A list is available (NRA 40397). The material covers constituency, national and international issues and complements the extensive Plaid Cymru party archive also held in the National Library of Wales.

ELKINS, VICE-ADMIRAL SIR ROBERT FRANCIS (1903–85) Naval officer. Held various commands in World War II. Flag Officer, Second-in-Command, Far East Station, 1955–56. Admiral, British Joint Staff Mission, Washington, 1956–58.

Sir Robert deposited a collection of correspondence and papers, 1940–75, in the National Maritime Museum. The material includes a first draft of his memoirs (ref. ELK/7). The post-war sections of the collection include a 1947 report and related papers on his wartime escape, 1940 (ref. ELK/6); papers relating to his command of a cruiser squadron in the Home Fleet, 1950–54; and correspondence following the publication of his book in 1974. Discipline and morale in the inter-war and post-war navy are detailed in court martial proceedings, correspondence and reports about the 1931 Invergordon Mutiny and the loss of the submarines, *HMS Seal* and *HMS Oswald* (ref. ELK/5).

ELLIOT, WALTER ELLIOT (1888–1958) MP (Con) Lanark, 1918–23; Kelvingrove, 1924–45; Scottish Universities, 1946–50; Kelvingrove, 1950–58.

Some papers are deposited in the National Library of Scotland (ref. Acc 6721). A list is available (NRA 29242). The material consists of ten boxes of pamphlets and correspondence together with 38 albums of newspaper cuttings for the period 1920–58 (mostly pre-war material).

ELLIOT, AIR CHIEF MARSHAL SIR WILLIAM (1896–1971) Served in World Wars I and II. Assistant Secretary, Committee of Imperial Defence, 1937–39; War Cabinet, 1939–41; Director of Plans, Air Ministry, 1942–44; Air Officer Commanding, Gibraltar, 1944; Balkan Air Force, 1944–45. Chief Staff Officer to Minister of Defence and Deputy Secretary (Military) to Cabinet, 1949–51. Chairman, British Joint Services Mission, Washington, and UK Representative, NATO, 1952–54. Chairman, Royal Institute of International Affairs (RIIA), 1954–58.

Six boxes of papers, 1928–71, have been deposited in the Liddell Hart Centre, King's College, London. A list is available (NRA 23649). They include extensive correspondence for the post-war period. There is considerable material on his wartime service in Yugoslavia including post-war correspondence with former partisans and reports and correspondence on the Balkan Air Force. The collection is also a useful source for the history of post-war defence

policy and Anglo-American relations. His correspondents include Dean Acheson, General Walter Bedell Smith, General Sir Harry Jackson and Air Chief Marshal Sir Karel Janousek. His post-retirement work for the Army League, 1955–57, and as head of the RIIA are also detailed. His articles and speeches, 1950–61, are included in the collection.

The papers of Sir Henry Tizard at the Imperial War Museum also include correspondence, 1938–57.

ELLIOTT, MICHAEL NORMAN (1932–) MEP (Lab) London West after 1984.

His political papers, 1985–99, have been placed in Ealing Local History Centre, Ealing.

ELLIS, JOHN (1930–) MP (Lab) Bristol North West, 1966–70; Brigg and Scunthorpe, Feb. 1974–79.

Some constituency papers and subject files, 1966–79, are held at the Brynmor Jones Library, University of Hull (ref. DME). A list is available (NRA 33412).

ELLIS, THOMAS IORWORTH (1899–1970) Educationalist and publicist for Welsh language and culture. Hon. Secretary, Undeb Cymru Fydd, 1941–66.

A collection of correspondence, working papers and material on local organisations is held at the National Library of Wales.

ELLISON, GERALD ALLISON (1910–92) Leading Anglican churchman. Bishop of London, 1973–81.

Lambeth Palace Library holds his correspondence and papers.

ELMHIRST, AIR MARSHAL SIR THOMAS WALKER (1895–1982) Air Attaché, Ankara, 1937–39. Deputy Director, Intelligence Section, Air Ministry, 1940. Assistant Chief of Air Staff (Intelligence), 1945–47. Chief of Inter-Service Administration, India, 1947. Commander-in-Chief, Indian Air Force, 1947–50. Lieutenant-Governor, Guernsey, 1953–58.

Seventeen boxes of memoirs and papers, 1904–64, are deposited in Churchill College, Cambridge. A list is available (NRA 14293). The collection consists of official files relating to World War II, Indian affairs and Guernsey. His personal correspondence includes letters to his wife and family, 1941–49; edited letters, 1940–59; a set of typescript memoirs; and draft articles, lectures and miscellaneous papers. Some sections of the collection may be closed to readers.

ELWORTHY, BARON Marshal of the Royal Air Force Sir (Samuel) Charles Elworthy (1911–93) Royal Air Force career. Served in Bomber Command during World War II. Commandant, RAF Staff College, Bracknell, 1957–59. Deputy Chief of Air Staff, 1959–60. Chief of Air Staff, 1963–67. Chief of Defence Staff, 1967–71.

Lord Elworthy informed the Liddell Hart Centre, King's College, London, in 1978 that there were no papers. An interview with Lord Elworthy regarding his entire career, including Aden, was recorded by the Air Historical Branch of the Ministry of Defence in 1975. Access to the recording and transcript is at the discretion of the Head of the Air Historical Branch, to whom queries should be directed.

ELWYN-JONES, BARON Sir (Frederick) Elwyn Jones (1909–89) MP (Lab) Plaistow, 1945–50; West Ham South, 1950–Mar. 1974. Attorney-General, 1964–70. Lord Chancellor, 1974–79.

The papers have been deposited in the Welsh Political Archive, National Library of Wales. The collection is reportedly closed.

EMMET OF AMBERLEY, BARONESS Evelyn Violet Elizabeth Emmet (1899–1980) MP (Con) East Grinstead, 1955–64. Chairman, Conservative Women's National Advisory Committee, 1951–54; National Union of Conservatives, 1955–56. British Delegate to the United Nations, 1952–53.

Eighteen boxes of papers have been deposited in the Bodleian Library, Oxford (ref. MSS Eng hist c 1053–69, d 485). They include material on the Conservative Party's Overseas Bureau during the 1960s; the United Nations, 1951–56; French and German political parties and elections, 1953–67; the European Community; India, Pakistan and Sri Lanka, 1960–72; social reform; and issues affecting women. Additional deposited papers are listed as MSS Eng hist c 5721–37, etc.). Further correspondence can be found in the main Conservative Party archive in the Bodleian.

EMRYS-EVANS, PAUL (1894–1967) MP (Con) Derbyshire South, 1942–45. Parliamentary Under-Secretary for Dominion Affairs, 1942–45.

A collection of correspondence and papers, 1914–67, some of which are closed to researchers, has been deposited in the British Library (ref. Add MSS 58235–58273). The open sections of the collection include general and political correspondence, 1916–67; constituency correspondence, 1934–47; papers relating to his memoirs (including drafts); and pre-war and wartime Foreign Office and Dominions Office files. There is a particularly useful series of correspondence with politicians and historians concerning Munich, its aftermath and World War II in retrospect, 1940–67. His correspondents include Lord Wakehurst (1924–67), Lord Howick (1943–60) and Sir Anthony Eden.

ENGLISH, MICHAEL (1930–) MP (Lab) Nottingham West, 1964–83.

Some constituency and parliamentary files are deposited in Nottinghamshire Record Office (ref. DD EN).

ERSKINE, GENERAL SIR GEORGE WATKIN EBEN JAMES (1899–1965) Served in World Wars I and II. General Officer Commanding, Land Forces, Hong Kong, 1946. Director-General, Territorial Army, 1948–49. General Officer Commanding, British Troops, Egypt and Mediterranean Command, 1949–52. Commander-in-Chief, East Africa Command, 1953–55. Lieutenant-Governor and Commander-in-Chief, Jersey, 1958–63.

A large collection of official papers, correspondence and press-cuttings from his World War II and post-war commands is deposited in the Imperial War Museum (ref. 75/134/1–17A). The papers include extensive material on his East African Command, 1953–55, including 69 letters to his wife and family. The collection also contains files on his period as General Officer Commanding, Egypt, 1949–52, and correspondence and memoranda regarding drafts for the North African sections of the *Official Histories of World War II*, 1950–53. A list is available (NRA 33304). Further papers are available at the National Archives (WO/236) (NRA 32918).

ETHERIDGE, RICHARD (DICK) ALBERT (1909–85) Trade union activist. Joined the Amalgamated Engineering Union (AEU), 1940. Senior Shop Steward, Austin Works, Longbridge.

His papers are held at the Modern Records Centre, Warwick University (ref. MSS 202). The material includes daily working notes, shop steward minutes, and some correspondence. There are also files on visits to Cuba, Romania and the USSR 1958– 65; speeches, writings and related papers, 1964–78; and miscellaneous Communist Party and trade union ephemera.

EVANS, ALFRED 'FRED' THOMAS (1914–87) MP (Lab) Caerphilly, 1968–79.

The papers have been placed in the South Wales Miners' Library, University of Swansea. There is material on the 1979 devolution referendum.

EVANS, GWYNFOR (1912–2005) MP (Plaid Cymru) Carmarthen, 1966–70; Oct. 1974–79. President of Plaid Cymru, 1945–81. Chairman, Union of Welsh Independents, 1954. Publications include *Plaid Cymru and Wales* (1950) and *Wales Can Win* (1973).

A substantial deposit of papers is held at the National Library of Wales. The papers cover his entire political career and include parliamentary and constituency correspondence, material on the history and politics of Plaid Cymru and various subject files, as well as some press-cuttings and pamphlets.

EVANS, STANLEY GEORGE (1912–65) Clergyman and Christian socialist. University of Oxford Extra-Mural Lecturer. Canon Residentiary and Chancellor of Southwark Cathedral from 1960.

The papers, correspondence and sermons (1930–65) are held at the Brynmor Jones Library, University of Hull (ref. DEV). A list is available (NRA 17262). The collection has subject files on Russia, China, India, Christian socialism, and ordination. The papers on Russia include material related to a number of organisations such as the Russia Today Society (1941–46), National Council for British–Soviet Unity (1944–46), British–Soviet Friendship Houses Ltd. (1945–49), and the British–Soviet Friendship Society (1951–56) as well as material on churches, Christianity, religion and Evangelical Christians in the USSR. There are also papers on other groups such

as the Society of Socialist Clergy and Ministers (1946–58), the British Peace Committee, the Christian Peace Group, the Movement for Colonial Freedom, the Christian Socialist Movement (1961–65), and the Campaign for Nuclear Disarmament.

EVANS, SIR (WILLIAM) VINCENT (JOHN) (1915–) Barrister. Judge, European Court of Human Rights after 1980. Legal Adviser, Foreign and Commonwealth Office. Chairman, European Committee on Legal Cooperation, Council of Europe, etc.

Papers on the European Court of Human Rights are in Essex University Library.

EVANS, STANLEY NORMAN (1898–1970) MP (Lab) Wednesbury, 1945–56. Industrialist.

There are papers in Walsall Archives Service, Local History Centre (ref. 247/964).

EVETTS, LIEUTENANT-GENERAL SIR JOHN FULLERTON (1891–1988) Military career. Served in World Wars I and II. Assistant Chief of Imperial General Staff, 1942. Senior Military Adviser, Ministry of Supply, 1944–46. Retired 1946. Head of British Ministry of Supply Staff in Australia, 1946–51, and Chief Executive Officer, Joint UK-Australian Long Range Weapons, Board of Administration, 1946–49.

The papers are in the Liddell Hart Centre for Military Archives, King's College, London. They include a complete diary of the first five years of the Woomera Project, 1946–51. There are also a number of photographic negatives of Palestine and the North West Frontier Province, India. An interview concerning pre-war service in the Middle East, 1936–39, is held in the Imperial War Museum's Department of Sound Records. Some World War I papers are in the Liddle Collection, Leeds University.

EWING, WINIFRED MARGARET (1929–) MP (SNP) Hamilton, 1967–70; Moray and Nairn, Feb. 1974–79; MEP (SNP) Highlands and Islands, 1975.

Mrs Ewing has retained her papers and is using them to write her memoirs.

F

FALKENDER, BARONESS Marcia Matilda Falkender (née Williams) (1932–) Political aide to Harold Wilson, 1956–76; Private Secretary, 1956–64; Political Secretary and Head of Political Office, 1964–76.

Lady Falkender has retained extensive papers and will make provision for their deposit.

FANSHAWE OF RICHMOND, LORD Sir Anthony Henry Fanshawe Royle (1927–) MP (Con) Richmond, 1959–83. Parliamentary Private Secretary to Under-Secretary of State for the Colonies, 1960; to Secretary of State for Air, 1960–62; to Minister of Aviation, 1962–64. Tory Opposition Whip, 1967–70; Parliamentary Under-Secretary of State for Foreign and Commonwealth Affairs, 1970–74.

Lord Fanshawe states that he has retained all his parliamentary papers which are unsorted and uncatalogued. The collection includes personal papers from his time in opposition and from his time as a Minister in the Foreign Office.

FARRAR-HOCKLEY, GENERAL SIR ANTHONY HERITAGE (1924–) Served in World War II. Palestine, 1945–46; Korea, 1950–53; Cyprus and Port Said, 1956; Jordan, 1958. Commanded Parachute Battalion in Persian Gulf and Radfan Campaign, 1962–65. Principal Staff Officer to Director of Borneo Operations, 1965–66. Commander, Land Forces, Northern Ireland, 1970–71. Director, Combat Development (Army), 1974–77. Commander-in-Chief, Allied Forces, northern Europe, 1979–82. Defence consultant and lecturer since retirement.

Sir Anthony informed the Liddell Hart Centre, King's College, London, in 1981 that he had retained his papers.

FAULDS, ANDREW MATTHEW WILLIAM (1923–2000) MP (Lab) Smethwick, 1966–74; Warley East 1974–97. Chairman, British branch of the Parliamentary Association for Euro-Arab Cooperation after 1974.

His political papers, including files relating to parliamentary and constituency matters, the arts and foreign affairs are in the LSE Library.

The Centre for Southern African Studies, University of York, holds documents, press-cuttings and speeches on African politics and refugees as well as one file of documents on the Israeli–Palestinian conflict.

FAULKNER OF DOWNPATRICK, BARON Arthur Brian Deane Faulkner (1921–77) Northern Irish Unionist politician. Stormont MP (UU) East Down, 1949–73. Member (UU) South Down, Northern Ireland Assembly, 1973–75. Member, Unionist Party of Northern Ireland (UPNI), South Down, Northern Ireland Constitutional Convention, 1975–76. Government Chief Whip and Parliamentary Secretary, Ministry of Finance, Stormont, 1956–59. Minister of Home Affairs, 1959–63; Commerce, 1963–69; Development, 1969–71. Prime Minister and Minister of Home Affairs, 1971–72. Chief Executive Member, Northern Ireland Executive, 1974. Leader, UPNI, 1974–76.

Lord Faulkner's papers have been placed in the Public Record Office of Northern Ireland (ref. D3591). They include press-cuttings covering his entire political career, including his split with Captain Terence O'Neill and his resignation in protest at the establishment of the Cameron Commission on the causes of violence in Northern Ireland, 1968–69; and Stormont Castle press-cuttings for his terms of office as Prime Minister and Chief Executive. The collection also includes extensive correspondence files, many of which are closed for fifty years from the termination dates. The closed sections mainly concern his work as Minister of Development, 1969–71; his clash with Captain O'Neill and resignation,

1969; the suspension of Stormont and the Darlington Conference on new forms of government for Northern Ireland, 1972; the Sunningdale Conference on power-sharing, 1973 and the ensuing short-lived Northern Ireland Executive, 1974. The remainder of the collection comprises constituency and party correspondence and files. Certain papers, including the originals of his correspondence with Captain O'Neill, 1969, and some unsorted correspondence, have been retained by his widow.

FEDDEN, SIR (ALFRED HUBERT) ROY (1885–1973) Aeronautical Engineer. Special Technical Adviser, Ministry of Aircraft Production, 1942–45. Research work for Ministry of Supply, 1945–47. Aeronautical Adviser to NATO, 1952–53.

The Imperial War Museum has a large collection of papers relating to many aspects of his long connection with British aircraft development in the 20th century. They include, in particular, schedules and detailed drawings for a number of his engine designs – including the Jupiter, Hercules, Taurus and Centaurus – as well as correspondence and reports concerned with post-war British and NATO air developments, especially reflecting his interest in the training of scientists and technologists for the British aircraft industry. Files containing NATO reports for 1952 and correspondence in 1966 on the future of the Royal Air Force College, Cranfield, may be restricted, and enquiries regarding access should be directed to the Museum.

FELL, DAME HONOR (1900–86) Prison administrator. Director, Strangeways Research Laboratory. Active in Society for Protection and Learning.

There are papers in the Contemporary Medical Archives Centre, to where enquiries should be directed.

FELL, CAPTAIN WILLIAM RICHMOND (1897–1978) Naval career.

Six boxes of papers are held at Churchill College, Cambridge (ref. FELL) (NRA 24832). The collection includes papers on his submarine service and salvage operations on the British coast, and Suez during the 1950s.

FENBY, CHARLES (1905–74) Journalist. Editor, *Leader Magazine*, 1944–48. Editor of the *Birmingham Gazette* from 1948; Editor-in-Chief, 1953–57. Editorial Director, Westminster Press Ltd. from 1957. Chairman, British Committee of the International Press Institute, and the Commonwealth Press Union.

A small series of papers is held at the Modern Records Centre, University of Warwick. They include files on his work with the Commonwealth Press Union and the International Press Institute; drafts and texts of articles and reviews; working notes relating to his research on W.T. Stead; and research papers relating to his various studies of Oxford politics and society in the early part of the century (ref. MSS 92).

FERGUSON, RICHARD (1935–) Stormont MP (UU) South Antrim, 1968–70. Joined Alliance Party, 1971. Founder member, New Ireland Movement. Queen's Counsel.

The Public Record Office of Northern Ireland has his papers for the 1968–70 period (ref. D2890).

FESTING, FIELD MARSHAL SIR FRANCIS WOGAN (1902–76) Served in World War II. General Officer Commanding, Land Forces, Hong Kong, 1945–46; British Troops in Egypt, 1952–54. Director of Weapons and Development, War Office, 1947–49. Commander, British Forces, Hong Kong, 1949. Commander-in-Chief, Far East Land Forces, 1956–58. Chief of Imperial General Staff, 1958–61.

Sir Francis left no papers relating to his career. A collection of photographs is deposited in the Imperial War Museum.

FIDLER, MICHAEL M. (1916–89) MP (Con) Bury and Radcliffe, 1970–74. Founder, Conservative Friends of Israel. President, General Zionist Organisation of Great Britain after 1973.

The papers are in the Hartley Library, University of Southampton (ref. MS 290).

FIELD, FRANK (1942–) MP (Lab) Birkenhead after 1979. Director, Child Poverty Action Group, 1969–79. Author of numerous works on social security questions, inequality, poverty, etc.

There are some papers in the Wirral Archives Service, Birkenhead. (ref. Acc. 1498). The collection includes files relating to articles, lectures, press-cuttings and personal notes.

FIELD, BRIGADIER LEONARD FRANK (1898–1978) Military career. Chief Chinese Liaison Officer on General Alexander's staff during Japanese invasion of Burma, 1942. Military attaché, China, 1945–49; Saigon, 1951–56.

A photocopied memoir covering his service in both world wars and his attachment to the staff of General de Lattre de Tassigny in Indo-China, 1951–52, is deposited in the Imperial War Museum (ref. X/LFF).

FINCH, SIR HAROLD JOSIAH (1898–1979) MP (Lab) Bedwellty, 1950–70. Parliamentary Under-Secretary, Welsh Office, 1964–66.

A few papers are deposited in the Library of University College, Swansea. His autobiography *Memoirs of a Bedwellty MP* (1972) was written largely from memory. The South Wales Miners' Library, University College, Swansea holds an interview and transcript.

FINNISTON, SIR (HAROLD) MONTAGUE ('MONTY') (1912–91) Industrialist and business consultant.

There are papers in the National Library of Scotland (ref. Acc. 11424).

FINSBERG, BARON Sir Geoffrey Finsberg (1926–96) MP (Con) Hampstead, 1970–83; Hampstead and Highgate, 1983–92.

In 1992, Lord Finsberg deposited a substantial collection of political and constituency papers in the LSE Library.

FIRTH, AUDREY (d. 1994) Conservative politician. Lord Mayor of Bradford, 1972–73.

The papers, 1972–94, have been placed in West Yorkshire Archives, Bradford (ref. 28D94). A list is available (NRA 40364).

FISHER OF LAMBETH, BARON Geoffrey Francis Fisher (1887–1972) Anglican clergyman. Bishop of London, 1939–45. Archbishop of Canterbury, 1945–61.

Lambeth Palace Library holds 54 boxes of correspondence for the period 1945–61, and additional miscellaneous correspondence and memoranda, 1937–66. Further papers have recently been deposited.

These include files on the 1968 Lambeth Conference, diaries of tours made as Archbishop and five volumes of personal papers, 1899–1972.

FISHER, SIR NIGEL (THOMAS LOVERIDGE) (1913–96) MP (Con) Hitchin, 1950–55; Surbiton, 1955–83. Parliamentary Under-Secretary, Colonies, 1962–63; Commonwealth Relations and the Colonies, 1963–64.

Sir Nigel stated that he had retained no papers of historical significance. Rhodes House Library, Oxford, holds the transcripts of interviews given between 1962 and 1964. Some papers relating to the political career of his wife, the former Patricia Ford (as MP for North Down, 1953–55) are in the Public Record Office of Northern Ireland.

FISHER, LADY PATRICIA (formerly Mrs P. Ford) (1921–95) MP (UU) North Down, 1953–55.

Some papers have been placed in the Public Record Office of Northern Ireland. They form part of a collection mainly relating to her father, Sir Walter Smiles, whom she succeeded as MP. The files relating to her political career include election correspondence, 1953–54; diaries and journals, 1935–39 and 1953; political speeches and notes for speeches, 1953–56; and miscellaneous press-cuttings.

FISHMAN, NINA (fl. 1980s) Political campaigner. Organiser of the tactical voting 87 campaign. Academic.

Papers concerning the 1987 tactical voting campaign are in the LSE Library (ref. M1820). This was a left-of-centre group whose aim was to educate the public about tactical voting in order to defeat the Conservatives at the general election in 1987. After the general election the group was wound up but some members went on to form Common Voice. The papers for this show the running and organisation of the group and its publications on electoral reform. Both groups contain ephemera.

FITT, BARON Gerard Fitt (1926–2005) MP (Republican Labour 1966–70, SDLP 1970–79 and Ind Socialist 1979–83) West Belfast, 1966–83. SDLP founder and leader. Stormont MP (Irish Labour Party) Belfast Dock Division, 1962–72. Deputy Chief Executive, Northern Ireland Executive, 1974. Resigned from SDLP leadership and party, 1979.

No information has been received regarding Lord Fitt's papers. He was believed to be writing his memoirs. SDLP party archives are deposited in the Public Record Office of Northern Ireland.

FLANNERY, MARTIN HENRY (1918–) MP (Lab) Sheffield Hillsborough, Feb. 1974–92.

A considerable amount of correspondence has been deposited in Sheffield City Library covering his career as an MP (ref. MPD). A list is available (NRA 22744). The collection is closed for 50 years.

FLETCHER, BARON Eric George Molyneux Fletcher (1903–90) MP (Lab) Islington East, 1945–70. Minister without Portfolio, 1964–66.

The surviving ten boxes of papers, including correspondence relating to his public offices and constituency matters, have been placed in the LSE Library.

FLETCHER-COOKE, SIR JOHN (1911–89) MP (Con) Southampton Test, 1964–66. Colonial Service, 1934–55. Prisoner of War, Japan, 1942–45. Served in Palestine, 1946–48. Counsellor (Colonial Affairs), UK Delegation to the United Nations, 1949–51. Colonial Secretary, Cyprus, 1951–55. Minister for Constitutional Affairs, Tanganyika, 1956–59; Deputy Governor, 1959–61.

A large collection of papers and documents (1934–89) is held at Rhodes House, Oxford. The material relates to his many colonial postings, to his UN work and his parliamentary career. His membership of a 1969 commission on the New Hebrides is also documented. There are tape recordings made by Sir John at Rhodes House and at St Antony's College, Oxford. Diaries and papers from his time as a prisoner of war in Java and Japan are at the Imperial War Museum.

FLORENCE, LELLA FAYE SECOR (d. 1966) Birth-control pioneer. President, Birmingham Family Planning Association.

There are papers, including files on her birth-control work, in Birmingham Central Library Archives (ref. MS 1571). A list is available (NRA 36667).

FLOUD, BERNARD FRANCIS CASTLE (1915–67) MP (Lab) Acton, 1964–67.

A few papers have been placed in the Brynmor Jones Library, University of Hull (ref. DLF). They include constituency correspondence and subject files, 1962–70.

FLOWERS, BARON Brian Hilton Flowers (1924–) Physicist. Worked on Anglo-Canadian Atomic Energy Project, 1944–46. On staff of Atomic Energy Research Establishment, Harwell, 1946–50; 1952–58. Professor of Physics, Manchester University, 1958–72. Rector of Imperial College, London, 1973–85.

The papers and correspondence have been deposited in Imperial College, London. The extensive collection (69 boxes, *c.* 2070 items) covers the period 1940s–98. A detailed list is available (NRA 42125).

FLYNN, PAUL PHILIP (1935–) MP (Lab) Newport West after 1987. Steelworker, 1955–84.

His political papers for the period 1974–88 have been placed in the National Library of Wales. These include three files of correspondence and papers, 1974–88; papers on the Newport West Constituency Labour Party; the 'M4 Group' of Labour Prospective Parliamentary Candidates, 1984–86; and material on local, general and European elections. A list is available (NRA 26130).

FLYNN, THOMAS VINCENT (fl. 1950s–80s) Trade unionist.

Papers covering the period 1943–91 are in the National Library of Scotland (ref. Acc. 11504).

FOOT, SIR DINGLE (MACKINTOSH) (1905–78) MP (Lib) Dundee, 1939–45; (Lab) Ipswich, 1957–70. Parliamentary Secretary, Ministry of Economic Warfare, 1940–45. Solicitor-General, 1964–67.

There are over 30 boxes of his political, personal and legal papers in Churchill College, Cambridge (ref. DGFT). The political papers include extensive constituency files and material relating to his career as a Liberal and Labour MP as well as his work for the Ministry of Economic Warfare and post-war industry. Certain files (mostly overseas correspondence) are subject to restrictions on access. There are legal case papers, including some on his defence of Bernadette Devlin MP for her alleged part in the 1969

Derry riots, and notes on the case of Dr Michael Abdul Malik, a leading Bangladeshi politician and prominent member of the Government in 1972–73. Sir Dingle Foot's advice was sought on many human rights cases, especially in Africa, and this is also documented in the collection.

The LSE Library holds three files from his time at the Ministry of Economic Warfare and also papers relating to the Liberal position on rearmament and civil liberties. There are also copies of some of his speeches on foreign policy (ref. COLL MISC 676). The remainder of his papers, mainly typescripts and printed material relating to his legal work, has been placed in the Institute of Advanced Legal Studies.

FOOT, MICHAEL (1913–) MP (Lab) Devonport, 1945–50; Ebbw Vale, 1960–83; Blaenau Gwent, 1983–92. Secretary of State for Employment, 1974–76; Leader of the House of Commons and Lord President of the Council, 1976–79. Deputy Leader of the Labour Party, 1976–80; Leader of the Labour Party, 1980–83.

The papers, 1926–92, have been deposited at the Labour History Archive and Study Centre, Manchester. Enquiries should be directed to the Archivist. The collection, which ranges from the 1930s to the 1990s, includes material as editor of *Tribune* and as party leader. The papers of his constituency agent, Ron Evans, are in the National Library of Wales.

FOOT, PAUL MACKINTOSH (1937–2004) Writer and campaigning journalist. Editor, *Socialist Worker*, 1974–75; *Daily Mirror* journalist after 1979.

Mr Foot informed the LSE that his papers consist of extensive files of letters sent to him from readers of the *Daily Mirror* throughout the Thatcher era.

FORBES, SIR ARCHIBALD FINLAYSON (1903–89) Deputy Secretary, Ministry of Aircraft Production, 1940–43; Member of the Aircraft Supply Council, 1942–45. Chairman, First Iron and Steel Board, 1946–49; Iron and Steel Board, 1953–59. President, Federation of British Industry, 1951–53. Director, Midland Bank, 1959; Chairman, 1964; President, 1975–83.

A collection of papers (*c.* 35 boxes, 1928–84), mainly on the Iron and Steel Board and his banking and other interests, is held at Churchill College, Cambridge (ref. FORB). A list is available (NRA 44031). Additional papers covering his presidency of the Federation of British Industry are held at the Modern Records Centre, Warwick University (NRA 23238).

FORD, BENJAMIN THOMAS (1925–) MP (Lab) Bradford North, 1964–83.

Mr Ford has retained extensive papers chronicling his career in the trade union movement, the Labour Party, the Social Democratic Party and the Liberal Democrats. The collection includes material relating to the Militant Tendency within the Labour Party and the Bradford North Constituency in the 1970s and early 1980s. Provision has been made for the deposit of the collection in Bradford.

FORD, EDMUND BRISCO (1901–88) Professor of Ecological Genetics, 1963–69, and Director of Genetics Laboratory, Zoology Department, Oxford University, 1952–69. On Wildlife Committee of the Ministry of Town and Country Planning, 1945–47. Governor, Nature Conservancy Council, 1949–59.

A collection of papers is held at the Bodleian Library, Oxford. A list is available (NRA 32671). The papers include biographical material, papers on his academic research, lectures and publications, correspondence, material on Oxford University, and on various visits and conferences.

FORD, JOSEPH FRANCIS (1912–93) Diplomat. Served Shanghai, Beijing, Saigon, etc. Consul-General, Hanoi, 1960–62. Director, Great Britain-China Centre, 1974–78.

His diaries, 1960–64, have been placed in Churchill College, Cambridge.

FORSHAW, JOHN HENRY (1895–1973) Architect. Chief Architect, Miners' Welfare Commission, 1926–39. Deputy Architect of London City Council, 1939–41; Architect, 1941–46. Chief Architect and Housing Consultant to Ministry of Health and later to Ministry of Housing and Local Government, 1946–59.

A collection of correspondence, circulars and reports is held by the Liverpool University Archives.

FOSTER, AIR CHIEF MARSHAL SIR ROBERT (1898–1974).
Served in World Wars I and II. Assistant Chief of Air Staff (Policy), 1947–49. Air Officer Commanding-in-Chief, Home Command, 1949–51. Commander-in-Chief, 2nd Tactical Air Force, 1951; 2nd Allied Tactical Air Force, 1952–53.

A collection of unlisted papers is deposited in the Royal Air Force Museum, Hendon (ref. AC 75/34).

FOX-PITT, THOMAS (b. 1897)
Secretary to the Anti-Slavery Society, 1953–63. Local Government official, Zambia, 1951–66.

There are 30 boxes of papers, covering the period 1953–62, in the Library of the School of Oriental and African Studies, University of London. The collection contains manuscripts, typescripts, press-cuttings, official documents and telegrams relating to his involvement with the campaign against the Central African Federation, 1952–63. Some of the material relates to his career in Zambia. A handlist is available.

FRANCIS, DAVID (fl. 1950s–60s)
Trade unionist. General Secretary, South Wales Area, National Union of Mineworkers.

Papers may be found within the South Wales Coalfield Archive at the University of Swansea. These include material on the British–Bulgarian Trade Union Association, and the British–Hungarian Friendship Society.

FRANCIS-WILLIAMS, BARON (Edward) Francis Williams (1903–70)
Author, journalist and broadcaster. Editor, *Daily Herald*, 1936–40. Controller of News and Censorship, Ministry of Information, 1941–45. Adviser on Public Relations to Prime Minister, 1945–47. Regents' Professor, University of California, Berkeley, 1961. Kemper Knapp Visiting Professor, University of Wisconsin, from 1967.

Churchill College, Cambridge, holds 42 boxes of manuscripts, typescripts and correspondence, covering the period *c.* 1929–70 (ref. FRWS). A list is available (NRA 23360). The collection includes material on his published works as well as the manuscript of his work on Ernest Bevin, the tapes of his interviews with Attlee and files relating to his publications (including reviews of his work). There are additional papers on the Advertising Commission; press freedom in the United States; correspondence on a libel action resulting from his autobiography; papers and cuttings concerning work on the *Daily Herald* and other Fleet Street newspapers; and two files on the Society of Authors. The collection also includes press-cutting files. His extensive correspondence includes letters from Clement Attlee.

FRANKLIN, SIR ERIC ALEXANDER (1910–96)
Indian Civil Servant, 1935–47. Administrative official, Government of Pakistan, 1949–57; Establishment Secretary, 1956–57. Chairman, Terms of Service Commission, Sudan Government, 1958–59. Civil Service Adviser to Jordanian Government, 1960–63; Acting Resident Representative, United Nations Technical Assistance Board, Jordan, 1961. Senior United Nations Administrative Adviser to the Nepal Government, 1964–66.

Sir Eric placed his papers in the India Office Library (ref. MSS Eur D 829). A list is available (NRA 25125). The collection includes a memoir of the Sudan and five files of official reports on his work there and in Jordan.

FRANKLIN, SIR MICHAEL DAVID MILROY (1927–)
Civil servant. Permanent Secretary, Ministry of Agriculture, Fisheries and Food, 1983–87.

One box of his papers is in Churchill College, Cambridge. The material includes a diary of the British negotiations to join the EEC, 1961–63 (when he was private secretary to the then Sir Christopher Soames), as well as a memoir. A list is available (NRA 44041).

FRANKS, BARON Sir Oliver Shewell Franks (1905–92)
Academic, diplomat and public servant. Professor of Moral Philosophy, Glasgow University, 1937–45. Temporary civil servant, Ministry of Supply, 1939–45; Permanent Secretary, 1945–46. Ambassador, United States, 1948–52. Chairman of Lloyds Bank, 1954–62. Provost of Worcester College, Oxford, 1962–76. Chancellor of University of East Anglia, 1965–84.

Lord Franks stated in 1991 that he had retained few papers. Material relating to his time in Washington (cited in a previous survey) is presumed to have been destroyed. The surviving papers are described in the biography by Alex Danchev, *Oliver Franks: Founding Father* (1993).

FRASER OF LONSDALE, BARON Sir William Jocelyn Ian Fraser (1897–1974) MP (Con) St Pancras North, 1922–29 and 1931–36; Lonsdale, 1940–50; Morecambe and Lonsdale, 1950–58.

A substantial collection of papers has remained in family possession. The material includes constituency correspondence and files relating to his business interests.

FRASER OF NORTHCAPE, 1ST BARON Admiral of the Fleet Sir Bruce Austin Fraser (1888–1981) Naval career. Third Sea Lord and Controller, 1939–42. Commander-in-Chief, Home Fleet, 1943–44; Eastern Fleet, 1944; British Pacific Fleet, 1945–46; Portsmouth, 1947–48. First Sea Lord and Chief of Naval Staff, 1948–51.

His papers are held in the National Maritime Museum (ref. MS 82/076 and MS 83/158).

FREEDMAN, LAWRENCE (1948–) Academic. Professor of War Studies, King's College, London after 1982. Author of numerous publications.

The Liddell Hart Centre for Military Archives, King's College, London, has 242 files of material concerning SALT, START, the 1982 Falklands War, the first Gulf war, etc.

FREELAND, LIEUTENANT-GENERAL SIR IAN (HENRY) (1912–79) Military career, 1931–71. Served in World War II. General Officer Commanding, East Africa Command, 1963; British Forces, Kenya, and Kenya Army, 1963–64. Vice Adjutant-General, Ministry of Defence, 1965–68. Deputy Chief of General Staff, 1968. General Officer Commanding and Director of Operations, Northern Ireland, 1969–71.

The papers are not at present open to researchers. Inquiries concerning their eventual availability should be directed to the Department of Documents, Imperial War Museum.

FREEMAN, JOHN (1915–) MP (Lab) Watford, 1945–55. PPS to Secretary of State for War, 1945–46; PUS for War, 1947; Parliamentary Secretary, Ministry of Supply, 1947–51. Editor, *New Statesman*, 1961–65. High Commissioner, India, 1965–68. Ambassador, United States, 1969–71. Chairman and Chief Executive, London Weekend Television, 1971–84; ITN, 1976–81.

Mr Freeman has retained few papers apart from certain packages of personal papers dating back to the 1940s. Relevant correspondence may be found in the archives of the *New Statesman*, now deposited at the University of Sussex.

FREYBERG, 1ST BARON Lieutenant-General Sir Bernard Freyberg (1889–1963) Military career. Served in World Wars I and II. General Officer Commanding, Salisbury Plain, 1939; New Zealand Forces, 1939–45. Commander-in-Chief, Allied Forces, Crete, 1941. Governor-General, New Zealand, 1946–52.

The papers have remained in family possession and are described in a recent biography.

FRY, SIR LESLIE ALFRED CHARLES (1908–76) Diplomat. Served in the Indian Army and Indian political service, 1928–47. Ambassador to Hungary, 1955–59; Indonesia, 1959–63; Brazil, 1963–66.

A collection of papers, including official and other correspondence, photographs, newspaper cuttings and memoirs is deposited in the India Office Library (ref. MSS Eur F 199). A list is available (NRA 39208). The collection includes material on Hungary.

G

GAGE, CONOLLY HUGH (1905–84) MP (UU) Belfast South, 1945–52.

Some political papers, covering the period 1945–69, have been placed in the Public Record Office of Northern Ireland (ref. D3211). They include letters received on his resignation in 1952 and an interesting correspondence, 1958–59, with Jack Sayers, editor of the *Belfast Telegraph*. This ranges from the development and management of the Ulster Unionist Party to relations between the party and the Orange Order and between Captain Terence O'Neill and Brian Faulkner.

GAIRDNER, GENERAL SIR CHARLES HENRY (1898–1983) Military career from 1916. General Officer Commanding, 6th Armoured Division, 1942; 8th Armoured Division, 1943; Chief of General Staff, North Africa, 1943. Head of UK Liaison Mission, Japan, 1945–46. Prime Minister's Special Representative in Far East, 1945–48. Governor, Western Australia, 1951–63; Tasmania, 1963–68.

According to information received by the Liddell Hart Centre, King's College, London, certain papers including his 1947 diary may have remained in private hands in Australia. His 1942–44 diaries are deposited in the Imperial War Museum. Some correspondence with Lord Ismay, 1945–47, is held within a series of Cabinet papers at the Public Record Office (ref. CAB127/51–52).

GAITSKELL, HUGH TODD NAYLOR (1906–63) MP (Lab) Leeds South, 1945–63. PUS, Ministry of Fuel and Power, 1946–47; Minister of Fuel and Power, 1947–50. Minister of State for Economic Affairs, 1950. Chancellor of the Exchequer, 1950–51. Leader of the Labour Party, 1955–63.

Some 181 boxes of papers are deposited in the Library of University College London. The material chiefly dates from the 1950s and includes committee papers, correspondence, speech notes, press-cuttings and files on Party conferences and election campaigns. There are 12 boxes of constituency papers, including a long correspondence with his agent. Enquiries concerning access should be directed to the UCL Archivist.

Five additional files of Leeds constituency correspondence, 1952–62, form part of the Leeds South Labour Party Archive, deposited with the West Yorkshire Archives Service in Leeds (ref. Acc 2845).

GALLACHER, WILLIE (1881–1965) MP (Comm) Fife West, 1935–50. Communist Party President, 1956–63.

There are 12 boxes of papers in the archives of the former Communist Party of Great Britain, now deposited in the Labour History Archive and Study Centre, Manchester. The collection (1918–65) includes personal and political correspondence, mainly with R. Page Arnot, Margot Parrish and Michael Shapiro (*c.* 1947–64); correspondence relating to *Rise Like Lions* (1950–51); with Communist Party officials and the *Daily Worker* (*c.* 1951–63); and with John Gordon, John Junor, the *Daily Express* and other newspapers (*c.* 1951–63). There is also a diary of his 1952 trip to Australia with related correspondence and Gallacher's 'Observations on Australia'; manuscript and typescript versions of his literary writings; correspondence on religious matters (1958–63); and letters received following his defeat in the 1950 general election.

The Marx Memorial Library holds 11 files of letters and documents on unemployment benefit cases raised by Gallacher in the House of Commons. Reference should also be made to the Robin Page Arnot papers.

GALLOWAY, LIEUTENANT-GENERAL SIR ALEXANDER (1899–1977) Military career. General Officer Commanding-in-Chief, Malaya, 1946–47. High Commissioner and Commander-in-Chief, British Troops in Austria, 1947–50.

There are 11 boxes of correspondence, c. 1960–77, deposited in Churchill College, Cambridge. A list is available (NRA 18561 Churchill). The material includes letters from Field Marshal Montgomery.

GAMMANS, 1ST BARON Sir (Leonard) David Gammans (1895–1957) MP (Con) Hornsey, 1941–57. Assistant Postmaster-General, 1951–55. Colonial service, Malaya, 1920–34. Director of Land Settlement Association, 1934–39. Ministry of Information official, 1939–41.

A few papers are deposited in the London Metropolitan Archives. A list is available (NRA 21958). They consist of four series of scrapbooks, a small file of correspondence, various election addresses and typescript articles. There are also papers related to campaign issues in the 1950 election.

His diaries (1926–56) are held at Rhodes House Library, Oxford (ref. MSS Brit Emp s 506).

GARBETT, CYRIL FORSTER (1895–1955) Anglican clergyman. Archbishop of York, 1942–55. Bishop of Winchester, 1932–42; Southwark, 1919–32.

The papers, correspondence and diaries are held at the York Minster Archives (ref. COLL 1973/1). A list is available (NRA 26607). The material includes correspondence, diaries, sermons and addresses and press-cuttings.

GARDINER, BARON Gerald Austin Gardiner (1900–90) Lawyer and politician. Lord Chancellor, 1964–70. Chairman, National Campaign for the Abolition of Capital Punishment.

A collection of 19 boxes of legal papers, reports and printed material, including some correspondence, is held at Churchill College, Cambridge (ref. GARD). A list is available (NRA 44042). The British Library also has nine files of papers relating chiefly to his activities in the campaign for the abolition of capital punishment, 1946–69 (ref. Add MSS 56455–63).

GARNER, BARON (Joseph John) Saville Garner (1908–83) Diplomat. Deputy High Commissioner, India, 1951–53. High Commissioner, Canada, 1956–61. Permanent Under-Secretary, Commonwealth Relations Office, 1962–65; Commonwealth Office, 1965–68.

The papers and diaries cited in his book *The Commonwealth Office, 1925–68* (1978) have not been located. Some correspondence, 1942–43, is in the Clement Attlee papers at the Bodleian Library, Oxford (NRA 27633).

GARRETT, JOHN LAURENCE (1931–) MP (Lab) Norwich South, Feb. 1974–83 and 1987–97. Consultant, Fulton Committee on Civil Service Reform, 1966–68. PPS to Minister for Civil Service, 1974; to Minister for Social Security, 1977–79.

Mr Garrett states that he has retained comprehensive files on issues such as Civil Service reform; parliamentary reform; and internal Labour Party organisation and proposed reforms since 1972.

GATLIFF, HERBERT EVELYN CAULFIELD (fl. 1960s–70s) Civil servant. Pioneer of the environmental movement.

His correspondence and papers have been placed in the Bodleian Library, Oxford. A list is available (NRA 43948). The collection (201 boxes) contains much material on such organisations as the Council for the Preservation of Rural England, the National Trust, the Youth Hostels Association, the Ramblers Association, etc.

GEDYE, GEORGE ERIC ROWE (1890–1971) Journalist. Central Europe correspondent, *Daily Herald*, 1945–50; *Observer*, 1950–52. *Manchester Guardian* correspondent for Central and South East Europe, 1953–54. Vienna correspondent of Radio Free Europe and Special Correspondent for the *Guardian*, 1956–61.

An extensive collection of papers covering the whole of his career, 1916–60, is held at the Imperial War Museum. A list is available (NRA 28545). The material includes newspaper articles, propaganda papers and typescripts of his autobiographical book, *Curtain Raiser*, and other works. The post-war section of the collection includes correspondence with eastern European dissidents; material on the Romanian spy trial, 1950; and weekly newsletters issued by Radio Free Europe, 1956. The archives of the *Manchester Guardian*, which are deposited in the John Rylands University Library, Manchester, include his correspondence with the newspaper, 1921–55.

GELLNER, ERNEST ANDRÉ (1925–95) Academic. Professor of Social Anthropology, University of Cambridge after 1984. Author of numerous major works.

A large collection of papers has been deposited in the LSE Library by his family. The collection was provisionally catalogued before the deposit was made.

GEOFFREY-LLOYD, BARON Geoffrey William Lloyd (1902–84) MP (Con) Birmingham Ladywood, 1931–45; Birmingham King's Norton, 1951–55; Sutton Coldfield, 1955–Feb. 1974. Secretary for Mines, 1939–40; Minister in Charge of Petroleum Warfare Department, 1940–45; Minister of Information, 1945; Minister of Fuel and Power, 1951–55; Minister of Education, 1957–59.

A collection of papers documenting his career during World War II is held at the Imperial War Museum (ref. 85/46/32). The collection comprises correspondence and memoranda as wartime Secretary for Mines, and includes details of negotiations between the British and American governments on oil allocations. No information regarding post-war papers has been obtained.

GEORGE-BROWN, BARON George Alfred Brown (1914–85) MP (Lab) Belper, 1945–70. Joint Parliamentary Secretary, Ministry of Agriculture and Fisheries, 1947–51; Minister of Works, 1951; First Secretary of State and Secretary of State for Economic Affairs, 1964–66; Foreign Secretary, 1966–68.

The papers have been deposited at the Bodleian Library, Oxford. Enquiries should be directed to the Archivist.

GIBB, PROFESSOR ANDREW DEWAR (d. 1974) Professor of Law, University of Glasgow, 1934–58.

The diaries, correspondence and papers for the period 1905–65 are held at the National Library of Scotland (ref. Dep. 217). A list is available (NRA 29072). The collection includes correspondence and papers on the Scottish National Party, drafts for political and other speeches and broadcasts, files on Home Rule and the 'Scottish constitution'. There is also material on the Scottish legal system, personal diaries (62 volumes), press-cuttings, and around 200 printed pamphlets.

GIBBS, AIR MARSHAL SIR GERALD ERNEST (1896–1992) Served in World Wars I and II; Director of Overseas Operations, Air Ministry, 1942–43; Chief Air Staff Officer to Lord Mountbatten, South East Asia Command, 1945–46. Chairman of UK Members of Military Staff Committee, United Nations, 1948–51. Chief of Air Staff and Commander-in-Chief, Indian Air Force, 1951–54.

The Liddell Hart Centre, King's College, London, has a collection of papers, 1928–63, mainly covering the development of airpower.

GIBBS, SIR HUMPHREY VICARY (1902–90) Governor of Rhodesia (Southern Rhodesia), 1959–69.

Some papers (8 boxes of correspondence) are reported to be in Zimbabwe. Initial enquiries are best addressed to BLCAS (Rhodes House Library), Oxford.

GIBSON, CHARLES WILLIAM (1889–1977) MP (Lab) Kennington, 1945–50; Clapham 1950–59.

The papers are deposited in Sussex University Library (ref. Sx MS 35). A list is available (NRA 21355). There are two boxes of diaries, notebooks and miscellaneous material for the period 1911–68 and a draft of an autobiography *Memoirs of a Cockney MP*.

GIBSON, D. (fl. 1920s–50s) National chairman of the Independent Labour Party in the post-war period.

The Imperial War Museum holds a large collection of papers relating to his career in the Independent Labour Party (ILP), 1924–55. The material includes files on the ILP's anti-war stance and conscientious objection. Gibson's period as a local councillor and ILP candidate in several by-elections is also documented. The collection includes ephemeral election material and copies of the *New Leader* and *Socialist Leader*.

GIBSON, T.H. (fl. 1923–68) Scottish nationalist and politician.

There are papers in the National Library of Scotland (ref. ACC 6058). A list is available (NRA 29288). The collection includes correspondence, 1923–68; agenda and minutes of meetings and conference proceedings, 1925–68; papers and correspondence relating to the Welsh Breton Committee, 1947;

miscellaneous press-cuttings and notes; pamphlets produced by the Scottish National Party and other groups; and periodicals.

GILCHRIST, SIR ANDREW (GRAHAM) (1910–93) Diplomat. Served as Ambassador to Iceland, Indonesia and Ireland.

Some papers have been placed in Churchill College, Cambridge.

GILL, STANLEY (1926–75) Computer and technology expert. Consultant, Ministry of Technology, 1966–69. Professor of Computing Science, 1964–70, and Director of Centre for Computing and Automation, Imperial College, London, 1966–70.

A large collection of papers is held at the Science Museum Library. A list is available (NRA 21399). The collection covers all aspects of computing and 'computing policy' and includes extensive press-cuttings and commercial and political reports. There are also records of various groups such as the Parliamentary Select Committee on Science and Technology, 1969–71.

GINSBERG, MORRIS (1889–1970) Sociologist. Editor of *British Journal of Sociology* and *Sociology Review*, London School of Economics, 1929–54. Author of *The Psychology of Society* (1921), *On Justice in Society* (1965), etc.

A collection of papers, correspondence and printed material (12 boxes) is held at the LSE Library. A list is available (NRA 30243). The collection includes material such as trade union pamphlets and papers, papers on the Association of University Teachers, anthropology, casual labour, eugenics, women in industry, social evolution and inequality. The correspondence dates chiefly from the 1940s to the 1960s with some earlier material concerning L.T. Hobhouse. There are also notebooks, questionnaires, examination papers, manuscript notes for some of his works, and university and school papers.

GLADWYN, 1ST BARON Sir Hubert Miles Gladwyn Jebb (1900–96) Diplomat, 1924–60. Counsellor, Foreign Office, 1943–46. Acting General Secretary, United Nations, 1946; Acting Under-Secretary and United Nations Adviser, 1946–47. UK Representative to the United Nations, 1950–54.

Ambassador to France, 1954–60. Deputy Leader of Liberal Party in the House of Lords and Liberal Spokesman on Foreign Affairs and Defence, 1965–88. MEP, 1973–76.

Churchill College, Cambridge holds 85 boxes of correspondence and papers covering the period 1956–96 (ref. GLAD). A list is available (NRA 43167). The collection includes much material on his work as Deputy Liberal Leader in the House of Lords and his work as an MEP and Vice-President of the European Parliament Political Committee. There are also pocket diaries.

GLUBB, LIEUTENANT GENERAL SIR JOHN BAGOT (1897–1986) Military career. Served in World Wars I and II. Transferred from Royal Engineers to Iraq Government, 1926. Administrative Inspector, Iraq and Transjordan. Chief of General Staff, Arab Legion, Jordan, 1939–56.

Some papers have been deposited in the Middle East Centre, St Antony's College, Oxford. They consist of memoranda, reports, telegrams and correspondence relating mainly to Iraq and Jordan, 1920–56. Additional material can be found in the H. St John Philby collection, also at St Antony's.

GLYN, 1ST BARON Ralph George Campbell Glyn (1885–1960) MP (Con) Stirlingshire East and Clackmannan, 1918–22; Abingdon, 1924–53.

Correspondence and papers for the period 1900–60 are held at the Berkshire Record Office (ref. D/EG1). A list is available (NRA 24810). The collection consists mainly of material on his earlier army career together with political and family correspondence. There are some post-war files on the Select Committee on Estimates (1946–53) as well as defence and foreign policy issues (including Suez, Cyprus and the Atomic Energy Commission). His correspondents include Sir Anthony Eden, Clement Attlee and Emanuel Shinwell. His memoranda on the Select Committee on National Expenditure are in the House of Lords Record Office.

GLYN HUGHES, HUGH LLEWELYN (1892–1975) Royal Army Medical Corps career. Vice-Director of Medical Services, British Army of the Rhine, 1945.

A substantial collection of correspondence, reports and photographs, 1916–72, is deposited with the

Wellcome Contemporary Medical Archives Centre, London (ref. 1218). The material includes his reports as the first medical officer to inspect Belsen Concentration Camp and copies of his lectures and articles on the medical aspects of the liberation of Europe, 1946–47. There are also extensive files on the post-war reorganisation of the Royal Army Medical Corps, 1946–64. These include material on the provision of medical services in Palestine, 1946–47.

GODBER OF WILLINGTON, BARON Joseph Bradshaw Godber (1914–80) MP (Con) Grantham, 1951–79. PUS, Foreign Office, 1960–61; Minister of State, 1961–63; Secretary of State for War, Jun.–Oct. 1963; Minister of Labour, 1963–64; Minister of State, Foreign and Commonwealth Office, 1970–72; Minister of Agriculture, Fisheries and Food, 1972–74.

According to *British Cabinet Ministers, 1900–51*, few papers have remained in the family's possession. An interview recorded in 1980 is held at the LSE Library.

GODFREY, CARDINAL WILLIAM (1889–1963) Roman Catholic clergyman. Archbishop of Westminster, 1956–63; Archbishop of Liverpool, 1953–56.

An extensive collection of correspondence and papers is held at the Westminster Diocesan Archives. An outline catalogue is available.

GOLLAN, JOHN (1891–1977) General Secretary, Communist Party of Great Britain, 1956–77.

A collection of papers is held with the archive of the former Communist Party of Great Britain, now deposited in the Labour History Archive and Study Centre, Manchester. The papers date from the 1930s to the 1970s, and include a file on China, European Community reports, typescript articles and speeches. An unpublished biography is held at the National Library of Scotland (ref. Acc 11479).

GOLLANCZ, SIR VICTOR (1893–1967) Publisher. Founded firm of Victor Gollancz Ltd, 1928. Launched Left Book Club, 1936. Organised 'Save Europe Now' campaign, 1945. Founder of the Jewish Society for Human Service, 1948. Founder of War on Want, 1951. Chairman, National Campaign for the Abolition of Capital Punishment, from 1955.

An important donation of papers was placed at the Modern Records Centre, University of Warwick in 1977 (ref. MSS 157). A list is available (NRA 40639). The papers reflect his wide range of interests in political and humanitarian causes, including the Left Book Club, the 'Save Europe Now' Movement, the United Europe Movement, the Association for World Peace and various Jewish organisations. Regular correspondents include Sir Richard Acland, Daphne du Maurier, Canon Collins, Harold Laski, Vera Brittain, Sir Basil Liddell Hart, Peggy Duff and Gilbert Murray. There are also files of correspondence covering visits to Germany, literary works, letters to the press and political activities.

Further additions have been made since the initial deposit. These papers document his involvement with organisations such as the Jewish Society for Human Service, the Labour Party, and the Association for World Peace. There are also drafts, letters and background material from his fourth volume of autobiography *Reminiscences of Affection*. The collection also includes personal and family correspondence and press-cuttings. Further details on sources are given in Ruth Dudley Edwards' work, *Victor Gollancz: A Biography* (1987).

GOODE, SIR WILLIAM ALLMOND CODRINGTON (1907–86) Colonial Service, 1931–63. Chief Secretary, Aden, 1949–53; Singapore, 1953–57. Governor, Singapore, 1957–59; North Borneo, 1960–63.

Five boxes of material concerning his years as Governor of North Borneo, 1960–63, are deposited in Rhodes House Library, Oxford (ref. MSS Ind Ocn s 323). The collection includes material relating to the formation of the Federation of Malaya, 1963 and to general political developments in the region, including the rise of Lee Kuan Yew and the People's Action Party in Singapore. A handlist to the collection is available at Rhodes House where transcripts and tapes of an interview concerning his career can also be consulted (ref. MSS Ind Ocn s 225). A list is available (NRA 35462)

GOODHART, ARTHUR LEHMAN (1891–1978) Lawyer and public servant. Professor of Jurisprudence, Oxford University, 1931–51. Master of University College, Oxford, 1951–63. Served on numerous public bodies, including the Royal Commission on the Police and the Monopolies Commission.

More than 300 boxes of correspondence and papers, 1906–78, have been deposited in the Bodleian Library, Oxford (ref. MSS Eng b 2040, c 2821–3113, d 2373–84 and e 2730–2731). They include extensive material on Anglo-American relations including files on the Warren Commission and on the Watergate scandal. His involvement with domestic politics and legal reform is also fully documented. A list is available (NRA 36176).

GOODMAN, BARON Arnold Abraham Goodman (1913–95) Academic, lawyer and public servant. Chairman, Newspaper Publishers Association, 1970–76; Housing Corporation, 1973–77. Master of University College, Oxford, 1976–86.

Lord Goodman retained extensive files. The papers were used in the biography by Brian Brivati.

GOODMAN, SIR VICTOR MARTIN REEVES (1899–1967) Clerk of the Parliaments, 1959–63.

There are 16 files of his official papers, covering the period 1939–62, at the House of Lords Record Office (ref. Hist Coll 321). A list is available.

GORDON-WALKER, BARON Patrick Chrestien Gordon Walker (1907–80) MP (Lab) Smethwick, 1945–64; Leyton, 1966–Feb. 1974. PUS for Commonwealth Relations, 1947–50; Secretary of State for Commonwealth Relations, 1950–51; Foreign Secretary, 1964–65; Minister without Portfolio, 1966–67; Secretary of State for Education and Science, 1967–68.

Fifteen boxes of diaries, correspondence and papers were given to Churchill College, Cambridge, in May 1981. A list is available (NRA 24835). Additional Private Office papers are held at the Public Record Office (ref. CAB 127/296–325) (NRA 32409). These reflect his responsibilities as Secretary of State for Commonwealth Relations. Other material held at the Public Record Office relates to his work as Chairman of Ministerial Committees on UK and overseas information services (ref. CP 51/136).

GORE-BOOTH, BARON Paul Henry Gore-Booth (1909–84) Diplomat. Served in Tokyo, 1938–42;

Washington 1942–45. Head of United Nations Economic and Social and Refugee Departments, 1947–48; European Recovery Department, Foreign Office, 1948–49. Director, British Information Services in the USA, 1949–53. Ambassador to Burma, 1953–56. Deputy Under-Secretary (Economic Affairs), Foreign Office, 1956–60. British High Commissioner in India, 1960–65. PUS, Foreign Office, 1965–69; Head of HM Diplomatic Service, 1968–69.

Over 200 boxes of correspondence and papers have been placed in the Bodleian Library, Oxford (ref. MSS Gore-Booth 1–223). The collection was substantially augmented in 1989 by the discovery of papers dating from the late 1940s and early 1950s, thought to have been lost in a fire (ref. MSS Gore-Booth Adds 1–44/2). The collection includes appointment and desk diaries, 1953–81, and files on his overseas postings and on his later reforms of the Diplomatic Service, 1968–70. There are also papers on the Middle East, 1970; the Soames affair, 1971; the House of Lords discussion group, 1975 and 1979; and the release of Rudolf Hess, 1976–78.

The material discovered in 1989 documents in greater detail his time as Director-General of the British Information Services in Washington and also covers trade with the East including Communist China, the Korean War, Suez, and the effect of the Anglo-Iranian oil nationalisation on Anglo-American relations. There are also additional files on his work as Ambassador to Burma; High Commissioner in India; the Ditchley Park Conferences, 1967–78; and his chairmanship of the Save the Children Fund. Most of the post-1970 files and some of the earlier material are subject to restrictions on access and all enquiries should be directed to the Archivist.

GORE-BROWN, SIR STEWART (1883–1967) Politician and settler in Northern Rhodesia.

His correspondence for the period 1911–56 is in Rhodes House Library, Oxford.

GRACEY, GENERAL SIR DOUGLAS DAVID (1894–1964) Indian Army career. Served in World Wars I and II; commanded 17th Indian Infantry Brigade, Iraq and Syria, 1941–42; 20th Indian Division, India, 1942–46; Allied Land Forces, French Indo-China, 1945–46. General Officer Commanding-in-Chief, Northern Command, India, 1946. Commanded 1st Indian Corps, 1946–47. Chief of Staff, Pakistan Army, 1947. Commander-in-Chief, Pakistan Army, 1947–51.

The Liddell Hart Centre, King's College, London has eight boxes of papers, 1941–47, relating primarily to Burma and Indo-China.

GRAFFTEY-SMITH, SIR LAURENCE BARTON (1892–1989) Levant Consular Service, 1914–51. Consul-General, Albania, 1939–40. Minister, Saudi Arabia, 1945–47. High Commissioner, Pakistan, 1947–51.

Some papers covering the period 1947–69 are held at the Middle East Centre, St Antony's College, Oxford. A list is available (NRA 20811). The papers relate to his time in Karachi, and as British delegate on the Governor-General's Commission in Khartoum, 1953–56.

GRAHAM, SIR JOHN (ALEXANDER NOBLE) (1926–) Diplomat. Principal Private Secretary to Foreign and Commonwealth Secretary, 1969–72. Ambassador to Iraq, 1974–77; Iran, 1979–80. Deputy Under-Secretary of State, FCO, 1980–82, etc.

His speeches and notes for the period 1972–94 are in the Liddell Hart Centre for Military Archives, King's College, London.

GRAHAM, MAJOR-GENERAL JOHN DAVID CAREW (1923–) Army career. Commander, Sultan's Armed Forces, Oman, 1970–72.

His papers concerning the Sultan's armed forces and Oman, 1970–72, are in the Middle East Centre, St Antony's College, Oxford. See NRA 43251.

GRANDY, MARSHAL OF THE ROYAL AIR FORCE SIR JOHN (1913–) Royal Air Force career, 1931–71. Served in World War II. Air Attaché, Brussels, 1949. Commander, Task Force Operation 'Grapple' (Nuclear Weapon Test Force), Christmas Island, 1957–58. Assistant Chief of Air Staff (Operations), 1958–61. Commander-in-Chief, Far East Command, 1965–67. Chief of Air Staff, 1967–71.

According to information supplied to the Liddell Hart Centre, King's College, London, the papers are to be deposited in the Royal Air Force Museum, Hendon. The Air Historical Branch of the Ministry of Defence has recorded an interview with Sir John covering his entire career.

GRANSDEN, SIR ROBERT (1893–1972) Civil servant, Northern Ireland, 1922–57. Permanent Secretary, Northern Ireland Cabinet, Clerk of the Privy Council and Secretary to Northern Ireland Prime Minister, 1939–57. Ulster Agent in Great Britain, 1957–62.

Some correspondence is held in the PM8 series of government files at the Public Record Office of Northern Ireland. His personal correspondence for 1957 and letters exchanged with two friends in the United States and Canada, 1951–58, are open to researchers (refs PM8/47 and PM8/48). His earlier correspondence, 1944–51, is subject to a 75-year closure rule (refs PM8/35 and PM8/41).

GRANT, BERNIE (BERNARD ALEXANDER MONTGOMERY) (1944–2000) MP (Lab) Tottenham, 1987–2000. Important figure in the Black Labour Movement.

The papers were deposited by his widow in the Library of the University of Middlesex (ref. GB 2925 BG). A list is available (NRA 44189). The collection (c. 70 boxes, mainly 1980 onwards) includes correspondence and subject files, papers of the African Reparation Movement, material on the Broadwater Farm affair, trade union activities, etc.

GREEN, BRIGADIER HENRY JAMES LINDSAY (1911–86) Served in France, North Africa and Italy during World War II. Officer Commanding, 2nd Battalion, Coldstream Guards, 1955–58. Officer Commanding, 1st Federal Infantry Brigade, Malaya, 1958–61. Chief of Staff, HQ London District, 1961–64.

Two boxes of papers and photographs, 1939–75, are deposited in the Liddell Hart Centre, King's College, London. Much of the material concerns counter-insurgency operations in Malaya and includes his account of his brigade's work there, 1959–61 (written in 1973), photograph albums, 1959–60, and a flying logbook, 1958–61. The collection also contains material on morale in the British Army of the Rhine in the immediate post-war period.

GREENBERG, IVAN MARION (1896–1966) Journalist. Editor, *Jewish Chronicle*, 1936–46.

A collection of papers and correspondence for the period 1936–49 is held at Southampton University (ref. MS 150). A list is available (NRA 22070). The collection includes extensive correspondence, articles, lectures, pamphlets, notes and reports from his time as editor of the *Jewish Chronicle*. There is a considerable amount of material relating to Palestine, the establishment of the State of Israel and Zionism. The subject files cover Palestine, Israel, Zionism, Herut, the Irgun, Shelach, refugees, and resettlement. There are also various articles submitted for publication, newspaper-cuttings and other material.

GREENE, SIR HUGH CARLETON (1910–87) Journalist, broadcaster and publisher. Director-General of the BBC, 1960–69. Chairman, The Bodley Head, 1969–81; President, 1981–87.

A collection of correspondence and papers has been deposited in the Bodleian Library, Oxford. Most of the material relates to the non-BBC aspects of his career, including his role as an adviser on broadcasting in Germany, Malaya, Israel and Greece. Other papers relate to his interest in anti-censorship issues and freedom of journalistic expression. Additional unlisted material includes printed matter, newspaper cuttings and photographs.

GREENIDGE, CHARLES WILTON WOOD (1889–1972) Colonial administrator and anti-slavery campaigner. Chief Justice of British Honduras, 1932–36; Solicitor-General, Nigeria, 1936–41. Secretary, Anti-Slavery and Aborigines Protection Society, 1941–56; Director, 1957–68.

Some 33 boxes of papers dating mainly from the 1940s and 1950s are available at Rhodes House Library, Oxford (ref. MSS Brit Emp s 285). A list is available (NRA 14913). Boxes 2–7 detail his work for the Anti-Slavery Society and other groups, and are arranged regionally, including files on South Africa, south-west Africa, other High Commission territories and the Seychelles. Boxes 8–10 contain papers on societies and committees related to race relations, the welfare of colonial peoples, human rights, post-war planning, etc. Boxes 11 and 12 deal with the Fabian Colonial Bureau and the Labour Party Advisory Committee on Colonial Affairs respectively. Boxes 13–20 hold files on the Settlement

Commission and related issues dating from the immediate post-war period. Boxes 21–25 contain draft reports as well as correspondence with MPs, officials and private individuals in the UK and the West Indies, mainly on colonial matters. Boxes 26–30 consist of lectures, articles, printed matter and private correspondence and papers. Boxes 31–33 contain papers concerning Lord Olivier and consist mainly of alternative draft versions of an incomplete published work, *The Dual Ethic of Empire*, with related material for appendices.

GREENWOOD OF ROSSENDALE, BARON Arthur William James (Anthony) Greenwood (1911–82) MP (Lab) Heywood and Radcliffe, 1946–50; Rossendale, 1950–70. Secretary of State for Colonial Affairs, 1964–65. Minister of Overseas Development, 1965–66. Minister of Housing and Local Government, 1966–70.

A collection of 151 boxes of papers has been deposited at the Bodleian Library, Oxford. A list is available (NRA 32908). The papers date from the 1930s and the major subject areas include World War II; the Labour Party; the Rossendale constituency; cotton; broadcasting; defence, disarmament and CND; Pakistan and Bangladesh; the European Community; the Colonial Office; the Foreign Office, especially relations with Israel; Ministry for Overseas Development; the Overseas Investment Bill, 1971–72; the Ministry of Housing and Local Government; the Universities of Lancaster and Guyana; and papers for biographies of himself and his father. There are also copies of some speeches, press-cuttings and various publications. The collection is not yet fully catalogued and there are some restrictions on access.

GREENWOOD, ARTHUR (1880–1954) MP (Lab) Nelson and Colne, 1922–31; Wakefield, 1932–54. Minister without Portfolio, 1940–42. Lord Privy Seal, 1945–47. Paymaster-General 1946–47.

There are 93 boxes of papers and correspondence in the Bodleian Library, Oxford. A list is available (NRA 32908). The collection spans his whole career covering major subject areas such as reconstruction policy after both World Wars; the Labour Party, including correspondence, 1948–54, and material on the National Executive Committee and Party Conferences during the 1940s and 1950s; Wakefield,

1948–54; health and education, especially adult education; employment (Juvenile Labour Exchanges); trade unions; housing; the European League for Economic Co-operation; and the Workers Education Association. The collection is not yet fully catalogued but an outline list is available.

GREER, LIEUTENANT-COLONEL ERIC ROBERTS (fl. 1940s–50s) Military career. Served as Military Attaché, Moscow, Ankara, Bucharest, etc.

His letters to his wife while Military Attaché in Moscow, Ankara and Bucharest, 1940–47, have been placed in the National Army Museum (ref. 1999–10–64).

GREER, GERMAINE (1939–) Lecturer and author of *The Female Eunuch* (1970), *The Obstacle Race* (1979) and *Sex and Destiny* (1984). Leading feminist.

Dr Greer states that the papers are in her possession, and that provision will be made for their eventual deposit. See NRA 43329.

GRETTON, VICE-ADMIRAL SIR PETER (1912–92) Naval career, 1926–73. Convoy escort commander during World War II. Commanded Naval Task Force during Operation 'Grapple' (British atomic bomb tests), Christmas Island, 1956–57. Deputy Chief of Naval Staff, 1961–63.

One box of autobiographical material has been deposited at Churchill College, Cambridge. A list is available (NRA 18561).

GREY, ANTHONY (1927–) (pseudonym of A.E.G. (EDGAR) WRIGHT) Campaigner for gay rights. Secretary, Homosexual Law Reform Society after 1962. Director Albany Trust etc.

The papers, covering the period 1958–92, have been deposited in the LSE Library. The collection comprises a mass of correspondence, reports, papers, minutes, etc. relating to the movement for homosexual law reform and related matters.

GRIERSON, JOHN (1898–1972) Documentary film producer. Involved in formation of the Empire Marketing Board and General Post Office film units. General Manager, Canadian Wartime Information Board, 1942–43. Director of Mass Communications, UNESCO, 1946–48. Controller, Films, Central Office

of Information, 1948–50. Professor of Communications, McGill University.

The John Grierson Archive was opened at the University of Stirling in 1977. A list is available (NRA 23838). The papers include manuscripts and typescripts of correspondence, lectures, speeches, memoranda and policy papers relating to his involvement with a large number of national and international agencies. Also included are press-cuttings, correspondence, and various publications by Grierson. Additional material on the Empire Marketing Board Film Unit can be found in the papers of Sir Stephen Tallents (NRA 29111). McGill University, Montreal, Canada, also holds some material (mainly for the latter part of his career).

GRIEVE, CHRISTOPHER MURRAY (1892–1978) (pseudonym HUGH McDIARMID) Poet and journalist. Active in communist politics, and a founder of the Scottish National Party.

A collection of correspondence and literary papers is held at Edinburgh University Library. The collection includes some 200 letters, 1922–64, together with typescripts of books and articles. Additional correspondence and papers are at the National Library of Scotland (ref. Acc 7361). This includes *c.* 4500 letters, 1929–78, with material on his candidacy as a Communist in the Kinross and West Perthshire election. A list is available (NRA 40776).

GRIEVE, JAMES MICHAEL (fl. 1930s–80s) Journalist, broadcaster and Scottish National Party activist.

His personal and political papers, including correspondence of and relating to his parents, 1933–93, have been placed in the National Library of Scotland (ref. Acc 11857).

GRIEVE, PROFESSOR SIR ROBERT (1910–95) Civil servant, 1946–54. Chief Planner, Scottish Office, 1960–64; Professor of Town and Regional Planning, Glasgow University, 1964–74. First Chairman of the Highlands and Islands Development Board, 1965–70.

An extensive collection of papers, *c.* 1945–64, has been placed in the National Library of Scotland. This material includes personal correspondence and papers; lectures and articles, 1942–65; reports, surveys and records of meetings concerning the

Clyde Valley Regional Plan, 1945–46; and files on general planning policy in Scotland. The papers are listed.

GRIFFIN, CARDINAL BERNARD WILLIAM (1899–1956) Roman Catholic clergyman. Archbishop of Westminster, 1943–56; Auxiliary Bishop of Birmingham, 1938–43.

Westminster Diocesan Archives holds a substantial collection of papers. They include files relating to post-war development work in Africa.

GRIFFITH, JOHN (1918–) Professor of Public Law, London School of Economics. Founding Chair, Campaign for Academic Freedom and Democracy.

A large number of files related to the Campaign for Academic Freedom and Democracy are held with the Saville papers at the Brynmor Jones Library, University of Hull.

GRIFFITHS, GWYN (fl. 1970s–80s) Welsh Liberal Party leader until formation of the Social and Liberal Democrats in 1988.

A collection of papers is held at the National Library of Wales. The papers include Liberal Party National Executive Committee agenda, minutes and correspondence, 1980–83; Liberal Party Council correspondence and papers, 1978–85; Campaigns and Elections Committee agenda, minutes and papers, 1980–83; Young Liberal Movement correspondence and papers, 1975–78; Liberal Party Assemblies, 1976–85; Liberal Party Standing Committee correspondence and minutes, 1979–84. Additional material consists of Welsh Centre for International Affairs correspondence and papers, 1979–88; Alliance Action Group for Electoral Reform papers and correspondence; Association of Liberal Councillors, 1981–88; Welsh League of Young Liberals, 1975–82; the Liberal Ecology Group, 1978–84; Liberal Agents Association, 1979–86; and also various Liberal Party pamphlets, 1970–81. Requests for access should be directed to the Archivist.

GRIFFITHS, JAMES (1890–1975) MP (Lab) Llanelli, 1936–70. Minister of National Insurance, 1945–50. Secretary of State for the Colonies, 1950–51. Secretary of State for Wales, 1964–66.

An extensive collection of letters, typescripts, memoranda and printed material has been deposited

in the National Library of Wales. A list is available (NRA 23695). The papers are divided into five main categories. Section A covers his early career, 1890–1936. Section B relates to political activities from the 1930s until his death, including material from his time as Minister of National Insurance, 1945–50; the Labour Party Conference of 1949; colonial affairs 1939–72; the visit of Bulganin and Khrushchev; the Suez crisis in 1956; the Council of Europe in 1958; the Nigerian-Biafra War of 1968–70; and National Superannuation and Social Insurance, 1969. Section C relates to Welsh affairs, including material on devolution; constituency affairs; education; local government reorganisation; and papers from his time as Secretary of State for Wales, 1964–66, including the Welsh White Paper of 1965. Section D contains papers relating to the autobiography, *Pages from Memory* (1969). Section E contains speeches, addresses, broadcasts, articles, reviews, reminiscences and press-cuttings.

GRIMOND, BARON Joseph Grimond (1913–93) MP (Lib) Orkney and Shetland, 1950–83. Leader of the Parliamentary Liberal Party, 1956–67.

Sixteen boxes of papers and correspondence, 1952–83, have been deposited at the National Library of Scotland (ref. Dep 363). A list is available (NRA 29120). Boxes 1–4 contain his engagement diaries as an MP, with related correspondence, 1952–83. Boxes 5–8 consist of drafts and copies of articles, reviews and broadcasts; press-cuttings of articles, book reviews, broadcasts and occasional writings, as well as related correspondence, 1967–83. Boxes 9–11 contain political speeches, 1968–83. Boxes 12 and 13 hold correspondence and papers concerning his publications. Boxes 14–16 contain photographs, correspondence, and material relating to the Local Government and Orkney and Shetland Bills. A later deposit of constituency correspondence, *c*. 1970–83, is currently closed (ref. Dep 364).

GRIMSTON OF WESTBURY, 1ST BARON Sir Robert Villiers Grimston (1897–1979) MP (Con) Westbury, 1931–64. Assistant Postmaster General, 1942–45; Parliamentary Secretary, Ministry of Supply, 1945; Deputy Chairman of the Ways and Means Committee, 1962–64.

Private Office papers (AVIA 11) can be found at the Public Record Office. No other papers have been located.

GRIST, IAN (1938–) MP (Con) Cardiff North, Feb. 1974–83; Cardiff Central, 1983–92. PUS, Welsh Office, 1987–90.

The papers were deposited in the Welsh Political Archive at the National Library of Wales in 1992. They include his entire constituency correspondence, 1974–92, together with files on wider issues such as abortion, devolution, immigration and west Africa.

GROCOTT, BRUCE JOSEPH (1940–) MP (Lab) Lichfield and Tamworth, Oct. 1974–79; The Wrekin, since 1987.

Constituency papers covering the period 1974–79 are held at the Staffordshire Record Office.

GROVES, REG (1908–88) Journalist, socialist activist and historian. Pioneer member of the British Section of the International Left Opposition.

There are papers at the Modern Records Centre, University of Warwick (ref. MSS 172). A list is available (NRA 26872). The bulk of the collection was acquired between 1978 and 1980 and relates to his various political campaigns. It also contains research material for his various books, articles and films. Among the files there are papers relating to the Beveridge Report and social insurance, 1936–52; a proposed film on the work of the Labour Government, 1946–47; correspondence; leaflets; and press-cuttings regarding his various Labour candidatures during the 1940s and 1950s.

Mrs Daisy Groves donated additional papers in 1989. These consist of notes and secondary material relating to his adult education work. There are also files on Christian Socialism; the National Union of Agricultural Workers; the International Socialists, 1973; a small amount on the No Conscription League and Socialist Anti-War Front; Victory for Socialism, 1943–45; and some research, publishing and political correspondence.

GULLAND, JOHN ALAN (1926–90) Fisheries ecologist. Senior Research Fellow, Centre for Environmental Technology, Imperial College, London, 1984–90. Adviser, International Whaling Commission, 1964–86; International Commission on Northwest Atlantic Fisheries, 1960–67; Canadian Royal Commission on Seals and Sealing, 1984–86.

Some papers relating to his time at the Centre for Environmental Technology are held at Imperial College, London. These include records of his consultancy work for the European Community, Canadian Government, International Centre for Ocean Development, the International Institute for Environment and Development, Natural Environment Research Council and Project Prospero (to improve management of living marine resources). There are also publications and related correspondence; papers on visits, lectures and meetings such as the 1985 Antarctic Treaty Conference, and correspondence, 1984–90. Enquiries regarding access to the collection should be directed to the Archivist.

H

HACKETT, GENERAL SIR JOHN WINTHROP (1910–97) Military career. Commanded Trans-jordan Frontier Force, 1947–48. Deputy Chief of General Staff, 1964–66. Commander-in-Chief, British Army of the Rhine and Commander, Northern Army Group, 1966–68. Principal, King's College, London, 1968–75.

The Liddell Hart Centre, King's College, London, has a collection of papers, 1944–74. A list is available (NRA 23070). They include correspondence on NATO strategy and German affairs, 1966–68, and research material on Arnhem, 1944. The Imperial War Museum's Department of Sound Records holds an interview concerning the Transjordan Frontier Force, 1933–48 (ref. 004527/06).

HAILES, 1ST BARON Patrick George Thomas Buchan-Hepburn (1901–74) MP (Con) Liverpool East Toxteth, 1931–50; Beckenham, 1950–57. Junior Lord of the Treasury, 1939 and 1944. Parliamentary Secretary, Treasury and Government Chief Whip, 1951–55. Minister of Works, 1955–57. Governor General and Commander-in-Chief, West Indies, 1958–62.

Some 50 boxes of papers, correspondence and newspaper cuttings were donated to Churchill College, Cambridge by Lady Hailes in 1978. A detailed list is available (NRA 24830). Among the more personal correspondence are letters from Sir Winston Churchill while Lord Hailes was his Private Secretary and then as Chief Whip. There are also constituency papers for East Toxteth, 1931–50, and Beckenham, 1950–57. Some of the correspondence is subject to restricted access. The newspaper cuttings chiefly record his time in the West Indies.

HAILEY, 1ST BARON Sir William Malcolm Hailey (1872–1969) Pre-war Governor of the Punjab and United Provinces, India. On Permanent Members Commission, League of Nations, 1935–39. Head of Economic Mission to Belgian Congo, 1940–41. Chairman, Governing Body, School of Oriental and African Studies, London, 1941–45 and International African Institute, 1945–47; Colonial Research Committee, 1943–48.

Several deposits of Lord Hailey's papers have been made in Rhodes House Library, Oxford. These include his correspondence, journals and papers, 1912–66 (ref. MSS Brit Emp s 334–340); an interview covering his career, 1931–63 (ref. MSS Brit Emp s 357); a survey of native affairs in Namibia, 1946; his diaries of various visits to Africa; Colonial Research Committee papers, 1940–43; and his lectures for the British Council, 1946–47.

Further African correspondence, 1947–55, is held at the Public Record Office (ref. CO 1018). A list is available (NRA 28777).

His Indian papers, 1898–1953, are deposited in the India Office Library (ref. MSS Eur E 220). A list is available (NRA 27482).

HAILSHAM OF SAINT MARYLEBONE, BARON Quintin McGarel Hogg, 2nd Viscount Hailsham (1907–2001) MP (Con) Oxford, 1938–50; St Marylebone, 1963–70. Joint Parliamentary Under-Secretary, Air Ministry, 1945. First Lord of the Admiralty, 1956–57. Minister of Education, 1957. Leader, House of Lords, 1960–63. Lord Privy Seal, 1959–60. Lord President of the Council, 1957–59 and 1960–64. Minister for Science and Technology, 1959–64. Secretary of State for Education and Science, 1964. Lord Chancellor 1970–74 and 1979–87.

Some 600 boxes of papers, correspondence and diaries have been deposited in Churchill College, Cambridge (ref. HLSM). A list is available (NRA 18561).

HAKEWILL SMITH, MAJOR-GENERAL SIR EDMUND (1896–1986) Served in World Wars I and II; commanded 52nd Lowland Division, 1943–46.

Presided at War Crimes Trial of Albert Kesselring, 1947.

The National Army Museum holds a collection of papers, 1917–82 (ref. 9012–28). A list is available (NRA 18641). The material includes his semi-official correspondence as a divisional commander in 1944; a diary and notebook, 1949; and miscellaneous correspondence and photographs. Three boxes of papers relating to the Kesselring trial are deposited in the Liddell Hart Centre, King's College, London.

HALDANE, JOHN BURDON SANDERSON (1892–1964) Geneticist and author. Professor of Biometry, London University, 1937–57. Research Professor, Indian Statistical Institute. Head of Genetics and Biometrics, Government of Orissa, India, 1962–64. Chairman, Editorial Board of *Daily Worker*, 1940–49.

Certain papers for the period 1907–64 are held at the National Library of Scotland (ref. MSS 20534–645). The collection, which chiefly relates to his postwar career, consists of diaries, correspondence, scientific research papers, lectures and texts of publications.

HALEY, SIR WILLIAM JOHN (1901–87) BBC Editor-in-Chief, 1943–44. Director General, BBC, 1944–52. Editor, *The Times* 1952–65.

There are extensive papers in Churchill College Cambridge (ref. HALY). The collection is listed (NRA 43589). There are diaries, 1922–86, correspondence for the period 1953–83 and also press-cuttings covering most periods of his career.

HALIFAX, 1ST EARL OF Edward Frederick Lindley Wood, 1st Baron Irwin (1881–1959) MP (Con) Ripon, 1910–25. Viceroy of India, 1926–31. Secretary of State, War, 1935. Lord Privy Seal, 1935–37. Lord President of the Council, 1937–38. Secretary of State, Foreign Affairs, 1938–40. Ambassador, United States, 1941–46.

The papers of Lord Halifax are held as a part of the Hickleton collection at the Borthwick Institute, York. A list is available (NRA 8128). These include various family papers, speeches and lectures and political correspondence. A microfilm of some of the papers relating to 1938–39 and to the period in Washington is kept at Churchill College, Cambridge. The same institution also holds his correspondence with Churchill, Bevin, Roosevelt and Eden, 1937–57. Foreign Office correspondence (1938–40) is held at the Public Record Office (FO 800/309–28). The India Office Library holds 38 volumes deposited by Lord Halifax in 1959, covering his time as Viceroy of India, 1926–31 (ref. MSS Eur C 152).

HALL, 1ST VISCOUNT George Henry Hall (1881–1965) MP (Lab) Aberdare, 1922–46. Civil Lord of the Admiralty, 1929–31. Parliamentary Under-Secretary, Colonial Office, 1940–42; Foreign Office, 1943–45. Financial Secretary, Admiralty, 1942–43. Secretary of State for the Colonies, 1945–46. First Lord of the Admiralty, 1946–51.

Photocopies of his trade union and political correspondence and other papers (from originals in family possession) are held by the Brynmor Jones Library, University of Hull (ref. DX/84/1–12). The collection comprises press-cuttings, correspondence with Ramsay MacDonald, Winston Churchill, Clement Attlee, Anthony Eden, Lord Mountbatten, Emmanuel Shinwell and others (ref. DX/84 1–12). There are also various election pamphlets, addresses and some photographs.

HALL, SIR ROBERT DE ZOUCHE (1904–) Colonial service, 1926–56. Member for Local Government, Tanganyika, 1950–52. Governor, Sierra Leone, 1953–56.

His unofficial diary of a visit to South Africa in 1944 to study African questions is in Rhodes House Library, Oxford (ref. MSS Afr r 92). His papers on Maori culture are deposited in the Gisborne Museum and Art Centre, New Zealand.

HALL-THOMPSON, MAJOR ROBERT LLOYD (1920–92) Stormont MP (UU) Clifton, 1969–72. Leader of Northern Ireland Assembly, 1973–74, and Chief Whip, Northern Ireland Executive. Unionist Party of Northern Ireland member of Northern Ireland Convention, 1975–76.

His papers relating to his own career together with those of his father, Colonel S.H. Hall-Thompson (Stormont Minister of Education, 1944–50) and grandfather, Robert Thompson, Westminster MP for North Belfast, 1910–18, have remained in family possession.

HALL-THOMPSON, COLONEL S.H. (1885–1954)
Stormont MP (UU) Belfast Clifton, 1929–53. Minister
of Education, Northern Ireland, 1944–50. Deputy
Speaker, Stormont, 1950–53.

The papers have remained in the possession of the
family. See entry above.

**HAMILTON, ADMIRAL SIR LOUIS HENRY
KEPPEL (1890–1957)**   Naval career; served in World
Wars I and II. First Naval Member and Chief of
Naval Staff, Commonwealth Naval Board, 1945–48.

A substantial collection of papers, 1903–56, is
deposited in the National Maritime Museum (ref.
HTN/201–51). A list is available (NRA 30121). The
post-war section consists of his journals, 1945–48
and 1950; correspondence, 1945–56; an account of
his mission to Australia, 1945–48; a journal of a trip
to Kenya, 1950; and letters of proceedings, signals
and orders, 1939–47. His earlier career is also fully
documented in the collection. Additional World
War I letters are contained among the papers of his
brother, Captain H. Hamilton, deposited in the
Imperial War Museum.

HAMILTON, WILLIAM WINTER (1917–2000)
MP (Lab) Fife West, 1950–74; Fife Central, 1974–87.

Certain papers, 1936–92, including some constituency correspondence, research notes and drafts
for published works have been deposited in the
National Library of Scotland (ref. Acc 10951). The
collection is listed. His memoirs were published in
1992.

HAMLING, WILLIAM (1912–75) MP (Lab)
Woolwich West, 1964–75. Assistant Government
Whip, 1969–70. Chairman, Defence of Literature and
the Arts Society.

The papers have been placed in the Modern
Records Centre, University of Warwick. The material
(mainly 1960s) consists of ten boxes of documents
covering both his public life and private interests.
Among the topics and organisations covered are
Amnesty International, the National Council for
the Single Woman and Her Dependants, education,
humanism, London planning and the Defence
of Literature and the Arts Society. There are also
minutes, leaflets and reports from a variety of
organisations (ref. MSS 136).

HAMM, JEFFREY (1915–92)   Leading Fascist sup-
porter of Mosley. National Secretary, Union
Movement and also of the Oswald Mosley
Secretariat.

Three boxes of papers (for the period 1960–79),
mainly consisting of correspondence and administrative files from his post as National Secretary, are
in the University of Birmingham Library. Reference
should also be made to the Mosley collection at
Birmingham (ref. GB 0150 OM).

**HAMMERSLEY, SAMUEL SCHOFIELD (1892–
1965)**   MP (Con) Stockport, 1925–35; East Willesden,
1938–45. Chairman, Parliamentary Palestine Committee, 1943–45. Executive Chairman, Anglo-Israel
Association, 1951–63. Chairman of cotton-spinning
and other industrial companies.

A collection of political and business papers,
1932–62, is held by Manchester Public Libraries
Archives Department. There are some 53 box files
and 12 bundles of papers. Most of the material is
business-related, but there is some correspondence
as Chairman of the Parliamentary Palestine Committee (1943–45) and as Executive Chairman of
the Anglo-Israel Association (1957–63). There are
also some minutes, accounts and publications of
the Association together with papers concerning
visits to Israel and five volumes of press-cuttings
(1922–63).

HANCOCK, SIR (WILLIAM) KEITH (1898–1988)
Historian. Professor of History, University of
Adelaide, 1924–33; Birmingham University, 1934–44.
Chichele Professor of Economic History, Oxford
University, 1944–49. Supervisor of Civil Histories,
War Cabinet Office, from 1941. Director of Institute
of Commonwealth Studies and Professor of British
Commonwealth Affairs, London, 1949–56. Professor
of History, Australian National University, 1957–65.

The Institute of Commonwealth Studies, London
University, has material relating to Africa. A list is
available (NRA 21997). The collection includes his
correspondence while working on the Smuts papers
and his report after the deportation of the Kabaka of
Buganda. Papers relating to General Smuts, collected
by Sir Keith Hancock, are in the National Library of
Australia (ref. MS 2886). Included are copies of letters
by General Smuts, a draft of Sir Keith's biography of

Smuts, and Sir Keith's correspondence with various people while researching the book.

HANKEY, 2ND BARON   Sir Robert Maurice Alers Hankey (1905–96) Diplomat. Chargé d'Affaires, Spain, 1949–51. Minister, Hungary, 1951–53. Ambassador, Sweden, 1954–60.

A collection of family papers and letters has been donated to Churchill College, Cambridge. Lord Hankey stated that as a public official he did not keep any papers. Some correspondence with Lord Avon is held at Birmingham University (ref. AP20/52).

HARBER, DENZIL D. (1909–66) Trotskyist. Secretary, Revolutionary Socialist League.

The papers have been placed in the Modern Records Centre, University of Warwick (ref. MSS 151). The collection comprises internal documents issued by various Trotskyist groups, primarily the Revolutionary Socialist League, the Workers' International League and the Revolutionary Communist Party, during the 1930s and 1940s. A photocopy of some of this is in the Brynmor Jones Library, University of Hull.

HARBOTTLE, BRIGADIER MICHAEL NEALE (1917–97) Served in World War II. Security Commander, Aden, 1962–64. Chief of Staff, United Nations Peacekeeping Force, Cyprus, 1966–68. Lecturer in Peace Studies, Bradford University, 1974–79. General Secretary, World Disarmament Campaign, 1980–82. Director, London Centre for International Peacekeeping, after 1983. Writer and broadcaster on peacekeeping and disarmament.

Brigadier Harbottle has deposited his papers relating to his peacekeeping duties with the United Nations project at the Bodleian Library, Oxford. Other papers, *c.* 1966–70, have been deposited at the Liddell Hart Centre for Military Archives.

The Department of Sound Records at the Imperial War Museum holds an interview which covers his British and United Nations military service and his subsequent involvement in the disarmament campaign, including his membership of Generals for Peace and Disarmament, 1975–88.

HARDING OF PETHERTON, 1ST BARON Field-Marshal Sir Allan Francis John Harding (1896–

1989) Military career. Served in World Wars I and II. General Officer Commanding-in-Chief, Southern Command, 1947–49. Commander-in-Chief, Far East Land Forces, 1949–51; British Army of the Rhine, 1951–52. Chief of Imperial General Staff, 1952–55. Governor and Commander-in-Chief, Cyprus, 1955–57.

Some papers, covering the period 1943–87, have been placed in the National Army Museum (ref. 8908–144). A list is available (NRA 33391). The collection consists mainly of press-cuttings and texts of speeches as well as a manuscript memoir and outline account of his service career, produced as the summary of a possible book. There is also a diary of the Italian Campaign in 1944; a file of semi-official correspondence while Chief of Staff at Allied Forces HQ, 1944–45; and press-cuttings, 1946–86. The later papers include an operations report and a press release on the Malayan Emergency; confidential reports on Cyprus; and the texts of broadcasts on Cyprus, 1949–63.

HARDY, GENERAL SIR CAMPBELL RICHARD (1906–84) Royal Marines career. Served in World War II. Commanded Third Commando Brigade, 1948–51. Chief of Staff, Royal Marines, 1953–55. Commandant-General of the Royal Marines, 1955–59.

According to information received by the Liddell Hart Centre, King's College, London, the papers have remained in the possession of his family.

HARKNESS, SIR DOUGLAS (ALEXANDER EARSMAN) (1902–80) Civil servant, Northern Ireland, 1924–63. Permanent Secretary, Ministry of Agriculture, 1948–52; Finance, 1953–61. Head of Northern Ireland Civil Service, 1953–61. Economic Adviser to Stormont Government, 1961–63.

A collection of papers, 1922–58, concerning his professional career and interest in economic and agricultural matters in the province, is deposited in the Public Record Office of Northern Ireland (ref. D3373 Add.).

HARRIS OF HIGH CROSS, LORD   Ralph Harris (1924–) General Director, then Chairman after 1986, Institute of Economic Affairs. Influential economist and author.

It is understood that Lord Harris has retained his papers.

HARRISSON, TOM (1911–76) Biologist, anthropologist and pioneer of social surveys. Founder (with Charles Madge) of Mass-Observation. Radio critic, the *Observer*, 1941–44. Government Ethnologist and Curator of the Museum, Sarawak, 1947–66. Visiting Professor, Cornell University, 1967–68. Visiting Professor and Director of the Mass-Observation Archive, University of Sussex.

Tom Harrisson's papers form the core of the Mass-Observation Archive, Sussex University. The collection amounts to over 700 boxes of diaries, observations, surveys and reports. Harrisson's books were also donated to the Archive. The National Archives of Malaysia have his books and papers relating to anthropological studies in Asia. The International Union for the Conservation of Nature and Natural Resources, 1110 Morges, Switzerland, has some papers concerning his long-time interest in conservation.

HARROD, SIR ROY FORBES (1900–78) Economist. Biographer of Keynes.

His correspondence, together with that of his wife, covering the period *c.* 1922–90, is in the British Library (ref. Add. MSS. 71181–71197).

HART OF SOUTH LANARK, BARONESS Judith (Constance Mary) Hart (1924–91) MP (Lab) Lanarkshire, 1959–83; Clydeside, 1983–87. Minister for Overseas Development, 1969–70, 1974–75, 1977–79. Minister for Social Security, 1967–68. Opponent of entry into Common Market.

The political papers (94 boxes, covering the period 1951–87) have been deposited in the Labour History Archive and Study Centre, University of Manchester. A list is available (NRA 41987). They reflect her many interests in international affairs, human rights and trade union matters, etc. The records of the Chile Solidarity Campaign are in the same repository. The bulk of her constituency correspondence and papers, 1964–87, is in Strathclyde Record Office.

HART, RICHARD (1917–) Jamaican trade unionist, politician and journalist. Member of People's National Party, 1938–52. Interned during World War II. Organiser of Jamaican People's National Party and

Trades Union Congress, 1943–53. Active in People's Freedom Movement, 1952–62. Editor of a Guyana newspaper, 1963–65. Active in the UK Caribbean Labour Solidarity movement since 1965.

Eight reels of microfilmed papers, 1937–66, are deposited in the Institute of Commonwealth Studies, London University. A list is available (NRA 22776). The collection is fully catalogued and indexed and consists of correspondence, reports and minutes of the various organisations with which he was involved, publications, newspaper cuttings and ephemera. The originals of the papers have remained in the West Indies.

HARVEY OF TASBURGH, 1ST BARON Sir Oliver Charles Harvey (1893–1968) Diplomat. Assistant Under-Secretary, 1943–46; Deputy Under-Secretary (Political), Foreign Office, 1946–47. Minister, France, 1940; Ambassador, 1948–54.

His papers have been deposited in the British Library (ref. Add MSS 56379–56402). The collection includes extensive diaries together with some memoranda and letters for the period 1937–46.

HARVEY, AUDREY (1912–97) Charity worker. Founder, Child Poverty Action Group (CPAG). Director, CPAG Citizen's Rights Office, 1970–72. Author of numerous articles and pamphlets on housing law, welfare rights, etc.

A collection of papers (12 boxes, 1960–96) was placed in the LSE Library in 1997 (ref M1844). The papers consist of drafts of articles, offprints, correspondence and press-cuttings.

HARVIE-WATT, SIR GEORGE STEVEN (1903–89) MP (Con) Keighley, 1931–35; Richmond, 1937–59. Assistant Government Whip, 1938–40. PPS to the Prime Minister, 1941–45.

There are three boxes of his papers, consisting of reports to Churchill on political events, in Churchill College, Cambridge (ref. HARV).

HASTINGS, SOMERVILLE (1878–1967) MP (Lab) Reading, 1923–24 and 1929–31; Barking, 1945–59. President, Socialist Medical Association.

The Brynmor Jones Library, University of Hull, holds a microfilm containing correspondence, notes and biographical material (ref. DSH).

HASTON, JOCK (1912–86) Socialist publicist. An early member of the Communist Party of Great Britain. Trotskyist from 1934 until 1949. A founder (and later secretary) of the Workers' International League, 1937. Secretary of the Revolutionary Communist Party from 1944. Tutor/organiser, National Council of Labour Colleges, 1950–63.

A large collection of papers is held at the Brynmor Jones Library, University of Hull (ref. DJH). A list is available (NRA 32030). The Haston papers constitute a unique source for the extreme left in British politics, particularly in the 1930s and 1940s. The collection includes minutes, correspondence, internal bulletins and other material on the following groups: Communist League, Militant Group, Militant Labour League, Marxist Group, Revolutionary Workers' League, Revolutionary Socialist League, Workers' International League, Revolutionary Communist Party, (US) Socialist Workers' Party, and the Workers' Party of the USA. There is also an extensive collection of radical journals and pamphlets.

HAWLEY, SIR DONALD (1921–) Sudan Political Service. After 1956, served Trucial States, Cairo, Baghdad, etc. Assistant Under-Secretary of State, Foreign Office, 1975–77. High Commissioner in Malaysia, 1977–81.

An extensive collection of papers, reflecting most aspects of his work, is in Durham University Library. A detailed 126 pp. list is available (NRA 43960).

HAWTREY, SIR RALPH GEORGE (1879–1974) Economist. Director of Financial Inquiries at the Treasury, 1919–45. President of the Royal Economic Society, 1946–48. Price Professor of International Economics, 1947–52.

His correspondence and papers were deposited in Churchill College, Cambridge, in 1975. A list is available (NRA 20291). The collection covers his entire career, including Treasury papers, 1904–45; the Treasury History of World War II; the Royal Institute of International Affairs; the Radcliffe Committee, 1957–58; the Committee on Economic Development, 1947–48; and the Council on Prices, Productivity and Incomes, 1957–59. There are also official publications together with published and unpublished articles, copies of reviews and correspondence with his publishers.

HAY, JOHN (1919–98). MP (Con) Henley, 1950–Feb. 1974. Parliamentary Secretary, Ministry of Transport, 1959–64; First Lord of the Admiralty, 1963–64; Parliamentary Under-Secretary, Ministry of Defence (Royal Navy), 1964.

Mr Hay retained his papers which include approximately 12 boxes of material relating to his public and political life. These include a large personal archive of the post-war Young Conservative movement and of the Council of Europe's activities during the late 1940s. His parliamentary papers include files on the re-organisation and break-up of the British Transport Commission in the early 1960s, the abolition of the Board of Admiralty in 1964–65, and the establishment of the Ministry of Defence. The collection also includes correspondence with and other items relating to his parliamentary colleagues, including his close friend, Enoch Powell.

HAY, LIEUTENANT-COLONEL SIR WILLIAM RUPERT (1893–1962) Indian Political Service. Political Agent, Malakand, 1931–33. Counsellor, British Legation, Kabul, 1933. Resident, Waziristan, 1940–41. Resident, Persian Gulf, 1946–53.

His papers and correspondence, together with four diaries, 1911–56, are in St Antony's College, Oxford. A list is available (NRA 41483).

HAYDON, MAJOR-GENERAL JOSEPH CHARLES (1899–1970) Military career. Chief of Intelligence Division, Allied Control Commission, Germany, 1948–50.

There are some papers, mainly for his wartime service, in the Imperial War Museum (ref 93/28/4). A list is available (NRA 36537). There is very little material on Germany.

HAYTER, SIR WILLIAM GOODENOUGH (1906–95) Diplomat, 1930–58. Ambassador, USSR, 1953–57. Deputy Under-Secretary, Foreign Office, 1957–58. Warden of New College, Oxford, 1958–76. Some papers relating to college administration and to his biography of W.A. Spooner are held in the library of New College, Oxford. Other papers may still be with the family.

HAYWARD, MARJORIE (1905–74) Businesswoman and expert on women's employment. Ministry of Labour HQ Staff, 1940–59.

Certain papers are held at the Women's Library (q.v.) A list is available (NRA 29390). The papers relate to the Ministry of Labour and issues of women's employment, including the 1953 Congress of the International Federation of Business and Professional Women. There are also reports and printed material on women's employment in the 1940s and 1950s.

HEAD, 1ST VISCOUNT Antony Henry Head (1906–83) MP (Con) Carshalton, 1945–60. Secretary of State for War, 1951–56; Minister of Defence, 1956–57. High Commissioner, Nigeria, 1960–63; Malaysia, 1963–66.

Lord Head's family have indicated (*British Cabinet Ministers, 1900–51*) that he left very few papers and that they are not available to researchers. His correspondence with Anthony Eden, 1957–82, is in the Avon papers at Birmingham University (ref. AP23/37). A list is available (NRA 28779). The papers of Lord Monckton, which are in the Bodleian Library, Oxford, include some correspondence, 1951–60 (NRA 20879).

HEALEY, LORD Denis Winston Healey (1917–) MP (Lab) Leeds South East, Feb. 1952–55; Leeds East, 1955–92. Secretary, International Department, Labour Party, 1945–52. Defence Secretary, 1964–70; Chancellor of the Exchequer, 1974–79; Deputy Leader of the Labour Party, 1980–83; Opposition spokesman on Foreign and Commonwealth Affairs, 1980–87.

Lord Healey stated that he was making plans for the eventual deposit of his papers.

HEALY, CAHIR (1877–1970) MP (Nat) Fermanagh and Tyrone, 1922–24, 1931–35; (Republican and Anti-Partition) Fermanagh and South Tyrone, 1950–55.

An extensive collection is held at the Public Record Office of Northern Ireland (ref. D2991). A list is available (NRA 24715). The papers include correspondence; literary papers; press-cuttings; pamphlets and publicity material; diaries, 1940–65, and photographs. His correspondents include leading nationalist figures such as Eddie McAteer, Senator Patrick McGill and Senator J.G. Lennon, and politicians from the Republic of Ireland, including Ernest Blythe. There is also correspondence with civil

rights groups such as the Campaign for Social Justice and with Irish-American lobbyists and organisations (among them the American Congress for Irish Freedom), 1964–69. The earlier material relates to the work of the Anti-Partition League during the 1940s and 1950s, the general elections of the 1950s, and includes extensive constituency correspondence. An unusual aspect of the collection are letters exchanged with former fellow internees of World War II, among them Sir Oswald Mosley and Admiral Sir Barry Domville, 1950–65. The collection is subject to a 75-year closure rule.

HEATH, SIR EDWARD RICHARD GEORGE (1916–2005) MP (Con) Bexley, 1950–74; Sidcup, 1974–83; Old Bexley and Sidcup, 1983–2001. Junior Lord of the Treasury, 1951; Joint Deputy Chief Whip, 1952; Deputy Chief Whip, 1953–55; Parliamentary Secretary, Treasury and Chief Whip, 1955–59. Minister of Labour, 1959–60; Lord Privy Seal, 1960–63; Secretary of State for Industry, Trade, Regional Development, and President of the Board of Trade, 1963–64; Prime Minister, 1970–74.

Sir Edward stated that he had retained a large personal archive of several hundred boxes of correspondence and papers. The eventual location of these papers is not yet known.

HECTOR, GORDON MATTHEWS (1918–) Colonial Service, 1946–58. Acting Governor of the Seychelles, 1953. Deputy Resident Commissioner and Government Secretary, Basutoland, 1956. Chief Secretary, Basutoland, 1964. Secretary, Basutoland Constitutional Commission, 1957–58. Secretary to the Assembly Council, General Assembly of the Church of Scotland, 1980–85.

Certain of his papers, 1940–65, have been given to Rhodes House Library, Oxford (ref. MSS Brit Emp s 381). A list is available (NRA 17376). They include memoranda and other papers concerned with wartime service in Abyssinia and colonial service in the Seychelles and Basutoland.

HEENAN, CARDINAL JOHN CHARLES CARMEL (1905–75) Roman Catholic Archbishop of Westminster, 1963–75; Archbishop of Liverpool, 1957–63; Bishop of Leeds, 1951–57.

Some papers are held in the Westminster Diocesan Archives and are subject to a thirty-year rule of access.

HEFFER, ERIC SAMUEL (1922–91) MP (Lab) Walton, 1964–91.

Provision has been made for the deposit of his papers at the Labour History Archive and Study Centre, Manchester. Other material is to be held in Liverpool.

HELMORE, HON. AIR COMMODORE WILLIAM (1894–1964) MP (Con) Watford, 1943–45. Royal Air Force career, including service in World Wars I and II. RAF war commentator, 1941–43. On Brabazon Committee on Civil Aviation, 1943–45. Scientific Adviser to Air Ministry and Ministry of Aircraft Production, 1941–45. Aeronautical inventor post-war.

A large collection of papers is held at the Air Historical Branch, Ministry of Defence. The material includes post-war correspondence relating to the aviation industry and Air Commodore Helmore's inventions. Access is at the discretion of the Head of the Air Historical Branch, to whom queries should be addressed. Further correspondence, 1942–50, is available in the papers of Lord Cherwell at Nuffield College, Oxford (NRA 16447).

HENDERSON, SIR HUBERT DOUGLAS (1890–1952) Economic Advisory Council, 1930–34. Economic Adviser, Treasury, 1939–44. Drummond Professor of Political Economy and Fellow of All Souls College, Oxford, 1944–51. Warden Elect of All Souls, 1951–52.

The papers are held at Nuffield College, Oxford. A list is available (NRA 15734). The collection relates to the Economic Advisory Council; the War Cabinet Committee on Reconstruction Problems, 1942–44; the War Cabinet, 1941–44; and various other commissions and committees, 1931–49. There are also various printed reports, memoranda, articles and lectures, 1932–51.

HENDERSON, JEAN (1900–97) Liberal Parliamentary Candidate for Barnet, 1945; Lincoln 1950 and Luton, 1955. Honorary Secretary of the Women's Liberal Federation, 1940s.

Four boxes of papers were donated to the LSE Library by her niece Mrs Sarah Graham in 1996 (ref. M1828). The bulk of the papers deals with her work as a parliamentary candidate and includes correspondence with the local parties, notes for speeches and election addresses and scrapbooks of the election campaigns. In addition to documenting her work as a Liberal candidate, this collection provides an insight into the political issues of the day, such as World War II, international relations, unemployment and social reform.

HENDERSON, SIR (JOHN) NICHOLAS (1919–) Diplomat. Ambassador, Poland, 1969–72; West Germany, 1972–75; France, 1975–79; USA, 1979–82.

Sir Nicholas informed the LSE in 1992 that he had retained a substantial collection of papers, diaries and correspondence, 1944–82. These include files relating to his work as the first British chairman of the Channel Tunnel Group. In addition, he has written his memoirs which are presently banned from publication under the Radcliffe rules. He will make provision for the deposit of his papers in due course.

HENRIQUES, SIR BASIL LUCAS QUIXANO (1890–1961) Author and publicist. Leader of the Anglo-Jewish community and Zionist supporter. Founder and Warden of Bernhard Baron St George's Jewish Settlement, 1914–47.

The Hartley Library, University of Southampton, holds a substantial collection of papers (ref. MS 132). The collection includes diaries, correspondence, addresses, articles and other miscellaneous items. There are also 50 files related to the biography of Sir Basil by Rose Louise (Lady Henriques), together with her 'Questionnaire to a Cross-Section of the Jewish Community', 1947–48.

HEREN, LOUIS PHILIP (1919–95) Journalist. *The Times* Foreign Correspondent from 1947 in Israel and the Middle East, 1948–50. Deputy Editor and Foreign Editor, *The Times*.

The Times archive holds papers which include material on the Middle East (1948–50), such as letters and cables from Tel Aviv.

HETHERINGTON, (HECTOR) ALASTAIR (1919–99) Editor, *Guardian*, 1956–75. Editorial Staff,

Glasgow Herald 1946–50. *Manchester Guardian*, 1950; Assistant Editor and Foreign Editor, 1953–56.

The John Rylands Library, Manchester University, holds 40 boxes of papers concerning his editorship of the *Guardian*. The collection includes correspondence with staff and contributors, internal office records and extensive reference files.

His own interview notes as editor of the paper (for the period from November 1958 to July 1975) are held at the LSE Library. These include detailed accounts of meetings with political leaders, including Hugh Gaitskell, James Callaghan and Jo Grimond. In addition, further material is in Stirling University Library. A list is available (NRA 43085).

HETHERINGTON, DR R.J. (fl. 1960s–70s) Medical practitioner and birth control specialist.

Twenty-six boxes of papers chiefly concerning oral contraception, drug abuse and the Thalidomide controversy (1960s and 1970s) are deposited in the Wellcome Contemporary Medical Archives Centre, London (ref. PP/RJH). The Thalidomide files include correspondence, documentation on its effects and the consequent litigation, and the arguments for and against pregnancy termination. Sections of the Thalidomide records are closed until 2007.

HEWITT, CECIL ROLPH (1901–94) (pseudonym C.H. ROLPH) Legal journalist. On editorial staff of the *New Statesman*, 1947–70; Director, 1965–80.

Eight boxes of papers were deposited in the LSE Library in 1989. They consist of material on the Obscene Publications Act and the 1960s Campaign Against the Death Penalty.

HEZLET, VICE-ADMIRAL SIR ARTHUR RICHARD (1914–) Naval career; submarine commander during World War II. Director, Royal Naval Staff College, Greenwich, 1956–57. Flag Officer (Submarines), 1959–61. Flag Officer, Scotland, 1961–62. Flag Officer, Scotland and Northern Ireland, 1963–64.

The Public Record Office of Northern Ireland holds a collection of papers, 1964–89. The material comprises research notes for his books on naval and Irish history and personal and financial correspondence. His career as a submariner is documented in the holdings of the Royal Navy Submarine Museum, Gosport.

HICKLING, REGINALD (1920–) Lawyer. Legal Adviser concerning Malaya, Aden and South Arabia, etc. Attorney-General, Gibraltar, 1970–72.

One box of papers, including a memoir concerning Aden and South Arabia, is in Churchill College, Cambridge.

HIGGINS, SIR TERENCE LANGLEY (1928–) MP (Con) Worthing, after 1964.

His correspondence and political papers have been placed in West Sussex Record Office (ref. Acc. 10839)

HILL OF LUTON, LORD   Charles Hill (1904–89) MP (Lib-Con) Luton, 1950–63. Postmaster-General, 1955–57. Chancellor of the Duchy of Lancaster, 1957–61. Minister for Housing and Local Government and Minister for Welsh Affairs, 1961–62. Chairman of the BBC.

It is understood that the surviving diaries were entrusted to the care of Lord Briggs. No collection of papers or correspondence has been located.

HILL, CAPTAIN DUNCAN C. (1900–77) Served in World Wars I and II; Naval Force Commander, Burma, 1944–45. British Naval Attaché, Moscow, 1946–48.

A collection of lectures, notes, and official memoranda (*c.* 85 pages) relating to his period in the USSR, is housed in the Imperial War Museum. The material includes his notes on the history of the Russian Navy.

HILL, HOWARD (1913–80) Communist activist. Full-time Secretary, Sheffield Communist Party. Communist Party candidate for Sheffield Brightside in post-war elections.

The Hill collection in the Brynmor Jones Library, University of Hull, includes Communist Party material, 1946–74, particularly relating to the Sheffield and Rotherham areas, and the Yorkshire District Communist Party (ref. DHH).

HILL, JOHN EDWARD BERNARD (1912–) MP (Con) Norfolk South, 1955–74. Participated in numerous parliamentary delegations to Europe. Member, European Parliament, 1973–74.

The papers have been deposited in the University of East Anglia Library, Norwich (ref JH). There is extensive material on agriculture and the European Union as well as on many of his other concerns. A detailed list is available (NRA 43375).

HILL, AIR CHIEF MARSHAL SIR RODERIC MAXWELL (1894–1954) Royal Air Force career. Air Officer Commanding, Palestine and Transjordan, 1936–38; Air Defence of Great Britain, 1943–44; Fighter Command, 1944–45. Member of Air Board for Training, 1945–46; and for Technical Services, 1946–48.

The Royal Air Force Museum, Hendon, has a collection of uncatalogued notebooks, photographs and publications, 1917–52 (ref. AC 72/18).

HILL-NORTON, ADMIRAL OF THE FLEET SIR PETER (JOHN) (1915–2004) Naval career. Naval Attaché, Uruguay and Paraguay, 1953–55. Assistant Chief of Naval Staff, 1962–64. Flag Officer and Second-in-Command, Far East Fleet, 1964–66. Deputy Chief of Defence Staff (Personnel and Logistics), 1966. Chief of Naval Personnel, 1967. Vice-Chief of Naval Staff, 1967–68. Commander-in-Chief, Far East, 1969–70. Chief of Naval Staff, 1970–71. Chief of Defence Staff, 1971–73. Chairman, Military Committee of NATO, 1974–77.

Photocopies of 60 speeches, 1968–73, are deposited with the Imperial War Museum. He has published two books, *No Soft Options* (1978), and *Sea Power* (1982).

HINDE, MAJOR-GENERAL SIR WILLIAM ROBERT (NORRIS) (1900–81) Military career, 1919–57. Deputy Military Governor, British Sector, Berlin, 1945–48. Deputy Commissioner, *Land Niedersachsen*, Hanover, 1949–51. District Commander, Cyrenaica, 1952–53. Deputy Director of Operations, Kenya, 1953–56. Chief Civil Affairs Officer to the Commander, Suez Expedition, 1956–57.

His personal, official and military papers, 1926–66, were deposited in the Lincolnshire Archives Office in 1982 (ref. 16 ELWES). Rhodes House Library, Oxford, holds 13 files of correspondence, 1953–61, kept during the Kenyan Emergency.

HINDEN, RITA (1909–71) Socialist journalist and anti-imperialist. Secretary of the Fabian Colonial Bureau, 1940–50. Secretary, Socialist Union. Editor of *Socialist Commentary* from 1948.

Some correspondence as Secretary of the Fabian Colonial Bureau is held at Rhodes House Library, Oxford (ref. MSS Brit Emp s 365). A list is available (NRA 16153). Rhodes House Library, Oxford, also has the papers of Arthur Creech Jones with whom Rita Hinden worked closely (NRA 14026) and correspondence with Margery Perham (NRA 14026). Reference should also be made to the records of *Socialist Commentary* which are deposited in the Modern Records Centre, University of Warwick.

HINTON OF BANKSIDE, BARON Christopher Hinton (1901–83) Scientist and government adviser. Deputy Controller, Atomic Energy (Production), Ministry of Supply, 1946–54. Managing Director, UK Atomic Energy Commission (Industrial Group), 1954–57; Chairman, Central Electricity Generating Board, 1957–64.

The correspondence and papers are deposited in the Institute of Mechanical Engineers Library. A list is available (NRA 29372). This extensive collection includes diaries, a memoir and papers on his work for ICI, the Ministry of Supply, the UK Atomic Energy Commission and the Central Electricity Generating Board. Other energy-related material includes correspondence and papers on atomic energy and electricity supply, and some on the mid-1970s investigation into the Dounreay prototype fastbreeder reactor project. There are also House of Lords speeches on engineering and energy, consultancy papers on the Electricity Council, Ministry of Transport investigation papers (1965) and extensive material on his work for the World Bank. The latter includes detailed project assessments and recommendations on Taiwan, Turkey, Brazil, East Africa and West Pakistan. The remaining sections concern societies and organisations and Lord Hinton's time as Chancellor of Bath University. There are also publications and lectures, photographs and sound recordings.

Five boxes of personal diaries are at Churchill College, Cambridge, as are various additional papers, an autobiography, and copies of lectures from the 1960s and 1970s. A list is available (NRA 29993).

Private Office papers are in the Public Record Office (ref. PRO AB19).

HINTON, JAMES (fl. 1980s) Academic and peace campaigner. Chair, CND Projects Committee, 1985–86. Chair, West Midlands CND, 1982–85.

Most of his papers relating to his CND work have been deposited in the Modern Records Centre, University of Warwick (ref. MSS 343). The deposit includes minutes and other papers of the various committees, material relating to the peace canvass, 1982–83, and material relating to particular events or campaigns, including the Greenham Common and Molesworth campaigns.

HIRSON, BARUCH (1921–99) South African revolutionary and historian.

His historical and political correspondence and papers have been placed in the Institute of Commonwealth Studies, University of London (ref. A133).

HOBBS, BRIGADIER GODFREY PENNINGTON (1907–85) Chief Staff Officer, British Military Mission to Polish Corps and Mission to Greece, 1942–47; Colonel, Liaison, British Military Mission to Greece, 1947–49; Deputy Director, Public Relations, War Office, 1950–54; Military Attaché, Athens, 1954–57; Director of Public Relations, Ministry of Defence, 1957–65.

Papers covering his career, 1926–67, are held at the Liddell Hart Centre, King's College, London.

HOBSON, BARON Charles Rider Hobson (1904–66) MP (Lab) Wembley North, 1945–50; Keighley, 1950–59. Assistant Postmaster-General, 1947–51. Lord-in-Waiting, 1964–66.

A small collection of papers is held at the LSE Library. Enquiries should be addressed to the Archivist.

HODSOLL, SIR ERIC JOHN (1894–1971) Civil servant. Inspector-General, Civil Defence, 1938–48. Director-General, Civil Defence Training, 1948–54. Chief Civil Defence Adviser, NATO, 1954–61.

There are 27 boxes of papers in Churchill College, Cambridge (ref. HDSL). A list is available (NRA 14443). The collection largely concerns his career in civil defence and consists of official correspondence,

transcripts and printed pamphlets, draft speeches and miscellaneous manuscripts. Special conditions of access apply to the collection.

HODSON, HENRY VINCENT (1906–99) Author, editor and economist. Assistant Editor, *The Sunday Times*, 1946–50; Editor, 1950–61. Author of *The Great Divide: Britain – India – Pakistan* (1969).

His correspondence relating to the partition of India, *c.* 1960–69, is in the Library of the School of Oriental and African Studies, University of London. Further correspondence, 1931–54, is contained in the papers of Lionel Curtis at the Bodleian Library, Oxford.

HOGGART, RICHARD (1918–) Academic and writer. Professor of English, Birmingham University, 1962–73, and Director, Centre for Contemporary Cultural Studies, 1964–73. Member, Pilkington Committee on Broadcasting, 1960–62; Assistant Director-General, UNESCO, 1970–75. Chairman, *New Statesman*, 1978–81; National Advisory Council on Adult and Continuing Education, 1977–83, and various other posts.

Professor Hoggart currently retains his papers and provision has been made for their eventual deposit at Leeds University. The collection includes drafts of various books; television and radio scripts; correspondence relating to his work at UNESCO; relevant files of the Broadcasting Research Unit; the *New Statesman*; and the National Advisory Council on Adult and Continuing Education.

HOLDERNESS, BARON Richard Frederick Wood (1920–) MP (Con) Bridlington, 1950–79. Joint Parliamentary Secretary, Ministry of Pensions and National Insurance, 1955–58; Ministry of Labour, 1958–59; Minister of Power, 1959–63; Minister of Pensions and National Insurance, 1963–64; Minister of Overseas Development, June–Oct. 1970; Minister for Overseas Development, Foreign and Commonwealth Office, 1970–74.

Lord Holderness states that he has retained a few papers, and is prepared to consider requests for access. Enquiries should be made direct to him.

HOLFORD, BARON Sir William Graham Holford (1907–75) Architect and planner. Professor of Civil Design, Liverpool University, 1936–47; Professor of Town Planning, University College, London, 1948–70. President, Royal Institute of British Architects, 1960–62; Director, Leverhulme Trust Fund, 1972–75.

Many of his papers have been deposited with Liverpool University Archives. A list is available (NRA 23191). The papers comprise some 700 files covering most aspects of his career and work. The three main categories are as follows. First, consultancy material such as plans for the post-war reconstruction of the Port of London, Cambridge and Carlisle, etc., and plans on the expansion of the universities in the late 1950s and early 1960s. Second, papers related to numerous government and professional councils and committees, often with complete agenda and minutes. Third, personal papers including diaries, notes and private correspondence, biographical notes, publications lists and press-cuttings. Additional papers cover the Royal Institute; Australia, South Africa and trips abroad; University College London; British architects; and financial affairs. There are also copies of his lectures and articles.

HOLLINGHURST, AIR CHIEF MARSHAL SIR LESLIE NORMAN (1895–1971) Served in World Wars I and II; Director, then Director-General of Organisation, Royal Air Force, 1940–43; Air Officer Commanding, 38th Group, 1943–44; Air Marshal Commanding Base Air Forces, South-East Asia, 1944–45. Air Member for Supply and Organisation, 1945–48. Inspector-General, RAF, 1948–49. Air Member for Personnel, 1949–52.

The main collection of papers, 1915–71, is held by the Royal Air Force Museum, Hendon (refs AC 73/23 and AC 73/35). The bulk of this material, comprising logbooks, correspondence, working files and notes, relates to his career until 1945. The post-war section of the collection includes material on the promotion structure for senior RAF ranks, 1947–50, and various photographs, 1949–60. The Imperial War Museum holds a smaller collection of official and semi-official reports of airborne and other operations in Holland, 1944–45.

HOLLIS, GENERAL SIR LESLIE CHASEMORE (1897–1963) Military career. Served in World Wars

I and II. Secretary of Chiefs of Staff Committee, 1939–46. Chief Staff Officer to Minister of Defence and Deputy Secretary (Military), 1946–49. Commandant-General, Royal Marines, 1949–52.

His typescript memoirs, 1914–52, are in the Imperial War Museum (ref. 86/47/1). The papers of Lord Beaverbrook, at the House of Lords Record Office, include correspondence, 1950–63 (ref. BBK C/172).

HOLMES, SIR HORACE EDWIN (1888–1971) MP (Lab) Hemsworth, 1946–59. Opposition Whip, 1951–59. Trade union official.

A collection of notebooks and diaries, 1915–59, is deposited in the University of Prince Edward Island, Canada. The material documents his parliamentary career and his earlier time as a miner and as a member of local bodies such as the South Yorkshire Wages Board and the West Riding County Council. There are also some printed minutes of the National Union of Mineworkers Executive Committee, 1969–70.

HOLMES, RICHARD J. (1928–) Diplomat. Served Western Aden Protectorate.

There is some material concerning the Arabian Federation in the Middle East Centre, St Antony's College, Oxford. A list is available (NRA 41211).

HOME OF THE HIRSEL, BARON Sir Alec (Alexander Frederick) Douglas-Home (1903–95) MP (U) Lanark South, 1931–45; (Con) Lanark, 1950–51; (U) Kinross and West Perthshire, 1963–Oct. 1974. In House of Lords, 1951–63, when he renounced his peerage. Joint PUS, Foreign Office, 1945. Minister of State, Scottish Office, 1951–55. Commonwealth Relations Secretary, 1955–60. Leader of the House of Lords, and Lord President of the Council, 1957–60. Foreign Secretary, 1960–63 and 1970–74. Prime Minister, 1963–64.

Lord Home's papers remain at The Hirsel, Berwickshire, where they were used by his biographer, D.R. Thorpe. Enquiries should be directed to the National Library of Scotland. The large collection reportedly consists of 111 boxes of private and political papers together with some loose and uncatalogued material, mostly relating to the post-war period, especially 1960–74. These papers will be fully catalogued in the future. There are 108 substantial scrapbooks collected by Lady Home and covering the period 1928–90. There are also many boxes of estate papers. In addition, Churchill College, Cambridge, has five boxes of D.R. Thorpe's papers accumulated whilst writing the biography.

HONE, MAJOR-GENERAL SIR (HERBERT) RALPH (1896–1992) Military career and Colonial Service. Secretary-General to Governor-General, Malaya, 1946–48. Deputy Commissioner-General, South-East Asia, 1948–49. Governor, North Borneo, 1949–54. Head of Legal Division, Commonwealth Relations Office, 1954–61. Constitutional adviser on Commonwealth administrative and legal systems.

A collection of papers, 1937–72, is held in Rhodes House Library, Oxford (ref. MSS Brit Emp s 407). It includes correspondence, reports and memoranda on the administration of Italian colonies in East Africa, on Malaya, North Borneo, Southern Rhodesia, Kenya, the East African Federation and the Bahamas. An additional collection of papers relating to the British military administration of Malaya, 1945–53, is also held in Rhodes House Library (ref. MSS Ind Ocn s 271).

HOOD, LIEUTENANT-GENERAL SIR ALEXANDER (1888–1980) Royal Army Medical Corps career. Served in World Wars I and II. Director-General of Army Medical Services, 1941–48. Governor, Bermuda, 1949–55.

A collection of papers, 1951–71, including an unpublished autobiography is held in the Wellcome Contemporary Medical Archives Centre, London (refs. 801 and 1338). This material was formerly in the Royal Army Medical Corps Library.

HOOLEY, FRANK OSWALD (1923–) MP (Lab) Sheffield Heeley, 1966–70 and Feb. 1974–83.

His political papers were deposited in Sheffield City Library in 1978 (ref. BMP 1–16). A list is available (NRA 22261). They include eight files of general correspondence (1977–78) relating to constituency issues, various legislation, and papers on environmental and conservation issues. These files are closed for 30 years. There are also five files of case papers (1976–77) which are closed for 50 years, and some files on South Africa and Rhodesia (1976–77), and on

the Windscale Enquiry (1976–78). The Brynmor Jones Library, University of Hull has further general and case files, and material on overseas aid and the United Nations Association (1968–70) (ref. DMH).

HOOSON, 1ST BARON (Hugh) Emlyn Hooson (1925–) MP (Lib) Montgomeryshire, 1962–79. Recorder of Swansea, 1971. Chairman, Welsh Liberal Party, 1966–79. President, Welsh Liberal Party, 1983–86.

The papers have been acquired in successive deposits by the National Library of Wales. A detailed inventory is available (NRA 34426). The collection includes constituency correspondence and House of Commons subject files covering his entire career. Among the many files are material on the 1962 by-election in Montgomeryshire, files relating to Jeremy Thorpe, 1967–79, files on the 1974 and 1979 elections etc. His prior consent is required for access to the papers.

HOOSON, TOM ELLIS (1933–85) MP (Con) Brecon and Radnor, 1979–85.

The National Library of Wales has certain papers. A list is available (NRA 26130). The deposit includes 26 boxes of constituency correspondence, House of Commons correspondence and papers, as well as subject files covering housing, transport, squatting, the Rates Support Grant, and the Warnock Report. Access to papers less than 20 years old requires the permission of the donor.

HOPKINSON, ARTHUR JOHN (1894–1953) Indian Political Service, 1924–50; United Provinces, Kathiawar, North-West Frontier Province and Tibet; Political Officer, Sikkim, 1944–48.

A collection of papers is held in the India Office Library (ref. MSS Eur D 998). A list is available (NRA 27475). There are papers on Sikkim, Bhutan, and Tibet, including letters from the Dalai Lama, as well as correspondence with his wife and mother, and photographs, 1921–51.

HORDERN, SIR PETER (MAUDSLAY) (1929–) MP (Con) Horsham (then Horsham and Crawley) after 1964.

The correspondence and papers have been placed in West Sussex Record Office (ref. Acc 10944).

HORNER, ARTHUR LEWIS (1894–1968) Trade Unionist and leading member of the Communist Party of Great Britain. President, South Wales Miners Federation, 1936–46. General Secretary, National Union of Mineworkers, 1946–59.

Certain papers are held in the Library of the University College of Swansea. A list is available (NRA 14694). The collection is mainly pre-war, but contains some later correspondence together with various press-cuttings, reports, addresses and speeches.

HORRABIN, WINIFRED (1887–1971) Feminist and socialist writer.

The correspondence, papers, journals and diaries of Winifred Horrabin are deposited in the Brynmor Jones Library, University of Hull (ref. DWH). A list is available (NRA 17258). Much of the material relates to the pre-1945 era. The journals include literary notes and descriptions of visits to Poland (between 1927 and 1952) and the USA (1949). There are also drafts of articles and other publications (1920s–60s) and some correspondence. The remainder of the collection consists of volumes of press-cuttings (1926–63), photographs and miscellaneous ephemera.

HORSBRUGH, BARONESS Florence Horsbrugh (1899–1969) MP (Con) Dundee, 1931–45; Manchester Moss Side, 1950–59. Parliamentary Secretary, Ministry of Health, 1939–45; Food, 1945. Minister of Education, 1951–Oct. 1954. Delegate to the Council of Europe and Western European Union, 1955–60.

Some scrapbooks, papers and correspondence are held at Churchill College, Cambridge. A list is available (NRA 21966). There is little of political significance in the collection.

HOSKYNS, SIR JOHN (1927–) Head of Prime Minister's Policy Unit, 1979–82. Director-General, Institute of Directors, 1984–89.

His political papers (8 boxes) are in Churchill College, Cambridge (ref. HOSK).

HOUGHTON OF SOWERBY, BARON Douglas Arthur Leslie Noel Houghton (1898–1996) MP (Lab) Sowerby, Mar. 1949–Feb. 1974. Chairman, Parliamentary Labour Party, 1967–74.

The papers have been placed in the Labour History Archive and Study Centre, University of Manchester.

HOWE, LORD Sir Geoffrey Howe (1926–) Conservative politician and Cabinet Minister.

The papers were placed in the Bodleian Library, Oxford, in 1997. The very extensive collection (*c.* 40 boxes) is best accessed via the Bodleian website. His constituency correspondence, 1982–91, has been deposited in Surrey Record Office (ref. Acc 6173).

HOWICK OF GLENDALE, 1ST BARON Evelyn Baring (1903–73) Colonial administrator. Indian Civil Service, 1926–34. Governor of Southern Rhodesia, 1942–44. UK High Commissioner, South Africa, Basutoland, Bechunaland Protectorate and Swaziland, 1944–51. Governor and Commander-in-Chief, Kenya, 1952–59. Chairman, Commonwealth Development Corporation, 1963–72.

There are 15 boxes of papers concerning his period as Governor and Commander-in-Chief Kenya, in Durham University Library. In addition, relevant material can be found in the papers of Charles Douglas-Home, his aide-de-camp in Kenya, which are held in the Liddell Hart Centre, King's College, London. Douglas-Home's biography *Evelyn Baring: The Last Proconsul*, was published in 1978. There is some correspondence, 1942–60, in the papers of Paul Emrys-Evans, at the British Library (ref. Add MSS 58235–58273) and in the Blundell papers at Rhodes House Library, Oxford. The transcript of his interview with Margery Perham regarding his time in Africa is also held in Rhodes House Library (ref. MSS Afr s 1574–1575).

HOWIE OF TROON, BARON William Howie (1924–) MP (Lab) Luton, 1963–70.

Some 74 case and subject files together with correspondence on constituency and local affairs, 1950–70, are held at the Brynmor Jones Library, University of Hull (ref. DMO).

HOWSON, REAR-ADMIRAL JOHN (1908–92) Royal Navy career, 1922–64. Served in World War II. British military representative, Supreme Headquarters, Allied Powers Europe, Brussels, 1955–58. NATO Commander, Allied Forces Northern Europe, 1961–62. Naval deputy to Commander-in-Chief, Allied Forces, Northern Europe, 1962–64.

The National Maritime Museum acquired a collection of papers in 1988 (ref. MS 88/021).

HUBBACK, DAVID FRANCIS (1916–91) Public servant. Principal Private Secretary, Chancellor of the Exchequer, 1960–62. Under-Secretary, Treasury, 1962–68. Served Department of Trade, etc.

The papers (5 archive boxes, 1956–88) have been placed in Churchill College, Cambridge. A list is available (NRA 44307).

HUBBACK, SIR JOHN AUSTEN (1878–1968) Indian Civil Service, 1902–41. Governor of Orissa, 1936–41. Adviser to Secretary of State for India, 1942–47.

A memoir of his time in India is deposited with the Cambridge South Asian Archive.

HUDDLESTON, (ERNEST URBAN) TREVOR (1913–98) Anglican clergyman. Bishop of Masai, 1960–68. Suffragan Bishop of Stepney, 1968–78. Chairman, International Defence and Aid Fund for Southern Africa, after 1983. President, Anti-Apartheid Movement, after 1981; Vice-President, 1969–81.

An important and extensive collection of his correspondence and papers has been acquired by BLCAS (Rhodes House Library), Oxford.

HUGHES, EMRYS (1894–1969) MP (Lab) Ayrshire South and Bute, 1946–69.

The correspondence and papers are deposited in the National Library of Scotland. Many concern his editorship of *Forward*. These include correspondence and draft articles from contributors (among them George Bernard Shaw and Leon Trotsky) and also complete files of *Forward*, 1932–51. The later material consists of working papers and drafts for his various articles, books and speeches. The surviving political correspondence and papers include letters on constituency affairs, general politics, journalism and broadcasting, 1950–59; election addresses, 1950–66; notes on defence policy; extracts from speeches and parliamentary questions by Hughes; a personal diary, 1961; a diary of the Sixty-Fourth Annual Party Conference, 1965; and also photographs and press-cuttings.

HUGHES, HERBERT DELAUNEY (1914–95) MP (Lab) Wolverhampton West, 1945–50. Principal, Ruskin College, Oxford, 1950–79.

Mr Hughes bequeathed his papers to Ruskin College. They include his constituency correspondence and extensive material on his later activities including Ruskin College, the Workers' Educational Association, the Russell Committee on Adult Education, the Civil Service Arbitration Tribunal and the Fabian Society.

HUME, CARDINAL (GEORGE) BASIL (1923–99) Roman Catholic Archbishop of Westminster after 1976. Abbot of Ampleforth, 1963–76.

Cardinal Hume's papers (over 600 boxes) are deposited in the Westminster Archdiocesan Archives under a thirty-year closure rule.

HUME, JOHN (1937–) MP (SDLP) Foyle 1983–2005. MEP (SDLP), Northern Ireland, 1989–2004. Leader of the SDLP after 1979. Stormont MP (Foyle) 1969–73. Minister of Commerce, Northern Ireland Executive, 1974. Civil-rights campaigner during the 1960s.

No recent information has been received regarding his papers. According to his biographer, Barry White, Mr Hume has never kept a diary. He has deposited a small collection of papers relating to the unsuccessful campaign to base the New University of Ulster in Derry, 1963–67, in the Public Record Office of Northern Ireland. The SDLP deposits its files with the same repository at regular intervals.

HUMPHREYS, MAJOR-GENERAL GEORGE CHARLES (1899–1991) Military career. Brigadier in charge of administration, Burma Command, 1946–48.

A memoir of his period in Burma is in Churchill Archives Centre (ref. MISC 53).

HUNT, SIR REX (MASTERMAN) (1926–) Diplomat, 1951–85. Counsellor, Saigon, 1974–75. Deputy High Commissioner, Kuala Lumpur, 1977–79. Governor and Commander-in-Chief, Falkland Islands, 1980–82; Civil Commissioner, 1982–85; Governor, October 1985.

Sir Rex's recently published account of the Falklands War, *My Falklands Days*, was based on the diary he kept at the time.

HUNTER, LESLIE STANNARD (1890–1983)
Anglican clergyman. Bishop of Sheffield, 1939–62.

The papers are deposited in Sheffield City Library. The collection includes extensive correspondence; sermons, addresses, lectures and House of Lords speeches; and typescripts of various published and unpublished works. There is material on German prisoners of war, his visits to Germany and his contacts with Bishop Dibelius of Berlin as well as personal papers and press-cuttings.

HUTCHINSON, REAR-ADMIRAL CHRISTO-PHER HAYNES (1906–90) Naval career, mainly in submarines. Senior Naval Adviser to UK High Commissioner, Australia, 1952–54. Director-General of Personal Services and Officer Appointments, 1959–61.

The Imperial War Museum holds a collection of uncatalogued papers, 1919–62.

HUTCHINSON, NINA (1943–94) (née Helweg)
Feminist activist.

There are 37 archive boxes of personal working and political papers as well as correspondence and other resource material in the Women's Library (Acc No 15/1998, ref. 7/NHH). The material includes education, Irish politics, and ethnic issues in London.

HUTTON, ALASDAIR HENRY (1940–) MEP (Lab) Scotland South, 1979–89.

His political papers as an MEP are in the University of Glasgow Library. The collection includes constituency correspondence, election correspondence, working papers of the European Parliament and correspondence with EU institutions.

HUXLEY, ELSPETH JOSCELINE (MRS GERVAS HUXLEY) (1907–97) Writer. UK independent member, Monckton Advisory Commission on Central Africa, 1959.

There are four boxes of diaries, correspondence and literary papers, 1919–59, in Rhodes House Library, Oxford (ref. MSS Afr s 782). A list is available (NRA 39155).

HUXLEY, SIR JULIAN SORELL (1887–1974)
Biologist and writer. Director-General of UNESCO, 1946–48. Fellow of the Royal Society, 1938 onwards.

A collection of correspondence and papers is housed at the Woodson Research Centre, Rice University. A list is available (NRA 27261). The papers include an extensive indexed correspondence; journals, diaries and notebooks; various manuscripts, notes and publications; and material relating to travel, conferences and various organisations. In addition, there are numerous clippings, photographs and memorabilia and box files on biological science issues.

HUXTABLE, (WILLIAM) JOHN (FAIRCHILD) (1912–90) Moderator, United Reformed Church, 1972–74. Executive Office, Churches' Unity Commission, 1975–78.

The papers have been placed in Dr Williams Library.

HYDE, HARFORD MONTGOMERY (1907–89)
MP (UU) Belfast North, 1950–59. Author and barrister.

Some manuscripts and research notes for his books on British Intelligence during World War II are held at Churchill College, Cambridge. A list is available (NRA 18561).

HYDE, AIR COMMODORE NOEL CHALLIS (1910–) Royal Air Force career from 1929. Served in World War II. Berlin Airlift, 1948–50. Director of Operations, Air Ministry, 1953–56. Air Officer Commanding, Royal Malayan Air Force, 1958–60. Commandant, RAF Staff College, Andover, 1961–62.

The Imperial War Museum holds a collection of papers covering his entire Royal Air Force career, 1929–62 (refs 88/14/4 and 4A). The material includes logbooks, reports and photographs.

HYMAN, RICHARD (fl. 1970s–) Academic. Professor.

Professor Hyman has deposited a variety of research and political papers at the Modern Records Centre, University of Warwick. Among the papers are two box files of material relating to the Conference of Socialist Economists, one file on International Socialism, 1975–80, a box file on industrial relations negotiating procedure, Sheffield City Council, 1984–85, and two ring binders of press-cuttings on industrial relations and the Coventry Toolroom Agreement (MSS.63, MSS.84). In addition, Professor

Hyman has deposited an NUR/RMT Research Collection. This includes minutes of Council of Executives, 1994–96; correspondence files including restructuring of the National Union of Railwaymen, railway workers' wage negotiations, 1970s–80s etc. (ref MSS. 380). A list is available (NRA 41292).

HYND, JOHN BURNS (1902–71) MP (Lab) Sheffield Attercliffe, 1944–70. Chancellor of the Duchy of Lancaster and Minister for Germany and Austria, 1945–47. Minister of Pensions, 1947.

A collection of papers is held at Churchill College, Cambridge. A list is available (NRA 31391). It includes an interesting series of papers on post-war relations with Germany, covering such issues as war crimes compensation, the German Social Democrats and the Anglo-German Association. Other files on foreign policy contain material on the USSR and Eastern Europe, Africa, Latin America, Suez, the European Economic Community, the Middle East and world communism. There are also some constituency and Labour Party files including correspondence, speeches, press-cuttings and photographs.

I

INCHYRA, 1ST BARON Sir Frederick Robert Hoyer Millar **(1900–89)** Diplomat. Minister, Washington, 1948. UK Permanent Representative, NATO Council, 1952. High Commissioner, Germany, 1953–55. Ambassador, German Federal Republic, 1955–57. Permanent Under-Secretary, Foreign Office, 1957–61.

Lord Inchyra indicated to a previous survey that on retirement he either destroyed his papers or returned them to the Foreign Office. He did not keep a personal diary. The LSE Library holds an interview recorded in 1980 for the British Oral Archive of Political and Administrative History. Applications for access to the transcript should be made to the Archivist. The papers of Lord Avon at Birmingham University Library include correspondence, 1957–65 (ref. AP23/40).

INGRAMS, WILLIAM HAROLD (1897–1973) Colonial service. Served Malaya, 1930; Aden and Yemen, 1940–45. Seconded to Allied Control Commission for Germany, 1945–47. On Colonial Office Missions to Gibraltar, 1949; Hong Kong, 1950; and Uganda, 1956. Adviser to Colonial Office, 1950–54. On research staff, Foreign and Commonwealth Office, 1960s.

A collection of papers, 1919–69, consisting of correspondence, despatches, reports and press-cuttings is in Rhodes House Library, Oxford (ref. MSS Brit Emp s 425–431). The papers include material on the suggested confederation of Malaysia and the Philippines and on Malaysia and Indonesia, 1962–64; the African franchise in East and Central Africa, 1953–56; African representation on the legislative council; and the political situation in Kenya, 1948–58. Access to the Kenyan material may be restricted.

Additional material is held at the Middle East Centre, St Antony's College, Oxford and at Churchill College, Cambridge. The Middle East Centre's collection covers the 1914–65 period (see NRA 20811).

The papers at Churchill College relate to his time with the Control Commission in Germany, 1945–47.

INVERCHAPEL, BARON Archibald Clark Kerr **(1882–1951)** Diplomat. Ambassador to the USSR, 1942–46. Special British Envoy to Java, 1946. Ambassador to the United States, 1946–48.

An extensive collection of papers has been deposited in the Bodleian Library, Oxford. The collection documents most aspects of British foreign policy from World War I to the Council of Europe, 1949. The post-war sections include files on the Allied Commissions to Romania, 1945–46, and to Indonesia, 1946. There are also reports on the Soviet Union, 1915–50, and on European Integration and the European Union, 1948. His correspondents include Harold Nicolson, 1910–50 and Madame Chiang Kai-shek, 1939–40.

IRELAND, DENIS (1894–1974) Northern Irish author, journalist and politician. Senator, Republic of Ireland, 1948–51; Irish representative, Council of Europe, 1949–51. Founder of Commonwealth Irish Association. Member, Clann na Poblachta until resignation, 1950.

The Public Record Office of Northern Ireland holds some papers, 1931–74 (ref. D3137). In addition to drafts and texts of his books and articles, they include some correspondence relating to Northern and Southern Irish politics. Two letters concerning Dominion Status for Northern Ireland, 1949 and 1959, are in the papers of Ernest Blythe, in University College, Dublin (ref. P24).

IRVINE, SIR BRYANT GODMAN (1909–92) MP (Con) Rye, 1955–83. Various ministerial posts. Deputy Speaker, 1976–82. Joint Secretary, 1922 Committee, 1965–68.

The papers (68 files) were placed in East Sussex Record Office by Mrs Carola Godman Law (ref. Acc 6866). A list is available (NRA 40623).

IRVING, SIR CHARLES GRAHAM (1924–95) MP (Con) Cheltenham after 1974.

The material in Gloucestershire Record Office includes press-cuttings, texts of speeches and photographs relating to his political career, *c.* 1945–91 (ref. D7264).

ISMAY, 1ST BARON General Sir Hastings Lionel Ismay (1887–1965) Chief of Staff to Minister of Defence, 1940–45. Deputy Secretary (Military), War Cabinet, 1940–45; Additional Secretary (Military), 1945. Chief of Staff to Viceroy of India, 1947. Commonwealth Relations Secretary, 1951–52. Secretary General, NATO, 1952–57.

A collection of papers (26 boxes) covering the whole of his career has been deposited at the Liddell Hart Centre, King's College London. A list is available (NRA 12103). The papers include extensive correspondence (including some material relating to Winston Churchill) as well as printed matter, subject files and notes written for an autobiography. Cabinet Office papers and correspondence, 1922–49, are held at the Public Record Office (ref. CAB 127/1–56) (NRA 32409).

J

JACKSON, SIR GEOFFREY HOLT SEYMOUR (1915–87) Various Diplomatic Service postings in Beirut, Cairo, Baghdad and Basra, 1937–46. First Secretary, Bogota, 1946–50; Berne, 1954–56; Minister, Honduras, 1956; Ambassador to Honduras, 1957–60; Consul-General, Seattle, 1960–64; Minister (Commercial) Toronto, 1965–69; Ambassador to Uruguay, 1969–72.

The papers have been placed at Churchill College, Cambridge (ref. JAKN). A list is available (NRA 32588). The collection relates mainly to his period as Ambassador to Uruguay, during which time he was kidnapped and held for eight months in captivity by the Tupamaros, and includes correspondence and press-cuttings. Also included are copies of speeches and press-cuttings from his diplomatic career, 1950s–70s; published and unpublished writings; material from an advisory group on the social effects of television; a file on education; and seven taped interviews.

JACKSON, PETER (MICHAEL) (1928–) MP (Lab) High Peak, 1966–70.

Some correspondence and other files are in the Brynmor Jones Library, University of Hull (ref. DMJ). The collection, 224 files, covering the period 1966–70, includes correspondence with constituents, material on the Select Committee on Agriculture and papers concerning the 1970 election.

JACOB, LIEUTENANT-GENERAL SIR (EDWARD) IAN CLAUD (1899–1993) Military Assistant Secretary, Committee of Imperial Defence, 1938; War Cabinet, 1939–46. Chief Staff Officer to Minister of Defence, and Deputy Secretary (Military) of the Cabinet, 1952. Director-General, British Broadcasting Corporation, 1952–60.

A collection of 27 boxes of papers, including diaries and correspondence relating to his service with Sir Winston Churchill, has been deposited in Churchill College, Cambridge. A list is available (NRA 44051). The LSE Library holds an interview recorded in 1980, which covers British Defence Policy from the White Paper of 1946 to his retirement in 1952, and includes some comments on developments after 1963.

JACQUES, MARTIN (1945–) Journalist, editor and writer. History lecturer, Bristol University, 1971–77. Editor, *Marxism Today*, after 1977. Political columnist, *The Times*, 1990–92; *The Sunday Times* since 1992.

Mr Jacques has retained extensive papers, including files on *Marxism Today* and transcripts and records of interviews, discussions and conferences organised by the magazine. He also holds papers relating to student politics, 1964–71, and to the Communist Party, 1963–91.

JAKOBOVITS, BARON Sir Immanuel Jakobovits (1921–99) Jewish rabbi. Chief Rabbi of the United Hebrew Congregations of the British Commonwealth, 1967–91; Rabbi of Fifth Avenue Synagogue, New York, 1958–67; Chief Rabbi of Ireland, 1949–58.

Researchers should make reference to the papers in the Hartley Library, University of Southampton. The collection covers the period 1967–91 (NRA 41475).

JAMES, MICHAEL (fl. 1980s) AIDS campaigner and Gay Rights activist.

A collection of papers was deposited at the LSE Library in 1990. These include his diaries, describing the impact of AIDS on the gay community in London and hospital visits during the 1980s. There are also *Body Positive* newsletters together with various related leaflets, papers and photographs. Further deposits have included additional diaries, correspondence, and material relating to Body Positive. Additional relevant material can be found in the

Hall-Carpenter Archive, also deposited at LSE. This archive is the major source for issues affecting the gay community in Britain.

JANITSCHEK, HANS (1934–) Journalist and International Socialist. London-based General Secretary of Socialist International (SI), 1969–77. Editor of *Who's Who in Social Democracy*, 1975–77.

His papers are in the International Institute of Social History, Amsterdam. The collection includes private correspondence, 1969–82; correspondence with journalists, 1970–76; press-cuttings, 1969–76; files relating to SI, 1969–82; publications of the United Nations Office of Public Information, 1977–82; and material relating to his editorial work.

JAY, BARON Douglas Patrick Thomas Jay (1907–96) MP (Lab) Battersea North, 1946–83. Economic Secretary, Treasury, 1947–50; Financial Secretary, 1950–51; President, Board of Trade, 1964–67. Chairman, Common Market Safeguards Campaign, 1970–77.

Lord Jay stated that he had retained a large collection of papers including letters, articles, reviews, and other official documents, as well as the typescript of a diary which mainly records his years in government. Many of these were used in his memoirs, *Change and Fortune*, (1980).

JEFFERYS, STEVE (fl. 1966–79) Leading student activist, London School of Economics, 1966–67; full-time Industrial Organiser, International Socialism/Socialist Workers' Party, 1974–79.

The Jefferys papers are held at the Modern Records Centre, University of Warwick (ref. MSS 244). The deposit relates to his work as an activist and organiser within International Socialism/Socialist Workers' Party, and includes Executive Committee and National Committee papers and incomplete handwritten notes on meetings from 1969 and 1979–80. There are also Glasgow North Branch minutes, 1969–71; subject files 1967–80, including material on Scotland and the Upper Clyde Shipbuilders; papers on LSE student politics, 1966–67; and leaflets and newsletters addressed to workers in various factories, companies and trade unions, 1970–79. The collection complements the Richard Kuper papers (q.v.).

JEFFREYS, SHEILA (fl. 1970s–80s) Feminist activist.

The Women's Library has *c.* 41 archive boxes and other material (ref. 7/SHJ). The collection includes personal working papers, campaigning and resource material, and other publications about radical feminism and lesbian issues, including Women Against Violence Against Women.

JEFFRIES, SIR CHARLES JOSEPH (1896–1972) Assistant Under-Secretary, Colonial Office, 1939–47; Joint Deputy Under-Secretary, 1947–56.

Rhodes House Library, Oxford, has a copy of an unpublished memoir of a visit to West Africa.

JEGER, BARONESS Lena May Jeger (1915–) MP (Lab) Holborn and St Pancras South, 1953–59, 1964–74; Camden, Holborn and St Pancras 1974–79. Member, Consultative Assembly, Council of Europe, 1969–71; WEU, 1969–71, etc.

The papers were placed in the LSE Library in 2005. The collection comprises mainly correspondence, reports, briefings, speeches, photographs and other papers relating to her work as a local councillor, MP and member of the House of Lords. Also included are draft articles, correspondence and other papers relating to her time as a journalist. For access apply to the Archivist.

JENKIN OF RODING, LORD Charles Patrick Fleeming Jenkin (1926–) MP (Con) Wanstead and Woodford, 1964–87. Financial Secretary to the Treasury, 1970–72; Chief Secretary to Treasury, 1972–74; Energy Minister, 1974. Secretary of State for Social Services, 1979–81; Industry, 1981–83; Environment, 1983–85.

The papers (61 boxes) have been deposited in Churchill College, Cambridge (ref. Acc 1309). They consist of copies of his outgoing letters, 1966–77; a complete set of constituents' correspondence and replies (for 1970 only); unsorted political correspondence; files relating to general elections, 1964–83; weekly and daily engagement diaries (dating back to the late 1970s); copies of his speeches, including those made as Environment Secretary; records of several foreign visits made as a backbencher or while in opposition; and personal letters of congratulation and support on his various appointments and his resignation.

JENKINS OF HILLHEAD, BARON Roy Harris Jenkins **(1920–2003)** MP (Lab) Central Southwark, 1948–50; Birmingham Stetchford, 1950–76; (SDP) Glasgow Hillhead, 1982–87. Minister of Aviation, 1964–65. Home Secretary, 1965–67 and 1974–76. Chancellor of the Exchequer, 1967–70. Deputy Leader of the Labour Party, 1970–72. President of the European Commission, 1977–81. First Leader of the SDP, 1982–83. Liberal Democrat Leader, House of Lords after 1988.

Lord Jenkins retained his papers and made provision for their deposit. The diary he kept at the European Commission was published in 1989 and his autobiography appeared in 1991.

JENKINS OF PUTNEY, LORD Hugh Gater Jenkins **(1908–2004)** MP (Lab) Putney, 1964–79. Minister for the Arts, 1974–76.

Lord Jenkins' papers have been deposited at the LSE Library. The collection reflects all aspects of his career but covers, in particular, the Putney Labour Party and his life-long interest in the arts. Subject areas covered include his early political career; London County Council; parliamentary duties; and publications, general papers and photographs. Of particular interest is his diary kept as Arts Minister, January 1975 to March 1976. Many of the papers deal with Lord Jenkins' writings and broadcasts, especially those concerning communications and the media. There are also minutes, papers and correspondence concerning Victory for Socialism, 1944–57.

JENKINS, (DAVID) CLIVE (1926–99) Joint General Secretary, 1968–70; General Secretary, 1970–88; Association of Scientific, Technical and Managerial Staffs. Member of the General Council of the Trades Union Congress, 1974–89.

His extensive papers are held with the ASTMS collection (ref. MSS 79) at the Modern Records Centre, University of Warwick. The collection contains correspondence and drafts of his writings and files on CND, and the anti-EEC and anti-Vietnam war campaign issues. Also included are papers concerning the Labour Party, particularly during his period as a Borough Councillor for St Pancras, and his service on various bodies such as the British National Oil Corporation, 1979–81, and the Labour

Party Commissions of Enquiry, 1979–80. A detailed list is available (NRA 42582).

JENKINS, SIR EVAN MEREDITH (1896–1985) Private Secretary to Viceroy of India and Secretary to Governor-General, 1943–45. Governor, Punjab, 1946–47.

The papers, 1947–72 are at the India Office Library (ref. MSS Eur D 807).

JENNINGS, SIR WILLIAM IVOR (1903–65) Lawyer and public servant. Expert on constitutional law. Adviser to Ceylon, Pakistan, Malaya, etc. on the drafting of constitutions. Vice-Chancellor, University of Ceylon, 1952–55. Chairman, Royal Commission on Common Land, 1955–58; Royal University of Malta Commission, 1956–57.

A collection of papers is held at the Institute of Commonwealth Studies. A list is available (NRA 30413). The collection includes advisory papers on constitutional arrangements for numerous countries including Ceylon, Eritrea, Malaya, Malta, Pakistan, the Federation of Rhodesia and Nyasaland and Sudan. There are also various papers relating to the social services and constitution of Ceylon, and his role in university administration. There are additionally various books, publications, and press-cuttings.

JOHN, BRYNMOR THOMAS (1934–88) MP (Lab) Pontypridd, 1970–88. Parliamentary Under-Secretary of State for Defence (Royal Air Force), 1974–76; Minister of State, Home Office, 1976–79.

His correspondence and papers, 1966–88, were deposited by Mrs Anne John at the National Library of Wales in 1989 (ref. A1989/181). A list is available (NRA 26130). The collection contains constituency and parliamentary correspondence and papers; correspondence on Welsh affairs; Pontypridd Divisional Labour Party papers, 1919–70; Labour Party material; local and national election material; foreign affairs papers; and various subject files and other material.

JOHN-MACKIE, BARON John Mackie **(1909–94)** MP (Lab) Enfield East, 1959–Feb. 1974. Chairman, Forestry Commission, 1976–79.

Lord John-Mackie retained his papers. Researchers should contact the LSE Library in the first instance.

JOHNSON, DONALD McINTOSH (1903–78) MP (Con) Carlisle, 1955–64.

His papers were deposited at the LSE Library in 1989 (ref. M1669). Enquiries should be addressed to the Archivist.

JOHNSON, HEWLETT (1874–1966) Anglican clergyman. Dean of Manchester, 1924–31; of Canterbury, 1931–63. Author of *The Socialist Sixth of the World* (1941) and *Christians and Communism* (1956). The leading Anglican exponent of Marxism.

A collection of sermons, diaries, correspondence and press-cuttings, 1930–63, is deposited at the University of Kent Library, Canterbury. Much of the correspondence concerns post-war relations with Eastern Europe, including the Berlin Blockade and the Hungarian uprising and developments within the Soviet Union, including persecution of the Jews, the position of women, education, youth policy, the secret police, psychiatric abuse, and slave labour. The collection also includes copies of *The Interpreter*, the journal he founded and edited, 1905–24.

JOHNSON, JAMES (1908–95) MP (Lab) Rugby, 1950–59; Hull West, 1964–83.

Some correspondence on colonial issues, 1950–59, can be found in the Fabian Bureau archive at Rhodes House Library, Oxford (NRA 16153). Rhodes House Library also holds a microfilm of letters from Tom Mboya on the political situation in Kenya in 1957 (ref. Micr Afr 586). Some further political papers, including a little correspondence, are in the Brynmor Jones library, University of Hull. (ref. DJJ).

JOHNSON, AIR VICE-MARSHAL JAMES EDGAR (JOHNNIE) (1916–) Royal Air Force career. Served in World War II. Attached to the United States Air Force, 1948–50, including service in Korea, 1950–51. Air Officer Commanding, Middle East, Aden, 1963–65.

The Department of Sound Records at the Imperial War Museum holds an interview which covers, in particular, his Korean War experiences (ref. 10347/3). A transcript is available. Two volumes of autobiography have been published, *Wing Leader* (1956) and *Full Circle* (1964).

JOHNSTON, SIR CHARLES (HEPBURN) (1912–86) Diplomat. Third Secretary, Tokyo, 1939; First Secretary, Cairo, 1945, and Madrid, 1948; Counsellor, Foreign Office, 1951, and British Embassy, Bonn, 1955. Ambassador to Jordan, 1956; Governor and Commander-in-Chief, Aden, 1960–63; High Commissioner for Aden and Protectorate of South Arabia, 1963. Deputy Under-Secretary of State, Foreign Office, 1963–65; High Commissioner, Australia, 1965–71.

There are 18 boxes of papers, correspondence and photographs, 1924–86, at the Liddell Hart Centre, King's College, London. They include files of correspondence, notes and press-cuttings on pre- and post-war Anglo-Japanese relations; correspondence and press-cuttings on events in Jordan, 1956–59 (including the stationing of British troops there in 1958); files on the merging of Aden with the Federation of Southern Arabia, 1962–63; and his despatches on the 1950 trials in Madrid of opponents of Franco. There is also material on his appointment as political adviser to the British High Commissioner in Bonn in 1953 and some correspondence with Sir Paul Gore-Booth on events in Australia, 1968.

JONES OF DEESIDE, BARON Stephen Barry Jones (1938–) MP (Lab) Flint East, 1970–83; Alyn and Deeside after 1983.

His political correspondence and papers have been placed in Flintshire Record Office. The collection includes correspondence, press-cuttings etc. with material on the Shotton Steel (workers) Campaign.

JONES, ARTHUR CREECH (1891–1964) MP (Lab) Shipley, 1935–50; Wakefield, 1954–64. Parliamentary Under-Secretary, Colonial Office, 1945–46. Colonial Secretary, 1946–50.

Sixty-one boxes of papers and correspondence have been deposited at Rhodes House Library, Oxford (ref. MSS Brit Emp s 332). A detailed list is available (NRA 14026). Boxes 1–5 contain biographical material. Boxes 6–8 hold correspondence from a variety of individuals including Winifred Holtby and R.H. Tawney. Boxes 9–11 hold writings and speeches; 12 and 13 visits to British dependencies, 14–17 the pre-war Labour Party. Boxes 18–33 hold large amounts of papers on specific territories in Africa, Asia, the Pacific, Europe, and four files on Palestine. Boxes 34–43 contain papers on the Advisory Committee on Education in the Colonies. Boxes 44–49 are on colonial development and welfare; 50–53 are printed material, and the remainder contain official papers on general issues and by territory.

There are additional papers relating to Creech Jones in the Greenidge Papers (ref. MSS Brit Emp s 285), and the Fabian Bureau Papers (ref. MSS Brit Emp s 365). Both of these collections are also at Rhodes House Library, and lists are available (NRA 14913 and 16153).

JONES, AUBREY (1911–2003) MP (Con) Birmingham Hall Green, 1950–65. Minister of Fuel and Power, 1955–57. Minister of Supply, 1957–59. Chairman, National Board for Prices and Incomes, 1965–70.

Churchill College, Cambridge, holds 190 boxes of papers, diaries and press-cuttings (ref. AUJO). A list is available (NRA 44035).

JONES, BENJAMIN GEORGE (1914–89) Chairman, Council for the Welsh Language, 1973–78; President, Honorary Society of Cymmrodorion, 1982–89.

Some papers are held at the National Library of Wales. They include personal correspondence and political scrapbooks, 1958–63; material on the Honorary Society of Cymmrodorion, 1939–88; files on the *Dictionary of Welsh Biography*, 1953–86; and miscellaneous papers and reports on the status of the Welsh language together with Council for the Welsh Language memoranda, reports and circulars, 1973–78. There are also various political pamphlets and lecture notes.

JONES, GENERAL SIR CHARLES PHIBBS (1906–89) Military career. Served in North West Europe, World War II, 1944–45; Chief of Staff, Malaya Command, 1945–46. Director of Plans, War Office, 1950. Vice-Adjutant-General, War Office, 1957–58. Director, Combined Military Planning Staff, Central Treaty Organisation, 1959. Master-General of the Ordnance, 1963–66.

His family informed the Liddell Hart Centre, King's College, London, that they have retained a collection of unsorted papers.

JONES, GWILYM (1947–) MP (Con) Cardiff North, 1983–97.

Some files relating to his political activities during the 1980s (mainly constituency files for Cardiff North) are held at the Welsh Political Archive, National Library of Wales.

JONES, IEUAN WYN (1949–) MP (Plaid Cymru), Ynys Môn, 1987–2001. Leader of Plaid Cymru in Welsh Assembly.

His constituency correspondence and papers, 1987–96, have been placed in the National Library of Wales. There are files on specific subjects including water, education, health, employment and Europe. The material is not available for 20 years without the permission of the donor.

JONES, JAMES IDWAL (1900–82) MP (Lab) Wrexham, 1955–70.

His papers, covering the period 1924–70, have been placed in Clwyd Record Office, Ruthin (ref. DD/DM/698). A list is available (NRA 34291). The collection consists of a series of scrapbooks which contain press-cuttings and other printed matter, as well as correspondence. Specific topics include the Welsh language, education and the creation of employment opportunities.

JONES, JAMES LARKIN (JACK) (1913–) Trade union leader. General Secretary, Transport and General Workers Union, 1969–75. Campaigner for pensioners' rights.

There are 45 boxes of material from the 1930s to the present now deposited in the Modern Records Centre, University of Warwick (ref MSS 126/JJ). The papers include his service in the Spanish Civil War, his membership of the Royal Commission on Criminal Procedure, and his post-retirement campaigning for pensioners' rights.

JONES, (WILLIAM) ERNEST (1895–1973) Trade unionist. General Secretary, Yorkshire Miners' Association, 1939. Regional Labour Director, Ministry of Fuel and Power, 1942–44. President, National Union of Mineworkers, 1954–60. Member of the General Council, Trades Union Congress, 1950–60. Secretary, Miners' International Federation, 1957–60. Chairman, Southern Regional Board for Industry, 1961–66.

A collection of papers is held at the Brynmor Jones Library, University of Hull. A list is available (NRA 20510). The papers and correspondence relate mainly to the National Union of Mineworkers and to Labour Party political issues.

JOSEPH, LORD Sir Keith Joseph (1918–94) Conservative politician, one of the key architects of the Thatcher era.

The papers have been placed in the Bodleian Library, to where enquiries concerning access etc. should be addressed.

JOSEPHY, FRANCES L. (1900–84) Liberal activist and Europeanist. Chairman, Federal Union.

A collection of papers has been deposited in the LSE Library. The collection contains Federal Union Committee minutes and papers, 1940–60, Executive Committee papers, 1941–58, and various publications including issues of *Federal News*, 1942–64. Also included are the committee minutes, papers and correspondence for the European Union of Federalists, 1946–55, the European Movement Congress (UK) and International Executive Bureau papers, 1947–52, Council of Europe conference papers and a diary, 1949–54, along with various Europa Union Congress papers, 1949–51. Other papers include the minutes and papers for a number of other European committees, various subject files, a collection of speeches, 1939–57, and other miscellaneous items. The LSE Library also holds a large collection of related material on the Federal Union.

JOUHL, AVTAR (fl. 1950s–90s) Trade unionist and shop steward. General Secretary, Indian Workers Association.

His papers concerning his work as a stop steward and as General Secretary of the Indian Workers Association, *c.* 1950–90s, are in Birmingham City Archives (ref. MS2142).

K

KAHN, BARON Richard Ferdinand Kahn (1905–89) Economist. Professor of Economics, Cambridge University, 1951–72; Fellow of King's College, Cambridge, from 1930.

The papers are held at King's College, Cambridge, to whom enquiries should be addressed.

KALDOR OF NEWNHAM, BARON Nicolas Kaldor (1908–86) Professor of Economics, University of Cambridge, 1966–75. Member, Royal Commission on Taxation of Profits and Income, 1951–55; economic adviser to successive governments, 1956–63; special adviser to the Chancellor of the Exchequer, 1964–68 and 1974–76.

Lord Kaldor bequeathed his economics papers to King's College Library, Cambridge. Enquiries regarding the collection should be directed to the Librarian.

KAPP, YVONNE (1903–99) Writer and communist.

Her correspondence and papers have been placed in the Women's Library, London Metropolitan University (ref. 7/YVK).

KEATING, REX (fl. 1930s–50s) Broadcaster with War Pictorial News, Egypt and Palestine, 1940–47. Employee of Egyptian State Broadcasting, 1935–45. Deputy Director, Palestine Broadcasting Service, 1945–48. Director-General of the Cyprus Broadcasting Corporation, 1951–54.

An interesting collection of papers covering his entire career, 1935–54, has been deposited in the Imperial War Museum. A full list is available at the Museum. There is material on War Pictorial newsreels, 1940–45; propaganda and censorship; the Arab–Jewish struggle in Palestine; and the Cyprus media in the 1950s. The Museum's Department of Sound Records has a recording and full transcript (108 pages) of an interview with him. Special conditions of access apply to this recording (ref. 8752/9).

KELF-COHEN, REUBEN (1895–1981) Civil servant, 1920–55. Under-Secretary, Ministry of Fuel and Power, 1946–55. Author of books on nationalisation.

His unpublished autobiography is in the LSE Library (ref. COLL MISC 677).

KELLETT-BOWMAN OF SLYNE, DAME (MARY) ELAINE (1924–) MP (Con) Lancaster, 1970–97. MEP, 1975–84.

Her constituency files have been placed in Lancashire Record Office (ref. DDX 2067, acc 7878). The collection is closed.

KELLEY, JOANNA (b. 1910) Prison administrator. Governor, HM Prison, Holloway, 1959–66. Assistant Director of Prisons (Women), 1967–74.

Seven boxes of papers were deposited in the LSE Library by Joanna Kelley in 1993 (ref. M1780). The papers consist mainly of research notes on the prison system, particularly the treatment of women and history of Holloway. Most of the notes were made between 1947 and 1952, with additions between 1952 and 1959. The collection is an important research resource for the history of women's prisons.

KELLOCK, THOMAS OSLAF (1923–93) Colonial legal career. Director, Legal Division, Commonwealth Secretariat, 1969–72. Constitutional Adviser, HM Sultan of Brunei, 1975–76. Chairman, Anti-Apartheid Movement, 1963–65. Circuit Judge, UK since 1976.

Some papers have been placed with the Centre for Southern African Studies, University of York. A list is available (NRA 19618). The collection includes papers relating to the Devlin Commission of Enquiry, Nyasaland, 1959; miscellaneous papers on South Africa, political trials in Malawi, the Boycott Movement of March 1964, the Rivonia Trials and the World Campaign for the Release of South African Prisoners.

KELLY, SIR DAVID VICTOR (1891–1959) Diplomat. Ambassador, Argentine Republic, 1942–46; Turkey, 1946–49; USSR, 1949–51.

Sir David's papers, earlier reported to be in the care of his widow, have recently been destroyed. His autobiographical works include *The Ruling Few* (1952) and *Beyond The Iron Curtain* (1954).

KEMP, ERIC WALDRAM (b. 1915) Anglican clergyman. Dean of Worcester, 1969–74. Long-serving Bishop of Chichester.

His papers concerning Anglican-Methodist Unity, 1956–72, are in Lambeth Palace Library.

KENNEDY, GAVIN (fl. 1970s) Economist and author.

There are papers concerning Scottish National Party committees and conferences, 1974–80, in the National Library of Scotland (ref. Acc 11565).

KENNEDY, MAJOR-GENERAL SIR JOHN NOBLE (1893–1970) Military career and colonial administrator. Served in World Wars I and II. Assistant Chief of the Imperial General Staff, 1943–46. Governor and Commander-in-Chief, Southern Rhodesia, 1947–54.

His account of the establishment of the Central African Federation is deposited in Rhodes House Library, Oxford (refs. MSS Afr r 209 and Micr Afr 631). Further papers are at the Liddell Hart Centre for Military Archives, King's College, London. They include diaries and papers concerning his service as Director of Military Operations, War Office 1940–43; papers relating to his governorship of Southern Rhodesia, 1946–54; and papers relating to the publication of his book *The Business of War* (1957).

KENNEDY, LUDOVIC HENRY COVERLEY (1919–) Writer and broadcaster.

Some papers have been deposited. Those on criminal matters are held at the Institute of Criminology, Cambridge. Those on naval subjects are held at the Naval Historical Branch of the Ministry of Defence. Other papers have been retained in his possession. All these collections are currently closed to researchers.

KENT, BRUCE (1929–) Chairman, Campaign for Nuclear Disarmament (CND), 1987–90; General Secretary, 1980–85. Roman Catholic clergyman, 1958–87.

The papers have been placed with the archives of CND at the Modern Records Centre, University of Warwick. Mr Kent retains a few additional papers. His autobiography was published in 1992. The Department of Sound Records at the Imperial War Museum has an interview concerning his CND role. The LSE Library holds a microfilm of his speeches and articles, 1981–89 (ref. M 1795).

KENT, NICHOLAS (fl. 1980s) Conservative activist. Vice-Chairman, Tory Reform Group.

There are papers, *c.* 1980–99, mainly relating to the Young Conservatives and the National Federation of Conservative Students, in the LSE Library (ref. KENT).

KENT, SIR PERCY EDWARD (PETER) (1913–86) Chief Geologist, British Petroleum, 1966–71. Member, Natural Environment Research Council, 1973–80; Chairman, 1973–77.

A large collection of papers is held at the Hallward Library, Nottingham University. The collection covers his entire career, including geological surveys and expeditions from the mid-1930s onwards and his work for various geological societies. A list is available (NRA 36387).

KERR, ANNE PATRICIA (1925–73) MP (Lab) Rochester and Chatham, 1964–70.

Certain case and subject files and press-cuttings, 1964–70, are in the Brynmor Jones Library, University of Hull (ref. DKM). A list is available (NRA 38979). The deposit includes material as Chair of Women Against the Common Market, and correspondence on the Vietnam War.

KERR, DAVID (1923–) MP (Lab) Wandsworth Central, 1964–70.

His political papers have been placed in Essex University Library.

KEY, CHARLES WILLIAM (1883–1964) MP (Lab) Poplar, 1940–64. Parliamentary Secretary, Ministry of Health, 1945–47. Minister of Works, 1947–50.

Ten boxes of papers are held at the Bodleian Library, Oxford. A list is available (NRA 18262). The papers include material on the Blitz, Civil Defence and Air Raid Precautions during World War II; his by-election victory in 1940; and his post-war ministerial career including rebuilding in London and the Lynskey Tribunal. The collection includes several sets of photographs. Further correspondence is available in the Attlee papers, also deposited at the Bodleian Library.

KEY, (SIMON) ROBERT (1945–) MP (Con) Salisbury after 1983.

His constituency papers, 1983–91 (not at present open), are in Wiltshire Record Office (ref. 2484).

KEYNES, 1ST BARON John Maynard Keynes (1883–1946) Economist. Fellow of King's College, Cambridge. Civil servant from 1906; Treasury 1915–19. Principal Treasury Representative, Paris Peace Conference. Member of the Committee on Finance and Industry, 1929–31. Editor of *Economic Journal*, 1911–44. Economic adviser to the Government during and after World War II.

The professional papers of Lord Keynes are held at the Marshall Library of Economics, Cambridge. These are arranged by subject and filed with related correspondence. The collection includes papers on official work, manuscripts of books, articles, lectures, broadcasts, etc., and papers on his work for various societies, business organisations and educational institutions. A list is available (NRA 10405). Official correspondence and papers, 1938–49, are held at the Public Record Office (ref. T 247).

Additional personal papers and correspondence are held at King's College, Cambridge. These include family letters and papers. There is also material on the Bursarship of King's College and his involvement in the arts, including his membership of the Arts Council and the Fine Arts Commission. The extensive correspondence, from *c.* 100 individuals to Keynes, is supplemented by various papers and correspondence at the British Library (ref. Add. MSS 55201–4) and includes letters to Duncan Grant (ref. Add. MSS 57930–1). The LSE Library also holds letters from Keynes to Professor Hayek, the editor of *Economica*, and an exchange with E. Rosenbaum.

KILFEDDER, SIR JAMES (1928–95) Ulster Unionist politician. MP (UU) Belfast West, 1964–66;

North Down after 1970. Leader, Ulster Popular Unionist Party after 1980.

His personal and political papers, 1964–95, have been deposited in the Public Record Office of Northern Ireland (ref. D/4127).

KILLEARN, 1ST BARON Sir Miles Wedderburn Lampson (1880–1964) Diplomat. Ambassador, Egypt and High Commissioner, Sudan, 1936–46. Special Commissioner, South-East Asia, 1946–48.

A series of diaries, 1934–51, is held at the Middle East Centre, St Antony's College, Oxford. A list is available (NRA 20811). Further papers are held at Rhodes House Library, Oxford (ref. MSS Afr s 1170).

KILMUIR, 1ST EARL OF Sir David Patrick Maxwell-Fyfe (1900–67) MP (Con) Liverpool West Derby, 1935–54. Solicitor-General, 1942–45; Attorney-General, 1945; Deputy Chief Prosecutor, Nuremburg trials, 1945–46; Secretary of State for Home Affairs, 1951–54; Lord Chancellor, 1954–62.

There are 27 boxes of diaries, speeches and correspondence at Churchill College, Cambridge (ref. KLMR). A list is available (NRA 14286). The collection, covering the period 1922–65, includes material on his legal work, his time in opposition, and as Deputy Chief Prosecutor in the Nuremberg trials. There are also speeches, papers relating to his memoirs, miscellaneous items and photographs. Enquiries regarding access should be addressed to the Archivist.

KING, CECIL (HARMSWORTH) (1901–87) Newspaper proprietor. Chairman, Daily Mirror Newspapers Ltd and Sunday Pictorial Newspapers Ltd, 1951–63; International Publishing Corporation, 1963–68. Director, Reuters, 1953–59; Bank of England, 1965–68.

Some papers are deposited in the Special Collections section, University of Massachusetts in Boston. Other papers are reported with his daughter, Lady Burton. His wartime diary and two volumes of diaries, 1965–74, have been published. His letters to Lord Beaverbrook, 1953–62, are in the Beaverbrook collection in the House of Lords Record Office.

KING-HALL, COMMANDER SIR (WILLIAM) STEPHEN RICHARD (1893–1966) MP (National

Labour) Ormskirk, 1939–42; (Independent National), 1942–45. Served in Ministry of Aircraft Production and Ministry of Fuel and Power during World War II. Founder of Hansard Society for Parliamentary Government, 1944. Author, naval historian, journalist and publisher.

Six boxes of papers have been deposited in the Liddell Hart Centre, King's College, London. The material includes personal letters, 1946–54, issues of the *King-Hall Newsletter* and *National Newsletter*, 1936–59, and various pamphlets. Further correspondence, 1930–54, is in the papers of Lionel Curtis, at the Bodleian Library, Oxford. A list is available (NRA 21614).

KINGSTON-McCLOUGHRY, AIR VICE-MARSHAL EDGAR JAMES (1896–1972) Royal Air Force career. Commanded various RAF Groups during World War II. Air Member, Government of India Frontier Defence and Reorganisation of Armed Forces Committees, 1945–46. Senior Air Staff Officer, RAF, India, 1946; Fighter Command, 1948–50. Chief Air Defence Officer, Ministry of Defence, 1951–53.

The Imperial War Museum holds 12 boxes of papers, 1917–72. A list is available (NRA 28549). The bulk of the material covers his career to 1945. The later part of the collection comprises addresses, copies and drafts of books, articles and lectures, and correspondence relating to his historical writings. A number of files relate to the immediate post-war period and include material on strategic bombing, 1946; a report on the reorganisation of the Army and Air Force in India, 1946; and intelligence reports on the Netherlands East Indies, 1946.

KINNOCK, LORD Neil Gordon Kinnock (1942–) MP (Lab) Bedwellty, 1970–83; Islwyn 1983–95. PPS to Employment Secretary, 1974–75; Member, National Executive Committee, Labour Party after 1978 and of Parliamentary Committee of the Parliamentary Labour Party after 1979. Leader of the Labour Party, 1983–92. European Commissioner, 1995–2004.

Some 450 boxes of papers concerning his period as party leader and leader of the opposition, 1983–92, have been deposited at Churchill College, Cambridge (ref. KNNK). In addition, Churchill College has more recent papers concerning his work as a European Commissioner. His constituency correspondence and papers are in the National Library of Wales.

KIRKPATRICK, SIR IVONE AUGUSTINE (1897–1964) Diplomat. Deputy Commissioner (Civil), Control Commission, Germany, 1944. Assistant Under-Secretary, Foreign Office, from 1945 and Deputy Under-Secretary, 1948. Permanent Under-Secretary (German Section), 1949. High Commissioner, Germany, 1950–55. Permanent Under-Secretary, Foreign Office, 1953–57.

A collection of letters and press-cuttings relating to his work in Germany is deposited in the Imperial War Museum. His correspondence with Lord Monckton, 1940–45, is in the Monckton papers at the Bodleian Library, Oxford (NRA 20879).

KIRKWOOD, 1ST BARON David Kirkwood (1872–1955) MP (Lab) Dumbarton Burghs, 1922–50; Dumbartonshire East, 1950–51.

The papers have remained in private hands. A list is available (NRA 20221). The collection contains an extensive set of newspaper cuttings, 1919–61, various speeches, notes, pamphlets and other election ephemera. There are also some correspondence and photographs.

KLEIN, VIOLA (1908–73) Sociologist. Czech refugee living in Britain from 1939. Held research posts at the Foreign Office, the London School of Economics and Manchester University. Sociology lecturer, Reading University.

The papers are held at Reading University Library and include correspondence, research notes and drafts for lectures and publications. Her research papers include correspondence, questionnaires and press-cuttings on a wide range of subjects, including her study of the family, 1944–48; marriage and the family in the Soviet Union, 1950; ageing; employment of married women and of women graduates, 1960–64; and the status of women. Further correspondence concerns her publications and the conferences and courses she addressed. There is a useful collection of press-cuttings on women's organisations, 1969–73. There are also press reviews of her books and conference papers including the International Council of Social Democratic Women, 1962; the International Seminar on the role of women in a changing society, 1961; and papers concerning meetings of experts organised by the Youth Institute of UNESCO, 1959–63.

KLUGMANN, JAMES (1912–77) Marxist writer and lecturer. Historian of the Communist Party of Great Britain.

Some papers have been placed in the Marx Memorial Library. In addition, the archive of the former Communist Party of Great Britain holds *c.* 40 files and three boxes of his papers. This includes working papers for the Communist Party's official history, including typescript drafts; notes made from Comintern material at the Central Party Archive, Moscow; papers of the commission on party history, 1956–58; and lecture notes and photographs. This archive has now been transferred to the Labour History Archive and Study Centre, Manchester.

KNATCHBULL-HUGESSEN, SIR HUGHE MONTGOMERY (1886–1971) Diplomat. Ambassador, China, 1936–37; Turkey, 1939–44; Belgium (and Minister, Luxembourg), 1944–47.

His diaries and papers, 1901–65, are in Churchill College, Cambridge (ref. KNAT). A list is available (NRA 20289). The correspondence dates from his China posting onwards and his diaries range from 1915 to 1952. There is practically no material on his time in Turkey. Further China correspondence, 1936–38, is available in the Private Office papers at the Public Record Office (ref. FO 800/297).

KNIGHT, DAME LAURA (1876–1970) Artist. Official war artist at Nuremberg trials.

Her Nuremberg diary, 1946–49, together with engagement diaries and later correspondence, 1969, are held in Nottinghamshire Archives Office.

KUPER, RICHARD (fl. 1966–79) Leading student activist, London School of Economics, 1966–67; activist member of International Socialism/Socialist Workers' Party.

The Kuper papers are held at the Modern Records Centre, University of Warwick (ref. MSS 250). The collection details his activities in revolutionary student politics and his membership of International Socialism/Socialist Workers' Party. The material consists of Executive Committee and National Committee minutes and papers, 1970–72; subject files, 1969–79, including reports on various factions within International Socialism/Socialist Workers' Party; papers on student politics at LSE, 1966–67, and Birmingham University, 1970; journals, internal bulletins, booklets and pamphlets, 1969–77; and leaflets and newsletters, 1965–79. In addition, there are copies of *Socialist Review* and photocopies of the Socialist Review Group minutes, 1950–53. The collection complements the Steve Jefferys papers (q.v.).

L

LAIRD, DR NORMAN D. (d. 1970) Stormont MP (UU), St Anne's Belfast, 1969–70.

A collection of papers, 1941–70, has been deposited in the Public Record Office of Northern Ireland (ref. D2669). It consists mainly of election material and newspaper cuttings concerning both Stormont and Westminster elections in Belfast constituencies and local Unionist politics in West Belfast. The collection also contains some correspondence, pamphlets and cuttings relating to political events in the late 1960s, in particular, the premiership of Captain Terence O'Neill. Dr Laird's correspondence with the Northern Ireland Attorney-General, Edmund Warnock, concerning Warnock's resignation in 1956, is open to researchers, but later files of correspondence with politicians, including Sir Knox Cunningham, Robert Foster, Basil Kelly and Mrs Patricia McLoughlin, 1959–70, are closed for 30 years from the file termination date. While the collection includes speeches made by his wife, Mrs Margaret Laird, as a local councillor in Belfast, 1962–69, it contains no material concerning his son, John Laird, who succeeded him as MP, 1970–72.

LAITHWAITE, SIR (JOHN) GILBERT (1894–1986) Diplomat. Served with the India Office, 1936–43. Under-Secretary (Civil), War Cabinet, 1944–45. Deputy Under-Secretary, Burma, 1945–47; India, 1947; Commonwealth Relations, 1948–49. Ambassador, Republic of Ireland, 1950–51 (UK Representative, 1949–50). High Commissioner, Pakistan, 1951–54. Permanent Under-Secretary, Commonwealth Relations, 1955–59.

His correspondence, papers and photographs, 1912–69, are deposited in the India Office Library (ref. MSS Eur F 138). A list is available (NRA 44006). The collection covers his entire career, including official and private correspondence, 1927–68. There are also Commonwealth tour diaries (1955–59) and other overseas tour diaries (1960–69). Of particular interest are the political reports and correspondence for the period following the 1949 declaration of the Irish Republic.

Lancashire Record Office holds an additional collection of correspondence and working papers relating to Indian administration, c. 1940–70 (ref. DDX 788 acc 6099).

LAKEMAN, ENID (1903–95) Campaigner for electoral reform. Liberal activist. Director, Electoral Reform Society, 1960–79.

There are many papers with the archive of the Electoral Reform Society at its London headquarters.

LAMBE, ADMIRAL OF THE FLEET SIR CHARLES EDWARD (1900–60) Assistant Chief of Naval Staff (Air) 1945–46. Commander-in-Chief Far East Station, 1953–54. Second Sea Lord 1955–57. Commander-in-Chief Mediterranean 1957–59. Chief of Naval Staff 1959–60.

His papers and correspondence, 1923–60, remain in family possession. A list is available (ref. NRA 24919). The collection includes personal diaries and correspondence, including two long series of letters to his wife and to Hugh Drake (1937–60). There are 40 letters from Earl Mountbatten of Burma covering 1955–60.

LAMBRICK, HUGH TREVOR (1904–82) Indian Civil Service, Sind, 1927–47; Special Commissioner for Sind, 1943–46. Historian and Fellow of Oriel College, Oxford, 1951–71.

Ten boxes of papers are held at the India Office Library (ref. MSS Eur F 208). A list is available (NRA 29403). The collection comprises copies of official and semi-official papers, correspondence, and also notes and drafts for his books.

LAMBTON, VISCOUNT Antony Claud Frederick Lambton (1922–) (Disclaimed Peerage 1970) MP

(Con) Berwick-upon-Tweed, 1951–73. Parliamentary Under-Secretary, Ministry of Defence, 1970–73. PPS to Foreign Secretary, 1955–57.

Lord Lambton has retained his papers.

LAMONT, ARCHIE (fl. 1925–84) Scottish Nationalist, ecologist and geologist.

His correspondence and papers, 1925–84, have been placed in the National Library of Scotland (ref. Acc 9290). The collection is currently closed.

LANCASTER, COLONEL ALEXANDER STALKER (1893–1967) Military career. Served in the British Army, 1914–17; transferred to the Indian Army, 1917. Military Attaché, Kabul, 1935–38 and 1940–48. Conducted Turkish Military Mission to India, 1941, and Afghan Military Mission to India, 1944–45.

An important collection of papers, 1917–58, was given to the National Army Museum in 1988 (ref. 8801–2). A list is available (NRA 31398). The bulk of the material relates to his lengthy service in Afghanistan and comprises intelligence, trade and transport reports, c. 1935–47; texts and notes for lectures, 1937–48; and correspondence files, including letters from Afghan friends, 1949–54. His later correspondents include (in 1956) the Soviet military attaché in Ankara, Major-General Nikolai Rubenko, who had been stationed in Kabul with him during the war.

LANE, SIR ALLEN (1902–70) Publisher. Founder of Penguin Books.

Reference should be made to the Special Collections Department, University of Bristol, which has his correspondence (ref. DM 1819). The collection (42 boxes) has been listed (NRA 43618). There is material on the *Lady Chatterley* trial.

LASCELLES, SIR ALAN FREDERICK (1887–1982) Public servant. Assistant Private Secretary (and from 1943 Private Secretary) to George VI, 1936–52.

The papers have been placed in Churchill College, Cambridge.

LASKI, HAROLD JOSEPH (1893–1950) Political scientist and politician. Taught at the London School of Economics, 1920–50; Professor of Political Science,

University of London, 1926–50. Member of the Labour Party Executive, 1936–49; Chairman 1945–46.

The papers and correspondence are dispersed throughout various archives in Britain, Europe and the USA. Full details are available from the National Archives.

The Brynmor Jones Library, University of Hull, holds a substantial collection of his correspondence with his wife and with academic and political colleagues. There are also research notes and papers collected for Granville Eastwood's 1977 biography of Laski. The International Institute of Social History, Amsterdam, holds some papers for the period 1910–50. A list is available (NRA 30443).

LASKI, NEVILLE JONAS (1890–1969) Lawyer. A leader of the Anglo-Jewish community. Recorder of Burnley, 1935–56. Vice-President, Anglo-Jewish Association. President, Board of Deputies, 1933–40, and also Chairman, Joint Foreign Committee. Chairman, Jewish Agency for Palestine. Author, *Jewish Rights and Jewish Wrongs* (1939).

The Laski family papers, 1887–1963, are deposited in the Hartley Library, University of Southampton (ref. MS 134). A list is available (NRA 13579). The papers are mainly pre-war but include correspondence, press-cuttings and other material on N.J. Laski, 1942–63, Jewish defence and British fascism. Further papers are available in Manchester Central Library and in the archive of the Board of Deputies, now deposited in the London Metropolitan Archives.

LATEY, MAURICE (1915–91) Broadcaster and journalist.

The papers have been placed in the Bodleian Library, Oxford.

LAWRENCE, REGINALD JAMES (fl. 1960s–70s) Political scientist, Queen's University, Belfast.

Material on the 1973 Irish border poll survey has been placed in the Public Record Office of Northern Ireland (ref. D3088). The collection includes his correspondence with the Stormont Ministry of Home Affairs, returning and registration officers, various political parties and Stormont and Westminster MPs.

LAWSON, BARON John James Lawson (1881–1965) MP (Lab) Chester-le-Street, 1919–49. Secretary of State for War, 1945–46.

There are papers, including journals, appointment diaries and correspondence, in Durham University Library. A list is available (NRA 37246).

LAWSON OF BLABY, LORD Nigel Lawson (1932–) MP (Con) Blaby, Feb. 1974–92. Financial Secretary to the Treasury, 1979–81; Secretary of State for Energy, 1981–83; Chancellor of the Exchequer, 1983–89.

Lord Lawson states that he has retained his papers and that provision will be made for their eventual deposit.

LAWSON, GEORGE McARTHUR (1906–78) MP (Lab) Motherwell, 1954–Feb. 1974; Motherwell and Wishaw, Feb. 1974–Oct. 1974. West Scotland organiser, National Council of Labour Colleges (NCLC), 1940–50; Director, Scotland is British Campaign, 1976–77.

The correspondence and papers, 1942–78, have been placed in the National Library of Scotland (ref. Acc 9588). The collection includes material on the Labour Party National Executive Committee, the Labour Party Scottish Council, 1971–74, and the Strathclyde Regional Party, together with Scottish Trades Union Congress correspondence, letters to the press and newspaper articles, 1950–67. There are also papers and pamphlets on education policy; Labour Party devolution policy 1962–70; EEC campaign papers including the Labour Campaign for Europe, 1972–78; correspondence with ministers and trade unionists and reports related to the steel industry; and committee papers and correspondence on the 'Scotland is British' Campaign. There are also various papers and reports on the Nature Conservancy Council Scottish Committee, 1972–77, the National Trust for Scotland, some press-cuttings and printed material, and notes from his work as an NCLC tutor.

LAWSON, HUGH McDOWALL (1912–97) MP (Common Wealth) Skipton, 1944–45.

A collection of Common Wealth records has been placed in the Library of the University of Sussex. This deposit includes the papers of Hugh Lawson. In addition to a very full collection of letters, press-cuttings, literature and documents relating to the Skipton by-election and to his subsequent time as

an MP, there is material from the Unser Kampf organisation and some other National Committee correspondence and records. There is also a comprehensive collection of letters and documents from his candidacy at Harrow West in 1945 and a set of Common Wealth conference agenda.

LAWTHER, SIR WILLIAM (1889–1976) Trade union leader. President, Miners' Federation of Great Britain, 1939–45; President, National Union of Mineworkers, 1945–54. President, Trades Union Congress, 1949–50.

A small collection of papers is deposited with Tyne and Wear Archives. A list is available (NRA 23329). The collection includes pamphlets, newspaper cuttings and ephemera relating to his political and trade union career as well as a few letters and photograph albums.

LAYCOCK, MAJOR-GENERAL ROBERT (1907–68) Army career. Chief of Combined Operations, 1943–47. Governor and Commander-in-Chief, Malta, 1954–59. Colonel Commandant, SAS Regiment.

There are papers in the Liddell Hart Centre for Military Archives, King's College, London.

LAYTON, BARON Sir Walter Thomas Layton (1884–1966) Economist, editor and Liberal politician. Served in the Ministry of Supply and the Ministry of Production during World War II. Leader of Liberal Party, House of Lords, 1952–55. Director of Reuters, 1945–53.

Some 200 boxes of correspondence and papers are deposited in the Wren Library, Trinity College, Cambridge. The collection includes correspondence, 1902–66; university papers, 1904–12; papers on World Wars I and II; the Liberal Party, 1912–65; the European Union, 1946–65 and the League of Nations, 1918–34. The collection also contains his memoirs and some speeches and articles, 1939–57.

LEATHER, SIR EDWIN HARTLEY CAMERON (1919–2005) MP (Con) Somerset North, 1950–64. Governor and Commander-in-Chief, Bermuda, 1973–77. Canadian Army officer during World War II.

Sir Edwin Leather stated that his exensive collection of papers had been bequeathed to the

Miller Memorial Library, McMaster University, Canada. His letters to Sir Anthony Eden, 1957–64, are in the Avon papers at Birmingham University Library (ref. AP24/42). Earlier correspondence with Lionel Curtis, 1942–54, is available in the Curtis collection at the Bodleian Library, Oxford.

LEATHERS, 1ST VISCOUNT Frederick James Leathers (1883–1965) Minister of War Transport, 1941–45. Secretary of State for the Co-ordination of Transport, Fuel and Power, 1951–53.

There are some Private Office papers at the National Archives (ref. MT 62/3–95, 62/130–46). No papers appear to have survived with the family.

LEE, BARONESS Jennie Lee (1904–88) MP (Lab) Lanark North, 1929–31; Cannock, 1945–70. Parliamentary Secretary, Ministry of Public Building and Works, 1964–65. Parliamentary Under-Secretary, Department of Education and Science, 1965–67; Minister of State, 1967–70.

Provision was made before her death for her large collection of papers (*c.* 80 boxes) to be housed at the Open University, Walton Hall, Bletchley, Bucks. Reference should also be made to material in the House of Lords Record Office.

LEE, SIR FRANK GODBOULD (1903–71) Civil Servant. Permanent Secretary, Board of Trade, 1951–59; Ministry of Food, 1959–61; Treasury (Joint) 1960–62.

The Public Record Office holds four files relating to the work of Sir Frank Lee and Sir J. Woods at the Board of Trade (ref. BT 91).

LEGGE-BOURKE, MAJOR SIR (EDWARD ALEXANDER) HENRY (1914–73) MP (Con) Isle of Ely, 1945–73.

His papers were deposited in 1985 by his widow in the Brotherton Library, University of Leeds (ref. MSS 742, 771). A list is available (NRA 30441). The first part of the collection deals with constituency organisation and election campaign planning. The second section consists of material on wider political and foreign policy matters, including files on scientific research and development, especially in aeronautics (civil and military); Middle East affairs including Suez; Gibraltar; and the European Economic Community.

LEGONNA, JOHN (1918–78) Welsh Nationalist, farmer and businessman.

There are correspondence and papers in the National Library of Wales (ref. A1989/119). A list is available (NRA 26130). The collection includes incomplete diaries, 1941–53, literary writings, correspondence (in English and Welsh) on Welsh, Breton, Scottish and Celtic nationalism, and some circulars and memoranda relating to the New Nation group within Plaid Cymru, 1964–66. His correspondents include Gwilym Prys Davies, Megan Lloyd-George, Compton Mackenzie, Cliff Bere, Huw Davies and Christopher Murray Grieve.

LEGUM, COLIN (1919–2003) Author and lecturer. Expert on African affairs.

A collection of papers relating to African issues, 1950–80, is held in Edinburgh University Library. Enquiries regarding the collection should be directed to the Special Collections Librarian. Other papers are in the Institute of Commonwealth Studies.

LEIGHTON, RONALD (1930–94) MP (Lab) Newham North-East after 1979. Secretary, Labour Committee for Safeguards on Common Market, 1967–70. Secretary, Get Britain Out campaign. National Organiser, National Referendum Campaign.

The papers are in the Labour History Archive and Study Centre, University of Manchester.

LEMKIN, JAMES ANTHONY (1926–) Bow Group Conservative. Opposed the British Government's June 1961 constitutional proposals for Northern Rhodesia. One of the founders of the London-based Rhodesia Committee of the Human Rights Advisory Service, established in 1965 to raise funds for the defence of Rhodesian political prisoners.

One box of papers is in the Centre for Southern African Studies, University of York. It contains the minutes of the London-based Rhodesia Committee, which lobbied for the withdrawal of the constitutional proposals, and related correspondence and memoranda received from Christopher Chataway, Jeremy Thorpe, James Callaghan, David Astor, Humphry Berkeley, James Chikerema and Sir John Moffatt, leader of the Northern Rhodesia Liberal

Party. The material on the Human Rights Advisory Service includes committee minutes, 1965–66, as well as notes on individual detainees.

LENNARD-JONES, SIR JOHN EDWARD (1894– 1954) Physicist. Professor of Theoretical Chemistry, Cambridge, 1932–53. Chief Superintendent of Armament Research, 1943–46; Chief Scientific Officer and Director-General of Scientific Research (Defence), 1952–54; Chairman, Scientific Advisory Council, Ministry of Supply, 1940–54.

Churchill College, Cambridge, holds four boxes of correspondence, journals and papers covering the period 1906–54 (ref. LEJO). A list is available (NRA 17356). The collection includes daily journals which cover his time as Superintendant of Armament Research and Director-General of Scientific Research at the Ministry of Supply. Additionally, there are files of scientific and personal correspondence, lectures, sermons and addresses. Special conditions of access apply.

LEONARD, RICHARD LAWRENCE (DICK) (1930–) MP (Lab) Romford, 1970–Feb. 1974. Writer and political consultant. Assistant Editor, *The Economist*, 1974–85. European Community and Brussels correspondent, *Observer*, after 1989.

Mr Leonard has retained a small collection of unsorted papers relating to his parliamentary career and in particular to his role as PPS to Anthony Crosland.

LESLIE, SIR (JOHN RANDOLPH) SHANE (1885– 1971) Biographer and poet.

The political and literary correspondence is deposited in the National Library of Ireland in Dublin (ref. MSS 22831–22864). It includes his 1945–65 correspondence with Sean T. O'Kelly (President of Ireland, 1945–59) and letters exchanged with leading Catholic clergymen and literary figures. Some of the papers concern the controversy over the publication of Sir Roger Casement's diaries, 1956–63.

Papers relating to his biography of Sir John Mahaffy are in Trinity College, Dublin, while those gathered for his biography of Lord Beatty are held in Churchill College, Cambridge.

LEVY, BENN WOLFE (1900–73) MP (Lab) Eton and Slough, 1945–50. Writer and dramatist.

His parliamentary papers are deposited in the House of Lords Record Office. The collection includes appointment diaries, 1946–50; constituency correspondence, 1945–50; files on National Health and National Insurance, the United Nations, the Union of Democratic Control, the Campaign for Nuclear Disarmament, and other peace organisations and campaigns.

Additional correspondence and papers, 1929–73, were placed in Sussex University Library in 1978 by his widow (ref. SxMs 37). A list is available (NRA 25064). The collection includes correspondence, committee minutes, parliamentary legislative files, press-cuttings, and various files on the arts, civil liberties and the peace movement. These include material on the Cinematography Films Bill 1948, Censorship of Plays (Repeal) Bill 1949, the Arts Council, Fabian Society, CND, the Labour Party, National Council for Civil Liberties, the Common Market, the Defence of Literature and Arts Society, the Entertainment Arts Socialist Association, and the Campaign for the Limitation of Secret Police Powers.

LEWIN, (GEORGE) RONALD (1914–84) Head of BBC Home Service, 1954–65. Military historian.

Thirty-six boxes of papers have been deposited in Churchill College, Cambridge (ref. RLEW). A list is available (NRA 29994). The material is largely composed of notes, drafts and correspondence for his books on World War II, and includes post-war correspondence with many senior commanders. Further correspondence, 1972–76, can be found in the papers of Lord Slim, also held at Churchill College.

LIDDELL HART, CAPTAIN SIR BASIL HENRY (1895–1970) Military historian and defence analyst. Military correspondent, *The Daily Telegraph*, 1925–35; *The Times*, 1935–39. Editor-in-Chief, *History of the Second World War*, 1968–70.

The Liddell Hart Centre, King's College, London, has 1000 boxes of correspondence and papers, 1913–70. A list is available (NRA 19291). Much of the collection concerns inter-war defence issues and assessments of the British, Allied and German military performances in World Wars I and II. His correspondents (some 780 individuals) include Lord

Attlee, Aneurin Bevan, Lord Boothby, Sir Winston Churchill, General Eisenhower, Michael Foot, Alistair Hetherington, Bernard Levin, Douglas Macarthur, Viscount Montgomery, Jawaharlal Nehru, Arnold Toynbee, G.M. Trevelyan, Hugh Trevor-Roper, and Lord Zuckermann. The collection includes research notes, drafts, proofs and reviews of his published writings. There are also lectures, speeches, broadcasts, interviews and a massive series of press-cuttings.

LIPSEY, LORD David Lawrence Lipsey (1948–) Labour politician and journalist.

Some papers for the period *c.* 1976–98 have been placed in the LSE Library to where enquiries concerning access should be addressed.

LISTOWEL, 5TH EARL OF William Francis Hare, Viscount Ennismore (1906–97) Parliamentary Under-Secretary, India Office, 1944–45. Postmaster-General, 1945–47. Secretary of State for India and Burma, 1947–48. Minister of State, Colonial Office, 1948–50. Parliamentary Secretary, Ministry of Agriculture and Fisheries, 1950–51. Governor-General, Ghana, 1957–60.

His correspondence with Lord Mountbatten on the transfer of power from Britain to India and Pakistan, April to August 1947, has been deposited in the India Office Library (ref. MSS Eur C 357). Further correspondence relating to India in 1947 is available in the papers of Sir Hubert Rance, which are also in the India Office Library (ref. MSS Eur F 169). There is also some correspondence in the Fabian Bureau archive at Rhodes House Library, Oxford (ref. MSS Brit Emp s 365).

A small collection of papers, mainly relating to his time in Ghana, remained in Lord Listowel's possession. These include correspondence with President Nkrumah and with the Queen's secretaries, some letters concerning Harold Macmillan's visit to Ghana in January 1960, and some notes of Macmillan's conversations with Ghanaian leaders. Material for the rest of his career is sparse, apart from a few letters concerning Burma, 1947 and some papers on the work of the 1961 Molson Committee on the boundary dispute between the Buganda and the Buryoro.

LISTOWEL, JUDITH COUNTESS OF (1903–2003) Author, journalist and anti-Communist. Campaigned against repression in Eastern Europe and Africa (on which she wrote widely).

Three files of papers, reports and press-cuttings on Rhodesia, 1971–72, and on Tanzania are deposited in the Centre for Southern African Studies, York University. The two files on Rhodesia include material on the African National Council, the Pearce Commission, the Centre Party, the Rhodesian Constitution, politics and the Catholic Church. There are also taped records of her conversations with Bishop Muzorewa and with Mr Pat Bashford (Centre Party) during 1974–75. The third file, on Tanzania, has miscellaneous papers on the period 1968–71 and includes material on Oscar Kambona and the opposition to President Nyerere and the TANU Party.

LIVINGSTONE, KEN (1945–) MP (Lab) Brent East 1987–2001. Member of Greater London Council, 1973–86 (Norwood, 1973–77; Hackney North, 1977–81; Paddington, 1981–86); Leader of Council and Labour Group, 1981–86. Mayor of London since 2000.

Mr Livingstone states that his Greater London Council (GLC) papers (*c.* 40 boxes) are held at the London Metropolitan Archives (ref. GLC XX/1). The collection covers his work with the GLC from the mid-1970s onwards and includes numerous subject files, material on internal GLC matters and the Labour Party, correspondence and committee minutes, etc. Requests for access should be directed to Mr Livingstone.

LLEWELLIN, 1ST BARON John Jestine Llewellin (1893–1957) MP (Con) Uxbridge, 1929–45. Civil Lord of the Admiralty, 1937–39. Parliamentary Secretary, Ministry of Supply, 1939–40; Aircraft Production, 1940–41; Transport (later War Transport), 1941–42. President of the Board of Trade, 1942. Minister of Aircraft Production, 1942. Minister for Supply (Resident in Washington DC), 1942–43. Minister of Food, 1943–45. Governor-General, Rhodesia and Nyasaland, 1953–57.

A small collection of papers, in the possession of Lord Llewellin's sister, is described in *British Cabinet Ministers, 1900–51.* Apart from material on his wartime work (including speech notes and copies of his 1943 letters), the remainder of the collection consists of 15 volumes of press-cuttings and photographs from his entire career. The bulk of these cover his term of office as the first Governor-General of the Federation of Rhodesia and Nyasaland. His sister has also retained a collection of mainly personal letters to herself and another brother. These were frequently quoted in Gilbert Thomas's book, *Llewellin* (1961). The Llewellin diaries, which Thomas also cited, have not been traced. Further material on his wartime career can be found in the AVIA 9 and AVIA 11 series of Private Office papers at the Public Record Office.

LLOYD, EDWARD MAYOW HASTINGS (1889–1968) Civil servant, economist and expert on nutrition. Economic Adviser to the Minister of State, Middle East 1942–44; United Nations Relief and Rehabilitation Administration (UNRRA), Economic and Financial Adviser for the Balkans, 1945; Food and Agriculture Organisation, United Nations Organisation, 1945–47; Permanent Under-Secretary, Ministry of Food, 1947–53.

Some papers are held at the LSE Library. A list is available (NRA 21432). The collection consists mainly of administrative papers, including material on the Middle East, UNRRA, and from his time as Economic Adviser to the Minister of State. There are also various subject files organised by region, some post-war papers, personal material and miscellaneous items.

LLOYD, SIR IAN (STEWART) (1921–) MP (Con), Portsmouth Langstone, 1964–74; Havant and Waterloo, 1974–83; Havant, 1983–92. Chairman and member of various parliamentary committees on shipping, energy, science and information technology.

Sir Ian has retained an extensive collection of papers dating from late 1962 onwards and will consider access by researchers. The collection includes all significant parliamentary papers, constituency, committee and ministerial correspondence.

LLOYD, JAMES HENRY (b. 1883) Ethical reformer and trade unionist. Chairman, Association of Public Health Lay Administrative Officers. President of the National Union of Clerks and Administrative Workers.

Some papers have been deposited in the Brynmor Jones Library, University of Hull (ref. DHL). The papers include a notebook of his essays and papers, a book of press-cuttings, a file of circular letters, correspondence on China, material on ethics, local government, and notes for lectures on Marxism, the Labour Party, town planning and pacifism. There is also a portfolio relating to Karel and Josef Capek; notes for lectures; articles by Lloyd on 'The Clerk in Literature', 'Trade Unionism for Clerks', letters on morals, humanism, socialism 1947–58; files relating to the Clerical and Administrative Workers' Union, and articles in *The Clerk*; material relating to the International Federation of Commercial, Clerical and Technical Employees; papers on the Health Service; material on the Co-operative Movement; papers on humanism and the Ethical Association, including a letter from G.B. Shaw, and lecture notes; miscellaneous other papers on trade unionism, wages, road safety; and various printed material including pamphlets, etc.

LLOYD, SIR THOMAS INGRAM KYNASTON (1896–1968) Colonial Office service. Secretary, Palestine Commission, 1929–30; West India Royal Commission, 1938–39. PUS, Colonial Office, 1947–56.

His private diaries and letters have not survived. Some Private Office papers and correspondence, 1948–56, are in the Public Record Office (ref. CO 967/169–238). A list is available (NRA 28778).

LLOYD-GEORGE, LADY MEGAN (1902–66) MP (Lib) Anglesey, 1929–51; (Lab) Carmarthen, 1957–66.

Certain papers of Lady Megan's have been acquired by the National Library of Wales as an addition to the extensive Lloyd-George collection (consisting of some 3500 items) (ref. MSS 20485C–20491E). These include letters from David Lloyd-George and Lady Megan, all pre-war; speeches and notes for speeches, 1920s to 1965; and six indexed volumes of press-cuttings, 1930–51. In 1993, the National Library of Wales purchased 554 letters to her from her lover, Philip Noel-Baker.

LLOYD-OWEN, MAJOR-GENERAL DAVID LANYON (1917–) Army career. Commander, Long Range Desert Group, 1943–45. Military Assistant to High Commissioner, Malaya, 1951–53. General Officer Commanding, Cyprus District,

1966–68. General Officer Commanding, Near East Land Forces, 1968–69.

An important collection of papers relating to his service as assistant to Field Marshal Sir Gerald Templer in Malaya, 1951–53, is held by the National Army Museum (ref. 8011–132). The collection includes material dating from 1948 to 1978. Apart from a folder of correspondence with Templer, March 1952 to September 1953, the collection also contains later correspondence and assessments of the Malayan situation. A file on the Services Kinema Corporation's publicity film on the Malayan emergency and Templer's command, made in 1976–77, is of particular interest. A second collection of Lloyd-Owen papers at the museum consists of further Malayan correspondence, 1952–53 (ref. 8301–6). Reference should be made to Templer's own papers, which are also deposited with the National Army Museum.

The Imperial War Museum holds a few papers relating to his World War II service.

LOCK, STEPHEN (1929–) Editor, *British Medical Journal*, 1975–91.

There are 11 boxes of papers at the Wellcome Contemporary Medical Archives Centre, London (ref. Acc 377). The collection includes correspondence with various contributors (1980s), files on the General Medical Council, Gay Medical Association, media, and the case of *S.L. Drummond-Jackson* v. *British Medical Journal* (1970–72).

LOCKHART, GENERAL SIR ROB MCGREGOR MACDONALD (1893–1981) Indian Army career, 1914–48. General Officer Commanding-in-Chief, Southern Command, India, 1945. Governor, North-West Frontier Province, India, 1947–48. Director of Operations, Malaya, 1951–52; Deputy Director, 1952–53.

Thirteen files and folders of papers concerning his career, 1914–53, and post-retirement activities with the Punjab Frontier Force Association, 1948–73, are available in the National Army Museum (ref. 8310–154). A list is available (NRA 40293). The collection includes material on Malaya, 1951–53. The papers of General Sir Roy Bucher, also at the National Army Museum, include some 1948 correspondence (ref. 7901–87).

LOCKSPEISER, SIR BEN (1891–1990) Aeronautical scientist. Director-General of Scientific Research, Ministry of Aircraft Production, 1945. Chief Scientist, Ministry of Supply, 1946–49. Secretary, Privy Council Committee for Scientific and Industrial Research, 1949–56.

No main collection of papers has been traced. Some correspondence is available in the papers of other scientists, including Lord Blackett (deposited in the Royal Society), Lord Cherwell (Nuffield College, Oxford) and A.V. Hill (Churchill College, Cambridge).

LOGAN, SIR DONALD (ARTHUR) (1917–) Diplomat. Assistant Private Secretary to Foreign Secretary, Selwyn Lloyd, 1956–58. Ambassador, Guinea, 1960–62; Bulgaria, 1970–73, etc.

The LSE Library has his account of discussions at Sèvres, 22 to 25 October 1956, between French, British and Israeli ministers, in connection with the Suez Crisis (ref. COLL MISC 0707). Logan was Assistant Private Secretary to the Secretary of State for Foreign Affairs, Selwyn Lloyd, who represented Britain at the meeting.

LONGDEN, SIR GILBERT JAMES MORLEY (1902–97) MP (Con) Hertfordshire West, 1950–Feb. 1974.

The papers were given by his executor to the LSE Library (ref. M 1858). They consist of 80 box files of constituency and parliamentary papers as well as material on the Council of Europe.

LONGFORD, 7TH EARL OF Francis Aungier Pakenham, Baron Pakenham (1905–2001) Politician and author. Parliamentary Under-Secretary, War Office, 1946–47. Chancellor of the Duchy of Lancaster, and Minister in Charge of the Administration of the British Zone in Germany, 1947–48. Minister of Civil Aviation, 1948–51. First Lord of the Admiralty, 1951. Lord Privy Seal, 1964–65; 1966–68. Secretary of State for the Colonies, 1965–66.

Hazlehurst (*British Cabinet Ministers, 1900–51*) reports that there are 22 boxes of Lord Longford's papers and correspondence in the possession of his son Thomas Pakenham, Tullynally Castle, Castlepollard, Co. Westmeath, Ireland. The papers, 1970–85, principally concern penal reform. There are also correspondence, speech notes, articles, book reviews, and papers of a more general political nature, e.g. Criminal Justice Bills, nuclear disarmament, the Official Secrets Act, and the All-Party Penal Affairs Committee. The collection has been listed by the PRONI (NRA 30594). Owing to the confidential nature of much of the material, enquiries regarding access should be directed to Thomas Pakenham.

LOTHIAN, SIR ARTHUR CUNNINGHAM (1887– 1962) Indian Civil Service, 1910–46. Resident at Hyderabad, 1942–46.

There are six boxes of papers, 1918–64, held on permanent loan at the India Office Library (ref. MSS Eur F 144). Further correspondence, 1946–57, is available in the papers of Lord Monckton at the Bodleian Library, Oxford.

LOVE, COLONEL STEPHEN (1931–99) Military career. Served Falklands War.

Two boxes of his papers concerning Argentina, etc. are in the Liddell Hart Centre for Military Archives, King's College, London.

LOVELOCK, JAMES EPHRAIM (1919–) Independent scientist and guru of the ecology movement. Visiting Professor, University of Reading, after 1967. Author of *Gaia* (1979) and *The Great Extinction* (1983).

Professor Lovelock states that he has retained his papers. Provision will be made for their eventual deposit.

LOYD, SIR FRANCIS ALFRED (1916–) Colonial Service, Kenya, 1939–63; Private Secretary to Governor, 1942–45; Permanent Secretary, Governor's Office, 1962–63. Commissioner, Swaziland, 1964–68.

It is understood that Sir Francis has kept extensive papers. The post-war sections include material on the Kenya–Ethiopia Boundary Commission, 1947; some confidential correspondence and minutes of meetings concerning developments in Nyanza Province, 1959–61; the Kenya Constitutional Conference, 1962; and handing-over notes on Kenyan independence, 1963.

LUCE, SIR WILLIAM (1907–77) Colonial administrator. Served Sudan, Aden, etc. Governor and Commander-in-Chief, Aden, 1956–60; Political Resident, Persian Gulf, 1961–66.

His papers relating to Sudan, 1930–56, are in the Sudan Archive, University of Durham.

LUSH, MAURICE STANLEY (1896–1990) Colonial and political administrator. Served Sudan, etc. Chief Political Officer, Ethiopia, 1941–42. Vice-President, Allied Commission, Italy, 1943–46, etc.

There are papers in the Sudan Archive, University of Durham. A list is available (NRA 42132). Most of the material is pre-war.

LUSTY, SIR ROBERT (1909–91) Publisher and BBC Vice-Chairman.

Sir Robert Lusty's working diaries, 1936–72, are held at Reading University Library. An additional file is held at the BBC Written Archives Centre, Reading (ref. S25) (NRA 31050).

LYDFORD, AIR MARSHAL SIR HAROLD THOMAS (1898–1979) Air Marshal. Air Officer Commanding, 28th Group, 1944; British Forces in Aden, 1945–48. Commandant-General, RAF Regiment, 1948–50. Air Officer Commanding, 18th Coastal Command, 1950–52. Air Officer Commanding, Home Command, 1952–56.

The Imperial War Museum holds a microfilm of official and semi-official correspondence, 1932–50. A list is available (NRA 28550). Much of the material relates to his Aden command and to the RAF Regiment's operations there and in Iraq and Malaya.

LYNE, MAJOR-GENERAL LEWIS OWEN (1899– 1970) Military career. Various commands in World War II. Military Governor, British Zone, Berlin, 1945.

There are seven boxes of papers in the Imperial War Museum. They mostly relate to World War II and include an unpublished autobiography covering the years 1937–45.

M

McALISKEY, (JOSEPHINE) BERNADETTE (1947–) (née Devlin) MP (Unity, 1969 and Independent from 1970) Mid-Ulster, 1969–74. Civil rights campaigner and People's Democracy activist, Northern Ireland, 1960s. Founder member, Irish Republican Socialist Party (IRSP), 1975. Chairman, Independent Socialist Party, Ireland.

Some papers concerning her involvement in the IRSP during the 1970s are deposited in the Public Record Office of Northern Ireland. The collection is closed. Her autobiography, *The Price Of My Soul*, was published in 1969.

McATEER, EDWARD (1914–86) Stormont MP (Nationalist) Mid-Derry (later Foyle), 1945–69. Opposition Leader, Stormont, 1965–69.

One file of correspondence, 1945–47, can be found in the papers of Anthony Mulvey, Westminster MP for Fermanagh and Tyrone, which are deposited in the Public Record Office of Northern Ireland (ref. D1862/F/2). PRONI also holds a recording of a 1978 BBC Radio Ulster interview with Mr McAteer and Captain (later Lord) Terence O'Neill concerning the events of 1968 (ref. TP18).

McAULEY, DEREK (fl. 1960s) Official Ulster Unionist Party official. Former student activist and Chairman of Young Unionists.

Mr McAuley has deposited 18 files of papers in the Public Record Office of Northern Ireland (ref. D3794). The papers comprise material relating to Official Ulster Unionist Party election campaigns and to Unionist student politics and academic administration in Queen's University, Belfast, 1978–85. The collection includes minutes and related papers of the executive committee of the Ulster Unionist Council, 1980–86; annual reports of the Ulster Unionist Council, 1979–82 and 1984–85; correspondence, reports and notices relating to Unionist Party branches in Larne and Antrim generally; corre-

spondence and related papers of the Conservative Students' Association, Queen's University, Belfast, 1978–86; and copies of the *Young Unionist*.

MacCALL, SEAMUS (1892–1964) Northern Irish politician.

The papers were deposited in the Public Record Office of Northern Ireland in 1967.

MacCARROLL, F.E. (fl. 1940s–50s) Nationalist politican and newspaper director, Derry, Northern Ireland. Secretary of the Catholic Registration Association.

Seventeen files of correspondence, 1942–52, have been placed in the Public Record Office of Northern Ireland (ref. T 2712 add). The material relates to both Westminster and local elections in Derry, his directorship of the *Derry Journal* and his involvement in the Catholic Registration Association and the anti-Partition movement in Ireland.

MacCOLL, JAMES EUGENE (1908–71) MP (Lab) Widnes, 1950–71. Joint Parliamentary Secretary, Housing and Local Government, 1964–69.

Some 72 boxes of papers were deposited by Mr Anthony MacColl at the LSE Library. The collection includes Labour Party and constituency papers, and subject files on housing, planning and local government, crime and delinquency, and race relations.

MacCOLL, RENÉ (1905–71) Foreign and war correspondent. Covered the Spanish Civil War for the *Daily Telegraph*, 1939. Director of Press and Radio Division, British Information Services, New York, 1941–45. Foreign correspondent, *Daily Express*, 1946–69; Washington, 1946–48; Paris, 1949–50; Chief American correspondent, 1951–52; Chief Foreign correspondent, 1959–69.

The Imperial War Museum has a collection of correspondence and newspaper cuttings concerning the compilation and reception of MacColl's 1956 book on Roger Casement together with press-clippings about Casement's diaries. The Museum also holds a small number of typescript synopses for articles written in Spain, 1939, and reports on his tour of American states, 1943.

McCOY, WILLIAM FREDERICK (1885–1976) Stormont MP (UU) South Tyrone, 1945–65. Senior Crown Prosecutor, Belfast, 1949–67.

A collection of papers and correspondence, 1904–75, is held at the Public Record Office of Northern Ireland (ref. D3333). A list is available (NRA 21973). The collection includes constituency case files (closed for 75 years from the date of termination); general political correspondence and papers, 1945–71; speeches; and press-cuttings. Several of the files concern his advocacy of Dominion Status for Northern Ireland and the rift this caused in the Ulster Unionist Party during 1952 and 1953. There is also material on Party administration, on the Orange Order and on the Shankill Road riots of 1970 and his role as President of the Shankill Road 'People's Tribunal'. Much of the collection is subject to restricted access.

McCUSKER, (JAMES) HAROLD (1940–90) MP (UU) Armagh, 1974–83; Upper Bann, 1983–90.

His political papers for the period 1962–90 have been placed in the Public Record Office of Northern Ireland (ref. D3716). They consist of over 10,000 documents, including correspondence and other files relating mainly to constituency matters. The papers are uncatalogued and currently closed to researchers. Further papers relating to the gas industry in Northern Ireland are deposited with the Northern Ireland Political Collection in the Linen Hall Library, Belfast.

MacDONALD, MALCOLM JOHN (1901–81) MP (Lab) Bassetlaw, 1929–31; (National Lab) 1931–35; (National) Ross and Cromarty, 1936–45. Health Minister, 1940–41. High Commissioner, Canada, 1941–46. Governor-General, Malayan Union and Singapore, 1946; Malaya, Singapore and British Borneo, 1946–48. British Commissioner-General,

South-East Asia, 1948–55. High Commissioner, India, 1955–60. Governor, Kenya, 1963–64; High Commissioner, 1964–65. British Special Representative in Africa, 1966–69.

An extensive collection of colonial, diplomatic and administrative papers was deposited in Durham University in 1986. A list is available (NRA 30832). The collection includes official and private correspondence, memoranda and reports, diaries, scripts of speeches, drafts of books, articles, and short stories. The later subject files cover the Labour Party; his parliamentary career; Palestine; Ireland; Canada; South-East Asia; India; Africa; China; and Voluntary Service Overseas (VSO). There are also copies of published and unpublished books and articles; the transcripts of interviews conducted by the Oxford University Colonial Records Project, 1969–72; diaries and autobiographical papers, printed papers and newspaper cuttings.

MacDOUGALL, SIR (GEORGE) DONALD (ALASTAIR) (1912–2004) Economist. Director-General, Department of Economic Affairs, 1964–68. Chief Economic Adviser to the Treasury, 1969–73. Closely involved with European Monetary Union.

His correspondence and papers, 44 boxes covering the period c. 1930–2002, have been placed in Churchill College, Cambridge (ref. MACD). A list is available (NRA 44052). The papers concern mainly economic policy and include diaries and a draft autobiography.

McFADYEAN, SIR ANDREW (1887–1974) Economist and Liberal politician. Joint Treasurer, Liberal Party Organisation, 1936–48; President, 1949–50. President, Free Trade Union, 1948–59.

A collection of c. 48 boxes is held in the LSE Library.

McFARLAND, SIR BASIL ALEXANDER TALBOT (1898–1986) Northern Irish politician, banker and businessman. Unionist Mayor of Derry, 1939 and 1945–50.

A substantial collection of papers relating to the political and commercial activities of the McFarland family has been deposited in the Public Record Office of Northern Ireland (ref. D3703). Much of the material concerns cross-border trade and transport in the Donegal–Derry region. In addition to files of correspondence, the collection also contains photographs and volumes of newspaper cuttings, 1939–70. A number of files are subject to a thirty-year closure rule: these include his correspondence with Sir Robin Chicester-Clark, MP, 1960–62, and 1968–69, and Lord Grey, the Governor-General of Northern Ireland, 1964–74; files on the appointment of Justices of the Peace and other Crown officials in Northern Ireland; and a volume of election results, 1900–66.

MacFARQUHAR, RODERICK LEMOND (1930–)
MP (Lab) Belper, Feb. 1974–79.

Mr MacFarquhar states that he has retained an unsorted collection of papers. The collection includes election addresses, constituency cases, local and national party material, and files on personal initiatives taken on foreign and domestic affairs.

MacGILLIVRAY, SIR DONALD CHARLES (1906–66) Colonial Service. Under-Secretary, Palestine, 1946–47. Liaison Officer, United Nations Special Committee, 1947. High Commissioner, Malayan Federation, 1954–58.

A collection of papers relating to Palestine, 1938–47, is held at St Antony's College, Oxford. A list is available (NRA 20811). The collection includes engagement books covering service in Palestine, 1938–45; papers on social ceremonies in Palestine, 1944–47; the British withdrawal, 1947–48; and the internationalisation of Jerusalem, 1947.

Rhodes House Library, Oxford, has files relating to his Malaya command. These include the records of the Committee on the Reorganisation of Agriculture, 1959.

McGIVAN, LORD   Alec John McGivan (1953–)
National Organiser, Social Democratic Party, 1981–88.

His political papers concerning the SDP have been placed in Essex University Library.

MACGOUGAN, JACK (1913–98)   Northern Irish trade unionist and Irish Labour Party politician. President, Irish Trades Union Congress, 1957–58 and 1963–64. On TUC General Council, 1970–79. General Secretary, National Union of Transport and General Workers, 1969–79.

Mr Macgougan deposited his papers in the Public Record Office of Northern Ireland (refs D3699 and D3699add). They mainly concern the organisation and activity of the Irish Labour Party in Northern Ireland, 1938–58. The collection includes campaign literature of both the Irish Labour Party and the Northern Irish Labour Party in various municipal, Stormont and Westminster elections, 1938–55; files of in- and out-letters relating to Irish Labour Party administrative work in Northern Ireland, 1950–53; articles, 1957–72; and photographs, 1951–78.

McGRATH,   GARRETT   (fl.   1960s–70s)   QC, Northern Ireland.

A collection of c. 300 documents accumulated by Mr McGrath and Michael Nicholson, barrister, during the 1969–71 proceedings of the Scarman Tribunal of Inquiry into the disturbances of August 1969, has been deposited in the Public Record Office of Northern Ireland (ref. D3789). The collection includes draft submissions, statements by witnesses, briefing papers, research material and press-cuttings.

McGUFFIN, JOHN (fl. 1960s–70s)   Civil rights campaigner in Northern Ireland during 1960s. Member of People's Democracy and the Northern Ireland Civil Rights Association.

Approximately 80 boxes of papers have been deposited with the Northern Ireland Political Collection at the Linen Hall Library, Belfast. The bulk of the collection consists of Irish newspapers and periodicals including many spawned by the Troubles, such as *Andersonstown News*, *Freedom*, *The Protestant Telegraph* and *Loyalist News*. There are also autobiographical accounts of the 1969 Burntollet March and the 1971 Falls Curfew; statements, photographs and other items relating to internees; files relating to People's Democracy, 1970–71 (minutes, agendas, policy documents, reports, circulation and membership correspondence, publicity material and copies of the People's Democracy newsletters *Unfree Citizen* and *Free Citizen*); papers relating to prisoners' rights in Northern Ireland and the Republic; and ephemera relating to the Northern Ireland Civil Rights Association, the anti-internment campaign, and various elections.

McINTOSH,   ALASTAIR   JAMES   (1913–73)
Colonial Service.

Rhodes House Library, Oxford, holds four volumes of diaries while McIntosh was Protectorate Secretary and Chief Adviser to the High Commissioner of Aden, 1948–63.

McINTOSH, MARY (1936–) Prominent sociologist and feminist. Supporter of numerous left-wing campaigns. Founding member, *Feminist Review*.

An extensive collection of papers (25 boxes) was placed in the LSE Library via Janet Foster in 1996 (ref. M1831). The collection consists of papers relating to gay and feminist politics mainly: minutes, leaflets and journals, 1960s and 1980s.

Represented are groups such as Feminists against Censorship, the Camden Prostitutes Safe House Project, etc.

McINTYRE, DR ROBERT DOUGLAS (1913–98) MP (Scottish Nationalist) Motherwell and Wishaw, 1945. Chairman, SNP, 1948–56; President, 1958–80. Physician.

The political correspondence and papers, covering the period *c*. 1930–88, are in the National Library of Scotland (ref. Acc 10090). The collection is now listed (NRA 39938).

McIVOR, (WILLIAM) BASIL (1928–) Stormont MP (UU) Belfast Larkfield, 1969–72. Minister of Community Relations, 1971–72. Minister of Education, Northern Ireland Executive, 1974.

His 1969–73 papers have been given to the Public Record Office of Northern Ireland (ref. D2962). The collection is closed.

MACKAY OF CLASHFERN, LORD James Peter Hymers Mackay (1927–) Lord Chancellor, 1987–97.

Correspondence and papers, 1987–97, mostly relating to his period of office as Lord Chancellor are in the National Library of Scotland (ref. Acc 12280). The collection is closed.

MACKAY, RONALD WILLIAM GORDON (1902–60) MP (Lab) Hull North West, 1945–50; Reading North, 1950–51.

A collection of Mackay's correspondence and memoranda is held in the LSE Library. The papers (1930s–51) relate to his parliamentary activities, especially on European Union. There are 15 groups of files including papers on the Council of Europe, the US Congress and Strasbourg, General Affairs, committee papers, and various subject files. These include Africa, the dominions, housing, education and electoral reform. The collection also holds some correspondence. Mackay's papers complement the archives of the Federal Union at the same location.

MACKINTOSH, JOHN PITCAIRN (1929–78) MP (Lab) Berwick & East Lothian, 1966–Feb. 1974; Oct. 1974–78.

His correspondence and papers, covering the period 1944–78, are deposited in the National Library of Scotland (ref. Dep 323). A list is available (NRA 24817/NRA[S] 2334). The collection contains biographical material, articles, reviews, broadcasts, and related correspondence (1952–78). There are also political papers on various subjects (1956–78) such as the EEC, local government, economic affairs, industrial relations, the Labour Party, devolution, Scottish affairs, the Helsinki Conference, and constituency files. Certain parts of the collection are closed until 2011.

MACLEHOSE OF BELOCH, BARON Crawford Murray Maclehose (1917–2000) Diplomat, 1947–82. Ambassador, Vietnam, 1967–69; Denmark, 1969–71. Governor and Commander-in-Chief, Hong Kong, 1971–82.

Lord Maclehose informed historians that he has been in contact with Rhodes House Library, Oxford regarding his papers. Inquiries should be directed in the first instance to the Librarian.

MACLENNAN OF ROGART, LORD Robert Adam Ross Maclennan (1936–) Labour, then SDP, politician. Leader of the SDP, 1987–88.

His political papers concerning the SDP have been placed in Essex University Library which also has the main SDP archive.

MACLEOD, IAIN NORMAN (1913–70) MP (Con) Enfield West, 1950–70. Minister of Health, 1952–55; Minister of Labour and National Service, 1955–59; Secretary of State for the Colonies, 1959–61; Chancellor of the Duchy of Lancaster, 1961–63; Chancellor of the Exchequer, June 1970.

According to the Bodleian Library, Oxford, very few papers have survived.

McLEOD, GENERAL SIR RODERICK WILLIAM (1905–80)

Military career. Commanded Special Air Services Brigade, 1944–45. Director of Military Operations, India, 1945–46. General Officer Commanding, 6th Armoured Division, 1955–56. Deputy Chief of Defence Staff, 1957–60. Commander, British Forces in Hong Kong, 1960–61. General Officer Commanding-in-Chief, Eastern Command, 1962–64.

His lectures and notes on the founding of the Special Air Services (SAS), 1944–49, are deposited in the Liddell Hart Centre, King's College, London. Other papers have been given to the Special Air Services Regimental Headquarters.

MACMILLAN OF OVENDEN, VISCOUNT Maurice Victor Macmillan (1921–84)

MP (Con) Farnham, 1966–83; Surrey South West after 1983. Cabinet Minister and prominent Europeanist.

The papers have been placed in the Bodleian Library, Oxford (which also has the papers of his father, Harold Macmillan, Earl of Stockton).

MACMILLAN, BARON Hugh Pattison Macmillan (1873–1952)

Lord of Appeal in Ordinary, 1930–39 and 1941–47. Lord of Appeal, 1947–52. Minister of Information, 1939–40.

His papers are deposited in the National Library of Scotland (ref. Acc 4849) and in the British Library (ref. Add MSS 54575–8). Both collections are described in *British Cabinet Ministers, 1900–51*. A list is also available for the National Library of Scotland papers (NRA 29056).

MacMILLAN OF MacMILLAN, GENERAL SIR GORDON HOLMES ALEXANDER (1897–1986)

Military career. Served in World Wars I and II. General Officer Commanding, Palestine, 1947–48; Scottish Command, 1949–52. Governor and Commander-in-Chief, Gibraltar, 1952–55.

A microfilm of papers relating to MacMillan's service in World War II and his post-war command in Palestine (1939–48) is held by the Imperial War Museum (ref. DS/MISC/15). The Palestine file includes a narrative of events from February 1947 to June 1948, the text of notes by the Chief of Staff on plans for evacuation, and a 'General Survey of Her Majesty's Government's Policy in Palestine'.

MACMILLAN, WILLIAM MILLER (1885–1974)

Historian. Specialist in African affairs. Professor of History, University of Witwatersrand, Johannesburg, 1917–34. Served in Empire Intelligence Section, BBC, 1941–43. Senior Representative of the British Council, 1943–46. Member, Colonial Labour Advisory Committee, 1946–52. Director of Colonial Studies, University of St Andrews, 1947–54.

A collection of papers, including correspondence, speech drafts, broadcasts, diaries and press-cuttings has been deposited in Rhodes House Library, Oxford (refs MSS Afr s 216–219 and MSS Afr s 1599).

MACNAB, BRIGADIER SIR GEOFFREY ALEX COLIN (1899–1995)

Military career, 1919–54. Member of Military Mission to Hungary, 1945. Director of Military Intelligence, Middle East, 1945–47. Military Attaché, Prague and Bucharest, 1938–40; Rome, 1947–49; Paris, 1949–54.

It is understood that Sir Geoffrey's papers were promised to be given to the Imperial War Museum. They are believed to consist of diaries, correspondence, press and photograph albums, covering the period 1938–68.

McNAMARA, (JOSEPH) KEVIN (1934–)

MP (Lab) Hull North, 1966–Feb. 74; Hull Central, Feb. 1974–83; Hull North, 1983–2005. Shadow Defence spokesman, 1982–87, Shadow Northern Ireland spokesman after 1987.

A very large collection of case and subject files is held at the Brynmor Jones Library, University of Hull (ref. DMC). Additional deposits have been made. The papers and correspondence cover constituency affairs, elections, Northern Ireland, Roman Catholic issues (including the debate on abortion), the European Community, the Council of Europe, the Commission for International Justice and Peace, the Select Committee on Overseas Development and the fishing industry. There is also a scrapbook of press-cuttings, 1965–75. The collection is subject to a thirty-year rule.

McNEIL, HECTOR (1907–55)

MP (Lab) Greenock, 1941–55. Parliamentary Under-Secretary, Foreign

Office, 1945–46. Minister of State for Foreign Affairs, 1946–50. Scottish Secretary, 1950–51.

According to *British Cabinet Ministers, 1900–51*, there are no political papers. His widow retained film and tape recordings of three speeches made at the United Nations, some personal correspondence, and a rough draft of an uncompleted biography. These are not available to researchers. Private Office papers relating to Scotland are held in the Departmental files at the Scottish Record Office. Some correspondence with Lord Beaverbrook is held at the House of Lords Record Office (ref. BBK C/236) (NRA 19284).

McNEILL, BRIGADIER-GENERAL ANGUS JOHN (1874–1950) Military career. Served Palestine, etc.

His diary of events, May 1948–May 1949, of the last period of the British mandate in Palestine is in the Middle East Centre, St Antony's College, Oxford. Other material relates to the 1929 disturbances. See NRA 41214.

MACPHERSON, SIR JOHN STUART (1898–1971)
Colonial Service. Chief Secretary, Palestine, 1939–43. Head, British Colonies Supply Mission, Washington, and Member of Anglo-American Caribbean Commission, 1943–45. Governor-General (Governor, 1948–54), Nigeria, 1954–55. Permanent Under-Secretary, Colonial Office, 1956–59.

A tape and transcript of an interview regarding his career, 1921–55, are available at Rhodes House Library, Oxford (ref. MSS Brit Emp s 487). Some correspondence, 1958–59, is available in the papers of P.G. Buchan-Hepburn, at Churchill College, Cambridge. Although Sir John was believed to have kept papers, this was not confirmed by his executors.

MACRORY, SIR PATRICK (ARTHUR) (1911–)
Ulster lawyer, businessman and writer. Chairman, Local Government Reorganisation Committee.

There are papers in the Public Record Office of Northern Ireland (ref. D.4025).

McSHANE, HARRY (1891–1988) Trade union activist.

An extensive correspondence with Raya Dunayevskaya, for the period 1959–88, has been donated to the Labour History Archive and Study Centre by the Raya Dunayevskaya Memorial Fund in Chicago. The exchange of letters, between 'the last of the Red Clydesiders' and 'the founder of Marxist Humanism' provides a useful commentary on the two veteran revolutionaries and on the resurgence of class conflict in the 1960s and 1970s.

MACKNEY, PAUL (fl. 1970s–90s) Socialist and trade unionist activist.

There are papers in Birmingham Central Library Archives (ref. MS 1591). The collection includes material on Birmingham Trades Council, *c.* 1970–90, as well as material on the International Socialists, the Troops Out movement, etc.

MADDOCKS, SIR KENNETH (PHIPSON) (b. 1907) Colonial administrator, Nigeria, 1929–58; Deputy Governor, Northern Region, Nigeria, 1957–58. Governor and Commander-in-Chief, Fiji, 1958–63.

Copies of his letters to Sir Arthur Benson regarding the 1953 Nigerian Constitutional Conference in London, together with records of meetings of heads of regional departments in Northern Nigeria, 1957, are in Rhodes House Library, Oxford (ref. MSS Afr s 1798).

MAGEEAN, BISHOP DANIEL (1882–1962) Roman Catholic Bishop of Down and Connor, 1929–62.

His correspondence, 1929–62, is deposited in the Down and Connor Diocesan Archives, Belfast.

MAINWARING, WILLIAM HENRY (1884–1971)
MP (Lab) Rhondda East, 1933–59. Miners' leader.

A collection of papers has been deposited by his daughter at the National Library of Wales. A list is available (NRA 34111).

MALLET, SIR VICTOR ALEXANDER LOUIS (1893–1969) Minister, Stockholm, 1940–45. Ambassador, Spain, 1945–46; Italy, 1947–53.

A collection of papers has been retained by his family. It is understood to include files on his pre-war posting in Tehran and Sweden during World War II; correspondence; notes for speeches; press-cuttings; and unpublished memoirs. A photocopy of the memoirs is held in Churchill College, Cambridge (NRA 18561).

MALVERN, 1ST VISCOUNT Sir Godfrey (Martin) Huggins (1883–1971) Prime Minister, Southern Rhodesia, 1933–53; Federation of Rhodesia and Nyasaland, 1953–56.

A collection of papers, 1933–56, is deposited in the National Archives of Zimbabwe. Further correspondence, 1933–58, can be found in the papers of C.J. Sibbett, deposited in the University of Cape Town Library; in the Lionel Curtis collection (1935–51) at the Bodleian Library, Oxford; and in the papers of Sir Michael Blundell (1946–53) at Rhodes House Library, Oxford.

MANBY, MERVYN (1915–) Colonial police service. Served Malaya, Kenya. Director of Intelligence and Security, Kenya, 1961–64.

Some papers are in Rhodes House Library, Oxford (ref. MSS Afr s 2159). A list is available (NRA 39158). There is material on the Mau Mau emergency in Kenya.

MANSERGH, GENERAL SIR (E.C.) ROBERT (1900–70) Military career. Served in World War II; commanded 5th Indian Division and 15th Indian Corps, 1945–46. Commander-in-Chief Allied Forces, Netherland East Indies, 1946. Military Secretary to Secretary of State for War, 1948–49. Commander-in-Chief British Forces, Hong Kong, 1949–51; Commander-in-Chief Allied Forces, Northern Europe, 1953–55; UK Land Forces, 1956–59. Master Gunner of the Royal Artillery, 1960–70.

His papers concerning the military administration of South East Asia during the later part of World War II are in the Imperial War Museum. The collection also contains post-war intelligence reports on the Japanese Army and some files on the occupation of the Netherlands East Indies, 1945–46. His papers relating to his time as Master Gunner are deposited in the Derbyshire Record Office (NRA 22989).

MANSFIELD COOPER, SIR WILLIAM (1903–92) Academic and university administrator. Professor of Industrial Law, Manchester University, 1940–70; Vice-Chancellor, 1956–70. President, Council of Europe Committee of Higher Education and Research, 1966–67.

His papers, 1948–70, are in the John Rylands Library, Manchester University. A list is available (NRA 20286). They chiefly consist of minutes, agendas and reports of the many public bodies on which he served, including the Fulbright Commission, the Independent Television Association, the Educational Advisory Council, the Western European Union and the Council of Europe.

MAREK, JOHN (1940–) MP (Lab) Wrexham, 1983–2001. Member, National Assembly of Wales after 1999 (Lab, then Ind).

There are papers in Wrexham Archive Service to where enquiries concerning the collection should be addressed.

MARKS OF BROUGHTON, 1ST BARON Sir Simon Marks (1888–1964) Businessman and Zionist. Chairman and Joint Managing Director, Marks and Spencer Ltd. Vice-President, English Zionist Federation.

Some private papers are deposited in the Central Zionist Archives (ref. A247). The archives of Marks & Spencer Ltd contain further relevant papers. The Weizmann Archives in Rehovot, Israel, include extensive correspondence, 1915–51.

MARLAND, PAUL (1940–) MP (Con) Gloucestershire West after 1979.

His constituency papers are in Gloucestershire Record Office (ref. D 7075). A list is available (NRA 38244). Access is subject to a 51-year rule.

MARQUAND, HILARY ADAIR (1902–72) MP (Lab) Cardiff East, 1945–50; Middlesbrough East, 1950–61. Parliamentary Secretary, Department of Overseas Trade, 1945–47. Paymaster-General, 1947–48. Minister of Pensions, 1948–51. Minister of Health, 1951.

Professor David Marquand (son) has informed the LSE Library that his father's papers contain little of interest on his life or political career. They are not available for research.

MARSH, ARTHUR (1922–99) Expert on industrial relations. Senior Fellow in Industrial Relations, St Edmund Hall, Oxford after 1964. Author of such works as *The Seamen* (1989) and *The Clerks* (1997).

The papers have been deposited in the Modern Records Centre, University of Warwick (ref. MSS 408). The collection includes arbitration files on industrial disputes, agreements and conference reports in the steel industry *c.* 1910–70s, and files on the National Union of Seamen, including the 1966 strike. Other subjects covered include engineering industry enquiry files for the 1960s and rates of pay and working conditions in the rubber industry.

MARRIS, ADAM DENZIL (1906–83) Diplomat.

His diary kept whilst attending the first meeting in 1943 of the United Nations Relief and Rehabilitation Administration (UNRRA) is in the Imperial War Museum.

MARSHALL, THOMAS HUMPHREY (1893–1982)
Sociologist. Professor of Sociology, London School of Economics, 1954–56. Educational adviser, British zone of Germany, 1949.

The LSE Library holds nine boxes of papers, 1930–80.

MARTEN, SIR NEIL (1916–86) MP (Con) Banbury, 1959–83.

Thirty-three boxes of papers, 1965–85, are deposited in the Bodleian Library, Oxford (ref. MSS Eng hist c 1130–59, e 385, misc a 29). The collection chiefly concerns his opposition to British membership of the European Community. Topics include the 1975 National Referendum Campaign; the Atlantic Free Trade Parliamentary Group, 1968–70; Commonwealth trade, 1969–76; fishing limits, 1970–72 and 1976–78; the Norwegian referendum, 1972, and European passports, 1975. There is also material on British policy towards Vietnam and Rhodesia during the 1960s, and copies of speeches by Enoch Powell. Restricted conditions of access apply to the collection.

MARTIN, (BASIL) KINGSLEY (1897–1969)
Socialist and journalist. Co-founder and joint editor, *The Political Quarterly*. Editor, *New Statesman* and *Nation*, 1930–60.

A large collection of papers and correspondence is held at Sussex University Library (ref. SxMs 11). A list is available (NRA 20303). There are extensive files on his editorship of the *New Statesman*. His correspondents include leading political and literary figures. The collection also contains notes and drafts for his books, broadcasts and lectures. Also included in the collection are a series of recorded memories of Martin which were collected by C.H. Rolph for his study *Kingsley: the Life, Letters and Diaries*. Among those interviewed were Richard Crossman, John Freeman, Edward Hyams, Paul Johnson, Arthur Koestler, Ivor Montagu, Raymond Mortimer, Malcolm Muggeridge, J.B. Priestley, V.S. Pritchett, Tom Harrisson, W.A. Robson, A.J.P. Taylor and Dame Rebecca West.

MARTIN, DENNIS (1919–98) Welsh communist activist in Rhondda Valley.

There are papers in the Welsh Political Archive, National Library of Wales.

MARTIN, SIR JOHN MILLER (1904–91) Home and Colonial Civil Service. Secretary, Palestine Royal Commission, 1936. Private Secretary to Sir Winston Churchill, 1940–45. Assistant (later Deputy) Under-Secretary, Colonial Office, 1945–65.

One box of diary and letter extracts from his time as Private Secretary to Sir Winston Churchill has been placed in Churchill College, Cambridge (ref. MART). A list is available (NRA 43511). Rhodes House Library holds the tapes and transcript of an interview on his colonial service, 1927–67 (ref. MSS Brit Emp S 419 (1–2)).

MARTIN, ROGER (1941–) Diplomat, 1964–86. Political officer, British Embassy, Saigon, Vietnam, 1968–70. First Secretary, Geneva, 1975–79. Deputy High Commissioner, Zimbabwe, 1983–86. Director, Somerset Trust for Nature Conservation since 1988.

Mr Martin informed the project that he has retained papers relating to Rhodesia, Saigon and South Africa. They consist of files relating to the UDI crisis, 1965–66; his personal letters, chiefly to his parents, written when stationed in Saigon, 1968–70; and various files kept while he was Deputy High Commissioner in Zimbabwe, 1983–86, including material on the case for sanctions against South Africa.

The Imperial War Museum's Department of Sound Records holds three recordings from a BBC radio programme in which he recalled his time in Saigon, 1968–70 (ref. U565/1–U567/1).

MASON OF BARNSLEY, BARON Roy Mason (1942–) MP (Lab) Barnsley, 1953–87. Secretary of State for Defence, 1974–76; Northern Ireland, 1976–79.

A collection of papers, 1953–84, has been placed in South Yorkshire County Record Office, Barnsley. This collection is uncatalogued and is not yet open to researchers.

MASON, PHILIP (1906–99) (pseudonym PHILIP WOODRUFF) Race relations expert. Director of Studies in Race Relations, Chatham House, London, 1952–58. Director of the Institute of Race Relations, London, 1959–69.

His typescript history of the Institute of Race Relations, together with related documents, is in the Centre for Southern African Studies, University of York.

MASON-MACFARLANE, LIEUTENANT-GENERAL SIR (FRANK) NOEL (1889–1953) Military career. Served in World Wars I and II. Military Attaché, Budapest, Vienna and Berne, 1931–34; Copenhagen and Berlin, 1937–39. Director of Military Intelligence with British Expeditionary Force, 1939–40. Head of British Military Mission to Moscow, 1941–42. Governor and Commander-in-Chief, Gibraltar, 1942–44. Chief Commissioner, Allied Control Commission for Italy, 1944. MP (Lab) Paddington North, 1945–46. Resigned seat in 1946.

A collection of papers covering his varied career is held at the Imperial War Museum. The material consists mainly of wartime diaries and engagement books, 1943–44 and 1946; papers kept as Governor of Gibraltar; files relating to his role in Italy, 1944; and a collection of miscellaneous papers, press-cuttings and drafts of articles written by him in the post-war years.

MATHERS, 1ST BARON George Mathers (1886–1965) MP (Lab) Edinburgh West, 1929–31; Linlithgowshire, 1935–50; West Lothian, 1950–51. Comptroller to the Royal Household, 1945–46.

The National Library of Scotland holds the papers (ref. Acc 4826). They include political and personal correspondence (1920–61), drafts of speeches and election addresses, press-cuttings (1919–58) and photographs (NRA 19290).

MAUDLING, REGINALD (1917–79) MP (Con) Barnet, 1950–Feb. 74; Chipping Barnet, Feb. 1974–79. Economic Secretary, Treasury, 1952–55. Minister of Supply, 1955–57. Paymaster-General, 1957–59. President of the Board of Trade, 1959–61. Colonial Secretary, 1961–62. Chancellor of the Exchequer, 1962–64. Home Secretary, 1970–72.

There are 28 boxes of constituency correspondence deposited at Churchill College, Cambridge (ref. MLNG) (NRA 18561). Rhodes House, Oxford, holds an interview on colonial problems as Secretary of State for the Colonies, 1961–62, including his impressions of Welensky, Kaunda and Kenyatta (ref. MSS Brit Emp s 484). See also *British Cabinet Ministers, 1900–51*.

MAXWELL, SIR REGINALD MAITLAND (1882–1967) Indian Civil Service. Home Member, Governor-General's Executive Council, 1938–44. Adviser to Secretary of State for India, 1944–47.

There are 17 boxes of miscellaneous papers, 1912–46, deposited in the Cambridge South Asian Centre.

MAXWELL, SIR WILLIAM GEORGE (1871–1959) Colonial civil servant.

Some papers are held at Rhodes House Library, Oxford. There is material on the Gold Coast (ref. MSS Afr s 141) together with correspondence, memoranda and other papers on the decentralisation of the Federated Malay States, 1958–59, the reconstruction of Malaya, 1963, and also miscellaneous papers and newspaper cuttings (ref. MSS Ind Ocn s 42 and MSS Ind Ocn s 146). Additional papers on the Malay Union are held at the Royal Commonwealth Society Library (now based in Cambridge University Library).

MAXWELL-HYSLOP, SIR ROBERT JOHN (ROBIN) (1931–) MP (Con) Tiverton, 1960–92.

His political papers, 1970–79, are in the Brynmor Jones Library, University of Hull.

MAYBRAY-KING, LORD Horace Maybray Maybray-King (1901–86) MP (Lab) Southampton Test, 1950–55; Southampton Itchen, 1955–70. Speaker of the House of Commons, 1965–70. Deputy Speaker, House of Lords, after 1971.

His diaries, correspondence and other papers are reported in Southampton Archives Office.

MAYBURY, MAURICE (1914–95) Adviser, Ministry of Overseas Development.

There are papers in the School of Oriental and African Studies, University of London.

MAYHEW, BARON Christopher Paget Mayhew (1915–97) Labour, then Liberal, politician. Served as Minister of Defence (RN) 1964–66.

There are papers in the Liddell Hart Centre for Military Archives, King's College, London, to where enquiries should be addressed.

MAYNARD, (VERA) JOAN (1921–98) MP (Lab) Sheffield Brightside, Oct. 1974–87.

Ms Maynard retained her political papers. Some early files for the period to October 1978 are held in Sheffield City Library (ref. MPA 1–26) (NRA 22260).

MEADE, LIEUTENANT-COLONEL C.J.G. (fl. 1940s–60s) Military career with 8th Hussars, 1940–67. Post-war service in Korea and Cyprus.

The National Army Museum holds a collection of papers reflecting his interesting career including attachments to Staff College, the Joint Services Staff College and the British Defence Staff, Washington (ref. 8009–79). Certain items on the Korean War and the 1959 Cyprus Emergency are subject to restricted access, and readers should initially consult a detailed catalogue held at the Museum.

MEADE, JAMES EDWARD (1907–95) Economist. Economic Assistant, 1940–45, and Director, 1946–47, Economic Section, Cabinet Office. Professor of Commerce, with special reference to International Trade, London School of Economics, 1947–57. Professor of Political Economy, Cambridge University, 1957–68.

Material deposited at the LSE Library includes notes and papers on various topics such as Government economic policy, economic growth, inflation, and correspondence relating to his various books and studies (ref. M165). A list is available (NRA 2511). A more recent deposit (by his widow in 1996) comprises 30 additional boxes of papers relating to his later economic writings and his work with the Social Democratic Party (ref. M1826).

MEADOWCROFT, MICHAEL (JAMES) (1942–) Liberal activist. MP (Lib) Leeds West, 1983–87. Liberal Party Local Government Officer, 1962–67. President of the (independent continuing) Liberal Party after 1993. Opponent of merger of Liberals and Social Democrats. Chairman, Electoral Reform Society, 1989–93.

His political papers (34 boxes, 1960s–94) were deposited in the LSE Library in 1997 (ref. M 1844). The papers relate to his career in the Liberal Party, including publications, Assembly papers and material relating to elections. There is also material on the SDP/Liberal Alliance. A further deposit, transferred from the Electoral Reform Society, contains material relating to the SDP Liberal Party merger negotiations (Files 171–179).

MEDLICOTT, SIR FRANK (1903–72) MP (Lib Nat) Norfolk East, 1939–50, (Nat Lib and Con) Norfolk Central, 1950–59. Treasurer of the Liberal Party, 1969–71.

It is understood that the surviving papers are with his son, Paul Medlicott.

MEGAHY, THOMAS (1929–) MEP (Lab) SW Yorkshire, 1979–99. Deputy Leader, British Group of Labour MEPs.

His constituency papers, 1979–99, are in the West Yorkshire Archive Service, Wakefield (ref. C976).

MELCHETT, 3RD BARON Julian Edward Alfred Mond (1925–73) Chairman, British Steel, 1967–73. Director, Confederation of British Industry, 1969–73.

The papers remain in family possession. They have been catalogued and provision is currently being made for their deposit in a suitable archive. In addition to several files on his role as the first chairman of the re-nationalised steel industry, the papers include correspondence, speeches and speech notes on his other roles in banking and agriculture.

MELLORS, BOB (d. 1996) Gay writer, biographer of Charlotte Bach.

The collection in the LSE Library (part of the Hall-Carpenter archives) consists of 9 boxes of the papers of Charlotte Bach (1920–81), sexologist, gathered by Bob Mellors while writing Bach's biography. Charlotte/Carl Bach, a man who lived the second half of his life as a woman, developed a number of philosophical theories relating to gender and sexuality. The papers consist of typescripts of Bach's work and drafts of Mellor's biography. There is also a box of pamphlets, many published by Quantum Leap.

MENAUL, AIR VICE-MARSHAL STEWART WILLIAM BLACKNER (1915–87) Royal Air Force career. Served in World War II. Commanded British Atomic Trials Task Force, Monte Bello and Maralinga, Australia, 1955–56. Air Officer Commanding, Administration, Aden, 1959–60. Commandant, Joint Services Staff College, 1965–67. Director-General, Royal United Services Institute, 1968–76. Media commentator on defence issues, including the 1982 Falklands War.

Some 74 boxes of papers are deposited in the Liddell Hart Centre, King's College, London. A detailed catalogue is available. The material includes correspondence, reports, memoranda, speeches and press-cuttings, and largely dates from his post-retirement career in the Royal United Services Institute and as a defence analyst. The collection is an important source for recent global defence policies, strategic and tactical planning and conventional and nuclear weaponry. The collection is now open.

MENDELSON, JOHN J. (1917–78) MP (Lab) Penistone, 1959–78.

An extensive collection of papers is held at the South Yorkshire Record Office, Sheffield, to which enquiries concerning access should be addressed. A list is available (NRA 24911).

MERCHANT, PIERS ROLF GARFIELD (1951–) MP (Con) Newcastle Central, 1983–87; Beckenham, 1992–97 (Oct).

His political papers have been placed in Bromley Central Library (ref. 1072) to where enquiries should be addressed.

MESSER, SIR FREDERICK (1886–1971) MP (Lab) Tottenham South, 1929–31, 1935–50 and Tottenham, 1950–59.

Copies of certain papers are held at the Brynmor Jones Library, University of Hull. There is some correspondence relating to the Victory for Socialism campaign together with newspaper cuttings and election addresses from 1929 and 1945.

MESSERVY, GENERAL SIR FRANK WALTER (1893–1974) Military career. Served in World Wars I and II. General Officer Commanding-in-Chief, Malaya Command, 1945; Northern Command, India, 1946–47. Commander-in-Chief, Pakistan Army, 1947–48.

Three boxes of material, 1941–54, have been placed in the Liddell Hart Centre, King's College, London. A list is available (NRA 23074). The collection comprises unit histories and miscellaneous propaganda publications produced by the Ministry of Information and the Indian War Department in World War II. The post-war items include a 1947 report on the Keren battlefield and two reports (1947 and 1951) to the Combined Chiefs of Staff on the 1943–46 campaign in South-East Asia.

MEYER, SIR ANTHONY JOHN CHARLES (1920–) MP (Con) Eton and Slough, 1964–66; West Flint, 1970–83; Clwyd North West, 1983–92. Diplomat, 1946–64; First Secretary, Moscow, 1956–58.

His correspondence and papers, 1979–91, have been deposited in Clwyd Record Office, Hawarden (ref. D/AM). There are papers relating to the Falklands War and also his challenge to Margaret Thatcher concerning the leadership.

MICHAELSON, DAVID (1912–75) Communist shop steward. Editor, *The Metal Worker*, 1953–63.

There are papers in the Modern Records Centre, University of Warwick (ref. MSS 233). A list is available (NRA 27052). The collection includes various subject files on *The New Propellor/The Metal Worker* (the official organ of the Engineering and Allied Trades Shop Stewards' National Council), together with back copies. There are also files on the engineering industry; the post-war shop stewards' movement; the Communist Party of Great Britain; the 1950 election campaign; and Communist Party controversies following de-Stalinisation. There are also literary papers and correspondence including drafts of unpublished novels and plays.

MIDDLETON, JAMES SMITH (1878–1962) Assistant Secretary (later General Secretary) of the Labour Party.

An extensive collection of correspondence and papers relating to his career and that of his wife, Lucy Middleton (q.v.) has been deposited at Ruskin College, Oxford. A list is available (NRA 27385). Further correspondence and papers, 1906–47, are in the Labour Party Archives at the Labour History Archive and Study Centre, Manchester.

MIDDLETON, LUCY ANNIE (1894–1983) MP (Lab) Plymouth Sutton, 1945–51.

A collection of papers has been deposited jointly with those of James Middleton (q.v.) at Ruskin College, Oxford. A list is available (NRA 27385).

MIDGLEY, HARRY (1892–1957) Stormont MP (NILP) Belfast Dock, 1933–38; (NILP, 1941–42, Commonwealth Labour Party, 1942–47, UU, 1947–57) Belfast Willowfield, 1941–57. Northern Ireland Minister of Public Security, 1943–44; Labour, 1944–45; Education, 1950–57.

The papers *c.* 1926–80, have been deposited in the Public Record Office of Northern Ireland (ref. D4089). His biographer, Graham Walker, made extensive use of them in *The Politics of Frustration: Harry Midgley and the Failure of Labour in Northern Ireland* (1984). The papers of the Northern Ireland Labour Party Secretary, Sam Napier, deposited in the Public Record Office of Northern Ireland, include notes and material (1941–69) gathered for a proposed biography of Midgley. These are now open (ref. D3702/D/7).

MIERS, REAR-ADMIRAL SIR ANTHONY CECIL CAPEL (1906–85) Royal Navy career, 1924–59, chiefly in submarines. Attached to the US Pacific Fleet, 1943–44. Commanded *HMS Theseus*, 1954–55. Flag Officer, Middle East, 1956–59.

Three boxes of papers covering his wartime service in the submarine *HMS Torbay* in the Pacific, and during the Cyprus Emergency, 1955–59, are deposited in Churchill College, Cambridge.

MIKARDO, IAN (1908–93) MP (Lab) Reading (and Reading South), 1950–59; Poplar, 1964–74; Bethnal Green and Bow, 1974–83; Bow and Poplar, 1983–87. Leading figure on the left of the party.

His papers, covering the period 1933–84, have been placed in the Labour History and Archives Centre, University of Manchester.

MILLARD, DR CHARLES KILLICK (1870–1952) Medical Officer of Health of the City of Leicester, 1901–35. Founder of the Voluntary Euthanasia Society, 1936.

His papers, 1931–50, are held in the Wellcome Contemporary Medical Archives Centre, London. The collection includes correspondence, speech notes, press-cuttings and printed material on euthanasia, birth control and vaccination. Some additional material is held at Leicestershire Record Office.

MILLER, SIR HILARY 'HAL' (1929–) MP (Con) Bromsgrove and Redditch, Feb. 1974–83; Bromsgrove, 1983–92. Vice-Chairman of the Conservative Party, 1984–87.

An extensive collection of papers has been deposited in Hereford and Worcestershire Record Office (ref. BA11701).

MILLER, MILLIE (1923–77) MP (Lab) Ilford North, 1974–77. Leader, Camden Council, 1971–73.

Her personal papers and correspondence, 1950–70, have been placed in London Metropolitan Archives (ref. LMA/4427).

MILLS, 1ST VISCOUNT Percy Herbert Mills (1890–1968) Conservative politician. Minister of Power, 1957–59; Paymaster-General, 1959–61; Minister without Portfolio, 1961–62; Deputy Leader, House of Lords, 1960–62.

According to *British Cabinet Ministers, 1900–51*, a small collection of papers is held by the grandson.

MILNER-BARRY, SIR PHILIP STUART (1906–95) Civil servant. Involved in World War II code-breaking. Under-Secretary, Treasury, 1954–66.

A few surviving papers (many early papers were destroyed) have been placed in Churchill College, Cambridge. A list is available (NRA 44053) but the papers mainly relate to code-breaking and intelligence.

MIRFIN, DERRICK (fl. 1940s–60s) Liberal activist.

His Liberal Party papers, 1940s–60s, are held at Bristol University Library (ref. DM 668). Material in the collection includes various papers on the Union of Liberal Students, 1949–59; the Liberal Party Organisation, 1951–61; the Radical Reform Group,

1953–60; and youth and international organisations. There are also 15 files of Liberal Party Organisation Executive papers covering policy issues such as constituency and parliamentary tactics, foreign affairs, the Commonwealth, defence and nuclear weapons, the economy, labour relations, education and housing.

MITCHELL, AUSTIN VERNON (1934–) MP (Lab) Grimsby, Apr. 1977–83; Great Grimsby since 1983.

Many of his early political and constituency papers are held at the Brynmor Jones Library, University of Hull (ref. DMM). The collection consists of over 200 files. These files reflect his interests in social, environmental and health matters as well as local constituency casework and other correspondence. A list is available (NRA 41128).

MITCHELL, JOSEPH STANLEY (1909–87) Cancer researcher. Regius Professor of Physics, University of Cambridge, 1957–75.

There are papers in Cambridge University Library (NRA 35398). Among the many committee papers etc. is material on the peaceful uses of nuclear energy.

MITCHELL, MAJOR-GENERAL SIR PHILIP EUEN (1890–1964) Colonial Service. Political Adviser to General Sir Archibald Wavell, 1941. British Plenipotentiary in Ethiopia and Chief Political Officer to General Officer Commanding-in-Chief, East Africa, 1942. Governor, Fiji (High Commissioner, Western Pacific), 1942–44; Kenya, 1944–52.

There are 23 volumes of diaries in Rhodes House Library, Oxford (1927–44 and 1953–59), relating to service in Tanganyika, Uganda and the Western Pacific. Relevant correspondence can be found in the papers of Lord Lugard, Arthur Creech Jones and Margery Perham, also deposited at Rhodes House Library. His Private Office correspondence, 1945–52, is available at the Public Record Office (refs CO 967/59 and CO 967/62–63). A list is available (NRA 28778).

MITCHISON, NAOMI MARGARET (1897–1999) Author. Member, Highlands and Islands Advisory Panel, 1947–65; Highlands and Islands Development Council from 1966. Tribal adviser to the Bakgatla, Botswana, from 1963.

The National Library of Scotland has some of her papers including some correspondence between herself and her husband, Gilbert (Lord) Mitchison, and with various literary figures. The library of the School of Oriental and African Studies, London University, has miscellaneous papers relating to Botswana, 1964–74. These include correspondence with Botswanan politicians, minutes of meetings, leaflets, reports relating to local community development and transcripts of speeches. The Imperial War Museum has the letters she received from her family, 1914–45. Additional papers can be found in the Columbia University Library, the University of Texas at Austin, and the Lockwood Library, State University of New York at Buffalo.

MITRANY, DAVID (1888–1975) Political economist. Professor in School of Economics and Politics, Princeton University, 1933–75. Attached to the Foreign Office during World War II.

A collection of working files and notes, correspondence, book reviews and letters to the press is held at the LSE Library. They form an important source for the history of 20th-century international relations and, in particular, the roles of the League of Nations, the United Nations and its agencies.

MOLYNEAUX, BARON James Henry Molyneaux (1920–) MP (UU) South Antrim, 1970–83; Lagan Valley after 1983. Leader of the Ulster Unionist Party after 1979.

Mr Molyneaux states that he has refrained from collecting correspondence and other papers. He has never kept a diary.

MONCKTON OF BRENCHLEY, 1ST VISCOUNT Sir Walter Turner Monckton (1891–1965) MP (Con) Bristol West, 1951–57. Minister of Labour and National Service, 1951–55; Minister of Defence, 1955–56. Paymaster-General, 1956–57.

More than 150 boxes of papers, 1896–1964, have been deposited in the Bodleian Library, Oxford (ref. MSS Dep Monckton 1–63 and MSS Dep Monckton Trustees 1–89). A list is available (NRA 20879). The post-war files include material on the Suez Crisis, 1956–57; the Birkett Committee on the Interception of Communications (telephone tapping), 1957; the Central African Federation, 1959–62; and the

Monckton Commission, 1959–60. Files relating to the Duke and Duchess of Windsor (1936–51) and to other members of the Royal Family are closed. Enquiries concerning access should be directed to the Bodleian Library.

MONKHOUSE, PATRICK JAMES (fl. 1950s–70s)
Northern Editor, *Manchester Guardian*

A collection of papers for the years 1952–75 is held with the *Guardian* Archives ('D' sequence) at the John Rylands University Library, Manchester. The collection includes extensive correspondence (1940s–60s); individual, general and editorial staff files; obituary files; and papers relating to areas of special interest such as East Africa. There are also files concerning the *Manchester Evening News*.

MONROE, ELIZABETH Mrs Humphrey Neame
(1905–86) Scholar and historian of the Middle East. Diplomatic correspondent, *The Observer*, 1944. British representative, United Nations Sub-Committee for Prevention of Discrimination and Protection of Minorities, 1947–52. Staff, *The Economist*, 1945–58. Fellow, St Antony's College, Oxford, 1963–73.

Five files of papers, mainly on Palestine, are held at the Middle East Centre, St Antony's College, Oxford. They contain correspondence with persons active in Middle Eastern affairs, as well as notes of interviews with Richard Crossman, John Hamilton, Francis Williams, Sir Alex Kirkbride, Eliahu Elath and Arthur Creech Jones regarding Bevin's Arab policy (1945–48).

MONTAGU, (ALEXANDER) VICTOR (EDWARD PAULET) 10th Earl of Sandwich (Disclaimed 1964) (1906–95) MP (Con) Dorset South, 1941–57; (Ind Con) 1957–58; (Con) 1958–62.

The papers are reported still in the care of the family.

MONTAGU, IVOR (GOLDSMID SAMUEL) (1904–84) Communist, author, film critic and producer.

The papers are held in the archives of the former Communist Party of Great Britain, now deposited in the Labour History Archive and Study Centre, Manchester. They are an important source for radical left politics in the inter-war period. The post-war material includes correspondence with leading Communist Party and Fabian Society figures. The collection includes material on Anglo-Soviet relations and on his career in the cinema. Further papers have been deposited at the British Film Institute Library.

MONTEATH, SIR DAVID TAYLOR (1887–1961)
Under-Secretary of State for India and Burma, 1941–47; Burma, 1947.

Correspondence and papers for the period 1942–47 are held at the India Office Library (ref. MSS Eur D 714). A list is available (NRA 27459).

MONTGOMERY OF ALAMEIN, 1ST VISCOUNT
Field-Marshal Sir Bernard Law Montgomery (1887–1976) Military commander. Served in World Wars I and II. Commanded 8th Army, 1942–44 (North Africa, Sicily, Italy); British Group of Armies and Allied Armies, North France, 1944; British Army on the Rhine and British Member of Allied Control Commission Germany, 1945–46. Chief of the Imperial General Staff, 1946–48. Chairman of Western European Commanders-in-Chief Committee, 1948–51. Deputy Supreme Allied Commander, Europe, 1951–58.

The papers were acquired by the Imperial War Museum in July 1982. The collection includes 44 volumes of diaries, 1942–58, in addition to extensive wartime and post-war correspondence with several of the leading Allied commanders and politicians, including Churchill, Attlee, Alanbrooke, Eisenhower and de Gaulle. His letters from the Western Front during World War I are included in the collection, which has been fully catalogued. Since 1982, the Museum has acquired additional correspondence with other figures, including his letters to Lieutenant-Colonel T. Warren, 1942–70, and to Sir Edgar Williams, 1954–72. Much more correspondence is available in the papers of contemporary statesmen and commanders, including Lord Avon (Birmingham University Library), Earl Attlee and Lord Monckton (Bodleian Library, Oxford), Lord Beaverbrook (House of Lords Record Office) and Field Marshal Lord Alanbrooke (Liddell Hart Centre, King's College, London).

MOON, SIR (EDWARD) PENDEREL (1905–87)
Indian Civil Service, 1929–44. Editor, *India Office Records on Transfer of Power*, 1972–82.

A collection of correspondence, papers, articles and photographs, 1929–85, has been given to the India Office Library (ref. MSS Eur F 230). A list is available (NRA 34759).

MOORE, SIR HENRY MONCK-MASON (1887–1964) Colonial Service, 1919–49. Governor and Commander-in-Chief, Kenya, 1939–44; Ceylon, 1944–48 (Governor-General, 1948–49).

Certain papers, including his letters and the diaries of his wife, Lady Daphne, have been deposited in Rhodes House Library, Oxford (ref. MSS Brit Emp s 466). Special conditions of access apply to the collection. Further correspondence regarding Kenya, 1930–47, is available at the Public Record Office (ref. CO 967)

MOORING, SIR (ARTHUR) GEORGE (RIXSON) (1908–69) Colonial service. Resident, Zanzibar, 1959–64.

There are papers concerning his career deposited in BLCAS (Rhodes House Library), Oxford.

MOORMAN, JOHN RICHARD HUMPIDGE (1905–89) Bishop of Ripon, 1959–75. Delegate-observer to Second Vatican Council, 1962–65.

His diaries are deposited in Lambeth Palace Library. The earlier volumes, 1921–58, are open to researchers. The library also holds his diary of the Second Vatican Council, 1962–65, and research papers on the Franciscan Order of St Deiniols.

MORAES, FRANCIS ROBERT (1907–74) Journalist, author and editor. First Indian editor, *The Times of India*.

The papers (17 boxes, 1935–74) have been deposited in the School of Oriental and African Studies, University of London (ref. PP MS 24). A list is available (NRA 43400). The collection includes his diary/notebooks.

MORGAN, LIEUTENANT-GENERAL SIR FREDERICK EDGWORTH (1894–1967) Military career. Chief of Operations, UNRRA, 1945–46.

There are papers in the Imperial War Museum. Details are available on the IWM website.

MORLEY, ELLIOTT (1952–) MP (Lab) Glanford and Scunthorpe after 1987.

His correspondence and subject files have been deposited in the Brynmor Jones Library, University of Hull (ref. DMY). They reflect his concerns over agriculture and animal welfare, nuclear disarmament, conservation, etc.

MORRELL, FRANCES MAINE (1937–) Labour activist. Leader, Inner London Education Authority. Secretary to the Speaker's Commission on Citizenship. Special Adviser to Tony Benn etc.

Her papers as Secretary of the Speaker's Commission on Citizenship (7 boxes, 1988–90) were placed in the LSE Library in 1994 (ref. M 1792). The Commission was established to consider how to encourage, develop and recognise Active Citizenship within a wide range of groups in the community, both local and national, including school students, adults, those in full employment, as well as volunteers. The papers consist of minutes of the meetings of the Commission, papers and other evidence submitted to it, correspondence and drafts of the final report including extensive comments by the members of the Commission and others.

MORRIS OF BORTH-Y-GEST, 1ST BARON John William Morris (1896–1979) Lawyer, arbitrator on industrial disputes and public servant. A Lord of Appeal in Ordinary from 1960.

A large collection of papers is held at the National Library of Wales. The collection includes correspondence on various Welsh subjects such as the proposals for a Welsh-language television channel (1959), a Parliament for Wales (1968), and the use of Welsh in legal cases. There is also some political and legal correspondence and various committee papers such as the Courts of Inquiry into Engineering and Shipbuilding Wage Disputes (1953–54) and the Coal Mining Conciliation Scheme (1955–65). Other papers relate to the growth of Plaid Cymru, Welsh Nationalism, and Welsh Independent support in Liverpool. Additional family correspondence is held at the Gwynedd Archives, Caernarfon (NRA 33211).

MORRIS OF WYTHENSHAWE, LORD Alfred Morris (1928–) MP (Lab and Co-op) Manchester Wythenshawe 1964–97. First Minister for the Disabled, 1974–79. Architect of the Chronically Sick and Disabled Persons Act, 1970.

A large deposit of papers (51 boxes, covering the period 1970–95) was placed in the LSE Library in April 1997 (ref. M1841). Most of the papers relate to disability and the care of the disabled, Labour Party policy and Manchester and Stanstead Airports.

MORRIS, JOHN (1931–) MP (Lab) Aberavon after 1959. Secretary of State for Wales, 1974–79. Member, UK Delegation, Council of Europe and Western European Union.

His political papers, covering the period 1960s–1994, have been acquired through successive deposits by the National Library of Wales.

MORRIS, SIR RHYS HOPKIN (1888–1956) MP (Ind Lib) Cardiganshire, 1923–32; (Lib) Carmarthen, 1945–56.

A substantial collection of correspondence and other papers is deposited in the National Library of Wales. A list is available (NRA 41933). There is material on the 1929 Palestine Royal Commission, but nothing on the Liberal Party.

MORRIS, SIR WILLIAM (BILL) (1938–) Trade union leader. General Secretary, Transport and General Workers Union, 1992–2003.

Reference should be made to the collection of his official papers in the Modern Records Centre, University of Warwick (ref. MSS. 126/BM). The papers (80 boxes) are mainly concerned with Sir Bill's term as General Secretary, and include appointment diaries, texts of speeches (including many made while Deputy General Secretary) and files on a wide range of subjects. The collection is now fully catalogued.

MORRISON OF LAMBETH, BARON Herbert Stanley Morrison (1888–1965) MP (Lab) Hackney South, 1923–24, 1929–31 and 1935–45; Lewisham East, 1945–50; and Lewisham South, 1950–59. Minister of Transport, 1929–31. Minister of Supply, 1940. Home Secretary, 1940–45; Lord President of the Council, 1945–51; Foreign Secretary, 1951.

A small collection of papers is deposited at Nuffield College, Oxford. For further details see *British Cabinet Ministers, 1900–51*. The LSE Library has the papers collected for the biography by Professor G.W. Jones and Lord Donoughue, *Herbert*

Morrison: Portrait of a Politician (1973). A list is available (NRA 30242). They include some original documents, research notes and typescript interviews with his associates. Some 1951 subject files are held at the National Archives (ref. FO 800/628–61) (NRA 23627).

MORRISON, DR GEORGE (fl. 1970s–80s) Welsh Liberal Party activist.

A collection of papers is held at the National Library of Wales. This includes various files on local elections, Liberal conferences and subject files. There are also correspondence, minutes and papers on the Welsh Liberal Party, 1968–82; the Ceredigion Liberal Association, 1971–83; and the Ceredigion and Pembroke North Liberal Association, 1980–83.

MORTIMER, JAMES EDWARD (1921–) Trade unionist. General Secretary, Labour Party, 1982–85.

A collection of papers has been placed in the Modern Records Centre, University of Warwick (ref. MSS 525).

MORTON, SIR DESMOND JOHN FAULKNER (1891–1971) Principal Assistant Secretary, Ministry of Economic Warfare, 1939. Personal Assistant to Prime Minister, 1940–46. UK Delegate to Inter-Allied Reparation Agency.

Morton kept no diary and burnt most of his personal papers. His letters to R.W. Thompson, written while Thompson was writing *The Yankee Marlborough*, offer a record of his personal relationship with Churchill. These letters, 1943–71, form part of the Thompson collection at the Liddell Hart Centre, King's College, London, and were published in 1976 as *Churchill and Morton*. Other papers, 1939–51, are available at the Public Record Office (ref. PREM 7). A list is available (NRA 28788). They include his minutes to Churchill, 1940–51; letters from Churchill concerning his memoirs; and some closed items, 1945–51.

MOSER, SIR CLAUS (ADOLF) (1922–) Professor of Social Statistics, London School of Economics, 1961–70. Director, Central Statistical Office and Head of Government Statistical Service, 1967–78. Chairman, Economist Intelligence Unit, 1979–83. Warden, Wadham College, Oxford, after 1984.

Sir Claus states that he has retained non-official papers and that provision will be made for their eventual deposit.

MOSLEY, SIR OSWALD ERNALD (1896–1980)

MP (Con until 1922, Ind, 1922–24 and Lab from 1926) Harrow, 1918–24; Smethwick, 1926–31. Leader of British Union of Fascists during 1930s. Interned during World War II.

Mosley's surviving papers, previously in the possession of his widow, Lady Diana Mosley, have been deposited in the University of Birmingham. They are closed pending listing. For the extensive pre-war files in the Public Record Office, see *British Cabinet Ministers*. Some correspondence, 1928–63, is available in the Beaverbrook papers in the House of Lords Record Office. The papers of Bob Boothby, which are still in the Boothby family's possession, include correspondence with both Oswald and Lady Diana Mosley. Reference should also be made to the Jeffrey Hamm papers (q.v.). An autobiography, *My Life*, was published in 1968.

MOULTON, MAJOR-GENERAL JAMES LOUIS

(1906–94) Military career, serving Royal Marines, Commandos, etc. Naval writer.

Five boxes of his papers, 1939–81, are in Churchill College, Cambridge (NRA 44347).

MOUNTBATTEN OF BURMA, 1ST EARL

Admiral of the Fleet Louis Francis Albert Victor Nicholas Mountbatten (1900–79) Naval Commander. Adviser on Combined Operations, 1941–42. Supreme Allied Commander, South East Asia, 1943–46. Viceroy of India, March–August 1947. Governor-General, India, 1947–48. Flag Officer Commanding, 1st Cruiser Squadron, Mediterranean Fleet, 1948–49. Fourth Sea Lord, 1950–52. Commander-in-Chief Mediterranean and Allied Forces, Mediterranean, 1952–54. First Sea Lord, 1955–59. Chief of UK Defence Staff and Chairman of Chiefs of Staff Committee, 1959–65.

Lord Mountbatten's extensive papers were deposited in the Hartley Library, University of Southampton, in 1987. A summary catalogue of the collection is available (*University of Southampton Library, Occasional Paper 9*, edited by L.M. Mitchell, K.J. Sampson and C.M. Woolgar)(NRA 34063).

Particularly significant are the series of papers dealing with his command of Combined Operations during World War II; the transfer of power in India while serving as the last British Viceroy; and the reorganisation of the Royal Navy and broader defence developments following the Suez crisis, 1956. The papers of his wife, Lady Edwina Mountbatten, form part of the collection, and are a valuable source for Anglo-Indian relations during the period of the transfer of power.

The sections of his papers which cover his time as Viceroy and Governor-General of India, March–August 1947, have been photocopied by the India Office Library (ref. MSS Eur F 200).

MOWSHOWITSCH, DAVID (1887–1957) Member, Jewish Board of Deputies in England. Secretary of the Foreign Department, Board of Deputies, 1945–57.

The Central Archives for the History of the Jewish People, Jerusalem, have a collection of his private papers, 1919–56. Further papers – the Lucien Wolf-David Movshovicz (Mowshowitsch) collection – are in the YIVO Institute, New York. The archive of the Board of Deputies, now deposited in the London Metropolitan Archives, includes his correspondence, 1916–50s, on Palestine and foreign affairs.

MOYLE, ROLAND (DUNSTAN) (1928–) MP

(Lab) Lewisham North, 1966–74; Lewisham East, 1974–83. Minister of State, Northern Ireland Office, 1974–76; Health, 1976–79.

Mr Moyle states that he has retained some files on his parliamentary work and speeches as Minister of State for Health, together with papers on election campaigns and press-cuttings covering the period 1966–91. About 135 files of constituency material (and papers on his campaigns against motorways) are held with other Labour Party records at the Lewisham Local History Centre. Enquiries should be directed to the Archivist.

MOYOLA, BARON Major James Dawson

Chichester-Clark (1923–2002) Prime Minister, Northern Ireland, 1969–71. Stormont MP (UU) South Derry, 1960–71.

Lord Moyola stated that he had no files relating to his time as Prime Minister. He had, however, retained some unsorted papers which include constituency correspondence and copies of parliamentary speeches.

MUDIE, SIR ROBERT FRANCIS (1890–1976) Governor, Sind, 1946–47; West Punjab, 1947–49. Head, (British) Economic Mission to Yugoslavia, 1951–54.

The India Office Library has 12 boxes of papers, 1914–70, covering many aspects of his career (ref. MSS Eur F 164). A list is available (NRA 27546). The collection includes official reports from 1927 onwards; correspondence concerning the Simla conference of 1945; and papers relating to his term as Governor of the West Punjab.

MUGGERIDGE, MALCOLM (1903–90) Journalist on the *Manchester Guardian, Calcutta Statesman* and *Evening Standard*, 1930–36. Washington Correspondent, *The Daily Telegraph*, 1946–47; Deputy Editor, 1950–52; Editor of *Punch*, 1953–57.

The large collection of papers (occupying 90 ft of shelf space) was purchased by the Buswell Library, Wheaton College, Illinois. The collection includes letters, journals, sermons, book reviews, videotapes and scripts for radio and television.

MUIRSHEIL, 1ST VISCOUNT John Scott Maclay (1905–92) MP (Nat Lib and Con) Montrose Burghs, 1940–50; Renfrewshire West, 1950–64. Parliamentary Secretary, Ministry of Production, 1945; Transport and Civil Aviation, 1951–52; Minister of State, Colonial Affairs, 1956–57; Scottish Secretary, 1957–62.

According to *British Cabinet Ministers, 1900–51*, after his death his papers were dispersed. Some political papers went to Glasgow University Archives (ref. DC371) whilst family papers and other correspondence passed to Lord Maclay. His Private Office papers are contained in the various departmental files held by the Scottish Record Office. An interview recorded in 1980 is held at the LSE Library.

MULLEY, BARON Frederick William Mulley (1918–95) MP (Lab) Sheffield Park, 1950–83. Aviation Minister, 1965–67; Joint Minister of State and Minister for Disarmament, 1967–69; Transport,

1969–70 and 1974–75; Education Secretary, 1975–76; Defence Secretary, 1976–79.

Lord Mulley retained some unsorted papers.

MULLIN, CHRIS (1947–) MP (Lab) Sunderland South after 1987. Campaigner against miscarriages of justice.

Files relating to his campaign work against miscarriages of justice, particularly the Birmingham Six and Guildford Four, are in Hull University Library (ref. DMU).

MULVEY, ANTHONY J. (1882–1957) MP (Irish Nat) Fermanagh and Tyrone, 1935–50; Mid-Ulster, 1950–51.

The Public Record Office of Northern Ireland holds a collection of correspondence and papers (ref. D1862). The papers include constituents' letters, family correspondence and speech notes. His correspondents include several Stormont Nationalist MPs (such as Cahir Healy and Eddie McAteer) and members of the British Labour Party 'Friends of Ireland' Group (including Geoffrey Bing, William Hannon and Hugh Delargy). There are some letters from Chuter Ede, when Home Secretary, 1946–47. The papers cover issues such as electoral and penal reform; his abstention from Westminster until 1945; British policy on Northern Ireland; the development of the Anti-Partition League's branches in Britain; and the revival of the Irish language. There is also a typescript autobiography of Mulvey.

MURPHY, SIR WILLIAM LINDSAY (1887–1965) Colonial Service. Ceylon Civil Service, 1910–37. Governor, Bahamas, 1945–49; Acting Governor, Southern Rhodesia, 1954; Governor, Rhodesia and Nyasaland, 1957.

Rhodes House Library, Oxford, has some papers, 1911–65 (ref. MSS Brit Emp s 483 t 6). They concern his service in Ceylon, Bermuda and the Bahamas. The only African material in the collection relates to his retirement activities in Rhodesia.

MURRAY, DAVID (fl. 1950s) Maverick Liberal and Nationalist candidate.

The papers have been acquired by the National Library of Scotland.

MURRAY, SEAN (1898–1961) General Secretary, later Chairman, of the Northern Irish Communist Party.

A large collection of his papers, 1930–67, has been deposited in the Public Record Office of Northern Ireland (ref. D2162). The material is unlisted and is not generally available. The collection was used extensively by Mike Milotte for his study *Communism in Modern Ireland*. It includes private and political correspondence; diaries; speeches; election ephemera; newspaper cuttings and photographs. The collection is a useful source also for the history of the Communist Party in the Republic of Ireland and of the Northern Irish Labour Party. His early political life and participation in the Irish War of Independence is also documented.

MURRAY, THOMAS (fl. 1920–68) General Secretary, Scottish–USSR Association.

A collection of papers is deposited at the National Library of Scotland (ref. Acc 9083). A list is available (NRA 29279). There is material on the Spanish Civil War, the International Brigades Association, the Scottish–USSR Association, and his various political and trade union activities.

MYERS, BRIGADIER EDMUND CHARLES WOLF (1906–97) Military career. Served in Palestine pre-war and as a Staff College instructor, Haifa, 1940–42. On Special Operations Executive (SOE) missions in Greece, Balkans and North West Europe, 1943–45. Served in Korea, 1951–52. Chief Engineer, British Troops in Egypt, 1955–56. Deputy Director, Personnel Administration, War Office, 1956–59.

Brigadier Myers deposited his papers, 1942–54, in the Liddell Hart Centre, King's College, London, in 1978. A list is available (NRA 23075). The collection contains his miscellaneous correspondence, signals and reports regarding his activities and general SOE operations in Greece, 1942–45. Some files concern political developments in Greece. There are also contemporary photographs of Greece and a revised manuscript of his book, *Greek Entanglement*, published in 1955. Relevant material can also be found in the Woodhouse papers in the same archive.

N

NAIRNE, SIR PATRICK (DALMAHOY) (1921–)
Entered Civil Service 1947. Deputy Under-Secretary
of State, Ministry of Defence, 1970–73; Second
Permanent Secretary, Cabinet Office, 1973–75;
Permanent Secretary, Department of Health and
Social Security, 1975–81. Member, Falkland Islands
Review Committee, 1982; Government Monitor,
Hong Kong, 1984.

Sir Patrick states that he has retained six boxes
of speeches and lectures covering his time at the
Ministry of Defence, Cabinet Office, and Department
of Health and Social Security (1973–81). He has
also kept papers relating to his Falkland Islands and
Hong Kong roles. He will make provision for his
papers in due course.

NAPIER, J. CHRISTOPHER (fl. 1970s) Northern
Irish solicitor.

His working papers on Lord Widgery's inquiry
into the Bloody Sunday deaths of 30 January 1972
have been deposited in the Public Record Office of
Northern Ireland (ref. D3907). The collection comprises transcripts from the preliminary and main
hearings, statements from witnesses, photographs,
street plans, British Army logs, forensic reports,
printed material and files compiled by the National
Council of Civil Liberties.

NAPIER, SAMUEL (fl.1940s–70s) Northern Ireland
Labour Party activist. Secretary, NILP, 1964–65.

Some 350 files relating to the labour movement in
Northern Ireland, 1940–77, have been deposited in
the Public Record Office of Northern Ireland (ref.
D3702). They include material on trade unions,
housing, education and local politics. There are
extensive press-cuttings on Northern Irish politics
during the 1960s and 1970s. In addition to conference
reports and policy statements of the NILP, there
is also a minute book of the Commonwealth Labour
Party, 1943–48. Mr Napier's article and notes,

1941–69, relating to a proposed biography of Harry
Midgley were subject to a thirty-year closure rule
(ref. D3702/D/7), as were his papers on the North–
South trade union *rapprochement* of 1944–56 (ref.
D3702/D/4). These include speeches and memoranda and articles by leading figures of the Left such
as David Bleakley and William Blease.

**NATHAN, 1ST BARON Colonel Harry Louis
Nathan (1889–1963)** MP (Lib) Bethnal Green North
East, 1929–35; (Lab) Wandsworth Central, 1937–40.
Parliamentary Under-Secretary, War Office, 1945–46.
Minister of Civil Aviation, 1946–48.

British Cabinet Ministers, 1900–51 stated that the
papers are in the possession of the family, but closed
to researchers.

**NEAVE, AIREY MIDDLETON SHEFFIELD (1916–
79)** MP (Con) Abingdon, 1953–79. Joint Parliamentary Secretary, Ministry of Transport and Civil
Aviation, 1957–59. Parliamentary Under-Secretary
of State for Air, 1959. Head of Leader of the
Opposition's Private Office, 1975–79.

Some 700 files of personal, political and business
papers, 1940–79, have been deposited in the House
of Lords Record Office (ref. Hist Coll 260). A list is
available. Special conditions of access apply to this
collection.

NEEDHAM, DOROTHY MARY (1896–1987)
Research biochemist, Cambridge University,
1920–63.

The papers have been deposited in Girton College,
Cambridge. In addition to extensive research papers,
they include material on numerous charities and
political causes with which she was involved.

NEEDHAM, JOSEPH (1900–95) Scientist. Director,
Needham Research Institute (East Asian History
of Science Library), Cambridge, from 1976. Head of

British Scientific Mission to China, 1942–46; Reader in Biochemistry, 1933–66, Stanford University. Master, Gonville and Caius College, Cambridge, 1966–76.

An extensive and varied collection of his scientific, personal and family papers was acquired by Cambridge University Library in 1976. A list is available (NRA 38808). The papers (including many from the pre-war period) comprise material on the moral, theological, social and theoretical aspects of biology; science and society, including anti-war activities; Russian science, the genetics controversy and the 200th anniversary of the USSR Academy of Sciences; theological writings; politics and religion; historical interests; wartime science; Anglo-Chinese relations and the British Indonesia Committee founded in 1970. His academic correspondence, research papers and lecture notes are included in the collection. The private papers will remain closed for 50 years after his death. Those on science, society and politics at Cambridge University Library are open. The history of science papers are held at the East Asian History of Science Library, Cambridge. Other post-war papers were deposited at the Imperial War Museum in 1992.

NEILL, MAJOR SIR IVAN (1906–) Stormont MP (UU) Belfast Ballynafeigh, 1949–72. Minister of Labour and National Insurance, Northern Ireland, 1950–61; Education, 1962; Finance, 1964–65; Development, 1968. Last Speaker of Northern Ireland House of Commons, 1969–72.

Sir Ivan informed historians in 1992 that many of his papers were lost when his home was destroyed in a terrorist attack. He has retained copies of his speeches and a few papers relating to his career. These may be placed in an archive in due course. His travel memoirs were privately published in 1990.

NELLIST, DAVID (1952–) MP (Lab) Coventry South East, 1983–92.

Mr Nellist has retained some 25 boxes of constituency papers, correspondence and subject files. The collection is promised to the LSE Library, where enquiries should be directed.

NELSON, JAYNE (fl. 1980s) Peace campaigner. Active in Greenham Common protest, etc.

There are papers in the Women's Library, London Metropolitan University, concerning Greenham Common, etc.

NEWALL, 1ST BARON Marshal of the Royal Air Force Sir Cyril Louis Norton Newall (1886–1963) Royal Air Force career. Served in World Wars I and II. Chief of Air Staff, 1937–40. Governor-General and Commander-in-Chief, New Zealand, 1941–46.

There are six boxes of correspondence and reports, 1918–56, at the Royal Air Force Museum, Hendon (ref. B391–B413 and A233–A239). The Museum also holds a set of photographs (ref. P708). Some papers can also be found at the Public Record Office (ref. AIR 8/235–299).

NEWE, DR GERALD BENEDICT (1907–82) Minister of State, Department of the Prime Minister, Stormont, 1971–72. Founder and Secretary of the Northern Ireland Council of Social Service, 1948–72. Founder member of the Protestant and Catholic Encounter Group. Editor, *The Ulster Farmer*, 1931–67.

A large collection (*c.* 300 folders) of correspondence and other material, *c.* 1950–82, has been deposited in the Public Record Office of Northern Ireland (ref. D3687).

NEWENS, ARTHUR STANLEY (1930–) MP (Lab) Epping, 1964–70; Harlow, Feb. 1974–83. MEP (Lab) Central London after 1984.

Mr Newens states that nine boxes of his Epping constituency correspondence have been deposited at the Essex Record Office (ref. A6449). Access is subject to his consent. He has retained a larger collection of personal and political material, including personal diaries, Harlow constituency papers and files relating to his work in the European Parliament. Of particular interest are minutes of the former Epping CLP, 1929–35 and 1945–74 and several files on Liberation (formerly the Movement for Colonial Freedom). He will make provision for their eventual deposit in due course.

NICHOLAS, PETER (fl. 1950s–70s) Trade union convener at Rover, Tyseley Works; Treasurer of the Rover Combine Shop Stewards' Committee and later of British Leyland Trade Union Combine Committee.

Some papers and correspondence, 1950–70, are held at the Modern Records Centre, University of Warwick (ref. MSS 309). The material includes papers on the shop stewards' organisation at the Rover company and on the changes and crises within British Leyland during the 1970s. A list is available (NRA 38385).

NICHOLSON, JOHN LEONARD (1916–90) Chief Economic Adviser to the Department of Health and Social Security and to successive Secretaries of State for Social Services, 1968–76.

A substantial collection of papers has been donated to the LSE Library.

NICHOLSON, MARJORIE (1914–97) Served, International Department, TUC, 1955–72. Author, *The TUC Overseas: The Roots of Policy.*

Her research notes and personal papers are in the Trades Union Congress Library Collection, London Metropolitan University. A list is available (NRA 41904).

NICOL, DAVIDSON SYLVESTER HECTOR WILLOUGHBY (1924–94) Diplomat. Under-Secretary-General of the United Nations.

There are papers in Churchill College, Cambridge (ref. NICL).

NICOLSON, SIR HAROLD GEORGE (1886–1968) Diplomat, 1919–29. MP (Nat Lab) Leicester West, 1935–45. Parliamentary Secretary, Ministry of Information, 1940–41. Journalist and author.

The Library of Balliol College, Oxford, holds a series of diaries, 1930 to 1964. Special conditions and charges for access apply to the collection. His correspondence with his wife, Vita Sackville-West, and other personal papers are held by their son, Mr Nigel Nicolson, to whom applications for access should be made.

NICOLSON, NIGEL (1917–2004) MP (Con) Bournemouth East and Christchurch, 1952–59. Involved with the 1989 Tolstoy libel case.

It is believed that Mr Nicolson retained his papers with correspondence and press-cuttings on the Suez crisis, 1956 and material relating to his constituency de-selection. The Imperial War Museum, Depart-

ment of Sound Recordings, holds an interview covering his experiences in Austria in 1945, and the repatriation of Russians and Yugoslavs in the same year (ref. 10552/3 Ax).

NOBLE, SIR ALLAN HERBERT PERCY (1908–82) MP (Con) Chelsea, 1945–59. Parliamentary and Financial Secretary, Admiralty, 1951–55. Parliamentary Under-Secretary, Commonwealth Affairs, 1955–56. Minister of State, Foreign Affairs, 1956–59. Special Ambassador, Ivory Coast, 1961.

Churchill College, Cambridge, holds his papers. A list is available (NRA 23365). The collection includes correspondence and journals. There are some files on the Bikini Atom Bomb Tests of 1946.

NOEL-BAKER, BARON Philip John Noel-Baker (1889–1982) MP (Lab) Coventry, 1929–31; Derby, 1936–50; Derby South, 1950–70. Parliamentary Secretary, Ministry of War Transport, 1942–44. Minister of State, Foreign Office, 1945–46. Secretary of State for Air, 1946–47; Commonwealth Relations, 1947–50. Minister of Fuel and Power, 1950–51.

Over 700 boxes of papers were deposited in Churchill College, Cambridge, by Lord Noel-Baker in 1978 (ref. NBKR). A further 400 boxes were discovered and deposited after his death. The material includes files from his various ministries as well as constituency papers, 1924–70. The collection is a valuable source for British foreign and domestic policy. A detailed list is available (NRA 24828).

NORMANBROOK, 1ST BARON Sir Norman Craven Brook (1902–67) Deputy Secretary (Civil), War Cabinet, 1942. Permanent Secretary, Ministry of Reconstruction, 1943–45. Additional Secretary to the Cabinet, 1945–46; Secretary, 1947–62. Joint Secretary, Treasury, and Head of the Home Civil Service, 1956–62.

A collection of papers is held at the Bodleian Library, Oxford. The papers include drafts of speeches, invitations, luncheon engagements, etc., but the purely political material is sparse. Additional Cabinet Office papers, 1945–49, are held at the National Archives, Kew (ref. CAB 127/338–44). A list is available (NRA 32409). These include files on the establishment of *ad hoc* committees of ministers; proposed ministerial appointments; and comments on Cabinet discussions on Hugh Dalton's Budget 'leak' as well as papers on defence and India.

NORRIE, 1ST BARON Lieutenant-General Sir (Charles) Willoughby Moke Norrie (1893–1977) Military career. Served in World Wars I and II. Formed and commanded 30th Corps (Middle East), 1941–42. Commanded Royal Armoured Corps, 1943. Governor, South Australia, 1944–52; New Zealand, 1952–57.

The Liddell Hart Centre, King's College, London has reported that the papers were returned by his family to the Army Historical Branch of the Ministry of Defence. Lord Norrie had informed previous surveys that his papers included extensive press-cuttings from his time in Australia and New Zealand.

Some correspondence, 1923–52, can be found in the papers of Major-General Sir Edward Spears, at Churchill College, Cambridge.

NORRIS, VICE-ADMIRAL SIR CHARLES (FRED WIVELL) (1900–89) Naval career. Director of Naval Training and Deputy Chief of Naval Personnel, 1950–52. Flag Officer (Flotillas), Mediterranean, 1953–54. Commander-in-Chief, East Indies Station, 1954–56.

According to information received by the Liddell Hart Centre, King's College, London, the papers are to be placed in Churchill College, Cambridge. Some papers relating to his service in the Caspian Sea, 1919–20, are deposited with the Liddle Collection, Leeds University.

NORTH, MAJOR JOHN (1894–1973) Military historian and novelist. Served in World Wars I and II. Attached to the Home Office, 1944. On missions to Belgium, Holland, Germany, Greece and Italy, 1944–45. Author of North West Europe volume of the *Official History of World War II*.

The Liddell Hart Centre, King's College, London, holds an extensive collection of papers, 1939–63, mainly concerning his books on Gallipoli and World War II and his edition of Field Marshal Lord Alexander's memoirs. A list is available (NRA 23076).

NORWICH, 1ST VISCOUNT Alfred Duff Cooper (1890–1954) MP (Con) Oldham, 1924–29, and Westminster St George's, 1931–45. Secretary of State for War, 1935–37. First Lord of the Admiralty, 1937–38. Minister of Information, 1940–41. Chancellor, Duchy of Lancaster, 1941–43. Representative, French Committee of National Liberation, 1943–44. Ambassador, France, 1944–47.

A large collection of papers and correspondence has been deposited in Churchill College, Cambridge. A list is available (NRA 31392). His diaries for 1952 and 1953 and his correspondence with Lady Caroline Duff are held in the British Library (ref. Reserved MS 94). The British Library also holds the papers of his wife, Lady Diana Cooper, which include his World War I letters (ref. Add MSS 70704–20). Further correspondence may be found in the papers of Lord Beaverbrook (1928–49) at the House of Lords Record Office and the papers of Major-General Sir Edward Spears (1933–54) at Churchill College, Cambridge.

NOTT, SIR JOHN (1932–) MP (Con) St Ives, 1966–83. Secretary of State for Trade, 1979–81. Secretary of State for Defence, 1981–83.

His political papers, 1952–98, are in Churchill College, Cambridge.

NUTTING, SIR (HAROLD) ANTHONY (1920–99) MP (Con) Melton, 1946–56. PUS, Foreign Office, 1951–54; Minister of State, Foreign Office, 1954–56.

Sir Anthony retained some correspondence.

NYE, LIEUTENANT-GENERAL SIR ARCHIBALD EDWARD (1895–1967) Military commander. Director of Staff Duties, 1940. Vice-Chief of Imperial General Staff, 1941–46. Governor, Madras, 1946–48. High Commissioner, India, 1948–52; Canada, 1952–56.

Sir Archibald Nye is believed to have left no papers. Some correspondence is available in the papers of Lord Cherwell at Nuffield College, Oxford (1941–48), and of Field Marshal Sir Roy Bucher at the National Army Museum (1949–51).

O

OAKESHOTT, MICHAEL JOSEPH (1901–90)
Political philosopher. Professor of Political Science, London School of Economics, 1951–69.

There are 8 boxes and 3 transfer cases of papers, deposited in the LSE Library in 1997 through the good offices of Professor Minogue and Oliver Letwin (ref. M 1853). A list is available (NRA 43323).

O'BRIEN, CONOR CRUISE (1917–) Irish diplomat, politician and writer. United Nations official, Congo, 1961. *Teachta Dala* (Lab), Dublin North-East, 1969–77; Minister for Post and Telegraphs, 1973–77; Senator, 1977–79. Editor-in-Chief, *Observer*, 1979–81.

No information has been received regarding Dr O'Brien's papers. His account of service in the Congo was published in 1962 as *To Katanga And Back*. The Department of Sound Records at the Imperial War Museum holds a 1961 interview regarding the United Nations' role in the Congo.

O'CONNOR, GENERAL SIR RICHARD NUGENT (1889–1981) Military commander. Military Governor of Jerusalem, 1938–39. Corps commander, Western Desert and France during World War II. General Officer Commanding-in-Chief Eastern Command, 1945, and North Western Army, India, 1946–47.

There are 16 boxes of papers, 1889–1976, deposited in the Liddell Hart Centre, King's College, London. These include some post-war correspondence, 1945–49 and 1960–70. His Desert War diary (1941) is in the National Army Museum (ref. 6312–29).

ODDY, CHRISTINE MARGARET (1955–) MEP (Lab) Midlands Central, 1989–94; Coventry and North Warwickshire, 1994–99.

Her political papers, *c.* 1980–99, have been placed in Coventry Archives (ref. PA 2230).

OGMORE, 1ST BARON David Rees Rees-Williams (1903–76) MP (Lab) Croydon South, 1945–50. Parliamentary Under-Secretary, Colonies, 1947–50; Commonwealth Relations, 1950–51. Minister of Civil Aviation, 1951. President, Liberal Party, 1963–64.

A collection of papers relating to his political career from 1959 (when he joined the Liberal Party) onwards has been deposited in the National Library of Wales. A list is available (NRA 26130). In addition to correspondence concerning the Liberal Party and the Welsh Liberal Party (1959–74), there are files on Welsh affairs including devolution and relations with the European Economic Community, some material relating to the 1970 General Election and a memoir. In addition, his son, the 2nd Lord Ogmore, has also retained many of his father's papers, including diaries.

OLIVER, ADMIRAL SIR GEOFFREY NIGEL (1898–1980) Naval career from 1915. Held various commands during World War II, including 21st Aircraft Carrier Squadron, 1944–45. Assistant Chief of Naval Staff, 1947–48. Commander-in-Chief East Indies Station, 1950–52; The Nore, 1953–55.

A collection of naval and personal papers, 1945–79, has been deposited at Churchill College, Cambridge (ref. OLVR). A list is available (NRA 24831). The papers relate mainly to naval issues during and after World War II, including his East Indies posting, and some correspondence on the possible ownership of Southern Sinai, 1947–49. Some additional papers are deposited in the Royal Naval Museum, Portsmouth.

O'NEILL OF THE MARNE, BARON Captain Sir Terence O'Neill (1914–90) Prime Minister, Northern Ireland, 1963–69. Stormont MP (UU) Bannside, 1946–70. Minister of Finance, 1956–63.

It is believed that the papers have remained in family possession.

O'NEILL, SIR CON DOUGLAS WALTER (1912–88) Director, Britain in Europe Campaign, 1975.

Some papers, acquired as Director of the Britain in Europe Campaign, are deposited, with other material relating to this pressure group, in the House of Lords Record Office. The collection includes detailed material on the referendum; representations made to the broadcasting authorities on campaign coverage; subject files for January–June 1975 (*c*. 100); and financial and administrative records. Other papers are in the Bodleian Library, Oxford.

ONSLOW, LORD Sir Cranley Onslow (1926–2001) MP (Con) Woking after 1964. Chairman of the 1922 Committee, 1984–92.

Lord Onslow stated that his constituency correspondence is deposited in the Surrey Record Office under a thirty-year rule of access. His other papers are likely to be deposited with the 1922 Committee Archive in the Bodleian Library, Oxford.

ORAM, LORD Albert Edward Oram (1913–99) MP (Co-op and Lab) East Ham South, 1955–Feb. 1974. Parliamentary Secretary, Overseas Development Ministry, 1964–69.

Lord Oram has deposited 13 boxes of parliamentary papers in the LSE Library.

ORME, STANLEY (1923–2005) Salford Labour MP and Cabinet Minister.

The surviving papers, including material on the miners' strike, are to be deposited in the LSE Library.

OSBORN, SIR FREDERIC JAMES (1885–1978) Town planner. Estate Manager, Welwyn Garden City, 1919–36. Hon. Secretary and Chairman, Town and Country Planning Association, 1936–61. Editor, *Town and Country Planning*, 1949–65.

The papers have been placed in Welwyn Garden City Central Library. A list is available (NRA 34633).

OSBORN, SIR JOHN HOLBROOK (1922–) MP (Con) Sheffield Hallam, 1959–87.

His papers have been deposited in Sheffield City Library (ref. MPC). A list is available (NRA 22694). The collection includes 7 files of correspondence (1961–); files of constituency correspondence (Aug. 1976–Apr. 1977); and boxes of speeches, press

releases, articles, and Commons questions. There are also files on the 1970 General Election and the 1977 local elections, and correspondence and minutes of meetings of the Hallam Conservative Association. The constituency correspondence is closed for 50 years. Other correspondence is closed for 30 years. Additional papers and diaries covering his more recent career have also been deposited. The minutes and correspondence relating to his work as Secretary of the 1922 Committee are with the Conservative Party Archive at the Bodleian Library, Oxford.

OSMOND, JOHN (fl. 1980s) Former Chairman, Parliament for Wales Campaign. Director, Institute for Welsh Affairs. Writer and journalist.

The Welsh Political Archive, National Library of Wales, has received a group of papers, 1982–98, accumulated by him concerning the Parliament for Wales Campaign. The papers include correspondence, minutes of meetings, strategy documents, press releases and press-cuttings. The correspondents include Alex Carlile MP, Tom Ellis, Gwynfor Evans, Peter Hain MP, Lord Hooson, Lord Prys-Davies, and Rhodri Morgan MP.

O'SULLIVAN, SUE Feminist activist.

There is extensive material in the Women's Library, London Metropolitan University (Acc. 4/1998, ref. 7/SUL2). The collection includes working papers, correspondence, periodicals, publications, material about *Spare Rib* magazine, women's health issues and educational work with women in Holloway Prison.

OWEN, LORD Dr David Anthony Llewellyn Owen (1938–) MP (Lab) Plymouth Sutton, 1966–74 and Plymouth Devonport, 1974–92 (Lab until 1981, SDP, 1981–90 and Independent Social Democrat, 1990–92). Parliamentary Under-Secretary of State for Defence, 1968–70; Minister of State, Foreign and Commonwealth Affairs, 1976–77. Foreign Secretary, 1977–79; SDP co-founder, 1981; SDP leader, 1983–87, resigned over merger with the Liberals, re-elected 1988. Co-chairman, International Conference on former Yugoslavia.

Around 400 boxes of his papers, covering the period *c*. 1943–92, have been placed in Liverpool University Library (ref. D709). The collection embraces most aspects of his political career.

P

PAGET, GENERAL SIR BERNARD CHARLES TOLVER (1887–1961) Military career including various commands during World War II. Commander-in-Chief, Middle East Forces, 1944–46.

The LSE Library understands that the papers are still in family possession and may be placed in a suitable archive in due course. They are understood to include diaries and photographs from his time in Palestine, 1945–46. His letters to Lord Glyn, 1941–46, are in the Berkshire Record Office.

PAISLEY, DR IAN RICHARD KYLE (1926–) MP (DUP) North Antrim since 1970. MEP for Northern Ireland 1979–2004. DUP Leader since 1971. Stormont MP (UU) Bannside, 1970–72. Free Presbyterian minister.

Dr Paisley states that his papers are not available at present. His biographer, Clifford Smyth, cited an interview with Dr Paisley together with other sources in *Paisley: Voice of Protestant Ulster*. Recordings of his sermons and issues of the various periodicals he has edited (including *Revivalist* and *Protestant Telegraph*) are held in the Northern Ireland Political Collection at the Linen Hall Library, Belfast, and in the Bob Jones University Library, South Carolina.

PALING, WILFRED (1883–1971) MP (Lab) Doncaster, 1922–31; Wentworth, 1933–50; Dearne Valley, 1950–59. Parliamentary Secretary, Ministry of Pensions, 1941–45. Minister of Pensions, 1945–47. Postmaster-General, 1947–50.

It is understood that any surviving papers were destroyed after his death. See *British Cabinet Ministers, 1900–51*.

PALLEY, CLAIRE (DOROTHEA TAYLOR) (1931–) Professor of Law, University of Kent, 1973–84. Former lawyer in South Africa and Rhodesia. Constitutional adviser to African National Council at the 1976 Geneva talks on Rhodesia. Author of *The Constitutional History and Law of Southern Rhodesia, 1888–1965*. Constitutional adviser to the Republic of Cyprus after 1980. Principal, St Anne's College, Oxford after 1984.

Some papers have been placed in the Centre for Southern African Studies, University of York. The collection includes files on the negotiations between the Rhodesian Government and the African National Council, correspondence on the 1972 Pearce Commission, extensive political and other ephemera, her draft proposals on constitutional issues, and an almost complete set of Rhodesian High Court judgements, 1965–70.

PALMER, ARTHUR MONTAGUE FRANK (1912–94) MP (Lab) Wimbledon, 1945–50; (Lab and Co-op) Cleveland, 1952–59; Bristol Central, 1964–Feb. 1974; Bristol North-East, Feb. 1974–83.

Mr Palmer stated that he had retained extensive papers and would make provision for their eventual deposit.

PANKHURST, (ESTELLE) SYLVIA (1882–1960) Suffragette and socialist. Hon. Secretary, Women's Social and Political Union. Founder member, Abyssinia Association. Editor, *Ethiopia News*, 1936–56; *Ethiopia Observer* from 1956.

The International Institute of Social History, Amsterdam, holds the papers of Sylvia Pankhurst and the Pankhurst family. A list is available (NRA 17176). The collection includes correspondence, minute books and ephemera of various suffrage and socialist organisations; and material relating to anti-fascist campaigns, especially her support for Ethiopia and its emperor and her editorship of the *New Times* and *Ethiopia News*.

PANNELL, BARON (Thomas) Charles Pannell (1902–80) MP (Lab) Leeds West, 1949–Feb. 1974. Minister of Public Buildings and Works, 1964–66.

A collection of papers, covering the period 1935–77, has been deposited at the House of Lords Record Office (ref. Hist Coll 124). Access to the collection is restricted. All enquiries should be addressed to the Clerk of the Records.

PARISER, SIR MAURICE (1906–68) Local politician. Leader, Manchester City Council, 1962–65.

The collected papers for the period 1953–68 can be found in Manchester Central Library. The collection reflects his interest in education, the arts, regional development, and the transition to comprehensive education in the 1950s. A list is available (NRA 28131).

PARKER, JOHN (1906–87) MP (Lab) Dagenham, 1945–83. Parliamentary Under-Secretary, Dominions Office, 1945–46.

The papers have been deposited in the LSE Library. A list is available (NRA 42849).

PARKES, DR JAMES WILLIAM (1896–1981) Advocate of Christian–Jewish reconciliation. Supporter of Zionism. National Committee, Common Wealth, 1942–43. President, Jewish Historical Society, 1949–51. Director, The Parkes Library, 1956–64.

The Parkes Library, University of Southampton, holds a large collection of material (ref. BZ 7051 PAR). A list is available (NRA 13844). The collection includes personal and professional papers, as well as documentation on the Parkes Library. There is also extensive correspondence with leading Jewish and Christian figures. Special topics covered include relations between Jews and Presbyterians, Palestine (1928–46), Arab–Israeli relations (1946–54), missions to the Jews, anti-Semitism, fascism in Britain, the Eichmann Trial, and visits to the USA and Israel. There are also correspondence and minutes of a great variety of Jewish committees and organisations.

PARKIN, BENJAMIN THEAKER (1906–69) MP (Lab) Stroud 1945–50; Paddington North, 1953–69. Served Executive Committee, Union of Democratic Control.

His surviving papers have been deposited in the Brynmor Jones Library, University of Hull (ref. DBP). A list is available (NRA 41116). The papers reflect two of his major political concerns, namely housing (and the activities of private landlords) and German re-armament after World War II. The collection includes a series of correspondence spanning 1953 to 1968 and material from constituency and national levels of the Labour Party.

PARRY, SIR DAVID HUGHES (1893–1973) Professor of English Law, London University, 1930–59; Vice-Chancellor, 1945–48. Director of the University of London Institute of Advanced Legal Studies, 1947–59. President, University College, Aberystwyth, 1954–64. Moderator of the Welsh Calvinistic Methodist Connexion (Presbyterian Church of Wales), 1964–65.

An extensive collection of papers is held in the National Library of Wales. The papers reflect his wide variety of interests and activities as a lecturer and academic administrator, legal expert, public servant, Welsh nationalist and church leader.

PARRY, SIR (FRANK) HUGH (NIGEL) (1911–92) Colonial administrator. Cabinet Minister in Rhodesia.

There are papers relating to Rhodesia and Nyasaland, 1948–65, in BLCAS (Rhodes House Library) Oxford.

PARRY, ADMIRAL SIR (WILLIAM) EDWARD (1893–1972) Naval career from 1905. Served in World Wars I and II, including posting as First Naval Member of New Zealand Naval Board, 1940–42. Deputy Head of Naval Division, Control Commission Germany, Berlin, 1945–46. Director of Naval Intelligence, 1946–48. Commander-in-Chief, Indian Navy, 1948–51.

An important and substantial collection of papers relating to Parry's career has been deposited in the Imperial War Museum (ref. 86/35/1). The papers, mainly personal diaries, letters and photograph albums, cover Admiral Parry's service in both wars, in addition to his diaries and correspondence when commanding the Indian Navy, 1948–51.

PARSONS, SIR ANTHONY (DERRICK) (1922–96) Diplomat. Ambassador to Iran, 1974–79; the United Nations, 1979–82. Special adviser to the Prime Minister on foreign affairs, 1982–83. Lecturer and Research Fellow at Exeter University after 1984.

Sir Anthony informed the LSE in 1992 that his papers were to be deposited with the United Nations Career Records Project. This project was established in 1989 by St Antony's College, Oxford, and its collections are deposited in the Bodleian Library, Oxford.

PARSONS, SIR MAURICE (1910–78) Assistant to Governor, Bank of England, 1955; Executive Director, 1957; Deputy Governor, Bank of England, 1966–70.

The Bank of England Archive has some 32 files of memoranda, letters and correspondence covering the period 1954–66 (ref. ADM 13) (NRA 33132).

PART, SIR ANTONY (1916–90) Civil servant. Deputy Secretary, Ministry of Education, 1960–63; Ministry of Buildings and Works, 1965–68; Board of Trade, 1968–70; Department of Trade and Industry, 1970–74; Permanent Secretary, Department of Industry, 1974–76.

There are eight boxes of papers in Churchill College, Cambridge (ref. PART). The collection is uncatalogued and currently closed. An interview recorded in 1980 is held at the LSE Library.

PATER, JOHN EDWARD (1911–89) Civil servant. Under-Secretary for Health, 1947–73.

One box of papers is in Churchill College, Cambridge (ref. PTER).

PATON-WALSH, BRIGADIER EDMUND JAMES (1898–1985) Military career. Served in post-war Germany.

His diaries and other papers relating to the Quadripartite Commission in Germany, 1946, are in the Liddell Hart Centre for Military Archives, King's College, London.

PAUL, SIR JOHN (WARBURTON) (1916–) Colonial service. Governor, The Gambia, 1962–65, British Honduras, 1966–72 etc.

There are papers in BLCAS (Rhodes House Library), Oxford.

PAWSEY, JAMES FRANCIS (1933–) MP (Con) Rugby, 1979–83; Rugby and Kenilworth, 1983–97.

His constituency correspondence has been deposited in Warwickshire County Record Office (ref. CR 2240). A list is available (NRA 41789).

PEACHEY, CAPTAIN ALLAN THOMAS GEORGE CUMBERLAND (1896–1967) Naval career from 1914. Various commands during World War II. Commodore, Palestine and Levant, 1947–48. On staff of British Embassy, Cairo, 1950–54.

An interesting collection of papers, 1916–54, is at the National Maritime Museum and includes material relating to his service in World Wars I and II, Palestine, Suez and NATO (ref. PCY).

PEARCE, BERT (fl. 1940s–50s) Prominent Welsh Communist activist.

There are papers for the post-war period in the Welsh Political Archive, National Library of Wales.

PECK, SIR JOHN (HOWARD) (1916–95) Diplomat, 1946–73. Civil servant, 1937–46; Assistant Private Secretary to Prime Minister, 1940–46. UK Permanent Representative to the Council of Europe, 1959–62. Ambassador to Senegal, 1962–66 and Mauritania, 1962–65; Republic of Ireland, 1970–73.

Some correspondence, 1941–50, is in the Attlee papers in the Bodleian Library, Oxford. The papers of Lord Cherwell at Nuffield College, Oxford, include some wartime correspondence, 1939–44. Sir John's memoirs of his Irish posting were published in 1978 as *Dublin From Downing Street*.

PEDDER, VICE-ADMIRAL SIR ARTHUR REID (1904–95) Naval career. Assistant Chief of Naval Staff (Warfare), 1953–54. Flag Officer, Aircraft Carriers, 1954–56. Commander, Allied Naval Forces, Northern Europe, 1957–59.

A tape and transcripts of his naval memoirs, 1936–60, are in Churchill College, Cambridge.

PEDLER, SIR FREDERICK JOHNSON (1908–91) Colonial Service, 1930–47; Secretary to Lord Hailey in Africa, 1939 and 1940; Chief British Economic Representative, Dakar, 1942. United Africa Company, 1947–68; Chairman, 1965–68.

Some correspondence, papers and diaries have been placed in Rhodes House Library, Oxford (ref. MSS Afr s 1814). A list is available (NRA 26285). The collection includes files on various economic missions to the Belgian Congo and French West Africa, 1942–72; the Colonial Office Recruitment Branch, 1946–47; the United Africa Company, 1948–72; and conferences on African affairs, 1958–81. There are also some pre-war and wartime diaries of and reports on Tanganyika, the Congo and Lord Hailey's African Surveys. Rhodes House Library also has a 1970 interview on his career, 1930–68 (ref. MSS Afr s 1718).

PEIERLS, SIR RUDOLF ERNST (1907–95) Scientist. Fellow of the Royal Society. Professor of Mathematical Physics, Oxford University, 1963–74. Served during World War II on the Atomic Energy Project, Birmingham, 1940–43; USA, 1943–46.

Sir Rudolf deposited thirty boxes of papers in the Bodleian Library, Oxford, in 1974. A list is available (NRA 20805). The collection documents his research and teaching career and, in particular, his role in the development of nuclear weapons during World War II, and his subsequent involvement with disarmament and the Pugwash movement.

PENHALIGON, DAVID CHARLES (1944–86) MP (Lib, then Lib Dem) Truro 1974–86.

His constituency correspondence, 1974–86, is in Cornwall Record Office (ref. AD 1010/1–267). A list is available (NRA 37638). Other papers are believed to remain with the family.

PENNEY, BARON Sir William George Penney **(1909–91)** Director, Atomic Weapons Research Establishment, Aldermaston, 1953–59. Chairman of the Atomic Energy Authority, 1964–67.

It is understood no papers have survived. Penney retained few papers and those that he had kept he destroyed before his death. Some correspondence is contained within the papers of several leading scientists. These include Lord Jackson (Imperial College, London), Sir Edward Bullard (Churchill College, Cambridge) and Lord Hinton (the Institute of Mechanical Engineering).

PENNEY, MAJOR-GENERAL SIR (WILLIAM) RONALD CAMPBELL (1896–1964) Military career. Served in World Wars I and II; various Signals Commands, Middle East, North Africa and Italy, 1941–44; Director of Intelligence, HQ Supreme Allied Commander, South East Asia, 1945. Assistant Controller (Munitions), Ministry of Supply, 1946–49, and attached to the Foreign Office, 1953–57.

Three boxes of papers, 1920–62, are deposited in the Liddell Hart Centre, King's College, London. They mainly concern his service in World War II and include correspondence, 1945–62, on Anzio. The earlier part of the collection includes material on his time in Shanghai, 1931–32.

PEPLER, SIR GEORGE LIONEL (1882–1959) Town Planner. Chief Technical Adviser, Ministry of Town and Country Planning, 1943–46. Chairman, Inter-Allied Committee for Physical Planning and Reconstruction, 1942–45. Planning Adviser to the Government of Singapore, 1950–54.

A collection of books, maps, drawings and correspondence is held in the Department of Urban and Regional Planning, Strathclyde University (NRA 12634).

PERHAM, DAME MARGERY (1895–1982) Academic and pioneer in African studies. Fellow of Nuffield College, 1939–63; Reader in Colonial Administration, Oxford University, 1939–48.

Some 771 boxes of diaries, correspondence and papers are held at Rhodes House, Oxford. A list is available (NRA 33434). Her research papers include 165 notebooks on twentieth-century Africa and the transcripts of several interviews with politicians and colonial civil servants. There are also copies of her lectures and teaching notes, including post-war training for the Colonial Service during decolonisation. The largest part of the collection (310 boxes) covers African countries in detail. For each country, there are separate personal correspondence series and files on administration, national affairs, and constitutional and political development. These files also hold Colonial Office fact sheets and large collections of press-cuttings on topics including agriculture, education, health and race relations.

There are additional files on other Commonwealth countries and on decolonisation and development policies of non-British colonial powers.

PEROWNE, STEWART HENRY (1901–89) Orientalist and historian. Served Baghdad, Cyrenaica, etc. Married to Dame Freya Stark.

There are papers on Iraq, etc. in the Middle East Centre, St Antony's College, Oxford. A list is available (NRA 42967). The collection includes Iraq correspondence, 1942–57.

PERRY, WALTER (1921–) Academic administrator. First Vice-Chancellor, The Open University.

The Open University has his papers relating to the Open University, his notes for speeches, lectures etc.

PESTELL, SIR JOHN (1916–2005) Colonial Service. Secretary/Comptroller to Sir Humphrey Gibbs as Governor of Southern Rhodesia.

His diaries and papers concerning Rhodesia in the crucial early years after UDI, 1965–69, are in Rhodes House Library (BLCAS), Oxford (ref. Mss Afr s 2208).

PETHICK-LAWRENCE, 1ST BARON Frederick William Pethick-Lawrence (1871–1961) MP (Lab) Leicester West, 1923–31; Edinburgh East, 1935–45. Secretary of State for India and Burma, 1945–47.

Correspondence and papers, including those of his wife, are held at Trinity College, Cambridge. The India Office Library has a small collection of additional papers on Burma and India (ref. MSS Eur D 540) (NRA 25125).

PHILIPS, SIR CYRIL (HENRY) (1912–) Professor of Oriental History, London University, 1946–80; Director of the School of Oriental and African Studies, 1957–76. Chairman, Royal Commission on Criminal Procedure, 1978–80.

Seventeen boxes concerning his chairmanship of the Royal Commission on Criminal Procedure are held at the LSE Library. The collection includes minutes, oral and written evidence, correspondence and copies of the Commission's final reports.

PHILLIPS, MORGAN WALTER (1902–63) Labour Party official. Secretary of Research Department, 1941–44. Secretary of the Labour Party, 1944–62. Chairman, Socialist International, 1948–57.

The papers are held in the Labour Party Archives at the Labour History Archive and Study Centre, Manchester. A list is available (NRA 14863 pt 3, General Secretary Papers, 1945–64). Of 37 boxes in the collection, 27 comprise subject files, 7 contain correspondence with trade unions, and 3 hold correspondence with regional offices. An additional 22 boxes contain correspondence with constituency branches of the Labour Party.

PHILLIPSON, SIR SYDNEY (1892–1966) Colonial Service. Financial Secretary, Nigeria, 1945–48. Financial and constitutional adviser to Southern Cameroons Government, 1959–61.

Some correspondence and papers are held at Rhodes House Library, Oxford (ref. MSS Afr s 2063). The collection covers his career from 1913 and includes papers on the Southern Cameroons, 1959–62.

PHIPPS, DR COLIN BARRY (1934–) MP (Lab) Dudley West, Feb. 1974–79. Founder member, SDP. Chairman, Clyde Petroleum after 1983.

Dr Phipps has retained his political and private papers. These include all files on his several election campaigns and period in Parliament, the Council of Europe, and the Western European Union. There are also papers on the formation of the SDP and his period on its National Committee and as an SDP candidate. Other documents relate to various working parties and to the UK oil and gas industry (especially the establishment of Britoil).

PICKERING, SIR EDWARD (1912–2003) Newspaper editor and executive. Editor, *Daily Express*, 1957–62. Executive Vice-Chairman, Times Newspapers Ltd after 1982; Chairman, Times Supplements Ltd after 1989.

Sir Edward stated that he had retained some personal correspondence with politicians and other leading public figures.

PIERCY, 1ST BARON William Piercy (1886–1966) Economist and industrialist. Principal Assistant Secretary, Ministry of Supply and Ministry of Production, and Personal Assistant to the Deputy Prime Minister during World War II. Chairman, Industrial and Commercial Finance Corporation, 1945–64. Director of the Bank of England, 1945–56. President, National Institute of Industrial Psychology, 1946–63. Chairman, Wellcome Trust, 1960–65.

A collection of papers is held at the LSE Library. A list is available (NRA 28048). The collection covers his career from 1915 to 1966, and includes a series of subject files from his time as Personal Assistant to Clement Attlee, 1943–45. There are also papers, memoranda, correspondence and press-cuttings on the Industrial and Commercial Finance Corporation, 1945–64; the Revolving Fund for Industry, 1953–57; the Acton Trust Society, 1962–66; the BBC; and the Committee of Inquiry on the Rehabilitation of Disabled Persons (official records of the 'Piercy Committee'). Further papers concern Ghana; the Institution of Works Managers; the Labour Party; the London School of Economics and London University, 1950–66; and the National Institute of Industrial Psychology, 1947–52.

PIEROTTI, A. MURIEL (d. 1982) Feminist and trade unionist.

Papers, including material relating to the Status of Women Committee and the Joint Standing Committee of Women's Organisations, have been placed in the Women's Library, London Metropolitan University (ref. 7/AMP). A list is available (NRA 33573).

PIKE, LIEUTENANT-GENERAL SIR WILLIAM GREGORY HUDDLESTONE (1905–92) Military career. Served in World War II. Chief of Royal Artillery, 1st Commonwealth Division, Korea, 1951–52. Director of Staff Duties, War Office, 1954–57. Chief of Staff, Far East Land Forces, 1957–60. Vice-Chief of the Imperial General Staff, 1960–63.

A large collection of papers relating to the Korean War is deposited with the Royal Artillery Institute, Woolwich. It includes his diaries, 1951–52; reports, unit strength and casualty statistics; maps; post-campaign disbandment and assessment papers; and material relating to battle honours awarded to the Commonwealth Division in Korea.

The Imperial War Museum's Department of Sound Records holds an interview with General Pike regarding his artillery command during the Korean War, including his memories of Operation 'Commando' and the defence of Imjin River (ref. 8995/3).

PIM, SIR RICHARD PIKE (1900–87) Police officer. Northern Ireland civil servant, 1922–39; in charge of

Churchill's War Room at the Admiralty and the Map Room at Downing Street, 1939–45; Inspector-General of the Royal Ulster Constabulary, 1945–61.

His memoirs are deposited in the Public Record Office of Northern Ireland (ref. T3620).

PINCHAM, ROGER JAMES (1935–) Liberal Party activist; Chairman, 1979–82; on National Executive, 1974–75 and 1978–87.

Mr Pincham holds extensive files of correspondence, minutes and other papers relating to Liberal politics. These include material on the 1981 establishment of the Alliance and the Liberal Party's negotiations with the SDP prior to the 1983 election. He also retains material from his candidacy in several elections. The papers are unsorted and currently unavailable to researchers, but he intends to make provision for them in due course.

PIRIE, AIR CHIEF MARSHAL SIR GEORGE CLARK (1896–1980) Royal Air Force career. Allied Air Commander-in-Chief, South-East Asia, 1946–47. Inspector-General, RAF, 1948. Air Member for Supply and Organisation, 1948–50. Head of Air Force Staff, British Joint Mission to United States, 1950–51.

His collected papers, correspondence and diary extracts, 1918–73, have been placed in the Liddell Hart Centre, King's College, London.

PITMAN, SIR (ISAAC) JAMES (1901–85) MP (Con) Bath, 1945–64.

Some correspondence, papers and press-cuttings have been deposited at the LSE Library. They concern monetary reform and the Bank of England, 1958–66; resale price maintenance, 1947–51; the Board of Trade Committee on Management, 1946; and the Standing Committee on Women's Organisations, 1950–51.

PITT, TERENCE JOHN (1937–86) MEP (Lab) Midlands West, 1984–86. Head of Labour Party Research Department, 1965–74.

The papers are in the Labour History Archive and Study Centre, University of Manchester. A list is available (NRA 30410). The collection includes minutes of the TUC Economic Committee as well as 94 files arranged alphabetically by subject.

PLATTS-MILLS, JOHN FAITHFUL FORTESCUE (1906–2001) MP (Lab, then Ind), Finsbury, 1945–50. President, Haldane Society. Vice-President, International Association of Democratic Lawyers.

His political papers, diaries and general files have been deposited in the Brynmor Jones Library, University of Hull.

PLAYFAIR, SIR EDWARD WILDER (1909–99) Treasury civil servant, 1934–56; seconded to Control Commission, Germany and Austria, 1946–47. Permanent Under-Secretary of State for War, 1956–59. Permanent Secretary, Ministry of Defence, 1960–61.

According to information received by the Liddell Hart Centre, King's College, London, Sir Edward kept no papers.

The British Oral Archive of Political and Administrative History at the LSE Library holds an interview, recorded in 1980. The papers of Stanley Gill, deposited in the Science Museum Library, include correspondence, 1964–71 (NRA 21399).

PLOWDEN, BARON   Edwin Noel Plowden (1907–2001) Public Servant.

Two boxes of his papers on the Common Market and the United States of Europe, 1961–73, are in Churchill College, Cambridge (ref. PLDN). A list is available (NRA 44271).

PLUMTREE, AIR VICE-MARSHAL ERIC (1919–90) Royal Air Force career. Personal Staff Officer to Commander-in-Chief, Middle East Air Force, 1947–49. Air Adviser to UK High Commissioner, Ottawa, 1965–67. Director, Air Plans, Ministry of Defence (Air), 1968–69. Co-ordinator of Anglo-American Relations, Ministry of Defence, 1977–84.

According to information received by the Liddell Hart Centre, King's College, London, the only surviving papers are logbooks which are to be given to the Royal Air Force Museum, Hendon.

POCHKIN, SIR EDWARD (1909–90) Medical specialist in radiation protection and risk estimation. Chairman, International Commission on Radiological Protection, 1962–69; UK representative, United Nations Scientific Committee on Effects of Atomic Radiation, 1956–82.

There are three boxes of working papers, 1948–90, at the Wellcome Contemporary Medical Archives Centre, London (ref. Acc 372). Most of the material is from the 1960s and 1970s and comprises notes, memoranda, reports and correspondence.

POLLITT, HARRY (1890–1960) Communist propagandist. General Secretary of the Communist Party of Great Britain, 1929–39 and 1941–56; Chairman from 1956.

Some 20 boxes of his papers form part of the archives of the former Communist Party of Great Britain, now deposited in the Labour History Archive and Study Centre, Manchester. The collection includes correspondence, speeches and articles, notes for speeches, pocket diaries, cuttings, photographs, memorabilia and printed material. The later material includes diaries and press-cuttings of visits to Eastern Europe and India, 1949–59. The collection is a rich source for the history of the pre-war Left in Britain and in particular the British involvement in the Spanish Civil War.

POLLOCK, JAMES HUEY HAMILL (1893–1982) Colonial Service. Chief Civil Adviser to General Officer Commanding British Troops in Palestine, 1948. Member, Senate of Northern Ireland, 1954–57.

A collection of family papers at the Northern Ireland Public Record Office includes Pollock's correspondence as District Commissioner and Chief Adviser in Jerusalem, 1944–48. The papers were subject to a 50-year rule of access. The Middle East Centre at St Antony's College, Oxford, holds engagement books together with various papers and notes on religion in Palestine.

PONSONBY, SIR CHARLES EDWARD (1879–1976) MP (Con) Sevenoaks, 1935–50.

Certain papers relating to his career are deposited at Rhodes House Library, Oxford. They mainly concern his commercial interests in Tanganyika, particularly in the sisal industry, but there are also miscellaneous notes and reports on labour unrest in Eastern Nigeria.

POPE, SIR GEORGE REGINALD (1902–82) General Manager, *The Times*, 1965–67; Director, Times Newspapers Ltd., 1967–76. Member, Newspaper Proprietors' Association, 1938–79.

A collection of papers is held at the Modern Records Centre, Warwick University (ref. MSS 271). The collection consists mainly of agendas, circulars, and minutes for meetings of the Newspaper Proprietors' Association's Joint Board, council, executive committee and other committees, 1944–79, and material on the NPA's Labour Executive and meetings with various unions in London and Manchester, 1965–71. There is also some general correspondence for the period 1938–69.

POPPER, SIR KARL RAIMUND (1902–94) Philosopher and political theorist. Author of *The Open Society and its Enemies* (1945). Professor of Logic and Scientific Method, London School of Economics, 1949–69.

A large collection of papers (463 boxes) has been deposited in the Hoover Institution, Stanford University, California. A microfilm of these papers is available at the LSE Library. The collection includes speeches and writings, course material, conference papers, sound recordings and photographs.

PORTAL OF HUNGERFORD, 1ST VISCOUNT Marshal of the Royal Air Force Sir Charles Frederick Algernon Portal (1893–1971) Served in World Wars I and II. Chief of Air Staff, 1940–45. Controller, Atomic Energy, Ministry of Supply, 1946–51.

Copies of his correspondence with Winston Churchill during World War II are held at Christ Church, Oxford. No recent details have been received regarding other private and personal letters believed to have remained in family possession. Further correspondence is available in the papers of Lord Cherwell at Nuffield College, Oxford (1940–56), and of Lord Avon at Birmingham University Library (1969–76). The Avon collection also includes letters from Lady Portal.

PORTER, RODNEY ROBERT (1917–85) Professor of Biochemistry, Oxford University, 1967–85. Joint winner of the 1972 Nobel Prize for Medicine.

The Bodleian Library, Oxford, has 57 boxes of correspondence and working papers (ref. MSS Eng misc c 995–1011, d 1398–1434, e 1534–36). They include files on the World Health Organisation, 1964–84, the Medical Research Council and the

House of Commons Education, Science and Arts Committee, 1982. The collection is subject to restricted access.

PORTER, DAME SHIRLEY (1930–) Leader, Westminster City Council after 1983.

Enquiries concerning papers relating to her court case should be directed to the LSE Library.

POWELL, (JOHN) ENOCH (1912–98) MP (Con) Wolverhampton South West, 1950–Feb. 1974; (UU) South Down, Oct 1974–87. Parliamentary Secretary, Ministry of Housing and Local Government, 1955–57. Financial Secretary to the Treasury, 1957–58. Minister of Health, 1960–63.

The main collection of his political papers (42 boxes) has been placed in Churchill College, Cambridge (ref. POWL). The archive was opened in 2003 and can be accessed via the Churchill website. Enoch Powell apparently never kept a diary.

Some papers relating to his years in Northern Irish politics have been deposited in the Public Record Office of Northern Ireland (ref. D3107add). They include a large series of correspondence with constituents and with the Northern Ireland Office, 1974–80. There are also transcript copies of some speeches given in 1984 (ref. D3107add). A collection of speeches covering the period 1969–74 is held at the University of St Andrews Library. An interview with Anthony Seldon, recorded for the Oral History Project, is held at the LSE Library.

POWELL, SIR RICHARD (ROYLE) (1909–) Civil servant, 1931–68. Under-Secretary, Ministry of Defence, 1946–48. Deputy Secretary, Admiralty, 1948–50; Ministry of Defence, 1950–56. Permanent Secretary, Ministry of Defence, 1956–59; Board of Trade, 1960–68.

The British Oral Archive of Political and Administrative History at the LSE Library holds an interview recorded in 1980.

POWER, ADMIRAL OF THE FLEET SIR ARTHUR JOHN (1889–1960) Naval Commander. Served in World Wars I and II. Second Sea Lord and Chief of Naval Personnel, 1946–48. Commander-in-Chief, Mediterranean Station, 1949–50; Portsmouth, 1950–52; Naval Commander-in-Chief, Home Fleet (designate), 1951–52. Allied Commander-in-Chief, Channel and North Sea Command, 1952.

A collection of diaries, notebooks and correspondence, 1905–50, is available at the British Library (ref. Add MSS 56093–8).

POWER, ADMIRAL SIR MANLEY LAURENCE (1904–81) Naval career. Served in World War II. Fifth Sea Lord and Deputy Chief of Naval Staff, 1957–59. Commander-in-Chief, Portsmouth, Allied Commander-in-Chief, Channel, and Commander-in-Chief, Home Station (Designate), 1959–61.

His autobiography has been deposited in Churchill College, Cambridge. A list is available (NRA 18561). Two folders of papers relating to World War II operations are deposited at the Imperial War Museum.

POYNTON, SIR (ARTHUR) HILTON (1905–96) Civil servant. Permanent Under-Secretary of State, Colonial Office, 1959–66.

A tape and transcript of an interview covering his time at the Colonial Office is in Rhodes House Library, Oxford. A separate interview recorded in 1980 for the British Oral Archive of Political and Administrative History is deposited at the LSE Library.

PRENTICE, LORD   Sir Reginald (Ernest) Prentice (1923–2001) MP (Lab) East Ham North, 1957–74; Newham North East, 1974–79 (joined Conservative Party, 1977); (Con) Daventry, 1979–87. Minister of State, Department of Education and Science, 1964–66; Minister of Public Building and Works, 1966–67; Overseas Development, 1967–69 and 1975–76; Secretary of State for Education and Science, 1974–75. Minister for Social Security and Minister for the Disabled, 1979–81.

His correspondence and papers, covering the period 1947–2000, have been placed in the LSE Library. They include correspondence, etc. on his de-selection by Newham North East, his joining the Conservatives, etc. There is also general correspondence, articles, speeches, notes and draft chapters.

PRESCOTT, JOHN LESLIE (1938–) MP (Lab) Hull East since 1970. Deputy Prime Minister after 1997.

A large collection of subject and case files dating from 1971 onwards (with regular subsequent deposits) is held at the Brynmor Jones Library, University of Hull (ref. DMR). The collection includes constituency and general correspondence (1971–89), especially on shipping and the fishing industry, material on the National Union of Seamen and files on his campaign for the deputy leadership of the Labour Party (NRA 41129).

PREST, ALAN RICHMOND (1919–84) Economist. Professor of Economics (with particular reference to the public sector), London School of Economics, 1970–84.

There are papers in the LSE Library, particularly concerning Personal Injury Compensation. A list is available (NRA 42239).

PRETTY, AIR MARSHAL SIR WALTER (PHILLIP GEORGE) (1909–75) Royal Air Force career. Director-General of Organisation, Air Ministry, 1958. Air Officer Commanding-in-Chief, Signals Command, 1961–64. Deputy Chief of the Defence Staff (Personnel and Logistics), 1964–66.

Some papers are available at the Royal Air Force Museum, Hendon. They consist of logbooks, notebooks and published material, 1928–56 (ref. AC 75/24); letters chiefly concerning his service appointments, 1951–66 (refs AC 75/25 and AC 76/12); and photographs and press-cuttings, 1950–75.

PRICE, SIR (CHARLES) ROY (1893–1976) Served in the Colonial Office and Dominions Office. Deputy High Commissioner, South Africa, 1940–42; Australia, 1948–50. High Commissioner, New Zealand, 1949–53.

Some correspondence, 1928–72, is available at the Bodleian Library, Oxford (ref. MS Eng Litt d 414).

PRICE, CHRISTOPHER (1932–) MP (Lab) Birmingham Perry Barr, 1966–70; Lewisham West, Feb. 1974–83.

His constituency correspondence and subject files for the period 1964–70 are held at the Brynmor Jones Library, University of Hull (ref. DMP). A later deposit includes files relating to miscarriages of Justice, 1969–99.

PRICE, MORGAN PHILIPS (1885–1973) MP (Lab) Whitehaven, 1929–31; Forest of Dean, 1935–50; Gloucestershire West, 1950–59.

The papers are held by the Gloucestershire Record Office. A list is available (NRA 30262). The papers include general political correspondence, 1906–73; foreign policy files and correspondence, including material on Russia, Eastern Europe, the Mediterranean and Kenya, 1930–73 (*c.* 28 files); files on domestic politics (*c.* 25 files); miscellaneous personal papers (37 files); and literary papers, scrapbooks and photographs.

PRIOR, BARON James Michael Leathes Prior **(1927–)** MP (Con) Lowestoft, 1959–83; Waveney, 1983–87. Minister of Agriculture, Fisheries and Food, 1970–72; Lord President of the Council and Leader of the House of Commons, 1972–74; Secretary of State for Employment, 1979–81; Northern Ireland, 1981–84.

Lord Prior states that he has retained some papers. These are unavailable to researchers at present.

PRITT, DENIS NOEL (1887–1972) MP (Lab, later Ind Lab) Hammersmith North, 1935–50.

His political and legal papers, 1938–61, are in the LSE Library. A list is available (NRA 25121) They include correspondence, printed material, occasional diary notes and press-cuttings on a wide variety of topics including the 1945 election; trips to socialist countries, 1946–61; Pritt's work as an MP; the Korean War; Jomo Kenyatta; China; Hungary; Ghana; the Reichstag fire; chemical warfare; the Munich agreement; and the Helsinki Conference.

PROFUMO, JOHN DENNIS (1915–) MP (Con) Kettering, 1940–45; Stratford-upon-Avon, 1950–63. Joint Parliamentary Secretary, Ministry of Transport and Civil Aviation, 1952–57. Minister of State, Foreign Affairs, 1959–60. Secretary of State for War, 1960–63.

The papers which he has retained are not available for research.

PROTHERO, CLIFF (1898–1990) Labour activist. Secretary, Welsh Regional Council of Labour.

His papers, 1917–89, are in the National Library of Wales.

PUCKEY, SIR WALTER CHARLES (1899–1983) Promoter of factory automation. Founder, Management Selection Ltd., 1957. Author of several works on management.

His papers are in the Institution of Electrical Engineers Archive, London. A list is available (NRA 40843).

PURDIE, ROBERT (BOB) (1940–) Historian and radical campaigner. Active in Young Socialists, Socialist Labour League and International Marxist Group, 1967–74. Organiser, Anti-Internment League, 1972–73. Ruskin College lecturer.

Some correspondence, papers and pamphlets are at the Modern Records Centre, University of Warwick (ref. MSS 149). A list is available (NRA 20684). The material includes files relating to the Irish Solidarity Campaign, the Troops Out Movement, and the Anti-Internment League, as well as various nationalist and socialist journals and publications. There are also some items concerning the Vietnam Solidarity Campaign, including leaflets and notes for articles and speeches, 1966–72, and some records of the International Marxist Group, particularly concerning Ireland. All unpublished material relating to the International Marxist Group is closed to researchers.

PURSEY, COMMANDER HARRY (1891–1980) MP (Lab) Hull East, 1945–70. Journalist and lecturer. Naval career, 1907–36.

A large collection of papers is held at the Brynmor Jones Library, University of Hull (ref. DPU). This includes his parliamentary and constituency papers for the period 1945–70. Enquiries regarding access should be directed to the Archivist. Commander Pursey's naval papers, including his correspondence with Lionel Yexley, have been acquired by the National Maritime Museum (ref. MS 80/098) (NRA 20623).

PYM, LORD Francis Leslie Pym **(1922–)** MP (Con) Cambridgeshire, 1961–83; Cambridgeshire South, 1983–87. Secretary of State for Northern Ireland, 1973–74; Defence, 1979–81. Chancellor of the Duchy of Lancaster, Paymaster-General and Leader of the House of Commons, 1981. Foreign Secretary, 1982–83.

Lord Pym has retained 20 box files of papers. Any enquiries should be made directly to him.

PYMAN, GENERAL SIR HAROLD ENGLISH (1908–71) Military career. Served in World War II. Chief of Staff, General Headquarters, Middle East Land Forces, 1946–49. Director-General, Fighting Vehicles, Ministry of Supply, 1951–53. Director of Weapons and Development, War Office, 1955–56. Deputy Chief of Imperial General Staff, 1958–61. Commander-in-Chief, Allied Forces, Northern Europe, 1961–63.

There are 19 boxes of papers and diaries, 1939–71, deposited at the Liddell Hart Centre, King's College, London. A list is available (NRA 23085). The diaries cover the years 1945–49, 1953–57 and 1961–63. There are also extensive post-war correspondence, lectures, speeches, articles and press-cuttings. His correspondence regarding the Royal Tank Regiment, 1920–68, includes letters exchanged with Sir Basil Liddell Hart, 1955–58. The section of the collection relating to his NATO role, 1961–63, includes material on Norwegian defence policy.

R

RAFFAN, KEITH WILLIAM TWORT (1949–)
MP (Con) Delyn, 1983–92.

Many papers are deposited with the Welsh Political Archive at the National Library of Wales. They include his House of Commons office papers on the Welsh Select Committee and two successful Private Members Bills. There are also constituency correspondence on local issues and subject files on national issues together with speeches and press releases. A list is available (NRA 35979). Permission of the donor is required to consult the collection.

RAISIN, JIM W. (1904–74) Labour Party official. Organiser, London and Home Counties Labour Party from 1946; Regional Organiser for the Northern Home Counties Region, 1958–69.

A collection of papers has been placed in the London Metropolitan Archives (ref. 2783/JWR). A list is available (NRA 33032). The papers constitute a significant addition to the London Labour Party records, also held at the LMA. They include London District Organiser's Reports for the National Agent, 1946–58; Regional Organiser's Reports, 1959–68; and correspondence, 1946–69.

RAMELSON, MARION (fl. 1940s) Communist Party organiser and historian of the women's movement.

A small collection of papers, including a diary of her 1949 London–Moscow–Peking–Prague trip, is held with the archives of the former Communist Party of Great Britain, now deposited in the Labour History and Archives Centre, Manchester.

RAMSBOTHAM, SIR PETER (EDWARD) (1919–) Diplomat. Ambassador, Iran, 1971–74; USA, 1974–77. Governor and Commander-in-Chief, Bermuda, 1977–80.

Sir Peter has retained some papers. These include despatches and lectures on Watergate, correspondence and press cuttings. He has never kept a diary. He is willing to make his papers available to researchers.

RAMSEY, (ARTHUR) MICHAEL (1904–88) Anglican clergyman. Professor of Divinity, University of Cambridge, 1950–52; Bishop of Durham, 1952–56; Archbishop of York, 1956–61. Archbishop of Canterbury, 1961–74.

The papers and correspondence are held in Lambeth Palace Library.

RAMSEY, IAN THOMAS (1915–72) Bishop of Durham, 1966–72.

A collection of papers is held at the Durham Dean and Chapter Library.

RANCE, MAJOR-GENERAL SIR HUBERT ELVIN (1898–1974) Military career. General Staff, Western Command, 1943–45. Director of Civil Affairs, Burma, 1945–46. Governor, Burma, 1946–48; Trinidad and Tobago, 1950–55.

Four boxes of letters and papers, 1945–72, are held at the India Office Library (ref. MSS Eur F 169). A list is available (NRA 25125). The collection consists of recollections and official documents by British officials and politicians involved in the events leading up to the transfer of power in 1948. Correspondents include Lord Mountbatten and Malcolm MacDonald. There are also correspondence, press-cuttings and related papers concerning his return to Burma in 1956 as an official guest of the Burmese government. Some are published in Hugh Tinker's two-volume documentary history of the transfer of power, *Burma: The Struggle for Independence, 1944–48*.

RANGER, TERENCE OSBORN (1929–) Professor of Race Relations and Fellow of St Antony's College, Oxford after 1987. Historian.

A microfilm of correspondence, notes, reports and memoranda, as well as publications on nationalist movements in Rhodesia, 1958–78, is available in the Institute of Commonwealth Studies, London University and in the John Rylands Library, University of Manchester. Rhodes House Library (BLCAS) Oxford also has papers, including correspondence and minutes of the Britain–Zimbabwe Society, 1981–96.

RANKIN, JOHN (1890–1973) MP (Lab) Glasgow Tradeston, 1945–55; Glasgow Govan, 1955–73.

There are some papers for the period 1946 to 1949 at the Mitchell Library, Glasgow. The material consists of correspondence and miscellaneous papers mostly concerning the Glasgow socialist, John Maclean.

RANKINE, SIR JOHN DALZELL (1907–87) Colonial Service. Colonial Secretary, Barbados, 1945; Chief Secretary, Kenya, 1947. British Resident, Zanzibar, 1952–54. Governor, Western Region, Nigeria, 1954–60.

A number of files on the Western Region, Nigeria, 1954, is deposited in Rhodes House Library, Oxford.

RAPP, SIR THOMAS CECIL (1893–1984) Diplomat. Head of the British Economic Mission to Greece, 1946–47. Ambassador, Mexico, 1947–50. Head of Middle East Office, Cairo, 1950–53.

A copy of his unpublished memoirs is deposited at St Antony's College, Oxford. A list is available (NRA 20811). Most periods of his service are covered, including events in the Canal Zone and Egypt during the early 1950s.

REDCLIFFE-MAUD, BARON Sir John (Primatt Redcliffe) Maud **(1906–82)** Second Secretary, Ministry of Food, 1941–44; Secretary, Ministry of Reconstruction, 1944–45; Office of Lord President of the Council, 1945. Permanent Secretary, Ministry of Education, 1945–52; Ministry of Fuel and Power, 1952–58. Ambassador, South Africa, 1961–63 (High Commissioner, 1959–61) and High Commissioner, Basutoland, Bechuanaland and Swaziland, 1959–63. Chairman, Royal Commission on Local Government in England, 1966–69.

The papers are held at the LSE Library. About half relate to his wartime activities in the Ministry of Food

and later the Ministry of Reconstruction. There are also files on the Ministry of Education, 1945–52; UNESCO conferences, 1946–52; the Ministry of Fuel and Power and the Ministry of Power, 1952–58; and South African affairs, 1959–63. Rhodes House Library, Oxford has speeches, press-cuttings and photographs from his time as High Commissioner, 1959–63, together with his wife's diaries. The papers of Sir Francis Hill, in Nottingham University Library, include one box of files on the Redcliffe-Maud Commission on Local Government.

REDDAWAY, (ARTHUR FREDERICK) JOHN (1916–90) Deputy Commissioner-General, United Nations Relief and Works Agency, 1960–68. Administrative Secretary, Cyprus, 1957–60. Director-General, Arab–British Centre, London, 1970–80.

There are papers concerning his involvement in Cyprus in Rhodes House Library (BLCAS) Oxford.

REDMAN, LIEUTENANT-GENERAL SIR HAROLD (1899–1986) Military career. In War Cabinet Secretariat, 1939–40; Secretary, Combined Chiefs of Staff Committee, 1943–44; Head of British Military Mission (France), 1945–46. Director of Military Operations, War Office, 1948–51. Deputy Supreme Allied Commander, Europe, 1951–52. Vice-Chief of Imperial General Staff, 1952–55. Governor and Commander-in-Chief, Gibraltar, 1955–58.

According to information received by the Liddell Hart Centre, King's College, London, the papers have remained in family possession. The papers of Lord Ismay, deposited in the Liddell Hart Centre, include correspondence, 1940–61.

REDMAYNE, BARON Sir Martin Redmayne **(1910–83)** MP (Con) Rushcliffe, 1950–66. Chief Whip, 1959–64.

His political papers have been deposited in the Bodleian Library, Oxford to where enquiries should be addressed.

REES, ALWYN D. (1911–74) Welsh nationalist, author and journalist. Editor of *Barn*.

The papers are deposited in the National Library of Wales. They include general correspondence, 1930s–74; material relating to the University of Wales; the Welsh language; disciplinary measures against students attending the Tryweryn trial, 1963; proposed defederalisation of the University, 1960–66; miscellaneous printed material, lectures, notes and reviews, and correspondence, 1955–75. There are articles and notes, 1966–74, relating to the Welsh periodical *Barn*, together with a substantial collection of correspondence. There are also files on broadcasting in Wales, *c.* 1960–74; the National Eisteddfod, 1972–74; and Welsh politics, *c.* 1960–74.

REES, MAJOR-GENERAL THOMAS WYNFORD (1898–1959) Indian Army career. Commanded various Indian Divisions, World War II. Commander, Punjab Boundary Force, Aug.–Sept. 1947. Head of Military Emergency Staff to Emergency Committee of the Cabinet, Delhi, Sept.–Dec. 1947. Chief of Staff to Governor General of India, 1947–48.

A collection of papers is preserved in the University of Sussex Library. The material mainly relates to the military and political situation in the Punjab during the transfer of power, 1947–48, and includes conference notes, situation and intelligence reports by the Punjab Boundary Force, 1947, and a report and letters on the Batala incident, Aug.–Sept. 1947. The collection also includes some World War II files. Other papers are in the British Library (India Office Records). A list is available (NRA 39211).

REES-MOGG, BARON William Rees-Mogg (1928–) Editor, *The Times*, 1967–81.

The main section of Lord Rees-Mogg's papers as editor of *The Times* is held in the News International Archive, London. In addition, he has retained a substantial collection of papers dealing with events since that period.

REID, BRIGADIER SIR FRANCIS (1900–70) Military career. Commander, Ceylon Army, 1952–55. Secretary to the Speaker, 1966–70.

His diaries and papers (mainly wartime) are in the National Army Museum (ref. 9103–119). A list is available (NRA 36740).

REILLY, SIR D'ARCY PATRICK (1909–99) Diplomat. Served Paris, Athens, etc. Deputy Under-Secretary, Foreign Office, during Suez Crisis. Ambassador to France, 1965–68.

His correspondence, papers and diaries have been placed in the Bodleian Library, Oxford.

REILLY OF BROMPTON, BARON Paul Reilly (1912–90) Director, Design Council, 1960–77. Architect, conservationist, etc.

His correspondence and papers, 1920–90, have been placed in the V&A Archives (ref. AAD6-1992).

REITH, 1ST BARON Sir John Charles Walsham Reith (1889–1971) First General Manager, BBC, 1922; Managing Director, 1923; Director-General, 1927–38. MP (Nat) Southampton, 1940. Minister of Information, 1940; Minister of Transport, 1940; Minister of Works, 1940–42. Director of Combined Operations Material Dept, Admiralty, 1943–45. Chaired various official bodies including Commonwealth Telecommunications Board, 1946–50.

A substantial collection of correspondence, diaries and papers is held at the BBC Written Archives Centre, Caversham Park, Reading (ref. S 60). A list is available (NRA 31050). The collection includes correspondence, 1940–71 (14 files), together with 23 volumes of enclosures, 1889–1971; one volume of press-cuttings, 1926–70, and one file on business interests. *The Reith Diaries* (ed. Charles Stuart) were published in 1975.

RENDEL, SIR GEORGE WILLIAM (1889–1979) Diplomat. Served on European Committee of United Nations Relief and Rehabilitation Administration, 1944–47. Ambassador, Belgium, 1947–50 (Minister, Luxembourg, 1947–49).

His papers and correspondence have been placed in the National Library of Wales. A list is available (NRA 31574). The collection includes material relating to his diplomatic postings and to the Catholic Union of Great Britain and also to his published memoir *The Sword and the Olive* (1957). There are also some family and personal papers. Further papers relating to pre-war Saudi Arabia and the Middle East are held in the Middle East Centre, St Antony's College, Oxford.

RENISON, SIR PATRICK (MUIR) (1911–65) Colonial Service, Trinidad and Tobago, 1948–52. Governor, British Honduras, 1952–55; British Guiana, 1955–59; Kenya, 1959–62.

His papers on colonial constitutional developments, 1949–62, are in Rhodes House Library, Oxford (ref. MSS Brit Emp s 404). A list is available (NRA

17622). Photocopying restrictions apply to the West Indian section of the collection.

RENNELL OF RODD, 2ND BARON Major-General Francis James Rennell Rodd (1895–1978) Diplomat, financier and explorer. Served in World War II as Major-General, Civil Affairs Administration, Middle East, East Africa and Italy.

A collection of papers, 1943–46, formerly held in the Library of Nuffield College, has recently been transferred to the Bodleian Library, Oxford. The papers include confidential reports relating to the British military administration in Malaya (1945–46), Eritrea (1945), the Dodecanese Islands (1945), and Tripolitania (1945); the finance and accounts of the Civil Affairs Branch, Middle East Forces (1944); and files on Somalia (1943).

RENTON, BARON Sir David Lockhart-Mure Renton (1908–) MP (Nat Lib, then Con) Huntingdon, 1945–79. Parliamentary Secretary, Ministry of Fuel and Power, 1955–57; Ministry of Power, 1957–58. Joint Parliamentary Under-Secretary, Home Office, 1958–61, Minister of State, Home Office, 1961–62.

His personal and political papers, covering the period 1948–84, are deposited at the House of Lords Record Office (ref. Hist Coll 209). These are not available without the permission of Lord Renton. A list is available.

RHODES OF SADDLEWORTH, LORD Hervey Rhodes (1895–1987) MP (Lab) Ashton-under-Lyne, 1945–64. Parliamentary Secretary, Board of Trade, 1950–51, 1964–67.

His surviving papers have been placed in Lancashire Record Office (ref. DDRS, accs 7790, 8201). The papers include material on parliamentary trade delegations to China, Japan and the Far East together with correspondence with universities, election addresses and papers 1945–64.

RHYL, BARON (Evelyn) Nigel (Chetwode) Birch (1906–81) MP (Con) Flintshire, 1945–50; Flint West, 1950–70. Parliamentary Under-Secretary, Air, 1951–52; Parliamentary Secretary, Defence, 1952–54; Minister of Works, 1954–55; Secretary of State, Air,

1955–57; Economic Secretary to the Treasury, 1957–58.

No papers have been located. An interview covering his period as Parliamentary Secretary to the Minister of Defence, 1952–54, is held at the Imperial War Museum (ref. 3951/1).

RHYS-WILLIAMS, SIR BRANDON (1927–88) MP (Con) Kensington South, Mar. 1968–Feb. 1974; Kensington, Feb. 1974–88. MEP, 1973–84.

The papers were deposited at the LSE Library in 1992. The collection includes files on reforms in tax, pensions, company law and property law. There is material on European economic and monetary union as well as more general political correspondence, constituency papers and election ephemera. Further material relating to election campaigns and to a long-running dispute with the Welsh Water Authority remained in his family's possession. A list is available (NRA 41200).

RHYS-WILLIAMS, LADY Juliette Evangeline Rhys-Williams (née Glyn) (1889–1964) Social worker and campaigner. Founder and Chairman of the National Birthday Trust. Founder member of the Economic Research Council. Hon. Secretary, United Europe Movement and British Section of European League for Economic Co-operation. Active Liberal.

Some medical papers of Lady Rhys-Williams are with the archives of the National Birthday Trust Fund at the Wellcome Contemporary Medical Archives Centre, London. A list is available (NRA 13792).

Further papers reflecting her political interests, especially in Europe, have been placed in the LSE Library (ref. M1789). A list is available (NRA 41138). There is much correspondence on Europe during the 1950s, especially the development of the European Movement and the European League for Economic Co-operation. The correspondents include Sir Winston Churchill, Harold Macmillan, Lord Eccles, Duncan Sandys, Peter Thorneycroft, Sir Piers Dixon and Sir Roger Makins. Her work as a Liberal candidate and publicity officer is also documented. There is also material on the other organisations with which she was involved, including the Married Women's Association, the Population Commission, the Economic Research Council, Christian Action, the National Council of Social Service and the BBC (as a governor).

Some papers, including some relating to her work on the Home Publicity Sub-Committee of the Ministry of Information, 1938–39, are in the Imperial War Museum.

RICHARD, BARON Ivor Seward Richard (1932–) MP (Lab) Barons Court, 1964–Feb. 1974. Ambassador to the United Nations, 1974–79. Labour Leader, House of Lords, 1992–98.

Lord Richard states that his papers will eventually be deposited with the Welsh Political Archive at the National Library of Wales.

RICHARDS, VERNON (1915–2001) (pseudonym Vero Recchioni) Anarchist and publisher. Editor of *Freedom*, 1945–64.

Some manuscripts and papers are deposited in the International Institute of Social History, Amsterdam. They include files on the anarchist periodical *Freedom* during the 1940s and 1950s and correspondence with leading intellectuals, writers and anarchists, among them Fenner Brockway, George Orwell, Sylvia Pankhurst and Bertrand Russell.

RICHARDSON, JO (JOSEPHINE) (d. 1994) MP (Lab) Barking after 1974. Chairperson, Tribune Group, 1978–79 (Secretary, 1948–78).

There are papers in the Labour History Archive and Study Centre, University of Manchester. These include minutes of the Keep Left Group, 1948–54 (predecessor of the Tribune Group).

RICHMOND, VICE-ADMIRAL SIR MAXWELL (1900–86) Naval career from 1918. Various commands during and after World War II. Naval Liaison Officer, New Zealand, 1948–50. Flag Officer (Air), Mediterranean, and Flag Officer, Second-in-Command, Mediterranean Fleet, 1955–56.

A microfilm of his papers is held in the Imperial War Museum (ref. DS/MISC/21). The material includes the texts of addresses and speeches given during the 1950s and 1960s on his naval experiences and modern naval policy (including a talk on 'Operations in Egypt', November 1956). The collection also includes papers from his early years in the navy, 1918–22. A full catalogue is available.

RIDLEY, BARON Nicholas Ridley (1929–93) MP (Con) Cirencester and Tewkesbury, 1959–92. Financial Secretary to the Treasury, 1981–83; Secretary of State for Transport, 1983–86; Environment, 1986–89; Trade and Industry Secretary, 1989–90.

Enquiries should be addressed to the Gloucestershire Record Office which already has some constituency correspondence, 1983–86 (ref. D 3893). Lord Ridley stated in 1992 that he had retained extensive papers.

RIDSDALE, SIR JULIAN ERRINGTON (b. 1915) MP (Con) Harwich, 1954–92. Chairman, British–Japanese Parliamentary Group, 1964–92.

The papers have been placed in Churchill College, Cambridge (ref. RIDS). A list is available (NRA 44034). The collection consists of *c.* 40 boxes of correspondence and papers, 1949–92.

RIPPON, LORD Geoffrey Rippon (1924–97) Conservative politician and Cabinet Minister. Key negotiator of Britain's EEC entry.

The papers have been placed in the Bodleian Library, Oxford, to where enquiries should be addressed.

RITCHIE, GENERAL SIR NEIL METHUEN (1897–1983) Military Commander, Middle East, during World War II. General Officer Commanding-in-Chief, Scottish Command, 1945–47; Far East Land Forces, 1947–49. Commander, British Army Staff, Washington, and Military Member of Joint Services Mission, 1950–51.

It is understood that General Ritchie had retained some papers but their present location is unknown. Material from his service in the Middle East, 1941–42, was destroyed by enemy action. A brief memoir of his earlier service in Palestine is held at the King's Own Royal Lancaster Regimental Museum, Lancaster. Some correspondence, 1941–42, is in the Auchinleck papers at John Rylands Library, Manchester University.

RITCHIE-CALDER, BARON Peter Ritchie-Calder (1906–82) Author. Scientific, social and political journalist. Professor of International Relations at Edinburgh University, 1961–67. United Nations consultant.

His correspondence and papers, 1940–82, have been placed in the National Library of Scotland. A list is available (NRA 29122). They include a number of files on UNESCO, the World Health Organisation and other international bodies. There are also files on oceanography and maritime law, 1970–82; energy issues, especially atomic power, 1958–63; the Political Warfare Executive, 1941–45; the peace movement; and race relations. There is also some personal correspondence, 1967–82, and the texts of various articles, speeches, broadcasts and lectures.

ROBB, AIR CHIEF MARSHAL SIR JAMES MILNE (1895–1968) Royal Air Force career. Served in World Wars I and II. Air Officer Commanding-in-Chief, Fighter Command, 1945–47. Vice-Chief of the Air Staff, 1947–48. Commander-in-Chief, Air Forces, Western Europe, 1948–51. Inspector-General of the RAF, 1951.

The Royal Air Force Museum, Hendon, has a collection of papers, 1914–63, including logbooks, diaries, files, letters, photographs, lectures and published material (ref. AC 71/9). A detailed catalogue is available at the Museum. His Great War and inter-war service are documented as are his war-time commands in North-West Africa and Europe. The files on his post-war responsibilities include records of Tactical Air Operations in Korea, 1950. The collection also contains a file of correspondence and papers of Air Marshal Sir Wilfred Freeman.

ROBB, JOHN (1928–) Northern Irish surgeon and politician. Founder of New Ulster Movement and New Ireland Movement. Senator, Irish Republic, 1983–86.

Mr Robb has deposited several boxes of papers with the Northern Ireland Political Collection at the Linen Hall Library in Belfast. They concern the many campaigns with which he has been involved since the 1960s. His correspondents include politicians, peace campaigners and clergymen from both parts of Ireland. The collection includes chronological albums of press-cuttings on the Northern Irish situation, including the 1981 hunger strikes and the 1985 Anglo-Irish Agreement. Of particular interest are the files relating to the New Ireland Forum in 1983. These include draft and final submissions made to the Forum by several bodies, including those by

Northern and Southern Branches of the New Ireland Movement. The collection also contains reports and correspondence dating from his membership of the Irish Senate and his other interests. These include reports on the Irish health services and the Law Reform Commission in Dublin and files relating to non-denominational primary education in Ireland and to cross-community groups in Northern Ireland such as the Corrymeela Centre. Requests for access to the collection should be addressed to the Linen Hall Library.

ROBBINS, LORD Lionel Charles Robbins (1898–1984) Economist and public servant. Professor of Economics, London School of Economics, 1929–61. Chairman, *Financial Times*, 1961–70. First Chancellor of Stirling University, 1968–78.

Some papers, including lectures on economic thought given in the early 1980s, are at the LSE Library. The main collection of papers is currently in the care of his biographer, Susan Howson. It is expected that these will be deposited in due course.

ROBENS OF WOLDINGHAM, BARON Alfred Robens (1910–99) MP (Lab) Wansbeck, 1945–50; Blyth, 1950–60. Parliamentary Secretary, Ministry of Fuel and Power, 1946–51; Minister of Labour and National Service, 1951.

It is understood that Lord Robens retained very few papers.

ROBERTHALL, BARON Robert Lowe Hall (1901–88) (Changed surname to Roberthall, 1969) Economist. Served in the Ministry of Supply, 1939–46. Adviser, Board of Trade, 1946–47. Director, Economic Section, Cabinet Office, 1947–53. Economic Adviser to the Government, 1953–61.

The transcript of an interview with Lord Roberthall is held at the LSE Library. An edited version of his diaries has been published (Alec Cairncross (ed.) *The Robert Hall Diaries, 1954–61*, 1991).

ROBERTS, ELWYN (1904–88) Welsh Nationalist. Secretary, Plaid Cymru, 1964–71.

The family and political papers have been placed in Gwynedd Record Office, Dolgellau. Some additional material, including files on the Parliament for

Wales Campaign, is held at the National Library of Wales (NRA 26130 NLW misc).

ROBERTS, EMRYS OWAIN (1910–90) MP (Lab) Merioneth, 1945–51. Chairman, Development Board for Rural Wales, 1977–81.

The papers are held by the National Library of Wales. The collection includes various committee minutes, correspondence and press-cuttings on the National Eisteddfod, 1959–76; Welsh Development Board policy papers, minutes and correspondence (as Chairman), 1973–83; and papers covering his other interests.

ROBERTS, SIR FRANK KENYON (1907–98) Diplomat. Minister, Moscow, 1945–47. High Commissioner, India, 1949–51. Deputy Under-Secretary of State, Foreign Office, 1951–54. Ambassador, Yugoslavia, 1954–57; USSR, 1960–62; Federal Republic of Germany, 1963–68.

His personal correspondence and papers (35 boxes, covering the years 1914–97) have been placed in Churchill College, Cambridge (ref. ROBT). A list is available (NRA 43164). The collection relates to postings in Bonn and Moscow and material on NATO, the British Atlantic Committee, etc.

ROBERTS, BRIGADIER MICHAEL ROOKHERST (1912–77) Indian Army officer and military historian. Served in World Wars I and II, including Burma campaign, 1942–43. Historian, Cabinet Office, 1956–68. Joint author, *Official History of the War Against Japan* (vols II–V, 1958–69).

One box of papers is deposited in Churchill College, Cambridge (ref. MRBS). A list is available (NRA 18561). The material comprises his Burma diary, 1942–43; papers relating to the Gurkhas in World War II and after; correspondence with Ronald Lewin relating to Lewin's biography of Field Marshal Lord Slim, 1972–77; and an article and related correspondence on the background to the Chindit operations.

ROBERTS, GENERAL SIR OUVRY LINDFIELD (1898–1986) Military career. GO Commander-in-Chief Southern Command, 1949–52. Colonel Commandant, Royal Corps of Engineers, 1952–62.

There are papers, including diaries, in the Liddell Hart Centre for Military Archives, King's College, London.

ROBERTSON OF OAKRIDGE, 1ST BARON General Sir Brian Hubert Robertson (1896–1974) Military career. Commander-in-Chief, and Military Governor, Germany, 1947–49. UK High Commissioner, Germany, 1949–50. Commander-in-Chief, Middle East Land Forces, 1950–53. Chairman, British Transport Commission, 1953–61.

The papers have remained in family possession. No other details are available.

ROBERTSON, SIR DENNIS HOLME (1890–1963) Economist. Professor of Political Economy, Cambridge, 1944–57. President of the Royal Economic Society, 1948–50.

A collection of papers and correspondence for the period 1914–63 is held at Trinity College, Cambridge. A list is available (NRA 39229).

ROBERTSON, SIR JAMES WILSON (1899–1973) Sudan Political Service, 1922–53; Civil Secretary, 1945–53. Governor-General, Nigeria, 1955–60.

There are 17 boxes of papers and correspondence, 1945–53, deposited in the Sudan Archive, Durham University Library. They include records of the Advisory Council for the Northern Sudan, 1946–48; the Juba Conference, 1947–48; constitutional developments, 1943–51; the Sudan Church Council; correspondence between the Civil Secretary and Sudan Agents in London and Cairo; monthly letters to provincial governors, 1945–53; letters from officals; his letters home, 1922–54; and various articles and speeches. In addition, Rhodes House Library, Oxford, has the transcript of two interviews concerning Sudan and Nigeria, and a memorandum (1957) on the Nigerian constitution. The Department of Sound Records, Imperial War Museum, holds an interview from the BBC series *Tales from the Dark Continent* (ref. 4731/6).

ROBERTSON, JOHN HENRY (1909–65) (pseudonym John Connell) Journalist, biographer and military historian. On the staff of the *Evening News* from 1932; leader-writer, 1945–49. Co-opted member, London County Council Education Committee, 1949–58; Deputy Mayor, St Pancras Borough, 1951–52.

McMaster University Library, Ontario, Canada, holds his literary manuscripts and an extensive series of correspondence with literary, political and military figures. In addition to the typescripts of his books, there are numerous articles and reviews for newspapers, radio and television, drafts of unpublished work and research notes.

ROBINSON, SIR ALBERT EDWARD PHINEAS
(1915–) Businessman. Member, Monckton Commission. High Commissioner for the Federation of Rhodesia and Nyasaland, 1961–63.

His papers as High Commissioner and as a member of the Monckton Commission are in BLCAS (Rhodes House Library) (ref. MSS. Afr. S. 2164). There is also a series of letters written between 1953 and 1960 to Sir Roy Welensky. See NRA 40207.

ROBINSON, SIR (EDWARD) AUSTIN
(GOSSAGE) (1897–1993) Economist. Served in the Ministry of Production, 1942–45; on Reparations staff, 1945; Board of Trade, 1946; Economic Planning Staff, 1947–48. Professor of Economics, Cambridge University, 1950–65.

A collection of papers (64 boxes) covering the period 1940–59 has been placed in Churchill College, Cambridge (ref. ROBN). A list is available (NRA 31394). There are extensive files on wartime and post-war economic planning. Some additional files on the economies of India, Pakistan and Bangladesh, 1926–80, are held at the Centre for South Asian Studies, Cambridge. Special conditions of access apply.

ROBINSON, JOAN VIOLET (1903–83) Professor
of Economics, University of Cambridge, 1965–71.

The papers have been placed in the Library of King's College, Cambridge. A list is available (NRA 33381). Section 1 contains drafts of her published work, work-in-progress papers and notes on other writings. Section 2 consists of correspondence with various left-wing academics and other figures. Section 3 holds personal papers including address books, engagement diaries, travel journals, field notebooks and other travel records as well as photographs. Section 4 contains publications by other writers, including reviews, obituaries and studies of her life and work, and copies of her own writings.

ROBINSON, JOHN ARTHUR THOMAS (1919–83)
Anglican clergyman. Lecturer in Theology and Dean of Chapel, Trinity College, Cambridge, 1969–83. Assistant Bishop of Southwark, 1969–80. Author of numerous works on theology, including the controversial *Honest to God* (1963).

His papers have been placed in Lambeth Palace Library. The deposit includes correspondence and other papers on social and political questions, as well as church reform, 1953–78.

ROBINSON, LIEUTENANT-COLONEL WILLIAM
ALLEYNE (fl. 1940s–60s) Military career. Commanded battalion of the King's Own Border Regiment on policing duties, South Cameroon, 1960–61.

Rhodes House Library, Oxford, has a memoir of his Cameroon command together with related reports, cuttings and photographs (ref. MSS Afr s 2033). The Imperial War Museum also has a photocopy of the memoir which describes social and political conditions in South Cameroon during the period of the plebiscite on whether to join Nigeria or Cameroon. A further collection of papers at the National Army Museum contains other material on the plebiscite (refs 9102–250 and 9104–9). This collection, covering his career from 1946 to 1971, also contains items on the establishment of the Joint Services Staff College.

RODGERS, BARON William Thomas Rodgers
(1928–) MP (Lab and from 1981 SDP) Stockton, 1962–83. One of the founders of the SDP. Vice-President, SDP, 1982–87. PUS, Department of Economic Affairs, 1964–67; Foreign Office, 1967–68. Minister of State, Board of Trade, 1968–69; Treasury, 1969–70; Ministry of Defence, 1974–76. Transport Secretary, 1976–79.

Lord Rodgers has placed his papers in Essex University Library. Those for his SDP years are particularly extensive. The earlier material includes files on his period as General Secretary of the Fabian Society (1953–60) and on his role in the Campaign for Democratic Socialism (1960–64). His ministerial career is also documented.

RODGERS, SIR JOHN (CHARLES) 1ST BT
(1906–93) MP (Con) Sevenoaks, 1950–79. Parliamentary Secretary, Board of Trade, 1958–60.

The papers have been placed in Kent County Record Office.

ROGERS, SIR PHILIP (1914–90) Civil servant. Assistant Under-Secretary, Colonial Office, 1953–61; Deputy Cabinet Secretary, 1964–67; Permanent Under-Secretary, Department of Health and Social Security, 1970–75.

A small collection of incoming letters, 1952 and 1964–75, has recently been deposited in the Bodleian Library, Oxford (ref. MS Eng c 2194). Some of the papers are closed. Additional papers, relating to Kenya and an interview concerning his years in the Colonial Office, are in Rhodes House Library, Oxford. The Kenyan papers are subject to restricted access.

ROGERSON, SYDNEY (1894–1968) Publicist. Served in World War I. Publicity Manager for Federation of British Industries, 1923–30. Publicity Controller, ICI Ltd., 1937–52. Publicity and Public Relations Adviser to Army Council, War Office, 1952–54.

The typescript and final drafts of Rogerson's book *Propaganda in the Next War* and his autobiographical works *Unorthodox Endeavour* and *Stirling Times* are held at the Imperial War Museum. The collection also includes some typescript articles and his diaries for the period 1939–47.

ROSE, PAUL BERNARD (1935–) MP (Lab) Blackley, 1964–79. Founder member, SDP.

Mr Rose has retained extensive papers. They include files on the civil rights movement in Northern Ireland during the 1960s and his role as chairman of the Campaign for Democracy in Ulster. He also retains copies of his articles and research notes for his published and unpublished work on Irish history, South African intelligence, race relations and pseudo-religious cults. He intends to make provision for the deposit of his papers in due course.

ROSKILL, CAPTAIN STEPHEN WENTWORTH (1903–82) Naval officer and historian. Various staff appointments during World War II. Deputy Director of Naval Intelligence, 1946–48. Official Naval Historian, Cabinet Office, 1949–60. Fellow of Churchill College, Cambridge, from 1961.

Some 180 boxes of papers covering his career and family life, 1919–82, are held at Churchill College, Cambridge (ref. ROSK). In addition to material on his own service career, the collection includes extensive research files on naval history and his correspondence with other historians. Special conditions of access apply to this collection, and enquiries should be directed to the Archivist at Churchill College.

ROSS, WILLIAM (1936–) MP (UU) Londonderry, 1974–83; East Londonderry, 1983–2001.

Mr Ross states that he has retained some unsorted papers. They are not currently available to researchers.

ROTHA, PAUL (1907–84) Film director, author and journalist. Produced documentary films for the Empire Marketing Board, UNESCO, the Scottish Office and the National Council of Social Service. Head of Documentaries, BBC Television, 1953–55.

A large collection is held by the University College of Los Angeles. The archive includes the original and annotated manuscripts and scripts of his books, films and television programmes. There are also files on unrealised projects. A separate section of the archive covers his career in journalism and includes copies of published and unpublished work, 1928–59. The archive also contains a unique collection of press-cuttings on contemporary cinema, 1920–62, and on Rotha himself.

ROWBOTHAM, SHEILA (1943–) Feminist writer and historian.

A small collection of her working notes on the women's movement, 1969–82, has been placed in the Women's Library London Metropolitan University (ref. 7/SHR).

ROWLANDS, LORD Edward (Ted) Rowlands (1940–) Welsh Labour politician. MP for Cardiff North, Merthyr Tydfil, etc.

The papers, 1972–91, have been placed in the Welsh Political Archive in the National Library of Wales.

ROWLEY, BARON Arthur Henderson (1893–1968) MP (Lab) Cardiff South, 1923–24, 1929–31; Kingswinford, 1935–50; Rowley Regis and Tipton, 1950–66.

Financial Secretary, War Office, 1943–45. Parliamentary Under-Secretary, India and Burma, 1945–47. Minister of State for Commonwealth Relations, 1947. Secretary of State for Air, 1947–51.

It is understood that no papers have survived. See *British Cabinet Ministers, 1900–51.*

RUBINSTEIN, MICHAEL (fl. 1960s) Lawyer specialising in publishing, libel, etc.

His papers relating to Penguin Books and the obscenity trial against *Lady Chatterley's Lover* have been placed in Bristol University Library (ref. DM 1679). A list is available (NRA 39438).

RUMBOLD, SIR (HORACE) ANTHONY CLAUDE (1911–83) Diplomat. Ambassador to Thailand, 1965–67; Austria, 1967–70.

The Bodleian Library, Oxford, holds his correspondence and papers, 1920s–80s. The collection, which consists of 50 boxes and volumes, is subject to restricted access. Additional family papers have remained with his son.

RUNCIE, LORD Robert Alexander Kennedy Runcie (1921–2000) Anglican clergyman. Bishop of St Albans, 1970–80. Archbishop of Canterbury, 1980–91.

Enquiries should be addressed to Lambeth Palace Library.

RUSSELL, 3RD EARL Bertrand Arthur William Russell (1872–1970) Philosopher and writer. Fellow of Trinity College, Cambridge. Lecturer at the London School of Economics, Cambridge, the Sorbonne and several other institutions. President of the Aristotelian Society. First Reith Lecturer. Awarded Nobel Prize for Literature, 1950. Founder member of No-Conscription Fellowship, the Campaign for Nuclear Disarmament and Committee of 100.

The massive Bertrand Russell Archive is located at McMaster University, Hamilton, Ontario. A list is available (NRA 12092). The material includes family papers, several drafts and versions of Russell's autobiography, and the manuscripts of books and articles on mathematics and political subjects, as well as some fictional work.

There is a vast correspondence (some 25,000 letters) with leading philosophers, politicians and other public figures. There are also *c.* 10,000 letters from members of the public worldwide.

RUSSELL, DORA W. (1894–1986) Writer, socialist, feminist and radical campaigner. Second wife of Bertrand Russell. Active in various progressive and civil rights organisations in the 1930s. Worked for the Ministry of Information, 1943–50, mainly as science editor of *Britanski Soyuznik*. Led Women's Caravan of Peace across Europe to Moscow and back in 1950.

A large collection of papers is held at the International Institute of Social History in Amsterdam. The papers cover virtually the whole of her career from 1912 onwards and include correspondence with Fenner Brockway, Sinclair Lewis, Rebecca West and Beatrice Webb. There are also diaries and other personal papers. The collection contains extensive files on the organisations and committees with which she was involved, including the World League for Sexual Reform and the Women's Caravan of Peace. The Feminist Archive, Trinity Road Library, Bristol, has the records of the journey through Europe of the Women's Peace Caravan, 1958 and some of her own papers.

RUSSELL-JOHNSTON, BARON David Russell-Johnston (1932–) MP (Lib, then Lib Dem) Inverness (subsequently Inverness, Nairn and Lochaber), 1964–97. Leader of the Scottish Liberal Party. Chairman of the Scottish Liberal Democrats.

His political correspondence and papers, 1964–97, have been deposited in the National Library of Scotland (ref. Acc 11682).

RYDER, RICHARD (1940–) Author and campaigner on animal welfare etc.

There are papers, including material on animal welfare, in the British Library.

RYMER-JONES, BRIGADIER JOHN MURRAY (1897–1993) Military and police career. Served in World War I; post-war service in Germany and Ireland. Metropolitan Police, 1935–59. Inspector-General and Brigadier Commanding Palestine Police, 1943–46. Assistant Commissioner, Metropolitan Police, 1950–59.

His unpublished memoirs, which cover his life

until 1946, have been deposited in the Imperial War Museum. The Museum's Department of Sound Records holds an interview recorded in 1990 which covers the same period (ref. 10699/24). Access to the recording is subject to certain restrictions. A collection of photographs is also available at the Museum. Brigadier Rymer-Jones is understood to have retained his Palestine diaries and letters.

S

SACKS, DR JONATHAN HENRY (1948–) Jewish leader. Chief Rabbi of the United Hebrew Congregation after 1991.

His official papers as Chief Rabbi, 1991–96, are in London Metropolitan Archives (ref. Acc 2805).

SALISBURY, 5TH MARQUIS OF Robert Arthur James Gascoyne-Cecil, Baron Cecil of Essendon (1893–1972) Conservative elder statesman.

The papers remain with the present (7th) Marquis of Salisbury. These papers are not open for research.

SALISBURY-JONES, MAJOR-GENERAL SIR (ARTHUR) GUY (1896–1985) Military career. Head of Military Mission to South Africa, 1941–44; on staff of Supreme Headquarters Allied Expeditionary Force, 1944–45. Head of Military Mission and Military Attaché, Paris, 1946–49.

Correspondence and other papers covering his service in World Wars I and II and his Paris appointment, 1946–47, are deposited in the Imperial War Museum.

SAMUEL, 1ST VISCOUNT Herbert Louis Samuel (1870–1963) MP (Lib) Cleveland, 1902–18; Darwen, 1929–35. Various Cabinet posts during World War I. High Commissioner, Palestine, 1920–25. Leader of the Liberal Parliamentary Party, 1931–35. Home Secretary, 1931–32. Leader of the Liberal Party in the House of Lords, 1944–55.

Lord Samuel's papers in the House of Lords Record Office are described in *British Cabinet Ministers, 1900–51*. The post-1945 papers include correspondence and press-cuttings from his time as Liberal Leader in the House of Lords. Additional papers on Palestine and Zionism can be found in the Israeli State Archive. A list of both collections is available (NRA 11187).

SAMUEL, RAPHAEL (1934–96) Historian and socialist.

The papers have been placed in the Bishopsgate Institute, London.

SANDELSON, NEVILLE (1923–2002) MP (Lab, then SDP) Hayes and Harlington, 1971–83. Treasurer of the Manifesto Group, 1975–80. Founder member of the SDP.

The papers (13 boxes, 1950–*c*85) have been deposited in the LSE Library. A list is available (NRA 41473). The papers include a series of scrapbooks relating to his election campaigns, and files relating to the Hayes and Harlington constituency party and membership of the Labour Party and the SDP as well as his interest in Afghanistan, Lebanon and Gibraltar.

SARA, HENRY (1886–1953) Socialist activist. Founder member of the Trotskyist Left Opposition in Britain.

Some papers relating to the British and international far left, 1922–55, are in the Modern Records Centre, University of Warwick (ref. Maitland/Sara MSS 15). A list is available (NRA 19094). They consist of correspondence; policy papers; ephemera; and press-cuttings, including some scrapbooks of the Moscow Trials, and political activity during and after World War II.

SARGENT, SIR ORME (1884–1962) Permanent Under-Secretary, Foreign Office, 1946–49.

Some papers, including diaries and correspondence, have remained in private hands and are not available to researchers. However, his Private Office correspondence, 1926–48, is held in the Public Record Office (ref. FO 800/272–9).

SAUNDBY, AIR MARSHAL SIR ROBERT HENRY MAGNUS SPENCER (1896–1971) Royal Air Force career. Served in World Wars I and II. Senior Air Staff Officer, Bomber Command, 1941–42;

Deputy Air Officer Commander-in-Chief, Bomber Command, 1943–45.

The papers are housed in the Royal Air Force Museum, Hendon, and are a valuable source for the history of the post-war development of air-power (ref. AC 72/12). In addition to material dating from his own service career, the collection contains files on gradual deterrence; strategic bombing; lectures and notes on the principles of war and on tactical bombing (1946 and 1952); seven files relating to the working party on the *Official History of the RAF in World War II*, 1948–51; a mid-1950s file on the Royal Air Force in the missile age; and press-cuttings, photographs and slides. His correspondents include Trenchard, Sir Sydney Camm and Sir John Slessor. The papers include some 1971 correspondence with Lord Harris relating to the Goebbels diaries.

SAUNDERS, ROBERT (fl. 1930s–50s) Fascist. Active in Dorset in British Union of Fascists and Union Movement.

There are papers, 1935–52, in the University of Sheffield (ref. MS 119). A list is available (NRA 43169). There is some correspondence with Mosley and almost complete administrative files of the Dorchester Constituency of the Union Movement.

SAVILLE, JOHN (1916–) Lecturer (and later Professor), Economic and Social History, University of Hull, 1947–82. Member, British Communist Party, 1934–56. Co-editor (with E.P. Thompson) of the *Reasoner* and *New Reasoner*, 1956–59; (with Asa Briggs) *Essays in Labour History*, 1960, 1971, 1977, etc.

A large collection of papers is held at the Brynmor Jones Library, University of Hull (ref. DX/70). The collection includes extensive material on the Communist Party from 1939 onwards. Subject files cover the Communist Historians Group, 1946–48; communist activity within the university sector; and considerable correspondence with intellectuals, including Christopher Hill, Eric Hobsbawm, Maurice Dobb and Dona Torr. The events of 1956, the publication of the *Reasoner* and the emergence of the New Left are all covered in detail. There is a large correspondence with Edward Thompson. There are also papers on the beginnings of the Campaign for Nuclear Disarmament and the attitudes of the New Left, especially neutralist foreign policy. Further documents relate to the political relationship between the *Reasoner* group and the Fife Socialist League, co-founded by Lawrence Daly. The remainder of the collection concerns his subsequent political and academic activities, including local politics; university affairs such as the 1968 'troubles'; Council for Academic Freedom and Democracy cases; the National Council of Labour Colleges and Ruskin College; and the National Unemployed Workers' Movement.

SAVORY, SIR DOUGLAS LLOYD (1878–1969) MP (UU) Queen's University, Belfast, 1940–50; Antrim South, 1950–55. Professor of French, Queen's University, Belfast, 1909–41.

The Public Record Office of Northern Ireland holds a collection of correspondence, writings, speeches and press-cuttings, 1900–69. A list is available (NRA 23522). His papers relating to Poland, 1941–55, are held at the Sikorski Institute, London (ref. KOL.9). These include files on the Katyn massacre; the Southern Tyrol, 1946–47; the Polish Resettlement Corps, 1947–49; and parliamentary speeches, 1945–47 and 1955. A list is available at the Institute.

SAVORY, LIEUTENANT-GENERAL SIR REGINALD ARTHUR (1894–1980) Indian Army career. Served in World Wars I and II. General Officer Commanding, Persia and Iraq, 1945–46. Adjutant-General, India, 1946–47.

A substantial collection of papers, 1914–48, was deposited in the National Army Museum in 1976 (ref. 7603–93). A list is available (NRA 27852). In addition to his letters to his parents and his wife, there are many official and semi-official papers.

SAWERS, MATTHEW (fl. 1990s) Police career. Chief Inspector, Western European Union Police Contingent, Bosnia.

His correspondence and papers relating to his service in Mostar, 1995–98, are in the Liddell Hart Centre for Military Archives, King's College, London.

SAYERS, JOHN (JACK) EDWARD (1911–69) Northern Irish journalist. Editor-in-chief, *Belfast Telegraph*.

The papers remain in family possession and are not available for research. Material from these papers is included in Andrew Bailey's edition of his writings, *Crying in the Wilderness: Jack Sayers, a Liberal Editor in Ulster, 1939–69*.

SCAFFARDI, SYLVIA (1904–2000) Co-founder and Assistant Secretary, National Council of Civil Liberties (NCCL).

There are papers in the Brynmor Jones Library, University of Hull. The collection includes material relating to Ronald Kidd.

SCAMP, SIR ATHELSTAN JACK (1913–77) Industrial arbitrator and conciliator. Chairman, Motor Industry Joint Labour Council. Member of numerous government inquiries. Seconded to Department of Economic Affairs as Industrial Adviser, 1965–66. Associate Professor of Industrial Relations, University of Warwick, 1970–75.

Certain papers have been deposited in the Modern Records Centre, University of Warwick (ref. MSS 178). The material consists of four boxes relating to his work in industrial arbitration, 1965–77, and as Chairman of the Motor Industry Joint Labour Council as well as proceedings and reports of inquiries with related documentation and correspondence. Access to some papers is restricted.

SCANLAN, JAMES DONALD (1899–1976) Roman Catholic Archbishop of Glasgow, 1964–74; Bishop of Motherwell, 1955–64; Bishop of Dunkeld, 1949–55.

A collection of correspondence and papers relating chiefly to the diocese of Dunkeld, 1948–55, is held in the Scottish Catholic Archives in Edinburgh (ref. DD11). In addition to administrative and financial files relating to various parishes, seminaries, schools and colleges, charities, hospital and prison chaplaincies and missionary orders, there are also some policy papers on religious instruction in schools, teacher training and the Catholic Church's relations with the Scottish Office. This collection is a valuable source for the history of post-war European immigrants in Britain and contains several files on Polish and Italian immigrants in Dundee and elsewhere in the diocese.

His papers for the 1964–74 period are deposited in the Archdiocesan Archives in Glasgow and access is subject to the Archivist's discretion.

SCHONFELD, DR SOLOMON (1912–84) Principal, Jewish Secondary Schools Movement from 1930. Executive Director, Chief Rabbi's Religious Emergency Council, 1938–46. Presiding Rabbi, Union of Orthodox Hebrew Congregations.

The papers are in the Hartley Library, University of Southampton. In addition to his own personal papers, correspondence, publications and working papers, the collection includes correspondence and papers of his father Dr Avigdor Schonfeld, his father-in-law Chief Rabbi Hertz and other family members. There are extensive records of the Jewish Secondary Schools Movement. The files of the Chief Rabbi's Religious Emergency Council detail the rescue of Jews from Germany and Eastern Europe during World War II, and immediately after. There is also related material on Polish Jewish refugees, the Committee for Austrian and German Jewry and the Jewish Committee for the Rescue of Jewry in Nazi Germany.

SCHONLAND, SIR BASIL FERDINAND JAMIESON (1896–1972) Deputy Director, Atomic Energy Research Establishment (AERE), Harwell, 1954–58; Director, 1958–60.

There are five boxes of papers relating to the AERE, Harwell, covering the period 1954 to 1960, at Churchill College, Cambridge (ref. SCHO)(NRA 18561).

SCHUMACHER, ERNEST FRIEDRICH (1911–71) Economist, conservationist and writer. Economic adviser, National Coal Board, 1950–70 and Director of Statistics, 1963–70. Advocate of intermediate technology. Founder Chairman, Intermediate Technology Development Group. Author of *Small is Beautiful* (1973).

An extensive collection of papers is in the care of his family. The papers (some in German) cover most aspects of his life and work. Enquiries concerning the papers should be addressed in the first instance to the Secretary, Intermediate Technology Development Group.

SCHUSTER, SIR GEORGE ERNEST (1882–1982)
MP (Liberal Unionist) Walsall, 1938–45. Interwar economist and civil servant. Member of Government Committee on Industrial Productivity, 1947–51. Economic adviser to Maltese Government, 1950 and 1956–57.

Over 200 boxes of correspondence and papers have been deposited in the Bodleian Library, Oxford. The collection is uncatalogued but a draft list is available at the library. The post-war sections of the collection include files on India, Kenya and the Sudan, 1920s–60s; Anglo-American relations; the World Bank; Voluntary Service Overseas, 1962–76; and the many committees and bodies he served on, including Oxfordshire County Council, 1952–74. Restricted conditions of access apply to his private correspondence and files relating to his work as a Chairman and Governor of Atlantic College.

SCOONES, GENERAL SIR GEOFFRY (ALLEN PERCIVAL) (1893–1975) Military career. General Officer Commander-in-Chief, Central Command, India, 1945–46. Principal Staff Officer, Commonwealth Relations Office, 1947–53; High Commissioner, New Zealand, 1953–57.

There are papers, covering the period 1947–75, in the Imperial War Museum.

SCOTT, REVEREND (GUTHRIE) MICHAEL (1907–83) Clergyman, author and campaigner for justice in South Africa.

There are papers in BLCAS (Rhodes House Library), Oxford.

SCOTT, PAUL HENDERSON (1920–) Diplomat and author. SNP activist.

There are papers in the National Library of Scotland (ref. Acc 11854). The collection includes papers concerning service in the Allied Military Government of Berlin, 1945–49 and also the 1999 Scottish Parliament elections.

SCOTT, SIR PETER (MARKHAM) (1909–89)
Leading ornithologist and conservationist, artist and broadcaster. Chairman, World Wildlife Fund International.

The correspondence and papers have been deposited in Cambridge University Library. The papers (*c.* 7800 items) cover the period 1916–93. A detailed list is available (NRA 42717).

SCOTT, SIR ROBERT (1903–68) Colonial Administrative Service, Uganda, Palestine, Gold Coast. Administrator, East African Commission, 1950–54. Governor, Mauritius, 1954–59.

Many papers used in writing his books *A Survey of Palestine* (3 volumes) and *Memorandum on the Administration of Palestine under the Mandate* (Jerusalem, 1947) were destroyed in 1946 at the King David Hotel. Rhodes House Library, Oxford, has his personal correspondence, 1928–58, and his incomplete reminiscences. St Antony's College, Oxford, has the proclamation (1945) prohibiting the carrying of arms.

SCOTT, SIR ROBERT HEATLIE (1905–82) Civil servant and diplomat. China Consular Service, 1927–47; then transferred to Foreign Office. Assistant Under-Secretary of State, 1950–53. Minister, British Embassy, Washington, 1953–55. Commissioner General for the UK in South-East Asia, 1955–59. Commandant, Imperial Defence College, 1960–61. Permanent Secretary, Ministry of Defence, 1961–63.

Some papers, including journals, scrapbooks, press-cutting books, photographs and other items for the period 1923 to 1982 are in the National Library of Scotland (ref. Acc 8181). A list is available (NRA 29213). The collection relates especially to his wartime imprisonment in Singapore. There are also various accounts by Rosamund Dewar Durie (Lady Scott) of visits to the USA and parts of South East Asia during his time as Commissioner General. A recorded interview is held at the LSE Library.

SCOTT, RUSSELL (fl. 1940s–50s) Supporter of European and internationalist movements.

His papers (1930s–50s) relating to his interests in Federal Union and other supra-nationalist movements, mainly print and ephemera plus a biography by his grandson John Russell Scott, have been placed in the LSE Library (ref. M 1814).

SCOTTER, GENERAL SIR WILLIAM NORMAN ROY (1922–81) Served in World War II with Gurkha Rifles in Burma; Malaya, 1948–51. On NATO duties, 1952–54. Instructor, Staff College, 1960–63.

Ministry of Defence, 1963–65. Commanded King's Own Royal Border Regiment, 1965–67; commanded 19th Infantry Brigade, 1967–69. National Defence College, 1969–70.

A small collection of papers, 1953–70, is held in the Liddell Hart Centre, King's College, London.

SCRIVENOR, SIR THOMAS VAISEY (1908–98)
Colonial Service, Tanganyika, Palestine, Malta, Nigeria. Deputy High Commissioner, Basutoland, Bechuanaland and Swaziland, 1953–60.

Rhodes House Library, Oxford, has a number of papers from the 1930s and the tape and transcript of an interview given to the Colonial Records Project. In addition, one box of his papers and speeches as Deputy High Commissioner for Basutoland, Bechuanaland and Swaziland is held at the Centre for Southern African Studies, York University.

SEDGEMORE, BRIAN CHARLES JOHN (1937–)
MP (Lab) Luton West, Feb. 1974–79; Hackney, 1983–2005.

His constituency correspondence and files from 1982 onwards are held in the Archives Department of the Rose Lipman Library, Hackney (ref. D/F/SED 1). A list is available (NRA 32669). The papers are subject to a thirty-year restriction on access.

SEEAR OF PADDINGTON, BARONESS (Beatrice) Nancy Seear (1913–97) Liberal Leader in the House of Lords, 1984–88. Sponsor of the 1973 Sex Discrimination Act.

The papers are divided among various archive centres. The Women's Library, London Metropolitan University, has some parliamentary papers including submissions relating to equal opportunities, pay and sex discrimination 1969–75. The LSE Library has received two large deposits (refs M1894 and M 1911) comprising 39 boxes. Some family correspondence is in the MRC, King's College, Cambridge.

SELKIRK, 10TH EARL OF George Nigel Douglas-Hamilton (1906–) Paymaster-General, 1953–55; Chancellor of the Duchy of Lancaster, 1955–57; First Lord of the Admiralty, 1957–59.

According to *British Cabinet Ministers, 1900–51*, some papers remained in the possession of the Earl of Selkirk.

SELWYN-CLARKE, HILDA (d. 1967) Anti-colonialist. Secretary, Fabian Colonial Bureau.

Relevant administrative and personal papers, 1950–62, can be found in the archives of the Fabian Colonial Bureau which are housed in Rhodes House Library, Oxford (ref. MSS Brit Emp s 365). A list is available (NRA 16153).

SELWYN-CLARKE, SIR PERCY SELWYN (1893–1976) Colonial Service in Gold Coast, Malaya and Hong Kong, 1919–47. Governor, Seychelles, 1948–51.

There are 11 boxes of correspondence, speech notes and other papers in Rhodes House Library, Oxford (ref. MSS Brit Emp s 470). (NRA 26286).

SELWYN-LLOYD, BARON John Selwyn Brooke Lloyd (1904–78) MP (Con) The Wirral, 1945–76. Minister of State, Foreign Office, 1951–54. Minister of Supply, 1954–55. Minister of Defence, 1955. Secretary of State for Foreign Affairs, 1955–60. Chancellor of the Exchequer, 1960–62. Lord Privy Seal and Leader of the House of Commons, 1963–64. Speaker of the House of Commons, 1971–76.

The papers have been deposited by his literary executors in Churchill College, Cambridge (ref. SELO) (NRA 18561). The deposit consists of 495 boxes organised by subject.

His Foreign Office correspondence, diaries and papers covering 1952–60 are held at the Public Record Office, Kew (ref. FO 800/691–746). A list is available (NRA 23627).

SENIOR, DEREK (1912–88) Expert on town planning and local government. Author of *Guide to the Cambridge Plan* (1966), *The Regional City* (1966) and *Memorandum of Dissent from the Redcliffe-Maud Report* (1969).

A collection of working papers was deposited in the LSE Library by his widow, Dr Helen Mair, in 1991. These include papers relating to the Redcliffe-Maud Royal Commission on Local Government in England, 1966–69.

SEROTA, BARONESS Beatrice Serota (1919–2002) Labour politician. Minister of State, Department of Health and Social Security, 1969–70. Deputy Speaker, House of Lords after 1985.

The correspondence and papers (ten boxes) have been placed in the LSE Library (ref M3187), to where enquiries should be addressed. The papers relate to her work as a social reformer and Deputy Leader of the House of Lords.

SEYMOUR, SIR HORACE JAMES (1885–1978)

Diplomat. Assistant Under-Secretary, Foreign Office, 1939–42. Ambassador to China, 1942–46.

There are six boxes of correspondence, papers and photographs, 1930–78, at Churchill College, Cambridge (ref. SEYR). A list is available (NRA 23859).

SHACKLETON, BARON Edward Arthur Alexander Shackleton (1911–94) MP (Lab) Preston, 1946–50; Preston South, 1950–55. Minister of Defence (Royal Air Force), 1964–67. Minister without Portfolio, 1967–68. Lord Privy Seal, Jan.–Apr. 1968. Lord Privy Seal, Oct. 1968–70. Minister, Civil Service Department, Nov. 1968–70. Opposition Leader, House of Lords, 1970–74.

The House of Lords Record Office holds Lord Shackleton's political and personal papers, 1933–93 (ref. Hist Coll 125). Access to the collection is restricted. All enquiries should be directed to the Archivist. An interview with Lord Shackleton is held at the LSE Library.

SHAFTESLEY, JOHN MAURICE (1901–81)

Editor, *Jewish Chronicle*, 1946–58.

There are papers, 1950–78, in the Hartley Library, University of Southampton (ref. MS 230). The Hartley Library also has the archive of the *Jewish Chronicle* itself.

SHAW, SIR JOHN VALENTINE WISTAR (1894–1982) Colonial Service. Chief Secretary, Palestine, 1943–46. Governor and Commander-in-Chief, Trinidad and Tobago, 1947–50.

The papers are deposited in Rhodes House Library, Oxford (ref. MSS Brit Emp s 456). They consist largely of newspaper cuttings and photographs recording his entire career and include material on the bombing of the King David Hotel in Jerusalem. Gramophone recordings of his 1947 inauguration and 1949 departure as Governor of Trinidad and Tobago form part of the collection.

SHAWCROSS, BARON Hartley William Shawcross (1902–2003) MP (Lab) St Helens, 1945–58. Attorney-General, 1945–51; President, Board of Trade, 1951.

Lord Shawcross stated that he had retained a small collection of papers.

SHEERMAN, BARRY (1940–) MP (Lab) Huddersfield East, 1979–83: Huddersfield after 1983.

Some papers, 1980s–90s, mainly reflecting his interests in criminal justice, have been placed in the Brynmor Jones Library, University of Hull.

SHELDON, LORD Robert (Edward) Sheldon (1923–) MP (Lab) Ashton-under-Lyne, 1964–2001. Financial Secretary to the Treasury, 1975–79. Chairman, Public Accounts Committee, 1983–97.

An extensive collection of papers relating to his work as Chairman of the Public Accounts Committee, 1983–97, has been placed in the LSE Library (ref. M 1854). A list is available (NRA 42850). There are 49 boxes of his files as Chairman, 1985–97, 13 boxes of Office of Public Accounts Reports and 15 boxes of National Audit Office Reports.

SHERFIELD, BARON Sir Roger Mellor Makins (1904–96) Diplomat and civil servant. Ambassador to the USA, 1953–56. Joint Permanent Secretary of the Treasury, 1956–60. Chairman of the UK Atomic Energy Authority, 1960–64.

The papers have been placed in the Bodleian Library, Oxford. Some papers for the 1947–52 period are available at the National Archives (ref. FO 800/614–26). Further correspondence can be found in the papers of Lord Cherwell at Nuffield College, Oxford, (1934–56), and Lord Jackson at Imperial College, London (1967–68). The British Oral Archive of Political and Administrative History at the LSE Library holds an interview recorded in 1980.

SHERMAN, SIR ALFRED (1919–) Journalist. Adviser on public affairs. Founder, Centre for Policy Studies.

There are papers concerning the Centre for Policy Studies deposited in the Library of Royal Holloway and New College, Egham.

SHINWELL, BARON Emanuel Shinwell (1884–1986) MP (Lab) Linlithgowshire, 1922–24, 1928–31;

Seaham, 1935–50; Easington, 1950–70. Financial Secretary, War Office, 1929–30. Parliamentary Secretary, Department of Mines at the Board of Trade, 1924 and 1930–31. Minister of Fuel and Power, 1945–47. Secretary of State for War, 1947–50. Minister of Defence, 1950–51.

A collection of correspondence, articles, speeches and press-cuttings is held in the LSE Library. No papers survive from his early trade union and Labour Party career and relatively few from his period of office in the 1945 Labour Government. Most of the files relate to his later years as a backbench MP and peer. These include political and general correspondence along with drafts and copies of his broadcasts and publications. Some photographs survive from the post-World War II period.

SHONE, SIR TERENCE ALLEN (1894–1965)
Diplomat. Minister, Syria and Lebanon, 1944–46. High Commissioner, India, 1946–48. Deputy Permanent Representative, United Nations, 1948–51.

Some papers are deposited in St Antony's College, Oxford. They include a report on events in Damascus and other parts of the Levant in 1945; an account by Prince Paul of the Yugoslav accession to the Axis; and notes by Lady Shone. A list is available (NRA 20811).

SHONFIELD, SIR ANDREW (AKIBA) (1917–81)
Economist, journalist and writer. Foreign Editor, *Financial Times*, 1947–57; Economics Editor, *The Observer*, 1958–61. Director, Royal Institute of International Affairs, 1972–77. Professor of Economics, European University Institute, Florence, 1978–82.

His papers have been placed at the LSE Library. The collection includes copies of his major publications on economics, reports on Commissions of Enquiry and literary papers as well as copies of articles written for *Tribune*, the *Financial Times* and *The Observer*, among others. Enquiries should be directed to the Archivist.

SHORE, LORD Peter David Shore (1924–2001)
Labour politician and Cabinet Minister. Leading anti-Europeanist.

His political papers, 1958–2001, have been placed in the LSE Library. There is material on the Wilson and Callaghan governments, his opposition to

Europe and the single currency and the 1983 leadership campaign as well as on constituency affairs. The collection covers the whole of Shore's career, including wartime correspondence and papers concerning his ministerial posts, along with material documenting his active involvement in campaigns against Britain's assimilation with the European Community and intermittent diaries detailing, most notably, the 1983 General Election and his attempts to become leader of the Labour Party.

SHORT, MAJOR JOHN McLOUGHLIN (1897–1969)
Indian Army career. Assistant to Stafford Cripps during the Cabinet Mission to India, 1946.

Some correspondence and papers, 1923–67, are held at the India Office Library (ref. MSS Eur F 189). They include files on Sikh discontent during the war and on the Cripps Mission.

SHORT, RENÉE (1919–)
MP (Lab) Wolverhampton North East, 1964–87.

The papers are to be deposited at the LSE Library. They include extensive files on Eastern Europe and the USSR, Israel, health and education, trade unions and industry, the Warnock Report and the Home Office. There are also constituency correspondence and files from several parliamentary committees including the Select Committee on Social Services and the Scientific Committee.

SHUCKBURGH, SIR (CHARLES ARTHUR) EVELYN (1909–94)
Diplomat. First Secretary, Prague, 1945–47; Private Secretary to the Foreign Secretary, 1951–54; Ambassador to Italy, 1966–69.

One box of correspondence and papers on British relations with Argentina, 1947–49, is held at the Bodleian Library, Oxford (ref. Dep c 713). It is understood that other papers remained in his possession, among them his 1951–56 diaries published in 1986 as *Descent to Suez*.

SIEGHART, PAUL (1927–89)
Human rights advocate.

There are papers in the Human Rights Archive, University of Essex, to where enquiries concerning access should be addressed.

SILKIN, BARON Lewis Silkin (1889–1972) MP (Lab) Camberwell (Peckham), 1936–50. Minister of Town and Country Planning, 1945–50.

It is understood that no body of papers has survived.

SILKIN, BARON Samuel Charles Silkin (1918–88) MP (Lab) Dulwich, 1964–83. Attorney-General, 1974–79.

There are 27 boxes of legal and political papers at Churchill College, Cambridge (ref. SILK). The collection includes papers as Attorney General and on his work in the House of Lords as well as material on the 1987 Criminal Justice Bill, freedom of information, and the Crown Prosecution Service (1985). There are also case files and some correspondence. Access to the collection is currently restricted.

SILKIN, JOHN ERNEST (1923–87) MP (Lab) Deptford, 1963–87.

A collection of 33 boxes of papers is held at Churchill College, Cambridge (ref. SLKN). A list is available (NRA 36542). Access to the collection is restricted.

SILLITOE, SIR PERCY JOSEPH (1888–1962) Colonial Service and British Police career. Chief Constable, Glasgow, 1931–43; Kent, 1943–46. Director-General, MI5, 1946–53.

The diaries and papers in private hands cited by his biographer, W.H. Allen, (1975) have not been located. An autobiography, *Cloak Without Dagger*, was published in 1955.

SILSOE, LORD Arthur Malcolm Trustram Eve (1894–1976) Businessman and public servant. Closely involved in local government.

Some papers have survived in the possession of his son. No further details are available.

SIMEY, BARON Thomas Spensley Simey (1906–69) Professor of Social Science, University of Liverpool, from 1939. Adviser on Social Welfare to the Comptroller for Development and Welfare in the West Indies, 1941–45.

The papers have been placed in Liverpool University Archives (ref. D396). A list is available (NRA 26885). The collection includes papers and correspondence on his work in the West Indies along with Royal Commission and Colonial Office reports on development and welfare in the West Indies, 1939–47. There are also letters and publications, lecture notes, 1934–64, articles, reviews and press-cuttings, 1935–75.

SIMMONS, CHARLES JAMES (1893–1975) MP (Lab) Birmingham Erdington, 1929–31; Birmingham West, 1945–50; Brierley Hill, 1950–59. Junior Lord of the Treasury, 1946–49; Parliamentary Secretary, Ministry of Pensions, 1949–51.

The papers have been deposited in the Social Sciences Department, Birmingham Reference Library. The collection consists of personal papers, notes for sermons and addresses and political memoranda.

SIMMS, GEORGE OTTO (1910–91) Archbishop of Armagh and Primate of All Ireland, 1969–80.

His papers are in the Representative Church Body Library (ref. MS 238).

SIMON, 1ST VISCOUNT John Allsebrook Simon (1873–1954) MP (Lib) Walthamstow, 1906–18; Spen Valley, 1922–40 (Lib Nat from 1931). Solicitor-General, 1910–13; Attorney-General, 1913–15; Home Secretary, 1915–16. Foreign Secretary, 1931–35; Home Secretary, 1935–37; Chancellor of the Exchequer, 1937–40; Lord Chancellor, 1940–45.

Nearly 300 boxes of correspondence, press-cuttings and papers, 1894–1953, have been deposited in the Bodleian Library, Oxford (ref. MSS Simon 1–284). Much of the collection concerns the inter-war Liberal Party and domestic and international crises including the 1926 General Strike, the abdication of Edward VIII in 1936 and the 1938 Munich Crisis. However, there are some files on wartime and postwar issues including the Burgess and Maclean spy scandal and the Suez Canal situation (1954).

SIMON, SIR FRANCIS EUGENE (1893–1959) Physicist. Closely involved with German refugee question in the inter-war period. Professor of Thermodynamics, Oxford University, 1945–56; Member, Atomic Energy Project, 1940–46.

The Royal Society holds a collection of papers. A list is available (NRA 13900).

SIMON, (WILLIAM) GLYN HUGHES (1903–72)
Anglican clergyman. Dean of Llandaff, 1948–54.
Bishop of Swansea and Brecon, 1954–57; Llandaff,
1957–71. Archbishop of Wales, 1968–71.

A collection of papers is held at the National
Library of Wales. Enquiries regarding access should
be directed to the Archivist.

**SIMPSON, GENERAL SIR FRANK (ERNEST
WALLACE) (1899–1986)** Military career. Served in
World Wars I and II. Vice-Chief of the Imperial
General Staff, 1946–48. Commandant, Imperial
Defence College, 1952–54.

Some papers are held at the Imperial War
Museum.

SIMPSON, FREDERICK VIVIAN (1903–77)
Stormont MP (NILP) Belfast Old Park, 1958–72.
NILP Chairman.

The papers have been placed in the Public Record
Office of Northern Ireland (refs D3223 and D3223-
add). The first part of the collection relates to the
events of 1972 (including the Darlington Conference,
internment, prison riots and the Diplock Report).
The second section consists of 60 files relating
to constituency matters and the NILP, 1958–76.
This material includes minutes of the NILP's executive committee and other committees; minutes of
the Women's Advisory Council, 1961–70; party conference papers, 1960–74; and correspondence, 1958–
71. At present the collection is uncatalogued and
closed to readers.

SIMPSON, WILLIAM WYNN (1907–87) General
Secretary, Council of Christians and Jews, 1942–74.

The Hartley Library, Southampton University,
holds 31 boxes of papers, 1927–87 (ref. MS 66). A
list is available (NRA 30685). The collection contains extensive correspondence, 1953–87, diaries,
1963–84, notes, 1957–75 and a draft history of the
Council of Christians and Jews. Other papers include
correspondence and statements from the Vatican
and from two Roman Catholic Archbishops of
Westminster, Cardinals Heenan and Hume, 1966–70
and 1975–85. There are also files on the Christian
peace conferences in Prague, 1959–68 and the Ten
Points of Seelisberg, 1947–68.

SINCLAIR, SIR GEORGE EVELYN (1912–2005)
MP (Con) Dorking, Oct. 1964–79. Colonial Service,
1936–60. District Commissioner, Gold Coast, 1943;
Senior Assistant Colonial Secretary, 1947; Principal
Assistant Secretary, 1950; Regional Officer, Trans-
Volta Togoland Region, 1952; Deputy Governor,
Cyprus, 1955–60.

Sir George Sinclair stated that he had retained an
extensive collection of papers. The Department
of Sound Records, Imperial War Museum, holds an
interview from the BBC series *Tales from the Dark
Continent* covering his colonial career, especially his
time in Cyprus (ref. 4736/2).

**SKRIMSHIRE OF QUARTER, BARONESS
Margaret Betty Harvie Anderson (1915–79)** MP
(Con) East Renfrewshire, 1959–79.

The constituency papers are held by Strathclyde
Regional Archive, Glasgow (ref. TD 1164).

**SKRINE, SIR CLAIRMONT PERCIVAL (1888–
1974)** Indian Civil Service, 1912–15. Indian Political
Service, 1915–48. Counsellor for Indian Affairs,
Teheran, 1946–48.

The India Office Library has some papers, 1912–52
(ref. MSS Eur F 154). They consist of weekly letters
to his parents, some personal and private correspondence, semi-official papers, official diaries and
notes and articles by him. The subject matter is
mainly Persia. A list is available (NRA 27544).

**SLESSOR, MARSHAL OF THE ROYAL AIR
FORCE SIR JOHN COTESWORTH (1897–1979)**
Royal Air Force career. Served in World Wars I and
II. Commander-in-Chief, RAF Mediterranean and
Middle East, 1944–45. Air Member for Personnel,
1945–47. Commandant, Imperial Defence College,
1948–49. Chief of the Air Staff, 1950–52.

The papers, formerly held at the Royal Air Force
Museum, Hendon, are now in the care of the
Ministry of Defence's Air Historical Branch to whom
queries concerning access should be addressed. The
bulk of the collection relates to World War II,
but there are a number of files of significance for
the post-war period covering the Fleet Air Arm and
carrier policy, 1952–55; RAF–RN controversies,
1943–54; British and NATO control of maritime
operations, 1945–51; India and Pakistan in the period

immediately prior to partition; Airborne Force policy and Land/Air Warfare, 1940–48; pay and working conditions for RAF officers and other ranks, 1945–52; bomber policy, 1946–52; Exercise Thunderbolt (strategic policy and planning for war against the USSR), 1947; and Chief of the Air Staff papers, including material on Korea.

SLIM, 1ST VISCOUNT Field-Marshal William Joseph Slim (1891–1970) Military career. During World War II commanded 1st Burma Corps, 15th Indian Corps and 14th Army; Commander-in-Chief, Allied Land Forces, South East Asia, 1945–46. Chief of Imperial General Staff, 1948–52. Governor-General and Commander-in-Chief, Australia, 1953–60.

An important collection of papers, 1914–76, has been acquired by Churchill College, Cambridge. The collection comprises 12 boxes of private correspondence, military papers, articles, etc. The correspondence includes letters to his aide-de-camp, Nigel Bruce, 1949–69, and photocopies of letters to his daughter, 1940–59, and to Field-Marshal Lord Birdwood and Colonel H.R.K. Gibbs. The originals of the Slim-Gibbs correspondence are held at the Imperial War Museum.

SMALLWOOD, AIR CHIEF MARSHAL SIR DENIS (GRAHAM) (1918–97) Royal Air Force career, 1938–76. Vice-Chief of the Air Staff, 1970–74; Commander-in-Chief, RAF Strike Command, 1974–76 and UK Air Forces, 1975–76. Defence Industry consultant, 1977–83.

The Air Historical Branch, Ministry of Defence, holds a transcript and tape of an interview recorded with Sir Denis in 1976, covering his entire Royal Air Force career. It is particularly useful for the details it reveals about Operation 'Musketeer' (Suez), 1956. Access to the interview is at the discretion of the Head of the Air Historical Branch.

SMILES, SIR WALTER DORLING (1883–1953) MP (Con) Blackburn, 1931–45; (UU) Down, 1945–50; North Down, 1950–53.

The papers have been deposited in the Public Record Office of Northern Ireland. The collection includes election ephemera, 1945–50, newspaper cuttings, 1930–53, and some brief notes for speeches. Some papers relating to his daughter, Mrs P. Ford

(later Lady Fisher), who succeeded him as MP for North Down, 1953–55, are included in the collection.

SMITH, ELLIS (1896–1969) MP (Lab) Stoke-on-Trent, 1935–50; Stoke-on-Trent South, 1950–66. Parliamentary Secretary, Board of Trade, 1945–46. General President, United Patternmakers' Association.

The papers are held at Salford Archives Centre. A list is available (NRA 33407). The collection includes considerable correspondence and publications relating to his work as an MP. Other files concern the United Patternmakers' Association and local trades councils and trade union issues. There is also election ephemera and newspaper cuttings, etc.

SMITH, GEORGE IVAN (1915–95) Senior United Nations official. Personal representative of U Thant (United Nations Secretary-General), Central Africa, 1964.

A large collection of correspondence and papers relating to the United Nations has been deposited with the UN project at the Bodleian Library, Oxford. A microfilm of papers relating to political developments in Southern Africa, 1962–65, is deposited in the Centre for Southern African Studies, University of York. This includes material on the Tanganyika mutiny, 1964; files on federal politics in Rhodesia and Nyasaland; correspondence with Robert Mugabe, Sir Roy Welensky and Sir Edgar Whitehead; and a file on the aircraft accident in which Dag Hammarskjöld was killed.

SMITH, JOHN (1938–94) MP (Lab) Lanarkshire North, 1970–83, Monklands East, 1983–94. Leader of the Labour Party, 1992–94.

The papers have been placed in the Labour History Archive and Study Centre, University of Manchester. Researchers should also consult the biography by Mark Stuart.

SMITH, RENNIE (1888–1962) MP (Lab) Penistone, 1924–31. Journalist and lecturer. Joint Editor, *Central European Observer*, 1940–46. Civilian officer, Germany, 1946–49.

Thirty-four boxes of correspondence and papers, 1920s–60s, are deposited in the Bodleian Library, Oxford (ref. MSS Eng hist c 467–469, d 286–302, e 230–239, f 14–20). They include diaries, 1910–58; material on Labour politics throughout this period and on post-war international relations, including German reconstruction 1946–47, Czechoslovakia, and the Suez Crisis; and notes and drafts of his articles and books. There are files on the work of organisations such as the Friends of Europe, the Interparliamentary Union and the Worker's Educational Association.

SMITH, TRAFFORD (1912–75) Colonial Office career. On staff of UK delegation, United Nations Special Assembly on Palestine, 1948. Lieutenant-Governor of Malta, 1953–59. Assistant Under-Secretary of State, Commonwealth Office (previously Colonial Office), 1959–67. Ambassador to Burma, 1967–70.

There are four boxes of papers chiefly relating to his time in the Commonwealth Office, 1959–67, deposited in Rhodes House Library, Oxford (ref. MSS Brit Emp s 490). A list is available (NRA 39154). They include correspondence, texts of talks and printed material relating to his pre-war service in Fiji, 1938–39 and to his tours of the Caribbean and Western Pacific, 1938–66.

SMITH, WILLIAM HARVEY SAUMAREZ (1911–) Indian Civil Service, Bengal, 1934–47. Deputy Private Secretary to the Governor of Bengal, 1946–47.

A typescript copy of a diary kept from June to August 1947 (with explanatory notes added in 1987) has recently been placed in the India Office Library (ref. MSS Eur C 409).

SOAMES, BARON Arthur Christopher John Soames (1920–87) MP (Con) Bedford 1950–66. Parliamentary Under-Secretary, Air Ministry, 1955–57; Parliamentary and Financial Secretary, Admiralty, 1957–58; Secretary of State for War, 1958–60; Minister of Agriculture, Fisheries and Food, 1960–64; Ambassador, France, 1968–72; Vice-President, Commission of the European Communities, 1973–77. Governor of Southern Rhodesia, 1979–80; Lord President of the Council and Leader of the House of Lords, 1979–81.

There are 94 boxes of papers at Churchill College, Cambridge (ref. SOAM). The collection consists of

diaries, 1973–86, and papers on the Conservative Party (including correspondence with Margaret Thatcher). There is also some general correspondence and personal papers, together with copies of speeches and articles. A list is available (NRA 43568). The collection is currently closed.

SOPER, LORD Donald Oliver Soper (1903–98) Methodist minister. Superintendent of the West London Mission, 1936–78. President of the Methodist Conference, 1956; Christian Socialist Movement; League Against Cruel Sports. Chairman, Shelter, 1974–78. Prominent CND campaigner.

Most of the papers have been deposited with the Methodist Church Archives in Manchester. Lord Soper retained some recent files.

SORENSEN, BARON Reginald William Sorensen (1891–1971) MP (Lab) Leyton West, 1929–31, 1935–50; Leyton, 1950–64. Lord-in-Waiting, 1964–68. Former Free Christian Church minister, Walthamstow.

A collection of personal and political material is held at the House of Lords Record Office (ref. Hist Coll 102). A list is available (NRA 18378). The papers cover his entire career, 1908–68. They include an unpublished autobiography, backbencher correspondence and press-cuttings, and reports and memoranda concerning his overseas visits (including that of the British Parliamentary Delegation to India in 1946). His extra-parliamentary activities are fully documented, especially his extensive involvement in Indian affairs. There are also drafts and typescripts of articles on Commonwealth and colonial issues. Further papers relating to India are deposited in the Centre for South Asian Studies, Cambridge. A copy of the autobiography together with sermons, theological papers and literary writings is held in the Local Studies Section of Vestry House Museum, Walthamstow.

SOULBURY, 1ST VISCOUNT Sir Herwald Ramsbotham (1887–1971) MP (Con) Lancaster, 1929–41. Chairman, National Assistance Board, 1941–48. Governor-General, Ceylon, 1949–51.

The papers, which consisted mainly of speeches, were lent by his son to a prospective biographer in the 1970s and not returned. Some correspondence,

1942–52, is available in the Violet Markham papers at the LSE Library.

SOWREY, AIR MARSHAL SIR FREDERICK (BERESFORD) (1922–) Air force career. Director, Defence Policy, Ministry of Defence, 1968–70. Commandant, National Defence College, 1972–75.

There are papers relating to his career, including personal correspondence files, lectures, articles and conference papers relating to defence, 1961–85, in the Liddell Hart Centre for Military Archives, King's College, London.

SPEARING, NIGEL JOHN (1930–) MP (Lab) Newham South, 1974–97; Acton, 1970–74.

Mr Spearing states that he has retained extensive papers. They chiefly concern various parliamentary committees on European Community legislation and foreign affairs. He will make provision for their deposit in due course.

SPEARS, MAJOR-GENERAL SIR EDWARD LOUIS (1886–1974) MP (Nat Lib) Loughborough, 1922–24; (Con) Carlisle, 1931–45. Head of British Mission to General de Gaulle, 1940. Head of Mission to Syria and Lebanon, 1941. First Minister to Syria and Lebanon, 1942–44.

Churchill College, Cambridge, holds 337 boxes of papers covering his career, 1915–73, especially his time in politics (ref. SPRS). Special conditions of access apply to this collection.

A large collection is held in the Middle East Centre, St Antony's College, Oxford. It includes files on post-war Palestine, 1945–51; the Anglo-American Commission of Enquiry, 1946; Count Bernadotte's report to the United Nations General Assembly on Palestine, 1948; and the Arab–Israeli conflict from the establishment of the State of Israel onwards.

Papers relating to his earlier role as Head of the British Military Mission to Paris, 1917–20, are deposited in the Liddell Hart Centre, King's College, London.

STALLARD, SIR PETER (1915–95) Colonial administrator. Secretary to the Prime Minister, Federation of Nigeria, 1958–61. Governor of British Honduras, 1961–66.

A tape and transcript of an interview concerning his career are in Rhodes House Library, Oxford.

STANSGATE, 1ST VISCOUNT William Wedgwood Benn (1877–1960) MP (Lib) Tower Hamlets, St George's, 1906–18; Leith 1918–27; (Lab) Aberdeen North, 1928–31; Manchester Gorton, 1937–41. Secretary of State for India, 1929–31. Served in World War II in the Royal Air Force, 1940–45. Secretary of State for Air, 1945–47.

The papers of Viscount Stansgate are held at the House of Lords Record Office (ref. Hist Coll 141). Access to the collection is restricted and all enquiries should be directed to the Clerk of the Records.

STARK, DAME FREYA MADELINE (1893–1993) Writer and traveller. Government official in the Middle East during World War II.

Some correspondence has been placed in the Middle East Centre, St Antony's College, Oxford, which is to receive further deposits of papers and photographs. Researchers should note that the papers of her husband Stewart Perowne are also at the Middle East Centre.

Her vast correspondence, 1914–80, was published in eight volumes between 1974 and 1980. The originals are deposited in the University of Texas.

STEEL, LORD Sir David Steel (1938–) MP (Lib, 1965–88, Lib Dem since 1988) Roxburgh, Selkirk and Peebles, 1965–83; Tweeddale, Ettrick and Lauderdale, 1983–97. Leader of the Liberal Party, 1976–88. Co-founder, Social and Liberal Democratic Party, 1988.

Fourteen boxes of papers concerning his period as leader of the Liberal Party, 1976–88, were deposited in the LSE Library in November 1989. A handlist is available. The collection includes correspondence with fellow Liberals, files on election arrangements and on the Lib–Lab pact, 1977–78, the alliance with the SDP, 1981–88, and the formation of the Social and Liberal Democrats. There is correspondence with Paddy Ashdown, Richard Wainwright, Bill Walker, Bryan Gould, William Wallace, David Owen, Ian Wrigglesworth, Jeremy Thorpe, Simon Hughes and Sir Russell Johnston. There is additional correspondence from 1986 with Michael Meadowcroft, Annette Penhaligon, Lord Mackie, Lord Tordoff, Laura Grimond, Lord Gladwyn, Lord Hooson, Richard Wainwright, Cyril Smith, and Alexander Carlile. Access to the collection is restricted under a twenty-year rule. Additional papers have been retained.

STEELE, GENERAL SIR JAMES STUART (1894–1975)
Military career, 1915–50. Commander-in-Chief and High Commissioner, Austria, 1945–47. Adjutant-General to the Forces, 1947–50.

Some papers are available in the Royal Ulster Rifles Museum, Belfast. They include photocopies of papers relating to his Austrian posting, 1946–47, including correspondence with Austrian officials, and a photograph album of his visit to Marshal Tito, 1947, to sign an agreement on displaced Yugoslavs in Austria and Germany (ref. M55).

STEIN, LEONARD JACQUES (1887–1974)
Lawyer and Zionist. Vice-President, Anglo-Jewish Association, 1939–49. Author of *The Balfour Declaration* (1961) and joint editor of the *Letters and Papers of Chaim Weizmann* (1968).

A substantial collection of papers (140 boxes) is held at the Bodleian Library, Oxford. The post-war material includes files on the Anglo-Jewish Association; the Council of Christians and Jews, 1954–55 and 1962–69; the National Committee for the Rescue of Refugees from Nazi Terror, 1942–46; the Central British Fund for Jewish Relief, 1946–47; and the Jewish Historical Society. The collection includes his research papers for his books on the Balfour Declaration and Chaim Weizmann.

Elsewhere, the Anglo-Jewish Archive at Southampton University holds six folders of statements, papers and correspondence related to his presidency of the Anglo-Jewish Archive (ref. AJ 37/16 34). There is some additional material on the Anglo-Jewish Association. Separate lists are available (NRA 21917 and 24655). The British Board of Deputies archive, now at the London Metropolitan Archives, has some additional papers. There are 78 files on inter-war Palestine and Zionism at the Central Zionist Archives (A185). An interview transcript on his life and career is held at the Oral History Archive, Institute of Contemporary Jewry, Hebrew University, Jerusalem.

STEPHENS, IAN MELVILLE (1903–84)
Civil servant, journalist and historian. Deputy Director, Bureau of Public Information, Government of India,

1930–32; Director, 1932–37. Editor of the Calcutta *Statesman*, 1942–51. Fellow, King's College, Cambridge, 1952–58. Army Historian, Pakistan Government, 1957–60.

Seventeen boxes of papers, 1931–80, have been given to the Centre for South Asian Studies, Cambridge.

STERN, MICHAEL (1942–)
MP (Con) Bristol North West, 1983–97. Paymaster-General. Chairman, Bow Group.

His constituency papers have been placed in Bristol University Library (ref. DM 1793). A list is available (NRA 41342). The collection is not yet open. The papers, 257 boxes covering the years 1968–97, include material on the Bow Group.

STEVENS, SIR ROGER BENTHAM (1906–80)
Consular and Diplomatic Service. Assistant Under-Secretary, Foreign Office, 1948–51. Ambassador, Sweden, 1951–54; Iran, 1954–58. Member, United Nations Administrative Tribunal, 1972–80.

Twenty boxes of papers have been placed in Churchill College, Cambridge (ref. STVS). The collection includes private correspondence as well as papers on Sweden, Iran and the United Nations. A list is available (NRA 43566).

STEWART, LORD (Robert) Michael Maitland Stewart (1906–90)
MP (Lab) Fulham East, 1945–55; Fulham, 1955–79. MEP, 1975–76. PUS for War, 1947–51. Parliamentary Secretary, Ministry of Supply, May–Oct. 1951. Education and Science Secretary, 1964–65; Foreign Secretary, 1965–66; Secretary of State for Economic Affairs, 1966–67; Foreign Secretary, 1968–70.

A large collection of personal and political papers (*c.* 180 boxes) has been deposited in Churchill College, Cambridge (ref. STWT). The collection includes papers relating to the career of his wife, Baroness Stewart of Alvechurch. Enquiries on access to the Archivist.

STEWART, (JOHN) ALLAN (1942–)
MP (Con) East Renfrewshire, 1979–83; Eastwood since 1983.

A collection of constituency papers is deposited in the Mitchell Library, Strathclyde Regional Archives (ref. TD 1164).

STOCKTON, EARL OF (Maurice) Harold Macmillan (1894–1986)

MP (Con) Stockton-on-Tees, 1924–29 and 1931–45; Bromley, 1945–64. Minister Resident in North West Africa, 1942–45. Secretary of State for Air, 1945; Minister for Housing and Local Government, 1951–54; Defence, 1954–55. Foreign Secretary, 1955. Chancellor of the Exchequer, 1955–57. Prime Minister, 1957–63.

The extensive papers have been deposited in the Bodleian Library, Oxford. Reference should be made to the Bodleian Electronic Catalogue. A survey of the papers can be found in the journal *British History* (Winter 1997).

STOCKWELL, GENERAL SIR HUGH CHARLES (1903–86)

Military career. Served in World War II. Commander, 6th Airborne Division, Palestine, 1947–48. General Officer Commanding, Malaya, 1952–54; 1st Corps, British Army of the Rhine, 1954–56; Ground Forces, Suez, 1956. Military Secretary to Secretary of State for War, 1957–59. Adjutant-General to the Forces, 1959–60. Deputy Supreme Allied Commander, Europe, 1960–64.

There are 16 boxes of papers and photographs covering his entire career deposited in the Liddell Hart Centre, King's College, London. The collection is a rich source for conflicts involving the British Armed Forces after 1945 and includes papers on internal security in Palestine, 1945–48, the Malayan Emergency, 1952–53, and the Suez Crisis, 1956. The Palestine material comprises army reports and field security logs; police orders and signals; intelligence records; immigration and deportation files; briefing and propaganda notes on various Jewish organisations; reports on bombing and other outrages; files on the protection of oil installations; and British evacuation papers. For the Malayan Emergency, the papers include directives, memoranda and reports on administrative and technical policy matters; District War Executive Committee papers, 1952; appointment diaries, 1952–53; papers relating to Operation 'Dictum' (psychological warfare); operations and intelligence reports; records of chaplains' conferences, 1952; and photographs. In addition to his personal correspondence during the Suez Crisis, the collection contains some operational reports and post-Suez material including queries on casualties and articles and press-cuttings. There is

also a very limited amount of material covering his SHAPE (Supreme Headquarters, Allied Powers, Europe) appointment, chiefly consisting of photographs and a few speeches and newsletters. His post-retirement activities are also documented in the collection.

STOKES, SIR JOHN HEYDON ROMAINE (1917–)

MP (Con) Oldbury and Halesowen, 1970–Feb. 1974; Halesowen and Stourbridge, Feb. 1974–92.

Sir John retained letters, memoranda and press-cuttings covering his political career since 1970.

STOKES, RICHARD RAPIER (1897–1957)

MP (Lab) Ipswich, 1938–57. Minister of Works, 1950–51. Lord Privy Seal, 1951. Minister of Materials, 1951.

The correspondence and papers are deposited in the Bodleian Library, Oxford (ref. Stokes Papers). The collection is catalogued and a draft list is available. There are files on election campaigns from the 1920s to the 1950s; press-cuttings, speeches and speech notes, 1938–57; and his secretary's engagement diaries, 1926–56. There are several files on issues affecting the Middle East including the Suez Crisis, 1956–57. There are also files on post-war Germany, Italy and Czechoslovakia; on the Central African Federation, 1952–53; and on economic policy and trade with Canada during the 1950s. His correspondents include Clement Attlee, Anthony Eden and Herbert Morrison.

STOKES, WILLIAM HENRY (1894–1977)

Trade unionist. Member of various public bodies. Chairman, Midland Regional Board for Industry, 1945–50; Iron and Steel Corporation.

The papers have been placed in the Modern Records Centre, University of Warwick (MSS 180). A list is available (NRA 21924). The papers cover the whole of his career but much of the material is pre-1945. Included are diaries, 1913–77 (incomplete); speaking notes, 1936–70; Midlands Regional Board for Industry minutes and papers, 1941–51; National Advisory Committee minutes and notes, 1942–50; and extensive files on the Iron and Steel Corporation of Great Britain, including daily notes on corporation matters, 1950–53. There is a volume of minutes of the Amalgamated Engineering Union Shop Stewards, Humber Works, Coventry, 1950–63, and various notes, press-cuttings and circulars relating to the Coventry Toolroom Dispute of 1971. An additional group of papers relates to his work in industrial relations and service on public bodies (ref. MSS 289). The Modern Records Centre also holds the diary and correspondence of Mrs Francis Stokes. Coventry City Record Office holds Stokes' files as Armstrong Siddeley Personnel Manager during 1955 (ref. RO Acc 1060/116/1–2).

STONE, SIR (JOHN) RICHARD (NICHOLAS) (1913–91) Economist.

The papers have been placed by his widow in the Modern Archives Centre, King's College, Cambridge. A list is available (NRA 42283). The collection reflects his involvement with OEEC, OECD, the UN Statistical Commission etc.

STOPES, MARIE CARMICHAEL (1880–1958) Scientist and birth control pioneer. Founder, Mothers' Clinic for Constructive Birth Control, 1921. President, Society for Constructive Birth Control and Racial Progress. Author of numerous works on contraception.

The British Library holds an extensive collection of mainly pre-war correspondence and papers (ref. Add MSS 58447–770).

The Wellcome Contemporary Medical Archives Centre holds some 70 box files of queries sent to Marie Stopes by readers of her books, 1918–48. A list is available (NRA 24915). The Centre also holds papers relating to the Marie Stopes Clinics and files concerning her publications and also media coverage of her work. A collection of correspondence with the Eugenics Society is also held at the Centre. An additional list is available (NRA 24905).

STOPFORD, ROBERT WRIGHT (1901–76) Anglican clergyman. Bishop of Peterborough, 1956–61; London, 1961–73.

The papers have been placed in Lambeth Palace Library (ref. MSS 3421–27).

STOTT, MARY CHARLOTTE (1907–) Journalist and author. Women's editor, the *Guardian*, 1957–72.

A collection of papers is held at the Women's Library (ref. 7/CMS). The collection includes her papers as Women's editor of the *Guardian*, and the manuscripts and drafts of her books. There are also various files on the women's movement, the ordination of women priests, education, and abortion. Other files concern the National Union of Townswomen's Guilds (1950s–70s) and the Co-operative Women's Guild (*c.* 1980).

STOW HILL, BARON Sir Frank Soskice (1902–79) MP (Lab) Birkenhead East, 1945–50; Sheffield Neepsend, 1950–55; Newport, 1956–66. Solicitor-General, 1945–51. Attorney-General, 1951. Home Secretary, 1964–65. Lord Privy Seal, 1965–66.

The surviving papers have been deposited in the House of Lords Record Office. A list is available (NRA 19657).

STOWE, SIR KENNETH RONALD (1927–) Civil servant. Assistant Under-Secretary, Department of Health and Social Security, 1970–73 and Permanent Secretary, 1981–87; Under-Secretary and Deputy Secretary, Cabinet Office, 1973–79; PPS to the Prime Minister, 1975–79; PUS, Northern Ireland Office, 1979–81.

There are 74 boxes of papers at Churchill College, Cambridge (ref. STOW). One envelope relating to Wilson's resignation remains closed during the donor's lifetime.

STRACHEY, (EVELYN) JOHN ST LOE (1901–63) Labour politician and socialist writer. MP (Lab) Birmingham Aston, 1929–31; Dundee, 1945–50; Dundee West, 1950–63. PUS, Air Ministry, 1945–46. Minister of Food, 1946–50. Secretary of State for War, 1950–51.

The main collection of papers has remained in private hands and enquiries regarding access should be directed to the National Archives (NRA). The collection is arranged chronologically and covers his whole career, with greater depth of detail on the 1930s and 1950s. There is extensive correspondence with intellectuals and members of the Labour movement, including Fenner Brockway, Arnold Toynbee, J.K. Galbraith and Victor Gollancz. There are also drafts of published work and other writings and lectures from 1946 onwards. The remainder of the collection consists of papers on military affairs and civil aviation, 1950–63; notebooks and draft memoranda; and obituaries and other papers gathered by his widow, 1963–72. The House of Lords Record Office holds additional papers.

STRANG, 1ST BARON Sir William Strang (1893–1978) Diplomatic Service, 1919–53. Assistant Under-Secretary, Foreign Office, 1939–43. UK Representative, European Advisory Commission, 1943–45. Political Adviser to Commander-in-Chief, Germany, 1945–47. PUS, Foreign Office (German Section), 1947–49; Foreign Office, 1949–53. Chairman, Royal Institute of International Affairs, 1958–65.

There are 14 boxes of papers, 1919–78, deposited in Churchill College, Cambridge (ref. STRN). A list is available (NRA 24829). The collection contains papers and correspondence relating to his work at the Foreign Office, with greater detail on his career after 1945. There are also letters to historians written during the 1970s concerning events connected to his career between 1945 and 1953. Special conditions of access apply. Papers for the earlier part of his career are held at St Antony's College, Oxford, and University College, London.

STRANGE, IRIS (fl. 1960s–70s) Campaigner for War Widows.

Reference should be made to the collection in the War Widows Archive, University of Staffordshire. See *History Workshop Journal*, Vol. 38, for a description of the papers.

STRAUSS, BARON George Russell Strauss (1901–93) MP (Lab) Lambeth North, 1929–31 and 1934–50; Lambeth Vauxhall, 1950–79. Parliamentary Secretary, Ministry of Transport, 1945–47. Minister of Supply, 1947–51.

Lord Strauss retained few papers. The only item was a copy of his untitled autobiography, which was not commercially published. It has been deposited in Churchill College, Cambridge (STRS). The North Lambeth Constituency Labour Party records at the LSE Library include one box of his papers. A transcript interview is held with the Nuffield Oral History Project.

STREET, MAJOR-GENERAL VIVIAN WAKEFIELD (1912–70) Military career. Military adviser, Jordan.

One box of papers, including material on his position when military adviser to King Hussein of Jordan, 1959–60, is in the Liddell Hart Centre for Military Archives, King's College, London.

STRINGER, SIDNEY (1899–1969) Midland Labour politician. Leader of the Labour majority, Coventry City Council, 1938–67. Mover of the controversial motion in 1954 for Coventry to abandon civil defence.

The Modern Records Centre, University of Warwick, holds some papers (ref. MSS 24). A list is available (NRA 29308). The collection includes over 200 letters concerning the civil defence controversy, 1954, and a small group of papers regarding Coventry City policy, mainly on housing and housing finance, 1958 and 1966–67. Some similar material has been deposited in Coventry Record Office.

STRONG, MAJOR-GENERAL SIR KENNETH WILLIAM DOBSON (1900–82) Career in military intelligence. Served in World War II as Head of Intelligence, Home Forces, 1942; Head of General Eisenhower's Intelligence Staff, 1943–45. Director-General, Political Intelligence Department, Foreign Office, 1945–47. Director, Joint Intelligence Bureau, Ministry of Defence, 1948–64. Director-General of Intelligence, Ministry of Defence, 1964–66.

The General informed the Liddell Hart Centre, King's College, London, that the papers used in writing his memoirs, *Intelligence at the Top* (1968) and *Men of Intelligence* (1970), were destroyed. The Imperial War Museum holds a microfilm of his correspondence with Dwight Eisenhower following the publication of *Intelligence at the Top* in which they discuss Allied Intelligence and relations with the USSR during World War II and afterwards.

STUART OF FINDHORN, 1ST VISCOUNT James Gray Stuart (1897–1971) MP (Con) Moray and Nairn, 1923–59. Junior Lord of the Treasury, 1935–41. Joint Parliamentary Secretary to the Treasury and Government Chief Whip, 1941–45. Secretary of State for Scotland, 1951–57.

Nineteen bundles of political correspondence and papers, 1916–64, are held by his nephew, the 20th Earl of Moray. A list is available (NRA 10983 and NRA (S) 0217 part 5). These include various notes on the future of the Conservative Party and on political appointments, both written in 1945, and some material on the Suez Crisis. Further details are given in *British Cabinet Ministers, 1900–51*.

Private Office papers as Secretary of State for Scotland are in the files of the relevant government departments.

SURRIDGE, SIR ERNEST REX EDWARD (1899–1990) Colonial Service in Kenya and Tanganyika, 1924–51. Chief Secretary to Government of Tanganyika, 1946–51. Salaries Commissioner, Cyprus, 1953–54; High Commission Territories (South Africa), 1958–59; Gibraltar, 1959–60. Financial Commissioner, Seychelles, 1957–58.

A tape and transcript of an interview covering his career is held in Rhodes House Library, Oxford (ref. MSS Afr s 1813). The same library also holds an interview with Lady Surridge (ref. MSS Afr s 1480). No other papers have been located.

SUTHERLAND, SIR GORDON BRIMS BLACK McIVOR (1907–80) Scientist. Director, National Physics Laboratory, 1956–64. Master, Emmanuel College, Cambridge, 1964–77.

The papers have been deposited in Cambridge University Library. Apart from scientific research papers, there are files on wider issues such as education and science policy, university expansion and the 'brain drain' in the 1960s.

SWANN, LORD Michael Meredith Swann (1920–90) Scientist and public servant. Chairman, BBC, 1973–80.

There are papers in Edinburgh University Library, to where enquiries concerning access should be addressed.

SWINLEY, CAPTAIN CASPER SILAS BALFOUR (1898–1983) Naval career. Chief Staff Officer, Commander-in-Chief, Malta, 1942. Chief of Naval Information, Admiralty, 1947. Commodore and Chief of Staff, Royal Pakistan Navy, 1953–54.

A collection of papers, formerly at Churchill College, Cambridge, is now housed in the Imperial War Museum. The collection covers the period 1916–51, and includes a memoir (1898–1941), copies of some of his diaries (1919–26), and correspondence. The post-war section of the collection includes material from his time as Chief of Naval Information, 1947–48.

SWINTON, 1ST EARL OF Sir Philip Cunliffe-Lister (formerly Lloyd-Graeme) (1884–1972) MP (Con) Hendon, 1918–35. President of the Board of Trade, 1922–23, 1924–29 and 1931; Secretary of State for the Colonies, 1931–35; Air, 1935–38. Cabinet Minister Resident in West Africa, 1942–44; Minister for Civil Aviation, 1944–45; Chancellor of the Duchy of Lancaster and Minister of Materials, 1951–52. Commonwealth Relations Secretary, 1952–55.

The papers (42 boxes) covering the period 1914–70 are held at Churchill College, Cambridge (ref. SWIN). A list is available (NRA 21107). A substantial proportion of the collection consists of post-1950 papers, including important political and private correspondence. Section 1 (ref. Acc no. 174) contains papers from his time in opposition; as Chancellor of the Duchy of Lancaster; and as Secretary of State for Commonwealth Relations. There are also personal letters, 1956–70; House of Lords papers on procedure and reform; and House of Lords papers on Rhodesia and other subjects, 1956–71. There is also some historical writing by Swinton and others; miscellaneous correspondence and papers; financial correspondence, and papers on the Anglo-Belgian Union. Section 2 (ref. Acc no. 270) includes some speeches and correspondence, 1945–59. Section 3 (ref. Acc no. 313) contains a draft autobiography, various papers on Indian Affairs; letters, 1951–59; files on security, 1950–51; and other correspondence and engagement diaries.

SYMON, SIR ALEXANDER (COLIN BURLINGTON) (1902–74) Deputy High Commissioner, India, 1946–49. Assistant Under-Secretary of State, Commonwealth Relations Office, 1949–52. High Commissioner, Pakistan, 1954–61.

Two volumes and three boxes of papers for the years 1930–74 are held at the India Office Library (ref. MSS Eur E 367). The collection also includes his wife's letters.

T

TALBOT, JOHN ELLIS (1906–67) MP (Con) Brierley Hill, 1959–67.

His political files, 1959–67, are in Dudley Archives and Local History Service, Coseley, Dudley.

TALBOT, MAJOR-GENERAL DENNIS EDMUND BLAQUIÈRE (1908–94) Military career. Chief of Staff, BAOR, and GOC, Rhine Army Troops, 1963–64.

There are papers in the Liddell Hart Centre for Military Archives, King's College, London.

TALLENTS, SIR STEPHEN GEORGE (1884–1958) Public servant. Imperial Secretary, Northern Ireland, 1922–26. Secretary, Empire Marketing Board, 1926–33. Principal Assistant Secretary, Ministry of Town and Country Planning, 1943–46.

A collection of papers is held at the Institute of Commonwealth Studies, London. A list is available (NRA 21999). The collection is mainly pre-war but also includes some later correspondence and press-cuttings. Some miscellaneous family papers are contained within the Violet Markham papers at the LSE Library. (NRA 30246)

TATCHELL, PETER (1952–) Australian-born, Labour Party, CND and gay rights activist. Fought February 1983 Southwark and Bermondsey by-election.

The early papers, deposited at the LSE Library in 1992, include copies of articles for various publications, letters to the press, correspondence with politicians, along with the papers of activist groups e.g. ACT UP and OutRage! They cover the period 1981 to 1992. Subsequent important deposits of more recent material have now been made.

TAYLOR, CHRIS (fl. 1970s–80s) Left activist.

There are papers in the Modern Records Centre, University of Warwick (ref. MSS 406). The collection contains various Trotskyite papers, including Workers' Fight minutes, correspondence, internal bulletins *c.* 1972–76; International Communist League minutes, internal bulletins, circulars, 1974–75; Intervention Collective minutes, circulars, discussion bulletins 1977–79; and Socialist Charter publications, discussion bulletins, etc.

TAYLOR, SIR THOMAS MURRAY (1897–1962) Academic and lawyer. Principal and Vice-Chancellor, University of Aberdeen, 1948–62; formerly Professor of Law, 1935–48. Executive Committee, World Council of Churches.

The papers have been placed in Aberdeen University Library. A list is available (NRA 19918 and NRA (S) 1229). The collection includes copies of published works, 1946–65, manuscripts and type-scripts of sermons and speeches, 1936–62, legal opinions, 1936–48, and papers relating to his public work. This latter group includes material on the Inquiry into Crofting Conditions, 1951–54, the Crofters' Commission, 1951–61, the World Council of Churches, 1948–59, and General Assemblies, 1931–58. There is also extensive correspondence relating to university administration.

TEMPLER, FIELD-MARSHAL SIR GERALD WALTER ROBERT (1898–1985) Military career. Served in World Wars I and II. Director of Military Government, 21st Army Group, 1945–46. Director of Military Intelligence, War Office, 1946–48. Vice-Chief of the Imperial General Staff, 1948–50. General Officer Commanding-in-Chief, Eastern Command, 1950–52. High Commissioner and Director of Operations, Malaya, 1952–54. Chief of the General Staff, 1955–58.

A large collection of papers, mainly relating to Malaya, 1951–54, has been deposited in the National Army Museum London (ref. 7410–29). It includes correspondence, drafts and texts of speeches and press-cuttings. Further material on his career can be found in the papers of his assistant in Malaya, Major-General David Lloyd-Owen, which are also deposited in the Museum. Additional correspondence as High Commissioner of Malaya, 1952–53, may be found in Rhodes House Library, Oxford.

TENBY, 1ST VISCOUNT Gwilym Lloyd George (1894–1967) MP (Lib) Pembrokeshire, 1922–24 and 1929–50; (Con) Newcastle-on-Tyne North, 1951–57. Parliamentary Secretary, Board of Trade, 1931–34 and 1939–41; Ministry of Food, 1940–42; Fuel and Power, 1942–45. Minister of Food, 1951–55. Home Secretary, 1955–57.

The small collection formerly held by his younger son has been purchased by the National Library of Wales. The material (which is very thin on the post-war period, except for some papers concerning the 1951 election) is more fully described in *British Cabinet Ministers, 1900–51*.

TENNANT, ADMIRAL SIR WILLIAM GEORGE (1890–1963) Naval career. Flag Officer, Levant and Eastern Mediterranean, 1944–46. Commander-in-Chief, America and West Indies Station, 1946–49.

The National Maritime Museum has a collection of papers, 1905–63 (ref. TEN). The post-war sections include correspondence with survivors of the Malayan campaign, 1945; incoming letters, 1945–50; files of correspondence, notes and speeches dating from his West Indies command, 1946–49; material on his chairmanship of an Admiralty Committee on Roving Commissions and the Fluid Fleet, 1949; and post-retirement correspondence, notes and speeches.

TERRINGTON, 5TH BARON Christopher Montague Woodhouse (1917–2001) MP (Con) Oxford, 1959–66 and 1970–Oct. 1974. Led British Military Mission to German-occupied Greece, 1942–44. Secretary-General, Allied Mission to supervise Greek elections, 1946. Director-General, Royal Institute of International Affairs, 1955–59. Parliamentary Secretary, Ministry of Aviation, 1961–62. Joint Under-Secretary of State, Home Office, 1962–64.

Three boxes of his papers, 1942–65, were placed in the Liddell Hart Centre, King's College, London, in February 1976. A list is available (NRA 23080). The material includes Special Operations Executive

documents, 1942–45; a report by Woodhouse on the Allied Military Mission to Greece, 1942–44; reports of the BBC Monitoring Service, 1948–50; and personal accounts of operations in Greece, written by Woodhouse and G.K. Wines. A later deposit includes additional papers relating to his service with the British Military Mission to Greek guerillas in German occupied Greece and the deposition of Hussein in Iran, 1942–76. The collection does not include any papers concerning his later career in politics.

THATCHER OF KESTEVEN, BARONESS Margaret Hilda Thatcher (1925–) MP (Con) Finchley, 1959–92. Joint Parliamentary Secretary, Ministry of Pensions and National Insurance, 1961–64; Secretary of State for Education and Science, 1970–74; Leader of the Opposition, 1975–79. Prime Minister, 1979–90.

The papers have been placed in Churchill College Cambridge, where they have been loaned in perpetuity by the Margaret Thatcher Archive Trust. The Thatcher archive amounts to more than 2500 boxes containing one million documents dating back to 1945, including photographs and film. Margaret Thatcher never kept a regular diary, only occasional aides-memoires. A detailed list is now available (NRA 43914) as well as electronic catalogues. The papers of Finchley and Golders Green Conservative Association for her time as MP are also at Churchill (NRA 43999).

THOMAS, SIR BEN BOWEN (1899–1977) Educationalist, author and UNESCO official.

His papers have been deposited at the National Library of Wales. The collection includes correspondence with Thomas Jones on Coleg Harlech and education in Wales, 1927–55; files relating to the Rural Development Board in Wales, 1968–69; the 1973 establishment of the Welsh Language Council; correspondence and diaries covering his journeys to the Far East, Europe and North and South America as member and chairman of the Executive Board of UNESCO, 1946–65; and miscellaneous material. A list is available (NRA 37030).

THOMAS, DAVID EMLYN (1892–1954) MP (Lab) Aberdare, 1946–54.

His papers, 1946–54, have been placed in the National Library of Wales. A list is available (NRA 26130). They include pocket diaries and constituency correspondence.

THOMAS, GRAHAM F. (fl. 1940s–80s) Welsh socialist, author and lecturer. Worked in the Sudan and Kenya.

The correspondence he maintained while living in Africa during the 1950s and 1960s has recently been deposited with the Welsh Political Archive at the National Library of Wales. The collection includes over 80 letters from the Llanelli MP, James Griffiths (1949–72) and 65 from the Cardiff and later Middlesbrough MP, Professor Hilary Marquand (1945–61).

THOMAS, IORWERTH RHYS (1895–1966) MP (Lab) Rhondda West, 1950–66.

A collection of correspondence, 1926–66, and miscellaneous other papers has been deposited in the Library of University College, Swansea.

THOMAS, JEFFREY (1933–89) MP (Lab and from 1981, SDP) Abertillery, 1970–83.

A collection of papers is held at the National Library of Wales. They include constituency correspondence, 1973–82; subject files on domestic politics, 1978–82, legal matters, 1978–80 and foreign affairs, 1978–81; correspondence and papers on the formation of the SDP, 1981–85 and his decision to join in 1981; and some early personal papers, 1936–57.

THOMPSON, EDWARD PALMER (1924–93) Historian and peace activist. Author of *The Making of the English Working Class* (1963), *Beyond the Cold War* (1982), *Customs in Common* (1991), etc.

The papers are promised to the Bodleian Library, Oxford (which already has his father's papers). There is some correspondence with Ernest Edward Dodd (who undertook research for Thompson) in the Modern Records Centre, University of Warwick (ref. MSS 369). A list is available (NRA 40028).

THOMPSON, SIR HAROLD WARRIS (1908–83) Professor of Chemistry, Oxford University, 1964–75. Foreign Secretary, Royal Society, 1965–71. Chairman, Great Britain–China Committee 1972–74; Great Britain–China Centre, 1974–80.

An extensive archive has been deposited in the library of the Royal Society. A list is available (NRA 31136). Section A consists of a few reports and some correspondence on his scientific research. Section B is the largest and deals with his work for the Royal Society as Foreign Secretary and on the International Relations Committee. The papers document how international crises such as the Cultural Revolution in China and the Prague Spring have hindered the promotion of international science. Section C includes material on his membership of various scientific and cultural organisations such as the Great Britain–China Committee (later the Great Britain–China Centre). Sections D and E relate to various visits and conferences and to his involvement with the Football Association.

THOMPSON, MARJORIE ELLIS (1957–) Peace activist. Chair, CND, 1987–93. Campaigner on numerous social issues.

There are papers in the Modern Records Centre, University of Warwick (ref. MSS 428). The collection includes papers relating to her work as an official of CND and its chair, 1987–93, and her work as Chair of the Committee to stop War in the Gulf, 1990–91. Some of the papers are closed for research.

THOMPSON, REGINALD WILLIAM (1904–77) War correspondent and author. Covered the Korean War for *The Daily Telegraph*.

Four boxes of correspondence with Sir Desmond Morton, 1943–71, Major-General Eric Dorman-O'Gowan (formerly Dorman-Smith), 1960–69 and Captain Sir Basil Liddell Hart, 1952–74 are deposited in the Liddell Hart Centre, King's College, London.

THOMPSON, MAJOR WILLOUGHBY HARRY (1919–) Army officer, 1937–47. Colonial administrator, Kenya, 1948–63. Colonial Secretary, Falkland Islands, 1963–69. Acting Administrator, British Virgin Islands, 1969. Commissioner, Anguilla, 1969–71. Governor of Montserrat, 1971–74.

Major Thompson wrote his memoirs in 1987 and has deposited them in the Imperial War Museum (ref. 89/13/1). They cover his varied career, including the Mau Mau years in Kenya; the Hola affair; the rise of Amin; the Falklands dispute with Argentina, 1963–69; and the British reoccupation of Anguilla following the 1971 revolution.

THOMPSON-McCAUSLAND, **LUCIUS PERRONET (1904–84)** Adviser to the Governor of the Bank of England, 1949–65. Attended the pre-Bretton Woods Conference with Lord Keynes in 1943 and the Havana Conference in 1948. Government consultant on international monetary problems, 1965–68.

There are some memoranda, correspondence and papers (91 pieces, 1941–65) in the Bank of England archive (ref. ADM14) (NRA 33132).

THOMSON OF MONIFIETH, BARON George Morgan Thomson (1921–) MP (Lab) Dundee East, July 1952–72. Minister of State, Foreign Office, 1964–66. Chancellor of the Duchy of Lancaster, 1966–67. Joint Minister of State, Foreign Office, 1967. Commonwealth Affairs Secretary, 1967–68. Minister without Portfolio, 1968–69. Chancellor of the Duchy of Lancaster, 1969–70. EEC Commissioner, 1973–77. Chairman, Independent Broadcasting Authority, 1981–88.

Lord Thomson has retained extensive papers relating to his political career since 1946. They are unsorted and unavailable to researchers at present.

THOMSON, SIR GEORGE PAGET (1892–1975) Nuclear physicist. Professor of Physics, Imperial College, London, 1930–52. Chairman, first British Committee on Atomic Energy, 1940–41. Master of Corpus Christi, Cambridge, 1952–62.

The papers and correspondence are deposited at the Wren Library, Trinity College, Cambridge. A list is available (NRA 24104). The collection includes records on his part in the British nuclear research programme at Associated Electrical Industries, Aldermaston, and at Harwell between 1946 and 1963. One box of papers concerning the Maud Committee is at Churchill College, Cambridge (ref. TMSN). Special conditions of access apply.

THORNETH, ALAN (1937–) Trade unionist. Shop steward, British Leyland. Founder member, Workers Socialist League. The British Leyland 'mole' of the 1970s.

There are some papers, 1951–c. 97, in the Modern Records Centre, University of Warwick (ref. MSS 391). A list is available (NRA 42682). The papers include branch minutes, correspondence files, political publications, etc.

THORNEYCROFT, BARON (George Edward) Peter Thorneycroft (1909–94) MP (Con) Stafford, 1938–45; Monmouth, 1945–66. Numerous Cabinet posts, including Chancellor of the Exchequer, 1957–58. Conservative Party Chairman, 1975–81.

His political papers, 44 boxes covering the period 1951–84, have been placed in the Hartley Library, University of Southampton (ref. MS 278). They include files relating to his time as President of the Board of Trade, as Chancellor of the Exchequer and as Secretary of State for Defence. The Bodleian Library has his files as Conservative Party Chairman.

THORPE, (JOHN) JEREMY (1929–) MP (Lib) North Devon, 1959–79. Leader of the Liberal Party, 1967–76.

A large collection of papers (c. 350 volumes) has been acquired by the British Library to where enquiries concerning access should be addressed.

THWAITES, BRIGADIER PETER TREVENEN (1926–91) Military career. Chairman, Joint Staff, Sultan of Oman's Armed Forces, 1977–81.

There are some papers, including material on Muscat, in the Liddell Hart Centre for Military Archives, King's College, London.

THYNE, WILLIAM (1901–78) Scottish banker and businessman. Active in Rhodesian affairs after 1948. Founded Scottish Study Group on the Federation of Rhodesia and Nyasaland.

His Rhodesian papers are in the Centre for Southern African Studies, University of York. The collection includes records and minutes of the Scottish Study Group and correspondence with, among others, Sir Roy Welensky, 1960–65, Garfield Todd, Sir Alec Douglas-Home, Sir Hugh Beadle, etc.

TILLEY, JOHN VINCENT (1941–) MP (Lab) Lambeth Central, Apr. 1978–83. Treasurer, Tribune Group, 1979–82.

Mr Tilley stated that he has retained a number of files relating to constituency matters, 1978–83, and to earlier candidacies in other London constituencies during the 1970s. He also retains papers from his time as Treasurer of the Tribune Group of Labour MPs (including an application by Tony Benn to join the Group); files relating to James Callaghan's

Election Team on which he served; and various papers on the 1981 British Nationality Bill.

TILNEY, SIR JOHN DUDLEY ROBERT TARLETON (1907–94) MP (Con) Liverpool Wavertree, 1950–Feb. 1974. Parliamentary Under-Secretary, Commonwealth Relations, 1962–64.

A collection of *c*. 100 boxes, deposited by Sir John in 1975, is held at the Picton Library, Liverpool (ref. Acc. 2805). The collection covers his career from 1950 onwards, and relates to his public and political life, including papers on various visits abroad on behalf of the Inter-Parliamentary Union and the Commonwealth Parliamentary Union.

TINKER, HUGH RUSSELL (1921–2000) Historian and author. Director, Institute of Race Relations, 1970–72. Liberal activist. Vice President, Ex-Services Campaign for Nuclear Disarmament.

There are six boxes of papers (1965–82) in the Institute of Commonwealth Studies, University of London. A list is available (NRA 43056). There is some material on the Institute of Race Relations and his Liberal Party involvement.

TITMUSS, RICHARD MORRIS (1907–73) Social theorist. Cabinet Office historian, 1942–49. Professor of Social Administration, London School of Economics, 1950–73. Deputy Chairman, Supplementary Benefits Commission, 1968–73.

Some 142 boxes of papers, *c*. 1939–73, have been deposited at the LSE Library. A list is available (NRA 30236). The papers, arranged in five categories, reflect his wide involvement in medical care, sociology, poverty and welfare. Further details are available from the Archivist. Some further papers collected by Margaret Gowing have also been deposited. An additional 11 files on poverty, social medicine and world health are held at the Wellcome Unit for the History of Medicine, Oxford.

TIZARD, SIR HENRY THOMAS (1885–1959) Academic career. Permanent Secretary, Department of Scientific and Industrial Research, 1927–29. Member, Council of Minister of Aircraft Production; Air Council, 1941–43. Chairman, Advisory Council on Scientific Policy and Defence Research Policy Committee, 1946–52.

Over 700 files of papers, 1891–1959, are deposited in the Imperial War Museum. A catalogue is available (NRA 24549). Special conditions of access apply to this collection, and applications to use it should be addressed to the Keeper of the Department of Documents. The papers record his role in scientific research and development, 1934–43; cooperation with the USA and Commonwealth countries on technological research during World War II; and British atomic policy, 1944–52.

Additional papers on defence research policy, 1945–49, are in the DEFE 9 series at the National Archives.

TODD, BARON Sir Alexander Robertus Todd (1907–97) Scientist. Professor of Organic Chemistry, Cambridge University, 1944–71. President, Association for the Advancement of Science, 1969–70. Chairman, Advisory Council on Scientific Policy, 1952–64; Royal Commission on Medical Education, 1965–68.

A collection of papers (*c*. 200 boxes) has been deposited at Churchill College, Cambridge (ref. TODD). The papers cover his career as Professor of Organic Chemistry at Cambridge, 1944–71; Master of Christ's College, 1963–78, and his work as a scientific adviser to successive governments. Special conditions of access apply. Further papers at Cambridge University Library include circulars, minutes, reviews and press-cuttings, 1963–71, relating to the Royal Commission on Medical Education, 1965–68. There is also correspondence with members of the Commission including Lord Platt, Sir George Godber, Sir Frank Lee, Sir John Wolfenden and T.S. Black-Kelly.

TODD, SIR (REGINALD STEPHEN) GARFIELD (1908–) Prime Minister of Southern Rhodesia, 1953–58. Arrested by Ian Smith Regime, 1965, and again in 1972.

There are some papers reported in the Commonwealth Resource Centre, Commonwealth Institute, London. They include letters explaining conditions under detention, confinement and imprisonment during the period of Unilateral Declaration of Independence after 1965.

TOFAHRN, PAUL (1901–79) Assistant General Secretary, International Transport Workers'

Federation (ITWF), 1956–68. UK resident from 1940. Member of the Fabian Society and the Railway Development Society; Executive Committee Member, Pedestrian Association for Road Safety.

His papers covering the period 1930–76 are held at the Modern Records Centre, University of Warwick (ref. MSS 238). A list is available (NRA 27428). The collection dates mainly from the 1940s and includes files on the International Transport Workers' Federation (based in London from 1945) covering the period 1940–68. Correspondents include Harold Wilson, Rita Hinden, Charles Lindley and Edo Fimmen. There are papers on differences of opinion within the ITWF administration; peace aims; the Joint Council of the Three Internationals; relations with the International Federation of Trades Unions, *c.* 1940–45; the New York office; and his private journals, 1941–43. There are also files on the Emergency International Trades Union Congress, 1941–45; the World Trades Union Conference/World Federation of Trades Unions, 1944–45; the International Union of Food and Drink Workers (English and German press reports, 1932–36); and the Public Services International. The collection also includes material on the post-war Belgian Socialist Party and on his later campaigning for road safety. The Modern Records Centre also holds part of an unpublished memoir of Harold Lewis, former ITWF General Secretary (ref. MSS 238x/6).

TONYPANDY, VISCOUNT Thomas George Thomas (1909–97) MP (Lab) Cardiff Central, 1945–50; Cardiff West, 1950–83. Joint Parliamentary Under-Secretary, Home Office, 1964–66; Minister of State, Welsh Office, 1966–67; Commonwealth Office, 1967–68. Secretary of State for Wales, 1968–70. Speaker of the House of Commons, 1976–83.

An extensive collection of papers (over 600 files) has been deposited in the National Library of Wales A list is now available (NRA 41954). Enquiries regarding access should be directed to the Archivist.

TOWNSEND, PETER (1928–) Expert on social policy. Senior academic posts at Bristol, Essex, LSE, etc. Numerous major publications on poverty, old age, etc.

The papers are part of the National Archive of Social Policy and Social Change, University of Essex, to where enquiries should be addressed.

TOYE, COLONEL CLAUDE HUGH MORLEY (1917–) Military career. Served in World War II. Acting Chief Intelligence Officer, Burma Command, 1947.

Some papers concerning political developments in Burma, May to September 1947, are in the India Office Library (ref. MSS Eur D 1108).

TOYNBEE, ARNOLD JOSEPH (1899–1975) Historian and writer. Director of Studies at the Royal Institute of International Affairs from 1925 and Research Professor of International History, London University. Director, Research Department, Foreign Office, 1943–46.

His library and personal papers have been deposited at the Bodleian Library, Oxford. The collection consists of correspondence, diaries and unpublished papers. The Royal Institute of International Affairs at Chatham House has papers relating to his time as Director of Studies.

TREACY, ERIC (1907–78) Anglican clergyman. Rector of Keighley, 1945–50; Archdeacon and Vicar of Halifax 1950–61; Bishop Suffragan of Pontefract, 1961–68; Bishop of Wakefield, 1968–78.

Some of his correspondence and papers, 1947–78, are held by the West Yorkshire Archive Service, Calderdale. A list is available (NRA 26592). The collection contains copies of various sermons, speeches and talks and a large set of photographs. Additional papers can be found in Lambeth Palace Library, including his papers and correspondence as Bishop of Wakefield, and his diaries and autobiographical notes (ref. MSS 3566–75).

TREVASKIS, SIR (GERALD) KENNEDY (NICOLAS) (1915–90) Colonial civil servant. British Military Administration, Eritrea, 1941–50. Political Officer, Western Aden Protectorate, 1951. High Commissioner for Aden and the Protectorate of South Arabia, 1963–65.

Six boxes of correspondence and memos, covering his service in Eritrea and Western Aden, 1944–65, are in Rhodes House Library, Oxford (ref. MSS Brit Emp s 367). A list is available (NRA 13845).

TRIFFIN, ROBERT (1911–) Economist. Economic Adviser to the Organisation for European Cooperation and Development and the European Economic Community.

A microfilm (34 reels) of his papers has been deposited at the LSE Library (ref. Coll Misc 739). The collection consists of papers on European Monetary Policy, 1969–74: *Robert Triffin, le CAEUE de Jean Monnet et les Questions Monitaires Européennes 1969–74*. The originals are in the European University Institute at Florence.

TUCKMAN, FREDERICK (FRED) (1922–) MEP (Con) Leicester, 1979–89. President, Anglo-Jewish Association, 1989–95.

There are papers in the Hartley Library, University of Southampton (ref. MS 270).

TUGENDHAT, BARON Sir Christopher Samuel Tugendhat (1937–) MP (Con) Cities of London and Westminster, 1970–74; City of London and Westminster South, 1974–76. European Community Commissioner, 1977–85; and Vice-President, 1981–85.

His papers relating to his time in the European Community are held at Cambridge University Library. There are extensive files on the work of each of the EC Directorates-General. Subject areas covered include trade agreements; financial and economic affairs; international legal jurisdiction; competition, regional and industrial aid to member states; social affairs, employment, poverty, unions and the movement of workers; agriculture; transport; development; consumer protection and the environment; scientific research and development; fisheries; regional development policy; financial institutions and taxation; energy; and EC budgetary control. There are also files on his visits and meetings throughout the UK. Enquiries concerning access should be directed to the Archivist. Lord Tugendhat retains some constituency correspondence.

TUKER, LIEUTENANT-GENERAL SIR FRANCIS IVAN SIMMS (1894–1967) Indian Army career. Served in World Wars I and II. Divisional Commander, 1941–44; Chairman, Frontier Committee, India, 1944; General Officer Commanding Ceylon, 1945; Corps Commander, 1945. General Officer Commanding-in-Chief, Eastern Command, India, 1946–47.

The Imperial War Museum has over 70 files of official and private papers, 1914–67, chiefly relating to Indian defence and frontier problems (pre-war and post-war), Indian independence, Indo-Pakistan relations, and Nepal and the Gurkha regiments. A list is available (NRA 28562). Certain sections of the collection are subject to restricted conditions of access.

TULL, THOMAS STUART (1914–82) Pre-war Indian Civil Service career. Served with the Royal Air Force in India and South East Asia during World War II. In charge of repatriating Allied prisoners of war, Indonesia, 1946. Post-war diplomat; Press Counsellor, Cairo, 1956; Consul-General, Durban, 1966–67; High Commissioner, Malawi, 1967–71. Founder Chairman of Philafrica Action Group, 1974.

A collection of papers is available in the Liddell Hart Centre, King's College, London. They relate mainly to operations in Java, 1945–46, and include material on the Indian Air Force; the repatriation of Allied POWs and the transfer of evacuees; situation reports on operations against Japanese troops and Indonesian Nationalists; and a typescript memoir, *Mission to Java*, written in 1980, which covers his experiences from 1938 until 1946. The papers do not cover his time in the Foreign Office and his post-retirement work in Third World Development.

TURNBULL, SIR FRANCIS FEARON (1905–88) Civil servant. Principal Private Secretary, Secretary of State for India, 1941–46.

His diary of the Cabinet mission to India, 1946 is in Churchill College, Cambridge.

TURNBULL, SIR RICHARD GORDON (1909–98) Colonial Service in Kenya from 1931. Governor and Commander-in-Chief, Tanganyika, 1958–61. Governor-General, 1961–62. High Commissioner for Aden and the Protectorate of South Arabia, 1965–67.

Tapes and transcripts of his work in Kenya, 1931–58, are in Rhodes House Library, Oxford. The Department of Sound Recordings, Imperial War Museum, holds a transcript interview from the BBC series *Tales from the Dark Continent* covering his career for the period 1931–62 (ref. 4742/5).

TURNER, ADMIRAL SIR ARTHUR FRANCIS (1912–91) Royal Navy career. Director-General, Aircraft (Navy), Ministry of Defence, 1966–67.

Two boxes of his correspondence and papers, 1931–67, are in Churchill College, Cambridge (ref. TRNR).

TURNER, SIR GEORGE WILFRED (1896–1974) Civil servant. Permanent Under-Secretary, War Office, 1949–56.

Five boxes of Sir George's papers, 1901–72, together with those of Engineer Vice-Admiral Sir Harold Brown, covering munitions production in the War Office and Ministry of Supply, 1936–45, are at the Liddell Hart Centre, King's College, London. The collection also includes personal reminiscences collected by Sir George and files kept as Permanent Under-Secretary at the War Office, 1956.

TUSA, JOHN (1936–) Broadcaster and presenter. Managing Director, BBC World Service, 1986–92 etc.

A large collection of papers (c. 250 volumes) has been acquired by the British Library, to where enquiries should be addressed.

TWEEDSMUIR OF BELHELVIE, BARONESS Priscilla Jean Fortescue Buchan (née Lady Grant of Monimusk) (1915–78) MP (Con) Aberdeen South, 1946–66. PUS for Scotland, 1962–64. Minister of State, Scottish Office, 1970–72; Foreign and Commonwealth Office, 1972–74.

A collection of correspondence and papers, 1937–78, has been placed in the National Library of Scotland (ref. Acc 11884). They include files on the European Movement, the Council of Europe, the United Nations and the United Nations High Commission for Refugees and various overseas visits. Constituency files include records of the Aberdeen South Unionist Association. There are also election ephemera and notes and copies of articles, speeches and broadcasts. Enquiries regarding access should be directed to the Archivist.

TWEEDY, OWEN MEREDITH (1888–1960) Journalist and civil servant. Special correspondent, Middle East, *Daily Telegraph*, 1951–52.

There are papers in the Middle East Centre, St Antony's College, Oxford. A list is available (NRA 42966). There is a diary for 1951–52.

TWYNAM, SIR HENRY JOSEPH (1887–1966) Governor, Central Provinces and Berar, 1940–46. Acting Governor, Bengal, 1945.

The India Office Library holds a microfilm of Twynam's papers, 1943–46 (ref. Photo Eur 53). This includes correspondence with the Viceroy, personal diaries, speeches and other official papers. The same library also holds two printed volumes of speeches (1940–42) and his typescript memoirs. The papers of Sir Robert Reid, also in the India Office Library, include additional correspondence (ref. MSS Eur E 278). A further copy of the memoirs, together with a diary, 1920–29, is available on microfilm at the Cambridge South Asian Archive.

TYLECOTE, DAME MABLE (1896–1987) President, National Federation of Community Associations, 1958–61; Adult Education Lecturer, Manchester University, 1935–51; various education and social services posts.

A collection of papers is held at John Rylands University Library, Manchester. The collection consists of correspondence, files on political and academic topics, and photographs. Subjects covered include her career in the Labour Party (she contested seats as a Labour candidate on five occasions), Manchester local politics, and adult education.

TYSON, SIR JOHN DAWSON (1893–1976) Indian Civil Service. Secretary to the Agent of the Government of India in South Africa, 1927–29. Private Secretary to the Governor of Bengal, 1930–35, 1938, and 1945–47.

One trunk of papers was deposited in the India Office Library on permanent loan in 1975 (ref. MSS Eur E 341). A list is available (NRA 27500). The material includes copies of detailed weekly letters written home, 1920–48.

U

URQUHART, SIR BRIAN (1919–) United Nations diplomat, 1945–86. Under-Secretary-General, United Nations, 1974–86. UN Representative in Katanga, Congo, 1960–62.

Transcripts of various interviews concerning his career are to be deposited with the United Nations project at the Bodleian Library, Oxford.

V

VALENTINE, JAMES (fl. 1927–96) Scottish Nationalist activist.

There are papers for the period 1927–96 (including material on the formation of the National Party of Scotland) in the National Library of Scotland.

VAN STRAUBENZEE, SIR WILLIAM RADCLIFFE (1924–99) MP (Con) Wokingham, 1959–87. Minister of State, Northern Ireland Office, 1972–74.

Sir William deposited the majority of his papers at the Bodleian Library, Oxford.

VERNEY, MAJOR-GENERAL GERALD LLOYD (1900–57) Military career. Armoured brigade and divisional commander during World War II. General Officer Commanding, Vienna, 1945–46.

Two boxes of papers, 1922–47, are deposited in the Liddell Hart Centre, King's College, London. A list is available (NRA 23079).

VERNON, WILFRID FOULSTON (1882–1975) MP (Lab) Dulwich, 1945–51.

The LSE Library holds two files of correspondence relating to the left wing of the Labour Party and to the left section of the Italian Socialist Party (ref. Coll Misc 521).

VICKERS, SIR CHARLES GEOFFREY (1894–1982) Lawyer, public servant and writer. Legal adviser, National Coal Board, 1946–48; Board Member, 1948–55; Chairman, Mental Health Research Fund, 1951–67.

A collection of papers has remained in family possession. A list is available (NRA 31755). Most of the papers relating to his career prior to 1955 have been destroyed. The remainder consists of family correspondence and papers along with drafts for published and other writings. Reference should also be made to *The Vickers Papers*, edited by the Open Systems Group, 1984.

VICKERS, D.B.H. (fl. 1960s–70s) United Nations legal counsel.

Some papers have been given to the United Nations project at the Bodleian Library, Oxford. They include files on the work of United Nations Relief and Rehabilitation Administration, United Nations Relief and Water Agency and various UN peace-keeping missions. There is also material on the UN's relations with South Africa and Rhodesia and on various African national liberation movements.

VICKERS, LIEUTENANT-GENERAL SIR RICHARD (MAURICE HILTON) (1928–) Military career. Served with tank units, British Army of the Rhine, Korea and Middle East, 1948–54; 4th Royal Tank Regiment, Borneo and Malaysia, 1964–66. Deputy Director of Army Training, 1975–77. Commandant, Royal Military Academy, Sandhurst, 1979–82. Director-General of Army Training, 1982–83.

Sir Richard has informed the Liddell Hart Centre, King's College, London, that he has retained some unsorted papers.

VIGNE, RANDOLPH (fl. 1970–95) Chairman, Namibia Support Committee, 1970s. Anti-apartheid campaigner.

His correspondence and papers, 1970–95, as chair of the Namibia Support Committee are in the BLCAS (Rhodes House Library) Oxford.

VILLIERS, SIR CHARLES HYDE (1912–92) Banker and industrialist. Chairman, British Steel, 1976–80.

Twenty boxes of papers, 1950–91, including his unpublished diaries, were deposited in Churchill College, Cambridge, in 1992. A list is available (NRA 44032).

W

WADDELL, SIR ALEXANDER (NICOL ANTON) (1913–99) Colonial Administrator. Malayan Civil Service, 1946; Principal Assistant Secretary, North Borneo, 1947–52; Colonial Secretary, Gambia, 1952–56; Sierra Leone, 1956–58. Deputy Governor, Sierra Leone, 1958–60. Governor and Commander-in-Chief, Sarawak, 1960–63.

Some material is held at Rhodes House Library, Oxford (ref. MSS Pac s 105). The papers relate to the development and economy of Foochow and Sarawak, and include his speeches for the period 1950–63.

WADDINGTON, LORD David Charles Waddington (1929–) MP (Con) Nelson and Colne, 1968–74; Clitheroe, Mar. 1979–83; Ribble Valley, 1983–90. Minister of State, Home Office, 1983–87; Parliamentary Secretary to the Treasury and Government Chief Whip, 1987–89. Home Secretary, 1989–90. Leader of the House of Lords, 1990–92. Governor of Bermuda after 1992.

Lord Waddington states that he has retained extensive papers. When these have been catalogued, he will make plans for their deposit.

WADE, MAJOR-GENERAL DOUGLAS ASHTON LOFFT (1898–1996) Military career. Served in World Wars I and II. Commander, Madras Area, India, 1944–47. General Officer Commanding, Malaya District, 1947–48. Member, Indian Armed Forces Naturalisation Committee, 1947–49. Member of War Crimes Review of Sentence Boards, 1948–49. Retired from army, 1950. Telecommunications Attaché, British Embassy, Washington, 1951–54.

General Wade has given papers to several repositories. Reports and recommendations of the War Crimes Boards, miscellaneous documents concerning prisons and prisoners in Germany, and a personal file as Chairman of one of the boards, 1948–49, are held in the Liddell Hart Centre for Military Archives, King's College, London. The National Army Museum has an important series of papers recording the work of the 1947 Indian Forces Naturalisation Committee established to facilitate the replacement of British officers with Indian nationals (ref. 8204–792). Papers relating to his service as a subaltern in World War I are deposited with the Liddle Collection, Leeds University.

WADSWORTH, ALFRED POWELL (1891–1956) Editor, *Manchester Guardian*, 1944–56.

Papers covering his editorship can be found in the *Guardian* Archives at John Rylands Library, Manchester University. A list is available (NRA 18162).

WAINWRIGHT, RICHARD SCURRAH (1918–2003) MP (Lib) Colne Valley, 1966–70, 1974–87.

The papers have been placed in the LSE Library.

WAITE, AIR COMMODORE REGINALD NEWNHAM ('REX') (1901–75) Royal Air Force career. On staff of Supreme Headquarters Allied Expeditionary Force, 1944; HQ Control Command, 1949. Chief of Staff, Allied Air Forces Central Europe, 1951–53.

Two boxes of his reports, manuals and other papers, 1944–52, have been placed in the Liddell Hart Centre, King's College, London, and are an especially useful source for the history of the Berlin Airlift, which he devised. A list of the collection is available (NRA 27839).

WAKEFIELD, SIR EDWARD BIRKBECK (1903–69) Indian Civil Service, 1927–47. MP (Con) Derbyshire West, 1950–62. Junior Lord of the Treasury, 1956–58. Commissioner for Malta, 1962–64; High Commissioner, Malta, 1964–65.

The papers are understood to have remained in family possession. They include his Indian correspondence and the papers he used in writing his memoirs, *Past Imperative: My Life in India, 1927–47* (1966). The collection also includes appointment diaries, press-cuttings and correspondence relating to his Maltese appointment.

WAKEHURST, 2ND BARON   John De Vere Loder (1895–1970) MP (Con) Leicester East, 1924–29; Lewes, 1931–36. Governor, New South Wales, 1937–46; Northern Ireland, 1952–64.

The papers were deposited in the House of Lords Record Office in 1976 by the Dowager Lady Wakehurst. The collection includes a typescript of his unpublished memoirs, accounts of visits to South America, Australia and French North Africa, copies of Intelligence Summaries from Turkey, 1918, personal scrapbooks, press-cuttings, election material and a few papers relating to Northern Ireland. The Northern Ireland papers are closed. In addition, a letter book and diary relating to the Gallipoli and Palestine campaigns, and a memorandum on the Zionist Commission (1918) are at St Antony's College, Oxford.

WALL, MAJOR SIR PATRICK HENRY BLIGH (1916–98) MP (Con) Haltemprice, Feb. 1954–83; Beverley, 1983–87.

The Brynmor Jones Library, University of Hull, has his papers (ref. DPW). The collection reflects his wide-ranging concerns at national and international level, as well as the usual focus on local constituency matters. Also covered by the papers are his numerous foreign visits, often as a British delegate of the Inter-Parliamentary Union, and his involvement in internal Conservative pressure groups, such as the Monday Club and the 92 Committee. There is also correspondence with various premiers of Rhodesia, including Sir Roy Welensky, in the 1960s and 1970s.

WALLACE, HARRY WRIGHT (1885–1973) MP (Lab) Walthamstow East 1929–31; 1945–55.

The LSE Library has one folder of papers (ref. COLL MISC. 693). They include press-cuttings of two foreign tours made by Wallace on behalf of the Attlee Government, notes on philosophical matters and a few letters. Rhodes House Library, Oxford, holds some correspondence relating to colonial trade unions, 1949–54 (ref. MSS Brit Emp s 365) (NRA 16253).

WALLACE, WALTER IAN JAMES (1905–93) Indian Civil Service 1928–47. Defence Secretary to the Government of Burma at Simla. Chief Secretary to the Government of Burma, 1946.

A memoir on Burma, 1945–47 and some correspondence and papers, 1930–57 are held in the India Office Library (ref. MSS Eur E 338) (NRA 25125).

WALLACE, WILLIAM (1891–1976) Businessman and philanthropist. Director, Rowntree and Company, 1931–52; Chairman, 1952–57. Chairman, Joseph Rowntree Memorial Trust, 1951–63; Joseph Rowntree Social Service Trust, 1959–69; Industrial Co-Partnership Association, 1954–57.

His papers are with the Joseph Rowntree Trust archives at York.

WALLIS, SIR BARNES (NEVILLE) (1887–1979) Aeronautical scientist. Invented Geodotic construction and the weapon which destroyed the Moehne and Eder Dams and penetration bombs.

Two boxes of his papers are in Churchill College, Cambridge. The papers consist of his aeronautical research files, 1940–58. The Royal Air Force Museum, Hendon, has his personal and general correspondence files, 1968–74 (ref. DB140–156). Additional research papers are held in the Science Museum Library (NRA 30555) and at the Brooklands Museum (NRA 34342).

WALLIS, LEONARD GEORGE COKE (1900–74) Indian Political Service. Deputy High Commissioner, Pakistan, 1947–52. Adviser on establishment of Nigerian civil service.

His papers, 1947–61, are in the India Office Library (ref. MSS Eur D 1002).

WALSH ATKINS, LEONARD BRIAN (1915–97) Colonial and diplomatic career. Principal, Burma Office, 1945–47. Commonwealth Relations Office, 1947. Counsellor, British Embassy, Dublin, 1953–56. Deputy High Commissioner, Pakistan, 1959–61. Assistant Under-Secretary of State, 1962–67. Seconded to Civil Service Selection Board, 1967. Retired 1970.

Some papers, kept during an official visit to Burma, November 1946, dealing chiefly with the political position of the Kachins, are deposited in the India Office Library (ref. MSS Eur D 1119).

WALTERS, SIR ALAN ARTHUR (1916–) Professor of Political Economy, Johns Hopkins University, after 1976. Personal Economic Adviser to Margaret Thatcher after 1983 (full-time secondment, 1981–83).

Sir Alan states that he has retained some papers but that these are not currently available to researchers.

WALTERS, SIR DENNIS (1928–) MP (Con) Westbury, 1964–92. Closely involved in Middle East matters, WEU, etc.

His constituency papers, 1984–91, are in Wiltshire Record Office (ref. Acc 2590). The collection is closed.

WARD, DAME IRENE (b. 1895) MP (Con) Wallsend, 1931–45; Tynemouth, 1950–74.

The political papers have been placed in the Bodleian Library, Oxford, to where enquiries should be addressed.

WARNER, SIR FREDERICK ARCHIBALD (1918– 95) MEP (Con) Somerset, 1979–84. Diplomat. Ambassador to Laos, 1965–67; Ambassador and Deputy Permanent UK Representative to the United Nations, 1969–72; Ambassador to Japan, 1972–75.

The papers relating to his time as an MEP have been deposited in the Bodleian Library, Oxford. The collection is closed pending the deposit of papers concerning his diplomatic career.

WATERHOUSE, CHARLES (1893–1975) MP (Con) Leicester South, 1924–45; Leicester SE, 1945–57.

It is understood that the papers have remained in family possession. No details of extent or access are available.

WATERHOUSE, SIR RONALD GOUGH (1926–) Judge of the High Court of Justice, Family Division, 1978–88; Queen's Bench Division after 1988. Chairman of various Committees of Inquiry.

A collection of correspondence, papers and press-cuttings was deposited at the Clwyd Record Office (Hawarden) in 1985 (ref. D/WA). A list is available (NRA 29784). The collection includes material on the Moors Murders case (1966), the Free Wales Army prosecution (1969), the Aberfan disaster (1966–67) and his work as Chairman of the Local Government

Boundary Commission for Wales (1976–78). There is also material on his role in local Labour politics in Flintshire in the late 1950s. His papers as adviser on terrorism to the Home Secretary (1974–78) are closed. Access to other parts of the collection requires permission from the depositor.

WATKINS, BARON Tudor Elwyn Watkins (1903–83) MP (Lab) Brecon and Radnor, 1945–70.

The papers have been placed in the National Library of Wales. Lists are available (NRA 26130 and 29618). The collection includes correspondence, papers and leaflets on Brecon and Radnor elections, 1924–66; printed constituency material, 1935–69; miscellaneous Labour Party papers, 1928–52; and papers and correspondence on Parliamentary questions, 1945–52. There are also pamphlets, papers and press-cuttings relating to the Parliament for Wales Campaign and the Government of Wales Bill, 1954, and papers on various visits abroad including Patagonia and the USSR.

WATKINS, DAVID JOHN (1925–) MP (Lab) Consett, 1966–83. Joint Chairman, Council for the Advancement of Arab-British Understanding (CAABU), 1979–83; Director, 1983–90.

Mr Watkins has retained an extensive collection of papers. Provision will be made for their eventual deposit. The papers include correspondence, press-cuttings and election addresses relating to his trade union and Labour Party activities in Bristol in the 1950s, and his parliamentary candidacy in 1964. His House of Commons papers include files on two Private Members Bills which he sponsored and on the closure of the Consett steel works in 1980. There are also papers on the Middle East from the late 1960s onward including material on his work as director of the CAABU, 1983–90. These include correspondence with government ministers and opposition spokespersons and extensive material on the United Nations Meetings of Non-Governmental Organisations on the Question of Palestine, 1984–91.

WATKINSON, 1ST VISCOUNT Harold Arthur Watkinson (1910–95) MP (Con) Woking, 1950–64. Parliamentary Secretary, Ministry of Labour and National Service, 1952–55. Minister of Transport and Civil Aviation, 1955–59; Defence, 1959–62.

British Cabinet Ministers, 1900–51, states that 9 box-files of papers were deposited at Ashridge Management College, while others had remained in the possession of Lord Watkinson.

WATNEY, SIMON (fl. 1971–98) Gay activist.

There are 83 boxes of papers, *c.* 1980–90, deposited in the Hall-Carpenter Archives, LSE Library (ref. M 1862). The collection includes correspondence, newsletters and publicity relating to gay activism and AIDS campaigning in Britain and the USA, with some material from the rest of the world.

WATSON, GRAHAM ROBERT (1956–) MEP (Lib Dem) after 1994. Head, Private Office, to David Steel 1983–87. Leader of the Liberal Democrats in the European Parliament.

Enquiries should be directed to the LSE Library, which has material relating to his period with David Steel and as an MEP.

WAVELL, 1ST EARL Field-Marshal Sir Archibald Percival Wavell (1883–1950) Military career. Served in World Wars I and II; Commander-in-Chief, Middle East, 1939–41; India, 1941–43; Supreme Commander, South West Pacific, 1942. Viceroy and Governor-General, India, 1943–47.

The main collection of papers remains in family possession and includes diaries, correspondence, and copies of speeches. Photocopies of his papers as Viceroy and Governor-General of India, 1943–47, are at the India Office Library (ref. MSS Eur D 977). Some personal and regimental correspondence, 1940–60, is available at the Black Watch Museum, Perth.

WEATHERHEAD, SIR ARTHUR TRENHAM (1905–84) Colonial Service, Nigeria, 1930–60; Deputy Governor, 1958–60.

Seven boxes of papers are deposited in Rhodes House Library, Oxford (ref. MSS Afr s 2028). In addition to his letters home, 1930–60, the collection includes some reports and memoranda on Nigeria and a typed memoir, 'Possessors of Power: Thirty Years to Independence in Nigeria, 1930–60' (ref. MSS Afr s 232(2)).

WEATHERHEAD, LESLIE DIXON (1893–1976) Methodist leader and author.

There are papers, including diaries, in the University of Birmingham (ref. Acc 2000/93). The diaries are closed until 2080.

WEATHERILL, BARON (Bruce) Bernard Weatherill (1920–) MP (Con) Croydon North East, 1964–83. Speaker of the House of Commons, 1983–92.

The papers have been placed at the University of Kent in Canterbury. The collection includes constituency correspondence, his wartime letters to his parents and summaries of business in the House of Commons written by the Speaker for the Queen over an 18-month period. Enquiries regarding the collection should be directed to the Librarian.

WEBSTER, SIR CHARLES KINGSLEY (1886–1961) Stevenson Professor of International History, London School of Economics, 1932–53. Served in World War II in the Foreign Research and Press Service, 1939–41; Director of the British Library of Information, New York, 1941–42; Foreign Office, 1943–46; British Delegation, Dumbarton Oaks and San Francisco, 1944–45. On staff of Preparatory Commission and General Assembly of the United Nations, London, 1945–46. President, British Academy, 1950–54.

The LSE Library has an extensive collection of papers, 1901–61. A list is available (NRA 20610). Several of the files concern the post-war settlement and the establishment of new international bodies. There are minutes, memoranda and conference papers concerning war time planning; the UK delegation to the Dumbarton Oaks conference; the San Francisco conference; the United Nations Conference on Internal Organisation, April–July 1945; the United Nations General Assembly, July 1945–March 1946; the final assembly of the League of Nations; and UNESCO. There are also files on other aspects of his post-war work including academic administration, the Anglo-Israeli Association, the Weizmann Archives, the Friends of the Atlantic Union and the Great Britain–USSR Society. His research notes, lectures, speeches and publications files are included in the collection, as are his pre-1949 diaries. His later diaries were left to Dr Noble Frankland.

WEETCH, KENNETH THOMAS (1933–) MP (Lab) Ipswich, 1974–87.

Some papers, 1981–84, have been placed in Suffolk Record Office (Ipswich Branch) (ref. HD 1644). A list is available (NRA 39701). The main political papers are closed for 30 years. There is extensive constituency material (sensitive material is closed for 75 years).

WEIR, DR ANDREW JOHN (JACK) (1919–) Irish clergyman and mediator. Clerk of Assembly and General Secretary, Presbyterian Church in Ireland, 1964–85.

Dr Weir retained unsorted papers. He stated he would make provision for them in due course.

WEIS, PAUL (1907–) Austrian-born international lawyer and human rights activist. Devoted to the cause of refugees. Legal Adviser, International Refugee Organisation Centre, Geneva. Director, Legal Division, UNHCR.

There are extensive papers in the Refugee Studies Programme Documentation Centre, University of Oxford. A detailed list is available (NRA 38404).

WEISZ, VICTOR ('VICKY') (1913–66) Cartoonist for the *Evening Standard* from 1958 and the *New Statesman* from 1954.

Various illustrated letters, notes, scrapbooks, press-cuttings and photographs, covering the period 1920–66, are held at the Brynmor Jones Library, University of Hull (ref. DX/165–166, DP/172).

WELENSKY, SIR ROY (ROLAND) (1907–91) Rhodesian politician, 1938–64. Prime Minister, Northern Rhodesia, 1953. Prime Minister and Minister of External Affairs, Federation of Rhodesia and Nyasaland, 1956–63.

A 2-volume printed catalogue is available of the papers now in BLCAS (Rhodes House Library) Oxford (NRA 39191). The collection includes material from the Office of Prime Minister and Minister of External Affairs, some of Sir Godfrey Huggins papers as Prime Minister of Southern Rhodesia and the office files of the (United) Federal Party. The collection is a key source, not just for Central Africa from the 1940s but for Britain in the 1950s and 1960s.

WEST, GENERAL SIR MICHAEL MONT-GOMERIE ALSTON ROBERTS (1905–78) Military

career. Served in World War II. Commanded Commonwealth Division, Korea, 1952–53. Head of British Defence Staff, Washington, 1962–65.

A collection of papers, 1952–66, chiefly concerning his command of the Commonwealth Division during the Korean War, is deposited in the Imperial War Museum. A list is available (NRA 28565). The material consists of orders, maps, memoranda, summaries, statistical returns of casualties and prisoners, press-cuttings, and a transcript of his televised press-conference held on New Year's Day, 1954.

WEST, ROBERT GEORGE RAYNARD (1900–86) Medical doctor, pacifist and Liberal activist. Author of *Conscience and Society* (1942) and *Psychology and World Order* (1948).

A collection of papers is held at the Wellcome Contemporary Medical Archives Centre, London (ref. PP/RRW). The collection includes political diaries, correspondence, 1930–86, notebooks and lectures. There are files on subjects such as psychology; international relations; conscientious objection; and the Liberal Party.

WESTWOOD, JOSEPH (1884–1948) MP (Lab) Midlothian and Peeblesshire, 1922–31; Stirling and Falkirk Burghs, 1935–48; PUS for Scotland, 1931 and 1940–45; Scottish Secretary, 1945–47.

According to *British Cabinet Ministers, 1900–51*, no papers have survived. His Private Office papers as Secretary of State for Scotland are in the relevant departmental files at the Scottish Record Office.

WHEELER-BENNETT, SIR JOHN WHEELER (1902–75) Historian and biographer. Assistant Director-General, Political Intelligence Department, Foreign Office, 1945. British Editor-in-Chief of Captured German Foreign Office Archives, 1946–48. Fellow of St Antony's College, Oxford, 1950–57.

Some papers relating chiefly to Germany and the 1944 plot to assassinate Hitler are deposited in St Antony's College, Oxford. There is also material on the German Army; peace moves; the US Navy; Yugoslavia; and post-war Germany and the war crimes trials.

WHEELER-BOOTH, SIR MICHAEL (ADDISON JOHN) (1935–) Clerk of the Parliaments, 1991–97.

There are 22 boxes of papers, 1999, relating to his work as a member of the Royal Commission on the Reform of the House of Lords, including papers, evidence, submissions, drafts, correspondence, press cuttings, etc. deposited in the House of Lords Record Office (ref. 4070).

WHISTLER, GENERAL SIR LASHMER GORDON (1898–1963) Military career. Served Palestine, 1937–38 and 1945–46. Major-General, British Troops in India, Feb.–Aug. 1947; General Officer Commanding, British Troops in India and Pakistan, Aug.–Dec. 1947. *Kaid*, Sudan Defence Force, 1948–50. General Officer Commanding-in-Chief, West Africa, 1951–53.

The West Sussex Record Office in Chichester holds a large collection of papers, 1917–63. A list is available at the record office. The Imperial War Museum has an official report on his appointment as commander of troops in India, 1947.

WHITE OF RHYMNEY, BARONESS Eirene Lloyd White (1909–99) MP (Lab) East Flint, 1950–70. Minister of State for Foreign Affairs, 1966–67; Welsh Office, 1967–70. Deputy Speaker, House of Lords, 1979–89.

The papers are now deposited with the Welsh Political Archive at the National Library of Wales. The collection is divided into six main divisions (incoming letters, political interests etc.).

WHITE, FRANK RICHARD (1939–) MP (Lab) Bury and Radcliffe, Oct. 1974–83.

His complete indexed files of constituency correspondence, 1974–83, are held in the Manchester Metropolitan University.

WHITE, (HENRY) GRAHAM (1880–1965) MP (Lib) Birkenhead East, 1922–24 and 1929–45. President of the Liberal Party, 1955.

The papers have been deposited in the House of Lords Record Office. Much of the material relates to Birkenhead during the 1930s. However, there are confidential correspondence and memoranda concerning Party organisation from the late 1930s to the mid-1950s. Correspondents include Clement Davies and Lord Meston. The wartime files include material on the campaign on behalf of German internees.

WHITEHEAD, SIR EDGAR CUTHBERT FREMANTLE (1905–71) Southern Rhodesian politician. High Commissioner in London, 1945–46. Minister of Finance, 1946–53. Representative of Federation of Rhodesia and Nyasaland in USA, 1957–58. Prime Minister of Southern Rhodesia, 1958–62.

An extensive collection of papers is deposited in Rhodes House Library, Oxford (ref. MSS Afr s 1482). The collection includes a typescript unpublished autobiography, 1928–46; papers on the United Federal Party 'Build a nation' tour of 1962; personal correspondence, 1949–65; speeches and circulars as Prime Minister, 1961–62; and extensive press-cuttings.

WHITEHOUSE, MARY (1910–2001) Campaigner against pornography and the 'permissive society'. Founder and Hon. General Secretary, National Viewers and Listeners Society (NVLA), 1965–80. President after 1980.

Enquiries should now be directed to the University of Essex Library, which also houses the archive of the National Viewers' and Listeners' Association.

WHITELAW, VISCOUNT William (Willie) Whitelaw (1918–99) Conservative Cabinet Minister and elder statesman.

Some papers are held by Glasgow University Library, to where enquiries should be directed. In addition, three boxes of material accumulated by Mark Garnett whilst writing his biography of Whitelaw are held by Churchill College, Cambridge.

WICKS, HARRY (fl. 1930s–80s) Communist until his expulsion from the Party in 1932. Subsequently involved with the Trotskyist movement.

Some papers have been deposited at the Modern Records Centre, University of Warwick (ref. MSS 102). The collection includes his writings, study notes and correspondence on Communism and Trotskyism (1940s–80s), as well as his journals, pamphlets and other printed material on radical politics since the 1920s.

WIGG, BARON George Edward Cecil Wigg (1900–83) MP (Lab) Dudley, 1945–67. Paymaster-General, 1964–67. Member, Racecourse Betting

Control Board, 1957–61; Horserace Totalisator Board, 1961–64; Chairman, Horserace Betting Levy Board, 1967–72. President, Betting Office Licencees Association, 1973–83.

The papers (now open) are; at the LSE Library. They consist mainly of correspondence and memoranda relating to the political positions held by Lord Wigg and have been divided into 8 sections: (1) Early life and personal papers (2) Early Political Career, 1945–51; (3) Labour Party in Opposition, 1951–64; (4) Paymaster General, 1964–67; (5) Later Political Career, 1967–83; (6) General Elections, 1945–66; (7) Constituency Papers, 1945–66; (8) Horserace Betting Levy Board. A further 80 boxes of papers relating to the Horserace Betting Levy Board remain closed and unlisted.

WIGGIN, SIR ALFRED WILLIAM (JERRY) (1937–) MP (Con) Weston-super-Mare, 1969–97.

Some papers relating to the Night Assemblies Bill, 1972, have been deposited in the Bodleian Library, Oxford.

WIGLEY, DAFYDD (1943–) MP (Plaid Cymru) Caernarvon, Feb. 1974–2001.

His constituency correspondence, 1974–83, has been placed in the National Library of Wales. Requests for access and enquiries concerning other papers should be directed to the Archivist.

WILES, SIR GILBERT (1880–1961) Indian Civil Service, 1904–46. Adviser to Secretary of State for India, 1941–46.

There are two boxes of papers, 1928–47, held in the Cambridge South Asian Archive. The material includes notes, letters, confidential telegrams and pamphlets.

WILKINSON, ELLEN CICELY (1891–1947) MP (Lab) Middlesbrough East, 1924–31; Jarrow, 1935–47. Parliamentary Secretary, Ministry of Pensions, 1940; Home Security, 1940–45. Minister of Education, 1945–47.

According to *British Cabinet Ministers, 1900–51*, the bulk of her papers were destroyed, though some press-cuttings and scrapbooks have been deposited with the Labour Party Archives at the Labour History Archive and Study Centre, University of Manchester.

WILLETT, ARTHUR (b. 1910) Trade unionist and Liberal activist.

Some papers are held at the Modern Records Centre, University of Warwick (ref. MSS 116). The collection includes minutes and reports of the Liberal Party Organisation Council, 1949–53; papers on his Chester candidacy in 1950; the Association of Liberal Trade Unionists; and the Liberal Commission on Trade Unions. There are also papers relating to the Society of Post Office Executives (SPOE), including conference minutes and papers, annual reports, subject and correspondence files, and copies of the SPOE *Review*. In addition, there are an incomplete set of diaries, 1938–74 (many badly damaged), and papers on his Home Guard service, 1939–46.

WILLIAMS OF BARNBURGH, BARON Thomas Williams (1888–1969) MP (Lab) Don Valley, 1922–59. Parliamentary Secretary, Ministry of Agriculture and Fisheries, 1940–45; Minister of Agriculture and Fisheries, 1945–51.

According to *British Cabinet Ministers, 1900–51*, a small collection of correspondence and press-cuttings has remained in family possession.

WILLIAMS, CICELY DELPHINE (1894–1992) Nutritionist and paediatrician.

The papers have been placed in the Wellcome Contemporary Medical Archives Centre. A list is available (NRA 38199).

WILLIAMS, DAVID JAMES (1897–1972) MP (Lab) Neath, 1945–64. South Wales miners' leader.

A substantial collection of papers has been deposited at University College, Swansea. The papers cover his entire career, including his trade union activities, 1919–45 and his time as an MP. The material relating to his parliamentary work includes constituency correspondence, 1961–64, speeches, election addresses, newspaper cuttings, broadcasts and notes. There are also obituaries and condolence letters sent to his widow. The South Wales Miners' Library, University College, Swansea, holds his library and an interview with his widow.

WILLIAMS, BRIGADIER SIR EDGAR TREVOR (1912–95) Historian. Served in World War II. Director, Enforcement Division, Security Council,

United Nations, 1946–47. Pro-Vice-Chancellor, Oxford University, 1968–80. Editor, *Dictionary of National Biography*, 1949–80. Member, Devlin Nyasaland Commission, 1959. UK Observer, Rhodesia elections, 1980.

The Imperial War Museum has his correspondence with Field-Marshal Viscount Montgomery, 1954–72. Some brief notes on his United Nations service have been given to the United Nations project at the Bodleian Library, Oxford.

WILLIAMS, JOHN LLOYD (b. 1895) MP (Lab) Glasgow Kelvingrove, 1945–50.

Correspondence, lecture notes and articles, 1950–79, are held at the National Library of Wales. Enquiries regarding access should be directed to the Archivist. An interview transcript is held at the South Wales Miners' Library, University College, Swansea.

WILLIAMS, PAUL (1922–) MP (Con) Sunderland, 1953–64. Chairman, Monday Club.

It is understood that a few papers have been retained by him.

WILLIAMSON, ROBERT KERR (ROY) (1932–) Anglican leader. Bishop of Bradford, 1984–91. Subsequently Bishop of Southwark, 1991–98.

The papers have been placed in West Yorkshire Archive Service, Bradford (ref. 64D94). They reflect his intervention over cuts in council services in Bradford and his attempt to build bridges with the Muslim community during the *Satanic Verses* controversy and the first Gulf War.

WILLINK, SIR HENRY URMSTON (1894–1973) MP (Con) Croydon North, 1940–48. Minister of Health, 1943–45.

There are two boxes of personal papers and memoirs deposited at Churchill College, Cambridge (ref. WILL).

WILLIS, ADMIRAL OF THE FLEET SIR ALGERNON USBORNE (1889–1976) Naval career. Second Sea Lord and Chief of Naval Personnel, 1944–46. Commander-in-Chief, Mediterranean Fleet, 1946–48; Portsmouth, 1948–50.

There are 13 boxes of papers, 1905–75, at Churchill College, Cambridge (ref. WLLS). A list is available (NRA 20290). The material includes his World War I diaries, memoirs of World War II, letters and newspaper cuttings. Further World War II memoirs are deposited with the Imperial War Museum.

WILLIS, BOB (fl. 1945–69) Trade unionist. General Secretary, National Graphical Association, 1945–69.

The National Graphical Association has deposited some papers with the Modern Records Centre, Warwick University (ref. MSS 28). These include his files as General Secretary of the London Society of Compositors/London Typographical Society and as General Secretary of the National Graphical Association 1945–69. There is also material on his Trades Union Congress activities and his membership of the National Board for Prices and Incomes (1965–67).

WILLOCK, AIR VICE-MARSHAL ROBERT PEEL (1893–1973) Air Attaché, British Embassy, China, 1933–36. Air Officer Commanding Iraq and Persia, 1943–44. Deputy Head, Royal Air Force Delegation, Washington, 1944–46. Civil Air Attaché, Washington, 1946–47. Civil Aviation Adviser to UK High Commissioner, Australia, 1949–59.

A collection of papers, 1914–60, has been placed in the Imperial War Museum. The post-war section of the collection documents his time in Washington, 1944–47, and in Canberra, 1949–59.

WILMOT OF SELMESTON, 1ST BARON John Wilmot (1895–1964) MP (Lab) Fulham East, 1933–35; Kennington, 1939–45; Deptford, 1945–50. Joint Parliamentary Secretary, Ministry of Supply, 1944–45. Minister of Supply, 1945–47.

According to *British Cabinet Ministers, 1900–51*, the papers were destroyed by his widow. Private Office papers (AVIA 11) survive at the Public Record Office.

WILSON, 1ST BARON Field-Marshal Sir Henry Maitland Wilson (1881–1964) Military career. Served in World Wars I and II; Supreme Allied Commander, Mediterranean, 1944; Head of British Joint Staff Mission, Washington, 1945–47.

Very few papers are believed to have survived. Some 1945 papers are in the Public Record Office (ref. CAB 127/47).

WILSON OF RIEVAULX, BARON James Harold Wilson (1916–95) MP (Lab) Ormskirk, 1945–50; Huyton, 1950–83. Parliamentary Secretary, Ministry of Works, 1945–47. Secretary, Overseas Trade, 1947. President of the Board of Trade, 1947–51. Prime Minister, 1964–70, 1974–76.

The papers were placed in the Bodleian Library, Oxford in 1993 after the completion of the biography by Philip Ziegler. There are over 200 boxes of papers, including some of Lady Wilson's correspondence.

WILSON, SIR GEOFFREY (1910–2004) Served Foreign Office, Treasury, Commonwealth Secretariat etc. Chairman, Race Relations Board, 1971–77. Chairman, Oxfam, 1977–83.

The papers have been placed in the Bodleian Library, Oxford. Researchers should consult the Bodleian website.

WILSON, LIEUTENANT-GENERAL SIR JAMES ALEXANDER (1921–) Military career. Private Secretary to Commander-in-Chief, Pakistan, 1948–49. Chief of Staff, United Nations Forces, Cyprus, 1964–66. Vice-Adjutant-General, Ministry of Defence, 1972–74.

The United Nations project at the Bodleian Library, Oxford, holds copies of the sections of Sir James' unpublished memoirs which deal with his peacekeeping duties. The same project also holds a transcript and tape of an interview on this topic.

WILSON, (ROBERT) GORDON (1938–) MP (SNP) Dundee East, Feb. 1974–87.

Mr Wilson states that he has retained substantial volumes of files extending over 30 years. Provision will be made for their eventual deposit at the National Library of Scotland.

WILSON, SIR TOM IAN FINDLAY (1904–71) Rhodesian politician. MP for Umtali from 1940. Speaker of the Southern Rhodesian House of Assembly, 1950–53; Federal Assembly, 1953–60.

Seven files of papers, 1940–68, are deposited in the Centre for Southern African Studies, University of York. They contain correspondence and speeches, 1942; constitutional papers, 1940–45, including correspondence regarding the Southern Rhodesia Labour Party and the Rhodesian National Farmers' Union; World War II and immediate post-war papers, 1941–48; political papers kept as Speaker, including material on African members of the Assembly, and a 60-page autobiographical account, 1952–60; personal correspondence; reports and correspondence on the dissolution of the Central African Federation; and items relating to the Winston Churchill Memorial Fund in Rhodesia. His correspondents include R.A. Butler, Sir Alec Douglas-Home and Lord Boyd. Special conditions of access apply to his correspondence with Sir Roy Welensky.

WILSON, WILLIAM (1913–) MP (Lab) Coventry South, 1964–Feb. 1974; Coventry South East, Feb. 1974–83.

Some 60 box files of papers have been deposited in the Modern Records Centre, University of Warwick (ref. MSS 76). Among the subjects covered are the Joint Committee on Theatre Censorship (1966–67), the Divorce Reform Bill (1969), two files on the 1974 General Elections, notes and publications relating to American and Dutch policy on race relations and one file on legislation against sexual discrimination (1971–75). A later deposit includes constituency and policy files up to 1983 (ref. MSS 371). The Coventry City Record Office holds his letters written on active service, 1942–45.

WIMBERLEY, MAJOR-GENERAL DOUGLAS NEIL (1896–1983) Military career. Served in World Wars I and II. Divisional Commander, 1941–43; Director of Infantry, War Office, 1944–46.

The main collection of General Wimberley's papers, 1914–83, has been deposited in the National Library of Scotland (ref. Acc. 8681). A list is available (NRA 29221). The papers consist of diaries, letters, press-cuttings, and a multi-volume typed auto-biographical account entitled *Scottish Soldier*. This covers his military career and later work as Principal of University College, Dundee. Copies of the pre-1946 sections of this account have been deposited in Churchill College, Cambridge, the Imperial War Museum (ref. PP/MCR/182) and Dundee University Library.

WINNICK, DAVID JULIAN (1933–) MP (Lab) Croydon South, 1966–70; Walsall North after 1979. Chairman, United Kingdom Immigrants' Advisory Service after 1984.

His constituency correspondence and subject files since 1966 are deposited in the Brynmor Jones Library, University of Hull (ref. DMW). The collection includes files on the Select Committee on Race Relations and Immigration, 1966–70. There is also more recent material.

WINSTER, 1ST BARON Reginald Thomas Herbert Fletcher (1885–1961) MP (Lib) Basingstoke, 1923–24; (Lab) Nuneaton, 1935–42. Minister of Civil Aviation, 1945–46. Governor, Cyprus, 1946–48.

The only papers that have survived are reported in *British Cabinet Ministers, 1900–51*, to be in the charge of the Management Committee at his former home, Winster Lodge. The papers consist of five volumes of press-cuttings, visitors' books and his midshipman's logbooks, 1901–03. The volume of cuttings from Cyprus includes material on the British proposals for limited self-government in Cyprus, the rejection of which led to his resignation in 1948.

WINTERBOTTOM, RICHARD EMANUEL (1899–1968) MP (Lab) Sheffield Brightside, 1950–68.

A few personal papers, covering the period 1955–67 and including material on the Clean Air Bill, are in Sheffield Central Library (ref. MD 4045–49) (NRA 23246). The records of the Sheffield Brightside Constituency Labour Party are also deposited in Sheffield Central Library.

WINTERTON, MAJOR-GENERAL SIR (THOMAS) JOHN WILLOUGHBY (1898–1987) Military career. Served in World Wars I and II; Chief of Staff to General Officer Commanding, Burma, 1942. Deputy Commissioner, Allied Commission for Austria, 1945–49; British High Commissioner and Commander-in-Chief, Austria, 1950; Military Governor and Commander, British–US Zone, Free Territory of Trieste, 1951–54.

A collection of papers, 1929–54, was given to the Imperial War Museum in 1988. The Liddell Hart Centre, King's College, London, holds the text of a 1970 interview, primarily concerning the Control Commission.

WISE, ALFRED ROY (1901–74) MP (Con) Smethwick, 1931–45; Rugby, 1959–66.

His correspondence files, 1959–66, have been placed in Warwickshire Record Office (ref. CR 3410).

WISTRICH, ERNEST (1923–) Pro-Europe activist and writer on European affairs. Director, Britain in Europe, 1967–69; European Movement (British Council), 1969–86; National Organiser, 'YES' campaign, 1975 referendum on British membership of the European Community; Vice-President, International European Movement, 1971–89; Chairman, International European Movement Commission on European Citizenship.

Papers relating to the 1967–86 period are available at the offices of the European Movement, 158 Buckingham Palace Road, London SW1. Documents relating to the 1975 referendum campaign have been deposited in the House of Lords Record Office. Background files on the referendum campaign, election campaigns and other political activities have been retained by Mr Wistrich.

WOLFF, MICHAEL (1930–76) Conservative Party activist. Special Adviser to Sir Edward Heath, 1970–74. Director General, Conservative Party Organisation 1974–75. Journalist.

The papers have been placed in Churchill College, Cambridge (ref. WLFF). A list is available (NRA 43912). The papers, 72 boxes, 1962–75, consist chiefly of political files, some containing information on Sir Edward Heath.

WOOD, JOHN BRADSHAW (1924–91) Economist and writer. Deputy Director, Institute of Economic Affairs.

His papers (20 boxes) covering the period 1946–91 have been placed in Churchill College, Cambridge.

WOODBURN, ARTHUR (1890–1978) MP (Lab) Clackmannan and East Stirlingshire, 1939–70. Parliamentary Secretary, Ministry of Supply, 1945–47. Secretary of State for Scotland, 1947–50.

His papers, 1907–78, are in the National Library of Scotland (ref. Acc 7656). A list is available (NRA 29192). The papers reflect his various interests such as economics, education, European unity, international relations, modern languages, and Scottish history and literature. In addition, they contain personal and family correspondence, speeches and lectures as well as a draft autobiography. Private Office papers as Secretary of State for Scotland are at the Scottish Record Office while those from his time at the Ministry of Supply are held at the National Archives (ref. AVIA 9).

WOODCOCK, GEORGE (1912–95) Trade unionist. General Secretary, Trades Union Congress, 1960–70. Chairman, Commission on Industrial Relations, 1971–74.

The papers were donated to the Modern Records Centre, Warwick University, by his daughter.

WOODS, CHRIS (fl. 1988–93) Gay rights activist.

His files, 1988–93, relating to gay organisations and campaigns (together with copies of gay journals) form part of the Hall-Carpenter Archive at the LSE Library (ref. M1790).

WOOLF, LEONARD SIDNEY (1880–1969) Author and publisher. Joint Editor, *Political Quarterly*, 1931–59. Founded Hogarth Press, 1917. Secretary of Labour Party Advisory Committee on International Affairs.

The University of Sussex Library has a collection of Woolf's papers. This includes miscellaneous correspondence from the 1930s to 1969; family correspondence and two boxes of letters from eminent persons; 11 boxes of work and business papers up to 1968; and papers relating to his volumes of autobiography. A list is now available (NRA 42924).

WOOLLEY, SIR CHARLES CAMPBELL (1893–1981) Colonial Service. Ceylon Civil Service, 1921–35; Secretary to the Governor; Colonial Secretary, Jamaica, 1935–38; Chief Secretary, Nigeria, 1938–41. Governor and Commander-in-Chief, Cyprus, 1941–46; British Guiana, 1947–53.

Rhodes House Library, Oxford, has some correspondence and papers, 1922–59, relating to service in Ceylon, Jamaica, Cyprus and British Guiana (ref. MSS Brit Emp s 276) (NRA 11222).

WOOLTON, 1ST EARL OF Sir Frederick James Marquis (1883–1964) Minister of Food, 1940–43. Minister of Reconstruction, 1943–45. Lord President of the Council, 1945 and 1951–52. Chancellor of the Duchy of Lancaster, 1952–55. Minister of Materials, 1953–54.

Some 122 boxes of correspondence and papers, 1906–64, are deposited in the Bodleian Library,

Oxford. There is extensive material on his ministries and his role in the Conservative Party, 1943–64. The files of particular post-war interest include those on arrangements for the coronation of Elizabeth II; reform of the House of Lords, 1946–55; the Liverpool University Settlement, 1906–59; and the British Red Cross Society, 1947–64. His diaries are currently being edited for publication.

WORLOCK, ARCHBISHOP DEREK JOHN HARFORD (1920–96) Catholic leader. Archbishop of Liverpool after 1976.

His papers are in Liverpool Archdiocesan Archives. A very extensive archive has survived, including his diary of Vatican II. For details see Clifford Longley, *The Worlock Archive* (London, 2000).

WORM, PAUL (fl. 1980s) Industrial relations expert.

There is material in the Modern Records Centre, University of Warwick (ref. MSS 356). A list is available (NRA 40072). The core of the collection consists of interviews with Rover trade unionists and management in 1982–83.

WRIGGLESWORTH, SIR IAN (WILLIAM) (1939–) MP (Lab, then SDP) Thornaby, 1974–83; Stockton South 1983–87. Close associate of Roy Jenkins.

A collection of his papers has been deposited in Essex University Library. Some of these papers have been incorporated into the SDP deposit, but ten boxes of this collection constitute the 'Wrigglesworth papers'.

WRIGHT, SIR DENIS (1911–) Diplomat. Chargé d'affaires, Persia, December 1953. Ambassador to Ethiopia, 1959–62. Ambassador to Iran, 1963–71.

The papers have been placed in the Bodleian Library, Oxford.

WRIGHT, DR HELENA ROSA (1887–1982) Pioneer advocate of birth control.

Many of her papers were destroyed on retirement. However some papers collected by her biographer, Dr Barbara Evans, are now deposited in the Wellcome Contemporary Medical Archives Centre, London (ref. PP/HRW). A list is available (NRA 36138).

WYATT OF WEEFORD, BARON Woodrow Lyle Wyatt (1918–98) Politician and journalist. MP (Lab) Aston, 1945–55; Bosworth, 1959–70.

His papers have been placed in the Bodleian Library, Oxford to where enquiries should be addressed.

Y

YARDE, AIR VICE-MARSHAL BRIAN COURTNEY (1905–92) Royal Air Force career. Served in World War II. Deputy Director of Bomber Operations, Air Ministry, 1945. Station Commander, Gatow, during Berlin Airlift, 1947–49. Provost-Marshal and Chief of the RAF Police, 1951–53. Air Officer Commanding, 62nd Group, 1953–54. Commandant-General of the RAF Regiment and Inspector of Ground Combat Training, 1954–57.

Papers concerning his service, 1948–57, have been deposited in the Imperial War Museum (ref. 87/27/2). The collection includes reports, correspondence and a memoir of the Berlin Airlift, 1948–49. There are also papers relating to the RAF Regiment in the 1950s, including his reports as Inspector of Ground Combat Training on the RAF Regiment's role in Aden, Malaya, Cyprus, the Middle East and Far East.

YORK, CHRISTOPHER (1909–99) MP (Con) Ripon, 1939–51; Harrogate, 1951–54.

Mr York stated that his papers and diaries would eventually be deposited at the North Yorkshire County Record Office.

YOUENS, SIR PETER (WILLIAM) (1916–) Colonial administrative service. Assistant Secretary, Nyasaland, 1951; Deputy Chief Secretary, 1953–63. Secretary to the Prime Minister and to the Cabinet, Malawi, 1964–66. Executive Director, Lonrho, 1966–69 and after 1981.

A tape and transcript of interview, concerning colonial administrative service in Sierra Leone and Nyasaland, 1938–66, is in BLCAS (Rhodes House Library), Oxford.

YOUNG OF DARTINGTON, BARON Michael Young (1915–2002) Director, Institute of Community Studies after 1953. Author (with Peter Willmott) of *Family and Kinship in East London* (1957), *Life After Work – The Arrival of the Ageless Society* (1991), etc.

Lord Young's papers (*c.* 135 archive boxes) have been placed in Churchill College, Cambridge. Churchill College also holds the papers of his wife, Baroness Young. A list is available (NRA 44076).

YOUNG OF FARNWORTH, BARONESS Janet Mary Young (1926–2002) Conservative politician. Leader of the House of Lords, 1981–83.

Her correspondence and papers, 1960–2002, are in the Bodleian Library, Oxford.

YOUNG, AMICIA M. (fl. 1960s) Peace campaigner, opponent of Vietnam War. Secretary of the British Council (later Campaign) for Peace in Vietnam (BCPV) after 1968.

The surviving papers have been placed in the Brynmor Jones Library, University of Hull (ref. DYO/11). The BCPV papers include minutes and reports of its Council and Working Committee, conference papers, records of the Trade Union Sub-Committee, publicity material, press releases and extensive correspondence. Young also accumulated a large collection of leaflets and posters issued by other British and American anti-Vietnam War groups. Some other Young papers are in the ASTMS archive at Warwick (ref. MSS 74).

YOUNG, SIR ARTHUR EDWIN (1907–79) Military and police career. Commissioner of the Federation of Malaya Police, 1951–54; Kenya Police, 1954; City of London Police, 1950–71; seconded to be Chief Constable, Royal Ulster Constabulary, 1969–70.

Rhodes House Library, Oxford, holds six boxes of police reports and correspondence on his police service in the Gold Coast, 1951; Malaya, 1952–53; and Kenya, 1954 (ref. MSS Brit Emp s 486).

YOUNG, ARTHUR PRIMROSE (1885–1977) Works Manager. Member, Factory and Welfare Advisory Board, Ministry of Labour, 1940–47.

Director of Labour Supply Committee, Ministry of Labour, 1940–41; Visiting Fellow, Nuffield College, Oxford, 1939–47.

The papers are held at the Modern Records Centre, University of Warwick (ref. MSS 242). A list is available (NRA 33301). They include correspondence, copies of articles, reports and talks, press-cuttings and printed material. Subjects covered include British Thomson-Houston Co. Ltd; BKL Alloys Ltd; the Institution of Works Managers; education; and overseas visits and contacts.

YOUNG, DOUGLAS CUTHBERT COLQUHOUN
(1913–73) Poet, playwright and Scottish Nationalist. Chairman of the Scottish National Party, 1942–45. Resigned from SNP, 1948.

Some 140 boxes of correspondence and papers, 1931–73, have been purchased by the National Library of Scotland with the help of the Arts Council of Great Britain (ref. Acc 6419, 7085). A list is available (NRA 29228). The material includes literary manuscripts and typescripts and correspondence and documents relating to PEN, the Scottish National Party and other political groups. Correspondents include C.M. Grieve, Naomi Mitchison and Edwin Muir. The papers document his role in the Scottish nationalist and labour movements, especially the 1942 schism in the SNP, nationalist politics during World War II, and the Covenant campaign thereafter.

YOUNG, COMMANDER EDGAR P. (1899–1975)
Peace activist.

The Brynmor Jones Library, University of Hull, holds 25 boxes of correspondence, diaries and papers (ref. DYO). The collection includes writings and notes on his involvement with various societies relating to Eastern Europe, Vietnam and the peace movement from the 1940s to 1968. These include the China Campaign Committee, Czech Society of Great Britain, International Peace Campaign, National Peace Council, and the Russia Today Council. Three boxes of papers relate to the Vietnam Solidarity Campaign, the Council for Peace in Vietnam and the British Vietnam Committee. Other subjects include the Admiralty, elections, Institute of Naval Architects, Labour Party, the Groundnut scheme and the Munich Pact. There are also various Union of Democratic Control pamphlets. Enquiries regarding access should be directed to the Archivist.

YOUNG, MAJOR-GENERAL PETER GEORGE FRANCIS (1912–72) Military career. Served in the British Army and Royal West Africa Frontier Force, 1932–40. Attached to Airborne Forces, 1941–48. Commanded 1st Brigade, Royal Nigeria Regiment, 1958–61. On War Office Staff, 1961–62. General Officer Commanding, Cyprus District, 1962–64. Director of Infantry, Ministry of Defence, 1965–67.

His Cyprus maps and papers, 1963–68, are deposited in the Liddell Hart Centre, King's College, London.

Z

ZAIDMAN, AZAR (1903–63) Communist and Jewish activist.

There are correspondence and papers, including some relating to the Workers' Circle Friendly Society, in Sheffield University Library.

ZILLIACUS, KONNI (1894–1967) Left-wing Labour MP. Suspended from Labour Party, 1961.

The bulk of his papers was destroyed before he entered hospital for the last time. However, a semi-autobiographical 300,000-word manuscript, appointments diaries and some other material was found in the possession of his widow. There is material concerning the 1949 Nenni telegram and his 1961 suspension from the Labour Party.

ZIMAN, HERBERT DAVID (1902–83) Journalist.

The papers have been placed in the Bodleian Library.

ZIMMERN, SIR ALFRED (1879–1957) Political scientist. Secretary General, Constituent Conference of UNESCO, 1945. Director, Greater Hartford Council for UNESCO, 1950.

A collection of correspondence and miscellaneous papers is held at the Bodleian Library, Oxford. Lists are available (NRA 21562 and 16865). The papers relate mainly to his work for international peace at his Geneva School for International Studies, UNESCO. There are also lectures, broadcasts, articles and pamphlets.

ZUCKERMANN, 1ST BARON Solly Zuckermann (1904–93) Chief Scientific Adviser to Secretary of State for Defence, 1964–71; to HM Government, 1964–71. Chairman of numerous committees of inquiry.

The University of East Anglia Library holds an extensive deposit of over 900 boxes of correspondence and papers covering his career since 1926. Several files provide an overview of developments in post-war government science policy. In particular, there is material on the work of the Advisory Council on Scientific Policy and the Committee on the Management and Control of Research and Development. There are also extensive research papers on the philosophy and sociology of science. A typescript diary, October 1964– February 1968, is also deposited. A list of the collection is available (NRA 43537).

Part II

A Guide to the Archives
of Selected Organisations

A

ABORTION LAW REFORM ASSOCIATION
Formed in 1936, the Association aims to obtain and publish information on the legal, social and medical aspects of abortion, to encourage research into these aspects, and to ensure the application and maintenance of the 1967 Abortion Act.

In 1982 the records of the Association were transferred from the Medical Research Council's Institute of Medical Sociology at Aberdeen to the Contemporary Medical Archives Centre of the Wellcome Institute (ref. SA/ALR). A certain amount of re-arrangement of the papers was made upon their transfer and access to some classes of material is restricted; researchers should therefore consult the Archivist in advance of any visit. A list is available (NRA 29789). Additional more recent records continue to be deposited.

The collection, which comprises 108 boxes and one folder, is divided into six categories, viz: Sections A and B – the records of the Association and its officers and members, which are largely concerned with reform of the law on abortion; Section C – an incomplete collection of the papers of the Lane Committee on the Working of the Abortion Act, 1971–74, including its agendas and minutes; Section D – a collection of articles, reprints and lectures on abortion and family planning matters, 1935–79; Section E – a collection of press cuttings, 1930–79; and Section F – copies of the Annual Report of the Brook Advisory Centres for the period 1965–81, which were received with the collection but do not form part of it.

Researchers should be aware that the papers of the National Abortion Campaign (q.v.), which were previously lodged at the Women's Library (q.v.), have now also been transferred to the CMAC.

ABYSSINIAN ASSOCIATION The Association was formally established in April 1936, with the economist Professor Herbert Stanley Jevons as Hon.

Secretary. Its declared aims were to counter pro-Italian propaganda regarding the situation in Ethiopia and to assist the Abyssinian Government by pressing for effective sanctions and financial assistance.

Certain records relating to the activities of the Association and of the Anglo-Ethiopian Society may be found in the Jevons Collection at the National Library of Wales. A list is available (NRA 34429). The relevant papers include files of notes on planning of the Association, typescripts of articles, memoranda, etc., 1935–51, together with certain pamphlets. In addition there is material on the Anglo-Ethiopian Society (of which Jevons was Treasurer from 1948 to 1955), including its account books for 1953–55, and Jevons' correspondence with Haile Selassie, 1937–53.

ACADEMIC WOMEN'S ACHIEVEMENT GROUP
The AWAG was formed in 1979 by a group of women academics based at University College London. It seeks to improve the representation of women in academic posts and to address the tendency of women to remain at the lower end of the university career structure. The group has retained minutes for the early period of its existence (1979–86) and maintains a press-cuttings file on relevant issues. Reports of its activities have been periodically published in the college magazine *UCL News*. Certain of AWAG's records have now been placed in the UCL archives and persons interested in consulting them should contact the office at University College London.

ACTION FOR VICTIMS OF MEDICAL ACCIDENTS A charity established in 1982, AVMA assists and advises persons who believe that they may have been victims of a medical accident (which is interpreted as including a failure to treat or a misdiagnosis as well as negligent practice). AVMA provides guidance on procedures for making formal complaints to the appropriate medical authorities and may assist plaintiffs in securing legal advice and representation.

The Association has retained its papers at its offices. The available records include minutes of the Steering Committee and the Committee (1981–82), of the Trustees (1982–), and of the Board of Directors from 1990 to date; Annual Reports (1981–); copies of the thrice-yearly *Newsletter*, published since 1981 and the quarterly *Medical/Legal Journal*, published since 1990; statutory financial records; and correspondence files. Access to the papers should be sought by written application to the Executive Director. Personal files may be examined only with the permission of the clients concerned.

ACTION ON SMOKING AND HEALTH ASH, a charity founded in 1971 by the Royal College of Physicians of London, is the United Kingdom's leading public information campaign on the issue of smoking. It maintains a headquarters in London and national offices in Scotland, Wales and Northern Ireland. The ASH Information Service publishes a bi-weekly *ASH Bulletin*.

The ASH archives were deposited on permanent loan at the Wellcome Contemporary Medical Archives Centre in October 1991. The material includes all committee minutes, research reports, financial records and correspondence since 1971.

The papers of ASH (Scotland) for the period after 1989 have been placed in the National Library of Scotland (ref. Acc. 12241).

ADVERTISING ASSOCIATION The Association was founded in 1926 to provide a focus for country-wide publicity and advertising business; subsequently it evolved into a federation of organisations representing individual sectors of the industry.

The Association's archive has been retained at its offices, with the exception of earlier committee reports and minutes which have been deposited with the History of Advertising Trust. In general, correspondence and subject files have not been retained and financial records have been kept only for the statutory period. Apart from the annual reports, which are held in the Association's library,

the material is confidential and requests for permission to examine it must be addressed in writing to the Head of Information.

ADVICE SERVICES ALLIANCE The ASA is an association of national advice organisations founded in 1980; it brings together Citizens Advice Bureaux, law centres and local and national independent advice agencies in order to address issues of common concern, such as improving standards of provision and securing adequate funding for member organisations.

The ASA has retained its own papers, which comprise recent minutes, copies of the annual and published reports, financial records (since 1986) and correspondence files. Researchers desiring access should apply to the Secretariat.

ADVOCATES FOR ANIMALS The organisation (formerly known as the Scottish Society for the Prevention of Vivisection) has retained its archives.

The collection includes minutes, 1911–57, annual reports, 1912–92, files, 1901–83 etc. A list is available (NRA 40225, NRA(S) 3652).

AFGHANAID Afghanaid is a registered British charity founded in 1983 which provides emergency humanitarian assistance to the people of Afghanistan. It developed from the Afghanistan Support Committee, a campaigning group established in 1980 which subsequently divided into the present organisation and a media resource centre, the Afghanistan Information Office; the information office closed in September 1989 and Afghanaid inherited most of its files. Afghanaid works to raise food production and restore the basic rural infrastructure by supporting small-scale agriculture and irrigation projects. It is assisted by the UK Overseas Development Administration and UN agencies.

The archive has been retained at Afghanaid's London office. Publicly available material includes annual reports and financial accounts (from 1988), press-cuttings files on Afghanistan (from 1984), and a series of published reports on relief work. These may be made available for study by contacting the Press and Information Officer at the above address. Confidential material consists of Management Committee minutes from 1984 to the present; AGM minutes of the Afghanistan Information Office, and the correspondence and subject files of both organisations. Any further enquiries should be directed to the Director of Afghanaid.

AFRICA BUREAU The Africa Bureau was founded in 1952 by Revd Guthrie Michael Scott to advise those Africans who wished by constitutional means to oppose the actions of colonial regimes in their own countries, and to educate public opinion on the nature of colonialism. It was wound up in December 1978 when its Trustees adjudged that they had completed their task and the surviving papers were placed in BLCAS (Rhodes House Library), Oxford (ref. MSS Afr s 1681). The deposit contains also the associated records of the Africa Educational Trust, the Africa Protectorates Trust and the Africa Publications Trust, as well as seven boxes of the records of the African Development Trust, which had been established by the Bureau in 1952. A list is available for the collections (NRA 24727).

The deposited papers run to some 320 boxes and are arranged as follows:

Boxes 1–36 Administrative records, including minutes of the Executive Committee, 1952–78; papers of the Consultative Council, 1973–75; AGM notices, correspondence and administrative papers and copies of the Annual Report, 1953–73; conference papers; press releases; and the correspondence of the Chairman (1952–76) and the successive Directors and Secretaries.

Boxes 37–67 Financial administration papers, including audited accounts, 1955–78; ledgers and bills and receipts; records of fundraising; and membership and publication subscription records.

Boxes 68–108 Papers on publishing activities, including incomplete lists of all Bureau publications and runs of periodicals and serials (particularly the *Anniversary Addresses* and *Africa Digest*), and numerous pamphlets and associated correspondence.

Boxes 109–146 Papers on the Study Projects, 1972–73, with their associated publications.

Boxes 147–313 Papers on Africa, arranged by territory (viz. South Africa, the High Commission Territories, Central Africa, East Africa and other African countries). These include correspondence

with persons in those territories, press-cuttings and background materials on the political situation in each.

Boxes 314–319 International Conference and Organisation papers, the bulk of which concerns the UN International Seminar on Apartheid at Kitwe in 1967.

AFRICA CENTRE The work of the Centre, which had its origins in the work of the Catholic organisation, the Sword of the Spirit (which later became the Catholic Institute for International Relations), is documented in 28 files amongst the papers of Patrick Wall MP. These are now deposited in the Brynmor Jones Library, University of Hull. These papers include correspondence, reports and memoranda about its foundation, annual reports, minutes of the Council of Management (of which Patrick Wall was the first Chair) and AGMs, newsletters, notices of meetings and accounts. There are two files relating to the 1958 conference on the future of Africa and its follow-up held in 1961.

AGE CONCERN: NATIONAL OLD PEOPLE'S WELFARE COUNCIL Age Concern was founded in August 1940 as an independent associated group of the National Council of Social Welfare under the name of the National Old People's Welfare Committee, which name it retained until 1955 when it became the National Old People's Welfare Council. In 1970 it became fully independent of the NCSW and in 1971 it added Age Concern to the title.

Age Concern has retained most of its records back to the date of foundation at its headquarters. The post-war material includes minutes, correspondence, copies of *Age Concern Today* and results of surveys.

Researchers should note that local branch records have been deposited in Essex Record Office and Wiltshire Record Office.

AID TO THE ELDERLY IN GOVERNMENT INSTITUTIONS (AEGIS) A collection of papers 1962–78 is in the LSE Library, in the papers of Barbara Robb, the founder of this campaigning organisation. A list is available (NRA 42338). The LSE Library also has some additional files of research papers compiled for C. H. Rolph (C. R.

Hewitt), the Editor of the *New Statesman* (ref. M1794).

AIR LEAGUE The League was founded in 1909 as the Aerial League of the British Empire and adopted its present title in 1965. It seeks to promote the contribution of aerospace activity to the overall security and economic and technological development of the United Kingdom.

The League has retained its own papers. The material consists of minutes of the Council, Executive and Sub-Committee meetings and Annual General Meetings from 1909 to the present; ledger books and printed annual audit reports from the same date, and correspondence and subject files. An annual report is issued to coincide with the AGM and there are available certain occasional reports, mainly produced for internal use, on aspects of the Air League's and the Air League Educational Trust's activities. All records are held at the League's offices and researchers should apply in the first instance to the Secretary-General for permission to view any archival material.

ALBANY TRUST The Albany Trust was the educational and counselling wing of the Homosexual Law Reform Society, established in 1958 to campaign for the implementation by legislation of the Wolfenden Report, which had recommended the decriminalisation of male adult homosexuality. The law was changed by the Sexual Offences Act of 1967. In 1970 the HLRS was reconstituted as the Sexual Law Reform Society. The Albany Trust was active up to 1983 and formally is still in existence. Its papers now form part of the Hall-Carpenter Archive (q.v.) at the LSE Library; they cover the period 1963–80 and include trustees' correspondence, administrative files and the records of counsellors and field officers. The Trust was involved in many projects in the area of sexual reform and material may be located on such topics as youth sexuality, religion, and transsexual and transvestite research. The collection also contains papers relating to associated organisations such as the HLRS and its successor, and the National Coordinating Committee against Censorship. Some of the records may be closed at present; further enquiries should be directed to the Archivist.

ALCOHOL CONCERN Alcohol Concern was founded in 1984 as a national charity to promote the responsible consumption of alcohol and to inform the public of the problems of alcohol abuse. It is partly supported by central government funding. It runs national educational campaigns; offers technical advice to local counselling and treatment agencies, and seeks to influence public policy on alcohol use. The archives of Alcohol Concern are retained at its offices, but the collection is presently closed.

ALLIED CIRCLE A group dating from 1941 (but formally constituted the following year), the Circle began as a series of informal meetings of exiled members of foreign governments and armed forces to discuss wartime problems and post-war reconstruction. Upon the acquisition of offices in London in 1943 the Circle held lectures, discussions and debates to further its aim of promoting 'among the peoples of the United Nations, fellowship and understanding, and a better knowledge of each other's problems and national life'. It published a journal and newsletter and and arranged exchange visits with other countries. The Circle ran into financial difficulties in the 1950s and was dissolved in 1963.

The records of Allied Circle were deposited in Westminster City Library in 1981 (ref. Acc. 1196). A list is available (NRA 26033). They include by-laws; minutes of the committee meetings (1950–51, 1954–63) and of the Younger Members Group (1949–61); membership records; copies of the bi-monthly *Journal* (1959–62) and letters to members (1946–58); financial records; press-cuttings (*c*. 1959–70); papers on social functions (including lists of speakers and a description of proceedings at a Conference of Allied Circles in July 1949), and some private correspondence, mainly relating to Mrs McNeil Robertson, at whose house early meetings were held.

ALL-PARTY PARLIAMENTARY GROUP ON AIDS The Group was started by MPs in the autumn of 1986. It exists to enable organisations in both the voluntary and statutory sectors to bring matters to the attention of Parliament and acts as a research and information service for MPs on the issues of

HIV/AIDS. A quarterly *Parliamentary AIDS Digest* is produced. Papers which have been retained comprise general administrative files and outgoing correspondence from mid-1988 onwards, copies of the *Digest* from November 1988 and an Annual Report from 1989. Enquiries should be addressed to the Research and Liaison Officer.

AMALGAMATED ASSOCIATION OF BEAMERS, TWISTERS AND DRAWERS The first amalgamation was formed in 1866 and reconstituted in 1889. The Association declined substantially in membership in the post-war era and was reorganised in 1969. The records for the period 1896–1978 have been deposited in Lancashire Record Office (ref. DDX 1269/1). A list is available (NRA 23239).

AMALGAMATED ASSOCIATION OF OPERATIVE COTTON SPINNERS The surviving records of the union have been placed in Preston District Library. A list is available (NRA 30946). The papers include Committee minute books 1944–60; reports, 1913–63 and 1966–68; cash and account books, 1945–67; piecers' contribution books, 1933–60; and amalgamation accounts, 1966–70. A miscellaneous collection of attached material includes a copy of the Association's rule book of 1955; an address book, 1895–1956; a list of members 'drawing under the Amalgamation rule', 1963–67; copies of the *Cotton Growing Review*, 1962–75, and the Annual Reports of the Cotton Growing Corporation for 1964–75.

AMALGAMATED ENGINEERING UNION In 1992 the Amalgamated Engineering Union merged with the Electrical, Electronic, Telecommunications, and Plumbing Union (EETPU) to form the Amalgamated Engineering and Electricians Union (AEEU). Owing to the recent nature of this merger, the two constituent parts of the AEEU are treated under separate headings in this Guide.

Engineering societies began to appear early in the 19th century but the first recognisably 'national' trade union was the Amalgamated Society of Engineers, Machinists, Smiths, Millwrights and Patternmakers (ASE), formed in 1851 from a number of these smaller societies. The ASE gradually promoted further amalgamations until nine unions were brought together to form the first Amalgamated Engineering Union (AEU) in 1920. Further

amalgamation in the post-war era brought in the Amalgamated Society of Glass Works' Engineers (1944); the Amalgamated Society of Vehicle Builders, Carpenters and Mechanics (1945); the Amalgamated Machine, Engine and Iron Grinders and Glaziers Society (1956); the Leeds Spindle and Flyer Makers' Trade and Friendly Society (1958); the United Operative Spindle and Flyer Makers' Trade (1962), and the Turners, Fitters and Instrument Makers' Union (Scotland) (1965). In 1967 the AEU merged with another large organisation, the Amalgamated Union of Foundry Workers, to form the Amalgamated Engineering and Foundry Workers' Union (AEF); however, this was effectively a federation of the two unions, because both retained their separate constitutions.

With the accession of the white-collar engineering union DATA (the Draughtsmen and Allied Technicians' Association) in 1970, and the Construction Engineering Union in 1971, the AEF was reconstituted as the Amalgamated Union of Engineering Workers (AUEW) with four federated sections representing different industrial sectors. However, the federation was not a success and there were significant disputes between the sections over the issue of proceeding to a full amalgamation. In 1984 the AUEW was reformed to become a two-section federation in which the engineers, construction and foundry workers formed one group (which in 1986 once again took the name of the Amalgamated Engineering Union), and the Technical, Administrative and Supervisory Section formed another section under the name of TASS (q.v.). In 1988 TASS severed all connections with the AEU and instead united with the Association of Scientific, Technical and Managerial Staffs (q.v.) to form the Manufacturing, Science, Finance Union.

The vast majority of the union's records have been deposited at the Modern Records Centre, University of Warwick. Some material pertaining to the Engineering Section of the union in Scotland, and certain district records, have been deposited at the National Library of Scotland (in addition to a substantial amount of pre-war material) and papers of the AEU in Northern Ireland for the period 1824 to 1951 are now at the Public Record Office of Northern Ireland (ref. D1050/8), although they are at present unlisted and unavailable.

The material deposited at the Modern Records Centre reflects the sectional organisation of the union by being divided into four separate collections: the Engineering Section (ref. MSS 259), the Foundry Section (ref. MSS 41), the Construction Section (ref. MSS 273), and the Technical, Administrative and Supervisory Section (ref. MSS 101). The records of the latter section are described separately in this Guide under a main entry for TASS. It should be noted that references to the AEU in the description below refer to the first union of that name and not to the 1986 foundation.

ENGINEERING SECTION

The post-war material deposited at the Modern Records Centre consists of the minutes of the Amalgamated Machine, Engine and Iron Grinders and Glaziers Society (see above) for 1936–56; Final Appeal Court reports for the years 1920–65 and 1971–75 for both the AEU and AUEW; AEU Council minutes for 1920–44 and the *Monthly Journal* for 1936–64, and various local branch records, viz: the Birmingham West District AEU/AUEW minutes for 1946–75; Pontypool District minutes for 1950–55 and 1969–74; the Humber Works Stewards' minutes for 1950–63 (in collection MSS 180); and Oxford District minutes for 1968–75 (ref. MSS 228). The Etheridge Papers (ref. MSS 202) contain records relating to the Austin Longbridge Shop Stewards' committee, the Midlands District and Birmingham City branches, and some nationally circulated material.

A list is available describing the AUEW Engineering Section deposit (NRA 33604).

FOUNDRY SECTION

The Amalgamated Engineering and Foundry Workers' Union (AEF) – the predecessor of the present union before the accession of DATA and the Construction Workers – had been formed in 1966 by the merger of the old AEU and the Amalgamated Union of Foundry Workers (AUFW) (itself created in 1946 from the National Union of Foundry Workers, the Ironfounding Workers' Association and the United Metal Founders' Society).

Many of the Section's records are now at the Modern Records Centre in collection MSS 41. Post-

war printed records include copies of national agreements and information pertaining to the same, 1922–54; a memo on 'Post-War Reconstruction in the Engineering Industry' (1946) by the National Engineering Joint Trades Movement; and an AEU report 'Amalgamation: Report of Meeting of Trade Unions in the Engineering Industry' (1956). Records of the AUFW include rulebooks for itself and predecessor organisations from 1837 to 1956; National Executive Committee minutes for 1946–64; circulated files of various joint union committees, 1949–52; a series of files on NUFW/AUEW amalgamation discussions with the Engineering Workers and other unions, 1924–73; and journals for the period 1946–67. For the post-1966 period, the Modern Records Centre has AGM reports and journals for 1968–83 of both the AEF and AUEW, and a number of local records for these and predecessor unions, viz: the Chester Branch minutes, 1921–71; the Consett Branch minutes, 1951–80; and the minutes of the Oxford District Committee and quarterly meetings of shop stewards for 1968–71 and 1974–75.

The records of the Foundry Section in Scotland for the period 1867–1947 have been deposited at the National Library of Scotland (ref. Acc 9095).

CONSTRUCTION SECTION

In 1986 the Modern Records Centre received the remaining records of the former Construction Engineering Union (established 1924), and some of those of the AUEW Construction Section. These papers contain Executive Committee minutes for 1939–84; biennial conference reports and proceedings for 1945–83; a file of returns to the Registrar of Friendly Societies, 1925–84; the journal for the period 1968–75 and the *Construction Worker* for 1925–84; and miscellaneous material such as union agreements or documentation on its history.

TECHNICAL, ADMINISTRATIVE AND SUPERVISORY SECTION

The records are described under the main entry for TASS in this Guide.

AMALGAMATED SOCIETY OF BRASS-WORKERS The Society was founded in 1886 as the

London Society of Amalgamated Brassworkers and Gasfitters, following the cessation of the National Society of Amalgamated Brassworkers (est. 1872). It adopted its present name *c.* 1919. The papers were listed by the Librarian of the TUC in 1961 and found to comprise the minutes of the annual and quarterly meetings and of the Executive Committee from 1888 onwards; copies of the rule book (latest issue 1955); and bound membership ledgers, 1939–61. A list is available (NRA 8969). The union ceased to exist in 1962 and the present whereabouts of the papers is unknown.

AMNESTY INTERNATIONAL Amnesty International, which is based in London, was founded in 1961 to inform public opinion on the position of 'prisoners of conscience' throughout the world and to organise campaigns for their release.

Amnesty (as it is commonly known) retains its own archive, but under an agreement of 1974 with the Modern Records Centre at Warwick University, it periodically deposits a comprehensive collection of its publications at the Centre (MSS 34). The relevant series are publications relating to particular countries from 1963 onwards; publications on imprisonment and prison conditions from 1965; publications on conscientious objection and torture from 1973; publications on the application of the death penalty; Amnesty's *Annual Reports* and other periodicals from 1961; and Amnesty News Releases from 1970. In 1988 Amnesty additionally deposited 14 bound volumes of photocopied press-cuttings for the period 1961–69.

The papers of the International Secretariat, 1961–2002, are in the International Institute of Social History, Amsterdam.

ANGLICAN EVANGELICAL GROUP MOVEMENT The records of this pressure group within the Church of England are now in the Brynmor Jones Library, University of Hull (ref. DEM). The archive covers the period 1926–70 and the post-war material comprises minutes, 1927–67; committee files, 1927– 51; finance, 1927–72; study outlines, 1948–66; correspondence, 1937–62; publications *c.* 1927–62 (including *The Liberal Evangelical*, 1933–62), and subject files, 1927–70. A list of the collection is available (NRA 23221).

ANGLICAN GROUP FOR THE ORDINATION OF WOMEN TO THE HISTORIC MINISTRY OF THE CHURCH This body held its first meeting in March 1933, although there appears to have been a working group before this date. It was wound up in the mid-1970s and in 1987 the records were deposited in the Fawcett Library (now the Women's Library). Surviving papers for the post-war era include minutes of the annual meetings (1948–49, 1957–69) and of the Executive Committee (1954–75), and an intermittent series of press-cuttings (1928–53, 1956–78). Further press-cuttings on women in the Church for an earlier period (*c.* 1919–50) may be found in the Cavendish Bentinck collection at the Women's Library.

ANGLICAN PACIFIST FELLOWSHIP The Anglican Pacifist Fellowship was formed in Great Britain in 1937. Its members are Christians of the Anglican Communion who believe that faith in Jesus Christ calls for the renunciation of all war and the preparation for war. The Fellowship produces and distributes literature, including a newsletter, and organises conferences and retreats.

The Fellowship's papers consist of the minutes of its Governing Body and Executive Committee; annual reports; and correspondence files arranged by subject or country. Copies of the newsletter *Challenge* and its predecessor *The Anglican Pacifist* are available. The Annual Report includes a financial account for the year and certain financial reports and budget statements are attached to the minutes; other financial records are retained by the Hon. Treasurer. The papers have been deposited in the Commonweal Collection at the Department of Peace Studies, University of Bradford.

ANGLO-ALBANIAN ASSOCIATION Correspondence of Mary Herbert, who was instrumental in founding the association in 1944, is in Somerset Record Office (ref. Acc G/2338). A short list is available (NRA 41703).

ANGLO-AUSTRIAN SOCIETY Founded in 1944 as the Anglo-Austrian Democratic Society, for the first two years of its existence the aims of the Society were largely political; in the spirit of the Allies' Moscow Declaration of 1943 which had rejected the

Nazi annexation as void, the Society sought to promote the restoration of Austrian independence and democracy. It was renamed in 1946 following Austria's liberation and has since been active in promoting cultural contacts between Britain and the new republic. The papers are retained at the Society's offices and consist of committee minutes from 1944 to the present, annual reports and accounts from 1946, and correspondence. A commemorative history by Frederick Scheu, *The Early Days of the Anglo-Austrian Society*, was published in 1969. Persons seeking access to the collection should apply to the Secretary.

ANGLO-CHILEAN SOCIETY The Society was founded in 1944 to further the education of the British people concerning Chile. It retains its own papers, which include minutes of the Executive Committee; copies of the publications (the annual or biannual *Bulletin* and the annual report and accounts); financial records; and selected correspondence. Persons interested in consulting the papers should apply to the Secretary.

ANGLO-GERMAN ASSOCIATION The Association was founded in 1951 as an independent charity to promote close understanding in social and cultural matters between the United Kingdom and Germany. The papers have been retained at the Association's offices. They consist of the minutes of the Executive Committee and file copies of its publications, namely the quarterly *Anglo-German Review* and a diary of the Association's events (including an annual seminar in Berlin). Correspondence has not been kept. Persons seeking access to the records should write in the first instance to the Hon. Secretary.

ANGLO-JEWISH ASSOCIATION The Association was founded 1871 to further the 'social, moral and intellectual progress' of the Jewish people, to educate others in Jewish matters, and to fight anti-Semitic discrimination. Until 1943 it conducted its work in the field of foreign affairs in conjunction with the Board of Deputies of British Jews, but then established its own Foreign Committee.

The papers for the period after 1871 have been deposited with the Anglo-Jewish Archives at the Hartley Library, University of Southampton (ref. MS 137). There is a list available (NRA 21917). A summary guide has been prepared. A large proportion of the archive relates to foreign affairs and some of this material is closed. The papers of Council which are available for the post-war era include minute books, 1871–1962; AGM minutes, 1953–56; and expenditure sheets and annual reports, 1950–51. The various committees of the Association have produced a large collection of papers. Financial records, including cash books and investment sheets, date from 1889 to 1983 and the papers of the Finance Committee itself cover 1948–62. The Foreign Affairs Committee papers include reports on Jewish communities throughout the world and correspondence with international organisations, and certain subject files relating to issues such as war criminals and refugees. The material largely dates from the 1940s and 1950s. The archive also incorporates a collection of correspondence, articles and press-cuttings on various countries covering the period 1947–69.

ANGLO-PALESTINIAN CLUB An independent non-party organisation, the Club was founded in 1920 to foster agreement among those interested in 'the welfare of Palestine' and sympathetic to the creation of a Jewish national home there. It ceased to function in 1956. Minutes and other materials of the Club have survived in the papers of Lord Janner (in private possession).

ANGLO-TURKISH SOCIETY The Society was founded in 1953 with the object of strengthening and developing the historical ties of mutual understanding between Britain and Turkey. It has retained its papers, which consist of the minutes of the Executive Council and of AGMs from 1980 to date; cashbooks and income and expenditure accounts; correspondence; and the records of social and cultural programmes since 1990. The above are in the care of the Secretary but are closed to non-members.

ANTI-APARTHEID MOVEMENT The records of the organisation (founded in 1959 as the Boycott Movement) have been placed in BLCAS (Rhodes House Library), Oxford. Over 1300 boxes of papers have been deposited. BLCAS also has the records of the End Loans to South Africa campaign. The records of the Welsh Anti-Apartheid Movement are in the National Library of Wales. The Scottish records, 1975–94, are in Glasgow Caledonian University Archive.

ANTI-CONCORDE PROJECT The Project was founded in 1966 to oppose the development of the Concorde supersonic aeroplane, largely on environmental grounds. Many of its papers consist of publicity material (largely reprints of and commentaries upon statements by both proponents and critics of Concorde); the bulk of the archive was held by the founding Secretary, Mr Richard Wiggs. The Modern Records Centre, University of Warwick, has examples of publicity material, 1967–81, and an incomplete set of Advisory Committee minutes, 1969–74, in its collection MSS 32, for which there is a list available (NRA 18530). A related organisation, the Campaign for Action on Supersonic Engineering, has also deposited material (e.g. booklets and bulletins) at the Modern Records Centre in collection MSS 146.

ANTI-POLL TAX CAMPAIGN One box of literature produced by national organisations, local authorities and anti-poll tax campaign groups, 1988–91, has been placed in the LSE Library (ref. M1779). The collection is open.

ANTI-SLAVERY INTERNATIONAL Anti-Slavery International was originally formed in 1909 by the merger of the Anti-Slavery Society (est. 1839) and the Aborigines' Protection Society. In 1957 it adopted the name of the Anti-Slavery Society for the Protection of Human Rights and took its present title in November 1990. The aims of the Society, in accordance with the United Nations Declaration of Human Rights of 1948, are the eradication of slavery, the abolition of forced labour resembling slavery, and the protection and advancement of minority cultures.

The archives of Anti-Slavery International are sent at periodic intervals to BLCAS (Rhodes House Library), Oxford (ref. MSS Brit. Emp. S. 16–24) and persons wishing to use them should apply there to the Librarian. A list is available (NRA 1095). Decennial deposits were made in 1971 and 1981, consisting of papers for the post-war period up to the mid-1970s. These are described below. More recent deposits have been made.

MSS Brit. Emp. S. 19

D.8/1–7	Secretary's incoming correspondence, 1925–50
D.9/1–7	Secretary's outgoing correspondence, 1940–47
D.10/1–11	Secretary's incoming and outgoing letter files, 1950–61
D.10/12	Chairman's correspondence and activities, 1944–67; Director's correspondence, 1957–62
D.10/13	Correspondence with the President and Vice-Presidents, 1961–68
D.10/14–24	General correspondence of the Secretary and assistants, 1955–71
D.10/25	Official files, being correspondence with and representations to the Foreign and Commonwealth Office, 1963–70
D.11/1–7	Papers concerning the Society's management, meetings, annual reports, journal (*Anti-Slavery Reporter and Aborigine's Friend*), and financial arrangements and appeals, 1951–61
D.11/8–18	Further management files, 1963–72

MSS Brit. Emp. S. 22

E.4/24–39	Account books and ledgers, 1937–69
G.518–811	Subject files for 1944–62 relating to anti-slavery activities in various parts of the world. These incorporate reports on the economic, political and social conditions of those areas. The files are arranged by general geographical area (e.g. Africa, the Americas, Australia and Australasia, and Asia) and are further subdivided. In addition there are files on the activities of the United Nations and its organisations and other humanitarian associations
G.812–831	Subject files as above for the 1960s
G.852–904	Files re the United Nations, particularly the Commission on Human Rights, 1953–1972

G.914–922   Speakers' notes and comments on meetings at which the Society provided speakers, 1961–70

G.923–932   Correspondence with overseas associations

J.52–110   Files of unmounted newspaper cuttings, for the period up to 1977

MSS Brit. Emp. S. 23

H.3/1–3   Letters to the Secretary and other officials and their replies relating to the welfare of Africans resident in the UK, 1940–56

APEX The airline staff organisation (not to be confused with the Association of Professional, Executive, Clerical & Computer Staff which is now part of the GMB) has deposited material at the Modern Records Centre, University of Warwick. The collection consists of files from its Harlington office on union organisation in civil aviation for the period 1972–81, and from its Hayes office relating to industrial relations with British Airways in particular.

ARAB CLUB The Club was an organisation for supporters of the Arabs in Palestine which was active in London in the 1940s. No extant archive is known of, but material concerning its finances is contained in the Spears Papers at the Middle East Centre, St Antony's College, Oxford (1945–59, ref. VII/4); other records are included with the Mansour Papers at the same location.

ARAB OFFICE, LONDON An organisation of Palestinian Arabs and their sympathisers, the Office was active in the 1930s and 1940s in opposing Zionist propaganda. An independent archive has not been located, but relevant material may be found in the Spears Papers at the Middle East Centre, St Antony's College, Oxford (i.e. correspondence for the period 1945–53 between the Office and Sir Edward Spears, ref. VII/4). Further enquiries should be directed to the Council for the Advancement of Arab-British Understanding.

ARCHBISHOPS' COMMISSIONS It is the established practice that the papers of those Commissions of the Church of England which operate under the authority of either or both of the Primates of the Church are deposited in Lambeth Palace Library upon the termination of the Commission. Among those of the post-war era which have deposited material are the Archbishop of Canterbury's Overseas Advisory Committee (ref. MS 2962), comprising minutes, correspondence and papers, 1931–47; the Archbishops' Commission on Divine Healing (ref. MS 2859), including minutes, memoranda and other papers, 1953–57; the Archbishops' Commission on Intercommunion (ref. MSS 2554–56), with papers including duplicated memoranda, draft reports, and minutes, 1965–68; and the Archbishop's Group on the Reform of the Divorce Law (ref. MS 3460), minutes, 1964–66. Further enquiries should be directed to the Archivist.

ARCHITECTS FOR PEACE The archive of the organisation, from its foundation in 1981 to 1994, has been placed in the RIBA British Architectural Library, London.

ARMY LEAGUE The League was active in the 1930s among a group of private individuals of military and industrial backgrounds who had become concerned at the weakness of the British Army. It sponsored a public campaign in favour of rearmament, a policy which was repeated during the 1950s. The papers of Sir Basil Liddell Hart have been identified as the most valuable source concerning the activities of the Army League. These cover the period 1913–70 and have been deposited at the Liddell Hart Centre for Military Archives, King's College, London. A list of the material is available (NRA 19291).

ARTISTS' INTERNATIONAL ASSOCIATION There are official records, together with correspondence covering the period 1933 to 1971, in the archives of Tate Britain, London. A list is available (NRA 19361).

ARTISTS LEAGUE OF GREAT BRITAIN There are papers in London Metropolitan Archives. A list is available (NRA 41907).

ARTISTS UNION Archives of the organisation, including agendas, minutes and newsletters, have been placed in the Tate Britain Archive (ref. TGA 2001/16).

ASH See under **ACTION ON SMOKING AND HEALTH**.

ASSISTANT MASTERS' AND MISTRESSES' ASSOCIATION The AMMA was formed in 1979 by the amalgamation of the Incorporated Association of Assistant Masters in Secondary Schools (commonly known as the Assistant Masters' Association or AMA) and the Association of Assistant Mistresses. The former organisation had been founded in 1891 to campaign for improved working conditions and a professional status for secondary teachers, and the latter in 1884 to seek the same for women teachers. The AMMA is now the third largest teachers' union in the UK and one of the largest unions not affiliated to the TUC.

The archive of the AMA was formerly held at its headquarters but since amalgamation it has been transferred to the library of the Institute of Education, University of London. The collection incorporates a printed series (including a run of the monthly journal since its foundation); Annual Reports; and records of the Joint Scholastic Agency (an AMA-sponsored recruiting agency active until the 1950s). An annual yearbook was also produced until 1955, containing Burnham reports and membership and teaching statistics. Access to certain papers is restricted. There is a list available (NRA 18866).

The Institute of Education also holds the minutes of the Northern Ireland Branch for the period 1948–62. The minutes and statements of account of the Northern East Anglia District of the AMA for 1923–60 are reportedly in the Cambridgeshire Record Office.

The records of the Association of Assistant Mistresses were extensively damaged by enemy action in 1940, but in 1984 most of the surviving papers were deposited at the Modern Records Centre, University of Warwick (ref. MSS 59). This material comprises the minutes of the Association's Executive Committee and other committees for the period 1938–78; Joint Four minutes, 1947–60; membership registers, 1953–78; correspondence and other files (including Burnham negotiations and relations with

other professional organisations) from the 1920s until 1981; annual reports from foundation until 1978; the *Journal* and *Newsletter* for 1950–78; various publications, and the minutes and accounts of several branches. A list is available for this collection (NRA 29895).

The Modern Records Centre also has the papers of the first ten years of the amalgamated AMMA, which consist of committee agendas and minutes of 1979–80 and printed reports, conference proceedings and publications (including the *Briefing*) for the period 1978–88.

ASSOCIATED SOCIETY OF LOCOMOTIVE ENGINEERS AND FIREMEN (ASLEF) The ASLEF papers, deposited in the Modern Records Centre, University of Warwick (ref. MSS 379), comprise annual reports, the papers of Percy Collick (1897–1984), Assistant General Secretary; papers re the Clapham Junction Crash Enquiry, 1989; and branch minute books.

ASSOCIATION OF AREA MEDICAL OFFICERS OF HEALTH Established as a result of local government reorganisation, the Association was the successor to the Association of County Medical Officers of Health (q.v.); its members were employed by each NHS Area Health Authority rather than by the old local authorities. The Association was established in 1974 and wound up in 1981 prior to the abolition of the Area Health Authorities themselves. Its papers, covering the period 1974/75–81, have been given on permanent loan to the Contemporary Medical Archives Centre of the Wellcome Institute (ref. SA/AMO). The material consists principally of agendas and notes of meetings, rather than actual minutes, and includes papers circulated to members. Papers for the period 1974–76 are copies, whereas later material comprises the signed originals. A list is available (NRA 25579).

ASSOCIATION OF BRITISH CHAMBERS OF COMMERCE The Association was established in 1860. Its archive has been deposited on indefinite loan in the Guildhall Library (ref. MSS 14476–88 and 17363–595); application for access to the papers should be made to the Keeper of Manuscripts, although no appointment is specifically required for consultation of the material. A list is available (NRA 16614) and there is a published history of the Association by A.R. Ilersic and P.F.B. Liddle entitled *Parliament of Commerce: The Story of the ABCC* (London, 1960). The Guildhall Library also holds the papers of the Federation of Commonwealth Chambers of Commerce for the period 1911–74 (see NRA 27304), and the International Chamber of Commerce for 1958–60 (ref. MS 16490; NRA 27303).

The main series of ABCC records comprise the following: Executive Committee minute books, 1860–1953, and a loose collection of draft minutes, reports, correspondence, memoranda and circulars, 1876–1976; General Purpose Committee minutes, 1956–64, and agendas and copy minutes, 1966–69; Finance and Taxation Committee minute books, 1921–52, with files of the Finance Division's administrative papers, 1954–72; Home Affairs and Transport Committee minute books, 1921–51, and administrative papers of the Home Affairs Division, 1963–72; Overseas Committee minutes, 1921–64, and divisional subject files, 1957–72; a revised edition of the articles of association, 1969; a list of affiliated chambers, 1955; statistical series re local chambers, 1962–70; general circulars (i.e. copy minutes of the Association's National Council), 1969–73; copy out-letter files, 1968–71, and numerous subcommittee files.

There are also available certain records of the Association of Secretaries of British Chambers of Commerce, namely minutes, 1922–53; an incomplete series of the papers of conferences and general meetings, 1960–69, and circulars, 1963–66.

ASSOCIATION OF BRITISH INSURERS A trade association for insurance companies, with membership open to any company authorised by the Department of Trade and Industry to transact business in the UK and to Friendly Societies (but not brokers or intermediaries), the Association was formed in 1985 by the merger of a number of specialist insurance company organisations. Its archive consists of the minutes of the various policy and technical committees of its predecessors, dating from the early 1970s, and the annual reports of the same. Financial records are retained for the statutory period only and technical reports, correspondence, and subject files are subject to regular weeding of

routine material. Copies of circular records have also been deposited at the City Business Library. Applications for permission to examine the papers should be addressed to the Chief Executive.

ASSOCIATION OF COMMONWEALTH UNIVERSITIES In 1913 the Universities Bureau of the British Empire was founded to encourage co-operation between its members. The present name was adopted in 1963 upon its incorporation by royal charter. It is the oldest inter-university association in the world and has several hundred member institutions throughout the Commonwealth.

The ACU retains its minute books from October 1919 to date and printed Annual Reports from 1923 onwards. The majority of pre-war records were destroyed by enemy action during World War II. Post-war records, with the exception of the minutes and reports, are retained according to the policy of each individual department of the Association. The collection is at present closed to researchers. Further details may be found in Adrian Allan, *University Bodies: A Survey of Inter- and Supra-University Bodies and their Records* (University of Liverpool Archives Unit, 1990).

ASSOCIATION FOR THE CONSERVATION OF ENERGY The Association for the Conservation of Energy (ACE) was established in 1981 by a number of energy conservation companies in order to stimulate national awareness of the need for energy conservation and to encourage the adoption of a consistent national conservation policy. The Association commissions research on the subject and publicises developments in its newsletter, *The Fifth Fuel*. ACE has retained its complete archive from the date of its foundation. The material includes minutes, agendas and correspondence of the Governing Council; membership files and correspondence; press releases; copies of ACE's research reports and newsletter; papers relevant to the activities of Parliament, such as the statements of political parties on conservation issues and publications of select committees; and subject files (including statistics, files on organisations active in and responsible for energy conservation such as government departments and utility companies, and papers emanating from international organisations). Persons wishing to consult the records should write to the Director of ACE.

ASSOCIATION FOR EUROPEAN MONETARY UNION

Enquiries should be directed to the Archivist at the LSE Library concerning the surviving papers.

ASSOCIATION OF COMMUNITY HEALTH COUNCILS

Sixty-three boxes of papers, covering the period from the 1970s to 2003, have been placed in the Contemporary Medical Archives Centre. The earliest material dates from the formation of the association in 1977.

ASSOCIATION OF COUNCILLORS

The Association was established in 1959 to represent elected members of all local authorities. It provides a forum for councillors to exchange views on matters of common concern; initiates action on matters affecting the responsibilities of local government; and assists in the training and education of councillors. In 1966 it was recognised by the Ministry of Housing and Local Government as an organisation to which local authorities could belong. Membership is open to councils on a corporate basis or to serving councillors of any local authority in England and Wales.

The Association's records are retained in the care of the Secretary and other Officers. Existing material includes committee minutes since inauguration (complete only from 1980 onwards); financial records since 1959; correspondence; and copies of reports published by the Association. Application for access to the papers should be made to the Secretary.

ASSOCIATION OF COUNTY COUNCILS

Following local government reorganisation in 1974 the ACC was established to replace the existing County Councils Association. The CCA had been set up in 1890 to represent at a national level the newly formed county councils and to advise members on legal matters and on the implications of legislation. It was administered by an Executive Committee (composed of the members' representatives and of clerks of the county councils), which met nine times per annum, usually to consider committee reports. Most of the CCA's work was conducted through its committees, the most important of which covered agriculture, education, highways, parliament, planning, police, public health and housing, and finance. After the passage of the Local Government Act of 1972, a new Association comprising all non-metropolitan counties was formed and this assumed the CCA's responsibilities in April 1974.

The surviving archive includes the minutes of the Executive Committee of the CCA and the ACC for the periods 1905–06 and 1908 to date. Minutes for 1891–1905 and 1906–07 are available unsigned and bound up with minutes of the AGMs, the Annual Reports, and the Association's Rules. The Executive Committee minutes and Annual Reports are also published in the annual volumes of the *Official Gazette* (renamed the *County Councils Gazette* in 1957) which have also been retained. The *Gazette* is published to provide relevant information to members; it contains minutes and articles and reports on the work of member councils and on developments in Parliament. Correspondence and administrative files survive in large quantities. Most date from 1945 and only those for Agriculture, Education, and the Police contain much earlier material. These files are organised by originating committee and consist mainly of correspondence, reports, and memoranda on legislation and government policy.

Administrative files for the period before 1960 have been deposited in Hertfordshire Record Office. All other material is retained at the Association's headquarters and a list is available (NRA 24456).

The records of the Association of County Councils in Scotland are in Edinburgh City Archives (NRA 43371).

ASSOCIATION OF COUNTY MEDICAL OFFICERS OF HEALTH

The Association was founded in 1902 and was formally constituted as the County Medical Officers' Group of the Society of Medical Officers of Health in 1945, whilst at the same time remaining a separate Association. Joint General Meetings of the Group and the Association were held until 1956 and separately thereafter, although a Joint Executive Committee existed for both.

The Association was wound up in 1974 following the reorganisation of local government and its papers transferred to the Wellcome Institute; in 1980 there were added to the new Contemporary Medical

Archives Centre the papers of Dr G. Ramage, Secretary of the Association from 1954 to 1972, which had previously been deposited in Staffordshire Record Office. The material now at the CMAC (ref. SA/CMO), which is in 59 boxes, comprises minutes of the Association's General Meetings and Executive Committee (1902–07, 1918–74) and the Secretary's correspondence (1939–74). There are also in the collection 20 boxes of circulated papers and correspondence of the Public Health and Housing/Health and Welfare Committee of the Association of County Councils, 1959–72. A list is available (NRA 25580).

ASSOCIATION OF DISTRICT COUNCILS Prior to local government reorganisation in 1974, five principal local authority associations existed in Great Britain: the Association of Municipal Corporations (AMC), the County Councils Association (CCA), the Urban District Councils Association (UDCA), the Rural District Councils Association (RDCA), and the National Association of Parish Councils (NAPC). Although the Redcliffe-Maud Report on reorganisation had proposed a single association to represent local government, this suggestion was not adopted and instead the individual bodies were succeeded by new ones representing each administrative level. The AMC was replaced by the Association of Metropolitan Authorities (AMA), which consisted of the metropolitan counties and district councils, the Greater London Council and the Inner London Education Authority, the London Borough Councils and the Corporation of the City of London. The CCA was replaced by the Association of County Councils (q.v.); and the UDCA and the RDCA amalgamated to form the Association of District Councils, comprising all non-metropolitan district councils in England and district councils in Wales. The NAPC in turn was replaced by the National Association of Local Councils.

The antecedents of the ADC run back to the foundation of the UDCA and RDCA in 1891 and 1895 respectively. Its function is to represent the district councils nationally; to express an opinion on legislation and executive decisions relating to their interests; and to provide legal advice to members. There are papers in London Metropolitan Archives. A list is available (NRA 42974).

ASSOCIATION OF FOREIGN BANKS The archive of the Association, formerly the Foreign Banks and Securities Association, has been placed in the Guildhall Library, London (ref. MS 34831–920). A list is available (NRA 44111). A 30-year restriction on access applies.

ASSOCIATION OF GYPSY ORGANISATIONS The Association was founded in 1975. Its papers may be consulted on application to the Secretary.

ASSOCIATION OF HEALTH AND RESIDENTIAL CARE OFFICERS The Association existed from 1898 until 1984. Its original function was 'to consider the duties, responsibilities and interests of Masters and Mistresses of Poor Law institutions'. The papers have been deposited in the Contemporary Medical Archives Centre of the Wellcome Institute (ref. SA/AHR). They comprise minutes and committee papers of the AHRCO and its predecessors from 1915 until c. 1980, in 18 boxes. A list is available (NRA 31787).

ASSOCIATION OF INDEPENDENT RADIO CONTRACTORS AIRC is the trade association for radio contractors and was founded in 1973 to represent the interests of local radio companies in their negotiations with trades unions, advertising trade bodies and copyright societies. The Association retains certain of its records at its offices and the remainder is in store. None of the material is presently available for research. Readers should be aware that a collection of records for the period 1973–83 previously deposited on loan with the History of Advertising Trust (for which there is a list, NRA 30150) has now been returned to AIRC.

ASSOCIATION OF JEWISH EX-SERVICEMEN AND WOMEN AJEX was founded in 1929 to foster communal activities amongst Jewish veterans; oppose anti-Semitism; and assist migration to Palestine. Certain papers are believed to be in the care of the Secretary of AJEX. Copies of the minutes, memoranda and correspondence for the period 1934–56 are also known to exist in the archives of the Board of Deputies of British Jews (ref. E1/11–12). The records of the Merseyside branch covering the 1946–82 period have been deposited in Liverpool

Record Office (Acc. 4407, 4419) and a list is available (NRA 2664).

ASSOCIATION OF JUTE SPINNERS AND MANUFACTURERS
The Association was established in 1918, initially as a cartel among jute companies in Dundee to protect their prices. It later developed into a trade association. The records for the period 1925–28 have been deposited in Dundee University Library (ref. MS 84). There is a list available (NRA 31388).

The papers include copies of the rules and bylaws, 1915–64; the annual report, 1919–82; minutes of the Meetings of Members and of the General Committee, 1918–78; minutes of the Governing Committee, 1945–78, and the Industrial Committee, 1924–69, amongst others, and the minutes of numerous subcommittees brought together in several single volumes (including minutes of joint meetings with trades unions, 1925–68). There is also a substantial series of general files, which include correspondence with official bodies (e.g. the Board of Trade) and copies of their circulars; reports on the condition of the jute industry (including papers arising from the Monopolies Commission's action against the Association for price-setting, 1960–62), and files on the Association's involvement with the Association of European Jute Industries, 1954–65.

ASSOCIATION OF METROPOLITAN AUTHORITIES
The records, for the period 1970–95, are in the University of Birmingham Library.

ASSOCIATION FOR THE PROMOTION OF CHRISTIAN KNOWLEDGE
The organisation was founded in 1792 as the Association for Discountenancing Vice and Promoting the Knowledge and Practice of Religion and Virtue; it was subsequently known by the short form above. In 1971 the papers were deposited in the Representative Church Body Library in Dublin (ref. MS 174). A list is available (NRA 27252). The material includes minutes for the period 1792 to 1970 in eight books; a rough minute book for 1962–78; an agenda book, 1927–45; reports of the Finance Committee, 1940–54, and membership ledgers, 1966–78.

Researchers should also be aware that the Library holds certain papers of the Island and Coast Society (ref. MS 161), which was established in 1833 to promote the religious education of children in the west and south of Ireland.

ASSOCIATION FOR SCIENCE EDUCATION
The records for the period c. 1900–79 have been placed in the Brotherton Library, University of Leeds (ref. MS Dep. 1984/1 and 1991/3). A list is available (NRA 34704). The ASE grew through the amalgamation of a number of predecessor bodies which were concerned with promoting the cause of scientific education in schools; these were the Science Masters' Association (formerly the Association of Public School Science Masters), the Association of Women Science Teachers, the Science Association and the Association of Science Teachers.

Collections of papers were deposited in the Brotherton Library in 1984 and 1991; bona fide scholars should write to the Librarian in advance giving details of their proposed research. Material relating to the ASE itself comprises committee minutes, 1963–73; agendas and programmes of the Annual Meeting, 1964–79; the general minute book of the North Western region, 1966–71, and a looseleaf file of agendas and minutes, 1969–75, and a scrapbook of the agendas, notices and reports of meetings of the Yorkshire region for the period 1964–74. Predecessor archives consist of the following:

SCIENCE MASTERS' ASSOCIATION

Minute books, 1900–63; Annual Reports with lists of members and rules, 1920–59; AGM programmes, 1924–63; lists of members, 1953–60; accounts for the *Social Science Review*, 1941–52; AGM programmes of the Scottish branch, 1948–53; and a copy of the published history of 1950, *Science Masters' Association 1900–1950*. There are also various minute books of the North Western and Yorkshire branches, 1934–73.

ASSOCIATION OF WOMEN SCIENCE TEACHERS

General meeting minutes, 1912–59; committee minutes, 1933–63; Annual Reports, 1921–62; miscellaneous committee papers, 1931–46; ledger, 1951–63; income and expenditure day books, 1961–63; and the assorted minute books of the Liverpool, London and Northern branches, 1930–62, with account books and lists of members.

ASSOCIATION OF SCIENTIFIC, TECHNICAL AND MANAGERIAL STAFFS ASTMS was established in 1968 by the amalgamation of the Association of Scientific Workers (AScW) and the Association of Supervisory Staffs, Executives and Technicians (ASSET), both of which had pre-war origins. The united Association was joined in 1971 by the Medical Practitioners' Union and subsequently by several other staff associations, particularly ones in the finance sector such as the Guild of Insurance Officials/Union of Insurance Staffs and the ASTMS Pearl Section (which had originated in a 1926 breakaway from the National Amalgamated Union of Life Assurance Workers). In January 1988 ASTMS merged with the manufacturing white collar-union TASS to form MSF, the Manufacturing, Science and Finance Union. The two constituent parts of MSF are described separately in this Guide.

The ASTMS archive is held at the Modern Records Centre, University of Warwick (ref. MSS 79) and incorporates the records of its predecessor organisations. A list is available (NRA 30501). The description below covers this main collection; the reader should be aware that certain continuous series of ASTMS records were begun by one or other of the preceding unions.

The AScW papers comprise various series of minutes from 1918 to 1968 (including those of the Executive Committee, 1952–62; the General Purposes Committee/Administrative Committee, 1945–60; and the Central London Branch); copies of the *Scientific Worker* for 1920–54; the *Journal* for 1955–68; assorted subject files; the papers of Dr Amicia Young (also known as Dr Melland), sometime president of AScW, which principally concern disarmament and the social consequences of scientific research and largely cover the decade 1961–71.

The principal records of ASSET preserved at the Modern Records Centre include signed minutes of the National Executive Council for the period 1942–60; the General Purposes and Finance Committee for 1961–67; the Industrial Relations Committee for 1946–48; the Organisation Committee for 1961; and the Political/Parliamentary Committee for 1946–69.

Other papers comprise microfilm copies of files concerning legal cases, superannuation, inter-union relations, and particular industries or employers for the period 1943–74; the *Annual Report* for 1954–55; various series of circulars for 1955–68; and National Industrial Relations Court files. There are also local branch minutes for the Hayes Branch for 1952–57.

Among the papers of the various financial sector unions subsequently incorporated in ASTMS are those of the ASTMS Pearl Section and the Guild of Insurance Officials/Union of Insurance Staffs. The Pearl Section originated in 1924 as the National Union of Pearl Agents, which in 1964 became the National Union of Insurance Workers Pearl Section before amalgamating with ASTMS. The records comprise the *Pearl Agents' Gazette* for 1926–59; NUPA/NUIW Pearl Section circulated minutes for 1961–68 and 1970–71; the records of deputations, 1964–66; and the NUIW Pearl Section negotiations files, 1965–72. There are also various series of minutes of the Guild of Insurance Officials from 1919 to 1966; its journals *Insurance Guild Journal*, 1920–63, and *Cover Note*, 1963–67; subject files on membership in various companies (mainly of the 1950s–60s); a jubilee history of the union (dated 1970); and the Bristol Branch minutes, 1922–74. There is a list available for the GIO material (NRA 31484). In addition the deposit includes the papers of an ASTMS predecessor organisation, the United Commercial Travellers' Association, which are principally the records of various West Midlands branches, 1949–81, and subsequent ASTMS UCTA section files for 1975–78.

The records of ASTMS itself are extensive, and include minutes, subject files, and the papers of its former general secretary Clive Jenkins (see below). The former series comprises principally the signed minutes of the ASSET/ASTMS Parliamentary Committee, 1947–84; the National Executive Committee, 1961–86; and the General Purposes and Finance Committee, 1969–83.

The numerous non-current subject files – some of which are continued from ASSET – cover relations with other unions (e.g. amalgamation, demarcation, etc.); ASTMS opposition to the European Community and involvement in the Get Britain Out campaign; environmental and health and safety issues (including the Flixborough Disaster and nuclear testing), 1968–83; ASTMS organisation in various companies etc., e.g. NHS (1970–83), universities (1970–83), British Airways (1970s), British Aerospace and Chrysler-Peugeot; the aircraft and motor industries and civil aviation; and women's issues. There is also a series of circulars for 1968–77; ASTMS press-cuttings books; recruitment posters and artwork for journals from the 1940s to the 1970s; and files related to libel cases for 1975–82.

The ASTMS deposit also contains two significant collections of personal papers. The first is that of the former general secretary Clive Jenkins and includes correspondence; drafts of his various writings; and files relating to political campaigns (e.g. anti-Vietnam War and EEC), the Shoreditch and Finsbury Constituency Labour Party, 1964–65, and Jenkins' service on various Royal Commissions and official bodies (e.g. British National Oil Corporation, 1979–81, and the Labour Party Commission of Enquiry, 1979–80). A more recent deposit of material includes the files used by Jenkins in writing his autobiography and his correspondence with Tony Benn covering the period 1972–76. It should be noted that certain access restrictions apply to the Jenkins material. There are also the papers of Dr J. Dore concerning his activity in the union, including chairmanship of the AScW Southern Region/ ASTMS Division No. 8 and of the ASTMS Standing Order Committee.

ASSOCIATION FOR TECHNICAL EDUCATION IN SCHOOLS ATES was founded in 1951 as the Association of Heads of Secondary Technical Schools. It assumed its later title in 1964 upon the adoption of a new constitution. In 1985 the papers were deposited in the Brotherton Library, University of Leeds (ref. MS Dep. 1985/3). The material includes the Council minute book, 1951–73; minutes of the General Meetings, 1951–54; reports and papers of the Annual Conference, 1954–58, 1960–69 and 1971–73; copies of the bulletin, 1964–73; and the minutes of the Association of Heads of Northern Secondary Technical Schools for the period 1950–63. There is a list available (NRA 27774).

ASSOCIATION OF UNIVERSITY TEACHERS The AUT was founded in 1919 and is the trade union for all academic and academic-related staff at UK university-level institutions. A Scottish Association of University Teachers was formed in 1922 and remained an entirely separate body until 1949 when its Annual Meeting voted to affiliate to the national organisation as the AUT (Scotland), a distinct Section with its own constitution and administration.

The archive of the national AUT has been deposited in the Modern Records Centre at Warwick University (collection MSS 27). It comprises a complete run of General Council and other printed minutes for 1919–75; circulated minutes of the Council, National Executive Committee and other national committees along with reports and papers for 1977–85; a large number of subject files running from the 1920s (but mainly from 1935) to 1974 covering educational associations, salaries, superannuation, university funding, and international affairs; files on local negotiations, 1972–79, and the papers of NEC members R.J. Price and J.D. Bennett. There is a list available for this collection (NRA 32493). A journal, the *AUT Bulletin* (known as *The University Review* from 1928–62), is published nine times a year. Further details of the AUT material may be found in Adrian Allan, *University Bodies: A Survey of Inter- and Supra-University Bodies and their Records* (University of Liverpool Archives Unit, 1990).

The papers of the AUT (Scotland) for the period 1922–72 are now in the Library of the University of Glasgow and include minute books and correspondence. Copies of the minutes of the Council and Executive Committee and of all circulars for the subsequent period have also been deposited and may be seen with the agreement of the Hon. Secretary of the AUT (Scotland).

ASSOCIATION OF YOUNG ZIONIST SOCIETIES The Association is the central body for Zionist youth organisations in the UK and as such is closely associated with the Zionist Federation of Great Britain and Northern Ireland (q.v.). Its purposes are mainly educational and are pursued via public meetings and its publication, *Young Zionist*. The records of the Association have been deposited in the Central Zionist Archives in Jerusalem.

AUTOMOBILE ASSOCIATION The AA was founded in 1905 to provide a comprehensive service to motorists. It provides information, breakdown services and road patrols, technical and legal services etc.; and lobbies Parliament on relevant legislation through the mechanism of the Standing Joint Committee of motoring organisations. The administrative archive of the association has been placed in Hampshire Record Office (ref. 73M94). A list is available (NRA 37522).

Although separate from the AA records, the W. Rees Jeffreys collection at the LSE Library should be noted. It contains useful information on the activities of the Motor Union and the Roads Improvement Association. There is a history by H. Barty-King, *The AA* (1980).

AVERT AVERT, the AIDS Research and Education Trust, was established in 1986 to fund medical research projects concerned with HIV/AIDS and to assist educational projects. At present the Trust retains its own papers, which consist of the minutes of the Trustees' meetings since 1988 and of the advisory groups established for individual research projects; copies of the Annual Report and reports from scientific advisers; correspondence files, including those with the Health Education Authority, and the Trust's publications. Bona fide researchers may be granted access to the papers at the discretion of the Trustees.

B

BABY MILK ACTION A British-based consumer pressure group, Baby Milk Action campaigns for changes in baby milk marketing and to foster correct infant feeding practices. It was established originally as the Baby Milk Action Coalition in 1979 under the sponsorship of major development charities to organise a boycott in the UK of Nestlé products. It is part of the International Baby Food Action Network (IBFAN), which unites over 100 groups in 60 countries. The papers of the group consist of the minutes of national and international committee meetings and the AGM; Annual Reports; Directors' Annual Reports; financial records; and all substantive correspondence arranged by subject (routine correspondence is weeded annually). Baby Milk Action also maintains an archive of information sources, including press-cuttings, its monthly newsletter, and the newsletter *Breaking The Rules*, which monitors violations of the WHO/UNICEF Code of Marketing of Breast-Milk Substitutes. Unpublished papers are largely confidential but may be made available to bona fide researchers, who should give full details of the nature of their enquiry in writing to the National Coordinator.

BAKERS, FOOD AND ALLIED WORKERS' UNION The union for workers in the baking industry and related trades was originally established in 1861 as the Amalgamated Union of Operative Bakers. The records are retained at the Union's head office. The material consists of various branch minutes for the whole period of the last century; annual conference minutes; executive council and regional and district minutes; annual reports of the Union and its executive council conference; and correspondence for the past five years only (except for that relating to special events). Subject files are also maintained on working conditions within the industry and on individual companies. Bound copies of the Union's journals since 1898 (now known as *The Food Worker*, published monthly) are also available at the head office. Applications for access should be made to the General Secretary. There is a published official history, *Bakers' Union: Our History 1859–1977*.

BALTIC COUNCIL IN GREAT BRITAIN The Council is a representative organisation established in 1947 by the Association of Estonians in Great Britain, the Latvian National Council in Great Britain, and the Lithuanian Association in Great Britain, with the object of combining the work of these bodies to further the interests of the Baltic States, largely by the lobbying of the British Government and the education of public opinion.

The papers of the Council have been retained partly at its offices and partly in the personal care of the Chairman. Most records date from 1984 (prior to which the Council operated only on an *ad hoc* basis) and include the minutes of the Council meetings; Annual Reports and conference reports; annual accounts; files of correspondence with government, parliamentarians, members of the European Parliament, universities and religious organisations, and Baltic organisations in other countries, and assorted subject files. Further enquiries should be addressed to the Chairman at the Council's registered office.

BAND OF HOPE The Union was founded in 1855 to coordinate and promote the work of the Band of Hope temperance organisations throughout the country. It is a Christian charity which concentrates on health education to reduce alcohol and drug-related problems.

The papers were transferred to Lambeth Palace Library in 1991. The post-war series of records includes various collections of minutes (Executive Committee, 1948–75; General Council, 1925–53; Finance Committee, 1943–74; Education Committee, 1927–58; *et al.*); committee agenda books, 1936–50,

1964–76; a general expenditure book for 1949–79 and other financial files; annual reports, 1855–1986; *Notes and News*, 1958–67, and *Trend*, 1967–82, and the Secretary's file of the National Youth Temperance Council for the 1970s.

BANK OF ENGLAND Established by Act of Parliament in 1694 as the first public bank in the country, the Bank of England acted as the government's own bank (managing the national debt and issuing banknotes) for some two centuries before it was nationalised in 1946. Since then it has assumed all the functions of a national central bank.

The records of the Bank are maintained by its Archive Section, where application should be made for access. Most of those papers over thirty years old are open to researchers. A comprehensive list is available (NRA 33132). Material is divided into the following record groups:

Governors and Secretaries, 1694– Records of the Court of Directors and Committee of the Treasury, and files maintained by the successive Governors and Secretaries.

Establishment Department, 1695– Staff and accommodation records, including staff lists, pension records and a complete run of the quarterly magazine *The Old Lady* for the period 1920– .

Administration Department, 1694– Records of the major facilitative functions of the Bank, including files of the Governor's correspondence with foreign central banks, 1928–74, and the Banking Department General Ledger (the main account book including details of all income and expenditure), 1695– .

Cashier's Department, 1694– Returns of notes issued, 1844– , and customers' correspondence and transaction summaries, 1794– .

Registrar's Department, 1694– Records concerning the registration of government stock issues.

Economic Intelligence Department, 1758– Records relating to the department's preparation of the balance of payments estimates and other economic statistics.

Overseas Department, 1800– Records concerning foreign financial and economic intelligence and relations with overseas central banks. This group contains papers relevant to the Bank's policy on post-war reconstruction (1941–64) and international monetary reform (1958–64).

Exchange Control Department, 1932– Records on the Bank's administration of the Exchange Control Act 1947, until the abolition of controls in 1979.

The remainder of the collection comprises the records of the Printing Works (1837–) and the Audit Department (1894–); the papers of the Bank's solicitors, Freshfields & Co. (1695–); the Bank Museum's printed and manuscript collections (1681–????); and the papers of a number of officials of the Bank.

BANKING, INSURANCE AND FINANCE UNION Prior to 1979, BIFU was known as the National Union of Bank Employees and the archive deposited at the Modern Records Centre, University of Warwick, is of this organisation. NUBE was created in 1946 by the merger of the Bank Officers' Guild (founded 1918) and the Scottish Bankers' Association. BIFU is now part of UNIFI.

The BIFU archive (ref. MSS 56) is comprehensive, but small; a large amount of correspondence was destroyed when NUBE moved its headquarters in 1964. The surviving records at Warwick include a large minutes series (e.g. National Executive Committee minutes for 1919–48; Sub-committee minutes for 1922–56; General Purposes Committee minutes for 1936–74; minutes of committees dealing with particular banks; annual delegate meeting minutes for 1941–74); an incomplete run of reports of annual meetings, 1919–73; cash books and other financial records for 1922–61; extensive correspondence files from the foundation of the Bank Officers' Guild until 1974 (much originating in the NUBE Research Department or with various banks); sets of union head office circulars from 1962 and banks' circulars from 1920; and NUBE's journal, the *Bank Officer*, for the period in which it was published quarterly (1919–69).

A subsequent deposit at the Modern Records Centre in 1976 comprised some local and sectional records to 1970 and subject files relating to individual banks, incomes policy, national negotiating arrangements, pensions, and safety at work – largely for the period from the late 1960s to the early 1970s.

BAPTIST PEACE FELLOWSHIP The Fellowship is composed of clergy and members of Baptist Churches in Great Britain who believe that the message of Jesus Christ requires only the use of non-violent methods to overcome evil. Items of its archive have been left on permanent deposit at the Angus Library, Regent's Park College, Oxford, to be freely available. These comprise a notebook with notes on the original history of the Fellowship from 1929; minutes of public and committee meetings up to 1946–47, and a printed membership list for the 1930s; a notebook with minutes of the general and standing committees, 1946–61; a notebook with minutes of the AGMs and committees, 1961–71; a folder with duplicated typescript minutes of committees, 1966–79; and a box file containing correspondence for the period 1976–86.

BARNARDO'S Founded in 1866, Dr Barnardo's Charity seeks to provide care for children and young people in need. It runs children's homes and residential schools for those with special needs and supports child care schemes in the wider community. It also carries out care work in Australia, New Zealand, and the Irish Republic.

The Barnardo's archive has been deposited with the University of Liverpool Archives Unit. A list is available (NRA 22753). The records include minutes of the Council since 1877 and of the Executive Committee since 1908; agenda books, 1917–49; annual reports since 1867 and the General Secretary's reports to Council, 1941–89; Finance committee and subcommittee minutes, 1877–1971; properties ledgers, 1890–1963, and accounts ledgers, 1962–73. In addition there is a substantial series of correspondence since 1901 (which includes circulars), and all relevant subject files relating to child care administration since 1872, including children's records. The approval of Barnardo's Director of Child Care is required before access to the archive can be granted; an application form is available from the Librarian.

BELFAST HOUSING AID SOCIETY Some 7000 files of this charitable organisation covering the period c. 1964–68 have been deposited in the Public Record Office of Northern Ireland (ref. D3761). The papers refer to the activities of the Society in relation to such matters as urban redevelopment, environmental health, rents and rates, and sectarian disputes.

BELFAST VOLUNTARY WELFARE SOCIETY Prior to 1974 this organisation was known as the Belfast Council of Social Welfare and before that as the Belfast Christian Civic Union. There is a collection of papers for the period 1903 to c. 1980 deposited at the Public Record Office of Northern Ireland. The material includes minute books of the Society itself for 1922–68, and of its subcommittee, the Voluntary Service Bureau (later Voluntary Service Belfast), which organised voluntary workers for charitable purposes, for the period 1967–79.

BLACK EDUCATION MOVEMENT There are records of this organisation including leaflets and minutes, 1968–99, together with records of such organisations as the Black Parents Movement, the Carnival Movement and the New Cross Massacre Action Committee in the George Padmore Institute, London. It is understood these archives are currently closed. (See NRA 42574.)

BOARD OF DEPUTIES OF BRITISH JEWS Established in 1760, the Board is the representative body of British Jewry. Its members are drawn from synagogues and secular organisations.

A description of the records, when retained by the Board, is given in *Sources, 1900–51*, vol. I, pp. 20–21. A list is available (NRA 19919). These records have now been placed in the London Metropolitan Archives.

Reference should also be made to the collections of the Hartley Library at Southampton University, which are a rich source for the history of Anglo-Jewry and include the papers of many of the Board's officials.

BODY POSITIVE Some papers (1985–87) of the organisation, formed in 1985 to provide support and information for individuals who were HIV-positive and to represent their views, were placed in the LSE Library in 1995 (ref. M 1816). The papers consist of the minutes of the task groups, the Body Positive newsletter, leaflets and organisational papers. Details have been entered on the CAIRS database.

BOW GROUP An association of Conservatives, independent of the Conservative Party itself, founded by ex-members of University Conservative Groups. The first meetings were held in Bow in East London, whence the group takes its name, and Bromley. Its main function is the organisation of research teams and the publication of research reports.

A collection of files has been retained. Enquiries should be addressed to the LSE Library.

BOY'S BRIGADE The Brigade was founded in Scotland in 1883 as a predominantly Presbyterian youth organisation. It now embraces all the main Protestant denominations and retains a fundamentally religious outlook. The Brigade's main archive is retained at its Activities and Training Centre in Hemel Hempstead, but additional records are also held at the Scottish Headquarters. All requests for access should be made to the Brigade Secretary. The papers include executive and Council minutes; annual reports since 1883; assorted correspondence; and some records of individual companies and battalions. A number of written histories of the Brigade are also available.

BREWERS ASSOCIATION OF SCOTLAND A major collection of surviving records, commencing in 1903, can be found in the Scottish Brewing Archive at the Business Record Centre, University of Glasgow.

BREWERS AND LICENSED RETAILERS ASSOCIATION A large archive has been placed in the Modern Records Centre, University of Warwick (ref. MSS 420). The papers include minutes, circulars and subject files. There are also photographs and publicity material. The deposit also includes minutes of the County Brewers' Society from the 1820s.

BREWERS' SOCIETY The Society, which is the national trade association of the brewing industry, was established in 1904 by an amalgamation of the County Brewers' Society (founded 1822), the London Brewers' Society and the Burton Brewers' Society. The objects of the Society are to encourage the rendering of good service by the industry and to maintain and improve the quality of its products,

and to represent the interests of brewers to the government and other authorities.

The Society maintains a library where published material is freely available to researchers with advance appointments. The library has complete bound volumes of trade magazines from about 1890 to 1970. It also contains the Society's Annual Reports from 1904 and the minutes of the Council and Committees of the Society up to about 1960. The minutes of the County Brewers' Society, the Society's predecessor, are also available from 1822, as are some of the County Brewers' Society's Annual Reports.

The Society's archives of correspondence and papers are organised on a subject basis, and are not freely available. Applications to see any of this material should be addressed to the Secretary of the Society.

BRITAIN IN EUROPE An all-party coordinating group, Britain in Europe was launched in March 1975 to facilitate the activities of those organisations campaigning for a vote in favour of continued membership of the EC in the national referendum of that year. It arose from a Steering Group formed in December 1974 (which became BIE's executive committee); incorporated bodies such as the European Movement and the European League for Economic Co-operation; and continued until November 1975. BIE's director was Sir Con O'Neill, a former diplomat who had led the official team negotiating UK entry into the Community from 1969 to 1972. The BIE's archive also includes papers relevant to the Council for Britain in Europe, and the European Movement's 'Early Campaign' in 1974–75.

In 1978 the papers of Britain in Europe were deposited by the Trustees in the House of Lords Record Office. They consist of some 350 boxes and comprise Historical Collection No. 225. Material is arranged by department as follows: Director's office subject files, January-July 1975; Deputy Director's office files (largely administrative); Administration, including general correspondence, February-August 1975, and papers concerning the production of *The Federalist* magazine; Director of the European Movement (responsible for local and regional organisation), office files including Campaign Committee minutes for May 1974–June 1975; Deputy for Local and

Regional Organisation (responsible for local fund raising), office files including papers on fund raising and information centres; London Regional Organiser, organisational files February-June 1975; Speakers' Service, including diaries of public meetings; Broadcasting Department, including correspondence with the BBC and IBA; Finance Director's files, including lists of campaign contributions; Food Advisory Committee correspondence and minutes, February– May 1975; Meetings Department, office files and proceedings of meetings; Conservative Group for Europe papers; Labour Campaign for Britain in Europe papers, including files of research material 1973–75; Liberal Europe Campaign papers, including correspondence with area federations and regional Liberal Parties; Publicity Department internal correspondence, March–May 1975, and literature and promotional material; Press Office files, including press-cuttings, press releases, and opinion poll results; Advertising Manager's office papers, including video copies of TV broadcasts; Research and Information Department, general correspondence March–June 1975, and subject files; Information Officer, correspondence and meetings' diaries; Women's Section papers, April–June 1975; and Youth Department files, including papers of the Youth Aid Scheme.

The Britain in Europe papers may be made available to bona fide students and all enquiries should be addressed to the Clerk of the Records, House of Lords Records Office.

BRITISH ACTORS' EQUITY ASSOCIATION

Equity, the professional association for actors, was established in 1930. The papers have been retained in the care of the General Secretary and are available to researchers with prior permission. The material comprises Council and Executive Committee minutes and Annual Reports (including published accounts) from 1930 onwards; other records are not available for consultation.

BRITISH ASSOCIATION FOR ADOPTION AND FOSTERING

Enquiries should be directed to the LSE Library which received the papers in 2005 (together with those of predecessor organisations).

BRITISH ASSOCIATION FOR THE ADVANCEMENT OF SCIENCE

The British Association was formed in 1831 with the aim of promoting the study of scientific research and the spread of knowledge. Since that date it has held an annual meeting or conference at which academic papers are presented. The most important archive of the Association's papers is now maintained at the Bodleian Library (ref. Dep B.A.A.S.). There is miscellaneous material in other repositories, such as the LSE Library. A list is available for the Bodleian collection (NRA 30130). The archive is arranged in three main groups: papers concerning the administration of the Association; papers concerning the annual meeting, and the minute books and files of the individual sections of the Association, which are classified by the letters A to M for scientific committees (e.g. Maths and Physical Science, Geology, etc.) and the letter X for corresponding societies. In addition there is a separate collection of press-cuttings arranged chronologically, the majority of which covers the period 1859–1972.

The administrative records of the Association include the minutes, 1832–1962, and agendas, 1912–49, of the General Committee; the agendas, minutes and correspondence, 1947–52 and 1961–62, of the Council; the correspondence and papers of the Secretary (including Sir George Allen, Secretary from 1954 to 1970) and the Secretary's subject files, 1872–1953; and financial records, such as ledgers, 1871–1953, and subscription records, 1862–1957. The papers in section II, i.e. those relating to the annual meeting, largely comprise correspondence concerning the arrangement of the conference, 1907–53. Section III, the papers of the individual sections, also contains records arising from conferences of the Division for Social and International Relations of Science (DSRS) for the years 1939 to 1946.

BRITISH ASSOCIATION FOR EARLY CHILDHOOD EDUCATION

BAECE was founded in 1973 by the merger of the National Society of Children's Nurseries and the Nursery Schools Association. The former had been established in 1906 (and until 1928 was closely linked with the National League for Physical Education and Improvement); the latter in 1923.

A quantity of material of both predecessor organisations has been deposited in the LSE Library. A list is available (NRA 30253). For the National Society of Children's Nurseries there are available the minutes of the Council, 1928–70, and of the AGMs, 1930–48, and *inter alia* minutes of the following: Executive Committee, 1935–73; Editorial Committee, 1947–58; Examiners' Meeting, 1943–46; and Training Committee, 1944–46. Other material includes financial ledgers, 1948–64; petty cash books, 1954–66; and an attendance book, 1970–73. The NSCN also deposited in the LSE Library office copies of its Annual Reports and of its journal, successively known as *The Creche*, 1907–10, *The Creche News*, 1915–32, *The Day Nursery Journal*, 1932–42 and *The Nursery Journal*, 1942–73. Other pre-war material is included in the collection.

The archive of the Nursery Schools Association at the LSE Library comprises minute books of the Executive Committee, 1940–76; Delegate Council, 1942–64; Building Advisory Committee, 1943–69; Course and Conference Committee, 1936–67; Finance Committee, 1938–60; Medical Advisory Committee, 1944–71, and its Residential Nurseries Subcommittee, 1949–57; Private Nurseries Committee, 1954–62; and the Publications Committee, 1936–67.

There is a run of the Annual Reports, 1923– 45 and1962/63–1972/73; an incomplete series of news sheets, 1941–74; and nos. 1–79 (n.d.) of the NSA pamphlet series. In addition, there is considerable pre-war correspondence on the early operations of the NSA.

Other records are retained by BAECE at its offices. The papers include series of the minutes of the following committees: the Executive from 1976; Finance from 1960; Conference from 1957; Research, 1960–61 and from 1987; Publications from 1967; Child and Family, 1974–89; Appeals from 1990; Chairman's Committee, 1987–88; and Building Advisory, 1970–81. There are also the minutes of the AGM since 1984; the Council, 1965–84 and from 1989; the Area Representatives from 1985; the Teachers Council, 1955–70, and of working parties on Primary Education (1963) and on the Child and Family (1980). Photocopies of the Annual Report for the period 1923–45 have been retained at the office. Copies of the newsletter for 1942–82, *News from BAECE* for 1982–86, and the journal *Early Education* from 1990 are also available. Audited accounts from 1970 onwards and copies of evidence submitted to government enquiries on educational issues, beginning

with the Plowden Report of 1964, have likewise been kept. Further enquiries should be directed to the Secretary at the above address.

BRITISH ASSOCIATION OF MALAYSIA AND SINGAPORE
The Association was founded in 1868 as the Straits Settlements Association by businessmen and others with interests in that region. It was subsequently renamed the Association of British Malaya (in 1920) and the British Association of Malaya. The above name was adopted in 1964. The Association itself was dissolved nine years later.

Collections of papers have been preserved in both the India Office Library (ref. MSS Eur F 168) and the Library of the Royal Commonwealth Society (q.v.). The former consists of a complete set of minute books for the period 1920–74 and *c.* 90 correspondence files for 1941–74. The subjects dealt with include war damage claims, British educational and cultural links with Malaysia and Singapore, correspondence with the Colonial Office, etc.

The material at present held at the Royal Commonwealth Society archive in Cambridge University Library consists of over 20 boxes of papers collected by the Association from 1960 onwards. The papers include the memoirs and correspondence of British officials, military personnel and businessmen. A full list may be consulted at the Library.

BRITISH ASSOCIATION OF SOCIAL WORKERS
The British Association of Social Workers was formed in 1970 by the amalgamation of seven existing specialist professional organisations, namely the Association of Child Care Officers (est. 1949), the Association of Family Case Workers (1940), the Association of Psychiatric Social Workers (1929), the Association of Social Workers (1935), the Institute of Medical Social Workers (1945), the Moral Welfare Workers Association (1938), and the Society of Mental Welfare Officers (1954). Certain of these organisations were themselves created by the merger of previous bodies.

An important collection of papers (*c.* 130 crates) has been placed in the Modern Records Centre, University of Warwick (ref MSS 378/BASW). The archive contains constitutional records; minutes and reports, including those of committees, working parties, groups and panels; circulars; records relating to the National Health Service, parliamentary and local government, conferences, finance and membership; correspondence, regional and branch records etc.

The archives of its predecessor bodies have also been placed in the Modern Records Centre, University of Warwick (ref. MSS 378). They include the Association of Child Care Officers, 1949–70; the Association of Family Case Workers, 1940–70; the Association of Psychiatric Social Workers, 1929–70; the Association of Social Workers, 1935–70; the Institute of Medical Social Workers, 1903–70; the Moral Welfare Workers Association, 1941–70; the Society of Mental Welfare Officers, 1954–70; and the Standing Conference of Organisations of Social Workers. A catalogue of the archives has been compiled by the BASW (NRA 39338).

BRITISH ASSOCIATION FOR SOVIET, SLAVONIC AND EAST EUROPEAN STUDIES

The Association was formed in 1988 by the merger of the British Universities Association of Slavists (founded in 1956) and the National Association of Soviet and East European Studies (1961). The BUAS archive consists of Annual Conference records; minutes of the AGM, Committee and Congress Committee meetings; and miscellaneous correspondence. It is intended that two predecessor collections will be deposited in the Leeds Russian Archive at the Brotherton Library, University of Leeds, where all enquiries should be directed. Further details may be found in Adrian Allan, *University Bodies: A Survey of Inter- and Supra-University Bodies and their Records* (University of Liverpool Archives Unit, 1990).

BRITISH BANKERS' ASSOCIATION The Association, founded in 1919, exists to represent publicly the interests of UK banks and to provide a forum for their discussions. It is affiliated to the European Banking Federation. The records have been placed in the Guildhall Library, London. The deposit includes records of the Committee of London Clearing Bankers.

BRITISH BROADCASTING CORPORATION Since its inception in 1926 the British Broadcasting Corporation (from 1922–26 the British Broadcasting Company) has occupied a central place in British public life. For the history of the BBC, reference should be made to the comprehensive multi-volume *History of Broadcasting in the United Kingdom* by Asa Briggs.

The BBC Written Archives Centre was established at Caversham in 1970 to meet a growing interest in the history of broadcasting. Since then, the Centre has been used for a remarkable range of projects large and small, and attracted an increasing range of researchers. An outline guide to the material is available (NRA 31050), from which the following description is taken.

The WAC's holdings are of two main kinds. One kind is material, amounting to over 200,000 files, produced in the administration of the BBC (policy files), the planning and execution of its broadcasts and related services (programme files), and its relationship with the many contributors to its programmes (contributors' files). Letters, memoranda and minutes of meetings record the BBC's policies and development as well as its dealings with other organisations. Much of this material is correspondence; about half of it is contributors' files. The other category of holding at the WAC is miscellaneous related material including scripts, logs, transcripts and indexes of broadcasts, press-cuttings, published books and periodicals, and special collections connected with the history of the Corporation.

Summary class lists, more detailed name and subject indexes for many of the holdings, and other finding aids may be found at the WAC. As far as possible, unpublished material earlier than 1975 is normally made available for consultation. Broadcast and published material is made available as soon as possible after transfer to the WAC.

It should be stressed very strongly that the Centre does *NOT* hold sound recordings, film, photographs and internal post-1975 files. The material at Caversham Park, with certain limitations, notably copyright, is open to bona fide researchers. The BBC charges for access at a daily rate with special terms for season-ticket holders. A fee is also charged for research undertaken by the staff. Students wishing to use the Centre should apply in writing to the Written Archives Officer.

BRITISH CLOTHING INDUSTRY ASSOCIATION This organisation, the principal employers' association for the British clothing industry, has experienced several amalgamations since World War II. Its archive is held at the Modern Records Centre, University of Warwick (ref. MSS 222). The records were deposited in January 1982, when the BCIA merged with the British Apparel Manufacturers' Association; the BAMA itself had been formed in 1978 by the merger of the Apparel and Fashion Industry's Association and the British Mantle Manufacturers' Association.

BRITISH COMMONWEALTH EX-SERVICES LEAGUE

This veterans' organisation represents the interests of Commonwealth citizens who have served with either the British or Commonwealth Forces. It was founded in 1921 (as the British Empire Service League) by Field Marshal Earl Haig and Field Marshal Smuts to link together the various ex-service organisations throughout the Commonwealth.

The archives of the League are retained at its headquarters. The papers include minutes of the Council from 1952 onwards and those of the Executive Committee; reports of the Triennial Conference since 1921; annual audited accounts; and subject and correspondence files referring to individual ex-servicemen's organisations in various countries. A full set of the magazine *Our Empire* is also available. Special permission is required for access to the papers and further enquiries should be addressed to the Secretary-General.

BRITISH COUNCIL

The British Council was established in 1932 and incorporated by Royal Charter in 1940. Its function is to promote a wider knowledge of the United Kingdom and the English language overseas and to develop cultural relations with other countries. It also administers educational programmes etc. on behalf of the Ministry of Overseas Development, the UN etc.

The National Archives hold the Council's records for the period 1932–*c*. 1963 (ref. BW 1–66). A list is available (NRA 20892). They include minutes, correspondence, financial and subject files (including topics such as relations with universities, empire policy, publications and broadcasting). There is a series of files on the various activities of the Council in each of nearly 60 countries. A great deal of the

material relates to the wartime and immediate post-war work of the British Council.

See also British Council Staff Association below.

BRITISH COUNCIL OF CHURCHES

The Council was founded in 1942 as a fellowship of the Church of England and the main Protestant Churches in the British Isles to promote ecumenical activities and greater unity among themselves. It provided a model for the international World Council of Churches, based in Geneva, of which the BCC was the national member for the United Kingdom. The international relief and development agency Christian Aid (q.v.) (whose archive has been deposited at the School of Oriental and African Studies, University of London) was originally established as a department of the Council. In August 1990 the BCC was superseded by a new body, the Council of Churches for Britain and Ireland, which included the Roman Catholic and Pentecostal Churches.

The BCC archive has been deposited at the Church of England Record Centre. A list is available (NRA 32688). Papers include correspondence of Council meetings from March 1949; minutes and reports submitted to the Council from April 1952; Executive Council minutes since December 1951; and Annual Reports from 1942 onwards. There is one box of papers of the General Secretariat covering 1942–48. The bulk of the collection consists of a vast series of subject files which cover the Council's deliberations on international and domestic social affairs as well as ecumenical issues. These include material relating to Inter-Church Aid (the predecessor of Christian Aid), South Africa, race relations in the UK, and education. Financial records have also been retained for the entire period of the Council's existence. Material at the Church of England Record Centre is usually subject to a thirty year rule and enquiries should be directed to the BCC Archivist.

BRITISH COUNCIL OF DISABLED PEOPLE

Formed in 1981 the Council is the national representative body of disabled people's organisations in the UK. Records retained include all committee minutes and financial records since 1981; annual reports; correspondence, and copies of research papers. A small library is also maintained. Researchers should apply to the Director.

BRITISH COUNCIL STAFF ASSOCIATION The Association has deposited files covering the activities of the BCSA and the Trade Union Side at the British Council during the period 1940s–80s in the Modern Records Centre, University of Warwick (ref. MSS 381). They include minutes of staff committees within the Council and office bulletins.

BRITISH DEAF ASSOCIATION Formerly the British Deaf and Dumb Association (its title was amended in 1971), the Association had its origins in the failure of the Royal Commission of 1889 on the education of deaf children to consult deaf people; this failure prompted a National Conference of Adult Deaf and Dumb Missions and Associations the following year to form a national society.

The papers of the BDA have been retained at the Association's headquarters. Available minutes comprise those of the Executive Council, Management Committee, Finance and General Purposes Committee, Delegates' Conference, Policy and Resources Committee, Standing Committee, and other advisory and sub-committees. Those of the Council meetings and the Delegates' Conference date from 1890, and the other series from the date of establishment of the relevant committee. A complete run of annual reports has been retained, as have copies of published special reports. Correspondence files are organised by subject, but general correspondence is weeded after seven years. Applications for permission to view the records should be made to the Chief Executive. A list is available (NRA 27778).

BRITISH DENTAL ASSOCIATION In 1876 the Odontological Society of Great Britain (founded 1863) set up a Dental Reform Committee to promulgate its political activities and following the Dentists Act of 1878, which established the regulation of the profession, the Committee sponsored the establishment of a British Dental Association in 1879. Following the establishment of the National Health Service, the BDA incorporated two other professional associations, the Incorporated Dental Society and the Public Dental Service Association, in 1949.

The BDA has retained its records at its London headquarters. They have been listed by the Business Archives Council's Company Archives Survey (NRA 28631). They include the minutes of the Council, 1919–57, and of the AGM, 1879–1960; the minutes and agendas of the Executive Committee, 1949–67; Finance Committee minutes, 1881–1956; the minute books of numerous other committees (e.g. Dental Health Education Subcommittee, 1956–63); a guard book containing notices, programmes, copies of papers read etc. relating to the AGM, 1946–77; copies of the Memoranda and Articles of Associations, 1879–1975; cash books, 1932–66; and the Annual Report and Accounts as published in the *British Dental Association Journal*. In addition the archive contains the records of certain of the BDA's branches and the papers of its predecessor organisations.

A small collection of relevant material is included among the papers of R.G. Torrens, deposited at the Contemporary Medical Archives Centre at the Wellcome Institute. The material comprises sets of minutes of committees on which Torrens represented the British Dental Association (covering the period 1944–51) and the Incorporated Dental Society (1942–49). A list is available (NRA 24913).

BRITISH ECOLOGICAL SOCIETY The Society was established in 1913 by the British Vegetation Committee, formed in 1904 to survey the flora of the British Isles. The new society, however, was given a wider remit to promote ecology and in the post-war era has had great influence upon government policy concerning the scientific conservation of nature (especially the establishment of National Parks in 1949). It is essentially a learned society and does not have permanent offices; the archive is retained by the various officers, principally the Hon. Secretary to the Council whose official papers are described below.

The extant papers, for which there is a list (NRA 24453), consist almost exclusively of minutes and administrative and correspondence files. Minutes exist for the British Vegetation Society (1904–12) and the BES Council from 1915; the latter are contained in two minute books up until 1965 and thereafter are continued in the administrative files. The second minute book contains also some correspondence and printed material such as AGM programmes and the minutes of the standing committee on publications from 1956. Annual reports and reports of meetings are printed in each of the Society's journals, the *Journal of Ecology*, the *Journal of Animal Ecology*, the *Journal of Applied Ecology* and the *Bulletin*; lacking central offices, the Society does not retain copies of its own publications. Correspondence and administration files are largely post-1960 in date and include minutes and papers of the Council and committees and reports of the former. Persons wishing to view the papers should write to the Hon. Secretary to the Council.

BRITISH EDUCATIONAL RESEARCH ASSO-CIATION The Association was founded in 1974 as an interdisciplinary forum. The records have been deposited at the Modern Records Centre, University of Warwick (ref. MSS 268) by the co-founder Professor Edgar Stone, a founding committee member of the Committee for Research into Teacher Education. Papers include the minutes since 1974; conference papers and various subject files. Further information concerning the organisation may be found in E. Stone, 'The development of the British Educational Research Association', *British Educational Research Journal*, vol. 11, no. 2 (1985), pp. 85–90.

BRITISH EMPIRE CANCER CAMPAIGN The archive has been deposited in the Contemporary Medical Archives Centre, Wellcome Institute. Enquiries should be directed to the Archivist.

BRITISH ENGINEERS' ASSOCIATION The BEA was established in 1912 as the national organisation for the UK engineering industry, dedicated to promoting its interests at home and abroad. The records were discovered at the London Business School and have been deposited in the Modern Records Centre, University of Warwick (ref. MSS 267). The post-war material consists primarily of Council minutes for 1958–60; records of the President's Advisory Committee, 1937–59, and subscription records for 1950–57. A list is available (NRA 28044). There are also extensive pre-war papers for each of these series.

BRITISH EVANGELICAL COUNCIL Since 1952 the Council has existed to coordinate the testimony of evangelical churches and church bodies which

were not affiliated to the then British Council of Churches. The Council's papers since its foundation have been retained at its offices. Extant material includes minutes of the Executive Council, sub-committees, and special projects since 1952; financial records; papers emanating from Theological Study Conferences, and correspondence since the 1950s (arranged in relation to Council committees, churches, relations with other bodies, government departments and individuals). Duplicates of reports and addresses since 1987 are held on computer disk, and audio tape recordings of teaching conferences exist for the post-1967 period. Researchers should apply to the General Secretary; applications for access will be considered individually on their merits.

BRITISH FEDERATION OF BUSINESS AND PROFESSIONAL WOMEN The Federation grew out of the Council of the Federation of British Business and Professional Women's Clubs, whose first meeting was held in 1933. It was agreed in January 1935 that professional groups organised in such clubs would qualify for membership of the International Federation of Business and Professional Women; the British Federation was founded in the same year and within the international body it had equal representation with the National Federation of Business and Professional Women's Clubs (NFBPWC). In the post-war era it experienced financial difficulties due to the withdrawal of certain constituent organisations and was wound up in 1969–71, partly because the NFBPWC continued to exist.

The archive of the British Federation has been deposited in the Women's Library. A list is available (NRA 20625). The material comprises Executive Committee minutes and those of assorted subcommittees, 1946–69; minutes of the Bridge Committee (which served as a link between the British Federation, the International Federation and the NFBPWC), 1949–65; minutes of the Officers' Meetings, 1953–59; AGM minutes and agendas, 1942–71; correspondence, circular letters, and papers on subjects such as equal pay, UN agency activities (e.g. 1951 UNESCO Conference on Education and 1965 UN Status of Women Commission), women's pensionable age, national insurance, and the NHS;

and various publications, mainly dating from the 1950s. Annual accounts are available for 1958–71 and there are runs of the quarterly bulletin, *Women at Work*, for 1940–51 and its successor, the *Newsletter*, for 1952–67. The collection also contains certain papers of the International Federation, namely copies of its journal *Widening Horizons* (nos. XIX–XL, n.d.); numerous pamphlets; and reports of its meetings and congresses for 1936, 1947, 1951, 1952, 1953, 1956 and 1965.

BRITISH FEDERATION OF UNIVERSITY WOMEN The BFUW was founded in 1907 with the aim of promoting cooperation among women graduates of both British and foreign universities. The Federation, which affiliated to the International Federation of University Women in 1919, consists of local associations which hold regular speaker meetings. A biannual newsletter, *BFUW News*, is published. The surviving papers, which had been placed in the University of Portsmouth, were transferred to the Women's Library, London Metropolitan University, in November 2000 (ref. 5/BFW). A list is available (NRA 39086). The rich and extensive archive reflects most aspects of the organisation's interests.

BRITISH FEDERATION OF WOMEN GRADU-ATES The papers, 41 boxes covering the period 1909–80s, have been placed in the Women's Library, London Metropolitan University.

BRITISH FIELD SPORTS SOCIETY The British Field Sports Society was founded in 1930 to defend the public reputation of field sports. It incorporated a separate organisation BFSS (Scotland) in 1931. It continues to lobby Parliament on legislative matters relating to both field sports and wildlife conservation, and seeks to counter abolitionist campaigns by press releases, public meetings, publications, etc.

Most of the Society's papers were destroyed in 1977 when its offices were vandalised. All that has survived are publications, including copies of its *Year Book* from 1931 onwards (excluding World War II) and bound volumes of all leaflets etc. issued since its foundation. The *Year Book* contains a detailed Annual Report. A list is available for the collection

(NRA 24454) and persons wishing access to use the papers should apply to the Administrative Secretary.

BRITISH AND FOREIGN SCHOOL SOCIETY The Society was formed in 1808 under the aegis of Joseph Lancaster to promote educational reform according to Nonconformist principles. It was particularly active in the 19th century. The papers have now been deposited in the British and Foreign School Archives Centre at the West London Institute of Higher Education. A list is available (NRA 30809). The bulk of the material dates from the 19th century, but papers of post-war provenance include the minutes of the Meetings of the Council, 1946–53; the Finance Committee, 1943–51; and the Annual Meetings, 1941–74. Surviving files of the Secretary's papers include correspondence with Council members, 1940–53 and 1974–78; with the Chairman, 1951–75; and with the Ministry of Education and the Department of Education & Science. Financial records have been retained, along with numerous series of papers concerning the former Borough Road College itself and associated schools and colleges.

BRITISH GAS STAFF ASSOCIATION The Association's records are held at the Modern Records Centre, University of Warwick (ref. MSS 20) and comprise signed National Council minutes for the period 1947–62; conference reports, 1954–62; and the Association's journal, *Thermfare*, for 1946–62. The deposit also includes the minutes of the former organisation, the Gas Staff Association, for the period 1943–46 (incorporating those of its own predecessors), and the records of the non-manual staff co-ordinating committee of the Gas Light and Coke Company Staff for 1944–47.

BRITISH HEART FOUNDATION The BHF is a charity conducting research on heart disease. It was founded in 1961. The existing records of the Foundation have been retained at its head office and persons seeking to have access to the papers should apply to the Secretary. The material presently consists of typewritten minutes and lists of members of Council and governing committees from the incorporation of BHF to date; annual reports and accounts for the period since 1964; reports on the outcome of research undertaken by holders of grants from BHF; financial records for the preceding seven years; and correspondence and subject files, still held by each relevant department.

BRITISH HOSPITALS CONTRIBUTORY SCHEMES ASSOCIATION

Formed in 1930 to co-ordinate the work of the Hospital Saturday Funds and other contributory schemes, which were collecting to help support voluntary hospitals, the Association changed its aims in 1948 upon the establishment of the National Health Service to provide contributors to the member schemes with benefits additional to those offered by the NHS.

The archive of the Association has been deposited in the LSE Library. A list is available (NRA 41205). The papers date from 1930 but mostly refer to the later years of the Association. They include Executive Committee minutes, 1946–49; reports, 1931–48; members' register; minutes of the various subcommittees (e.g. Special Purposes, Publicity, Planning, etc.), and also of the several regional areas; correspondence, 1948–67, and circulars, 1948–67. In addition the collection incorporates papers arising from the British League of Hospital Friends.

BRITISH INSTITUTE OF HUMAN RIGHTS

An independent self-governing association established to act as a focal point for all aspects of human rights in the UK, BIHR was founded in 1970 as an executive agency of the Human Rights Trust. Its objectives are the promotion of respect for human rights by means of research and the education of public understanding (by the organisation of lectures and via the Human Rights in Education Network). The Institute is the British national correspondent of the Council of Europe and as such is responsible for furnishing the Council with information concerning civil liberties within the UK.

The BIHR is presently attached to the Department of Law at King's College, University of London. The department has a list of the earlier records which have been deposited in the College Archives. The papers retained by the BIHR include a complete series of the minutes of the Board of Governors and of the Executive Committee since 1990; annual reports from 1989; and correspondence, arranged by subject. BIHR publishes research papers and lectures and a bi-monthly *Case Digest*.

BRITISH INSURANCE ASSOCIATION

The records have been placed in the Guildhall Library, London (ref. MSS 29131–51). A list is available (NRA 37782). The deposit includes minutes, circulars to members etc.

BRITISH LACE OPERATIVES FEDERATION

Established in 1918 to include all trade unions in the lace industry, both craft and non-craft, the Federation was founded under the auspices of the Nottingham-based Amalgamated Society of Operative Lace Makers. However its effectiveness, particularly as a negotiating body, was compromised from the beginning by disputes between the Nottingham union and the Scottish Lace and Textile Workers' Union. Certain papers relating to the Federation (e.g. minutes, 1917–72; cash book, 1919–71) may be found among the records of the Amalgamated Society of Operative Lace Makers and Auxiliary Workers, deposited at the University of Nottingham Library (ref. LM, LM2, LM3).

BRITISH LEATHER CONFEDERATION

A trade association formed in 1984 by the merger of the former British Leather Manufacturers' Research Association and the former British Leather Federation, the Confederation retains a substantial number of records of its predecessor organisations. These comprise the papers of the National Leathergoods and Saddlery Manufacturers Association (1923–69); minutes of the Leather Trades Mutual Insurance Association (1921–57); sectional records and committee minutes of the United Tanners Federation (1942–61); minutes of the London and District Leather Producers Association (1936–61); papers of the Northern Leather Producers Association and the Northern Tanners Federation (1948–61); records of the Midland District Tanners Federation (1935–61); the Leather Institute's Management Committee and Council minutes (1954–61); the Leather and Hides Trades Benevolent Institution minutes and register (1933–71); and the papers of the Joint Standing and Central Committees of the Leather Producers Association for England, Scotland and Wales (1939–61). The Council Minutes of the British Leather Manufacturers Research Association also exist from October 1919 to date.

In some cases the above series of papers are not continuous owing to enemy action during World

War II and subsequent fire damage. Bona fide researchers should apply to the Chief Executive.

BRITISH LEYLAND TRADE UNION COMMITTEE The Committee was formed in 1968 as a co-federal body of trade unionists in the nationalised vehicle manufacturing company to unite the existing shop stewards committees of Leyland-Triumph and British Motor Holdings (formerly BMC).

Certain of the Committee's files have now been deposited at the Modern Records Centre, University of Warwick (ref. MSS 228). These comprise minutes for the period 1968–77; correspondence for 1968–76; agreements for 1970–76; and factory reports, 1972–76, in 26 files. The papers also cover records of predecessor organisations, viz: Morris Motors Amalgamated Union of Engineering and Foundry Workers Shop Stewards' Committee (minutes, 1968–69); Morris Motors Joint Shop Stewards' Committee (minutes, 1960, 1968–71); Morris Motors Joint Works Production and Advisory Committee (minutes and related papers, 1968–70); National Motor and Ancillary Trades Shop Stewards' Committee (minutes, 1955–60; circulars, 1957, and correspondence, 1975); and Nuffield Combined Shop Stewards' Committee/ British Motor Corporation Joint Shop Stewards' Committee (minutes, 1949–54, 1958–78, and correspondence, 1958–78). These records should be studied in conjunction with the papers of Richard Etheridge, AUEW convenor at the Longbridge factory, which are also at the Modern Records Centre (ref. MSS 202).

The BL Committee was succeeded by the Rover Company Shop Stewards following the privatisation of the company. A further deposit of records includes subject files from the early 1950s to the late 1970s and comprises material on such topics as rates and conditions, job evaluation, and the Leyland reorganisation of the 1970s (including the Employee Participation and Joint Management Council).

BRITISH MARINE INDUSTRIES FEDERATION The Federation was established in 1913 as the Boat and Yacht Builders' and Proprietors' and Allied Trades Protection Association, and later became the Ship and Boat Builders' National Federation. It acts on behalf of firms engaged in the manufacture of smaller boats.

Certain older papers of the Federation have been deposited at the Modern Records Centre, University of Warwick (ref. MSS 53). A list is available (NRA 36917) These include Executive Committee minutes for the period 1913–52. Other archival material is at present retained at the Federation's offices. The attention of readers is also drawn to the entry for the Shipbuilders' and Repairers' National Association in this Guide.

BRITISH MARITIME LAW ASSOCIATION The records for the period c. 1947–71 are available at the DMS Watson Library, University College London.

BRITISH MEDICAL ASSOCIATION The Association developed out of the Provincial Medical and Surgical Association, founded in Worcester in 1832. It moved to London in 1855, when it assumed the name of the British Medical Association.

The principal archive of papers is retained by the BMA itself at its offices. The records, which are voluminous, are stored either in the Registry or with the Accounts Department. They have recently been surveyed by the Business Archives Council and a list is available (NRA 28631). The description below follows that survey's findings.

The majority of papers is composed of the records of the individual committees of the Association, which usually begin in the early part of the twentieth century. Most of the committees are exclusively medical in scope but this series does include the reports of the Annual Representative Meeting, 1903–80; and the minutes and agendas of the General Medical Services Committee, 1929–80; the General Purposes Committee, 1961–76, and the Public Health Committee, 1904–74. In addition there are records of the BMA's governing body, the Council, and its own committees. These papers include the minutes and agendas of the Council, 1884–1980; the minutes, agendas and reports of the Executive Committee, 1939–80; an incomplete series of the Association's handbook, 1904–70, and yearbook, 1950–62; and copies of the annual reports of the individual Divisions and branches of the Association, 1930–77. Accounts of the BMA have been retained, including the Council's general ledger for the period 1866–1952. Correspondence files are more limited but do include copies of circulars to the Divisions and branches, 1910–75. The Library at BMA House holds a complete run of its journal, the *British Medical Journal*, since 1857; this is an invaluable source for the Association's history as the annual report of the Council is published as a supplement to the *Journal*. Applications to use the records should be made in writing to the Secretary.

Another valuable collection of papers emanating from the Association has now been deposited at the Contemporary Medical Archives Centre of the Wellcome Institute (ref. SA/BMA). The material, which runs to 280 boxes, consists mainly of miscellaneous committee files from the BMA Registry, *c.* 1915 to *c.* 1960, but in addition there is an incomplete set of copies of the minutes of the Council, its Committees and the Annual Representatives' Meetings and Special Representatives' Meetings for the period *c.* 1907 to *c.* 1982. A list is available for this collection also (NRA 34847). The privately held records of the BMA Scottish Council have been listed (NRA 35583).

BRITISH-NIGERIA ASSOCIATION Two files of the Association's records, consisting of bulletins, minutes, reports and miscellaneous material for the years 1965–82, may be found among the papers of the former colonial government officer H.H. Marshall, now deposited at BLCAS (Rhodes House Library), Oxford (ref. MSS Afr s 1911).

BRITISH OLYMPIC ASSOCIATION The British Olympic Association, founded in 1905, is the body responsible for the development of the Olympic movement in the United Kingdom. It consists of organisations which manage the sports included in the Olympic Games; representatives of armed services; student sports organisations; and certain other affiliates.

The archive, which is retained by the Association at present, consists of its committee and sub-committee minutes and those of the International Olympic Committee; official reports of the Olympic Games since 1904; photographs, slides, newspaper cuttings, posters, badges, programmes and miscellaneous ephemera relating to the Olympic Games (especially the London Games of 1904 and 1948); and the proceedings of the International Olympic Academy from 1968 to date. The Association also

maintains a library of books on all aspects of sport, but especially the Olympic Games, the Commonwealth Games and other sporting festivals.

Researchers wishing to examine the collection should apply to the General Secretary.

BRITISH PEACE COMMITTEE An assortment of papers, mainly ephemera, has been acquired by the Modern Records Centre, University of Warwick (ref. MSS 21).

BRITISH PENSIONERS AND TRADE UNION ACTION ASSOCIATION The first branch of BPTUAA was formed in Camden in London in 1972 and the Association now comprises 400 affiliates throughout the UK. Its object is to 'maintain and enhance the dignity and living standards of pensioners and to create understanding among all age groups of the problems associated with ageing.' BPTUAA's Annual Convention is sponsored by the Trades Union Congress and it is a founder member of the National Pensioners' Convention, an umbrella body of the major pension campaigning organisations. A journal, *British Pensioner*, has been published quarterly since 1980.

The Association's papers are retained at its offices. Extant material includes committee minutes from 1986 onwards and some correspondence, mainly with government departments and other bodies of a campaigning nature. Earlier papers have been destroyed. Further enquiries should be directed to the General Secretary.

BRITISH PHARMACOLOGICAL SOCIETY The Society was founded in 1931. Eleven boxes of papers have been deposited in the Contemporary Medical Archives Centre at the Wellcome Institute (ref. SA/BPS). They comprise minutes of the General Meetings, 1931–76, and of committee meetings, 1953–79, and correspondence, photographs and miscellaneous material. Access will be granted only upon the written permission of the General Secretary of the Society.

BRITISH PLASTICS FEDERATION The Federation exists to promote the growth and profitability of the UK plastics industry and was formed in December 1933 from the British Plastics Moulding

Trade Association, which had been established three years earlier. At present over 500 companies – principally polymer and additive suppliers, processors, and equipment suppliers – are members, representing nearly three quarters of the industry by turnover. As a trade association the Federation undertakes research and statistical surveys and liaises on members' behalf with national government and EU institutions. Its archive incorporates minutes of both the Council and Finance and General Purposes Committee since 1929, and copies of the annual reports and accounts. Financial records are retained only for the statutory period and correspondence and subject files usually for not more than the past three years. Enquiries should be directed to the Company Secretary.

BRITISH PORTS FEDERATION Prior to 1988 the Federation was known as the British Ports Association. It was founded in 1920 to represent the interests of port authorities in the UK. The records of the organisation have been added to the existing archive of the papers of the British Ports Association, which has been deposited in the Library of the Museum of Docklands (a division of the Museum of London). The records begin in 1911 and include material relating to the port transport industry nationally as well as to the Port of London. The collection is very large (at present occupying nearly 300 feet of shelving) and is catalogued only up to 1970.

Researchers should also be aware that the Museum of Docklands also holds the papers of all employers' organisations which operated under the aegis of the London Port Employers' Association. However this material has not yet been catalogued.

BRITISH PRINTING INDUSTRIES FEDERATION The BPIF was founded in 1898 as the manufacturers' association for the printing industry. The records are retained at the Federation's offices, but are unsorted and may be substantially incomplete. Series of minutes are known to exist for the 1980s but not for any period beforehand. However, copies of the members' circular, which later became the Federation's monthly magazine *Printing Industries*, have been kept from 1898 onwards as has the yearbook (since 1910). These may be examined on application to the Director General.

BRITISH RED CROSS SOCIETY The British Red Cross was founded in 1870 as the National Society for Aid to the Sick and Wounded in War. In 1898 the permanent Central Red Cross Committee was formed (under the auspices of the International Committee of the Red Cross based in Geneva) to unite the work of the National Aid Society, the St John Ambulance Association and the Army Nursing Reserve. In 1905 a renamed Central British Red Cross Council amalgamated with the National Aid Society to form the present organisation. A Royal Charter of Incorporation was granted in 1908. The fundamental principles of the Red Cross were redefined by the International Red Cross Conference of 1965 to be the prevention and alleviation of human suffering wherever it occurs, without discrimination; the British Red Cross is pledged to act in accordance with these.

The Society maintains its own Archives Section in its National Training Centre. The collection is extensive and includes the minutes of the Council from 1905; Annual Reports from 1924; reports of the International Conference from 1864 to date; reports, bulletins and the Review of the International Committee of the Red Cross from 1859 to the present day; a run of the official journal from 1914; County Branch records (which include minutes, annual reports, personnel and other records) from *c.* 1909 to date; and departmental files covering all aspects of the Society's work from 1905. In addition to these administrative records the Archives Section has collections of personal papers of past officers of the Society; official records relating to humanitarian assistance activities during both World Wars; a photographic archive covering every aspect of humanitarian relief work, domestic and international, since 1870; and records concerning Prisoners of War. The Archives Reference Library contains books on all aspects of the Society and the International Red Cross.

Current records (i.e. post-1979 material) are maintained at the Society's National Headquarters. Researchers should in the first instance write to the Archivist for further advice about access to the papers.

BRITISH RETAIL CONSORTIUM The British Retail Consortium is an umbrella organisation for the existing sectoral groups in the retail trade. It was formed in 1992 by the amalgamation of the former Retail Consortium and the British Retail Association.

The BRC presently retains its own papers, but the records of the former Retail Consortium are in the process of being transferred to the Oxford Institute of Retail Management. Existing material is largely confined to subject files dating from the 1970s on such topics as town and country planning, economic development, and shop legislation and hours. The minute books of a predecessor organisation, the Retail Distributors Association, also exist for the period since 1912. Enquiries should be addressed to the Company Secretary.

BRITISH ROAD FEDERATION LTD The Federation was founded in 1932. It existed to promote the interests of all concerned with the construction of roads. The records were retained at the Federation's offices. The collection included a complete set of minutes of the Council and committees since 1932; annual reports and accounts from 1946 until the present day; other financial records retained for the statutory period only, and a limited series of correspondence and subject files (mostly containing material covering the last five years only). The material was deposited in the Institution of Civil Engineers in 2001.

BRITISH SOCIAL HYGIENE COUNCIL The records of the organisation (formerly the National Council for Combating Venereal Diseases) are in the Contemporary Medical Archives Centre, Wellcome Institute (ref. SA/BSH). The collection (42 boxes) consists mainly of minutes. A list is available (NRA 40668).

BRITISH SOCIOLOGICAL ASSOCIATION The archival collection of the Association, which was founded in 1951, has now been deposited at the LSE Library. The records include series of minutes (e.g. Executive Committee, 1972–79; Professional Ethics Committee, 1975–77; Publications Committee, 1970–75; Finance Committee, 1976–77; Research Subcommittee, 1975–81; Teaching and Programmes Subcommittee, 1975–81; Social Science Action Committee, 1981–82) and correspondence, a large sequence of which relates to the International

Sociological Association in the period 1970–79. There are also files of administrative papers relating to such subjects as membership, careers information, research supervision in universities, other associations (e.g. Regional Studies Association, Social Studies Federation, Standing Committee of Sociologists, etc.) and the Association's journal, *Sociology*. The papers of a number of working parties, such as those on the employment of sociologists (1973–74) and the reorganisation of the Association (1977), have also been retained.

The records of the Medical Sociology Group for the period 1970–82, which consist mainly of annual files on conferences, have been deposited in the Modern Records Centre, University of Warwick.

BRITISH-SOVIET FRIENDSHIP SOCIETY The Society was founded in 1946 as a successor to the Anglo-Soviet Friendship Committee, formed in 1940. Earlier predecessor organisations were the Russia Today Society, founded in 1934, and the Friends of the Soviet Union, established in 1930. The Society aimed to strengthen peace and friendship, understanding and trade between Great Britain and the USSR.

Nearly all early correspondence and other records were lost in 1958 when the offices of the Society were transferred. No information is available about the Society's recent history and records. However, there is relevant material in the papers of Revd Stanley Evans which are now deposited in the Brynmor Jones Library at Hull University (ref. DEV). A list is available (NRA 17262). Reference should also be made to the archive of the Communist Party of Great Britain (q.v.).

BRITISH TELECOMMUNICATIONS UNION COUNCIL BTUC, the confederation of trade unions whose members are employed by British Telecommunications plc, was formed in 1981 when that company was set up independently of the Post Office. It assumed the functions of the former Council of Post Office Unions (q.v.) with respect to telecommunications staff. Certain relevant papers have been deposited at the Modern Records Centre, University of Warwick (ref. MSS 260), namely the minutes, reports and related papers of the Experimental Changes of Practice Committee for

1967–82, and subject files for 1972–81. A list is available (NRA 38221).

BRITISH TRUST FOR CONSERVATION VOLUNTEERS Founded in 1959 as the Conservation Corps, the Trust works in partnership with landowners, statutory authorities, businesses and charities to create and maintain woodlands, rare habitats and nature trails and to organise education projects. Its members include 760 local affiliated groups and the Trust maintains an International Conservation Action Network (ICAN) to encourage community-based conservation activities world-wide. BTCV has retained all its papers, including relevant committee minutes and copies of the annual report and staff conference report. Requests to consult the papers should be addressed to the Chief Executive at the Head Office.

BRITISH UNION FOR THE ABOLITION OF VIVISECTION The archives of the organisation, predominantly material from the 1960s, have been placed in the Brynmor Jones Library, University of Hull. A detailed list is available (NRA 41117) which has a valuable introduction on the history of the anti-vivisection movement. There are some minutes etc for the early pre-war period. Many of the campaigns waged by the society are documented as well as its lobbying efforts.

BRITISH UNIVERSITIES INDUSTRIAL RELA-TIONS ASSOCIATION BUIRA was established in 1950 as the Inter-University Study Group in Industrial Relations. The following year it was renamed the University Industrial Relations Association and the present name was adopted in 1967. It exists to further the academic study of industrial relations.

A collection has been established at the Modern Records Centre, University of Warwick (ref. MSS 52), to which all non-current files are periodically added. The deposited papers consist of minutes and reports of business for 1950–73 and 1978–80 (including minutes of annual meetings for the later years); financial statements, 1952–80; membership lists, 1955–80; details of conference programmes, 1952–80, and some subject files. Other material is in the care of the Secretary of the Association, including

for the period since 1950 copies of the AGM agenda and minutes; annual accounts; the Secretary and Treasurers' Annual Report; records of office holders, and the bi-annual newsletter. The papers deposited at the Modern Records Centre remain closed and the material retained by BUIRA is open only to its members. Further details may be found in Adrian Allan, *University Bodies: A Survey of Inter- and Supra-University Bodies and their Records* (University of Liverpool Archives Unit, 1990).

BRITISH UNIVERSITIES SPORTS FEDERA-TION The archives of the federation (and related student sporting bodies) have been deposited in Liverpool University Archives (ref. D741). A list is available (NRA 41874). There is also material on international competitions (e.g. World Student Games).

BRITISH VIGILANCE ASSOCIATION AND NATIONAL VIGILANCE ASSOCIATION The British Vigilance Association had its antecedents in the late 19th-century movement to amend the criminal law to prevent female and child prostitution. Reformers had founded the National Vigilance Association in 1885 and, following the example of other British moral reform agencies (particularly those against contagious diseases), held a Congress in London in 1899 to form an International Bureau in conjunction with societies abroad. The National Vigilance Association provided the original secretariat. The Bureau's operations were suspended during the First World War but it was reconstituted in 1919 and was very active in the inter-war period. In 1939 it absorbed the Travellers' Aid Society (an organisation formed in 1885 under the auspices of the YWCA to assist women travellers); this ceased to function as a separate operating body in 1952. The International Bureau was revived in 1949 and reconstituted in 1953; thereafter it worked closely with the relevant agencies of the United Nations. In 1953 the National Vigilance Association amalgamated with its own British executive committee, the National Committee for the Suppression of Traffic in Women, which included representatives of other similar bodies, to form a more broadly-based organisation, the British Vigilance Association. This was wound up in 1971 owing to financial difficulties, but the National Vigilance Association nominally still exists.

The papers of the three related organisations were transferred to the Women's Library (q.v.) in 1972–73. A list is available (NRA 20625). The material comprises the following:

NATIONAL VIGILANCE ASSOCIATION Executive Committee minutes, 1886–1956; reports of AGMs, 1953–55; annual reports, 1929–69; report of the Executive Committee, 1950–51; correspondence files on sex education, venereal disease, female migration, domestic service, courts, prisons and probation, prostitution, the age of consent and censorship; and assorted publications. It should be noted that much of the correspondence is pre-war.

BRITISH VIGILANCE ASSOCIATION Council minutes, 1956–68; Executive Committee minutes, 1956–69, AGM minutes, 1955–65; annual reports, 1952–69, and the papers of various subcommittees (particularly relating to the welfare of Irish girls in Great Britain, 1953–57).

TRAVELLERS' AID SOCIETY The post-war papers are contained within those of the National Vigilance Association.

INTERNATIONAL BUREAU Reports and files of International Congresses and preparatory conferences, 1899–1965; minutes of Bureau meetings, 1899–1968; annual reports, 1952–53, 1965–66 and 1968–69; the journal *Revue Abolitioniste*, 3rd series, 1951–52; and other publications.

BUILDING EMPLOYERS' CONFEDERATION

The Confederation was founded in 1878 and until March 1984 was known as the National Federation of Building Trades Employers. It acts as the central organisation of employers in the building trade, dealing with all commercial and industrial aspects, and has retained copies of its annual reports from 1948 and minutes since inception. Certain papers have also been deposited at the Modern Records Centre, University of Warwick (ref. MSS 187), namely the annual report and bulletin series for the period 1936–78; the NFBTE journal *National Builder* (which includes reports of meetings) for 1928–57; other NFBTE and trade union publications; and the histories of some individual member companies. In 1989 BEC deposited at the Modern Records Centre the signed minutes of the National Joint Council for the Building Industry and its committees for 1921–84, which contain various agreements and reports.

The papers of a constituent organisation, the Central Association of Master Builders of London, for the period 1872–1950 are now in the London Metropolitan Archives. These include minutes, records of the Conciliation Boards, and membership records. Also in this collection are the records of the Builders Benevolent Institution, 1847–1959, and Builders Clerks Benevolent Institution, 1883–1963.

BURMA CAMPAIGN Some records, 1991–2000, for the British section of the Burma Campaign are in the International Institute of Social History, Amsterdam. The organisation campaigns against the repressive regime in Burma.

C

CAMBRIDGE REFUGEE COMMITTEE The minutes of the Committee for the period 1938–53 have been deposited in Cambridge University Library. Further enquiries should be directed to the Librarian.

CAMPAIGN AGAINST THE ARMS TRADE The Campaign Against The Arms Trade was founded in 1974. It is a coalition of groups and individuals who seek to end the international arms trade and the United Kingdom's role as a significant exporter, and who campaign for the conversion of military industries to 'socially-useful production'. CAAT has retained all its records since its inception; these may be made available to researchers on a case-by-case basis and applications for access should be made to the Joint Coordinators at the offices of the society.

Copies of the bi-monthly newsletter are available on file at the CAAT information library, which is open to the public by appointment.

CAMPAIGN AGAINST DOUNREAY Records, including minutes, newsletters, press cuttings and photographs, *c.* 1980–99, have been deposited in Shetland Archives, Lerwick.

CAMPAIGN AGAINST PORNOGRAPHY Some records for the period 1985–94 are in the Women's Library, London Metropolitan University.

CAMPAIGN FOR THE ADVANCEMENT OF STATE EDUCATION Formerly known as the Confederation for the Advancement of State Education, CASE was founded in 1962 to serve as the national co-ordinating body for local Associations, the first of which had been formed in Cambridge two years earlier. The local groups were established as a result of public concern about the quality of state and commercial education and the Campaign acted as the national lobbying organisation for member Associations.

The archive of the national body for the period after 1961 is now at the Modern Records Centre, University of Warwick (ref. MSS 236). When deposited the papers were uncatalogued but most material has now been listed, namely an incomplete series of Executive Committee minutes for 1963–75; AGM minutes; and correspondence which has been rearranged into four series: administrative, subject (e.g. special education), relations with other organisations, and local Associations (incorporating some of their publications for the period 1963–73). In addition there are CASE circulars, press-releases, and other published materials. Recent material continues to be deposited.

CAMPAIGN FOR DEMOCRATIC SOCIALISM The CDS was a Gaitskellite pressure group of the early 1960s within the Labour Party. A collection of over 50 files, accumulated by Bill Rodgers, who was the Secretary and main organiser of CDS, has survived in his possession.

CAMPAIGN FOR HOMOSEXUAL EQUALITY CHE was formed in 1969 when the North-Western Committee of the Homosexual Law Reform Society (see Albany Trust) became the Committee for Homosexual Equality. In 1971 CHE was renamed the Campaign for Homosexual Equality and within a short period had become the biggest gay organisation in Britain. In the same year the Campaign founded its own counselling division, Friend (Fellowship for the Relief of the Isolated and in Need and Distress). It was very active until the late 1970s, when it was overtaken by other organisations such as the Gay Community Organisation, OLGA and Stonewall. CHE had two main roles: to encourage further legal reform (e.g. equalising the age of consent for homosexuals and heterosexuals) and to influence public opinion in favour of reform, and to act as a national body in support of local groups throughout the country.

CHE has deposited certain of its papers within the Hall-Carpenter Archive (q.v.) at the LSE Library. The material covers the period 1970–96 and comprises minutes, newsletters, Annual Reports, correspondence, financial records, conference papers, papers of the working parties, committee reports and leaflets and pamphlets Subject files include the age of consent debate, AIDS, local groups, Clause 25, Clause 27, law reform and discrimination. Further details are available from the Archivist.

CAMPAIGN FOR LABOUR PARTY DEMOC-RACY Four bundles of papers of the Campaign for the period 1973–91 have been deposited in the Brynmor Jones Library, University of Hull (ref. DX/222). The material includes minutes of the Executive Committee and the AGM, and reports and discussion papers arranged chronologically.

CAMPAIGN FOR NUCLEAR DISARMAMENT Founded in 1958, CND is the successor to the National Committee for the Abolition of Nuclear Weapons which had been established the previous year. The early history of the organisation is given in Christopher Driver, *The Disarmers* (London, 1964); reference should also be made to Richard Taylor, *Against The Bomb, The British Peace Movement 1958–1965* (Oxford, 1988). Militant members of CND later formed the Committee of 100 (q.v.).

The main archive of CND is held at the Modern Records Centre, University of Warwick (ref. MSS 181). The material includes Executive Committee minutes 1958–74; National Council minutes 1961–75; Income and Expenditure Accounts 1958–68; Annual Conference papers; the publications *Sanity* (1961–68, 1975–78), *Bulletin* (1958–60), *Monthly Notes* (1963–65, 1967), *The Month* (1963–66), and *Briefing* (1967–71); various other journals and pamphlets, and two files of ephemera. Also in the collection are a cash book (1965–67) and letters and lists of supporters (1968) of the British Council for Peace in Vietnam/National Vietnam Campaign Committee. Further selected material was deposited in 1990 covering the General Secretaryship of Bruce Kent (1980–85), with additional records from the National Committee, Trade Union CND and the Nuclear Warfare Tribunal. Further copies of various CND publications and papers of the International Confederation for Disarmament and Peace and the Committee for Peace in the Balkans are also at Warwick.

There is also a large deposit of CND material at the LSE Library. A first deposit of 31 boxes made in 1973–74 includes minutes of the Council and the Executive Committee; a very large collection of correspondence, duplicated leaflets and handouts; press-cuttings, and copies of various CND publications such as *Sanity* (1961–70), *Youth Against The Bomb* and *Resurgence*. Other subject files cover the annual conferences (1959–70), Easter Campaigns, the National Committee, the youth movement, administration, advertising, finance, material for magazines, Vietnam, the 'Ministry of Disarmament', the Committee of 100, and other peace groups. In 1988 a further deposit of 27 boxes was made consisting of National Council and Executive Committee minutes; annual conference papers; Trade Union CND papers; materials relating to national campaigns, specialist sections, and CND regions; local group newsletters, and assorted publications (from 1976). Most of this material covers the period 1981–85. It has been microfilmed by Harvester Press in the series *Primary Social Sources Programme. The Left in Britain*, Part V, Section 3 (reels 26–45).

A smaller collection of CND material exists at the National Library of Wales. There are the records of CND Cymru itself for the period 1983–86 (including minutes of the Council and papers relating to the AGM in 1985), and papers of various dates of the Aberystwyth CND, such as correspondence, posters, and press-cuttings for 1982–86 and the records of a predecessor organisation, the Aberystwyth Nuclear Weapons Committee (e.g. a minute book for 1958–60, correspondence, notes of the Secretary Dr Mansel Davies, scientific papers, pamphlets and posters, press-cuttings, and journals). The CND collection also incorporates subject files on other associated groups (e.g. Campaign against the Arms Trade, Medical Campaign Against Nuclear Weapons, Friends of the Earth, Green Party, Greenpeace, etc.). In addition the National Library has certain papers emanating from the Aberystwyth Peace Network, which was established in 1982 to coordinate various peace groups in the county of Ceredigion, including the Anti-Falklands War Campaign and Aberystwyth CND. The collection consists of the Network's correspondence and minutes for 1982–84, and a run of the *Newsletter* for February 1982 to May 1984. Other printed material, including copies of the publication *Peace News*, have been transferred to the Department of Printed Books.

Records of certain local CND branches are held at the appropriate record offices. Records of the North West CND have been deposited in the Working Class Movement Library in Salford and there is a list available for these papers (NRA 31932).

CAMPAIGN FOR A WELSH ASSEMBLY Relevant material concerning this group, which existed to further the case for devolution in Wales during the 1970s, may be found among the papers of D. Leslie Davies, now deposited at the National Library of Wales. These are not to be consulted without the permission of the donor and further enquiries should therefore be directed to the Keeper of Manuscripts at the National Library of Wales.

CAPRICORN AFRICA SOCIETY Founded in 1948 to campaign for constitutional reform in the British colonies in East and Central Africa, the Society was not a political party but did seek to establish a multi-racial electoral system in Kenya, Tanganyika, Rhodesia and Nyasaland, as stated in its Capricorn Declaration of 1952. Its president was Col. David Stirling, founder of the British Army Special Air Service Regiment (SAS). In the mid-1950s it was weakened by the defection of African members to more militant nationalist organisations. Before dissolution in 1963 it confined its work to educational and welfare projects.

Records of the London office of the Society have been deposited at the Centre for Southern African Studies, University of York, with a small number coming from the Salisbury (Southern Rhodesia) office. Other papers of the Salisbury branch, together with material emanating from the United Central Africa Association, are reported to be in the National Archives of Zimbabwe. The London office records are arranged in three series: the organisational files of the office and the personal files of David Stirling; papers from individuals relating to CAS; papers from branches in Southern Rhodesia; as well as several unnumbered articles about CAS. The London office records include committee minutes and agendas, although most is out-going mail. The

papers were microfilmed for the Cooperative Africana Microform Project and are available (without the Southern Rhodesian material) as *Papers of the Capricorn Africa Society held at the J.B. Morrell Library, University of York*, published in 20 reels by the University Library in 1977.

Additional material on the Society's work is held at BLCAS (Rhodes House Library), Oxford.

CAREERS FOR WOMEN Some papers (11 boxes) of the organisation, for the period 1933–93, are in the Women's Library (ref. Acc 23/1998). The organisation was formerly known as the Women's Employment Federation and subsequently as the National Advisory Centre on Careers for Women.

CARNEGIE TRUST FOR THE UNIVERSITIES OF SCOTLAND Certain papers have been deposited in the National Library of Scotland (ref. Acc 9587), including minutes of the Executive Committee for 1969–79. The permission of the Secretary of the Trust is required for access to the collection.

CATHOLIC COMMISSION FOR JUSTICE AND PEACE IN RHODESIA Some papers have been deposited at the Centre for Southern African Studies, University of York and comprise mostly pamphlets and publications of the 1970s. The material covers *inter alia* abuses by the Rhodesian security forces and political trials.

CATHOLIC EDUCATION SERVICE Founded in 1847 as the Catholic Poor Schools Committee, the organisation was reconstituted in 1905 as the Catholic Education Council for England and Wales and subsequently adopted the present title. The papers are retained at the head offices of the Service. A complete set of the Annual Report (which includes published accounts) has been retained since 1847 and these and other published reports would be available to researchers upon application. Otherwise only the most recent material has survived: there is a file of press-cuttings from 1935 and minutes and correspondence from 1949. Access to this material would be possible only by arrangement and would depend upon the character of the papers in question. Further enquiries should be addressed to the Director of the Service.

CATHOLIC TRUTH SOCIETY It is understood the Society has retained its archive, but no further details are available.

CATHOLIC UNION OF GREAT BRITAIN Founded in 1872, the Catholic Union is a voluntary association of the English, Welsh and Scots Catholic laity established to defend Catholic principles and express a Christian standpoint in public affairs. Its particular sphere of operation is the representation, where necessary, of Catholic interests in Parliament, to government departments, and to other national organisations or public authorities.

An assortment of early records has been deposited in the Westminster Diocesan Archives, whilst contemporary material is retained by the Secretary of the Union. A significant number of papers, including the minutes of the AGMs and Committees and the Annual Report, are regularly published as reports for members.

CELTIC LEAGUE Records for the period 1963–91 are in the National Library of Wales.

CENTRAL BRITISH FUND FOR WORLD JEWISH RELIEF The organisation was founded in 1933 as the Central British Fund for German Jewry. It was active until 1948 in rescuing German and Austrian refugees. Its case files are reported now to have been deposited at the London Metropolitan Archives. A microfilm of the CBF archive is available at the Hartley Library, University of Southampton. Other relevant material may be found in the archives of the Board of Deputies of British Jews (q.v.), including correspondence, 1933–49, with the Fund concerning the European situation and refugees; and minutes, notices, memoranda, financial statements etc. of the 'Central Council for Refugees', 1940–41.

Researchers should also be aware that the Schonfeld Papers, also deposited at the Hartley Library, University of Southampton, contain much material relevant to contemporary refugee work; it has papers emanating from the Committee for Austrian and German Jewry, the Jewish Committee for Relief Abroad and the Committee for the Rescue of Jewry in Nazi Germany. Reference should also be made to the Jewish Refugee Committee (q.v.).

CENTRAL CHURCH READING UNION The minutes of the Central Church Reading Union for the period 1926–52 have been deposited in Lambeth Palace Library (ref. MS 2659). It was founded in 1892 by the Revd Arthur Carr as the Central Society for Higher Religious Education in order to encourage the study of Christianity by the laity of the Church through diocesan associations.

CENTRE FOR ENVIRONMENTAL STUDIES The CES was set up in 1966 as an independent body with the object of promoting research and education in the planning and design of the physical environment. It was financed by grants from the Ford Foundation and the British Government, but was wound up in 1981. The papers were then deposited in the National Archives (ref. PRO 30/87), where they are open for research. A list is available (NRA 28792).

The collection includes minutes and papers of the Governing Body (which was responsible for policy and funding as well as for administration during the early years of the Centre); the minutes and papers of the Centre (later Executive) Committee which was established in 1970 to assume responsibility for the administration; the papers of the various other committees, e.g. Fellowships, Planning Exchange, etc., and a selection of CES working notes compiled by staff or fellowship scholars. A complete set of these has been retained by the Bartlett School of Architecture, University of London. The final part of the archive consists of the publications of the Centre, including Annual Reports, 1967–79, reviews, 1977–80; conference papers, 1970–79, and several series of academic papers.

CENTRE FOR POLICY STUDIES The Centre for Policy Studies is a right-wing research institute established in 1974 by the Conservative politician Sir Keith Joseph (later Lord Joseph). A description of the Centre's origins may be found in Michael J. Todd, *The Centre for Policy Studies: Its Birth and Early Days* (University of Essex: Essex Papers in Politics and Government No. 81, 1991).

The papers have been placed in the LSE Library (ref. M1878). The collection, deposited in 1993, includes minutes, correspondence and papers from the CPS's study groups, particularly the Health

Study Group, and the CPS's administration. Also deposited are papers concerning the Westwell Report. There is also additional material from Sir Alfred Sherman.

CENTRE FOR REFORM Some minutes and printed items of the Centre, 1998–99, have been placed in the LSE Library. The Centre was established by the Liberal Democrats in 1998 to provide a forum for broad debate on policy issues.

CHAIN MAKERS AND STRIKERS ASSOCIATION It is reported that the records of the Association for the period 1870–1970 have been placed in the Library of the University of Birmingham. Further enquiries should be directed to the Sub-Librarian (Special Collections).

CHAMBER OF SHIPPING An extensive archive has been placed in the Modern Records Centre, University of Warwick (ref. MSS 367). The deposit includes the archives of the Chamber itself, which was founded in 1877 to pursue commercial interests, as well as those of the Shipping Federation (later the British Shipping Federation), which pursued seagoing personnel matters. The Chamber combined with the BSF in 1975 to form the General Council of British Shipping. That name was changed to the Chamber of Shipping in 1991. All these bodies are represented in the archive.

CHANNEL TUNNEL ASSOCIATION The papers of this pressure group, together with the papers of the Channel Tunnel Company, were deposited at Churchill College, Cambridge in 1980. A list is available (NRA 25829). The majority of the collection is composed of Company papers which, because they relate to the 1930 tunnel scheme, are pre-war in date with the exception of material emanating from the Parliamentary Channel Study Group, 1947–60. The Channel Tunnel Association was formed in 1962; its papers form section 6 of the deposit and consist of correspondence, 1962–80, and copies of its publications, 1969–74. The last part of the collection is composed of the Association's library of relevant books, press articles and government publications.

CHARTER '87 This organisation was launched in 1987 to campaign for the human and legal rights of asylum seekers in the United Kingdom, and as a response to stricter Home Office policy regarding the treatment of such refugees and their applications for asylum. It seeks to enshrine in law a charter endorsing the principles of the 1951 UN Convention Relating to the Status of Refugees.

The group's records are retained in private hands. The relevant material includes minutes of Steering Group; a complete run of Charter '87's *Newsletter* and its occasional publication *News Updating*; financial records (bank statements, receipt books, and ledgers); correspondence, largely with the Home Office; and clippings files relating to asylum-seekers and refugees.

CHARTER '88 The original Charter '88 was published in 1988 as a declaration of intent for persons who favoured a written constitution for the United Kingdom. In June 1989 those who had signed the Charter supported the proposal to transform it into a continuing organisation; in the formative years Charter '88 sought the incorporation of the European Convention on Human Rights into law, electoral reform, the establishment of a Scottish Assembly and a Freedom of Information Act.

Enquiries concerning access to the papers should be directed to the University of Essex Library, which now houses them.

CHARTERED INSTITUTE OF BANKERS The records, covering the period 1878–1980, have been placed in the Guildhall Library, London.

CHILD ACCIDENT PREVENTION TRUST The Trust was founded in 1979 as the successor to the Joint Child Accident Prevention Committee, established under the Medical Research Council one year earlier by a group of paediatricians with the objective of reducing the incidence of childhood accidents. CAPT seeks to encourage research into childhood accidents, to promote a safer environment for children and to educate the public in accident prevention.

Certain papers of the Trust have been deposited in the Contemporary Medical Archives Centre at the Wellcome Institute (ref. SA/CAP). There are copies of the minutes of meetings of the Medical Commission on Accident Prevention and its finance committee, 1979–81, relating to the establishment of the Child Accident Prevention Committee, with the relevant correspondence; the minutes of the AGM, 1982–90; the Council of Management, 1984–90; the Executive Committee, 1979–88; the Trustees' meetings, 1982–91; and the Professional/Management Committee, 1989–90. General financial records (e.g. accounts, balance sheets) are preserved for 1981–82 only, along with correspondence related to funding, 1979–84. Personal correspondence files include those of Dr Gordon Avery, member of the Council of Management, 1977–86; Dr Hugh Jackson, Medical Secretary, 1979–83; other CAPT Council members, 1977–86, and past committee members, 1979–83. Administrative papers include several series of correspondence relating to publicity and education (e.g. road safety education, 1979–85; the BBC TV programme *Play It Safe*, 1980–83; fact sheets, 1984–87, etc.) and the records of working parties on individual aspects of child safety. There is also within the archive a collection of CAPT's publications, including occasional papers, fact sheets, published conference reports and copies of video-tapes.

The Trust's own Resource Centre also holds copies of conference papers and of annual reports since 1988 (which contain financial summaries), as well as examples of all CAPT's research publications. Researchers wishing to use the Resource Centre should contact the Information Officer. Access is free for individuals and non-profit organisations.

CHILD POVERTY ACTION GROUP The group was established in 1965 to campaign for the relief of poverty among children, particularly by ensuring that families of low income with children receive their full statutory entitlement of income benefits. The papers of CPAG are not available to non-members for research purposes but its history, *Campaigning for the Poor* by Michael McCarthy, was published by Croom Helm in 1986.

CHILD WELFARE ASSOCIATION Papers for the period 1870–1970 are reported to have been deposited in Merseyside Record Office (ref. 364 CWA).

CHILDLINE ChildLine, a registered charity, is the national telephone helpline for children or young people in danger. It was set up in October 1986,

following an investigation by BBC TV's *That's Life* programme into child sexual abuse.

The papers of ChildLine are at present retained at its national offices. Minutes of committees and conferences have been kept since inception, but are for internal use only. There is no policy on keeping correspondence beyond its immediate usefulness; some correspondence relating to campaigns is retained but is at present closed to researchers. An annual report is available from 1987 onwards. A library is kept of books, articles and other publications in ChildLine's field of interest but is for staff use only, although members of the public may request information in writing. A database and archive of counselling records is likewise maintained, but is highly confidential and access to those outside ChildLine is strictly limited to authorised researchers. Further enquiries should be directed to the Development Officer.

CHILE SOLIDARITY CAMPAIGN The organisation was founded in 1973. Papers covering the period to 1991 have been deposited at the Labour History Archive and Study Centre; the collection is closed at present but may be made available for research to persons applying in due course. Five boxes of material have also been deposited in the Brynmor Jones Library, University of Hull (ref. DX/185/1–5). The collection covers 1974–88 and includes minutes of the Executive Committee (1975–82); copies of the Affiliates' Newsletter, nos. 6–51 (1974–81); papers of the Campaign's Trade Union Conferences during the 1970s; internal political statements and discussion documents (1976–78); subject files on political conditions in Chile and British Government policy towards that country (1974–84), and papers relating to the AGM (1974, 1976–81). The attention of researchers is also drawn to the papers of the Chile Committee for Human Rights, likewise at the Brynmor Jones Library (ref. DX/185/6–7), which comprise an incomplete series of the Newsletter, nos. 1–55 (1975–84); subject files, and reports of Amnesty International.

CHINA ASSOCIATION The Association was established in London in 1889 by a group of businessmen with interests in China, Hong Kong and Japan (although these latter two areas are now represented by the Japan Association, established in 1950, and the Hong Kong Association, set up in 1961).

The papers of the China Association, in 116 volumes, have now been deposited in the Library of the School of Oriental and African Studies, University of London, although some documents of the period 1948–49 have been retained. The material includes 13 volumes of the Association's Annual Report (1889–1962); minutes of the General and Executive Committees (1889–1950); general circulars (1907–28); other papers of the General Committee such as circulars, agendas and resolutions (1927–45); correspondence with, among others, the Foreign Office (1945–56) and the Board of Trade (1958–70); and an incomplete series of the *China Association Bulletin*. The collection also includes the minutes, papers and correspondence (1946–53) of the British Community Interests Committee, relating mainly to Shanghai, and minutes, memos and correspondence (1960–69) of the Sino-British Trade Council.

CHRISTIAN ACTION Christian Action was founded in 1949 to encourage involvement of Christians in social and political affairs. One of its offshoots was the Defence and Aid Fund, established in the 1950s as a 'treason fund' for defendants accused of treason in South Africa. There is relevant material in the papers of J.L. Collins, sometime Canon of St Paul's Cathedral, London, which have now been deposited at Lambeth Palace Library (ref. MSS 3287–3319). Until 1973 Collins was chairman, and subsequently the president, of Christian Action.

The Collins Papers include the records (1942–50) of the Fellowship of the Transfiguration of Our Lord, the predecessor of Christian Action which Collins had founded in 1943; papers relating to a meeting, 'A Call to Christian Action', held by Collins in 1947; the minutes of the Council and the AGM of Christian Action, 1949–78, and from 1966 onwards those of its Finance and Establishments Committee. There is other useful material in the Gollancz (q.v.) papers at Warwick.

A further deposit of minutes and papers, 1976–96, has now been received by Lambeth Palace Library.

CHRISTIAN AID An international relief and development agency. During World War II the Churches in the United Kingdom established a

committee under the name of Christian Reconstruction in Europe to raise funds for relief in those countries affected by war. The organisation was later established on a permanent basis as the Department of Inter-Church Aid and Refugee Service within the British Council of Churches (q.v.). It adopted the name Christian Aid in 1964, and constitutionally it remains a division of the Council of Churches for Britain and Ireland, the successor to the BCC.

The papers of the BCC, which include material relating to the Department of Inter-Church Aid, are available at the Church of England Record Centre (q.v.). However the archive of Christian Aid itself, which runs to 70 boxes, has been deposited at the School of Oriental and African Studies, University of London. A list is available (NRA 27886). The files, which date mainly from the 1960s, are boxed and listed according to each regional area: Africa, Asia, Europe/UK, Global and Middle East. No material relating to Christian Aid's work in Latin America has yet been deposited. Papers dated after 1970 are retained for the use of the present administration. A sixth file group concerns the administration of Christian Aid and comprises Directors' papers up to 1970, correspondence with other fundraisers, and Christian Aid Week papers.

CHRISTIAN CONCERN FOR SOUTHERN AFRICA A collection of papers, including minutes, correspondence, files etc., 1972–92, was deposited in 1993 in the Library of the School of Oriental and African Studies, University of London.

CHRISTIAN ECONOMIC AND SOCIAL RESEARCH FOUNDATION There is relevant material in London Metropolitan Archives (ref. Acc LMA/4006). The organisation, founded in the 1950s, produced many publications on social welfare (especially drink offences). The archive, mainly pamphlets, is listed (NRA 41327).

CHRISTIAN SOCIALIST MOVEMENT There is material relating to the Movement (founded in 1960) during the years 1961–65 in the papers of the Revd Stanley George Evans (1912–65), which have been deposited in the Brynmor Jones Library, University of Hull (ref. DEV). A list is available to this collection (NRA 17262).

CHRISTIAN UNITY ASSOCIATION It is reported that the records of the Association for the period 1904 to 1956 have been deposited in the Ecumenical Collection at Edinburgh University Library. Further enquiries should be directed to the Librarian, Special Collections.

CHRYSLER SHOP STEWARDS RECORDS There is a significant deposit in the Modern Records Centre, University of Warwick (ref. MSS 315). A list is available (NRA 35310). The deposit includes Joint Shop Stewards' minutes, 1960–74, a single volume of AEU Shop Stewards' minutes, 1964–86; company documentation and other material on pay and conditions, productivity, participation and pensions, between 1968 and 1984; also documents re solidarity action, and press-cuttings. These records cover a particularly important period in the development of what was originally the Rootes Group: its operation as the UK division of the Chrysler Corporation (1964–78), the purchase of Chrysler Europe by Peugeot in 1978 and the closure of the Linwood plant in 1981.

CHURCH ACTION ON POVERTY A Christian ecumenical organisation committed to a programme of education and campaigning on poverty issues in Britain, CAP was established in 1982. It was a founder member of the Churches National Housing Coalition and in June 1991 of Poverty Action, which sought to raise the political profile of the issue of the disadvantaged. Enquiries about the papers of CAP should be directed to the National Coordinator.

CHURCH ARMY Founded by Prebendary Wilson Carlile in 1882, the Army is an Anglican body of Evangelists. Among its activities the Church Army runs welfare hostels, youth centres, old people's homes etc. Many of its officers work with clergy in the parishes and others hold missions. It is reported that certain papers of the Church Army have been deposited in the Bible Society Library, housed at Cambridge University Library. Researchers should address further enquiries to the Society's Librarian, at the CUL.

CHURCH MISSIONARY SOCIETY The Church Missionary Society was founded in 1799 under the auspices of the Church of England to conduct Christian missions throughout the world. Its archive, which consists of over half a million items, has now been deposited at the University of Birmingham Library. The majority of the material relates to the 19th century and details of pre-1945 records (and those of auxiliary societies) may be found in *Sources, 1900–51*, vol. I, pp. 38–39.

Papers are closed according to a forty year rule and, it should be noted, are opened in decennial series (i.e. materials for the 1950s were opened in 1999). Also available are sets of the *CMS Proceedings/ Annual Report/Yearbook* for 1801–1971, the *CMS Historical Record* (volumes from 1922–23 to 1956–57), the *CMS Register of Missionaries and Native Clergy* and various published histories of the Society.

Researchers wishing to use the collection should contact the Special Collections Archivist at the University of Birmingham Library.

CHURCH OF ENGLAND CHILDREN'S SOCIETY Founded in 1881 as the Church of England Waifs and Strays Society, the organisation cares for children in need by means of adoption, foster homes and children's homes. The Society, otherwise known simply as the Children's Society, adopted its present name in 1946 and now complements the work of the local authorities in this field.

The Society has retained its recent records and enquiries from researchers should be addressed to the Director. Earlier material has been deposited at the London Metropolitan Archives. The later papers which have not been deposited incorporate a considerable quantity of volumes of material emanating from the head office. Records which have been identified and listed include Executive Committee minutes, 1944–55, agendas, 1943–56, correspondence, 1912–73, and papers concerning the Society's reorganisation, 1966–75; the Homes Committee agenda book, 1947–65, and agendas and minutes, 1968–71; the Finance Committee agenda book, 1946–67; the Case (Adoption) Committee agenda book, 1946–68; the Case (Admissions) Committee agenda book, 1900–58; agendas and minutes for Annual Meetings, 1948–57; head office circulars and memoranda sent to homes, 1922–61; bulletins, 1952–59; head office policy files and general correspondence, 1935–47; and application registers,

1947–72. There are also papers relating to the head office's administration of the children's homes, such as quarterly returns (of numbers of children etc.), donor lists, registers, records of leases etc., and medical records.

A considerable number of volumes within the archive consists of the records of the various homes themselves. These include minutes of the local executive committees; reports of inspection; the Annual Reports of each home; medical registers; home diaries, etc. In some cases these papers run up to the 1980s in date. There is available a list (NRA 27642), which carries an appendix advising users how to trace information within the collection on particular subjects or on the various activities of the Society.

CHURCH OF ENGLAND MEN'S SOCIETY The Society was founded in 1899 by the amalgamation of the Church of England Young Men's Society, the Men's Help and the Young Men's Friendly Society. Deposited at Lambeth Palace Library (ref. MSS 3364–84) are the minutes of the Council, 1899–1986, and of the Executive Committee, 1901–80 (both partially indexed); minutes of various committees, 1913–83; and miscellaneous papers, 1917–85, including the minutes, presented evidence and other papers of the CEMS Development Commission, 1977–78.

CHURCH OF ENGLAND MISSIONARY COUNCIL The papers, which have been deposited in Lambeth Palace Library (ref. MSS 3121–28), comprise annual reports to the Missionary Council of the Church Assembly from the bishops of dioceses in Africa, Australia, Canada, the Far East, India, South America and the West Indies. They cover the period 1929–55.

CHURCH OF ENGLAND RECORD CENTRE Established in 1989, the Record Centre incorporates the former archives of the Church Commissioners, the General Synod of the Church of England and the National Society for Promoting Religious Education (q.v.), and serves as an information centre for all Anglican records.

In addition the Record Centre holds records of a number of ecumenical bodies, such as the British Council of Churches (q.v.) and the Churches' Council for Covenanting (q.v.), and the collections of smaller voluntary bodies connected with the Church of England. The latter include the papers of the Association of Church Social Work Administrators (formerly Association of Diocesan Organising Secretaries; 1930–76); Association of the Clergy (1975–79); Christian Evidence Society (1915–81); Church Reform League (including secretary's correspondence, 1940–55); Clergy Pensions Institution (1912–81); Partners-in-Mission (1974–81), and the William Temple Association (1955–84). The records of the Overseas Bishoprics Fund, deposited at the Centre, are overwhelmingly 19th century in origin. Material is usually subject to a thirty year rule and enquiries should be directed to the Archivist. The Centre is separate from Lambeth Palace Library, which also holds extensive Anglican archives.

CHURCH OF ENGLAND TEMPERANCE SOCIETY The records have been deposited at Lambeth Palace Library (ref. MSS 2030–72 and 2775–82). The material is largely pre-war in date apart from the following series of minutes: the Council, 1880–1967; the Central Executive Committee, 1935–67; the Central Women's Union Board, 1892–1947; the Central Education Board, 1929–1966, and the Finance Subcommittee, 1958–63.

CHURCH SOCIETY The Church Society is devoted to ensuring that the Church of England remains a Protestant institution and the established church of the United Kingdom. It was established in 1950 by a merger of the Church Association (founded in 1865) and the National Church League (established 1906).

The papers of the Society for the period from the foundation of its first constituent (the Protestant Association) in 1835 until 1950 have been deposited in Lambeth Palace Library. These include minutes of the Council, the Directors and all subcommittees from 1867 onwards and the records of the Finance Committee (1867–95) and its successor the Finance and General Purposes Committee (1895–1953). An annual report is not produced and correspondence is unavailable. A list is available (NRA 36519). Material for the post-1950 period is retained by the Society, but access to such papers is restricted to members only. Enquiries concerning membership may be directed to the Assistant Secretary of the Society. Further details of the papers may be found in C.J. Kitching, *The Central Records of the Church of England* (1976).

CHURCH UNION The Church of England Protection Society was formed in 1859 and renamed the English Church Union in 1860, when it incorporated several local Church societies. In 1934 it united with the Anglo-Catholic Congress to form the present Church Union. It seeks to defend and promote High Church principles. An archive has been deposited at Lambeth Palace Library, but the overwhelming bulk of the material is pre-war in date, with the exception of the final series of the minutes of the Legal Committee of the English Church Union for 1868–1947; minutes of miscellaneous committees of the Anglo-Catholic Congress for 1921–52; and an analysis of parochial returns from English dioceses concerning the extent of the Reservation of the Sacrament, 1949, and the returned questionnaires and analysis of the same for 1954.

CHURCHES' COUNCIL FOR COVENANTING An ecumenical organisation founded in November 1978, the Council was composed of representatives of the five Churches (the Church of England, the Methodists, the United Reformed Church, the Moravians, and the Church of Christ) which had accepted the ten propositions of a predecessor body, the Churches' Unity Commission (1974–78). The Council aimed to draw up a covenant by which the participants would commit themselves to seek closer unity, particularly in the mutual recognition of each other's sacraments and ministries. It was dissolved in March 1983.

The papers of both the Churches' Council for Covenanting and its predecessor have been deposited at the Church of England Record Centre (q.v.). The former collection consists of ten boxes of memos, correspondence and agendas. The papers of the Churches' Unity Commission fall into three groups: those of the Commission itself; the records of its Executive Committee, and the papers of its working parties. The Commission's papers form the bulk of the collection and may be divided into correspondence (1974–78) and documents (being

unsigned minutes for a similar period); annual reports, 1975–78; printed papers, 1965–77; documents for meetings, 1974–78; and press-cuttings, 1974–78. Executive Committee papers include correspondence (1975–78) and minutes (1974–78). The remaining papers comprise correspondence and documents of the five working groups for the 1970s.

Collections at the Church of England Record Centre are usually subject to a thirty-year rule; enquiries should be directed to the Archivist.

CHURCHES' COUNCIL ON GAMBLING The minutes of the Council for the period 1947–78 have been deposited in Lambeth Palace Library (ref. MSS 3155–58). Established in 1933 as the Christian Social Council Committee on Gambling, and dissolved in 1978, it was composed principally of representatives of the Church of England and the Free Churches.

CHURCHES' MINISTRY AMONG THE JEWS Founded in 1809 as the London Society for Promoting Christianity among the Jews, the society undertook Christian evangelisation among Jewish people. Today its object is to remind the Christian Church of its Jewish origins and its continuing obligations to the Jewish people. A very full archive has been deposited in the Bodleian Library. The records comprise minute books of the General Committee and its subcommittees, and administrative papers concerning the society's finances, its property, its staff and general mission work. Further enquiries should be directed to the Keeper of Western Manuscripts at the Bodleian Library.

CIVIL AND PUBLIC SERVICES ASSOCIATION Formerly known as the Civil Service Clerical Association (CSCA), it adopted this title in 1969. The earliest precursor of the union was the Assistant Clerks Association, formed in 1903, which became the Clerical Officers Association in 1920 and the CSCA two years later following a spate of mergers with smaller bodies. In the post-war period there have been amalgamations with the Ministry of Labour Staff Association (est. 1912) in 1973 and the Court Officers' Association (est. 1881) in the following year. In 1985 the Post Office Group withdrew from the CPSA and was affiliated to the National Communications Union.

The archive of the Union (now part of the Public and Commercial Services Union) has been placed in the Modern Records Centre, University of Warwick (ref. MSS 415).

Researchers should be aware that relevant material is available among the Norman Jacobs Papers also deposited at the Modern Records Centre, University of Warwick (ref. MSS 199). These include copies of minutes circulated by the national committees (1979–85); departmental sections' circulated minutes, reports and memoranda (1979–85); minutes and subject files of the London No.2 Area (1972–77), and other papers of various branches. The collection also contains material from a number of CPSA political groups (e.g. Broad Left minutes, publications and ephemera, 1977–82; and National Moderate Group publications and ephemera, 1974–82), and the circulated minutes and reports of the Council of Civil Service Unions – the central negotiating body for non-industrial civil servants – for 1982. There is also deposited at the Modern Records Centre (ref. MSS 48) a file of personal papers of Ernest J. Hicks, former President of the CSCA, relating to the years 1947–48.

CLERGY AGAINST NUCLEAR ARMS An interdenominational movement, CANA seeks to publicise the theological grounds for opposition to nuclear weapons and all strategies of defence based upon nuclear arms and deterrence. It has publicly called on the Government to subscribe to a doctrine not to use nuclear weapons first in the event of war and to renounce their possession. Its papers, including minutes and a published annual lecture, are currently held by the officers of the society and permission to consult them should be sought from the Secretary.

COAL MERCHANTS' ASSOCIATION OF SCOTLAND It was reported by the Business Archives Council of Scotland in 1980 that the records of the Association had been retained at the head office. A list is available to the collection (NRA 23867). The CMA was established in 1909 to promote the interests of the wholesale and retail coal merchants in the domestic trade. It negotiates on its members' behalf with the statutory authorities and other organisations.

The surviving records include Director's Office minute books, 1909–49; Executive Committee papers, 1949–79; Finance Committee minutes, 1967–79; and post-war records of the Wholesale and Retail Committees. Other records of the central administration include ledgers, 1950–76; cash books, 1950–78; annual accounts and balance sheets, 1964–79; and copy letters, 1971–79. There are also available the minutes of the National Joint Industry Council for the Distributive Coal Trade, 1946–76; various series of administrative files on marketing agreements from 1950 to the 1970s; and a run of the Association's journal for 1950–78. Following the passage of the 1956 Clean Air Act the Association established a special committee to examine the impact of the legislation on the coal trade and the collection includes the returns of questionnaires sent out by the committee to the residents of Glasgow and nearby towns, c. 1966–78.

COLONIAL CIVIL SERVANTS ASSOCIATION Certain papers of the Association for the years 1947–61 have been deposited at BLCAS (Rhodes House Library), Oxford (ref. MSS Brit Emp S 100–121). These include the constitution, minutes of conferences, circulars, bulletins and correspondence. Further enquiries should be directed to the Librarian.

COLONIAL SOCIAL SCIENCE RESEARCH COUNCIL The Council was established by the British Government at the end of World War II to undertake research into the economic development of the colonies. The LSE Library holds a collection of material which appear to be private sets of the Council's papers collected by several of its leading members, including Sir Alexander Carr-Saunders and Sir Arnold Plant. The majority of these are research proposals and technical reports to the Council's committees, and date from 1943 to 1963. The Council was subsequently superseded by the Overseas Development Committee. The papers at the LSE Library are open to researchers upon application to the Archivist.

Official Colonial Office records deposited at the National Archives may contain the Council's central archive.

COMMISSION ON THE FUTURE OF THE VOLUNTARY SECTOR Five boxes of papers concerning the work of the Commission, 1995–96, have been placed in the LSE Library by Jane Kershaw. A handlist is available and the collection is open.

COMMITTEE FOR ARAB AFFAIRS Although no surviving archive has been located for this pro-Arab pressure group, which was active in London in the 1940s, there is relevant material in the Spears Papers in the Middle East Centre, St Antony's College, Oxford. This includes minutes and agenda (1945–46), correspondence (mainly 1946) and membership records (1945–48).

COMMITTEE FOR THE LIMITATION OF SECRET POLICE POWERS Material relating to this organisation, which was active in the 1950s, is available in the papers of the writer and dramatist Benn Wolfe Levy (1900–73), who was Labour MP for Eton and Slough from 1945 to 1950. His papers have been deposited in Sussex University Library (ref. SxMs 37) and a list is available (NRA 25064).

COMMITTEE OF DIRECTORS OF POLY-TECHNICS Administrative records of this now defunct body have been placed in the Modern Records Centre, University of Warwick (ref. MSS 326). The deposit (38 shelf metres) includes the CDP's own minutes and related papers, 1972–91, and the minutes of its various standing committees. There are a large number of subject files, covering the administration of the committee itself and its convergence into the CVCP; the activities of several sub-groups, such as the Polytechnic Academic Registrars' Group; relations with other organisations such as the Department of Education and Science and the Council for National Academic Awards, the British Council, and related trade unions. There are files relating to the employment prospects of polytechnic graduates, conditions of employment of polytechnic lecturers, students' grants and accommodation, and fees for overseas students. The Modern Records Centre also has records of the Committee of Vice-Chancellors and Principals.

COMMITTEE OF 100 The Committee of 100 was formed in October 1960 by those members of the

Campaign for Nuclear Disarmament (q.v.) who wished to adopt a strategy of mass civil disobedience. A major role in its formation and activities was taken by Ralph Schoenman, an associate of Bertrand Russell, and his correspondence with the latter is preserved in the Russell Archive at McMaster University, Hamilton, Ontario, Canada (ref. VI/1). The main archive of the organisation, founded in 1960 as a movement of non-violent resistance to nuclear war and nuclear weapons, is in the International Institute of Social History, Amsterdam. The deposit includes agenda and minutes of national committee meetings with annexes 1961–66; documents relating to the national conference 'The Way Ahead' 1963; minutes of meetings of working groups and sub-committees 1962–66 and documents on the demonstration at Greenham Common US Air Force Base, the Aldermaston march and demonstrations against the Vietnam War 1962–66 and some circulars and leaflets on elections 1963.

COMMITTEE FOR PEACE IN NIGERIA The records are preserved among the papers of Liberation (q.v.; formerly the Movement for Colonial Freedom), now deposited in the Library of the School of Oriental and African Studies, although the Committee was technically a separate organisation. There are available for the period 1967–69 minutes, correspondence, copies of the newsletter, press releases, press cuttings and miscellaneous correspondence. In addition the Committee's files incorporate papers emanating from the North American Coalition for Biafran Relief and the Co-ordinating Committee for Action on Nigeria/Biafra. A list is available to the main collection (NRA 27885).

COMMITTEE OF VICE-CHANCELLORS AND PRINCIPALS OF THE UNIVERSITIES OF THE UNITED KINGDOM The Committee of Vice-Chancellors and Principals (CVCP) as it is commonly known was formally established in 1930 and until 1969 was linked with the Association of Commonwealth Universities (q.v.), whose Secretary served as the secretariat of the CVCP. The Committee's members comprise amongst others the Vice-Chancellors or Principals of the universities in England, Scotland and Wales and the Vice-Chancellors of the universities in Northern Ireland. The functions of the CVCP are advisory.

A large collection of administrative records (638 boxes), and several shelves of minutes, has been placed in the Modern Records Centre, University of Warwick (ref. MSS 399). The files are arranged by topic, from A for Academic Salaries or Adult Education to Y for relations with Yugoslavia. The Centre's holdings of higher education archives are now one of the most important in the country.

COMMITTEE OF WELSH DISTRICT COUNCILS
The papers of the Committee, which existed until 1989, were deposited at the National Library of Wales in 1990 by the Welsh Area Office of the Association of District Councils (q.v.). A list is available (NRA 33274). They complement the records of the Association of Welsh Local Authorities, deposited in 1981, and the papers of the Council for the Principality (q.v.), also at the National Library. The papers are open only with the permission of the Under Secretary (Wales) at the Welsh Area Office of the Association of District Councils.

The collection comprises papers of the Committee for the period 1983–89 (principally a large series of subject files on such topics as the economy and environmental health, housing, leisure, organisations and societies, finance and planning, and the Representative Body for Wales, 1974–88); and assorted records of the Association of District Councils, namely Welsh Office general correspondence (1983–89), Welsh Office circulars (1983–87), senior staffs' meetings papers (1983–89), and various subject files and branch records.

COMMITTEE ON ONE PARENT FAMILIES
There are records in the LSE Library.

COMMONS, OPEN SPACES AND FOOTPATHS PRESERVATION SOCIETY
The papers have been placed in the House of Lords Record Office (ref. Hist Coll 109). A list is available (NRA 35843). There are post-1945 files arranged by county.

COMMONWEALTH AND CONTINENTAL CHURCH SOCIETY
The Society was founded in 1861 as the Colonial and Continental Church Society by the amalgamation of two predecessor bodies – the Colonial Church Society and the Church of England Society for the Education of the Poor in Newfoundland and the Colonies. The surviving records have been deposited in the Guildhall Library, London. A considerable quantity of the material dates from before World War II, but the collection does include a complete set of the Annual Report since 1905 and of the magazine, *Greater British Messenger*, 1902–60. The surviving correspondence and Chaplain's books (registers) are also understood to be post-war in date.

COMMONWEALTH COUNTRIES LEAGUE
The Commonwealth Countries League was founded as the British Commonwealth League in 1925; it adopted its present name in 1952. Established by British suffragettes in recognition of the support their cause had received from other Commonwealth states, the League aimed to assist women throughout the Commonwealth to secure equality of status and opportunity. It declined during World War II but was later revived by Alice Hemming, largely as a social organisation to encourage links between different groups of Commonwealth women. It also took on a charitable role supporting secondary education for girls in Commonwealth countries.

The papers of the League have been deposited in the Women's Library (q.v.). A list is available (NRA 20625). Available material includes committee minutes for part of the period since 1950; reports of the annual conference, in bound volumes for the early 1960s but subsequently incorporated into the *Newsletter* (of which a complete set up to the end of 1990 has been deposited); and some miscellaneous correspondence. The files of Gloria Davies, a former Secretary of the League, are also available and these consist of Executive Council copy minutes for 1970–72 and 1978–79; minute books, 1971–81; correspondence from overseas organisations, 1970–72; and printed papers from various organisations concerning the equal opportunities campaign of the 1970s. The archive includes the Sadd-Brown library, an important collection of published works about women in Commonwealth and former Commonwealth countries.

COMMONWEALTH INDUSTRIES ASSOCIATION
Founded in 1926 as the Empire Industries Association, this organisation merged with the British Empire League in 1947 and subsequently

adopted the title of the Commonwealth and Empire Industries Association in 1958. In 1960 it was renamed the Commonwealth Industries Association and five years later merged with the Commonwealth Fellowship and the Commonwealth Union of Trade.

The Association's original aims were to promote Imperial economic co-operation in the inter-war period and, as a result, it had strong ties to the main UK industrial organisations. However in the post-war era of free trade its activities were directed towards the issue of Britain's entry into the EEC, which it opposed on the grounds that this would discriminate against exports from the Commonwealth to the UK.

The records of the Association have been deposited in the Modern Records Centre, University of Warwick (ref. MSS 221). A list is available (NRA 24412). The collection includes minute books for the whole period of the Association's existence, and these comprise a very important source for the study of British economic policymaking. Incorporated within them are the minutes of the Executive Committee, 1931–67; the Parliamentary Committee, 1945–47; the joint meetings between the Empire Industries Association and the British Empire League, 1947–55; and of the Council of the present Association, 1967–73. Annual reports exist for the Empire Industries Association and the British Empire League from 1927 to 1957, and for the present Association under its various names since 1958. Deposited publications consist of the *Monthly Bulletin*, 1941–70, and the journal *Britain and Overseas* from 1971 onwards. There is also a register of members, 1967–75, and financial records for the period 1945–77.

COMMONWEALTH PARLIAMENTARY ASSOCIATION

The Association, which was founded in 1911, has evolved with the Commonwealth. Starting as the Empire Parliamentary Association, administered by the UK branch, it changed its name in 1948 to the Commonwealth Parliamentary Association and the direction of its affairs came under the control of a General Council on which all branches are represented. The CPA remains an association of Commonwealth parliamentarians and exists to promote mutual understanding and co-operation and respect for parliamentary institutions.

A collection of the earlier papers of the CPA has been deposited in the House of Lords Record Office. The material extends from 1912 to 1972, but the majority of records date from the 1920s and 1930s. Those records which cover the post-war period do however include reports presented to the AGM, 1914–46; membership books, 1912–61; visitors' books, 1951–61, and overseas members' registers (giving details of visits), 1941–72. Among the financial records there are cash books, 1924–47, and ledgers, 1919–65. There is also film of a BBC transmission covering the Seventh Parliamentary Conference in 1961. It should be noted that the deposited papers contain very few committee minutes but do incorporate many series of printed committee reports.

It is understood that later papers have been retained by the Association itself.

COMMONWEALTH PRODUCERS' ORGANISATION

Originally established in 1916 as the British Empire Producers' Organisation, the CPO existed to promote the interests of primary producers overseas and the development of reciprocal trade within the Commonwealth and Preference Area. It was latterly involved in the debate over UK membership of the EEC, but did not adopt a particular stance for or against the Community. It was dissolved in 1975.

Upon its dissolution the surviving records of the CPO were deposited in the Library of the Royal Commonwealth Society, now in Cambridge University Library. The papers include the minutes of the Council, 1916–74, and of the Executive Committee, 1916–19 and 1941–75; the records of subsidiary bodies (including the Tobacco Federation, 1930–46); the *Newsletter*, 1948–67; and a run of the journal (known in its last format as *Commonwealth Producer*), which appeared biennially from 1946–47 to 1972–73. A list is available for the collection (NRA 25316).

COMMUNICATION MANAGERS ASSOCIATION

Prior to 1981, the association was known as the Post Office Management Staffs' Association (POMSA). Some records have been deposited in the Modern Records Centre, University of Warwick (ref. MSS 225). The deposit includes minutes, 1906–64; agendas, 1921–66; selected subject files, 1900s–70s;

Shrewsbury Branch records; publications; and two POMSA journals, *Supervising*, 1952–66 and *New Management*, 1978–80. In addition to POMSA records, the collection also includes conference proceedings of the Postal Inspectors' Association, 1951–59, its journal, *Postal Inspector*, 1952–59 and the Postmasters' Association journal, *The Quest*, 1921–72.

COMMUNICATION WORKERS UNION The CWU, formed in 1995, has deposited some of the records of its predecessors in the Modern Records Centre, University of Warwick (ref. MSS 148). For the Union of Post Office Workers, the deposit includes *The Post* (1921–41, incomplete) and *Branch Officials Bulletin* (1963–79); and also two report books for the 1971 postal strike. The Modern Records Centre also has some CWU publications from the 1990s, including material from the campaign against the privatisation of the Post Office.

COMMUNIST PARTY OF GREAT BRITAIN The party was founded in July 1920 as a fusion of various left-wing movements: the British Socialist Party, the larger part of the Socialist Labour Party, and individuals from the South Wales Socialist Society, the Shop Stewards' Movement, the Independent Labour Party and the National Guilds League. In March 1991 the party renamed itself the Democratic Left.

The archive of the party has been placed in the Labour History Archive and Study Centre, University of Manchester. A detailed list is available (NRA 40877). The collection can now be accessed electronically. The surviving records include both national and branch and district records, and the papers of a number of prominent Communist and socialist activists. It was formerly the practice of the CPGB to transfer its records to the care of the Communist International (Comintern) in Moscow, and the Political Bureau and Central Committee records of the period 1920–39 are currently held by the Russian Centre for the Storage and Identification of Documents of Recent History (formerly the Central Party Archives of the Communist Party of the Soviet Union). These records have, however, been microfilmed and a first instalment of microfilms of minutes and stenograms has been received by the library of the party in London.

The CPGB Executive Committee and Political Committee records which stayed in London (i.e. those for the period 1943–90) include minutes and supporting papers, correspondence, subject files, reports, circulars, press statements, weekly letters and membership records; records of the Cultural Affairs Committee, 1940s–70s; Economic Committee papers; Executive Committee *Morning Star* subcommittee papers; National Jewish Committee records, 1950s–60s; student organisation papers; and various records of the commissions on the *British Road to Socialism*, 1950s–70s. In addition there are the records of the Communist Party History Group *c.* 1945–80s, including minutes, accounts, correspondence, letter books, agendas, membership records, conference papers and reports and a file on the 1979 conference *1939: The Communist Party and the War*, the proceedings of which were published in 1984. Correspondents whose papers survive in this section include Maurice Dobb, Christopher Hill, John Simon, John Saville and Edward Thompson.

The central party archive incorporates certain papers emanating from other ancillary organisations, including the British Peace Committee (minutes, 1953–57, and membership records); the British-Soviet Friendship Society (papers of the 1950s); the *Daily Worker* editorial board (minutes, 1946–48); *Marxist Quarterly* board (minutes and papers, 1953–56); Society for Cultural Relations with the USSR (minutes, correspondence and papers, 1920s–80s), and the Young Communist League (minutes, reports, papers, publications etc., 1940s–80s). It is likely that similar conditions of access would be attached to these papers as to the CPGB.

Records of the Scottish Committee of the CPGB are in Glasgow Caledonian University.

COMPASSION IN WORLD FARMING A public trust founded in 1967, Compassion in World Farming is a campaigning organisation whose ultimate objective is to end the exploitation of farm animals and to convert agriculture to non-animal based production. Its short-term aims are to abolish factory farming, achieve reform of slaughterhouse practices and proper regulation of genetic engineering, and ensure the humane treatment of animals in agriculture throughout the European Community. Its educational wing, the Athene Trust, publishes reports and sponsors conferences. The papers of CWF which have been retained include minutes of Trustees' meetings and financial records (both of which are confidential); copies of special reports and an incomplete run of the members' magazine *Agscene*; and confidential correspondence and subject files. Persons wishing access to the papers should apply in writing to the Director.

CONCERN (NATIONAL COUNCIL FOR SOCIAL CONCERN)

There are papers *c.* 1980–2000 of this campaign for the homeless mentally ill in the Contemporary Medical Archives Centre, Wellcome Institute (ref. SA/CON).

CONFEDERATION OF BRITISH INDUSTRY

The CBI was established in 1965 as the national representative body for the manufacturing industry. It is now the premier employers' organisation in the UK and the sectoral equivalent of the Trades Union Congress. The Confederation was created by the amalgamation of the Federation of British Industries (established in 1916 to represent industrialists on all matters other than industrial relations); the British Employers' Confederation (founded as the National Confederation of Employers' Organisations in 1919 to meet employers' responsibilities for industrial relations), and the National Association of British Manufacturers (established as the National Union of Manufacturers in 1915 to represent smaller companies). Further details of the CBI's history and of its archive may be found in W. Grant and D. Marsh, *The Confederation of British Industry* (London, 1977); and A. Crookham, *The Confederation of British Industry Predecessor Archive* (Warwick, 1997).

The CBI archive has now been deposited at the Modern Records Centre, University of Warwick (ref. MSS 200); the Centre may therefore be regarded as the primary location for the study of British industrial policy, because it also holds the papers of the TUC. Researchers should be aware, however, that duplicates of the printed material in the collection have also been placed in Glasgow University Archives.

The post-1965 CBI material at Warwick consists largely of administrative papers of the officers; circulars and publications, and departmental subject files. It includes an extensive collection of CBI

Presidents' papers; circulars issued by the various directorates for the period 1984–87; bound copies of journals, *CBI Review* (1971–79), *CBI Overseas Trade Bulletin* (1965–74), *British Industry Week* (1967–74), and eight other titles, and minute books of the Fuel/Energy Committee (a series continuing from the Federation of British Industries). Also in the collection are the papers of the Devlin Commission on Industrial and Commercial Representation, which was established in 1970 to investigate the structure and efficiency of employers' representation in the UK; in 1974 an Advice Centre on the Organisation of Industrial and Commercial Representation was created, whose functions the CBI assumed in 1977. The records of the Commission deposited at the Modern Records Centre include papers circulated to the chairman and committee members, 1971–72; correspondence and subject files describing British and European industrial organisations (mainly for the period 1971–72); minutes and papers of the Advice Centre Consultative Board, 1975–77; and its subject and administrative files for 1974–81. Certain restrictions on access apply to this material. More recent material continues to be added.

The collections of the CBI's predecessors are described below.

FEDERATION OF BRITISH INDUSTRIES

The records cover the whole period 1916–65 and incorporate the minutes of the Grand Council and its various committees (including the Industrial Research Committee for 1949–63); papers of the Presidents, Directors-General, and Secretaries; annual reports, 1917–65; the journal *British Industries/FBI Review*, 1917–64, and other publications; and the subject files of the economic, overseas, technical, education and training, information and administration Directorates. Additionally there are minutes for the several regional branches: Midlands, 1918–65; North Midlands, 1947–55 (and office accounts, 1948–64); North Western, 1947–65; and East and West Ridings, 1960–65.

BRITISH EMPLOYERS' CONFEDERATION

The BEC papers include minutes of the Council and various committees, 1922–65; annual reports,

1919–64; the *Bulletin*, 1954–64; two large collections of miscellaneous subject files organised by pre- and post-1958 material; pamphlets for 1955–65, and a complete set of circulars distributed to members.

NATIONAL ASSOCIATION OF BRITISH MANUFACTURERS

The NABM records comprise its minutes for 1956–65 (including the National Union of Manufacturers' Executive Council minutes for January-September 1952); ledgers, 1925–65; legal documents, 1917–61; annual reports, 1947–65; the *Journal*, 1917–65; some correspondence and subject files, and minutes of the Midland Area Council for 1952 and the Coventry Area Committee for January-September 1952 (with a members' list).

CONFEDERATION OF EMPLOYEE ORGANISATIONS The Confederation was founded in June 1973 to act as a national representative organisation for non-aligned trades unions, and staff and professional associations, to negotiate with government and employers. It was disbanded in 1979 and the archive deposited at the Modern Records Centre, University of Warwick (ref. MSS 61). The papers consist of minutes of the Council and Executive Committee for 1973–80 and of the Insurance Division for 1977–79; various files by subject (e.g. administration; Council and European Community affairs; finance and membership; member associations; CEO Insurance Division; Managerial, Professional and Staff Liaison Group); CEO circulars, and press-cuttings. A list is available (NRA 36918).

CONFEDERATION OF HEALTH SERVICE EMPLOYEES The association was formed in 1946 by the amalgamation of the Mental Hospitals and Institutional Workers' Union and the Hospital and Welfare Services Union. It has developed the second largest membership of nurses and midwives (after the Royal College of Nursing) and has recruited all grades of staff within the health and social services profession. The official history of COHSE by Mike Carpenter has been published in three volumes, *All For One: Campaigns and Pioneers in the Making of COHSE* (COHSE, 1980); *They Still Go Marching On* (1985); and *Working For Health – The History of COHSE* (Lawrence and Wishart, 1986). In 1993 COHSE joined with NALGO and NUPE to form a new union, UNISON.

The COHSE archive has been deposited at the Modern Records Centre, University of Warwick (ref. MSS 229). It includes the minutes of the pre-war predecessor organisations. The COHSE records themselves consist of the minutes of the NEC for 1946–62, the Finance and Organisation Committee for 1951–69 and the Legal and Parliamentary Committee for 1946–51; the file relating to the amalgamation of the predecessor unions, 1945–46; files on the post-war staffing crisis, and an incomplete run of the *Health Services Journal*, 1946–63. In addition there are the papers of the union's official historian, deposited in 1985, which include MH1WU/COHSE Ryhope Mental Hospital branch minutes, 1932–64, and various COHSE materials such as rule books and papers relating to staffing in the post-war era.

CONFEDERATION OF INDIAN ORGANISATIONS (UK) The Confederation was set up in 1975 by a number of groups concerned with discrimination against the Asian community and is the national umbrella body for Indian organisations throughout the UK. It acts as a lobbying group, and campaigns through the media and by means of research and conferences for equal opportunities for Asian citizens.

The Confederation of Indian Organisations retains the minutes of its general meetings. Reports are produced after conferences or seminars (e.g. Disability Conference 1987, Equal Opportunity Conference 1985, Mental Health Seminar 1991) and the Confederation has produced a number of publications on different areas of work. In addition a quarterly newsletter has been published since 1988. Annual reports have also been produced from 1989 and annual audited accounts are retained on file. Correspondence is filed by subject, except for that with government departments and larger organisations, which is filed by originator. Press releases and miscellaneous mail are maintained separately. All documents are kept at the Confederation's offices, and access to non-public documents is subject to the management committee's approval.

CONFEDERATION OF SHIPBUILDING AND ENGINEERING UNIONS The Confederation was founded in 1890 as the national representative of the major unions in the shipbuilding and engineering industries. A substantial collection of non-current records has been deposited at the Modern Records Centre, University of Warwick (ref. MSS 44). These consist of an incomplete printed series of proceedings of annual meetings, 1949–68; the printed proceedings of special conferences, 1934–58; the minutes of the Railway Shopmen's National Council, 1928–68 (also incomplete); and an extensive series of post-war subject files. In addition the minutes of the Conventry District branch for the period 1943–81 are available in collection MSS 208.

CONFERENCE OF BRITISH MISSIONARY SOCIETIES The Conference, which represented most Protestant missionary societies in Great Britain, was founded in 1912 following an appeal by the 1910 World Mission Conference that members should form national cooperative councils for missionary work overseas. The organisation merged with the former British Council of Churches (q.v.) in 1977 and is now known as the Conference for World Mission.

An archive has been deposited at the School of Oriental and African Studies, University of London. The papers comprise Standing Committee minutes, 1939–49, and papers, 1930–60; Finance Committee minutes, 1944–60; an incomplete set of Annual Reports, 1912–60; papers relevant to the Annual Meetings, 1952–60; Home Council minutes, 1917–60 (the series is incomplete but does however include Executive Group minutes and papers, 1956–60; Annual Conference papers, 1953–60; and subject files on conferences and exhibitions); Schools Committee papers, 1946–65; Youth Committee papers, 1939–59; the minutes of the United Council for Missionary Education, 1937–52; and subsequent subcommittee papers. The archive also holds copies of books published by the Conference in the period 1916–67. The archives of the Overseas Department are arranged by originating Regional Committee (Africa, the Near and Middle East, the West Indies, and Asia) and cover the period from the late 1930s up to c. 1960. The collection also incorporates minutes, correspondence and finance and policy papers of the Christian Literature Committee (later Council) for 1943–60, and minutes, reports and pamphlets of the International Missionary Council, 1920–60, arising from its joint work overseas with the Council.

CONFLICT RESEARCH SOCIETY The CRS was officially inaugurated in 1963 with the object of bringing together researchers in conflict studies throughout the United Kingdom and to provide a forum for meetings with colleagues in other disciplines and professions, such as lawyers and civil servants. The CRS aims to disseminate the findings of academic conflict research to the widest possible audience; between AGMs it is administered by an elected Council. The Society is a corporate member of both the International and the European Peace Research Associations. The CRS also maintains a library, on the study and practice of conflict resolution, at the University of Kent and this is open to the public.

The minutes of the Council and the AGMs since 1988 are in the care of the present Secretary. Earlier records are held by the Information Officer, as is an archive of research papers and newsletters. The correspondence of the Society has been retained but is not systematically archived. Access to the papers is conditional upon the permission of the Council; applications may be addressed c/o the CRS Librarian, The Library, University of Kent, Canterbury.

CONSCIENCE There are minutes and correspondence of the chairman, Alan Howard, for the period 1973–89, in the Hartley Library, University of Southampton (ref. MS 276). Conscience was the Interdenominational Committee for Soviet Jewry.

CONSERVATIVE CHRISTIAN FELLOWSHIP The Fellowship was founded in December 1990 as an association of Christians within the Conservative Party who seek to encourage the formulation of public policies consistent with Christian values, and who wish to ensure that parliamentary legislation is in accordance with divine law. The papers are at present in the care of the Chairman and comprise committee minutes, conference reports, correspondence (principally between the Fellowship and MPs and various professional bodies) and financial records. A magazine, *The Wilberforce Quarterly* (September 1991 to date), is published. Access to the magazine and to published discussion papers is unrestricted; permission to examine the other records may be sought from the Chairman of the CCF.

CONSERVATIVE FRIENDS OF ISRAEL There are relevant papers in the M.M. Fidler papers in the Hartley Library, University of Southampton (ref. MS 290). They consist of 13 files of material, 1974–89.

CONSERVATIVE GROUP FOR HOMOSEXUAL EQUALITY (TORCHE) Some papers of the group (4 folders) including the Constitution, Executive and AGM minutes, newsletters and correspondence, 1977–92, were donated by Dr David Starkey to the LSE Library in 1993 (ref. M 1790). They form part of the Hall-Carpenter Archives (q.v.).

CONSERVATIVE PARTY

NATIONAL RECORDS

In 1978 the papers of the Conservative Party nationally were deposited in the Bodleian Library, Oxford. Previously they had been divided between the Party's Central Office in Smith Square and Newcastle University Library (where the papers of the Conservative Research Department were transferred upon the closure of Swinton Conservative College in the early 1970s). The inclusion of the Conservative Party Archive (CPA) within the Department of Western Manuscripts means that the Bodleian has a particularly rich collection of materials relating to Conservative politics; it already holds the private papers of Disraeli, Viscount Milner, the second and third Earls of Selbourne, and Lord Woolton (who was Party Chairman, 1946–55). The earliest records in the CPA date from 1867, although the deprivations of war and several moves of headquarters mean that most material dates from after 1945. Files are being continually accessioned upon their removal from Central Office.

The papers are organised according to the particular branch of the Party which produced them. Unlike the Labour Party, which is a truly national organisation, the Conservative Party is a federation of local parties with a national body (Central Office) at its head, as well as a parliamentary party. The CPA includes the records of the extra-parliamentary party only, with the exception of some papers of the Whips Office and the 1922 Committee (the organisation of Tory backbenchers). In general the records of the parliamentary party remain in its own care and are not available to researchers. Dr. Stuart Ball

of the University of Leicester has reported that the minutes of its committees prior to 1945 have probably been destroyed.

It should be understood that the records which are in the CPA are those of the federal organisation (i.e. Central Office and its regional branches; the National Union; and the Research Department) rather than the papers of individual constituency parties. Where the latter have been deposited, they are frequently to be found in the relevant county Record Office. The indexes of the National Register of Archives hold up-to-date information on these records. The central records nonetheless contain a great deal of correspondence between the Central and Area Offices and the constituency parties.

Given the nature of the material, access to the CPA is restricted. Documents dated up to and including 1975 are now available to all Bodleian readers without permission except for documents relating to Party finance, which are closed; papers from the Chairman's Office, which may be consulted only with the Chairman's permission whatever their date, and candidates' papers, which are available only with the permission of the Chairman and if this is forthcoming, the permission of the candidate in question if he or she is living. Documents dated 1 January 1965 to 31 December 1973 can only be seen with the Chairman's permission; those dated 1974 and after are closed. The records of the 1922 Committee for the post-1950 period may be consulted only with the agreement of the current Secretary of the Committee. Additional conditions relate to quotation from the CPA and further information should be sought from the Archivist.

A number of the CPA papers have however been commercially microfilmed and are available from Research Publications Ltd. A guide, *Archives of the British Conservative Party 1867–1986: A Detailed Guide to the Microform Collections* (Reading, 1989), has been published. It should be noted that this publication provides a useful introduction both to the archive retention policy of the Conservative Party and to the organisation of the CPA.

Readers wishing to consult the CPA should in the first instance write to or telephone the Archivist with details of their work. Catalogues are available for consultation in the Modern Papers Reading Room of the New Bodleian Library.

A number of collections documenting the activities of Conservative student groups have recently been deposited in the CPA. These include records emanating from the National Association of Conservative Graduates (1971–78), the Federation of Conservative Students (1971–81), and Conservatives Against Racialism (1970s).

AREA RECORDS

In 1991 an extensive deposit of the papers of the Scottish Conservative and Unionist Association was made at the National Library of Scotland (ref. Acc 10424). The material covers the period 1885–1987 and includes Western Divisional Council minutes, 1945–56, a cash book, 1944–59, and Organising Secretary's papers, 1949–65; Eastern Divisional Council Committee minutes, 1946–56, agendas, 1945–51, and pension fund papers, 1924–56; records of the salaries of trainees and missioners, 1950–55; accounts, 1892–1952, and bank books, 1948–52; election addresses, 1945–64; press-cuttings relating to general elections, 1955–71, and various issues of the *Campaign Guide* between 1950 and 1971. The permission of the Association is required for access to the papers. Other Scottish Conservative Party records which are known to have been deposited include miscellaneous papers of the Western Divisional Council for 1837–1960, which are in the University of Glasgow Archives (ref. DC/115; there is a list, NRA 21083), and the papers of the Scottish Universities Conservative Association for 1906–47, which are in the University of Glasgow Library.

The National Library of Wales has a major collection of records relating to the Conservative Party in Wales. The most important of these are microfilm copies of files from the Conservative Party Archive at the Bodleian Library, Oxford (see section above) relating to the Party in Wales during the period 1948–64. Specifically these are copies of the CPA series CCO2 and CCO4. In addition the National Library has the papers of the Wales North Association for 1953–85 (see list NRA 26130); the minute book for 1951–85 of the North Wales Group of the Wales Area Conservative Women's Committee (ref. NLW ex 917), and papers emanating from the Glamorgan and Monmouthshire Group of the Advisory Council of Wales and Monmouthshire

Provincial Area, which include an attendance book (1951–78) and minutes (1953–77). List NRA 26130 also has a description of this group.

CONSTITUTIONAL REFORM CENTRE Some records of the organisation (and the earlier National Committee for Electoral Reform) are in the LSE Library (ref. M 1777).

CONSUMERS ASSOCIATION This Association is one of the leading consumer pressure groups in Britain. A useful guide to its history, background and resources can be found in M. Hilton, *Consumerism in 20th Century Britain* (2003).

Researchers should note that the papers of Mary Adams, Deputy Chairman of the CA, 1958–70, form part of the Tom Harrisson Mass-Observation Archive at the University of Sussex. The Association retains its main archive.

CO-OPERATION FOR DEVELOPMENT Co-operation for Development was established as a UK charity in 1983 to support and sponsor small-scale enterprise development in the Third World. Its object is to promote self-sustaining projects which may continue to exist without future aid, and thus assist the reduction of poverty even in countries where the national or regional economy may be underdeveloped. Its papers are retained by the head office in the UK and comprise minutes of the AGM and Finance and General Purposes Committee; Annual Reports and evaluation reports; financial records and correspondence files organised by country and by project. All records date from 1983–84 onwards and permission to examine them should be sought from the General Secretary.

CO-OPERATIVE PRODUCTIVE FEDERATION LTD. The Federation was established in 1882 to bring together some 15 co-operative productive societies which had developed under Owenite and Christian Socialist influence. It sought to promote common action among its members and to assist them by securing access to markets and capital funding, etc.

The papers of the Federation have now been deposited in the Brynmor Jones Library, University of Hull (ref. DCF). Minutes of the following are included in the collection: the Federation (1896–1961); Co-operative Co-partnership Propaganda Committee (1918–60); Footwear Commodity Committee (1943–62); Management Committee and Advisory Subcommittee of the Co-operative Productive Federation Footwear Ltd. (1946–54), and the Stanton Memorial Scholarship Committee (1918–48). There are two volumes of press-cuttings relating to the Federation for the period 1961–68 and a visitors' book of 1947–52.

CO-OPERATIVE WOMEN'S GUILD The Guild was founded in 1883 as the Women's League for the Spread of Co-operation. The present title was adopted in 1963, prior to which the organisation was known as the Women's Co-operative Guild. The Guild was of importance in its early years for breaking the male monopoly of co-operative organisations. In 1921 an International Women's Co-operative Guild was formed and this remained as an independent body until 1963, when it was incorporated into the International Co-operative Alliance (q.v.).

Certain post-war records of the Guild are included among the collection of its papers deposited in 1974 at the Brynmor Jones Library, University of Hull (ref. DCW). A list is available (NRA 20163). The archive includes Central Committee minutes, 1888–1970; minute books of the Annual Congress, 1956–61, and resolutions and amendments, 1952–58, 1961–67, 1971; Reception Committee minutes, 1947–56 (and minutes of the South East Section, 1919–50); Annual Reports, 1946–59, 1962–64, 1967, 1970, and a series of Notes for Speakers up to 1962. There is a substantial collection of photographs in the archive, including those of the members of the Central Committee, 1923–51, and many examples of the Guild's publications, especially pamphlets, for the period up to 1959. However, the bulk of the collection is composed of a large series of subject files relating to the administration of the Guild (e.g. the election of General Secretaries, papers on training courses, files concerning various Commissions of Enquiry into the work of the Guild, a schedule analysis relating to branch activities from the 1950s, policy statements, and papers relating to the 'Caravan of Peace' of 1958 and the Guild Development Year, 1965–66).

The archive also includes certain papers of both the Scottish and the Irish Co-operative Women's Guilds Other records of the Scottish Co-operative Women's Guild for the period 1892–1984 are reported to have been deposited in the Strathclyde Regional Archives.

COTTON RESEARCH CORPORATION The Corporation was a government-sponsored independent industrial research organisation which had agricultural stations around the world. Further details may be found in M.H. Arnold (ed.) *Agricultural Research for Development* (CUP, 1976). Papers have been deposited in the University of Nottingham Library and consist of staff newsletters, 1952–76; General Cotton Advisers' reports, 1969–75; reports of the Ministry of Overseas Development, 1968–75; ledgers, 1957–77; salaries sheets, 1952–76; cash books, 1962–75, and copies of papers circulated to officers and committees of the Corporation, 1923–66.

COUNCIL FOR ACADEMIC FREEDOM AND DEMOCRACY Case and subject files of the Council for the period 1967–82 may be found in the papers of John Saville and those of Prof. John Griffith, its first chairman, which have been deposited in the Brynmor Jones Library, University of Hull (ref. DAF). A number of duplicate documents, press-cuttings, membership forms and individual case files relating to the Council for the period 1969–73 are preserved among the papers of Liberty (q.v.; formerly the National Council for Civil Liberties), likewise in the Brynmor Jones Library.

COUNCIL FOR THE ADVANCEMENT OF ARAB-BRITISH UNDERSTANDING (CAABU) This organisation was established in 1967 and seeks to promote friendship and understanding between Britain and the Arab world. Its principal activities are political, carried out through the lobbying of the British and European parliaments, the British government and the European Commission, and educational, e.g. providing speakers to schools. In particular CAABU is concerned to foster a sympathetic awareness in Britain of the Palestinian cause, and to work for the maintenance of human rights throughout the Middle East.

CAABU retains its own archive. Material comprises committee minutes from 1967 to date, which are however closed; annual reports since 1973, and (uncatalogued) correspondence and subject files from the Council's formation. The latter series contains a small amount of material on the UK; the bulk concerns political, social and economic aspects of the Arab countries, Israel and Palestine. Financial records are not available. Copies of publications, including briefings and edited conference speeches, have also been retained; there is a library open to the public at the Arab-British Centre. Persons seeking access to the papers should apply to the Information Officer.

COUNCIL FOR THE AMELIORATION OF THE LEGAL POSITION OF THE JEWESS The Council was founded in 1922 by Miss L. Hands in order to consult with the appropriate religious and communal authorities and produce suggestions for the improvement of the position of women under Jewish religious law. Two boxes of papers, consisting of minutes, correspondence and other papers of the Council for the period 1919–46, have been deposited in the Hartley Library, University of Southampton (MS 123).

COUNCIL FOR BRITAIN IN EUROPE The Council was formed in 1975, with the object of demonstrating to the public that continued British membership of the European Community was supported by significant figures of all descriptions.

The papers of the Council, comprising largely correspondence dated March to May 1975 and memoranda, have been included among those of Britain in Europe (q.v.) deposited in the House of Lords Record Office (ref. BIE/9/1–3). Also included with the collection is miscellaneous correspondence relating to the groups City in Europe and Kensington and Chelsea in Europe. The Britain in Europe papers may be made available to bona fide students and all enquiries should be addressed to the Clerk of the Records, House of Lords Record Office.

COUNCIL OF BRITISH SOCIETIES FOR RELIEF ABROAD Certain records have been deposited in the Bodleian Library (ref. BAG). These include a file index for the period 1942–50 on 'Home Societies', which holds material on the British Red Cross, the Foreign Office, the International Refugee Organisation and the Catholic Committee for Relief Abroad. There are also the papers (such as agendas, minutes and notices) of the various committees and the files of the chairman, deputy chairman and treasurer, together with documents relating to the Relief Supplies Fund of 1947–48. The collection includes financial records dated up to 1951, and a file index (1942–50) on 'Home-finance' including auditors' reports, financial statements, Treasury grants, which details subsidies to the Council and conference. Papers within the collection relating to the overseas work of the Council are arranged in a series of 'general' files on various countries, including Greece, Austria, Italy, Holland, Malaya and Palestine. A separate collection relates to relief in Germany in the period 1949–50, including minutes and agenda of various meetings, files on policy, a diary and circulars.

COUNCIL OF CHRISTIANS AND JEWS Formed originally in 1942, the Council's founder members included Archbishop William Temple and the Chief Rabbi, Dr J. H. Hertz. The Council exists to bring together the Christian and Jewish communities in Britain in a common effort to fight the evils of prejudice, intolerance and discrimination between peoples of different races and religions. Its pioneering work in the fields of inter-faith education and ecumenical relations includes the arrangement of lectures, conferences, study groups and publications. A history of the Council by Marcus Braybrooke, *Children of One God*, was published in 1991.

An archive of the Council's papers for the years 1940–84 has now been deposited at the Hartley Library, University of Southampton (ref. MS 65). A list is available (NRA 30683). It is composed of Executive Committee minute books and correspondence, 1941–78, and correspondence files of the AGM, the Standing Conference of Local Councils of the Council of Christians and Jews and of local associations of the Council. There is also a sequence of subject files which incorporates papers of related organisations such as Aid to Christian Lebanon (1976–80), the Association of Nazi Camp Survivors (1960–67), and the Rainbow Group (1978–80).

The archive also includes minute books for the management board of the Christian Council of Refugees, 1940–51, and the minutes of the Christian Council of Refugees from Germany and Europe Continuation Committee, 1951–53. Researchers should be aware that the Hartley Library holds the papers of the Revd William Wynn Simpson (1907–87), General Secretary of the Council from 1942 to 1974 and subsequently Honorary Chairman of the International Council of Christians and Jews (ref. MS 66).

COUNCIL OF CIVIL SERVICE UNIONS The Council, a confederation of unions within the Civil Service, originated as the Staff Side of the National Whitley Council for the Civil Service (more commonly known as the National Staff Side), which was founded in 1920. Its principal purpose was to co-ordinate the activities of those staff associations which were represented on the National Whitley Council, with the exception of the industrial civil servants. Reference should be made to H. Parris, *Staff Relations in the Civil Service: Fifty Years of Whitleyism* (London, 1973).

A collection of papers, consisting of the contents of the registry filing system, was deposited at the (former) Kingston Polytechnic in 1979, where preliminary sorting was undertaken. In 1988 the papers were transferred to the Modern Records Centre, University of Warwick, where they form collection MSS 296. A list is available (NRA 33003). The majority of the material comprises an extensive series of subject files covering such areas of the association's work as recruitment, pay, hours of work, sickness, National Insurance, superannuation, training, welfare etc. from the 1920s to the 1960s. Within these files may be found signed agreements of the Joint Council of the National Whitley Council for 1949–74; an incomplete series of minutes of the National Staff Side for 1964–69 and its general correspondence, 1953–63; the records of its committees, and papers arising from Royal Commissions to which evidence was presented (e.g. the Priestley Commission of 1953–55).

Researchers should also refer to the main entry in this Guide for the Inland Revenue Staff Federation whose papers, also at the Modern Records Centre, contain material relevant to the National Staff Side.

COUNCIL OF THE CORPORATION OF FOREIGN BONDHOLDERS The Council was formed in 1868 and incorporated in 1873 under licence from the Board of Trade and reconstituted in 1898 by Act of Parliament. Its function is to represent the interests of holders of bonds issued in the UK on behalf of overseas governments and statutory authorities. The papers for the period 1868 to *c.* 1979 have been deposited in the Guildhall Library, London. Researchers are advised by the Council to consult in the first instance the annual reports which reproduce public announcements made by the Council and details of all debt settlements; complete sets of the report are available at depository libraries in the UK.

COUNCIL FOR FREEDOM IN PORTUGAL AND THE COLONIES Relevant material covering the period 1961–62 may be found among the papers of the Liberal Party activist Derek Mirfin, which have been deposited in the University of Bristol Library (ref. DM 668).

COUNCIL OF MARRIED WOMEN Founded in 1952 under the auspices of Helena Normanton QC, the Council sought to promote the institution of marriage and the equality of the sexes therein, and to reform the legal position of divorced and separated women. After the publication of the report of the Royal Commission on Marriage and Divorce in 1956, the Council sponsored a parliamentary private bill to establish the wife's legal right to a portion of the family income. The Council ran into financial difficulties in the 1960s due to a decline in the number of members, and was wound up in 1969.

The archive has been deposited in the Women's Library (q.v.) and a list is available (NRA 20625). The collection consists of Executive Committee minutes, 1952–59, AGM minutes, 1952–61, 1962, and 1967; Chairman's reports, 1953 and 1956–59, and bank statements, 1961–67. There is a considerable series of subject files on relevant subjects or consisting of evidence to official enquiries, e.g. to the Royal Commission on Marriage and Divorce (1952–56). The surviving correspondence consists of general files, 1953–61, and correspondence with other groups and campaigns (such as the Marriage Law Reform Society, Six Point Group, Status of Women

Committee and the British section of the European Union of Women). Printed material includes copies of the *Bulletin*, 1952–59; collected pamphlets of other organisations, and various government publications (e.g. Acts of Parliament, White Papers, and public reports) on topics of interest to the Council.

COUNCIL FOR NATIONAL ACADEMIC AWARDS The minutes of the CNAA are in the National Archives (PRO). An extensive administrative archive is in the Modern Records Centre, University of Warwick (ref. MSS 322/CA). The archive, which fills 8 shelf metres, mainly comprises correspondence files with professional, governmental and educational bodies, 1965–92. In addition to its own archives, the CNAA has deposited the archives of the National Council for Technology Awards (MSS 322/TA) and the archives of the National Council for Diplomas in Art & Design. (MSS 322/AD).

COUNCIL FOR NATIONAL PARKS The records have been placed in the Rural History Centre, University of Reading (ref. Acc DX 172).

COUNCIL OF POST OFFICE UNIONS COPOU was dissolved in January 1982, to be replaced by the British Telecommunications Union Council and the Post Office Union Committee. The archive was subsequently deposited at the Modern Records Centre, University of Warwick (ref. MSS 89). It consists of COPOU committee minutes and circulars, 1969–81; correspondence files, 1960–77; subject files (including those on industrial democracy in the Post Office), 1966–81; *Annual Reports*, 1972–76 and 1978–80, and the publications of affiliated unions, 1972–81. In addition this collection includes minutes of the Post Office Engineering Federation for the period 1922–68; papers of the Federation's Departmental Whitley Council, namely minutes, 1932–69, *Whitley Bulletins*, 1954–55 and 1960–69, and correspondence and subject files (1930s to 1960s).

Reference should also be made to the British Telecommunications Union Council (q.v.) and the Society of Telecom Executives (q.v.; formerly the Society of Post Office Engineers).

COUNCIL FOR THE PRINCIPALITY The papers were deposited at the National Library of Wales by the Association of District Councils (q.v.) in 1985. The Council was formed in 1974 in the course of local government reorganisation in order to co-ordinate the work of the new District Councils. It held its first meeting in May 1974 and was superseded by the Committee of Welsh District Councils (q.v.) in April 1983.

The records deposited comprise individual subject files, 1976–83; management files (including agendas and minutes of meetings, reports and circulars and general correspondence files), 1975–83; minutes, memoranda and circulars of the Welsh Consultative Council on Local Government Finance, 1978–82, and the same of its Official Committee, 1978–81.

COUNCIL FOR THE PROTECTION OF RURAL ENGLAND Established in 1926 as the Council for the Preservation of Rural England to co-ordinate the activities of various bodies already involved in rural protection, CPRE exists to protect the natural condition of the countryside, monitor changes in the use of land and promote legislation on conservation. Its 22 original constituent members, which include bodies such as the National Trust and the County Councils Association, have more than doubled in number but much of its lobbying strength derives from the number of its county and district branches. CPRE was very influential in the national parks movement in the 1930s and its sister organisations, the Council for the Preservation of Rural Scotland and of Rural Wales, were founded in 1926 and 1929 respectively. The Council adopted 'Protection' in place of 'Preservation' in its title in 1969 and was reorganised in the following year to increase the representation of local branches.

A substantial archive of CPRE's papers survives from the earliest period. These include the complete minutes of the Executive Committee and of a number of subcommittees from 1926, and a complete series of AGM proceedings. Annual reports run from 1926; copies of the bi-monthly bulletin and other publications have also been retained. Financial records do not exist save for bank statements for the period 1960–75. The bulk of the archive is a vast series of administrative files, which consist of: correspondence with branches, constituent and affiliated bodies, and individuals; files on each county; files on internal administration, and papers relating to campaigns, etc. These include the working papers of committees and records of evidence given to public enquiries. Some files – mostly branch records – have been microfilmed.

The administrative files have been deposited at the Rural History Centre, University of Reading, and the permission of CPRE must be sought prior to consultation. A list is available (NRA 24450). The remaining material is retained at CPRE's national office.

COUNCIL FOR THE PROTECTION OF RURAL WALES
There are papers in the National Library of Wales. A list is available (NRA 38318). Some other older records of the Council, up to about 1950, are included among the papers of the public servant Dr. Thomas Jones, now deposited at the National Library of Wales. They include an incomplete run of the Annual Report for 1928–50; Executive Committee correspondence with members from the 1920s to 1950, and a one-volume record of members, 1934–50. A list is available (NRA 30994). Some later records for 1945–55 are reported to be available at the Ruthin Branch of Clwyd Record Office, and for 1968–75, at Pembrokeshire Area Record Office, Dyfed Archives.

COUNCIL OF WELSH DISTRICTS
There are papers in the National Library of Wales. A list is available (NRA 37942). The deposit includes correspondence, papers and financial records.

COUNCIL FOR THE WELSH LANGUAGE
Relevant material is available in the papers of the Liberal politician Ben G. Jones (1914–89), which have now been deposited at the National Library of Wales. Jones was chairman of the Council from 1973 to 1978. The records relating to the Council include minutes, 1973–77; memoranda, reports and circular correspondence, 1973–78; published reports, 1975–78 (e.g. 'Welsh for Adults' of 1976); Education Panel papers, 1974–76, and Communication Panel papers, 1974–76. Researchers should also be aware that the National Library has certain papers of the Committee to Clarify the Legal Status of the Welsh Language for the years 1963–65 and reference should also be made to the principal entries in this Guide for Cymdeithas Yr Iaith Gymraeg (Welsh

Language Society) and Undeb Cymru Fydd (New Wales Union).

COUNCIL OF WOMEN CIVIL SERVANTS
Founded in 1920, the Council covered the administrative, professional, and higher executive grades of the civil service. Its object was solely to work for equality of opportunity within the service. It was dissolved on 31 December 1958.

The Council's records have been deposited in the Women's Library (q.v.). They include minutes of the Executive Committee, 1920–58; the Committee of Representatives, 1932–52; the Equal Opportunities Subcommittee, 1951 and 1955–56, and the AGMs, 1923–58. Also available are various annual report series, 1940–54; correspondence files on subjects such as the admission of women to the Foreign Office and Diplomatic Service (1938–57), equal pay, family allowances and conditions of service (e.g. the marriage bar), and a run of the *Quarterly Bulletin*, 1934–57.

COUNCIL FOR WORLD MISSION
The Council for World Mission was formed in 1966 when the London Missionary Society (established 1795) merged with the (Congregational) Commonwealth Missionary Society (known as the Colonial Missionary Society prior to 1956) and the Presbyterian Church of England Overseas Mission. It is an international Council which now includes 30 member churches in 28 countries around the world, mainly of the Reformed tradition. Its function is to act as an international community of evangelism and service.

The archives of the Council and its predecessors prior to 1960 were deposited in the Library of the School of Oriental and African Studies, University of London, in 1973 (ref. CWM). Later papers are retained by the Council. The papers of the London Missionary Society at SOAS include the minutes of the Board of Directors, 1943–48 and 1953–59; the Consultative and Finance Committee, 1939–61; the Foreign and Occasional Committee, 1948–55; the Funds and Agency Committee, 1937–66; the Education Subcommittee, 1948–64, and the various regional committees. There is also a large series of correspondence and reports regarding the Society's overseas activities arranged by each geographical area; material is available relating to Central Africa,

Australia, China and Hong Kong, India, Madagascar, the Pacific and Papua New Guinea.

The Commonwealth Missionary Society's papers now at SOAS incorporate Board minutes, 1928–67; Finance Committee papers, 1932–50; Ministerial Committee papers, 1917–60; assorted subject files, and correspondence on its work in Australia, Canada, Guyana, Jamaica, New Zealand, South Africa and the USA. The papers of the Presbyterian Church of England Foreign Missions Committee are arranged into two groups: Overseas papers (Boxes 1–61) concerning six foreign missions; and in addition, Home papers (Boxes 62–99) relating to the head office administration. Boxes 64–76 contain minutes, office copies and reports of the Foreign Missions Committee for the period 1933–56. All other classes of record run up to 1960 in date.

The material retained by the Council itself relates to the more recent period.

COUNTRY LANDOWNERS' ASSOCIATION
The Association was founded in 1908. It adopted its present name in 1949, having previously been known as the Central Land Association until 1918 and thereafter as the Central Landowners' Association. It exists to promote and protect the interests of the owners of agricultural and other rural land.

A collection of the papers of the Association is deposited at the Rural History Centre, University of Reading. There is a list which refers to the material (NRA 20987). The collection has been arranged in four main parts: A (administrative), B (legal), C (social and personal) and D (publications and publicity material). The more important records include the minutes of the Council, 1922–55, and the Executive Committee, 1908–58, and 26 box files relating to branch and regional offices, sub-committees etc., which mainly date from the 1950s and 1960s. In addition there are AGM reports, a typescript of the history of the first forty years of the Association, and a run of the *Journal* for the period 1923–50. Enquiries concerning the conditions attached to access should be addressed to the Librarian.

COWETHAS FLAMANK Cowethas Flamank is a current affairs and research group formed in 1964 which seeks to encourage a wider awareness of Cornwall. It is named after Thomas Flamank, one of the leaders of the Cornish Host of 1497. There is no formal structure (membership is by invitation), but the group publishes a quarterly newsletter *Kerren-Link*. Its correspondence files for the period 1969–83 were donated to the National Library of Wales in 1987. A list is available (NRA 38327).

CRAFTS COUNCIL The papers have been placed in the Library of the V&A (ref. AAD 1991/4, AAD 1994/15). A detailed list of the papers (from its origins as the Crafts Advisory Committee established in 1971) is available (NRA 39807).

CRISIS AT CHRISTMAS Crisis at Christmas was founded in 1967 to assist those who are homeless and alone, both by providing food and shelter in London during the Christmas period and by funding projects throughout the country which help the single homeless.

Crisis presently retains its own records, which consist of minutes of the Executive Committee and of Trustee meetings since *c.* 1981; miscellaneous publicity material since 1969 (including a number of published reports, e.g. 'Women and Homelessness', 1977) and Annual Reports, annual financial reports, and correspondence for a preceding five year period, which is arranged by subject. Applications for access should be addressed to Crisis.

CRUSADE FOR WORLD GOVERNMENT Relevant material is available among the Beveridge papers deposited in the LSE Library (ref. Beveridge VII 55–59), namely correspondence, 1947–54; National Executive Committee minutes, 1948–50, and memoranda, 1948–54.

CRUSE Founded in 1959 as the National Organisation for the Widowed and their Children, Cruse exists to provide both a counselling service to the bereaved and a training service for those who provide care to such persons. Cruse retains its own papers, which consist of council minutes, annual reports, financial records, correspondence and subject files, and copies of its three journals, the monthly *Cruse Chronicle* for members, *Cruse Bulletin* for workers, and *Bereavement Care* for professional care givers. Applications for access to the material should be made to the Director.

CYCLISTS' TOURING CLUB Founded as the Bicycle Touring Club in 1878, the group adopted its present name in 1883. The Club retained a substantial archive of administrative records, photographs, press-cuttings, books and artefacts, which has now been listed (see P. Bassett, *List of Historical Records of the Cyclists' Touring Club*, Centre for Urban and Regional Studies, University of Birmingham, 1980). It is now in the National Cycle Archive in the Modern Records Centre, University of Warwick. Enquiries should be directed there.

CYMDEITHAS YR IAITH GYMRAEG (WELSH LANGUAGE SOCIETY) Records for the period 1885 to 1983 have been deposited in the National Library of Wales. A list (in Welsh) is available (NRA 26130). The papers were accumulated by Tom Ellis whilst he was MP for Wrexham (1970–83), and include his own correspondence with Raymond Garlick for the years 1971–79 and 1988, relating to the activities of the society and to court cases arising from the public campaign on behalf of the Welsh language during the 1970s. Also deposited in the National Library of Wales are some press-cuttings and related material (ref. NLW ex 1045) and the records of the Newport branch of the society for the period 1972–79.

D

DAIRY TRADE FEDERATION The present Federation is an incorporated body which took over the functions of a previously unincorporated organisation of the same name in December 1985. It exists to represent primary milk producers in the UK and has a statutory duty to negotiated prices, etc. with the Milk Marketing Board. As a member of various European trades associations, it represents the UK dairy industry to the European Commission.

The records of the Federation are retained at its headquarters. They include the minutes of the Council from the formation of the Federation in 1932, and of other committees since the 1950s. Annual reports and accounts are available from the early 1970s. The volume of records increased substantially upon the UK's accession to the EEC in 1973 and is particularly full from that date. Any person wishing to have access to the papers should apply to the Company Secretary.

DEBDEN COMMITTEE Seven files of the papers of the Committee for the period 1949–65, comprising minutes etc., may be found in the archive of the Bank of England (q.v.). A comprehensive list is available (NRA 33132).

DEFENCE MANUFACTURERS ASSOCIATION DMA is a non-profit trade association, established in 1976, which represents and advises all UK companies connected with selling products or services to government defence agencies and the principal defence contractors at home or abroad. It keeps its member companies informed of changing technical requirements and procedures in defence procurement and provides marketing advice and support.

Files for a preceding three-year period are retained by the DMA at its offices, whilst older material is stored off-site. The Association publishes an extensive series of reports, of which copies are retained, and in addition to the Annual Report there is issued yearly a short financial report. Correspondence and the minutes of the DMA's various committees (such as Contracts, Quality Assurance and Marketing) have been retained but access to this material may be restricted.

Further advice should be sought from the Association.

DEMOCRACY FOR SCOTLAND CAMPAIGN Some correspondence, minutes and other papers, 1992–97, have been deposited in the National Library of Scotland (ref. Acc 11497).

DEMOCRATIC LEFT The Labour History Archive and Study Centre has the records of this left-wing political think-tank.

DEMOCRATIC PARTY The main source for records of the party is the collection of papers deposited by its founder, Desmond Donnelly, in the National Library of Wales. See p. 62.

DIRECT ACTION COMMITTEE (AGAINST NUCLEAR WAR) The Emergency Committee for Direct Action Against Nuclear War was established in 1957. It was subsequently renamed the Direct Action Committee Against Nuclear War. Until it was disbanded following the demonstrations at Holy Loch in May 1961 the Committee was the principal driving force behind the strategy of direct action within the British peace movement. It was reported in Richard Taylor, *Against The Bomb* (Oxford, 1988), that the papers remain in private hands.

DISABLEMENT INCOME GROUP Certain records of the Group, which exists to promote the financial welfare of the disabled, have been deposited at the Modern Records Centre, University of Warwick (ref. MSS 108). These include the Coventry branch minutes (1970–75) and some correspondence files (1968–75) and publications, and the papers of National Executive member Dr Frank Reid, which largely comprise minutes, agendas and correspondence.

DONOVAN COMMITTEE ON TRADE UNIONS AND EMPLOYERS' ASSOCIATIONS The papers, which cover the period 1965–68, have been deposited at Nuffield College, Oxford.

E

EDUCATION AID SOCIETY The Society was founded in 1896 to support the cases of poor students of exceptional academic ability and to provide loans for their education in professional or artistic pursuits. A collection of papers has been deposited in the Hartley Library, University of Southampton (ref. MS 135). A list is available (NRA 13581). The bulk of the collection is pre-war in date, but among the post-war papers there are ledgers, 1938–50; files of applications, 1939–51; a copy of the Forty Third Report of 1947/48, and a series of correspondence, 1939–64.

EDUCATIONAL INSTITUTE OF SCOTLAND The Institute was founded in 1847 by Leonard Schmitz to promote 'sound learning' in Scotland and is now the oldest teachers' institute in the world. The papers for the period up to 1973 have been deposited in the Scottish Record Office (ref. GD 342) and a list is available to the collection (NRA 18885; NRA(S) 969).

The archive is comprehensive and includes minute books (incorporating reports of proceedings of the AGM), 1847–1973; lists of members, 1920–51 and 1966–69; the correspondence files of the Parliamentary Committee on the general elections of 1951 and 1955; Salaries Committee files, 1952–55; minutes of the Joint Committee on Religious Education, 1941–56; minutes of the Joint Advisory Committee with the National Union of Teachers, 1939–49; minutes of the Central Advisory Committee on Commerce, 1934–63; proceedings of the Ministry of Labour Juvenile Employment Committee, 1937–47; minutes of the National Committee on the Training of Teachers Central Executive Committee, 1920–1959, and its reports, 1944–52; and minutes of the Scottish Committee for the Training of Teachers, 1961–67.

Papers of a subsequent date are retained by the Institute itself and enquiries concerning this material should be directed to the General Secretary. The collection includes some duplicates of earlier records now at the SRO.

EIGHTY CLUB Founded in 1880, shortly before the general election of that year, the Club worked to promote Liberal education and to stimulate Liberal organisation. By the 1960s its influence had declined and reorganisation of the Party (particularly the development of the Party headquarters) lessened its importance. Despite several attempts to re-found the Club in the period 1965–67 it was decided to wind it up, a process which was completed by 1978. The name of the Eighty Club is now preserved in the annual lecture organised by the Association of Liberal Democrat Lawyers.

In 1989 a collection of papers was deposited in the Bodleian Library, and researchers should direct further enquiries concerning the records to the Keeper of Western Manuscripts at the Bodleian.

EL SALVADOR SOLIDARITY CAMPAIGN Papers covering the period 1980–87 were presented in 1989 to the Brynmor Jones Library, University of Hull, by Colin Creighton of the Department of Sociology and Social Anthropology. The classmark of the collection is DX/185/8.

ELECTORAL REFORM SOCIETY OF GREAT BRITAIN AND IRELAND Founded in 1884 as the Proportional Representation Society, the association aims to promote the use of the single transferable vote form of proportional representation, especially in the United Kingdom, in parliamentary and local government elections. In 1959 the present name was adopted.

A very full set of records has been preserved. These include a complete run of minute books, a great deal of uncatalogued correspondence (with members of the Society) on elections and other matters, reports, submissions to Parliament, press-cuttings and pamphlet material. The House of Lords has microfilms of certain of the more important material. Enquiries should be addressed to the Secretary. It should be noted that the Society also has papers of individuals associated with electoral reform (e.g. Dr J.F.S. Ross) as well as significant non-manuscript material.

ELECTRICAL, ELECTRONIC, TELECOMMUNICATIONS AND PLUMBING UNION
In 1992 the EETPU merged with the Amalgamated Engineering Union to form the Amalgamated Engineering and Electricians Union (AEEU). Owing to the recent nature of this merger, the two constituent parts of the AEEU are treated under separate main headings in this Guide.

The original Electrical Trades Union was formed in 1889. In 1968, following several takeovers of smaller unions, it merged with the Plumbing Trades Union (originally founded in 1865 and known by the name of PTU since 1946). Upon this last amalgamation the above title was adopted. The EETPU was expelled from the TUC in 1988 for refusing to comply with Congress' instructions concerning recruitment of members, at which point a number of members withdrew to form a new association, the Electrical and Plumbing Industries Union (EPIU). The EETPU was foremost during the 1980s in reaching single-union, no-strike agreements with employers.

An extensive archive of ETU papers has now been placed in the Modern Records Centre, University of Warwick (ref. MSS 387). The deposit includes minutes, circulars etc. The Modern Records Centre, also holds extensive records of the United Operative Plumbers' Association. It also has a collection (ref. MSS 137) of the papers of Sir Leslie Cannon (1920–70), sometime General President of the ETU, which mainly relates to the campaign against the Communist leadership of the union. A list is available (NRA 29717).

EMPLOYMENT INSTITUTE
The Employment Institute was established in 1985 with the objective of carrying out research into employment and labour market policy. It publishes a series of special reports and a regular bulletin, the monthly *Economic Report*. The Institute has retained its own records, which may be available to researchers upon written application to the Director. The papers consist of the minutes of the Executive Committee and of the AGM since 1987; copies of the Annual Report and accounts; working papers referring to individual published studies; and certain correspondence held in rough files.

ENGINEERING EMPLOYERS' FEDERATION
Founded in 1896, the Federation exists to promote the employer's right to manage and to further industrial relations in the engineering industry by establishing a negotiated code of wages and conditions and assisting in the settlement of disputes. Furthermore it seeks to help its member firms by lobbying government and by advising on training, safety and other issues related to industrial development. The Federation's history is recounted in E. Wigham, *The Power To Manage* (London: Macmillan, 1973).

The main records of the Federation have been deposited at the Modern Records Centre, University of Warwick (ref. MSS 237) and are described in *Information Leaflet* No. 7 (1982). More recent records have now been deposited. The records of the Scottish Engineering Employers' Federation for *c.* 1912–72 are now in Strathclyde Regional Archives.

The Warwick records consist of the minutes of the principal committees of the Federation (e.g. Executive/Management Board, Parliamentary, Policy etc.) for the period 1896–1950; two series of minutes of negotiating conferences with trades unions, 1919–74, and the verbatim minutes of the Central and Special Conferences, 1951–74; a large microfilmed series of subject and case files (including financial and membership records) for 1899–1959 with an index, and an original format series of subject files, 1897–1947; case registers, 1892–1950; records of national ballots by member firms, 1918–53; assorted publications, 1898–1961; national agreements, 1894–1947, and wage statistics, 1862–1965 (with more general workforce statistics for 1910–50).

The Modern Records Centre also has an important collection of area Federation records, principally those of the Engineering Employers' East Midlands Association (EEEMA), which was established in

1968 by the amalgamation of the Derby, Leicester, Lincoln and Nottingham district organisations (ref. MSS 288). A list is available to this (NRA 31486). The papers include the minutes of the constitutents for the following periods: Derby, 1923–69; Leicester, 1896–1968; Lincoln, 1947–59, 1968–72, and Nottingham, 1897–1968, 1948–72, and a series of files on intra-company negotiations covering the late 1960s to early 1980s.

In addition the collection contains records of certain other constituent organisations. For the post-war period these papers comprise the minutes of the Bridgebuilding and Constructional Engineering Employers Area Committee for the East Midlands, 1927–73, and the circulars, 1939–65, and other records, 1911–65, of the Federated Admiralty Contractors. A deposit by the West Midlands Association (MSS 265) includes Birmingham and District and Coventry and District minutes and other West Midlands material.

ENGLISH-SPEAKING UNION OF THE COMMONWEALTH   Originally established in 1918, the English-Speaking Union obtained a Royal Charter in 1957. It is an independent, non-political body which aims to promote mutual trust and friendship between the English-speaking peoples of the world, and traditionally between the British Commonwealth and the United States.

The ESU has retained the minutes of a variety of committees dating back to 1918, including the Board of Governors' meetings, and committees concerned with educational scholarships and conference reports. Little material exists for the pre-war period but there is a substantial amount from the 1940s and 1950s onwards. Also held in the collection are annual reports, tapes and films of speeches and events, photographs, copies of ESU periodicals dating back to the early 1920s and copies of reports of scholars who travelled on exchange programmes to the USA. A limited amount of correspondence has also been kept. Further enquiries should be directed to the Librarian.

EQUAL PAY CAMPAIGN COMMITTEE   This body was founded by the British Federation of Business and Professional Women and the National Association of Women Civil Servants in 1944 to press for equal pay within government service. On the achievement of its aims in 1956, the Committee was wound up and the records were deposited in the Fawcett Library (now the Women's Library). A list is available for the collection (NRA 20625). Deposited papers include the minutes and agendas of the Executive Committee, 1944–56, and various papers of its subcommittees for the period 1947–56. There are also a substantial series of files of correspondence, principally with government departments and political parties; finance files and accounts, 1949–56, and a pamphlet collection.

EUROPEAN MOVEMENT   The United Kingdom Council of the European Movement was established in July 1948 under the chairmanship of the Liberal peer Lord Layton, in succession to Winston Churchill's United Europe Movement. The function of the Council was to coordinate the activities of British organisations, or British sections of international organisations, working for the cause of European unity. In 1969 the United Kingdom Council merged with a sister organisation, Britain in Europe (q.v.). It was subsequently reorganised during the period 1987–90: the National Council was abolished and the Executive Committee became the Management Board. Reference should also be made to the entry in this Guide for the Federal Union.

The British section retains its own papers at its offices. The earliest material dates from 1959, previous records having been lost during office moves in 1972 and 1987. An incomplete set of the minutes of the Executive Committee survives for the period since 1948, but no Annual Report is published and only the most recent correspondence has been retained at the offices, along with an incomplete set of the published pamphlet series Facts. Audited accounts from the mid-1950s are available at Companies House, but there is nothing at the offices of an earlier date than 1980. Persons wishing to consult the records should apply in writing to the Assistant Director.

Researchers should also be aware that an archive of international papers of the European Movement has now been deposited at the library of the Collège d'Europe, Bruges, Belgium. The collection includes documents emanating from the London International Secretariat (1947–50) and the Secretariat International, Paris (1948–50), as well as assorted documents of committees, member associations and congresses.

EUROPEAN NUCLEAR DISARMAMENT (END) It is expected that the papers will be deposited in the LSE Library. Enquiries should be directed to the Archivist.

EUROPEAN TRADE UNION CONFEDERATION (ETUC) There are papers in the International Institute of Social History, Amsterdam. A published list and electronic guide are available.

EUROPEAN UNION OF FEDERALISTS Copies of the committee minutes, correspondence and other records for the period 1946–55 are to be found in the papers of Liberal activist Miss F.L. Josephy at the LSE Library. In addition, within this collection there is material from other related organisations such as the European Movement Congress (UK), the Europa Union Congress and also the International Executive Bureau.

F

FABIAN COLONIAL BUREAU The Fabian Colonial Bureau was formed in October 1940 as a special department of the Fabian Society. It became an important organ for research, information and policy proposals, particularly during the period of Labour government, 1945–51. During the later part of the 1950s, with the growth of the colonial independence movement, its influence waned somewhat and in 1963, to avoid overlapping of interest, the Bureau merged with the Fabian International Bureau.

The records of the Bureau covering the whole period of its independent existence have been deposited at BLCAS (Rhodes House Library), Oxford. The collection consists of a large correspondence, committee papers, files on various countries, and publications, sorted into some 180 boxes. The collection is described in *Sources, 1900–51*, vol. I, pp. 94–95. Additional material connected with the work of the Bureau occurs in two other collections in Rhodes House Library: the papers of Arthur Creech Jones and of C.W.W. Greenidge.

FABIAN SOCIETY Founded in 1884 as a socialist society, the Fabian Society has played a central role in left-wing politics, most particularly in the first half of the 20th century. The Society now concentrates on the sponsoring and publishing of individual research on matters of political and social importance.

The older records, formerly in Nuffield College, Oxford, have now been transferred to the LSE Library (ref. M1823). The collection, which can be accessed electronically, is open subject to a 30-year rule.

FAMILY CARE The archive of the organisation, founded in 1911 as the National Vigilance Association for Scotland, is now deposited in the National Library of Scotland (ref. Acc 11191).

FAMILY PLANNING ASSOCIATION The FPA was founded as the National Birth Control Council in 1930. It became the National Birth Control Association in 1931 and was joined by several other organisations established since 1924 to provide birth control advice for married women. In 1939 it adopted its present title.

The records of the FPA are now in the Contemporary Medical Archives Centre of the Wellcome Institute (ref. SA/FPA). They comprise over 600 boxes and 11 volumes and include the minutes of the National Council, Executive and other committees and subcommittees from 1930 to date; annual reports; accounts and other financial records (incomplete), and correspondence with individuals, government departments and other organisations. Full sets of publications to date and press-cuttings for the period up to 1975 are deposited in the CMAC, and further cuttings up to 1983 are held at the David Owen Centre for Population Growth Studies, University College, Cardiff. Subject files at the CMAC include papers relating to organisation and supplies for clinics and branches, as well as their records of meetings and the annual returns from clinics, branches and federations *c.* 1932–75; and papers concerning contraceptive testing (including those of the Council for Investigation of Fertility Control) and early contraceptive trials, 1931–70.

The archives include a large set of papers of the North Kensington Women's Welfare Clinic (established by the Society for Provision of Birth Control Clinics, which merged with the NBCA in 1938), 1924–67, and of its first superintendent, Margery Spring Rice, 1921–65. There are also available the papers of Caspar Brook, director of the FPA, for 1968–73. The archive is in two sections: 1930–75, which with the exception of a limited number of documents is open to researchers, and 1975–91, which is closed. Readers wishing to use the FPA collection should apply in advance to the Archivist of the CMAC.

The papers of the Family Planning Association (Scotland) are in Glasgow University Archives. A list is available (NRA 36242).

The papers of the Northern Ireland Family Planning Association of Belfast, which was established in 1965, have been deposited in the Public Record Office of Northern Ireland (ref. D3543). They include the articles of association, 1965; minutes of the executive committee and AGMs, 1965–71; annual reports and accounts, 1966–76; correspondence with the Northern Ireland Hospitals Authority and other statutory bodies, 1965–76, and correspondence, reports, accounts, etc. concerning family planning clinics, 1965–75.

FAMILY POLICY STUDIES CENTRE The Family Policy Studies Centre was established in 1983 as a successor to the Study Commission on the Family. It is an independent research trust with charitable status, dedicated to the study of the impact of demographic trends and of public policy upon the family. The Centre incorporates Family Forum.

Papers have been retained at the Centre's offices. They include minutes of the Governing Council, financial records, and files of the most important correspondence organised by subject. No annual report is produced but the Centre has a well-established publications programme of its research findings; copies of such material are available in the Library, which may be visited by appointment. Persons wishing for access to the papers must seek the written permission of the Director.

FAMILY WELFARE ASSOCIATION Formed in 1869 as the Charity Organisation Society, the present name was adopted in 1946. The association aims to preserve and protect the good health (in particular the mental health) of families, individuals and groups within the community. The work of the association includes provision of a casework service, the promotion of education and research, the creation and administration of charitable trust funds, and the establishment, support or assistance of charitable centres for giving advice and guidance. The association publishes annually the *Guide to the Social Services* and the *Charities Digest*.

The main archive has been deposited with the London Metropolitan Archives. A list is available (NRA 28510). The papers have been arranged by the origin of their deposit, i.e. the central office and the several area offices. The papers include Council and committee minutes and agendas; reports of Council and district committees, 1871–1961; casework files; press-cuttings and other printed material, and local area records.

A sixty-year rule applies to this material, except for publications such as annual reports, which are open.

FAMILY AND YOUTH CONCERN A national organisation without political or religious affiliation, Family and Youth Concern has since its formation in 1971 campaigned to advance public education in matters of family and personal welfare. It sponsors and publishes research into the social and medical consequences of the dissolution of families. The papers of the organisation have been retained at its offices. All classes of material are included, although correspondence is generally kept for the preceding six years only. Researchers should apply in writing to the Director.

FAWCETT LIBRARY *See* **WOMEN'S LIBRARY**.

FAWCETT SOCIETY A movement for social and political equality for women, the Society was founded as the London Society for Women's Suffrage in 1867. It was renamed the Central Society for Women's Suffrage in 1900; the London Society (again) seven years later; the London Society for Women's Service in 1919 (following the achievement of partial female suffrage), and then took the title of the London and National Society for Women's Service in 1926. In 1953 it adopted its present name in honour of Dame Millicent Fawcett (1847–1929).

The archive of the Society has been deposited in the Women's Library (q.v.). Lists are available to the papers (NRA 20625, 33544). Surviving material includes Executive Committee minutes, 1903–80; copies of the annual report, 1945–52; ledgers and cashbooks, 1930s–60s; conference papers for 1966, 1967 and 1969, and 21 boxes of correspondence subject files, largely of the 1950s–70s.

FEDERAL UNION Formed in 1938, the organisation aims for a regional Federal Union to include Great Britain, as an intermediary step towards full world government. The Research Institute of the Union, under the chairmanship of Sir William Beveridge, set out to explore the technical difficulties and, since these were considerable, it grew into a semi-autonomous body. The Federal Educational and Research Trust (later the Trust for Education and Research) was set up after World War II as a separate entity.

The records of both organisations, 1938–73, were formerly deposited at the University of Sussex Library but were transferred to the LSE Library in 1984 (ref. M1703 and M1722). A list is available (NRA 20019). The collection is supplemented by the personal papers of R.W.G. Mackay, MP, 1947–64. The collection consists of files on internal central and regional administration; relations with other organisations; records of conferences, seminars and other activities; publications and research papers; press-cuttings, and records of the London and Hendon branches. In addition to documenting the debate on federalism, the collection also includes material on other issues such as the revision of the UN charter, international monetary reform, disarmament and Britain's entry into the EC.

Further records of the Union and the Trust were placed in the LSE Library in 1998 (ref. M1902). Reference should also be made to the Cavanagh deposit in the Modern Records Centre, University of Warwick (ref. MSS 350).

FEDERATION OF CATHOLIC PRIESTS Six boxes of papers have been placed in Pusey House, Oxford.

FEDERATION OF COMMONWEALTH CHAMBERS OF COMMERCE The records, 1911–74, have been deposited in the Guildhall Library, London. A list is available (NRA 27304).

FEDERATION OF JEWISH RELIEF ORGANISATIONS The Federation was founded in 1919 and is an umbrella group for organisations which aid Jewish victims of war and persecution.

Ten boxes of correspondence and papers, 1945–54, are in the Anglo-Jewish Archives at the Hartley Library, University of Southampton (ref. MSS 183).

They concern donations and supply of food, clothing and other items to Israel and European countries.

Researchers should note that the papers of Rabbi Solomon Schonfeld, also deposited in the Anglo-Jewish Archives, contain correspondence with the Federation, 1945–70 (ref. MSS 198).

FEDERATION OF MASTER BUILDERS The largest trade association in the building industry, the Federation of Master Builders was originally established in 1943 in order to assist building firms comply with regulations concerning the reconstruction of buildings damaged during the war. Today the Federation, which has 10 regional offices throughout the UK, represents its members' interests before government and local authorities and provides an information service regarding statutory and industrial regulations. The FMB is the employers' representative on the Building and Allied Trades Joint Industrial Council and is a member of the European Builders Confederation.

The records of the FMB are retained at its head office. Its minutes, including those of the National Council and the various executive committees, are closed. Correspondence is kept for the past two years only. The Annual Report and accounts are incorporated in the August issue of the monthly journal *Masterbuilder*, and the AGM report in the October issue. Researchers seeking access to the papers should apply to the Research Executive at the head office.

FEDERATION OF TRADE UNIONS OF SALT-WORKERS, ALKALI WORKERS, MECHANICS AND GENERAL LABOURERS The Federation was effectively a regional organisation and its records, now deposited in the Cheshire Record Office (ref. LOU 6), cover its activities in Cheshire, Worcestershire, South Durham and North Yorkshire, in which counties the Annual General and Representative Meetings were held in turn. The papers include a minute book covering the period 1933–64. A list is available for the collection (NRA 33437).

FEDERATION OF WOMEN ZIONISTS OF GREAT BRITAIN The papers were placed in London Metropolitan Archives in 1988. A list is available (NRA 42200). The archives consist mainly of minutes (and some minutes of affiliated groups) with some material on Rebecca Sieff and the early history of the organisation.

FINANCE AND LEASING ASSOCIATION The Finance and Leasing Association was formed in January 1992 by the merger of the Finance Houses Association (founded in 1945) and the Equipment Leasing Association (formed 1971). The FLA is the major UK representative body for the finance and leasing industry; its members are companies offering business finance and leasing, consumer credit and motor finance. Annual reports of both predecessor organisations were published from 1972 onwards. The FLA's committee minutes are private, but requests for access from researchers would be considered on an individual basis. Further enquiries should be directed to the Public Relations Secretary.

FIRE BRIGADES UNION Founded in 1913 as the Fireman's Trade Union, the FBU adopted its present name in 1918. Its membership comprises some 90 per cent of uniformed personnel in the 68 brigades in the country. An official history of the union, *Forged in Fire*, edited by Victor Bailey, was published by Lawrence and Wishart in 1992.

Many of the union's records were destroyed by enemy action during World War II and by a fire at its head office during the subsequent decade. However, some more recent material has been deposited at the Modern Records Centre, University of Warwick (ref. MSS 346). A list is available (NRA 40314). The deposit consists mainly of printed series; reports to and proceedings of annual conferences, bound volumes of the *Firefighter* and publications, also some collected material. It retains minutes at its head office. Subsequent deposits have included publications, 1960s–90s, officers' speeches, 1995–98, a correspondence file on disarmament, 1987–88, the reminiscences of John Horner as General Secretary, files on the Merseyside dispute etc.

FOOD AND DRINK FEDERATION The Federation was formed in 1986 by the merger of the Food Manufacturers' Federation (FMF) and the Food and Drink Industries Council (FDIC). The FMF had been founded in 1913 as the Confectionery and Preserved Food Manufacturers' Federation,

to represent UK food manufacturers; it adopted its present name in 1947.

The Food and Drink Federation retains the archive of the Food Manufacturers' Federation in addition to its own records. These include minute books of the Executive Committee and Council of the FMF since 1913, as well as those of the present Federation, and a number of minute books relating to member organisations (in certain cases complete from the time of their formation). In addition there is a virtually complete set of the annual reports and statistics of the FMF and FDF, and copies of the monthly bulletin, which was produced by the FMF from 1914 onwards. Persons wishing for access to the papers should apply to the Librarian. Some sections of the collection are stored in other sites and therefore it is imperative that as much notice as possible must be given.

FOOTBALL ASSOCIATION The Association has retained a comprehensive archive, consisting of minutes from 1870 onwards and a photographic collection beginning in 1901 (e.g. team pictures, portraits, facilities etc.). The Association also maintains a library containing books and magazines on all aspects of the game dating back to the early 19th century and a historical collection of programmes. Access to the material is restricted and those wishing to consult the papers should apply in advance to the Association.

FRANCO-BRITISH SOCIETY Founded in 1924 the Society is a registered charity for the encouragement of better relations and mutual understanding between Great Britain and France. It has retained certain of its own papers, including committee minutes from 1944, copies of the newsletter from 1947 (originally entitled the *Franco-British Society Magazine* and subsequently the *Journal*) and correspondence files arranged by subject for the period of the 1980s. Financial records are retained for the statutory period only. Persons wishing to consult the papers should apply to the Executive Secretary.

FREE CHURCH FEDERAL COUNCIL OF ENGLAND AND WALES This was established in 1940 by the amalgamation of the National Council of Evangelical Free Churches (1896) and the Federal

Council of the Evangelical Free Churches of England (1919). Also incorporated in the organisation is the National Free Church Women's Council. The FCFC represents the interests of twelve English and Welsh denominations, including the Baptist Union, the Methodist Church and the United Reformed Church. The Council enables the Free Churches to act together in matters affecting the responsibilities and rights of the Federated Churches.

The records of the Council have now been deposited in Dr Williams' Library, London. They include minute books and annual reports. A list of the material can be consulted at the library.

Many records relevant to the history of the Free Churches have been deposited in London Metropolitan Archives. Those of the Liberation Society and the National Education Association are of particular interest. Other material includes deposits made by the Congregational and Methodist churches and the FCFC itself. These records are described in an article, by Alison C. Reeve, 'Free Church Records and the GLRO', *Free Church Chronicle*, December 1973.

FRIENDS OF THE EARTH This environmental pressure group was established in 1971. It is understood that the organisation retains its papers.

FRIENDS OF REUNION The Friends of Reunion was founded in 1933, following the Lausanne Conference of 1927 and the Lambeth Conference of 1930. The Society's members included both clergy and laity and it aimed to promote 'organic unity' within the Church, initially among non-Roman Catholics. The papers have been deposited at Lambeth Palace Library (ref. MSS 3225–28) and incorporate minutes of the Executive Committee and the Council, 1933–69; miscellaneous papers, 1936–76 (including lists of officers); a list of members of 1968; records of the Annual Conference for the period 1936–64, and correspondence, 1948–70, which covers among other subjects negotiations with other ecumenical bodies. The collection includes a copy of *The Friends of Reunion – An Historical Survey* (1976), by the sometime Secretary, the Revd Robert Jeffery.

FURNITURE, TIMBER AND ALLIED TRADES UNION The union, the major national body in the furniture and upholstery trade, was formed in 1971 by the merger of the Amalgamated Society of Woodcutting Machinists (founded 1866) and the National Union of Furniture Trades Operatives (itself a result of the amalgamation in 1947 of the National Amalgamated Furnishing Trades Association and the Amalgamated Union of Upholsterers). In the period since 1971, the National Union of Musical Instrument Makers, the National Union of Funeral Service Operatives and the National Society of Brushmakers and General Workers have all joined the FTAT.

The records of the union, which became part of the GMB in 1994, have been placed in the Working Class Movement Library. Some duplicate material is in the Modern Records Centre, University of Warwick (ref. MSS 192).

G

GALTON INSTITUTE The Galton Institute derives from the Eugenics Education Society, founded in 1907. The term 'eugenics' had been coined by the biologist Sir Frederick Galton, who became the Honorary President of the Society in 1908. The word 'Education' was dropped from the title in 1926 and the present name adopted in 1988. The Institute supports interdisciplinary research into the biological, genetic, social and cultural factors relating to human reproduction, development and welfare.

The Institute retains the minutes of its Council Meetings and copies of the Annual Report; all other papers have been deposited in the Contemporary Medical Archives Centre of the Wellcome Institute. The deposited material includes series of committee minutes, correspondence files, and a large collection of press-cutting albums dating back to 1907, which provide an important guide to the Institute's activities. The albums are organised chronologically and by subject; the subjects covered include population, genetics, psychology, national health, birth rate, birth control, sterilisation, etc. The Eugenics Society published a journal, *Eugenics Review*, in the period 1908–68, at which point it was superseded both by the *Journal of Bio-social Science*, published by the autonomous Galton Foundation, and by a quarterly *Bulletin* published by the Society. The bulk of the material at the CMAC covers the period up until the 1960s. A list is available (NRA 24905), as is an article by Lesley Hall on the Institute's archive and history, published in *Medical History*, vol. 34 (1990). The deposited papers may be consulted by bona fide researchers who have first obtained the permission of the General Secretary.

GCHQ CAMPAIGN The GCHQ campaign began in 1984 when unions were banned from the intelligence gathering centre at Cheltenham. The issue rapidly became one of the most important trade union issues of the 1980s. The campaign ended in 1997 with the partial restoration of trade union rights to GCHQ workers. Mike Grindley and Brian Johnson, two of the leaders of the campaign, have deposited its papers at the Modern Records Centre, University of Warwick (ref. MSS 384). A list is available (NRA 42684). The deposit includes minutes of members' meetings, 1984–97; National Co-ordinating Committee minutes, 1987, etc.

GEMMA GEMMA is a national lesbian support group which was formed in 1976 to lessen the isolation of disabled lesbians. It has retained its papers, which consist of correspondence for a preceding three-year period and financial records since 1980. Copies of GEMMA's newsletter are regularly deposited at the Lesbian Archive and Information Centre. Researchers should also be aware that material relating to GEMMA, 1977–83, forms part of the Hall-Carpenter Archive (q.v.) at the LSE Library.

GENERAL DENTAL COUNCIL The Council was established by legislation in 1956 as the successor to the Dental Board of the United Kingdom, set up under the General Medical Council in 1921. Its principal statutory functions are to maintain a register of those legally qualified to practise dentistry in the UK; to promote high standards of professional conduct and education, and to maintain professional discipline.

Since its inception the Council has kept bound minutes of its committees and sub-committees, which remain unpublished except for the minutes of the six monthly meetings of the Council and of its Professional Conduct Committee, which are published annually. There is no annual report. Financial records are retained for at least ten years, and the annual accounts are included with the published minutes and tabled before Parliament. Correspondence is organised by subject, but is not retained for more than the past ten years. All the above records are available at the Council's offices upon application to the Registrar. The Council is prepared to consider requests for access but not to records of the more recent past.

GENERAL, MUNICIPAL, BOILERMAKERS' AND ALLIED TRADES UNION The General, Municipal, Boilermakers' and Allied Trades Union, the second largest union in the UK, was formed in 1982 by the amalgamation of the General and Municipal Workers' Union (GMWU) and the Amalgamated Society of Boilermakers, Shipwrights, Blacksmiths and Structural Workers (ASB). Three years later it was joined by the Amalgamated Textile Workers' Union, and in 1989 by APEX (Association of Professional, Executive, Clerical and Computer Staff). The following year the National Union of Tailors and Garment Workers (NUTGW) transferred its engagements as well. The short title of the union – GMB – was formally adopted in 1987 to replace the less convenient acronym GMBATU, which had come into use after the 1982 merger.

Researchers should refer to *Sources, 1900–51*, vols. I and VI for a fuller description of the predecessor organisations of the GMB. Publications relevant to the history of the union include H.A. Clegg, *General Union in a Changing Society* (Oxford, 1964) and H.A. Turner, *Trade Union Growth, Structure and Policy* (London, 1962).

The GMB's main archive has been retained at its national training college in Manchester. Additionally, a significant amount of papers has been deposited at the Working Class Movement Library in Salford, the Lancashire Record Office (for the textile unions) and the Modern Records Centre, University of Warwick (ref. MSS 192). The latter includes material originating with the present union, rather than its predecessors, namely files relating to the water industry dispute of 1982–83 (e.g. daily progress reports, press releases, circulars, minutes, and correspondence). Other collections of papers are described below according to the originating union.

AMALGAMATED SOCIETY OF BOILERMAKERS, SHIPWRIGHTS, BLACKSMITHS AND STRUCTURAL WORKERS

The union was created in 1966 by the amalgamation of the Shipwrights' Union; the Associated Blacksmiths, Forge and Smithy Workers' Society, and the Boilermakers' Society. A significant collection of papers has been deposited at the Modern Records Centre. The post-war material in this holding includes a bound series of monthly and annual reports, and some ephemera and General Secretary's circular letters, for 1927–54, 1956–58, 1960–61, 1963, 1965–68 and 1971–73; the membership register for 1873–1948; death benefit lists for 1949–55, and a register of branch secretaries covering the 1960s. Papers emanating specifically from the Associated Blacksmiths comprise quarterly reports, 1927–60; financial reports, 1960–61, rule books, 1857–1968; correspondence files and some branch records. Further papers have been deposited at the Working Class Movement Library, namely Executive Committee minutes, letter books, circulars, annual reports and conference reports for the period 1912–60. A list is available (NRA 31932). The Library also holds the records of the South Wales District for 1915–81.

AMALGAMATED TEXTILE WORKERS' UNION

Assorted publications for 1976–79 have been deposited at the Modern Records Centre. Records of the Southern Area of the Union for 1886–1975 (including the minutes for 1944–66 and a series of annual reports) are with Tameside Archive Service (ref. TU/3).

AMALGAMATED WEAVERS' ASSOCIATION

The main archive of the union, in 24 volumes and covering the period 1918 to 1976, has been deposited in the Working Class Movement Library. A list is available (NRA 31932). The records include the Central Committee and Executive Committee minutes. An incomplete series of annual reports, 1908–75, and a collection of assorted wage agreements and piece-rate lists has also been deposited at the Modern Records Centre, and minutes, agendas and correspondence of *c.* 1890–1967 may be found in Lancashire Record Office (ref. DDX 1123).

APEX

The union was established in 1890 as the National Union of Clerks. The words 'and Administrative Workers' were added to the title in 1920, and in 1940 it adopted the name Clerical and Administrative Workers' Union to become the Association of Professional, Executive, Clerical and Company Staff in 1972. A collection of papers is deposited at the Modern Records Centre including conference reports, 1947–88 (incomplete); annual reports 1950–69; copies of the Presidential addresses, 1948–87; and runs of several of the union's periodicals: *The Clerk*, 1943–74, 1985–89; *Engineering Clerk*, 1955–60, etc.

GENERAL AND MUNICIPAL WORKERS' UNION

The forerunner of the GMB was established in 1934 by the amalgamation of three existing unions: the National Union of General Workers; the National Amalgamated Union of Labour, and the Municipal Employees' Association. This amalgamation produced the National Union of General and Municipal Workers (NUGMW), which subsequently adopted the title of the General and Municipal Workers' Union (GMWU) in 1979. The Modern Records Centre holds a series of the printed National Executive Committee minutes for 1947–53; an incomplete series of annual congress reports for 1950–77 and some subject files, including correspondence of the National Joint Industry Council for the Water Industry for 1970–80.

NATIONAL UNION OF TAILORS AND GARMENT WORKERS

The NUTGW was formed in 1932 by the amalgamation of the Amalgamated Society of Tailors and the Tailors' and Garment Workers' Union. In the post-war period the NUTGW did not experience any amalgamations until 1982 when it was joined by two minor unions, the Amalgamated Society of Journeymen Felt Hatters and Allied Workers (certain of whose earlier records are available in

the Local Studies Unit of Manchester Central Library), and the Amalgamated Felt Hat Trimmers', Woolformers' and Allied Workers' Association.

Certain papers of the NUTGW have been deposited in the Working Class Movement Library, including minutes of the Executive Board for 1933–52, 1955–61 and 1964–84; circulars to the Executive Board, 1936–60 and 1963–89; yearly reports and balance sheets of the Tailors and Garment Workers, Section, 1932–75, and the official journal *The Tailor and Garment Worker*, 1932–89. The Modern Records Centre holds an incomplete series of Executive Board minutes to 1964 and of circulars to branches etc. for 1937–89, and copies of *The Garment Worker*, 1928–38 and 1945–89. The papers of the Northern Ireland District of the union for the period 1884 to 1977, incorporating minutes of the Executive Board and committee minutes of the Belfast branch, have been deposited at the Public Record Office of Northern Ireland (ref. D1050/17). This material has not been catalogued and is therefore closed to researchers. One box of papers has also been deposited at the LSE (ref. Coll. Misc. 674). It includes papers of the Amalgamated Society of Tailors; the United Clothing Workers Union (a pre-war breakaway established by London members of the Tailors and Garment Workers, which was a rare revolutionary trade union formed in Britain, and affiliated to the Red International of Labour Unions), and the NUTGW itself, for which the only post-war material is a duplicated collection of rates of pay agreements, 1937–53. The Rollin papers at Warwick (MSS 240) include material on the London District.

NATIONAL UNION OF TEXTILE AND ALLIED WORKERS

The union was established in Rochdale in 1886. The Modern Records Centre has a collection of various reports and publications, including those of the Rochdale District for the period 1918–83.

PENWORKERS' FEDERATION

The surviving records of this small trade union, which transferred its engagements to the General and Municipal Workers' Union in 1974, have been deposited in the Modern Records Centre (ref. MSS

42). The collection includes minutes, 1918–54 and 1960–73; correspondence, 1968–73; and annual reports, 1936–73.

GERMAN EDUCATIONAL RECONSTRUCTION GROUP This organisation was founded by German and British academics who sought to rebuild and reform the German educational system after World War II. The Group's records have been deposited in the Institute of Education Library, University of London, and consist of 47 files, 1941–58, of correspondence, minutes, and reports. The collection is almost entirely post-war. A detailed list is available (NRA 20822).

GINGERBREAD Gingerbread is the leading association of self-help groups for one parent families. The national organisation, founded in 1970, exists to represent the interests of such families to the authorities and to provide an expert information and advice service for individual single parents. The papers, including minutes, publications and other papers, 1970–99, have been placed in the Women's Library, London Metropolitan University (ref. 5/GBN).

GIRL GUIDES ASSOCIATION The Association was founded in 1910 by Lord Baden-Powell to provide a female counterpart to the Boy Scouts. The national records are retained at the Commonwealth Headquarters. In addition local records are held by each Regional and County office. Not all the national material has been catalogued at present, but it is known to include committee minutes since 1910; annual and conference reports, 1916–90; unpublished research reports; financial records since foundation, and correspondence organised by person and subject. Subject files date from 1910 and cover such topics as training centres and historical events within the Girl Guides. Newspaper cuttings and log books of the Commonwealth Headquarters have also been retained. Enquiries should be addressed to the General Secretary at the Association's headquarters.

GRAPHICAL, PRINT AND MEDIA UNION This union was formed in 1991 by the merger of the National Graphical Association and SOGAT 82.

SOGAT 82 had itself been formed in 1982 by the merger of the previous SOGAT (itself established only in 1972) and NATSOPA. The records of SOGAT 82 have now been added to the GPMU deposit in the Modern Records Centre, University of Warwick (ref. MSS 39). The following outlines the position regarding the archives of most of the other predecessor unions:

SOGAT

The original SOGAT was formed in 1972. This was the name of the organisation known as the National Union of Printing, Bookbinding and Paper Workers until 1966. In that year the National Union amalgamated with the National Society of Operative Printers' Assistants to form the Society of Graphical and Allied Trades. This amalgamation was dissolved in December 1971 and the old NUPBW resumed its separate existence under its present title. For the early history of the NUPBW, see *Sources, 1900–51*, vol. 1, pp. 189, 246.

NATSOPA

For the background history of NATSOPA and a description of records which were believed to have been retained by NATSOPA, see *Sources, 1900–51*, vol. 1, p. 189.

NATIONAL GRAPHICAL ASSOCIATION

The NGA itself was founded in 1964 by the union of the previously independent Typographical Association and the London Typographical Society. It subsequently amalgamated with the Association of Correctors of the Press and the National Union of Press Telegraphists in 1985; the National Society of Electrotypers and Stereotypers in 1967, and the Amalgamated Society of Lithographic Printers and Auxiliaries in 1968. In 1979 the National Union of Wallcoverings, Decorative and Allied Trades (which itself resulted from the merger of the Wallcoverings Staff Association and the Wallpaper Workers' Union) was absorbed into the NGA. Finally, in 1982, after several attempts there was a merger with the Society of Lithographic Artists, Designers, Engravers and Process Workers (SLADE).

Most records of the NGA, its London Region and

its predecessor organisations have been deposited in the Modern Records Centre, University of Warwick. A list is available (NRA 24668).

Among records of predecessor unions which are lodged at the Modern Records Centre are:

Amalgamated Society of Lithographic Printers and Auxiliaries
Association of Correctors of the Press
London Typographical Society
National Union of Wallcoverings, Decorative and Allied Trades
Society of Lithographic Artists, Designers, Engravers and Process Workers
Typographical Association

Elsewhere, the records of the National Society of Electrotypers and Stereotypers (mainly minutes of the executive and national council) are in Cambridge University Library. The papers of the Belfast Typographical Society are at the Public Record Office of Northern Ireland (ref. D1050/18).

GREAT BRITAIN-CHINA CENTRE The Centre, which exists to promote cultural, economic, and academic links with China, was founded in 1974 as the successor to the Great Britain-China Committee. It is an independent organisation offering advice to individuals and organisations wishing to establish relations with China, and it maintains a reference and lending library and information service.

The Centre retains existing papers at its offices. These consist of minutes of the Executive Committee to date (and those of the preceding Great Britain-China Committee); annual reports since 1974/75; the newsletter *Britain-China*, published since autumn 1974; correspondence files arranged by originator and subject, and copies of any publicity material. Financial records are not available. The archive is not yet presently organised for research and, in particular, access to correspondence is unlikely. The Centre receives a grant-in-aid from the Foreign Office, whose permission is necessary for any examination of the Executive Committee minutes; researchers should therefore understand that requests for access will be forwarded to the Foreign Office. Further enquiries should be directed to the Librarian.

GREAT BRITAIN-RUSSIA CENTRE (SCOTLAND) The records for the period 1963–2001 have been placed in the National Library of Scotland (ref. Acc 12142).

GREEN ALLIANCE The Green Alliance was founded in 1979 to advocate the inclusion of environmental considerations in governmental and industrial policymaking, and to increase public awareness of the implications of such decisions for the environment.

Existing records have been retained at the premises of the Alliance. These consist of the minutes of the Executive Committee and AGM minutes; annual reports, 1983, 1987–89; a number of published reports on environmental questions; cash books; in-coming correspondence for the previous year, and subject files. Persons wishing to study the records should apply to the Director.

GREEN PARTY Founded in 1973 as the People's Party, becoming the Ecology Party in 1975, the party adopted its present name in September 1985. The party campaigns to raise public consciousness about environmental and peace issues and promote an ecological or 'green' perspective on economic matters. The party's origins and work are described in Sara Parkin's *Green Parties: An International Guide* (London 1988).

It is understood that a substantial archive has been placed in the University of Teesside. No further details are available. Some records of the Scottish Green Party, including minutes, policy papers etc. for the period 1977–2002 are reported in the National Library of Scotland (ref. Acc 12144). Other Scottish Green records, 1987–92, are reported deposited in the University of Bristol (ref. DM 1796).

GREENPEACE Greenpeace was founded in 1971 to protect the environment through peaceful direct action on land and sea. It has been prominent in its efforts to prevent whaling, nuclear power, and industrial pollution. There is no central archive of material and every unit within the organisation keeps its own records. The records of the campaign units consist mainly of reports, and those of the marketing units are largely composed of public appeals. Researchers with specific enquiries should address them to Greenpeace at its offices.

The main archive of Greenpeace International was deposited in the International Institute of Social History, Amsterdam, in 2005.

GUARDIAN Founded in 1821 as the *Manchester Guardian*, the newspaper changed its name to its present form in 1959.

The main archives of the *Guardian*, the *Manchester Evening News* and their parent company – the Manchester Guardian and Evening News Ltd – have been deposited with the John Rylands University of Manchester Library. The archives include commercial records and correspondence, accounts, minutes of meetings and editorial records, together with bound volumes of both newspapers and of the *Evening Chronicle*. The bulk of records pertaining to the *Guardian* are commercial and financial but there is also a large correspondence with staff journalists, outside contributors and other individuals connected with the newspaper. A list of the earlier material is available (NRA 18162). Handlists of the more recent material are available at the John Rylands Library. Researchers should also note that the LSE Library has transcripts of interviews conducted by Alastair Hetherington, editor of the *Guardian*, 1956–75.

H

HALDANE SOCIETY The Society was founded in 1929 by a group of left-wing lawyers and served as the UK affiliate of the International Association of Democratic Lawyers. It was later taken over by Communist sympathisers, which in 1949 prompted the Labour Party members to secede and form the Society of Labour Lawyers. The latter's papers have been deposited at the LSE Library and contain some records pertaining to the Haldane Society.

HALL-CARPENTER ARCHIVE The Hall-Carpenter Archive, which is named in honour of the lesbian novelist Radclyffe Hall and Edward Carpenter, the writer on social and sexual reform, exists to publicise and preserve the records and publications of gay organisations and individuals. It was founded in 1982 and transferred to the LSE Library in 1988. The Archive contains deposits from over 400 organisations, and priority is given to material from groups and individuals in the UK and the Republic of Ireland. The largest collections are those of the Albany Trust, the Campaign for Homosexual Equality and the Lesbian and Gay Christian Movement, each of which has a separate entry in this Guide. It should be noted that the Archive also contains papers emanating from a number of non-gay national organisations whose work brings them into contact with various issues of sexual reform; the Albany Trust is an example, as is the British Youth Council.

Material was collected systematically up until 1986, but the Archive remains an open-ended collection to which original depositors may have continued to add later records. Users should, however, be aware that subsequent papers may have been retained by the organisations themselves; certain major lesbian and gay bodies have never deposited records in the Hall-Carpenter Archive, e.g. OLGA (Organisation of Lesbian and Gay Activists) and the Stonewall Trust. More recent organisations not included in the list below may also have contacted the Archive about the possible deposit of papers; further details should be sought from the Archivist at the LSE Library. Prior to its transfer to the LSE, the Hall-Carpenter Archive initiated an oral history project, and the tapes and transcripts arising from this have been deposited with the National Sound Archive, where a handlist is available. The Hall-Carpenter Archive also holds extensive runs of gay and lesbian journals from the UK and overseas.

The following organisations which have deposited papers within the Archive may be broadly defined as being political in their scope. In most cases the material collected between the given dates comprises minutes, correspondence and publications.

Beaumont Society, 1963–80
Belfast Gay Liberation Society, 1970–74
Black Lesbian and Gay Centre, 1980–87
Conservative Group for Homosexual Equality/ Torche, 1977–92
Friends Homosexual Fellowship, 1973–85
Gay Activists Alliance, 1976–80
Gay Christian Movement, 1973–90
Gay Community Organisation, 1973–89
Gay Humanist Group, 1979–86
Gay Labour Group (Labour Campaign for Gay Rights), 1975–81
Gay Left Collective, 1977–81
Gay Liberation Front, 1971–79
Gay News, 1980–83
Gay Pride, 1977–80s
Gay Switchboard, 1976–89
Gay Youth Movement, 1976–85
Gays in Media, 1975–89
Gemma (q.v.), 1977–83
GLC Gay Rights Working Party, 1980–87
Homosexual Law Reform Society, 1964–70
International Gay Association, 1970–86
Irish Gays in London, 1981–83
(CHE) Joint Council for Gay Teenagers, 1976–83

Labour Campaign for Lesbian and Gay Rights, 1980–86

Liberal Gay Action Group, 1982–84

London Gay Campaign Group, 1981–86

London Gay Switchboard, 1974–82

London Lesbian and Gay Centre, 1983–90

Metropolitan Community Church, 1973–80

Northern Ireland Gay Rights Association, 1975–85

Paedophile Information Exchange, 1974–84

Scottish Homosexual Rights Group, 1978–84

Scottish Minorities Group, 1970–81.

Outside the LSE Library, researchers should note the existence of other important sources for gay and lesbian history. These include the Birmingham Gay Centre, Bristol Gay Centre and the Out Right Scotland material in the Scottish Record Office (GD 467). The archive of the National Lesbian and Gay Survey is in Sussex University Library.

HEADMASTERS' CONFERENCE The HMC, as it is usually called, was founded in 1869 by the head-masters of the leading public schools and now serves as the national representative body of the major independent secondary schools in Great Britain and a number overseas. A history of the HMC by Dr Alicia Percival, *The Origins of the Headmasters' Conference*, was published in 1969. The proceedings of the Headmasters' Conference are recorded in printed committee bulletins and the report of the AGM. Enquiries should be directed to the HMC.

HEALTH VISITORS' ASSOCIATION The Asso-ciation was established in 1896, as the Women's Sanitary Inspectors' Association, but was not regis-tered as a trade union until 1918. The words 'and Health Visitors' were added in 1915; it was changed in 1929 to Women Public Health Officers' Association, and in 1962 to its present name.

The records of the organisation (now part of the MSF trade union) have been transferred to the Contemporary Medical Archives Centre, Wellcome Institute.

HOWARD LEAGUE FOR PENAL REFORM The League was formed as the Howard Association in

1866, and adopted its present title following its amalgamation with the Penal Reform League in 1921. It exists to work for an improvement in prison conditions, mainly through acting as a specialised library and information service for other parties interested in penal reform. The surviving records of the League are limited with respect to the pre-war period. The Modern Records Centre, University of Warwick has the minutes for 1927–55; an incomplete set of annual reports, 1931–73; some correspondence files, and various publications and illustrations (ref. MSS 16). This collection was subsequently added to by the deposit of a group of files covering the directorship of Martin Wright (1971–81); among the subjects covered by the papers are the Floud Committee, Control Units, the Centre for Crime Problems, and children and young persons. In addi-tion there are League press statements for 1972–77 and press-cuttings for 1957–65.

The papers of the Floud Committee itself for 1976–80 have been deposited in Northamptonshire Record Office (ref. ZB148) and a list is available (NRA 4039). There is also a list (NRA 16356) for the numerous local records of the period 1895–1949, which have been deposited in several different locations.

HUMAN RIGHTS SOCIETY The Society was founded in 1969 to uphold the dignity of individual human beings by supporting in particular the UN Declaration on Human Rights and by defending the right to life of the sick and disabled. It has been active in opposing the legalisation of volun-tary euthanasia. Papers have been retained at the Society's offices. They consist of committee and AGM minutes; copies of the Annual Newsletter, press releases and tapes of meetings and confer-ences; annual accounts; subject files relating to euthanasia and hospice care, and copies of project material supplied to students. Correspondence has not been kept. Ordinarily the papers are available only for use by the Society's members, but the Committee will consider requests from other researchers and all enquiries should be addressed to the General Secretary.

I

IMPERIAL CANCER RESEARCH FUND The Fund was founded in 1902, and its objects (as laid down in the Royal Charter) are research into the causes, prevention, treatment and cure of cancer, including assistance in the development of research in hospitals and other institutions. Further details may be found in Joan Austoker, *A History of the Imperial Cancer Research Fund* (Oxford Science Publications, 1988).

The archives, maintained by the Fund's Secretariat, were surveyed in 1987 by the Wellcome Institute for the History of Medicine. Surviving papers consist principally of the minutes, correspondence and memoranda of the Council (1956–88) and of a number of the Fund's committees, including Appeals and Income Review (1986–91); Establishment (1981–86); Finance (1957–85); Scientific Advisory (1960–91); Cancer Research Campaign (1962–88), the Health Education Council (1981–88), and the Committee of Chairmen (1982–90). It should be noted that some of these records are available only on microfilm. In addition a certain amount of material is held in the Fund's own Library, such as Annual Reports (including accounts) from 1902; Scientific Reports; the Staff Reprint Collection, and press-cuttings and scrapbooks from the Public Relations Department. Persons wishing to use the archive should apply to the Assistant Secretary of the Fund.

INDEPENDENT LABOUR PARTY The Independent Labour Party was founded in 1893 and was affiliated to the Labour Representation Committee in 1900. It retained its affiliation to the Labour Party until 1932, while holding its own conferences and developing its own policies. In 1932, after growing differences between the two parties, the ILP disaffiliated. It then maintained an independent existence before losing its remaining political significance after World War II.

Most of the surviving records of the ILP are of primary interest for the period prior to 1945. These are discussed in *Sources, 1900–51*, vol. I, pp. 109–110 and the supplementary vol. VI, pp. 37–38.

The Imperial War Museum has received the papers of David Gibson, the national chairman in the immediate post-war period. These include material on the ILP's performance in elections between 1945 and 1955 and copies of *The Leader* and *Socialist Leader*. Other post-war material can be found at the LSE Library, including minutes of the National Administrative Council up to 1950 (ref. Coll Misc 464).

Coventry ILP Minutes, 1944–46, are in Coventry City Record Office.

INDEPENDENT TELEVISION ASSOCIATION The ITV Association is the central secretariat and co-ordinating organisation for the UK independent television companies.

The records of the ITV Association date from 1954. Council minutes are the main statutory records, and are supported by correspondence, papers and reports. The Association has various committees, including Finance & General Purposes, Regional Principals, Regional Controllers, Regional Planners, Grants Review, Rights, Copy Clearance, Technical, Film Purchase, Industrial Relations, Marketing, etc.

The records of the Association, which are managed and maintained by the company archivist, are not available to the public. Both non-current and archive materials are housed in an off-site records centre.

INDIA, PAKISTAN AND BURMA ASSOCIATION The Association placed certain of its surviving records on permanent loan in the India Office Library (ref. MSS Eur F 158) in 1972. These papers, running to over 1000 files, largely consist of subject files (principally relating to issues of trade and politics) for the period 1941–70. A further collection of material exists at the Modern Records Centre, University of Warwick (ref. MSS 200), namely Association minutes, 1942–63, and those of the Executive Committee for 1945–64; copies of the weekly bulletin, 1946–65, and monthly reports, 1949–71.

INDIAN TEA ASSOCIATION An important collection of records, comprising 1,000 volumes and 600 files, was deposited on permanent loan in the India Office Library in 1977 and 1980 (ref. MSS Eur F 174). A list is available (NRA 29779). The collection comprises files, *c.* 1900–74, on a wide variety of subjects including tea taxes, labour relations, wage boards and family planning, production figures etc. There are annual reports not only of the Association itself but of other organisations which shared its Secretariat, e.g. the Indian Tea Association (Calcutta), the Dooars Planters Association, the United Planters Association of Southern India and the British Tea Producers Association.

INDIAN WORKERS ASSOCIATION The records have been placed in Birmingham City Archives (ref. 2141), which also houses the papers of Avtar Jouhl.

INDUSTRIAL CHRISTIAN FELLOWSHIP This organisation was founded in 1877 as the Navvy Mission and reconstituted in 1919.

The records have been deposited in Sion College Library. A list is available (NRA 27076). The material includes minutes and annual reports from 1877 onwards; missioners' reports; records of 'crusades'; policy documents and working papers since 1920, and pamphlet and photograph collections. Access to the collection is subject to the discretion of the librarian and the secretary of ICF.

INDUSTRIAL COMMON OWNERSHIP MOVE-MENT LTD ICOM was founded in 1971 to promote the principle of worker cooperatives within British industry, in succession to DEMINTRY (the Society for the Democratic Integration of Industry). It now serves as the National Federation of Worker Co-operatives and acts as a national lobbying organisation for the local co-operatives.

ICOM's archive is held at its offices. The papers comprise minutes of the General Council and its various committees and working parties since ICOM's incorporation in 1978, and an incomplete series of the minutes of both DEMINTRY and the unincorporated ICOM. In addition there are annual reports (for most years); research reports on legal, financial and training matters affecting co-operatives; financial records since the late 1970s; correspondence files arranged according to topic, specific project or originating organisation, and files regarding the incorporation of over 2000 individual co-operatives. It should be understood that much of the material, being of a commercial nature, is confidential but persons conducting research in the interests of the co-operative movement may apply to ICOM at the above address.

INDUSTRIAL LIFE OFFICES ASSOCIATION The organisation was established as the Association of Industrial Assurance Companies and Collecting Friendly Societies in 1901. Its present title was adopted in 1950. It played a prominent part in the organisation of national health insurance in 1911 and in the campaign against nationalisation in 1949.

The archive was deposited in the Guildhall Library, London in 1994 (ref. MS 29801/11). A list is available (NRA 41516). The records consist of minute books, annual accounts and files.

INDUSTRIAL SOCIETY The Society, which adopted its present title in 1965, was founded in 1918 by the Revd Robert Hyde. Its objective is to promote the fullest involvement of persons in their work by encouraging the active cooperation of the leaders of trades unions and industry. The earliest campaigns were for improved working conditions, the creation of pension schemes and the establishment of personnel departments within firms. Today the Society focuses upon personal development (particularly that of the young) and on improving industrial relations. An account by C. Mailer and P. Musgrave, *The History of the Industrial Society 1918–1986*, was published in 1986.

Following a fire at the Society's headquarters in 1989, some of the records were transferred to the Modern Records Centre, University of Warwick. No material was lost in the fire. The Society has retained its minutes. The records now at Warwick (MSS 303) include annual and other reports (including directories and other items) for the period 1918–85; biographical files of prominent members and officials; a run of the journal (known as *Industrial Welfare* from 1922 until 1965 and as *Industrial Society* thereafter) and other titles, 1918–84; training course prospectuses and programmes, 1920–84; press-cuttings, 1918–88, and the records of the 'I'm Backing Britain Campaign' (mainly covering the period 1968–69). Other material, including photographs of official functions and Robert Hyde's own papers, has been retained by the Society.

INLAND REVENUE STAFF FEDERATION The organisation which was to become the IRSF was formed in 1936 when the Association of Officers of Taxes incorporated the National Association of Taxes Assessing and Collecting Services and the Valuation Office Clerical Association. It became a single union in the following year but retained the title of Federation.

Most of the IRSF's extensive archive was unfortunately lost when it moved headquarters in 1982, but a small quantity of material was discovered in 1988 when the records of the Council of Civil Service Unions (q.v.) were transferred to the Modern Records Centre, University of Warwick and the Federation papers were likewise deposited there (ref. MSS 297). A list is available (NRA 32570). This collection contains some post-war material, namely AOT/IRSF annual delegate conference files, 1927–52; subject files, 1929–56; rules revision files, 1957–79, and copies of Federation rules, 1923–78.

A more extensive collection of material at the Modern Records Centre (ref. MSS 304) relates to the Inland Revenue Departmental Whitley Council, which was formed in 1920 during the introduction of the Whitley system of industrial negotiation throughout the Civil Service (see J.D. Thomas, *Fifty Years of Whitleyism in the Inland Revenue, 1920–70*, 1970). This collection includes the Whitley Council's minutes for 1939–75 and its General Purposes Committee minutes for 1926–82, with an index. In addition there are minute books covering the period 1921–81 for the National Staff (later Trade Union) Side; annual conference proceedings, 1920–47; circulars, 1946–77; subject files for the 1920s to 1980s

(which include files on unrecognised associations and the 1970s management review), and an incomplete set of annual reports for 1922–76.

INLAND WATERWAYS ASSOCIATION The organisation was founded in 1946 to campaign for the restoration, retention and development of inland waterways. Some records, together with some from the Inland Shipping Group, have been deposited in the LSE Library. The Inland Shipping Group advises the IWA and campaigns to encourage freight carriage on Britain's inland waterways. The ISG deposit includes minutes, 1971–81, and correspondence. A list is available on application to the archivist.

INSTITUTE OF ADMINISTRATIVE MANAGEMENT A collection of papers of the Institute (formerly the Office Management Association) is available in the Modern Records Centre, University of Warwick (ref. MRC 337). A list is available (NRA 40027). The records include minutes, 1927–84, journals and other publications, some subject files, press cuttings etc.

INSTITUTE OF DIRECTORS Founded in 1903, the Institute was incorporated by Royal Charter three years later. It aims to raise the standards and status of directors of companies and to promote the interests of free enterprise. The records of the IOD, which largely begin from its reorganisation in 1949–50, include the Policy and Executive Committee minutes and the published Annual Report and Annual Convention Report and Speeches, although the minutes of the Council do exist from 1903 onwards. The IOD maintains its own library, which houses a run of the journal *The Director* (first published in 1921) and copies of the IOD's various publications, such as business books and policy research reports. Enquiries concerning access to the papers should be directed to the Head of the IOD's Information and Advisory Services.

INSTITUTE OF ECONOMIC AFFAIRS The Institute was founded in 1957 by Sir Antony Fisher, under the inspiration of Professor Friedrich von Hayek. It has campaigned to promote the causes of monetarism and free market economics, under such persons as Arthur Seldon and Lord Harris of High Cross.

The surviving archive of the early years of the Institute has been preserved by Mrs Linda Whetston (daughter of Sir Antony Fisher). Enquiries should be directed to the LSE Library.

INSTITUTE OF EDUCATION The Institute houses a wide range of archives of educational organisations, including the General Teaching Council (GTC), the Assistant Masters Association, The Moat, the Society of Teachers Opposed to Capital Punishment etc. It also has papers, 1991–95, of the National Commission on Education.

INSTITUTE OF EMPLOYMENT RIGHTS An independent organisation to promote the development of new theories and policies in the field of labour law, the Institute was established in February 1989. It is not a campaigning organisation but a research body partially funded by trade unions to promote the academic study of employment policy. The majority of its work is therefore concerned with the production of published reports on various aspects of the law.

The archive has been retained at the Institute's offices. Available material comprises minutes of the monthly Executive Committee meeting since February 1989 and of the Publications Subcommittee and the Sex Discrimination and Health and Safety working parties since 1990. AGM reports and annual financial records since 1989 are also available.

INSTITUTE FOR EUROPEAN ENVIRON-MENTAL POLICY IEEP was established in 1980 as the London office of the Institut für Europäische Umweltpolitik, founded in Bonn in 1976. Until 1990 IEEP was an integral part of its Dutch parent body, the European Cultural Foundation (ECF), but in that year it became legally independent and the London office was established as a British limited company and a charity. IEEP monitors the implementation of EU environmental directives and undertakes research on environmental policymaking.

IEEP's papers are presently retained at its offices. They consist of the annual report (produced by the International IEEP) from 1978 onwards, committee minutes, and correspondence and subject files related to the Institute's fields of interest. Copies of IEEP's publications are also held, including the bulletin *The Environment in Europe*, which was produced from 1979 to 1988. Minutes and correspondence are not open to the public, but the Institute will consider applications for access from bona fide researchers.

INSTITUTE OF JEWISH AFFAIRS There are papers of the Institute, which monitors Jewish affairs worldwide, in the Hartley Library, University of Southampton (ref. MSS 23741).

INSTITUTE OF MEDICAL SOCIAL WORKERS The papers for the period 1945 to 1970 have been deposited with the West Yorkshire Archives Service at Wakefield. They include minutes, miscellaneous papers, and annual reports for 1952–67.

INSTITUTE OF PERSONNEL MANAGEMENT The Institute was founded in 1913, but the main series of its records dates from 1917. A large proportion of material was destroyed during World War II but the surviving papers have been placed in the Modern Records Centre, University of Warwick (ref. MSS 97). The collection incorporates various series of minutes, 1917–64; annual reports, 1920–64; the journal, 1921–62, and bulletin, 1952–64, and certain records of related organisations, 1916–63. In addition there are the personal papers of four officials of the Institute, but this material largely relates to the pre-war period.

Two other collections at the Modern Records Centre contain local material of the Institute: the records of the Birmingham branch (minutes, 1951–72; correspondence, 1969–72; annual reports, 1964–69; a copy of the constitution, 1958; and study group papers) are in MSS 112; papers of the Manchester branch (minutes, 1967–71, and correspondence, 1965–72) are in MSS 211.

The Institute is now the Chartered Institute of Personnel and Development.

INSTITUTE OF WELSH AFFAIRS Enquiries should be directed to the National Library of Wales, which has received some papers.

INSTITUTION OF PROFESSIONALS, MANA-GERS AND SPECIALISTS A professional organisation for higher-grade civil servants, the IPMS was founded in 1919, on the initiative of the engineers of the Admiralty Department, as the Institution of Professional Civil Servants (IPCS). In 1989 the union was reconstituted as the Institution of Professionals, Managers and Specialists. It has regional offices in Scotland, Birmingham and Liverpool. An account of the history of the predecessor organisation, J.E. Mortimer and Valerie Ellis, *A Professional Union: The Evolution of the Institution of Professional Civil Servants*, has been published by Allen and Unwin (London, 1980).

IPMS retains its archival collection at its headquarters in London. Papers include bound volumes of minutes of the National Executive Committee from 1942 to date; Negotiations Committee, 1947–79; Pay and Conditions Committee, 1980–85; Organisation and Membership Committee, 1967–88; General Purposes Committee, 1942–88; Personnel Management Committee, 1985 to date, and Finance and Membership Organisation Committee, 1988 to date. In addition there are copies of the Annual Report from 1951 onwards and Annual Delegate Conference verbatim reports from 1948. Financial records are retained for the statutory period of seven years only. Correspondence files are organised by branch (e.g. government department), by subject (e.g. grading or pay), or by personal case. IPMS also has copies of its journals *State Service*, 1921–82; *IPCS Bulletin*, 1965–75, and *The Right Angle*, 1949–68. The papers are open to staff and members, but outside researchers may be given access on a reference-only basis. Interested persons should contact the Research Officer at the London headquarters.

In addition a quantity of IPCS material has been deposited at the Modern Records Centre, University of Warwick (ref. MSS 37), namely National Executive Committee minutes, 1965–70; and papers concerning the union's affiliation to the TUC.

INTERNATIONAL AFRICAN INSTITUTE Founded in 1926 as the International Institute of Languages, this is an international, independent and non-political organisation for the study of African people, their language and culture. The Institute's Library has been transferred to the John Rylands University Library of Manchester. Its archives for the period *c.* 1930–70 have been placed in the LSE

Library (ref. M1630 and M1655). More recent material (13 boxes, covering the period up to 1997) has now been deposited (M1908). However, researchers may apply direct to the Secretary of the IAI for access. The Africa Bureau (q.v.) is a quite separate institution.

INTERNATIONAL ALLIANCE OF WOMEN The records of the Alliance (formerly the International Woman Suffrage Alliance) have been placed in the Women's Library, London Metropolitan University. They are not yet fully catalogued. A subsidiary deposit (of the Alliance's Resource Files) has been listed (NRA 40660).

INTERNATIONAL ASSOCIATION FOR RELIGIOUS FREEDOM There are papers in the Hartley Library, University of Southampton (ref. MS 256).

INTERNATIONAL BRIGADE ASSOCIATION The Association is the organisation for British veterans of the International Brigade of the Spanish Civil War. In the post-war era until 1975 the IBA was active in supporting Spaniards exiled in Great Britain and in campaigning against the Franco regime; in particular it sought to focus international attention on the plight of political prisoners. Upon the restoration of democracy in Spain the principal archive was donated to the Marx Memorial Library; additional material has subsequently been received. A full catalogue has been published by the Library, *International Brigade Memorial Archive, Catalogue 1986*.

The archive is extensive and incorporates Working and Executive Committee minutes and agendas, 1942–55 (IBA Archive Box 37); AGM papers including Secretary's Reports, 1945–65 (Box 37); general correspondence (1946–55), including circular appeals letters and correspondence with trade unions and constituency Labour Parties (Boxes 42–43); branch correspondence, largely of the late 1940s and early 1950s; special correspondence (e.g. with Spaniards in the UK), mainly for the period 1944–50 (Box 41); campaign papers, 1962–65 (Box 3), and correspondence with organisations abroad arranged by country, largely from the late 1940s and early 1950s (Box 24).

There are also numerous papers emanating from other organisations, which were either established by or were otherwise closely associated with the International Brigade Association. The Archive includes the financial papers (1945–47), general correspondence (1946–47) and minutes (1946) of the Emergency Committee in Aid of Democratic Spain (Box 39); the papers of the Aid to Spanish Youth Committee for 1941–55 including the *Bulletin* of 1952–54 (Box 4), and the overseas papers of the Aid Spain Movement, arranged by country of origin (Box 26). Within this latter group, material referring to the Movement's activities in Great Britain is exclusively pre-war in date; a large number of the post-war papers cover the United States, including the publication *Volunteer for Liberty* (1940–54) and the papers of the Joint Anti-Fascist Refugee Committee (1951–54).

The Archive also incorporates the personal collections of Jack Brent and Lon Elliott, and the A. Rothstein Newscutting Collection (compiled from French and English papers).

INTERNATIONAL COMMITTEE OF INTEL-LECTUAL COOPERATION OF THE LEAGUE OF NATIONS Correspondence and papers relating to the International Committee and its various sub-committees for the period 1919–54 may be found among the Murray papers (1866–1957), now deposited in the Bodleian library (ref. MSS. Gilbert Murray 265–341). The papers contain a considerable quantity of material emanating from related organisations such as the League of Nations Union, the bulk of which is pre-war in date. A list is available (NRA 16865).

INTERNATIONAL CO-OPERATIVE ALLIANCE The Alliance was founded in London as an outcome of the International Cooperative Congress of 1895, to serve as a worldwide confederation of cooperative organisations of all kinds. It is therefore one of the oldest existing international voluntary bodies. A history of the ICA by William Pascoe Watkins, *The International Co-operative Alliance*, was published in 1970. Its headquarters are presently located in Switzerland.

Enquiries concerning the ICA's archive (which is described in *Sources, 1900–51*, vol. I) should be directed to its head office. However, researchers should be aware that a collection relating to its affiliate, the International Co-operative Women's Guild, has been deposited in the Brynmor Jones Library, University of Hull (ref. DCX) by the British national organisation, the Co-operative Women's Guild (q.v.). A list is available (NRA 20164).

The papers at Hull include an incomplete series of the minutes of the Central Committee (1932–62) and Executive Committee (1952–54, 1956–57); files relating to conferences (1946, 1951) and examples of papers submitted thereto (1948–60); reports of the International Co-operative Women's Committee (1921–59); circular letters (in English, French and German, 1947–50, 1953–57); an incomplete series of *The International Women Co-operator* (1945–61), and copies of the Guild's pamphlets (1921–61). The archive also contains a number of important subject files such as copies of Presidential addresses (1937, 1946, 1954, 1960); questionnaires (1927–54); memoranda and reports (1930–61); papers relating to the Campaign for World Government (1947–55), and the records of the Liaison Committee of the International Co-operative Alliance and the International Co-operative Women's Guild for the period 1951–58.

INTERNATIONAL COUNCIL OF WOMEN Records, including minutes, policy and administrative files and conference reports have been placed in the Women's Library, London Metropolitan University (ref. 5/ICW).

INTERNATIONAL DEFENCE AND AID FUND FOR SOUTHERN AFRICA It has been reported that the papers have been placed in the University of the Western Cape (located in Belville, Cape Town, Republic of South Africa). The IDAF collection includes copies of its publications and a photographic and film archive. It is understood that the records of the African National Congress have also been deposited in this new archive.

Researchers should also note that the papers of the late Canon Collins, a former President of the Fund, are now deposited in Lambeth Palace Library.

INTERNATIONAL FUND FOR ANIMAL WELFARE The IFAW was established in 1969 to campaign against the commercial slaughter of seals in the Gulf of St Lawrence in Canada. An archive of papers has been retained at its offices. The bulk of the material, including published and internal reports, financial records, and correspondence, is available to researchers with permission, but at present the minutes of the Trustees' meetings remain closed.

INTERNATIONAL GEOGRAPHICAL UNION The archive is in the care of the Royal Geographical Society (q.v.), where further enquiries should be directed. Other material relating to the IGU may be found in the papers of the late Professor Sir Dudley Stamp, which have been deposited at the University of Sussex Library. A list is available (NRA 20462).

INTERNATIONAL INSTITUTE OF SOCIAL HISTORY Founded in 1935 under the inspiration of Dr N. W. Posthumus, Professor of Economic and Social History in the University of Amsterdam, the Institute, still located in Amsterdam, has acquired a mass of material on left-wing and socialist persons and organisations across all countries of modern Europe. The material on early socialism in Britain is outlined in *Sources, 1900–51*, vol. I, pp. 117–120. The Institute also houses a mass of archive material on international organisations since 1945 (especially international trade unions), which is of value to the historian of post-war Britain. A check list of these is given below (with covering dates). Very good descriptions of the history and archives of these bodies are given in Atie van der Horst and Elly Koen (eds), *Guide to the International Archives and Collections at the IISH, Amsterdam* (1989).

Organisations with records deposited include:

International Bookbinders' Union (1907–53)
International Confederation of Free Trade Unions (1949–93)
International Federation of Chemical, Energy and General Workers Unions (1946–86)
International Federation of Industrial Organisations and General Workers' Unions (1923–64)
International Federation of Trade Unions (1919–53)
International Graphical Federation (1949–72)
International Metalworkers' Federation (1948–80)
International Sociological Association (1949–82)
International Union of Socialist Youth (1946–82)

Miners' International Federation (1933–79)
Postal, Telegraph and Telephone International (1922–68)
Socialist International (1951–88)
Socialist Youth International (1923–46)
War Resisters International (1921–89)
World Federation of Trade Unions (1945–87)
World Union of Free Thinkers (1883–1959)

Enquiries concerning access etc. should be directed to the Institute's website.

INTERNATIONAL MANAGEMENT RESEARCH ASSOCIATION Some papers of the association up to 1959 (formerly known as the Management Research Group) have been deposited amongst the Ward papers in the LSE Library. A handlist is available. The papers generally refer to Group 1 of the MRG but Groups 2 to 8 are also included. The collection consists of MRG bulletins (1932–59); the minutes of Directors' Dinner Discussions (1931–58); the papers of the Governing Council; miscellaneous annual reports; the minutes and reports (1934–45) of individual Groups 2–9; the general papers (mainly reports) of the MRG headquarters research staff (1929–58), which comprise half the archive; the papers of Group 1 Executive Committee (1929–59) and the minutes of Group 1 General Meetings (1928–59); the minutes (1928–34) of eleven Group 1 sub-committees on a variety of topics, e.g. Budgetary Control, Insurance, Labour, Office Management, Organisation of Companies; subject files on topics such as Civil Defence Insurance, Industrial Planning and the TUC; the working papers of Groups 1–8 (1929–39), and miscellaneous press-cuttings, etc.

INTERNATIONAL MARXIST GROUP (IMG) There is relevant material, *c.* 1969–86, in the LSE Library (ref. M 1796). The collection consists of six boxes of ephemera, conference papers and cyclo-styled journals of IMG, plus circulars and publications of other organisations including Red Camden and Am Phoblacht. A list is available (NRA 41201).

There is material in the Whelan and Purdie papers (qq.v.) at Warwick.

INTERNATIONAL PEN A worldwide association of writers, International PEN exists to promote goodwill among writers everywhere, regardless of political differences; to agitate for freedom of expression, and to campaign on behalf of writers who are suffering persecution by oppressive regimes. The movement was founded in London in 1921 by the novelist Mrs C.A. Dawson Scott.

The archive of International PEN for the period prior to 1974 is held by the University of Texas and further details should be sought from the Research Librarian, Harry Ransom Humanities Research Center, University of Texas at Austin. More recent material is retained by the International Secretariat at its offices. This comprises a complete set of the minutes of the International Executive Committee (or Assembly of Delegates from 1979) since 1934; reports of selected PEN conferences and International Congresses, beginning with the fourteenth, held in Buenos Aires in 1936; copies of the biannual report of the Writers in Prison Committee from 1988; recent financial records, and correspondence files for the post-1974 period. Researchers should be aware that the papers of the Scottish Centre of International PEN, including correspondence for the period 1936–83, have now been deposited at the National Library of Scotland (ref. Acc 9364). A list is available (NRA 40824).

INTERNATIONAL PLANNED PARENTHOOD FEDERATION

The International Planned Parenthood Federation (IPPF) is the world's leading voluntary family health care organisation. It was founded in 1952 in Bombay, India; since then its headquarters has been in London.

A complete record of IPPF Committee minutes, namely Central Council, Central Executive Committee, Members' Assembly, Budget and Finance Committee, International Programme Advisory Panel, and International Medical Advisory Panel, has been kept. Annual Reports have been published since 1951–52. Reports of conferences have been published whenever they are held. Other publications are: *IPPF News* (1952–80); *People* magazine (quarterly, 1973–92); *IPPF Medical Bulletin* (bi-monthly, 1966 to date); *Planet and People* (quarterly, 1992); *Research in Reproduction* (1969–90); a series of *Medical Handbooks*, and numerous periodicals.

The earlier part of the IPPF archive, consisting of some 300 boxes of mainly correspondence and dating from the late 1940s until 1975, has been deposited at the David Owen Centre for Population Growth Studies, University College, Cardiff. The collection is uncatalogued and deals principally with the establishment of Family Planning Associations around the world. Other records are retained at the IPPF's headquarters.

INTERNATIONAL STUDENT CONFERENCE

The ISC was established in 1950 as the Western counterpart of the Communist aligned International Union of Students. The function of the organisation was to organise congresses of its members, which were the individual National Unions of Students in each European country. The secretariat of the ISC was located in Leiden in Holland. It was disbanded in 1969.

Five boxes of papers covering the activities of the International Student Conference for the year 1969 have been deposited at Churchill College, Cambridge, but the main archive is located at the International Institute of Social History in Amsterdam. The papers comprise the records of the first to thirteenth International Student Conferences, including correspondence, circulars, reports and lists of members. Within the archive there are the records of the ISC's main committees, such as the Supervisory Commission (SUPCOM) and the Research and Information Commission (RIC). The correspondence in particular details the ISC's relations with a host of other international and political organisations, such as the International Union of Socialist Youth, the International Union of Students and the International Confederation of Free Trade Unions.

INTERNATIONAL TRANSPORT WORKERS' FEDERATION

The Federation was founded in 1896 by representatives of seafarers' and dockers' unions who were attending a Socialist International congress in London. Its headquarters, originally in England, was transferred to the Continent during the inter-war period and only returned to the UK immediately before the outbreak of World War II. In the post-war era the ITWF has had particularly close links with the industrial agencies of the United Nations and has been active in developing countries. A study by Herbert R. Northrup and Richard L.

Rowan, *The International Transport Workers' Federation and Flag of Convenience Shipping* (Philadelphia, 1983) is available.

The ITWF Secretariat has now deposited all but its most recent records at the Modern Records Centre, University of Warwick (ref. MSS 159). The collection is described in detail in a booklet by Nicholas Baldwin (University of Warwick Library Occasional Publications No. 13, 1985). Among the records are various series of minutes (including those of the Congresses), 1896–1977; sectional reports; *Reports & Proceedings*, 1906–76; other assorted publications (e.g. circulars and newsletters), 1923–85, and correspondence files, including material on the Federation's activities against the Nazis and during World War II.

In the late 1960s part of the ITWF archive was given to the Friedrich Ebert Stiftung (the research foundation of the German Social Democratic Party) in Bonn. Full reference is made to the contents of this collection in the above mentioned *Source Booklet*. Researchers should also be aware that the papers of the former ITWF Assistant General Secretary Paul Tofahrn, likewise deposited at the Modern Records Centre (ref. MSS 238), contain material on its activities during World War II.

INTERNATIONAL UNION OF SOCIALIST YOUTH An important archive is deposited in the International Institute of Social History, Amsterdam, to where enquiries should be addressed.

INVOLVEMENT AND PARTICIPATION ASSOCIATION Founded in 1884 as the Labour Association for Promoting Co-operative Production based on the Co-partnership of Workers, the purpose of the IPA is to promote employee involvement in companies by encouraging the implementation of suitable practices within organisations. In 1972 the name was changed to the Industrial Participation Association, and the present title was adopted in 1989. Upon moving office in January 1992 certain of the IPA's papers were deposited in the Modern Records Centre, University of Warwick (ref. MSS 310). These records include the Chairman's agenda books; a small number of Committee and Council minutes, 1887–1972; a run of its journal *Co-partnership*, 1894–1980; annual and conference reports, 1884–1980, and a small reference library.

IRISH ASSOCIATION FOR CULTURAL, ECONOMIC AND SOCIAL RELATIONS This body was established in 1938 to promote mutual understanding between Irish peoples of different traditions. It has members in Northern Ireland and the Republic (each of which has a committee under the council of IACESR), and in Great Britain.

A large collection of papers covering the period from 1938 to 1983 has been placed in the Public Record Office of Northern Ireland (ref. D2661). It includes the agenda and minutes of the council and of the Northern Committee's AGM, and the secretary's reports, 1959–82; accounts, 1972–81; membership lists, 1965–83; reprints of papers delivered at meetings, 1969–79, etc. The collection is at present closed and further enquiries concerning access should be addressed to the Deputy Keeper. Some miscellaneous correspondence regarding the association's work can also be found in the John Robb collection at the Linen Hall Library, Belfast, the Le Broquoy papers in the National Library of Ireland, Dublin and the papers of Ernest Blythe in University College Dublin.

IRISH CHRISTIAN FELLOWSHIP Papers for the period 1915–86, comprising 24 volumes and 1000 documents, have been deposited in the Public Record Office of Northern Ireland (ref. D3921). The records include minutes, secretary's notes, membership records, publicity material, conference papers, correspondence, and papers concerning the work of various civic and youth groups.

IRISH CONGRESS OF TRADE UNIONS Within the Republic of Ireland the ICTU is the equivalent of the Trades Union Congress in Great Britain.

A collection of the records of the Northern Ireland Committee of ICTU for the period *c.* 1950–76 is now available on microfilm at the Public Record Office of Northern Ireland (ref. MIC 193). This microfilm series also contains a collection of papers emanating from the Belfast and District TUC for 1900–70, including minutes, agendas, annual reports and correspondence. Reference should also be made to the extensive holdings of the Irish Labour History Archive, Beggars Bush Barracks, Dublin 4. Relevant material can also be found in the Labour History Archive and Study Centre in Manchester and at the Modern Records Centre, University of Warwick.

IRISH CO-OPERATIVE ORGANISATION SOCIETY The Society, usually known by its abbreviation ICOS, has deposited papers at the National Archives of Ireland in Dublin. These records, which include material of relevance to Northern Ireland, comprise files on affiliated co-operatives for the period 1891 to 1970 (ref. 1088), and general subject files for the 20th century (ref. 1089).

IRON AND STEEL TRADES CONFEDERATION The Confederation was formed in 1917 to facilitate the amalgamation of unions operating in the iron and steel industry. It is the largest union in the sector and incorporates the British Iron, Steel and Kindred Trades Association (BISAKTA), with which certain of the constituent unions amalgamated. In 1985 the National Union of Blastfurnacemen, Ore Miners, Coke Workers and Kindred Trades (NUB) transferred its engagements to the ISTC.

Several large deposits of the Confederation's archive have been made at the Modern Records Centre, University of Warwick (ref. MSS 36). Part of the collection is described in detail in S. Coyne, 'The deposited subject files of the Iron and Steel Trades Confederation', *Bulletin of the Society for the Study of Labour History*, 45 (1982). The majority of the material consists of very extensive correspondence and subject files for the period from the 1880s to the 1990s. Among the correspondents are John Brown, D.H. Davies, Sir Harry Douglass and Sir Robert Hadfield; the subjects covered include benevolent funds, co-partnership and profit-sharing, education, industrial relations, nationalisation and privatisation, and pensions. International subjects covered range from apartheid in South Africa to human rights in Argentina. The collection also incorporates the complete records (minutes and reports) of BISAKTA from 1917.

The ISTC has now deposited records of the National Union of Blast Furnacemen at the Modern Records Centre, University of Warwick. The collection includes Executive Committee minutes, 1925–85; Delegate Board minutes, 1921–82; Annual General Council minutes, 1927–83, and a large series of subject files, which includes papers relating to such matters as the negotiations prior to amalgamation, industrial accidents, the disputes of 1975 and 1977 at the Llanwern steel works, the national steel strike of 1980, and the plant closures of the 1970s and 1980s.

IRON AND STEEL TRADES EMPLOYERS' ASSOCIATION (ISTEA) An extensive archive has been deposited by British Steel plc in the Modern Records Centre, University of Warwick (ref. MSS 365). The initial deposit comprised some eighty boxes of indexed stencils, minute books, agreements, arbitration dispute files and other records. Later deposits include minutes and correspondence relating to negotiating meetings with various unions, 1934–74. There are also files relating to the closure of several steel plants 1977–80 (MSS 365B).

J

JAPAN SOCIETY The Japan Society, which was established in 1891 to promote the study of Japan in the United Kingdom, retains its own papers. These comprise the minutes of the Council, Executive Committee and other Committees from 1891 onwards, and the Proceedings/Transactions (in which the annual accounts are published) of the Society from the same date. The latter are available in the Society's Library, which is open to the public. There is no policy for retention of correspondence beyond six years and the material which is retained is closed. Further enquiries should be addressed to the Director.

JERUSALEM AND THE EAST MISSION Extensive records for the period 1827–1976 have been placed in the Middle East Centre, St Antony's College, Oxford. A list is available (NRA 41213).

JEWISH CARE Jewish Care is a recent organisation formed on 1 January 1990 by the amalgamation of the Jewish Welfare Board and the Jewish Blind Society. Its object is to assist the relief of persons of the Jewish faith who are in need or suffering sickness or distress. A collection of papers has been deposited at the Hartley Library, University of Southampton (ref. MS 173) covering the years 1759 to 1989 and incorporating the archives of three constituent organisations within Jewish Care: the Board of Guardians for the Relief of the Jewish Poor (founded in 1859 and commonly known as the Jewish Welfare Board); the Jewish Blind Society, founded in 1819, and the Jewish Association for the Protection of Girls, Women and Children, established in 1855 as the Jewish Ladies' Society for Preventive and Rescue Work to counter the white slave trade. The latter merged with the Jewish Welfare Board in 1947 and its own papers within the collection are pre-war in date.

The papers of the Jewish Welfare Board include the minutes of the Executive Committee, 1869–1978;

the Industrial Committee, 1894–1968 (along with other papers of the Committee); the Finance Committee, 1931–74, and the Women's, Girls' and Children's Welfare Committee, 1947–50. In addition there are many sets of administrative papers concerning the running of the Board's convalescent homes in the period 1897 to 1971. The surviving papers of the Jewish Blind Society include minute books of the General Court (and later of the Council) and its various committees, 1837–1989; records of its Housing Associations, incorporating minutes and correspondence, 1959–85, and copies of the Annual Report, 1945–88.

Researchers should be aware that access to some of the more recent records of Jewish Care is restricted, and further enquiries should be directed to the Archivist at the Hartley Library. A list is available for the collection (NRA 34717).

JEWISH CHRONICLE Some surviving records of this leading Jewish newspaper, including post-war material, are in the Hartley Library, University of Southampton (ref. MS 224).

JEWISH MEMORIAL COUNCIL There are papers in London Metropolitan Archives (ref. Acc 2999). A list is available (NRA 36331). The collection includes archives of the Jewish Memorial Council itself, with material on the Central Council for Jewish Religious Education *c.* 1950–89, the Jewish Committee for HM Forces, 1939–87, the Union of Jewish Women etc.

JEWISH REFUGEE COMMITTEE The Jewish Refugee Committee was formed in Manchester in 1938. It was set up to assist German Jews seeking to emigrate to the USA and other countries to move to Britain temporarily while awaiting visas. The Guarantee Sub-committee served both to assist the refugees financially whilst they were in Britain, and to transfer money from British Jews to their relatives in need around the world. The papers of the Committee have been deposited in Manchester Central Library (ref. M102) and include the accounts for the period 1939–53 and individual refugee case-files.

Researchers should also be aware that there is much relevant material deposited in the Anglo-Jewish Archive in the Hartley Library, University of Southampton. For example, the Schonfeld papers include records of the Committee for Austrian and German Jewry, the Jewish Committee for Relief Abroad and the Committee for the Rescue of Jewry in Nazi Germany. Reference should also be made to the Central British Fund for Jewish Relief (q.v.).

JEWISH SECONDARY SCHOOLS MOVEMENT There is a considerable quantity of material relating to the Jewish Secondary Schools Movement available in the papers of Rabbi Dr. Solomon Schonfeld (1912–84), deposited at the Hartley Library, University of Southampton. The Movement, which was founded by Schonfeld's father and of which he himself was Principal from 1930 onwards, forms the largest section of these personal papers, and the material allows researchers to follow the development of the JSSM up to the 1980s.

JOINT AFRICA BOARD Formed in 1923 as the Joint East African Board, this was a commercial organisation which aimed to provide an unofficial channel of communication between the authorities and individuals in both the UK and Central and Southern Africa, in order to promote British agricultural and industrial interests. It changed its name in 1949 to include Central Africa and in 1965 adopted the above title.

The Joint Africa Board was dissolved on 31 December 1973 and the records were deposited with the Royal Commonwealth Society. The confidential files were destroyed at that time and the only surviving papers are the minutes of the Executive Council (later the Council) for 1926–74; Board minutes of 1923–26, and a series of Annual Reports for 1924–64 (1944 missing). Included in the latter series are some pamphlets and, in the later issues, reports of the Annual Meetings.

Researchers should note that the library and archive of the Royal Commonwealth Society have been deposited in Cambridge University Library.

JOINT COUNCIL FOR THE WELFARE OF IMMIGRANTS (JCWI) The records, held in the Brynmor Jones Library, University of Hull, comprise two extensive deposits dating from 1967. These contain numerous correspondence and case files, policy papers and JCWI publications. Topics cover immigration, nationality, refugee status, prisons, etc.

JOINT FOUR SECONDARY TEACHERS' ASSOCIATIONS From 1921, the four principal secondary teachers' associations, the Incorporated Association of Head Masters (IAHM), the Association of Head Mistresses Incorporated (AHMI), the Association of Assistant Mistresses, Incorporated (AAMI) and the Assistant Masters' Association (AMA), while retaining their existence as separate bodies, federated for certain purposes under a joint committee, known as the Joint Committee of the Four Secondary Associations (frequently known as the Joint Four).

Some records of the Joint Four, 1973–76, have been deposited in the Hartley Library, University of Southampton (ref. MS 67). The material consists of correspondence, committee papers and other papers for the Humberside Committee for the Joint Four, together with some general papers.

Researchers should note that the Modern Records Centre at the University of Warwick holds the archives of the Association of Assistant Mistresses (ref. MSS 59).

JOSEPH ROWNTREE FOUNDATION The Quaker philanthropist Joseph Rowntree (1836–1925), who developed the cocoa and confectionery firm of that name in the 19th century, founded three trusts in 1904. These were the Joseph Rowntree Charitable Trust; the Joseph Rowntree Social Service Trust, for benevolent purposes which were not however charitable in law; and the Joseph Rowntree Village Trust, which managed the model village of New Earswick founded by Rowntree outside York in 1902. The aim of all three was to pursue philanthropic activities which might address the fundamental causes of need rather than simply ameliorate its symptoms. In time, however, the Village Trust was concerned to satisfy its founder's objectives in a wider ambit than New Earswick itself and by Act of Parliament in 1959 it was refounded as the Joseph Rowntree Memorial Trust. Its widened powers enabled the JRMT to develop an extensive programme of research in areas which were particular concerns of Joseph Rowntree and his son Seebohm. This it continues today, mostly by contact with academic institutions and other research organisations. The Policy Studies Institute is an example of the latter, formed in 1979 by the merger of the Trust's Centre for Studies in Social Policy (founded 1975) and an older institute, Political and Economic Planning. In 1990 the Trust was renamed the Joseph Rowntree Foundation.

The Joseph Rowntree Charitable Trust (JRCT) continues to support through its grants certain charitable activities, in particular those which, in keeping with the aims of its founder, seek to resolve communal conflicts, promote racial tolerance and understanding, and advance social justice.

The Joseph Rowntree Social Service Trust was renamed the Joseph Rowntree Reform Trust in 1990. It supports radical and reforming work which is not eligible for charitable status.

It should be clearly understood that the three Trusts are legally and operationally separate of each other and have no connection with the existing Rowntree confectionery business.

PAPERS OF THE JOSEPH ROWNTREE FOUNDATION

The Foundation maintains at its offices, effectively two separate archives: (1) the internal records relating to the Trust and Foundation since 1904, and (2) the Rowntree Archive, being private papers of various Rowntree family members most closely associated with the Trusts, which are jointly owned with the JRCT. This latter collection includes personal papers of Joseph Rowntree and his son Seebohm, Joseph's nephew Arnold (sometime MP for York), and the Rowntree manager William Wallace. The Wallace and Seebohm Rowntree papers do contain post-war material; and the schedules from Seebohm's second and third poverty surveys of York are available at the Borthwick Institute of Historical Research, University of York. A proportion of the Rowntree Collection has been catalogued and work continues on material more recently deposited.

The Trust and Foundation's own records, which are not yet catalogued, include the minutes of all its decision-making committees since 1904; triennial reports, issued since 1960; copies of special reports; audited accounts since 1906; and collected correspondence. Access to papers is at the discretion of the Foundation and application should be made to the Librarian and Archivist. Material may be consulted at the Library.

PAPERS OF THE JOSEPH ROWNTREE CHARITABLE TRUST

The JRCT retains its own papers at its offices. These comprise unpublished minutes of all Trust meetings and committees since 1904; triennial reports, published since 1973; financial records, and correspondence, arranged by project and organisation. Applications for permission to view the material should be addressed to the Secretary.

JOSEPHINE BUTLER SOCIETY The Society was previously known as the Association for Moral and Social Hygiene, which was established in 1915 by the amalgamation of two existing associations for the abolition of the state regulation of prostitution. It changed its name to the Josephine Butler Society, in honour of the social reformer and moral campaigner, in 1953. The Society is the British and founding branch of the International Abolitionist Federation and is associated with the Josephine Butler Educational Trust. The objective of the Society is to seek the removal of sex discrimination from the laws relating to prostitution and the adoption of a single moral standard for both men and women.

The papers of the Society have been deposited in the Women's Library (q.v.) and a list is available (NRA 20625). More recent records are retained by the Society itself, but enquiries concerning these should be made via the Library.

Deposited material comprises Executive Committee minutes, 1915–48, and duplicates in part to 1965 (the originals being with the Secretary of the Society); executive committee finance subcommittee minutes, 1951–58; correspondence and subject files on such subjects as venereal disease in the armed forces, solicitation, employment of women police officers, the work of the League of Nations, and the

1960 Cambridge Conference of the International Abolitionist Federation; papers of a subcommittee on international work, 1936–50; a file of UN publications, 1945–54; and ten folders of extracts from Hansard concerning bills in the House of Commons, 1918–59.

Researchers should be aware that the Women's Library also has a series of the journal *The Shield*, which was published by the British Committee of the Federation for the Abolition of the State Regulation of Vice and appeared intermittently until 1970. It is now published by the Josephine Butler Society.

JUSTICE (BRITISH SECTION OF THE INTERNATIONAL COMMISSION OF JURISTS)

Records of the organisation, from 1956 to the early 1990s, have been placed in the Brynmor Jones Library, University of Hull. The deposit comprises correspondence files relating mainly to the establishment and early history of Justice, 1956–85; minutes of the Council and Executive Committee, 1957–78; some 169 files of correspondence, minutes, reports, memoranda and other papers generated by Standing Committees on Administrative Law, Civil Justice, Colonial (later Commonwealth) Affairs and Criminal Justice, as well as various ad hoc and joint committees, 1950–91. There are 79 files on individual countries. A list is available (NRA 41119).

K

KESTON COLLEGE Keston College is an independent religious education foundation established in 1969. The two principal collections of archives retained by the College are those of religious samizdat literature and the press archive. The former consists of over 4000 items of correspondence, newsletters, petitions and memoirs, and covers the principal religious groups of the former Soviet Union. There is an index and a select bibliography which has been published in the college journal, *Religion in Communist Lands*. The press archive has been maintained since the college's foundation and includes press-cuttings from Soviet and foreign publications, pamphlets, and references to articles in periodicals held in the college library; it is arranged by subject and concentrates upon information relating to religious life in the countries of the former USSR.

KNITTING INDUSTRIES FEDERATION The Knitting Industries Federation Limited (KIF) was formed in 1970 by the amalgamation of two existing employer's bodies, the National Hosiery Manufacturers Federation (NHMF) and the Hosiery and Knitwear Employers Association (HKEA), whose function and responsibilities KIF assumed.

Certain of the older records of the KIF have been deposited in Nottinghamshire Archives Office (ref. DD KIF). The material includes minutes of the Federation, 1971–79, its predecessors and various associated trades bodies, including the National Joint Industrial Council for the Hosiery Industry (an industry-wide negotiating body for employers and trades unions, 1957–80), the Knitted Textile Dyers Federation (1967–79), and the British Knitting Export Council. Associated files of correspondence, circulars and statistical reports are also available, mostly dating from the 1960s and 1970s. This category of material incorporates KIF papers relating to the international Multi-Fibre Agreement and the lobbying of Parliament.

The Federation also retains in its own care the Council minutes of its predecessors from the late 19th century onwards; annual reports of the preceding 20 years; financial records since 1960, and copies of the annual statistical review of the industry from 1980. Enquiries regarding these papers should be addressed to the Director.

L

LABOUR ACTION FOR PEACE A pressure group within the Labour Party, Labour Action for Peace was founded in 1940 as the Labour Pacificist Fellowship. It is composed of individual party members and affiliated organisations. The group seeks to ensure that issues of internationalism and disarmament are given proper consideration in party policy at all times. The papers are in the care of the Hon. Secretary. Committee minutes have only been kept since *c.* 1980, but there are available a complete set of the quarterly (originally monthly) newsletter and copies of policy statements on international issues since 1945. Some annual reports have also been kept. Researchers should apply in writing to the Secretary.

LABOUR CAMPAIGN FOR BRITAIN IN EUROPE The Labour Campaign (originally Committee) for Britain in Europe was associated with the organisation Britain in Europe (q.v.), whose papers have been deposited in the House of Lords Record Office. Material emanating from the Labour Campaign for Europe (ref. BIE/15/1–72) comprises the agendas and minutes of, and reports to, its Executive Committee for the period April 1974 to March 1975; press releases; Labour Party campaign literature; and files of research material, 1973–75. The Britain in Europe papers may be made available to bona fide students, and all enquiries should be addressed to the Clerk of the Records, House of Lords Record Office.

LABOUR CAMPAIGN FOR CRIMINAL JUSTICE Some records of the Campaign, 1993–98, which was founded in 1978 by Alex Lyon MP, are in the LSE Library. The aim of the Campaign is to encourage discussion and campaigning on criminal justice issues within the Labour Party. In 1999 it became the Labour Criminal Justice Forum.

LABOUR CAMPAIGN FOR ELECTORAL REFORM The Campaign, which seeks to commit the Labour Party to reforming the present electoral system by the adoption of proportional representation, has retained all its papers since its formation in 1976. Persons wishing to consult these records should apply to the Secretary.

LABOUR COMMITTEE FOR EUROPE There are some records, 1964–90, in the Labour History Archive and Study Centre, University of Manchester.

LABOUR COMMON MARKET SAFEGUARDS COMMITTEE There are some records, 1972–81, in the Labour History Archive and Study Centre, University of Manchester.

LABOUR HISTORY ARCHIVE AND STUDY CENTRE (LHASC) The Labour History Archive and Study Centre (LHASC) is the only specialist repository for the political wing of the labour movement. It holds records of working-class political organisations from the Chartists to Tony Benn. LHASC holds the archives of the Labour Party and the Communist Party of Great Britain. It also holds the papers of numerous Labour politicians, Communists and other left-wing activists. Some of the more important collections are described briefly in this guide, but researchers are urged to visit the LHASC web site.

LABOUR PARTY The archives of the national Labour Party, which were formerly in the care of the Party itself at its successive London headquarters at Smith Square and Walworth Road, were transferred to the National Museum of Labour History (now the Labour History Archive) in Manchester in March 1990. It is understood that there are regular deposits of archival material over fifteen years old. The description given in this entry is divided into two sections, the first part pertaining to the records of the national party; the second to the papers of the regional organisations.

NATIONAL RECORDS

The collection now in the Labour History Archive and Study Centre consists of all material collected within the Labour Party archives since the foundation of the Labour Representation Committee in 1900. It therefore includes, for example, a complete set of the minutes of the National Executive Committee and its correspondence from 1900 onwards up to the date of last deposit, and copies of all reports of the Party Conference from a similar date. The correspondence of the General Secretaries forms a particularly valuable source within the archive: the archive holds a continuous set of collections from Ramsay MacDonald onwards.

The Library also has examples of all pamphlets published by the Labour Party, as well as a large collection of election material. Details of more recent acquisitions and of the conditions of access in force at any particular time should be sought from the Labour Party Archivist.

Following the description of the national Party archive there may be found details of the papers of the individual Regional Parties. Although the Labour Party is a truly national organisation (unlike the Conservative Party, which is technically a federation of local parties), the records of Labour's regional organisations are individually deposited at appropriate repositories around the country. The records of the national Labour Party should also be distinguished from those of both the Parliamentary Party and the European Parliamentary Party. The Labour History Archive at present holds the records of the latter since 1979, and a continuous set of minutes of the former from 1906 to 1976 (with the exception of those for 1937–40 which have now been lost), with the expectation that further deposits of minutes will be received annually. Details of the conditions of access regarding these papers should be sought directly from the Labour Party Archivist.

Committee Minutes

1. *National Executive Committee* A complete set of minutes from 1900 onwards; papers are to be deposited continuously after fifteen years. Researchers should be aware that the minutes and related papers of the NEC subcommittees are not included on any systematic basis.
2. *Organisation Committee* Minutes, 1931–57
3. *Finance and General Purposes Committee* Minutes, 1933–37
4. *Elections Sub-Committee* Minutes, 1932–38
5. *Home Policy Committee* Minutes, 1950–56; 1967–71
6. *International Committee* Minutes, 1919–67
7. *Commonwealth Committee* Minutes, 1950–62. Correspondence and papers, 1947–68
8. *National Joint Council* (prior to 1934 National Council of Labour) Minutes, 1921–56

NEC POLICY COMMITTEES AND STUDY GROUPS

The Labour History Archive has minutes, correspondence and documents of various policy committees and study groups of the National Executive Committee, including the Home Policy Committee (1937–69); Social Policy Committees (1952–73); Health Committees (1958–59); Finance and Economic Policy Committees (1948–73); Industrial Policy Committees (1947–73); Education Committees (1951–72); Local Government and Planning Committees (1954–74); Housing Committees (1956–75); Agriculture Committees (1952–76); Energy Committees (1959–75); Broadcasting and Communications Committees (1948–74); Common Market Committees (1962–76); Defence Committees (1954–55); Social Issues (1955–72); Immigration and Race Relations (1964–71); and Celtic Affairs and Devolution Committees (1957–74).

Other Papers

The Labour History Archive holds a substantial collection of the general correspondence and subject files of the Labour Party, the very large majority of which are pre-war in date. Further details of this material may be found in the volume *Labour Party: Guide to the Archives*. There is also a limited number of papers relating to party organisation, including agents' half-yearly reports for 1955 (ref. LP/CONS) and the papers of J.W. Raisin, the Regional Organiser for Home Counties North, which cover the period 1946–69.

REGIONAL RECORDS

1. *Eastern Region* Executive committee minutes for 1947–71 are available in Essex Record Office (ref. D/Z215). There is a list (NRA 34511).

2. *East Midlands Region* Assorted records for 1948–72 are available at the Modern Records Centre, University of Warwick. There is a list (NRA 20259). Seven boxes of papers have also been deposited at Nottinghamshire Archives Office (ref. DD LPC). These consist of Regional Organisers' papers, 1942–63, and financial papers, 1953–59; Women's Organisers' papers, 1943–47, with miscellaneous correspondence *c.* 1956–59 and files of individual sections; League of Youth papers, 1948–54; and unsorted correspondence.

3. *Greater London Labour Party* Minute books, 1919–64 (ref. Acc 2417), and correspondence files, reports and printed material, 1965–80 (ref. Acc 2959) have been deposited at the London Metropolitan Archives. There is a list available (NRA 33597). District Organisers' reports for 1946–68 are incorporated in deposit Acc. 2783, for which reference should be made to list NRA 33032.

4. *Hertfordshire Labour Federation* Minute books for 1932–59 have been deposited in Hertfordshire Record Office.

5. *Home Counties Labour Association* Miscellaneous material may be found among the Garnsworthy Papers deposited at the LSE Library (ref. Coll Misc 540).

6. *Kent Federation of Labour Parties* Minute books for 1932–72 are available at West Kent Archives Office.

7. *Somerset Federation of Labour Parties* Minute books and accounts for 1950–59 have been deposited in Somerset Record Office (ref. A/AAW).

8. *South West Region* The records for *c.* 1945–75 are in Bristol Record Office.

9. *Labour Party Wales* Early members of the Independent Labour Party (q.v.) had tried to establish a South Wales Federation as early as 1894 but it was not until 1937 that a South Wales Regional Council of Labour was formed. The Regional Council acquired responsibility for the whole Principality in May 1947. In 1959 the word 'Regional' was dropped from the title, and in May 1975 the Welsh Council of Labour was renamed the Labour Party Wales.

Since 1985 it has been the practice of the Labour Party Wales to make periodic deposits of papers at the National Library of Wales. Papers less than 15 years old (with the exception of microfilmed or printed material) may not be consulted without the permission of the Organiser, Labour Party Wales.

10. *West Midlands Region* Records for the period 1960–72 have now been deposited at the Modern Records Centre, University of Warwick. There is a list (NRA 17826).

11. *Yorkshire Region* Copy papers have been included among the deposit made by the Hull Labour Party at the Brynmor Jones Library, University of Hull (ref. DX/222).

12. *Scotland* All enquiries should be directed to the National Library of Scotland which has a microfilm of much relevant material.

LABOUR RESEARCH DEPARTMENT The Fabian Research Department was founded in 1912, developing out of the Control of Industry Committee, founded by Beatrice and Sidney Webb under the aegis of the Fabian Society. In 1916 the Department became a separate organisation with individual membership, and shortly afterwards invited trade unions and other labour bodies to affiliate to it. In 1918 it changed its name to the Labour Research Department. The continuing functions of the Department are to carry out research into problems of importance to the labour movement.

The Department has retained records dating back to its foundation, although much valuable material was destroyed during World War II. The archive includes complete sets of Executive minutes and annual reports; miscellaneous manuscript collections, and copies of the Department's pamphlets and other publications.

Enquiries about the records should be directed to the Secretary.

LABOUR AND SOCIALIST INTERNATIONAL Papers covering the period 1917–57 are reported to have been deposited in the Labour History Archive and Study Centre.

LABOUR SOLIDARITY CAMPAIGN Some records of the Campaign, which was established after the special Labour Party conference held at Wembley in February 1981, can be found in the papers of its joint chairman, Roy Hattersley. These are in the Brynmor Jones Library, University of Hull. The papers of Peter Shore are in the LSE Library.

LAMBETH CONFERENCES The Lambeth Conference is a decennial meeting of the bishops of the Anglican Communion, held under the chairmanship of the Archbishop of Canterbury. The first Conference met in 1867 and the papers are retained at Lambeth Palace Library, the depository for all records of the Province of Canterbury. Researchers may wish to consult NRA 36518. Further enquiries concerning the papers should be directed to the Librarian and Archivist at Lambeth Palace.

LAND SETTLEMENT ASSOCIATION LTD This group was established in 1934 to investigate whether unemployed industrial workers could be successfully redeployed as self-supporting smallholders. It worked in cooperation with Government departments, particularly the Commission for Special Areas, and with voluntary organisations, in purchasing land. From 1947, it served as the agent of the Ministry of Agriculture for the administration of smallholding estates which are its property. Since the beginning of World War II the Association has worked for the general development of smallholdings, rather than on the redeployment of industrial workers. Various services in marketing are provided on a co-operative basis.

The Association has retained very full records, including minutes, reports and publications. Access to non-published material is at the discretion of the Information Officer, to whom queries should be addressed.

The Rural History Centre at Reading University holds a microfilm of the annual reports, and other publications are deposited in the British Library. Researchers should also note that a large deposit of papers of the Welsh Land Settlement Society Ltd (including estate plans and other records dating from the inter-war years) has been placed in Glamorgan Record Office.

LAW CENTRES FEDERATION The LCF was founded in 1976 as a reconstitution of the Law Centres Working Group, established three years earlier to co-ordinate efforts made by the individual centres to secure funding and develop their own activities. All the LCF's papers have been retained for the period since 1976, including minute books and conference reports with submitted policy papers, but the material is at present unsorted. Earlier papers remain in the care of individual centres, of which North Kensington in London was the first. Enquiries should be addressed to the Legal Services Worker at the Law Centres Federation.

LEAGUE AGAINST CRUEL SPORTS The League, which was founded in 1924, exists to campaign for legislation which will outlaw hunting (particularly of foxes, hares or deer), and to educate the public in the issues of cruel sports. To this end it liaises with politicians of all parties to press for government action; lobbies local authorities to ban hunting on land which they own; and organises private prosecutions of those participating in already illegal hunting activities. The records of the League are maintained at its offices. Committee minutes and correspondence files remain closed but the files of press-cuttings and publications such as special reports and the Annual Reports are available for consultation by researchers. Application should be made to the Executive Director.

LEAGUE FOR DEMOCRACY IN GREECE Founded in 1945, the League has campaigned to secure the release of political prisoners, the banning of torture, illegal arrests and military tribunals, and the restoration of democratic freedom and justice in Greece.

A collection of papers, 1945–87, has been deposited in King's College, London. It includes minutes, reports, circulars, press-cuttings, published material and photographs.

Students of modern Greece should note that King's College, London, also holds the papers of the

Greek Relief Fund, 1948–84, and of the Anglo-Hellenic League, 1915–44.

LEAGUE OF JEWISH WOMEN The League was founded in 1943 as a Jewish voluntary welfare body, not only to serve the Jewish community but also to co-operate with other women's organisations for the advancement of humanitarian causes generally. The League has retained its own records since its inception but at present the collection remains closed.

LEGAL ACTION GROUP A company limited by guarantee and a registered charity, LAG was founded in 1972 to seek the improvement of local community legal services. The papers, which are retained at LAG's offices, comprise committee minutes and copies of the monthly magazine *Legal Action* (which includes the Annual Report where this is not published separately) from 1973 to date; subject files covering all aspects of the group's work, in particular legal aid and the legal profession itself, and copies of miscellaneous reports. Correspondence is kept in the subject files. Financial records are closed. Persons wishing for access to the papers should apply to the Director.

LESBIAN AND GAY CHRISTIAN MOVEMENT The LGCM was founded in April 1976 as the Gay Christian Movement, with the object of promoting acceptance of homosexual persons within the Christian churches. It adopted its present name in 1987.

The papers have been deposited at the LSE Library within the Hall-Carpenter Archive (q.v.). The first deposited material includes copies of the Annual Reports since 1976; AGM minutes for 1977, 1980 and 1981; committee and subcommittee minutes for 1976–83; copies of the *Gay Christian*, 1979–86 and a significant collection of offprints and pamphlets (including some published by other gay religious groups); campaign and working party papers (including LGCM submissions to the Home Office), and the papers of certain local groups of the LGCM. These records comprise lists of their convenors and newsletters, local committee minutes and correspondence. More recent papers have also now been deposited, but these remain closed.

Certain other of its more recent papers have been retained by LGCM and enquiries should be directed to the General Secretary, Richard Kirker. The General Secretary should also be approached for permission to view closed material at the LSE Library.

LIBERAL EUROPE CAMPAIGN The Liberal Europe Campaign was associated with the organisation Britain in Europe (q.v.), whose papers have been deposited in the House of Lords Record Office. Material emanating from the Liberal Europe Campaign Committee (ref. BIE/16/1–44) comprises correspondence, memoranda, minutes and the reports of the Campaign Director for the period October 1974 to June 1975; correspondence with the Liberal Party Area Federations and regional parties, and copies of the accounts. The Britain in Europe papers may be made available to bona fide students, and all enquiries should be addressed to the Clerk of the Records, House of Lords Record Office.

LIBERAL MOVEMENT Four boxes of papers, 1988–93, have been placed in the LSE Library by David Morrish, a Devon Liberal Movement activist. The Liberal Movement was a Liberal splinter group opposed to amalgamation with the SDP.

LIBERAL PARTY The description of the papers of the Liberal Party given in this entry is divided into two sections, the first part pertaining to the records of the national party; the second to the papers of the regional organisations. Because of the merger with the SDP, reference should be made to the SDP entry (see pp. 386–7).

NATIONAL RECORDS

Many records of the modern Liberal Party were deposited in the LSE Library in 1987. More recent deposits have been made. The initial deposit related mainly to the period 1945–87. Owing to divisions within the party after 1916 and the frequency with which it moved headquarters, the surviving pre-war material is slight. The papers referred to here principally cover the organisation and administration of the party. The more recent material fully covers the formation of the Social Democratic

Party, the creation of the Liberal/Social Democratic Alliance, and the merging of the two parties. All material older than twenty years is available to researchers; persons wishing to use later papers should consult the Archivist. The collection, which comprises 180 boxes, is described below by the 23 headings into which it has been divided.

1. *National Executive Committee* Minutes, 1954–85 (including agendas for 1981–85). Working papers, 1972, 1974, 1977, 1979, 1980, 1981–82, and 1987. Steering Group minutes and working papers, 1977–80. Correspondence, 1978–86. Financial correspondence, 1978–81. Records of campaigns on political donations and media promotion, 1985.

2. *Liberal Party Organisation* Minutes, 1958–79. Finance Committee minutes, 1983. Correspondence, 1978–87. The majority of this section comprises subject files on *inter alia*: Wainwright Report on internal organisation (1972–75); Sir David Steel's correspondence (1977–86); membership (1980s); political fundraising (1980s); Parliamentary Party (1983–87); Labour Party (1984–87); Conservative Party (1985–86); presidential rulings on the powers of the National Executive Board, Finance and Administration Board, etc. (1984–88); affiliation of regional parties (1986–87); planning and research (1986–87), and internal party elections (1976–80, 1982).

3. *Party Council* Working papers, 1972–86. Correspondence, 1970–76. Party Council Agenda Committee, minutes and working papers, 1973–82. Submissions to Party Council, 1974–83.

4. *Standing (later Policy) Committee* Minutes, 1960–87 (including agendas and reports for 1977–80). Working papers, 1980–86 (including minutes and correspondence for 1982–83 and 1985–86). Correspondence, 1986–87. Policy panel papers (on NHS, energy, agriculture and defence), 1984–86.

5. *Central Committees* Organising Committee: minutes, 1961–63, and memoranda and correspondence, 1962–65. General Election Committee: minutes, 1963 and 1978–83. Political Directorate: minutes, 1966–67. Constitutional Review Committee: working papers, 1967 and 1979–80; report, *c.* 1968, and copies of Party

Constitution, 1936–87. Publicity Subcommittee: minutes and papers, 1983; party political broadcast transcripts and correspondence, 1980–81, and *Liberal News* correspondence 1981–82. Leader's (heads of committees) meetings, 1967–68. Officer's Committee: minutes, 1976–77, and papers, 1975–77. Corporate Appeals Committee: minutes, papers, and correspondence, 1977–79. Staff Association: minutes, 1982–85. Candidates Committee: minutes, 1986–87; correspondence, 1982–87; candidates' mailing, 1985–87, and candidates' briefings, 1981–83. Ethnic Minorities Committee: papers, 1986. Press Spokesmen's Group: minutes and correspondence, 1981. Membership Committee: minutes, 1983; working papers, 1983 and 1985–87; correspondence, 1985–87. Policy Division: correspondence (mainly on internal party organisation), 1983–85. Strategy Working Group: minutes and working papers, 1979–81. Campaigns and Elections Committee: minutes and papers, 1979–84; *Campaign Bulletin*, 1965–67, and *Headquarters Bulletin*, 1967–69; campaign materials, 1980s, and subject files on Two Year Programme for the Liberal Party (1981–82), Trade Union Campaign with SDP (1984–85), Youth Campaign (1985), Poll Tax Campaign (1987) and Campaign for Social Democracy (1987).

6. *Annual Reports and Accounts* Liberal Party Annual Report and Accounts, 1961–67, 1969, 1971, 1974, 1976–87.

7. *Finance* Finance and Administration Board minutes, 1971–87. Finance and Administration Board reports to National Executive Committee, 1977–83. Finance and Administration Board correspondence, 1981–87. Subject files, including: Fundraising Group minutes, correspondence and papers etc. (1977–87); budgets (1975–83); parliamentary party finances (1983); By-election Guarantee Fund (1977–78, 1984–85); parliamentary deposits (1980–83); 'cashflow' (1977–79); Joseph Rowntree Social Services Trust correspondence (1969–71, 1977, 1981–85), and Treasurer's Conference (1982–86).

8. *Assemblies* Agendas and Programmes, 1912–87. Resolutions adopted at Conference, 1961–86. Subject files relating to individual conferences (including Assembly Committee papers,

Secretary's and Chairman's briefs, budgets and receipts, etc.): Scarborough, 1967; Edinburgh, 1968; Brighton, 1969; Scarborough, 1971; Margate, 1972; Southport, 1973; Brighton, 1974; Scarborough, 1975; Llandudno, 1976; Brighton, 1977; Blackpool (Special Assembly), 1978; Southport, 1978; Margate, 1979; Blackpool, 1980; Llandudno, 1981; Bournemouth, 1982; Harrogate, 1983; Bournemouth, 1984; Dundee, 1985; Eastbourne, 1986, and Harrogate, 1987.

9. *General Elections* Files (usually including General Election Committee minutes and reports, correspondence, lists of candidates and agents, campaign bulletins, candidates' briefings, party publications, and press-cuttings) for the elections of 1945, 1950, 1951, 1955, 1959, 1964, 1966, 1970, February and October 1974, 1979, 1983 and 1987.

10. *By-Elections* Files of press-cuttings and leaflets for the elections at Gloucester (Sept 1957); Ipswich (Oct 1957); Leicester (Nov 1957); Liverpool Garston (Dec 1957); Rochdale (Feb 1958); Glasgow Kelvingrove (March 1958); Harrow West (March 1960); Bolton East (Nov 1960); Mid-Bedfordshire (n.d.); Carshalton (Nov 1960); Ludlow (Nov 1960); Petersfield (Nov 1960); Oswestry (Nov 1961); Blackpool North (March 1962); Lincoln (March 1962); Middlesbrough East (March 1962); Orpington (March 1962); Derby North (April 1962); Montgomery (May 1962); Derbyshire West (June 1962); Middlesbrough West (June 1962); Leicester North East (July 1962); Dorset South (Nov 1962); Chippenham (Nov 1962); Glasgow Woodside (Nov 1962); Norfolk Central (Nov 1962); Northamptonshire South (Nov 1962); Dumfries (Feb 1963); Colne Valley (March 1963); Rotherham (March 1963); Swansea East (March 1963); Leeds South (June 1963); Deptford (July 1963); West Bromwich (July 1963); Bristol South East (Aug 1963); Stratford-upon-Avon (Aug 1963); South Belfast (Oct 1963); Dundee West (Nov 1963); Kinross & West Perthshire (Nov 1963); Luton (Nov 1963); Manchester Openshaw (Dec 1963); St Marylebone (Dec 1963); and Sudbury & Woodbridge (Dec 1963).

11. *Liberals and Europe* Liberal International papers, 1976–87. Federation of Liberal and Democratic Parties in the European Community (FLIDEPEC) papers, 1979. European Liberals and Democrats, programmes, financial records, election correspondence, etc., 1977–84. Files on European Elections of 1979 and 1984 (candidates' and agents' mailings, press releases, survey of seats, negotiations with SDP, correspondence, etc.). European Elections Working Group papers, 1983. European and International Co-ordinating Group minutes, 1979–83, 1983. European Liberal, Democratic and Reform Parties minutes, 1986–87, and bulletin *Liberal Flash*, Feb-March 1987. Liberal European Action Group *Bulletin*, vol. 1, 1982.

12. *Party Political Broadcasts* Correspondence files, 1982–87. Transcripts of Liberal, SDP/Alliance, Conservative, Labour, SNP, British Nationalist and Green Party broadcasts, various dates 1981–88.

13. *Press-Cuttings* Cuttings re Liberal Party (1960–80); electoral reform (1962–76); Jeremy Thorpe MP (1966–71); Margaret Thatcher MP (1972–79), etc. Press releases, 1977–87. Press correspondence, 1983–86.

14. *Publications Contact* (Journal of Liberal Candidates Association), 1976–83. *Liberator*, vols. 9–122, 1970s–80s. *Headquarters Bulletin*, Dec 1970 – Nov 1971. *Liberal Monthly Bulletin*, Feb 1972 – Jan 1975. *Regional Bulletin*, July 1975. *LPO Campaign News*, July 1980 – Oct 1983. *Liberal Centenary Publication*, 1977. *Liberal News* correspondence, 1983–86, and sales file, 1986.

15. *Speakers' and Candidates' Handbook*, 1945, 1950, 1951, 1959, 1964 (*Partners in Progress*), 1966, 1970 (*The Way Ahead*) and 1974 (*Pathways to Power*). Liberal Information Service, vols. 6–8, 11–12 and 14–23, 1950s–60s. *Election Agents Handbook*, 1951, 1955 and 1969. Speakers' notes, 1958–69.

16. *Policy Summaries* An extensive series of subject files summarising Party policy, almost exclusively post-war. The series includes summaries relating to civil liberties, defence, education, employment, energy, finance, foreign affairs (the largest series), health, housing etc.

17. *Regional Organisation* Regional mailings, Eastern Region (1984–87); Greater Manchester (1979–82); Greater Merseyside (1981–86); Home Counties (1986–87); London (1986–87); Northern

Area (1986–87); North West England (1986–87); Western Counties (1986–87); West Midlands (1978–87); Yorkshire (1986–87). Constituency surveys, 1963–66, 1984. Boundary Commission Reports for Wales, 1985–87. Action Programme for Counties, Districts and Boroughs, papers, 1981–86. Liberal Agents Association papers, 1984–87. Area agents reports and correspondence, 1980–87.

18. *Liberal Organisations* Alliance Action Group for Electoral Reform, 1977–86. Association of Liberal Trade Unionists, 1977–87. Association of Liberal Councillors, 1983, 1986. Labour Unit, 1985–86. Liberal CND and Peace Group, 1986. Liberal International, 1982–87. Liberal Lesbian & Gay Group, 1987. Liberal Parliamentary Association, 1983, 1985–87. Liberals Abroad, 1986–87. National League of Young Liberals, 1981–82, 1984–87. National Liberal Club, 1951–71, 1986–87. National Union of Liberal Clubs, 1977–87. Scottish Liberal Party, 1979–87 (including *Liberal Bulletin* and Annual Report and Accounts, 1986–87). Tory Unit, 1985–86. Ulster Liberal Party, 1986. Union of Liberal Students, 1982–87. Welsh Liberal Party, 1979–87. Women's Liberal Federation, 1976–87.

19. *Lib-Lab Pact* Papers relating to the agreement between the parliamentary Liberal and Labour parties, including letters to candidates and press releases, 1977–78.

20. *Social Democratic Party* Correspondence, 1985–87. Publications, 1986–87. Conference literature, 1987. Press releases and cuttings (mainly by and about David Owen, MP), 1987. *Campaign Update*, nos. 23–59, June 1986 – April 1987.

21. *Liberal/SDP Alliance* Joint Co-ordinating Committee minutes, 1982–83. Joint Campaign Committee/Group papers and minutes, 1983, 1986–87. Alliance Campaign Group papers, 1986–87. Joint Priorities Group papers (including policy statements), 1985–87. Liberal Party Standing Committee and SDP Policy Committee joint meetings, minutes and working papers, 1985–86. Alliance Fund correspondence, 1981–86. Joint selection of candidates, 1981–82, and Alliance Candidates' Handbook, 1983. Joint Negotiating Group papers, 1981–82. Seat negotiations (including assessment panel papers,

appeals procedures, and arbitrations), 1981–86. SDP/Alliance publications (*Britain United* and *The Time Has Come*), 1987. Press releases and cuttings re formation of SDP and Alliance, 1979–87. Subject files re Alliance policy etc.

22. *Tapes* Videocassettes, including tapes of party political broadcast of June 1970; Liberal Assemblies of 1979, 1984, 1986 and 1988, and Independent Television News coverage of local elections and by-elections, May 1984.

23. *Miscellaneous* Includes files on Party constitutional rulings (1985–86); legal actions against national and local parties (1985–87); CND and nuclear disarmament (1983–86); ecology (1987), and the Red Book (1962–68), a collection of briefs and memoranda regarding conduct of elections, standing orders, and Party policy.

The material deposited at the LSE Library largely runs from 1948 onwards. The most important individual source for historians of the Liberal Party for the preceding period is the records of the National Liberal Club, whose membership records, minute books, letters and papers for the period 1882 to 1973 have been deposited at Bristol University Library. A list is available (NRA 33764). This collection effectively forms the predecessor archive for that at the LSE Library. Bristol University Library also has the papers of a number of other national Liberal Party organisations, such as the Liberal Social Council (minutes and accounts, 1914–65); National League of Young Liberals (minutes, 1957–71), and Women's Liberal Federation (ref. DM 1193). The papers of the latter, for which a separate list is available (NRA 31778), form an extensive collection for the period 1888 to 1988 and include Executive Committee minutes, 1949–88; Annual Reports, 1952–54, 1956–87; Council meeting agendas etc., 1950–63, 1965, 1968–88; accounts, 1943–71; correspondence files *c.* 1912–84; press-cuttings, 1960–64; photographs, 1914–88; and publications.

Bristol University Library also holds a collection of the papers of the activist Derek Mirfin (ref. DM 668), which incorporates material emanating from a number of Liberal Party organisations. Among these are papers of the Union of University Liberal Societies (including a list of UULS officers, 1949–56; Assembly and Executive minutes, 1950–52;

other minutes and reports, 1952–53; Chairman's correspondence, 1952–53, and Secretary's correspondence, 1952–53); Union of Liberal Students (Executive Committee minutes, 1964–68); World Federation of Liberal and Radical Youth; and the Radical Reform Group (including the *Newsletter* for 1956–60).

In addition to these above collections of national party organisations, it is known that papers of the Association of Liberal Councillors for 1980–84 have now been deposited at Cheshire Record Office (ref. LOP 4) and that the records of the Society of Certified and Associated Liberal Agents for 1895–1951 are at Leeds District Archives. A list is available (NRA 14315). Minutes and accounts of the North Western District of the Society for 1903–51 are at Manchester Central Library (see list NRA 24631).

REGIONAL RECORDS

1. *Eastern Counties Liberal Federation* Records for the period 1920–88 are in Cambridgeshire Record Office (ref. R91/32).
2. *Lancashire, Cheshire and North West Federation* Minutes for the period 1913–71 are at Manchester Central Library. A list is available (NRA 24632).
3. *Leeds Federation* Minutes for 1894–1957 are at Leeds District Archives (NRA 14315).
4. *London Liberal Federation* Records, 1890–1970, are in the London Metropolitan Archives.
5. *Manchester Federation* Assorted papers for the period from 1878 onwards are at Manchester Central Library (NRA 21667).
6. *Scottish Liberal Club* Records for the period 1879–1953 have been deposited at the National Library of Scotland (ref. Dep 275 and Acc 7107). A list is available (NRA 29088). These papers include Management Committee minutes for 1947–53 and an agenda book for 1936–50.
7. *Welsh Liberal Party* The National Library of Wales holds an extensive collection of papers of the Welsh Liberal Party for the period from 1963 onwards and reference should be made to the list NRA 26130. A final deposit was made in 1988 by Gwyn Griffiths, the last Chairman of the Welsh Liberal Party prior to its merger with the Social Democratic Party. This deposit includes correspondence and papers regarding the

Constitutional Review Working Group's Report, 1980; the Boundary Commission Review, 1981–82, and papers relating to the AGMs of the Welsh Liberal Party for the period 1980–82. There is also a substantial collection of publications, papers and circulars dating from the 1970s. In addition the National Library holds the minutes of the Welsh Committee of the Social Democratic Party/Liberal Party Alliance for the period 1985–87. It is understood that papers within the archive are subject to a ten-year rule; further enquiries should be directed to the Director of the Welsh Political Archive.

Certain collections of personal papers deposited at the National Library also contain relevant material. The most important of these are the papers of Gwyn Griffiths, which contain records arising from the Welsh League of Young Liberals for the period 1978–84, and the minutes of joint meetings of the SDP Policy Committee and Liberal Standing Committee for 1985–88; and the papers of George Morrison, which include the correspondence and minutes of the Executive Committee of the Welsh Liberal Party for 1976–84 and correspondence of its General Council for 1968–82.

8. *West Midlands Federation* Assorted records for the period 1894–1962 are available at Birmingham University Library (see list NRA 13206).
9. *Western Counties Federation* Papers for the period 1922–67 have been deposited at Bristol University Library (ref. DM 1172). A list is available (NRA 28088). The collection includes Executive Committee minutes 1927–66; Finance and General Purpose Committee minutes, 1927–64, and accounts, 1922–67.
10. *Yorkshire Federation* A collection of papers, 1979–88, has been deposited at Bristol University Library (ref. DM 1411).

LIBERAL WRITERS' ASSOCIATION Relevant material covering the period 1956–60 may be found among the papers of the Liberal Party activist Derek Mirfin, which have been deposited in Bristol University Library (ref. DM 668).

LIBERATION Formerly known as the Movement for Colonial Freedom, Liberation was founded in

1954 to campaign for self-determination for colonial peoples. Its original constituents were the British branch of the Congress against Imperialism, the Central Africa Committee, the Kenya Committee and the Seretse Khama Defence Committee. It adopted its current name in 1970.

An archive has been deposited at the School of Oriental and African Studies, University of London. It runs to some 75 boxes of papers and a list is available (NRA 27885). All classes of material have been preserved, but up to approximately 1961 the records are intermittent on account of the number of moves of premises made during the early years of the organisation. However, it is possible that relevant papers may also be found among the private papers of Lord Brockway, the sometime President, and among those of a founder member, J. Murumbi, now deposited in the Kenya National Archives. The Movement's records in the Murumbi collection are understood to cover the period 1948–58.

The archive at SOAS is rather fuller for the period 1961–67 and is substantially complete for 1967–72. The division between groups of records within the collection is arbitrary, but it does include papers of the Executive Committee, 1956–72; the Central Council, 1957–72; Annual Delegate Conference, 1954–55, 1959, 1961–72; and the Area Councils. There are also sets of the Secretary's Report, 1965–72; the Annual Report for 1955 and 1958–71; general correspondence, 1960–72; a run of the *Journal*, 1960–73; press releases, 1961–72; and an extensive series of subject files arranged by individual country. In addition there are files relating to affiliated organisations such as trades unions, which contain correspondence, affiliation details, and papers on various campaigns conducted by the organisation.

Researchers should be aware that the archive of Liberation also incorporates the papers of the Committee for Peace in Nigeria (q.v.).

LIBERTY Formerly known as the National Council for Civil Liberties, Liberty was established in 1934. It works to promote the rights of the individual and to oppose racial, political, religious or other forms of discrimination and abuses of power. NCCL was prominent in the 1930s in opposing Fascism and anti-Semitism in the United Kingdom, but its level of activity declined somewhat during the 1950s; however, following the appointment of Tony Smythe as General Secretary in 1966 its work increased substantially. The collection may now be considered to cover all aspects of civil liberties in Great Britain and Northern Ireland. A history of Liberty by Mark Lilley, *National Council For Civil Liberties: The First Fifty Years*, was published in 1984.

Since the mid-1960s the papers of Liberty have been deposited on a periodic basis in the Brynmor Jones Library, University of Hull (ref. DCL). The collection now comprises some 450 cases of papers in total and extends up to 1977. Due to the personal nature of a large proportion of the material, not all of the collection is open at present and intending researchers should seek the advice of the Archivist. Included within the archive are the minutes of the NCCL Executive Committee for 1944–72, and files relating to the AGM for 1963–73 and its minute books for 1952–69. There is a run of the journal *Civil Liberty* for 1937–51. The bulk of the collection is made up of subject files covering all aspects of the work of Liberty such as police activities, women's rights, censorship, freedom of speech and of assembly, the position of minorities in the UK, mental health legislation, defence regulations, immigration etc. The majority of these series commence in the mid-1930s. A considerable number relate to foreign and Commonwealth affairs (chiefly dating from the 1940s). 'United Kingdom' and 'Ireland' files contain considerable information on Scottish and Welsh nationalism, the situation of Northern Ireland, the activities of the IRA, etc. Later files on individual legal cases or persons whose cases involved mental health regulations, are not open for research.

It should be noted that a number of papers (cases 429–440) comprise duplicate documents, press cuttings, membership forms and individual case files of the Council for Academic Freedom and Democracy (q.v.) for the period 1969 to 1973.

LIBRARY ASSOCIATION The Library Association, the professional association for British librarians, was founded in 1877. The majority of its papers are retained at its headquarters: older files are held in a basement store whilst current files are kept within each department. Some material was lost during World War II, but the existing collection includes the minutes of the Council and of the Standing Committees and their working parties; Annual Reports and Annual Conference Proceedings, and what the Association has described as 'normal office ledgers and accounts'. Correspondence of more recent years has been retained, in theory, according to Civil Service guidelines. In practice, files have been weeded less thoroughly. The Association is now called the Chartered Institute of Library and Information Professionals.

LICENSED VICTUALLERS' CENTRAL PROTECTION SOCIETY OF LONDON LTD The Society represents the interests of businesses licensed to sell alcohol. It was founded in 1833 and incorporated under its present title in 1893. Since 1892 the Society's London Central Board has been the central organisation for a number of affiliated societies of licensed victuallers in Greater London and adjoining counties. The Board gives advice, guidance and assistance to its affiliated societies and their individual members, and lobbies in Parliament and elsewhere to protect the licensed trade.

The records have been placed in the Guildhall Library, London (ref. Mss 21439–60).

LIFE OFFICES ASSOCIATION The association has deposited its records in the Guildhall Library, London (ref. MSS 28376). The most recently deposited material covers the period 1976–85.

LONDON MUNICIPAL SOCIETY The Society was formed in 1894 as a front organisation for the Conservative Party in London local government politics. Its principal aim was to win control of the London County Council; it fought local elections firstly as the Moderate and later as the Municipal Reform Party. Until its dissolution in 1963, the Society was closely associated with the National Union of Ratepayers' Associations.

A number of the surviving records of the Society were deposited in the Guildhall Library. These papers include three volumes of Executive Committee minutes, 1894–1963; two volumes of LMS Council minutes and two volumes of AGM minutes of the same date; and a large collection of printed material, pamphlets and typescript notes, including copies of the magazines *Ratepayer* (1924–48) and *The Londoner* (1948–63).

LONDON POSITIVIST SOCIETY The Positivist Society of London was founded in 1867 to propagate positivist social principles. It sponsored regular public meetings and publications and its influence is now continued through the Auguste Comte Memorial Lectures held at the London School of Economics.

The records of the society have been deposited in the LSE Library. For the pre-1945 papers, reference should be made to *Sources, 1900–51*, vol. I, p. 157. There is some post-1945 material including committee minutes to 1951, cash books, membership and subscription lists and a limited amount of correspondence, 1940s–50s. The collection is open and a handlist is available.

LONDON SOCIETY OF JEWS AND CHRISTIANS The papers have been placed in London Metropolitan Archives (ref. Acc/3686). A list is available (NRA 41525). The collection includes minutes, correspondence, administrative records and some publicity material. Access requires written permission of the Liberal Jewish Synagogue.

LORD'S DAY OBSERVANCE SOCIETY The Society was founded in 1831 by Joseph Wilson and his cousin the Rev Daniel Wilson (later Bishop of Calcutta). It has been in continuous existence since then and is today the sole surviving example of the influential movement which campaigned to preserve the Sabbath. It seeks particularly to promote the observance of the Lord's Day for worship and to oppose the spread of Sunday trading. In 1920 the Society united with the Working Men's Lord's Day Rest Association, with the Lord's Day Observance Association of Scotland in 1953 and finally with the Imperial Alliance for the Defence of Sunday in 1965.

The papers of the Society consist of minutes, reports and journals dating back to the inception of the Society in 1831, although some material was destroyed by enemy action during World War II. The minutes of the Council since the Society's foundation and a complete run of its magazine *Joy and Light* from the publication of the first edition in

1948 are available at the Society's headquarters. Copies of the annual report are retained for the period 1926–51, after which date the reports were incorporated in the magazine. Annual accounts exist from 1978 to date and some correspondence with government and local authorities has been retained. Certain records of the predecessor societies are also available. Enquiries should be directed to the General Secretary.

LOW PAY UNIT The Low Pay Unit has been in existence since 1974. It is a campaigning, research and advice organisation which seeks to bring to public attention the problems of the low paid and to advise such persons of their legal rights. Since 1983 it has assisted initiatives by local authorities on low pay and has established autonomous regional Units in England and Scotland. The Unit has retained its own papers, which comprise minutes of the AGM since 1986 and of the Management Committee since 1988; copies since 1974 of its press releases and publications (including the *New Review* from 1989); financial records; and correspondence and subject files. Permission to view the records must be obtained from the Director.

M

MALTHUSIAN LEAGUE The League was founded in 1877 with the object of promoting the understanding of Malthusian doctrine and its bearing on social problems, i.e. the necessity of restricting births in order to eliminate poverty, social unrest and wars. The League was the founder member of the International Federation of Neo-Malthusians and Birth Control Leagues.

The chief source of information for the activities of the League is its journal. This was published as *The Malthusian* (1879–1921, 1949–52) and as *New Generation* (1922–49). Annual reports were also published. No formal collection of records has been located, but the LSE Library has some notes, drafts etc. for C.V. Drysdale's published works on the Malthusian doctrine.

MANCHESTER COTTON ASSOCIATION The Association was a grouping of cotton merchants and brokers established to import cotton directly, following the opening of the Manchester Ship Canal in 1894. At the peak of activity in the 1920s one million bales were imported each season, but the contraction of the trade prompted the Association's liquidation in 1965. The records of the Association were subsequently deposited in Manchester Central Library (ref. M26). A certain amount of material was lost due to enemy action in 1940 but the surviving papers comprise minutes of the Board (1926–52, 1959–63), the Finance Committee (1937–54, 1961–65) and shareholders' meetings (1895–1961); cash books and ledgers (1940–65); circular books (1933–53); and miscellaneous records including Registers of Members (1894–1962) and Directors (1920–60).

MANIFESTO GROUP A political pressure group on the right of the Labour Party. Neville Sandelson, successively Labour and SDP MP for Hayes and Harlington from 1971 to 1983, was Treasurer of the Manifesto Group in 1975–80. His papers are in the LSE Library. Other Manifesto Group papers, 1976–90, are in the Labour History Archive.

MANUFACTURING, SCIENCE AND FINANCE UNION MSF was formed in January 1988 by the amalgamation of the Association of Scientific, Technical and Managerial Staffs (ASTMS), and the Technical, Administrative and Supervisory Staffs (TASS) section of the engineering union AUEW (see Amalgamated Engineering Union). Owing to its recent foundation, the records of the constituent unions within MSF are described separately in this Guide. The current files of the union, however, will be maintained by MSF itself.

MARINE SOCIETY The oldest public maritime charity in the world, the Marine Society was founded in 1756 to recruit men for the Royal Navy. Over the intervening two centuries it has continued both to train boys for the service by providing scholarships and maintaining training ships, and to care for the moral and physical welfare of seafarers. The Society was influential in the formation of such organisations as King George's Fund for Sailors, the Sea Cadet Corps and the Sail Training Association. In 1976 it merged with a number of other charities with which it was closely connected, including the Sailors' Home and Red Ensign Club (founded 1830), the London School of Nautical Cookery (1893), the Incorporated Thames Nautical Training College (1862), the Seafarers Education Service (1919) and the College of the Sea (1938).

The papers of the Society and its associated charities have been retained in part at its offices. The earlier material has been deposited at the National Maritime Museum.

MARRIED WOMEN'S ASSOCIATION Founded in 1938, the Association was an offshoot of the more feminist Six Point Group (q.v.). Its primary aim was to make marriage legally a financial partnership but its campaign statements were vague about how this was to be achieved in cases of persons who were co-habitees rather than those who were married to one another. The Association is still in existence but the papers for the period *c.* 1938–82 have been deposited in the Women's Library (q.v.). The material is presently unlisted and is unavailable, but it is known to comprise minutes, correspondence, annual reports, press-cuttings and assorted printed papers, arranged in three boxes. The Library also holds the papers of the late Nora Bodley (*d.* 1983), sometime Secretary of the Association.

MARX MEMORIAL LIBRARY The Library was founded in 1933 as a working-class library for the study of social science. It contains one of the richest collections in Britain of material of every kind connected with the working-class movement. Though it specialises in Marxist literature, its holdings include an important collection of printed ephemera relating to radical and socialist history. From time to time the papers and books of prominent radicals and left-wing activists have been acquired by the Library, so that it now holds a significant archival collection. Most of this material is relevant for the period prior to 1945. For these papers, see *Sources, 1900–51*, vol. I, pp. 61–62.

MASS-OBSERVATION Mass-Observation (M-O) was founded in 1937 by Tom Harrisson, Charles Madge and Humphrey Jennings. Their aim was to give a 'true picture of Britain in the late 1930s', since they felt that the media did not adequately reflect prevailing public feelings. More detail on the scope and methods of this early survey, which lasted from 1937 to the early 1950s is given in *Sources, 1900–51*, vol. I, p. 163. This material, housed at the University of Sussex since 1970, is fully listed (NRA 24301).

A new 'Mass-Observation in the Eighties' project was established in 1981. More than 1000 volunteer respondents were recruited nationwide to record their everyday lives in diaries and respond to specific questions or 'directives' sent to them three or four times each year. This material is also at Sussex University. Access is given to bona fide researchers at the discretion of the Trustees on application to the Archivist.

MEDICAL AID FOR VIETNAM The records of this body and those of the British Hospital for Vietnam have been deposited in the Working Class Movement Library. A list is available of the library's complete manuscript holdings (NRA 31932).

MEDICAL ASSOCIATION FOR PREVENTION OF WAR The Medical Association for Prevention of War was formed in 1951, during the Korean War. Its aims are to study the causes and consequences of war; to oppose the use of medical science for any end other than relief of suffering; to contemplate the ethical responsibilities of the profession in wartime; and to campaign for increased spending on health care rather than military pursuits. It is the British affiliate of the International Physicians for Prevention of a Nuclear War (IPPNW).

Records of the Association (which is now known as MedAct) have been placed in the Contemporary Medical Archives Centre, Wellcome Institute (ref. SA/MED). The collection covers the period 1951–96.

MEDICAL JOURNALISTS' ASSOCIATION There are papers in the Contemporary Medical Archives Centre, Wellcome Institute. The collection (some of which is closed until 2020) includes minutes, newsletters, membership records etc. A list is available (NRA 40678).

MEDICAL OFFICERS OF SCHOOLS ASSOCIATION The papers for the period *c.* 1884 to *c.* 1980 have been deposited with the West Yorkshire Archives Service at Wakefield. They include minutes, 1884–1980; agendas and notices of meetings; attendance books, 1908–83; annual reports and proceedings; newsletters, 1969–85; conference and symposium reports, 1973–77; general correspondence; and a variety of medical journals and reports.

MEDICAL WOMEN'S FEDERATION An extensive archive of the organisation, founded in 1917, has been deposited in the Contemporary Medical Archives Centre, Wellcome Institute (ref. SA/MWF). A detailed list is available (NRA 36148). There are extensive minutes, annual reports, correspondence files etc. and material relating to the Medical Women's International Federation etc.

MEN OF THE TREES The Men of the Trees had its origins in colonial Kenya when, in 1922, a forestry officer, Richard St Barbe Baker, founded the Watu-Wa-Miti to teach Kenyans the value of the proper management of the tree stock. On his return to England in 1924 Baker formed the Men of the Trees (the name is a direct translation of the Swahili original) to encourage tree preservation. Since World War II the Society has been concerned with promoting the scientific management of trees and educating public opinion about growing desertification.

Little of the archive of the Society has survived, but it is known to include minutes of the Council and AGM from 1957, and of the Executive Committee from 1969. No other administrative material has been kept. The principal reference source for the society is its journal, *Trees* (known as *Trees and Life* from 1957 to 1960 and again in 1965, and as *Trees and New Earth* for the year 1950); complete sets are available on deposit in the British Library and Cambridge University Library. The journal was first issued in 1936 and contains reports of all the Society's activities (including Council meetings, conferences and expeditions), Annual Reports and financial statements, and branch reports. The British Library also holds a near complete set of Annual Reports from 1934 and of copies of publications from 1948, and a full set of reports of the summer schools from 1938.

Administrative records are held by the society at its headquarters and enquiries should be addressed to the Secretary/Treasurer to the Council. A list is available (NRA 24461). The personal papers of Richard St Barbe Baker have been deposited in the Hartley Library, University of Southampton (ref. MS 92).

MENTAL HEALTH FOUNDATION The Foundation is a grant-making organisation which supports medical research and community-based projects in the voluntary sector. It was established in 1949 as the Mental Health Research Fund and adopted its present name in 1972 upon merging with the Mental Health Trust.

A substantial archive exists, including records of the former Research Fund (although not of the Mental Health Trust prior to 1972), which is in the process of being catalogued. The majority of papers consist of reports produced by research organisations under contract to the Foundation, a number of which are confidential, although access may be granted to bona fide researchers. Originally these reports were solely in the field of medical and psychiatric research and were issued under the aegis of the Research Committee, whose papers have been retained from 1954 to date; subsequently the Foundation's work has grown into the area of community-based projects under the direction of four new committees: General Projects (established 1973), Substance Abuse (1989), Learning Disabilities (1987) and Committee for the Mentally Disordered Offender (1989). The papers of these committees have also been retained. In addition the Foundation holds records relating to all its grant holders; archive correspondence from the 1970s onwards; and minute books of each of the above committees and of the Trustees and the Executive Committee since 1949. An annual report is also produced. All enquiries should be directed to the Information Officer.

METHODIST CONFERENCE Relevant records relating to Anglican-Methodist unity and ecumenical affairs, 1955–82, have been placed in the Methodist Archives and Research Centre, Deansgate, Manchester. A list is available (NRA 41928). The Methodist Archives are the basic starting point for all research in recent Methodist history. They possess numerous records of Methodist groups and organisations (e.g. minutes of the Methodist Peace Fellowship, 1937–77).

METROPOLITAN COUNTIES ANTI-ABOLITION CAMPAIGN It has been reported that the records of the London office for the period 1983–85 have now been deposited with the Tyne and Wear Archives Service.

MID-WALES INDUSTRIAL DEVELOPMENT ASSOCIATION It is understood that the papers of the Association have been deposited in the South Wales Coalfield Archive at the University College of Swansea Library.

MILITANT A collection of material for the period 1965–92 was deposited in 2004 in the Modern Records Centre, University of Warwick (ref. MSS 529). It is not yet listed.

MIND The principal voluntary mental health agency for England and Wales, MIND was established in 1946 (as the National Association for Mental Health) by the amalgamation of three existing mental health bodies: the Central Association for Mental Welfare, the Child Guidance Council, and the National Council for Mental Hygiene. In 1970 the name MIND was formally adopted for the Association as a whole to emphasise its new primary function as a lobbying group and advisory service. Today MIND focuses attention on the quality of care available to the mentally ill and co-operates with the responsible authorities and professional associations to improve and develop services.

The papers of MIND are presently retained at its offices. They include the minutes of various committees, e.g. child guidance clinic, clinical and social services, and the steering committee from 1945 onwards. The minute books are all stored off the premises and two weeks' notice is required to examine them. In addition there exist the annual reports of MIND and its predecessors from 1939 onwards, and reports of the Conference of Mental Welfare from 1918 and of the Child Guidance Conference from 1935. Copies of all publications issued by MIND are retained at its headquarters. Financial records are not available. The library maintains a series of information files on a wide range of mental health issues, including notices from official publications, covering the period from the 1920s onwards. Those wishing for access to the papers should apply to the Director at the above address.

MINORITY RIGHTS GROUP An educational charity and independent human rights research and information organisation. MRG's archive consists of an incomplete run of Executive Committee minutes from the mid-1960s to date; financial records (including ledger books), and edited correspondence and subject files. These papers are presently closed to researchers. Publicly available material includes annual reports, conference reports and published papers on minority groups worldwide (including the newsletter *Outsider*), copies of which have been retained. The papers have largely been kept at the Group's offices.

MISSION TO LONDON The papers for the period 1948–52 were given to Lambeth Palace Library by the Revd Dr. G. Huelin in 1966 (ref. MSS 1948–60). The Mission was started by the Bishop of London in 1949 to restore the religious life of the capital after World War II. The papers include minutes of the Executive Committee; minutes, reports and papers of the Advisory Council; financial accounts, 1947–52; a history of the Mission by its organising secretary the Revd Frank Tylery; monthly letters to incumbents and local representatives; a collection of press-cuttings; and an extensive number of records of its operations.

MISSIONARY SOCIETIES Missionary societies played a very major role in the history of Britain and British expansion overseas prior to 1945. Since 1945, although their influence has often much diminished, they have played an important part in many areas of the world (as in the liberation movement in Southern Africa or the crusade against apartheid in South Africa itself). Sometimes, the missions themselves have been under threat (as in China after the Communist takeover). The archives of very many of these societies are described in an extremely useful, compact published guide: Rosemary Seton and Emily Naish (compilers), *A Preliminary Guide to the Archives of British Missionary Societies* (SOAS, 1992). Further details of the archives listed below (and many others) can be found in this publication. Where an organisation is described in this volume, a cross-reference is given below.

Current Name of Society	*Records Held At*
Africa Evangelical Fellowship	Society HQ (Newbury)
Africa Inland Mission International	Society HQ (London N19)
Baptist Missionary Society	Society HQ (Didcot)
British and Foreign Bible Society	Society HQ (Swindon)
Church Missionary Society	(See p. 262.)
Church of Scotland Board of World Mission and Unity	NLS

Current Name of Society	Records Held At
Commonwealth Missionary Society	SOAS
Conference for World Mission	SOAS
Council for World Mission	(See p. 279.)
Foreign Mission of the Historical Society of the Presbyterian Church of Wales	NLW
Free Church of Scotland Foreign Missions Board	NLS
International Committee for Christian Literature for Africa	SOAS
International Missionary Council and Conference of British Missionary Societies Joint Archive: Africa	SOAS
International Nepal Fellowship	New College (Edinburgh)
Interserve	Society HQ (London SE11)
Jerusalem and East Mission	MEC, St Antony's College
Korean Mission	Birmingham. See NRA 43314
Lakher Pioneer Mission	IOL
Melanesian Society	SOAS
Methodist Church Overseas Division (Methodist Missionary Society)	SOAS
National Bible Society of Scotland	Society HQ (Edinburgh)
Overseas Missionary Fellowship	(See p. 363.)
Presbyterian Church of England (United Reformed Church) Foreign Missions Committee	SOAS

Qua Iboe Fellowship	PRONI
Quaker Peace and Service (now Quaker Peace and Social Witness)	Friends' Library, London
Regions Beyond Missionary Union	New College (Edinburgh)
Salvation Army	(See p. 379.)
Society of Catholic Medical Missionaries	Society HQ (London W3)
Society for Promoting Christian Knowledge	Cambridge University Library
South American Missionary Society	Society HQ (Tunbridge Wells)
St Joseph's Missionary Society (Mill Hill Fathers)	Society HQ (London NW7)
Trust Society for the Furtherance of the Gospel (Moravian)	Moravian Church Archive, London
United Mission to Nepal	New College (Edinburgh)
United Society for Christian Literature	(See p. 405.)
United Society for the Propagation of the Gospel	(See p. 406.)
Universities Mission to Central Africa	BLCAS (Rhodes House Library)

MIXED SERVICES ORGANISATION The records of this organisation, which represented the interests of Yugoslav and Polish POWs working for the Allied forces in post-war Germany, have now been deposited in the National Army Museum. The papers cover the period 1946–71 (ref. 8701–33).

MODERN CHURCHPEOPLE'S UNION Records for the period 1898–1977 have been deposited in Lambeth Palace Library

MONDAY CLUB A most useful source for the records of this right-wing Conservative organisation is the archive of Patrick Wall MP, a founder member. His papers, deposited at the Brynmor Jones Library, University of Hull, (ref. DPW), include 76 files on the Monday Club, 1961–80s. The collection includes minutes of the Executive Committee

Council, and Annual General Meetings, correspondence, reports, notices of meetings, memoranda and notes.

MOTHERS FOR PEACE In 1980 the founders of Mothers for Peace, Lucy Behenna and Marion Mansergh, began a fund to send mothers to the USA and USSR with messages of friendship. A series of international visits by other parties subsequently led to the establishment of a secretariat to maintain contacts with women overseas and to popularise the organisation's work and beliefs. Mothers for Peace retains its own records, which include minutes of the Committee and of AGMs since 1980; copies of newsletters (incorporating reports of visits) and miscellaneous publications, and correspondence (largely relating to the arrangement of visits). Copies of the publications have been deposited in the Commonwealth Collection at the University of Bradford. Applications for access to other material should be made to the National Co-ordinator.

MOTHERS' UNION The Mothers' Union was founded in 1876. It is a society of the Church of England whose aim is the advancement of the Christian religion in the sphere of marriage and family life. Membership is open to all baptised Christians (including men) who declare support for the aim and objects of the Society.

The archive has been retained at the Union's headquarters. Material includes minutes of the Central Council and the Executive Committee from 1896 to date and of the Departmental Committees from their inception, a run of the *Official Handbook* since 1911, and the following series of magazines: *Mother's Union Journal* (1898–1953), *Mothers in Council* (1891–1951), *Workers's Paper* (1915–61), *Mothers' Union News* (1962–75), and *Home and Family* (1954–). Other records have been retained but are presently uncatalogued. Applications for access to the papers should be made to the Secretary.

Reference should also be made to the entry in this Guide for the Scottish Mothers' Union, a separate organisation to the above.

MOTOR CYCLE ASSOCIATION OF GREAT BRITAIN LIMITED The trade association for UK motor cycle makers, the MCA was incorporated in 1901 as the Cycle & Motor Cycle Manufacturers' and Traders' Union Ltd. At present its membership comprises some one hundred firms.

The Association's papers have now been deposited at the Modern Records Centre, University of Warwick (ref. MSS 204). A list is available (NRA 28058). The collection is extensive and consists of the minutes of general meetings, committees, and subsidiary sections of the Association (cycle, proprietary article, and motor cycle manufacturers) in 44 volumes for the period 1909–73; Finance Committee minutes, 1949–71; a register of members' subscriptions, 1954–59; filebooks of duplicated and printed circulars and miscellaneous material, including agendas and reports to meetings, 1911–73; a substantial series of circulars, correspondence, subject files, filebooks etc.

The collection also includes the records of the Cycle Trade Union, namely minute books, 1914–62; ledgers, 1939–61; the register of members and subscriptions, 1954–58; filebooks of circulars, reports, etc., 1914–57, and annual reports and balance sheets, 1915–57.

MOVEMENT FOR CHRISTIAN DEMOCRACY An all-party non-denominational group dedicated to establishing Christian values in politics and developing relations with Christian political parties in Europe, the Movement for Christian Democracy was formally established in 1990 following meetings in the previous two years of an Epiphany Group convened by MPs David Alton and Ken Hargreaves. It has kept its own papers, which include minutes of the National Steering Group since its establishment in January 1990; minutes of the original drafting and organisation subcommittees; papers relating to the Epiphany Group meetings since 1989 and the National Conferences since 1991; financial records such as ledger books and bank statements; working group research papers, and correspondence files. A monthly bulletin is issued to members. Applications from researchers wishing to examine the material should be made to the General Secretary.

MOVEMENT FOR THE ORDINATION OF WOMEN MOW was founded in July 1979, following a resolution of the 1975 General Synod of the

Church of England that there were no fundamental objections to the ordination of women to the priesthood. The previous year an attempt to remove the legal bar to women's ordination had been rejected by the General Synod and this failure had stimulated the formation of MOW. The papers, around 100 boxes, which include the minutes of the AGM, Central Council and Executive Committee, copies of all MOW's publications, yearly financial statements and correspondence and subject files have been placed in the Women's Library (q.v.). It is understood that the papers are closed until the year 2022. The Women's Library also has some of the papers of Dame Christian Howard. Others are in the Borthwick Institute, which also has the York Diocesan MOW papers.

MOVEMENT FOR SOLIDARITY WITH THE WORKERS OF SPAIN The records of this pro-Spanish Republican organisation are incorporated within the Will Poynter Collection in the South Wales Coalfield Archive at the University College of Swansea Library. A list is available to the whole Archive (NRA 14694).

MUSEUMS ASSOCIATION The Museums Association was established in 1889 to promote the establishment and better administration of museums and galleries. Its papers have been deposited in the National Archives but are not open to researchers at present.

N

NAMIBIA SUPPORT COMMITTEE Part of the archive of the organisation, formed in 1969 as the Friends of Namibia, was deposited in BLCAS (Rhodes Library), Oxford in 1996 (ref. MSS Afr s 2300). A list is available (NRA 43081). The Rhodes House collection covers mainly the period 1985–93. Some earlier archival and printed material is in the Namibian State Archive. Rhodes House has a later accession of papers from Randolph Vigne. Likewise Vigne's earlier papers (1969 to mid-1980s) are also in Namibia.

NATIONAL ABORTION CAMPAIGN The National Abortion Campaign, whose aim is to build a mass campaign to oppose all legislation restricting a woman's right to terminate a pregnancy, has been largely organised around each successive parliamentary bill on abortion (e.g. the Benyon Bill of 1977 and the Corrie Bill of 1979). The archive, which has now been transferred to the Contemporary Medical Archives Centre at the Wellcome Institute, largely reflects this organisation inasmuch as there are few formal records. The deposited material consists largely of subject files relating to each bill, and minutes and a day-book covering the period 1982–83. Researchers should also be aware that the papers of the Abortion Law Reform Association (q.v.) are likewise available at the CMAC.

NATIONAL ADVISORY CENTRE ON CAREERS FOR WOMEN This body was previously known as the Women's Employment Federation (WEF). During World War II it assumed the functions of the Women's Service Branch of the Fawcett Society (q.v.), which had been established to advise women on opportunities for voluntary work. The National Advisory Centre deposited the papers of the WEF at the Women's Library (q.v.) in 1983. A list is available (NRA 29385). The material includes Executive Committee minutes, 1934–79; Advisory Department committee minutes, 1934–56, and reports, 1951–73 and 1976–79; AGM reports, 1951–64; extensive financial records (including ledgers, cash books, auditors' balance sheets, bank statements, and correspondence with the Inland Revenue); and miscellaneous reports, circular letters and pamphlets, 1939–83.

NATIONAL ANTI-RACIST MOVEMENT IN EDUCATION NAME has as its main aim the eradication of racism from education and society at large, which it seeks to bring about through campaigns, conferences, publications and other promotional activities. It was founded as the Association of Teachers of English to Pupils from Overseas in 1960 and changed its name to the National Association for Multiracial Education in 1972; it adopted its present title in 1985. NAME retains its own records. Available papers include most Executive Committee minutes from 1984 onwards, and most conference, AGM reports and financial records from the same date. Retained correspondence is organised into three series, i.e. with government departments, with trades unions and local education authorities, and with other bodies, especially in relation to incidents of racial discrimination. Certain conference reports have been separately published. NAME also holds copies of its journal *Multiracial Education*, up to vol. 13, no. 1 (March 1985), and of its newsletter *Arena* from 1983 to date. Persons wishing to use the papers should apply to the Secretary. A fee is payable for permission to use the published material.

NATIONAL ARCHIVE OF SOCIAL POLICY AND SOCIAL CHANGE Essex University Library holds the National Archive of Social Policy. All enquiries should be directed there.

NATIONAL ASSEMBLY OF WOMEN Founded in 1952 under the sponsorship of the Communist

Party, the National Assembly of Women had strong links with other internationalist 'progressive' women's organisations. Its stated aim was equal opportunities for women, although this was selectively interpreted depending upon prevailing CPGB policy (e.g. it was not active in the Equal Pay Campaign). The papers have been been deposited in the Women's Library (q.v.) and comprise minutes, correspondence and printed material (including papers relating to the Women's International Democratic Federation and the National Campaign for Nursery Education). The material largely covers the period 1963–81.

NATIONAL ASSOCIATION FOR THE CARE AND RESETTLEMENT OF OFFENDERS
NACRO is a national charity specialising in the rehabilitation, particularly through job training, of former prisoners and non-custodial offenders. It was founded in 1966 and offers a research and information service on all aspects of crime and its perpetrators.

The records of the association together with those of its predecessor, the Central Discharged Prisoners Aid Society, have been deposited in the Modern Records Centre, University of Warwick (ref. MSS 67). These consist of annual reports, 1933–63; minutes for 1968; some subject files; very many local and sectional reports; collected publications; and the files of Lord Donaldson of Kingsbridge from his period as chairman of NACRO and its predecessor (1961–78). A list is available for the collection (NRA 23021).

NATIONAL ASSOCIATION OF CITIZENS ADVICE BUREAUX
The need for a national information and advice service in Great Britain emerged in the years between the two World Wars, although the first Citizens Advice Bureaux were not established until 1939 to meet the national emergency.

The NACAB is responsible both for the policy of the CAB Service and for guidance in day-to-day work. The Association retains a large proportion of the material it publishes, which is held by the Administration Department at the Central Office and covers a preceding three-year period. In addition an archive of papers is held off-site. Internal committee records which have been retained include minutes and agendas of the Council from 1957 and its general correspondence from 1960; minutes and agendas of the Constitution Committee, 1973–80; and minutes and agendas of the Executive Committee from 1971. Annual reports for the period 1959–78 are also available and an extensive series of financial records, policy and development papers, evidence papers, and representations to Government are included amongst the archived subject files. Further details should be sought from the Research and Development Department of the NACAB.

Earlier papers have been deposited at the London Metropolitan Archives. They comprise five series of files covering c. 1940–60. One series comprises subject files, another national statistics for the Service. The remainder relate to closed and current bureaux, and are arranged by name of the bureau or by geographical region.

There is also a significant collection of material at PRONI (ref. D3485add), consisting largely of day books for local bureaux in the Northern Ireland Association (e.g. Belfast, East Belfast, Downpatrick and Lurgan) for the period of the 1970s and early 1980s.

NATIONAL ASSOCIATION OF COUNCILS FOR VOLUNTARY SERVICE
In 1945 the National Council for Voluntary Organisations set up a Standing Conference of Councils of Social Service to act as a national forum for the Councils for Voluntary Service which operate in rural and urban communities in England. The name was changed to the Councils for Voluntary Service National Association in 1981, and the above title adopted in April 1991 when the Association became independent of NCVO.

Retained material consists of the minutes of committees and of AGMs since 1945; copies of conference papers; correspondence arranged by subject and by organisation; annual reports from individual CVS (dating from whenever these were founded); examples of mailings to members since 1981; and copies of all publications. Financial records are unavailable, having been retained by NCVO. Persons wishing to examine any papers should write to the Information Officer.

NATIONAL ASSOCIATION OF DIVISIONAL EXECUTIVES FOR EDUCATION An extensive collection of records (101 boxes) covering the period 1934–74 is in the Hartley Library, University of Southampton (ref. MS 68). The collection includes correspondence regarding its establishment and constitution (1946–69); minutes (1947–74); miscellaneous correspondence; and numerous subject files (including topics such as secondary and religious education, staffing of schools, post-war education policy and planning and local government reorganisation). There are also extensive correspondence files with bodies such as the Association of Education Committees, the Association of Municipal Corporations, the National Union of Teachers and the County Councils' Association. For further details, see the *Guide to the Archive and Manuscript Collections of the Hartley Library* (1992).

NATIONAL ASSOCIATION FOR ENVIRONMENTAL EDUCATION NAEE was founded in 1960 to promote environmental education in schools and colleges, which it assists by the publication of teachers' aids and by organising conferences and advising on curriculum content. NAEE has retained its own papers, which include committee minutes, financial records and annual reports since 1975, and correspondence files from 1983 onwards. The Association also publishes the journal *Environmental Education*. Permission for access to the material should be sought from the General Secretary of NAEE.

NATIONAL ASSOCIATION OF ESTATE AGENTS The National Association was established in 1962 to represent the interests of professional practitioners. It has retained the complete minutes of its Council, Executive Committee and Subcommittees since that date; AGM notices and financial records from 1963 onwards, and files of correspondence with government departments, which are particularly full with respect to the period leading to the passage of the Estate Agents Act of 1979. Routine correspondence is preserved for a preceding seven-year period only. The records are retained by the National Association's secretariat and applications for access should be addressed to the General Secretary.

NATIONAL ASSOCIATION OF HEAD TEACHERS NAHT was set up in March 1897, originally as the National Federation of Head Teachers' Associations. Its membership is confined to head and deputy head teachers of schools, and recruitment is principally in the state education sector. It is understood that the union has retained a large archive itself but the papers of the London Association, the largest branch and one which was instrumental in establishing the National Association, have been deposited at London Metropolitan Archives. A list is available (NRA 34618).

NATIONAL ASSOCIATION OF LABOUR TEACHERS The records of this association, and of the later Socialist Educational Association, covering the period 1926–80, have been deposited in the London Metropolitan Archives. The collection includes minutes, financial and membership records, correspondence, publications and records relating to campaigns and enquiries. For further details, see *Sources, 1900–51*, vol. VI, p. 68.

NATIONAL ASSOCIATION FOR MATERNAL AND CHILD WELFARE This association evolved from the late 19th-century Infant Welfare Movement, established to combat child mortality. In 1938 the Association of Infant, Welfare and Maternity Centres merged with the National Association for the Prevention of Infant Mortality and for the Welfare of Infancy to form the National Association of Maternity and Child Welfare Centres and for the Prevention of Infant Mortality. This name was later changed to the National Association for Maternal and Child Welfare.

The association has retained its records at its headquarters, but an outline list can be consulted (NRA 26460).

NATIONAL ASSOCIATION OF PENSION FUNDS NAPF is the principal national body for those involved with occupational pensions. Its membership is divided into fund members, such as companies and organisations in both the public and private sectors which provide pensions for their own employees, and other bodies such as firms providing professional, legal, administrative or investment services to pension funds. The principal objective of NAPF is to encourage employers to provide and develop their own pension provision. The Association has retained its own archive, comprising minute books for the Council and Committees, annual reports and accounts, and some special reports, consultation documents, etc., but the collection is at present closed to researchers.

NATIONAL ASSOCIATION OF POWERLOOM OVERLOOKERS

The Association began in November 1865 at Pendleton, Lancashire as the Pendleton Powerloom Overlookers' Mutual Assistance Association. With the opening of more branches it was renamed the National Association of Powerloom Overlookers in 1879.

The papers for the period prior to 1982 have been deposited in Manchester Central Library (ref. M490). Material includes minutes (1945–82); annual reports (1871–1978); rules (1904–76); financial records; and a substantial number of branch records. Papers of certain associated bodies, such as the General Union of Associations of Loom Overlookers (for 1948–82), the Northern Counties Textile Trades' Federation (1949–82), the British Federation of Textile Technicians (1975–81), and the United Textile Factory Workers' Association (1947–72), are included in the deposit. Access to correspondence and minute books less than thirty years old is restricted and permission must be sought from the General Secretary.

It is reported that further records of the General Union of Associations of Loom Overlookers, covering the period 1875–1974, are available at the Bury Archive Service.

NATIONAL ASSOCIATION OF PRISON VISITORS

The Association was formed in 1924, but traces its origins to 1901 when prison visiting was first officially recognised. The NAPV coordinates the work of those members of the public who volunteer to visit prisoners as a humanitarian service, and membership is open to all on payment of an annual subscription. The papers have been retained in the care of the General Secretary. The material comprises minutes of the Executive Committee and the Annual Conference (in part back to 1924), an Annual Report printed in the newsletter,

and correspondence files, which include papers relating to the national and regional conferences. Financial records are held by the Treasurer.

NATIONAL ASSOCIATION OF ROUND TABLES

In 1927 the young Rotarian Louis Marchesi set up the first Round Table in Great Britain in Norwich, with the object of providing a forum in which young businessmen might meet to contribute to civic life.

The National Association has retained its own papers, which with the exception of the National Membership Directories are available to bona fide researchers by prior appointment. Papers which may be consulted include AGM minutes from 1929 to date; National Council minutes, annual accounts (circulated to members with the above minutes), and subject files, which incorporate papers relating to the formation of most individual Tables and copies of the magazine the *Tabler* (formerly *News and Views*) from 1929 to date. Enquiries should be made to the General Secretary.

NATIONAL ASSOCIATION OF SCHOOLMASTERS AND UNION OF WOMEN TEACHERS

The National Association of Schoolmasters was formed (as the National Association of Men Teachers) in 1919 within the National Union of Teachers, but it seceded from that union in 1922. It entered a 'Joint Two Alliance' with the Union of Women Teachers in 1970 and the two organisations merged in 1975. The UWT itself had been formed in 1966 and should not be confused with a previous organisation, the National Union of Women Teachers (q.v.), which existed from 1906 to 1961. The union has now discontinued its former usage of displaying the short form of its title with a diagonal character between the names of its constituents, and is now known simply as the NASUWT.

The records of both the NAS and the UWT have been and will continue to be transferred to the Modern Records Centre, University of Warwick (ref. MSS 38), following the archive of the NAS, the bulk of which was deposited in 1961. Many of the earlier records were destroyed by enemy action in World War II. The surviving and post-war material includes miscellaneous Conference reports and proceedings, 1927–70; copies of the NAS journal, *The*

New Schoolmaster, 1944–73; over 400 pamphlets and leaflets of the NAS and NASUWT for the 1920s–80s; local associations' publications, 1918–60; and photographs. Most of the Burnham Reports regarding salary negotiations are also available. Subsequent deposits have added much local material.

Researchers should be aware that the papers for 1972–73 of the Northern Ireland branch of the National Association of Schoolmasters (est. 1970) have now been deposited in the Public Record Office of Northern Ireland (ref. D1050/14).

NATIONAL ASSOCIATION OF SOCIAL WORKERS IN EDUCATION NASWE is the national professional organisation for education welfare officers and social workers. It does not confine its work solely to schools but embraces the social and legal aspects of schooling and problems of the school-age child such as truancy, child benefits, and juvenile offending. It was previously known as the Education Welfare Officers' National Association (EWONA).

The archive of the predecessor organisation has been deposited at the Modern Records Centre, University of Warwick (ref. MSS 71). It includes National Council and NEC minutes, 1897–1976; Conference Journals, 1948–69; certain branch records, 1936–59; national account books, 1922–78; some correspondence and subject files, 1961–75 (including files on the Children and Young Persons Bill of 1963, the Plowden Committee of 1968, and the Seebohm Committee of 1970); the publication *Education Welfare Officer*, 1946–76; and various editions of the *Rulebook*, 1965–73. A copy of the Association's centenary history by F. Coombes and D. Beer, *The Long Walk From The Dark* (Birmingham, 1984), has also been deposited. The papers of the sometime president R. Grimoldby are available in collection MSS 122; these include items relating to the Yorkshire and Lincolnshire Federation of EWONA and a run of the *Education Welfare Officer* for 1960–75.

NATIONAL ASSOCIATION OF TEACHERS IN FURTHER AND HIGHER EDUCATION NATFHE was formed in 1975 by the amalgamation of the Association of Teachers in Technical Institutions (founded 1904) and the Association of Teachers in Colleges and Departments of Education (founded 1943). It is the professional association for lecturers in every public sector of further and higher education in the UK.

At present the NATFHE head office retains National Council minutes, Executive Committee papers, conference reports, copies of publications and some correspondence. Persons wishing to consult this material, some of which has been microfilmed, should apply to the Librarian of NATFHE.

Certain records of NATFHE's predecessors have now been deposited at the Modern Records Centre, University of Warwick (ref. MSS 176). The post-war material relating to the Association of Teachers in Colleges and Departments of Education comprises various series of committee minutes, 1943–75 (including Executive Committee and Council minutes and papers of the Joint Standing Committee with the NUT, 1950–63); extensive subject files, 1951–71; conference reports, 1964–75; the *Year Book*, 1944–64; an incomplete series of the *Bulletin of Education*, 1943–53; and the *News Sheet*, 1953–71. Papers of the Association of Teachers in Technical Institutions consist of minutes of the Council (1904–69), the Executive Committee (1913–75), the Annual Meeting (1918–57) and the Burnham Committee (1944–57) amongst others; some branch records, 1909–75 (including many papers of the London Branch/Division); subject files, 1926–60, particularly on salaries, superannuation and National Certificates; and press-cuttings, 1923–63. A limited amount of specifically NATFHE material is available, namely nine transfer cases of files concerned with Burnham Committees and superannuation, among other subjects. Copies of *ATTI/NATFHE* circulars for the period 1961–79 are to be found among the papers of Cyril Collard of the NATFHE Solihull Branch, also at Warwick (ref. MSS 155).

NATIONAL ASSOCIATION OF TEACHERS OF HOME ECONOMICS LTD Until 1983 this organisation was known as the Association of Teachers of Domestic Science. It originated in 1896 as a technical subcommittee of the National Union of Women Workers.

The records have been deposited at the Modern Records Centre, University of Warwick (ref. MSS

177). A list is available (NRA 23183). The papers consist of the minutes of the Executive Committee, 1896–1949; annual reports, 1944–48; audited accounts, 1929–71; a large volume of correspondence, 1936–74 (the bulk of the pre-war series having been destroyed by enemy action in 1940); and some branch records for 1915–62. The correspondence covers such subjects as relations with other teachers' unions (e.g. with the National Union of Teachers on the issue of joint membership), international congresses, travelling scholarships, and various aspects of domestic science teaching. A thirty-year closure rule applies to the records of the Walter Hines Travelling Scholarship.

NATIONAL ASSOCIATION OF WELSH MEDIUM NURSERY SCHOOLS AND PLAY-GROUPS (MUDIAD YSGOLION MEITHRIN)
The records for the period 1971–96 have been placed in the National Library of Wales. A list (in Welsh) is available (NRA 35821).

NATIONAL ASSOCIATION OF WOMEN CIVIL SERVANTS
NAWCS was formed in 1932 by the amalgamation of the Federation of Women Civil Servants and the Civil Service section of the Association of Women Clerks and Secretaries. Within the civil service women's professional organisations traditionally tended to follow the same pattern as men's, i.e. to be based on grades. Although the admission of women into the general grades of the service in 1920 had obviated the need for a union purely on a gender basis, NAWCS continued as an effective pressure group for equal pay by obliging other unions to give more attention to the needs of women members to ensure they did not leave to join NAWCS. The Association was wound up in 1959 when the objective of equal pay had been achieved. A useful history of women's organisations in the service is given in B.V. Humphreys, *Clerical Unions in the Civil Service* (1958).

The archive has been deposited in the Women's Library (q.v.). It comprises Executive Committee minutes, agendas and general secretary's annotated copies, 1939–59; Finance Committee minutes, 1943–59; Officers' Meetings minutes and agendas, 1953–59; Foreign Office Departmental Whitley Council minutes, 1952–55, and annual reports, 1951–54, and general reports, annually for 1933–58. In addition there are membership records, 1955–58; three files of reports and resolutions relating to the conferences of 1952–54; personal case files, 1949–58; General Secretary's papers on the association's dissolution, 1958–59; and correspondence files and papers including press-cuttings for the period 1948 to 1953 on equal pay (the only post-war series). An incomplete run of the newsletter exists for 1935–52; there are also assorted pamphlets, and memos and circulars relating to claims and arbitration awards, 1948–53.

NATIONAL ASSOCIATION OF WOMEN'S CLUBS
The Association was formed in 1942 as a non-sectarian body to advance education and provide for recreation and leisure activities for women. It retains its papers, which consist largely of minutes, at its head office. The collection is for the use of members only.

NATIONAL BIRTHDAY TRUST FUND
The Fund was established in 1928 as the National Birthday Fund to campaign for improvements in maternity provision, antenatal care and maternal health. The complete archive of the NBTF from its foundation until 1987 has now been deposited in the Contemporary Medical Archives Centre of the Wellcome Institute (ref. SA/NBT); it comprises 190 boxes and 16 folders. A list is available (NRA 31792). The collection includes records of the Joint Council on Midwifery for the 1930s and 1940s and some personal papers of Lady Rhys-Williams, one of the founders of the Fund. Permission for access to the archive will only be granted with the prior permission of the NBTF.

NATIONAL BOARD OF CATHOLIC WOMEN
The Board is a co-ordinating organisation for 21 Catholic women's organisations in the UK and a consultative body to the Roman Catholic Bishops Conference of England and Wales. It was founded in 1938 and the papers are retained by each successive Hon. Secretary and Hon. Treasurer. They include minutes of the Board, its Annual Report and special reports (including a history from 1938 to 1985), financial records and correspondence. Permission to view the material must be sought from the Executive Committee, c/o the President.

NATIONAL BUSWORKERS' ASSOCIATION
The only known surviving material on this association, covering the period 1950–54, can be found in correspondence in the administrative files of the former National Union of Railwaymen, deposited in the Modern Records Centre, University of Warwick (ref. MSS 127). The Association was founded in October 1950 and was centred on Hampshire and Dorset Motor Services Ltd.

NATIONAL CAMPAIGN FOR THE ABOLITION OF CAPITAL PUNISHMENT This pressure group was established in 1955 and succeeded various organisations campaigning (since the early 19th century) to abolish the death penalty. In the immediate post-war years, this aim was pursued by the Death Penalty Sub-Committee of the Howard League for Penal Reform (q.v.).

The National Campaign for the Abolition of Capital Punishment has retained a file of minutes dating back to 1955, together with correspondence and press-cuttings from 1957. Researchers should address their enquiries to the Chairman of the Campaign.

Reference should also be made to the papers of the Rt. Hon. Lord Gardiner, a former Chairman of the Campaign. These are deposited in the British Library (ref. Add MSS 56455–56463). These record his involvement with the campaign (and related issues), 1946–69, and consist of nine volumes of correspondence.

NATIONAL CAMPAIGN FOR THE ARTS The National Campaign for the Arts was formed in 1984 by artists and arts administrators as an independent agency. It seeks to raise public awareness of the cultural and educational benefits of a strong artistic tradition in Great Britain and, to maintain that tradition, campaigns for increased public funding for the arts and an established place for arts education in school curricula.

The records of the NCA are held at its offices. Access to the material is only by appointment with the Director or Information Officer. The NCA has retained the minutes of its Interim Executive Meetings (1985), Council Meetings (since 1986) and Board Meetings (since 1991); the correspondence of its officials and membership records since foun-

dation; copies of its quarterly publication, *NCA News*, from the first issue in Spring 1986 onwards; full financial records; and correspondence files. The NCA has also a library of more than 1500 reports and publications covering all arts issues; most of the material relates to the period since 1984, but some items of historical interest are also held (e.g. Arts Council Annual Reports).

NATIONAL CAMPAIGN FOR NURSERY EDUCATION The National Campaign for Nursery Education was founded in 1965 to press for a rapid increase in nursery education provision. It exists to promote local authority nursery schools as the most suitable basis for the general education of children. The papers, which comprise committee minutes, reports, published pamphlets and correspondence, but which are extant only from 1988, remain at present in the care of the Hon. Secretary. Enquiries concerning access to the material should be addressed to the Campaign.

NATIONAL CHAMBER OF TRADE The archive of the organisation, which amalgamated in 1993 with the Association of British Chambers of Commerce (q.v.) has been deposited in the Guildhall Library, London. The records, covering the period 1927–93, have been listed (NRA 41512).

NATIONAL CHILDBIRTH TRUST The National Childbirth Trust (NCT) is the United Kingdom's largest parenthood education charity, supporting 350 voluntary branches nationwide. It was established in 1946 to modernise the practices of antenatal care and childbirth in hospital. It sponsors medical research and education on maternity issues. The papers have been retained at the NCT's head office. They include council minutes, annual reports, a limited series of recent correspondence and subject files, financial records and copies of its publications. The research collection of the Trust's founder, Dr Grantly Dick-Read, has been deposited in the Wellcome Contemporary Medical Archives Centre, London (NRA 28599).

NATIONAL CHILDCARE CAMPAIGN The NCCC was inaugurated in 1980 to campaign for the greater provision of childcare facilities by the state and employers, particularly for the benefit of working mothers. Its sister organisation, the Daycare Trust, received charitable status in 1986; the NCCC itself now has primarily a function of providing information via publications, conferences, etc. All records since the Campaign's inception have been retained at the national offices. They comprise committee minutes; a full set of annual reports, newsletters and publications, and correspondence, particularly with the Department of Health, the former Greater London Council (which is arranged by subject), and the London Boroughs Grants Unit. Subject files are organised on the basis of those relating to fundraising, reports for the Department of Health, and press releases/campaigns. Persons wishing access to the papers should apply to the Administrator; material from the Department of Health Archive and correspondence with the LBGU may not be published.

NATIONAL CHILDMINDING ASSOCIATION
The Association was founded in 1977 in order to campaign for the proper regulation and wider provision of childminding facilities in the UK, and to represent and assist registered childminders. Related Associations now exist for Northern Ireland and Scotland. NCMA retains its records at its offices. These include full sets of committee minutes, annual reports, financial records, and correspondence since 1977. The Association also maintains a library on childminding matters. Persons interested in consulting the papers should apply to the Information Officer at the head office.

NATIONAL CHILDREN'S BUREAU The National Children's Bureau was established as a registered charity in 1963 with the purpose of identifying and promoting the interests of all children and young people, and improving their status in a multiracial society. The Bureau's members are drawn from local authorities, voluntary and statutory bodies, and professional associations; it seeks to disseminate information about both children and good practice in children's services.

The NCB has retained its own archive. Surviving papers include minutes of the governing body, annual reports, and copies of all publications (including the journals *Concern* and *Children and*

Society and the parliamentary digest *Children and Parliament*), and unpublished papers since 1963. Correspondence is retained for a period of five years only, but an extensive series of subject files is kept by the Library and Information Service. Persons wishing to use the papers should contact the Head of the Library and Information Service.

NATIONAL CHRISTIAN EDUCATION COUNCIL This inter-denominational body was established in 1803 as the National Sunday School Union and adopted its present name in 1966. It aims to promote education on Christian principles, and offers practical training in religious education and publishes religious textbooks.

The Council has retained records dating back to its foundation in the early 19th century. They include minutes of various committees, annual reports, correspondence, issues of the *Sunday School Chronicle*, 1878–1966, and local records. Records of the Council's sister group, the Robert Raikes Historical Society, are also preserved at its headquarters. For access to both collections, researchers should contact the NCEC.

NATIONAL COUNCIL FOR THE ABOLITION OF THE DEATH PENALTY A few records for this organisation (mainly pre-war) are deposited in the Modern Records Centre, University of Warwick (ref. MSS 16). The records (consisting of minute books, 1923–48, some annual reports and a journal) form part of the archive of the Howard League for Penal Reform (q.v.).

NATIONAL COUNCIL OF BUILDING MATERIAL PRODUCERS This construction industry association was established in 1942. The papers have been retained and include minutes of the Council and the Committee of Management from October 1942 onwards; other committee minutes for a shorter period; all published annual reports; financial records for the statutory period, and correspondence and subject files. Complete sets of its publications (*BMP Information*, *BMP Statistical Bulletin*, and *BMP Forecasts*) are also available. Applications for access should be made to the Director General.

NATIONAL COUNCIL OF INDUSTRY TRAINING ORGANISATIONS

The Council was created in 1988 to represent the UK's 120 Industry Training Organisations, the employer-led voluntary bodies which promote training activities in their respective industrial sectors. The function of the NCITO is to represent them both to government and to the principal national institutions concerned with vocational education and training. The NCITO is managed by a bi-annual Council on which every ITO member is represented, and by an Executive Committee.

The papers have been retained and are known to include the minutes of the Council and the Executive Committee (which meets approximately six times per year); conference reports and papers; copies of its own research reports and a catalogue of the reports compiled by member ITOs; financial records; and correspondence and subject files. The papers are held at NCITO's head office. Requests to examine them should be directed in the first instance to the Director of Development.

NATIONAL COUNCIL ON INLAND TRANSPORT

Papers have been deposited at Doncaster Archives Department. A list is available (NRA 33914). The material includes correspondence with the Railway Development Association (see Railway Development Society) and the Scottish Association for Public Transport.

NATIONAL COUNCIL FOR JEWS IN THE FORMER SOVIET UNION

The surviving papers of this umbrella organisation (founded as the National Council for Soviet Jewry in 1975), have been placed in London Metropolitan Archives (ref. Acc 3087). A detailed list is available (NRA 38776). The deposit consists of minutes of the National Council and of many committees, correspondence files etc. Access to much of the material requires written permission.

NATIONAL COUNCIL OF LABOUR

This was established in 1921 as a National Joint Committee linking the Labour Party and the Trades Union Congress. In 1942 the Co-operative Party joined the Council, which then adopted its present form. Minutes, correspondence, agendas and other docu-

ments can be found within the archive of the Trades Union Congress (q.v.), now deposited in the Modern Records Centre, University of Warwick. The archive of the Labour Party (q.v.), held in the Labour History Archive and Study Centre, University of Manchester, also has relevant material.

NATIONAL COUNCIL OF LABOUR COLLEGES

The National Council of Labour Colleges was established in 1921 as the culmination of a movement for 'independent working-class education'. Its precursors had included Ruskin College in Oxford and the Plebs' League (1908–27), which had been instrumental in the establishment of the Central Labour College, first at Oxford, and later based in London. The Council continued the work of this residential college (closed in 1929), and co-ordinated the attendant local activities. The NCLC survived without the aid of state grants, and came frequently into conflict with the Workers' Educational Association (q.v.). The NCLC's educational work was merged with the Education Department of the Trades Union Congress (q.v.) in 1964. An NCLC Publishing Society was founded in 1929.

Records of the National Council of Labour Colleges, including material relating to the Plebs' League and the Central Labour College, have been deposited at the National Library of Scotland (ref. Acc 5120). A list is available (NRA 29145).

NATIONAL COUNCIL FOR ONE PARENT FAMILIES

The need to protect the rights of single mothers and their children led in 1918 to the establishment of the National Council for the Unmarried Mother and Her Child. In 1973 the organisation changed its name to the National Council For One Parent Families to emphasise its representation for all parents bringing up children alone. The NCOPF lobbies on behalf of such families and provides information, training and consultancy services for parents and employers.

The papers of the NCOPF are retained at its offices. There are available the minutes of the Executive Committee of Management since 1945; an incomplete series of the annual reports for the post-war period; financial records; and correspondence and subject files, usually for a preceding period of five years. The NCOPF's own library holds copies of its publications and maintains the UK's largest single computerised database of material relating to one parent families. Persons wishing to use the Library's research facilities or consult the annual report should apply to the Librarian. The records of One Parent Family (Scotland) are in Glasgow Caledonian University.

NATIONAL COUNCIL OF VOLUNTARY CHILD CARE ORGANISATIONS The NCVCCO, known as Child Care for short, was established in 1942 as a grouping of those voluntary organisations which exist to serve the needs of children and families. It seeks to promote their cooperation and interests and to consult the statutory authorities regarding the planning and provision of child care services. The NCVCCO is composed of a Council which meets biannually and to which all member organisations belong, and an administrative General Purposes Committee; beneath the national organisation is a structure of regional groups.

The papers of the NCVCCO are retained either at its offices at 80–82 White Lion Street, London N1 9PF or at the National Children's Home at Highbury. The material includes from 1942 onwards all national committee minutes, annual and special reports, financial records and correspondence; permission to consult the papers should be sought from the Director at the White Lion Street address.

NATIONAL COUNCIL FOR VOLUNTARY ORGANISATIONS The Council (formerly the National Council of Social Service) was founded in 1919 to promote the systematic organisation of voluntary social work, both at national and local level. It adopted its present name in 1980. The Council deposited its records in 1989 in the London Metropolitan Archives. They include minutes, correspondence and other papers dating back to the Council's foundation. The papers include material on the development of the Welfare State, unemployment in the 1930s, the National Health Service, the formation of Rural Community Councils and such specific projects as the International Year of the Disabled. A published history is also available, *Voluntary Social Action* by M. Brasnett (London, 1969).

NATIONAL COUNCIL FOR VOLUNTARY YOUTH SERVICES The NCVYS was founded in 1936 under the auspices of the National Council of Social Services as the Standing Conference of Juvenile Organisations. It adopted its present name in 1972 and became independent of the NCSS in 1980.

The principal objective of the NCVYS is to promote cooperation and co-ordination between the major national youth organisations, for which it is the national representative, and the local councils for voluntary youth service throughout England.

The records of the NCVYS are retained at its offices. The papers include committee minutes, annual reports, and correspondence (which is subject to regular weeding). The only financial records which are retained are those required for audit purposes.

The majority of older material is housed on behalf of the Council by the National Federation of Young Farmers Clubs and as much notice as possible should be given by persons wishing access to the archive. Applications for access should be addressed to the Executive Officer.

NATIONAL COUNCIL OF WOMEN OF GREAT BRITAIN The National Council of Women functions as a co-ordinating body for several national women's organisations. It had its origins in the 1870s, with the foundation of Ladies' Associations for the Care of Friendless Girls, and in the subsequent decade, with the various Unions of Women Workers. A National Union of Women Workers of Great Britain and Ireland was established in 1895; the present title was adopted in 1929. From 1897 it has been the British section of the International Council of Women.

The National Council's aims, as an independent and voluntary organisation, are through education and information to enable the participation of women in public life.

Records of the organisation are in the Women's Library, London Metropolitan University (ref. Acc 3613). The extensive collection is listed and open. See NRA 42202.

NATIONAL CYCLE ARCHIVE The archive is in the Modern Records Centre, University of

Warwick (ref. MSS 328). The extensive deposit also includes records of the Cyclists Touring Club (including Finance and Rights and Privileges committee minutes, legal documentation etc.), the minutes of the British Cycling Federation and the papers and collections of various individuals.

NATIONAL CYRENIANS Some records for the period *c.*1970–*c.*86 have been placed in Liverpool University Archives (ref. D612). See also Simon Community entry.

NATIONAL FAMILY CONCILIATION COUNCIL The NFCC, which co-ordinates the work of local conciliation services and establishes and promotes common standards of practice, was set up in 1981. It was later called the National Association of Family Mediation and Conciliation Services. Its work arises from the recommendations of the Finer Report of 1974, which advocated a national conciliation service as a means of resolving disputes between divorcing partners, particularly matters concerning their children, without recourse to law.

There have been retained since the formation of the NFCC its committee minutes; annual reports; copies of its *Newsletter* (1982–90) and *Journal* (1991–); financial records; correspondence and subject files; copies of published and unpublished reports, which include responses to White Papers; NFCC officers' reports; and papers relating to the professional standards and training programmes. The records of the organisation, now called National Family Mediation, have now been deposited. Some 74 boxes of papers, for the period 1981–2000, have been deposited in the LSE Library (ref. M 3170). The collection includes material concerning the administration of central and local branches, training courses and workshops, involvement in the shaping of Government legislation, casework material and the arrangements and proceedings of conferences.

NATIONAL FARMERS' UNION OF ENGLAND AND WALES The union was founded in 1908, with the aim of promoting and protecting the interests of those engaged in agriculture and horticulture.

Records retained include Council minutes since foundation and General Purpose Committee min-

utes from 1919 onwards. The union also keeps copies of its publications including the *Yearbook*, 1910 to date; the *Broadsheet*, 1921–47; the *Record*, 1922–47, and the *British Farmer* from 1948.

The union's archives have been deposited with the Rural History Centre at Reading University.

NATIONAL FARMERS' UNION OF SCOTLAND The NFU Scotland was formed in 1913, five years after the Union in England and Wales. In 1938 it amalgamated with the Scottish Chamber of Agriculture, which represented the larger tenant farmers and landlords. As well as acting as a trade union for farmers, the NFU Scotland has been active in promoting general agricultural development.

NFU Scotland retains its archive at its office. A list is available (NRA 24460). The papers include various minute books from 1919 to date (including those of the Council from 1938, the AGM from 1919, and the General Purposes Committee from 1945). The minutes of a large number of other committees also survive from the earliest date, including those of the Organisation and the Law and Parliamentary Committees (known as the Legal and Commerical Committee from 1956) and of other committees relating to particular agricultural products. More recent committees for which minutes survive include the Press and Publicity (now Organisation and Publicity) from 1946; Labour Committee (re-named Labour and Machinery in 1961) from 1945; Crofters' from 1962; and Highlands and Islands' from 1966. Files of copy letters have been retained since 1951 but nearly all surviving correspondence files are post-1960. Annual Reports exist from 1919 and the union has a complete set of its official publication, the monthly *Scottish Farming Leader*, from 1948.

The NFU is willing in principle to allow access for academic research. Interested persons should apply in writing to the Organiser and Publicity Officer.

NATIONAL FEDERATION OF CONSTRUCTION UNIONS A strong movement to form a federation of trade unions in the building industries had existed in Great Britain since the end of the 19th century; during World War I a working agreement was reached among the leading unions to establish such an organisation and in February 1918 the

National Federation of Building Trades Operatives was formed. The name was changed to the National Federation of Construction Unions in 1969 but in 1971, following the establishment of the Union of Construction, Allied Trades and Technicians (q.v.), it was agreed to wind up the Federation at the end of that year.

The main archive of the Federation has now been deposited in the Modern Records Centre, University of Warwick (ref. MSS. 78/NFBTO). The majority of records are pre-war in date but the collection does include Executive Committee minutes, 1940–64; head office circulars, 1922–72, and numerous other minutes and records relating to amalgamations, disputes, etc. There is a list available (NRA 32062). Other papers are available at the Modern Records Centre, University of Warwick, along with the papers of UCATT in collection MSS 78. This material includes Executive Committee minutes, 1951–66; General Council papers, 1951–61; an incomplete set of annual conference reports, 1930–71; copies of rulebooks, 1918–70; various financial records; a run of the journal *Operative Builder*, 1947–62; regional and branch circulars, 1936–57; miscellaneous reports and memoranda, 1932–55; miscellaneous pamphlets, 1926–57, etc. Likewise there is a list available (NRA 32040).

The minutes of the London Region of the Federation for the period 1922–69 are also retained at the Modern Records Centre in collection MSS 170. The records of the North West Regional Office for 1896– 1973 have been deposited at Greater Manchester Record Office. There is material pertaining to the Irish section of the union for 1956–63 available at the Public Record Office of Northern Ireland (ref. D1050/2).

NATIONAL FEDERATION OF CONSUMER GROUPS The NFCG is the national association of local Consumer Groups and was established in 1963. All of its papers have been retained at the head office. They include minutes, annual and special reports, financial records, and correspondence and subject files. However, researchers should be aware that access to the material is limited and a charge may have to be made. Further details may be obtained from the Secretary. It is the Federation's policy to recommend that, should a local Consumer Group be closed, its papers be deposited at the appropriate County Record Office.

NATIONAL FEDERATION OF HOUSING ASSOCIATIONS The Federation was established in 1935 as the central agency for Housing Associations, trusts and societies in the UK, those voluntary organisations which provide homes for rent or through housing cooperatives. It is a wholly independent body which represents its members before central government and local authorities. A weekly newspaper, *Housing Associations Weekly*, and a monthly magazine, *Voluntary Housing*, are published. The papers of the NFHA remain in its own care at the head office. The available material includes minutes of the AGM from 1964 to date and copies of the Annual Report from 1980 onwards and annual accounts from 1983. Further enquiries should be addressed to the Director.

NATIONAL FEDERATION OF RETIREMENT PENSIONS ASSOCIATIONS The Federation was founded in February 1940 as the National Federation of Old Age Pensioners Associations to campaign for improved state provision for the elderly and in particular for adequate state retirement pensions. It publishes a monthly newsletter, *Pensioners' Voice* (which also serves as the short title of the organisation), and is a founder member of the National Pensioners' Convention, the representative body of all major pensions pressure groups in the UK.

There are minutes and correspondence, covering the period 1943–94, in the Labour History Archive and Study Centre, University of Manchester.

NATIONAL FEDERATION OF VILLAGE PRODUCER ASSOCIATIONS It is reported that the papers for 1951–84 have been deposited in the Rural History Centre, University of Reading.

NATIONAL FEDERATION OF WOMEN'S INSTITUTES The first Women's Institute was founded in Ontario, Canada, in 1897 and the first in Great Britain in Anglesey in 1915. The National Federation of Women's Institutes, established two years later, is an independent voluntary association of over 9000 local WIs in the United Kingdom, which are organised in 70 county federations. It was originally – and is still predominantly – rurally based and its objectives are to develop the quality of rural life and further the education of country women.

The papers of the Federation remain in its own care, partly at the head office and partly at the NFWI's own residential adult education institution, Denman College at Marcham in Oxfordshire. The records are largely complete since 1917 and comprise minutes of the Executive Committee and all Sub-Committees; verbatim reports of the General Meeting; annual reports and copies of the reports of the county federations; copies of its magazine *Home and Country* (first published in 1919), and subject files, consisting of one for each individual WI and federation. The Press Office maintains a collection of agency press-cuttings as well as the Federation's own press releases. Each of the administrative departments publishes pamphlets on its own theme (e.g. crafts, public affairs, music etc.) and records of these are on file since 1948. The correspondence of the Federation is at present unsorted. The county federations retain their own papers. Further details should be sought from the General Secretary.

NATIONAL FOUNDATION FOR EDUCATIONAL RESEARCH IN ENGLAND AND WALES

The National Foundation for Educational Research in England and Wales was set up in 1946 and is Britain's leading educational research institution. It is an independent body undertaking research and development projects on issues of current interest in all sectors of the public educational system.

NFER retains its own archive. Committee minutes have been kept since 1946. There are also complete sets of conference papers from all members' conferences and one copy of each annual report and of all book reports and journals that the Foundation has published. The collection holds a limited number of confidential reports and data from projects (which are retained for the period specified by the project leader), and an archive of various tests produced by the Foundation. Financial records are maintained for seven years and correspondence is kept for varying periods which are specified by the originating department. Those wishing access to the collection should apply to the Director; it should be understood that certain items of project data remain confidential.

NATIONAL FRONT

There is material in the Patrick Harrington papers formerly in the Modern Records Centre, University of Warwick (ref. MSS 321). The papers (1976–88) of this NF activist relate to both national and local activity and include some minutes and much political ephemera, as well as cuttings-albums concerning Patrick Harrington and the Polytechnic of North London, 1984–85. The papers have now been returned to the depositor.

NATIONAL GRAPHICAL ASSOCIATION

The National Graphical Association merged in September 1991 with the other industry union SOGAT '82 to form the Graphical, Print and Media Union. The constituent parts are treated separately in this Guide and details of the papers of SOGAT may be found on p. 296.

The NGA itself was founded in 1964 by the union of the previously independent Typographical Association and the London Typographical Society. It subsequently amalgamated with the Association of Correctors of the Press and the National Union of Press Telegraphists in 1965; the National Society of Electrotypers and Stereotypers in 1967, and the Amalgamated Society of Lithographic Printers and Auxiliaries in 1968. In 1979 the NGA received the engagements of the National Union of Wallcoverings, Decorative and Allied Trades (itself formed four years earlier by the amalgamation of the Wallcoverings Staff Association and the Wallpaper Workers' Union). Finally, in 1982, after several attempts there was a merger with the Society of Lithographic Artists, Designers, Engravers and Process Workers (SLADE) to form a newly constituted union, the NGA.

Most surviving records of the NGA and its predecessor organisations have been deposited in the Modern Records Centre, University of Warwick. A list is available (NRA 24668). The papers of the NGA *per se* in collection MSS 28 comprise minutes, 1969–78; some publications, 1968–80, and files on negotiations and agreements with the Advertisement Production (later Typesetting and Foundry) Employers Federation, 1960–72. The papers of

R. (Bob) Willis, joint general secretary, covering the period 1939–62 are available in collection MSS 39.

The papers of the NGA's London Region held at the Modern Records Centre are particularly full. They include the minutes for 1902–59 of the *Daily Telegraph* Graphical Chapel and some of its financial records, and the composite record books of the *Daily Telegraph* Imperial Chapel. These record books incorporate minutes of union meetings and notes on regulations and disputes for 1977–87; the diaries of the Deputy Father of the Chapel, 1977–79; and various files concerning new technology, 1974–85. In addition there are the minutes of the *Daily Express* Machine Managers Chapel, 1948–79; the records of Walker & Co. (Printers) Ltd Compositors Chapel (consisting of subject files, 1973–84; the Father of the Chapel's working occurrences diaries for 1973–78 and 1981–82; and the Father's reports file, 1979–83), and the Barnet Advisory Committee's minutes from 1969 until its dissolution in 1987.

Deposited with the London Region records are three compendium files on the craft processes of electrotyping and stereotyping, compiled by H.G. Smart, former chairman of the London branch of the National Society of Electrotypers and Stereotypers. These supplement the NSES section of the NGA London Region records, which comprise minutes and correspondence (to 1967); annual reports, 1915–58; committee reports, 1919–67; a file on its amalgamation, 1967; printed notices, 1901–56; and an incomplete series of National Society reports, 1901–56. The Society's executive minutes for 1912–63 and national council minutes for 1918–63 are available in Cambridge University Library.

The NGA London Region deposit also includes the minutes of the London Printing and Kindred Trades Federation for 1939–50. Other deposited local NGA minutes include the Newcastle Branch records, 1867–1959, at the Tyne and Wear Archives Department; and, at the Modern Records Centre, the minute and correspondence books for 1973–80 and 1961–79 of the NGA Chapel at Edwards Printers of Coventry.

The post-war papers within other collections of material in MSS 28 and MSS 39 are best described by constituent organisation:

AMALGAMATED SOCIETY OF LITHOGRAPHIC PRINTERS AND AUXILIARIES

Triennial General Council and Delegate Meetings, agendas and reports of meetings, 1907–66; quarterly and half-yearly reports, 1880–1948; files on amalgamation, 1968–69; copies of the monthly journal *Lithographer*, 1949–68; financial statements, 1948–66; copies of the rules, 1887–1966, and the office files of R.A.W. Emerick, last ASLP General Secretary, from the 1960s and 1970s which cover relations with companies and other unions, and matters of ASLP administration. A list is available (NRA 22527).

ASSOCIATION OF CORRECTORS OF THE PRESS

Records 1880–1965 including minutes, 1953–65, and agenda books. A list is available (NRA 9334).

LONDON TYPOGRAPHICAL SOCIETY

Miscellaneous papers, mainly printed reports dated 1869–1972, comprise MSS 39A/CO. A list is available (NRA 22527). Other records for the period 1785–1965, including minute books of 1827–1964, committee minutes, reports, agenda books etc., are in MSS 28. The relevant list for this latter material is NRA 9334.

NATIONAL UNION OF WALLCOVERINGS, DECORATIVE AND ALLIED TRADES

A list is available (NRA 24668). The collection contains the following: Signed minutes, 1933–68, of the Print Block Roller and Stamp Cutters' Society. Accounts, 1929–47; other financial records, 1929–47; copies of the rules, 1928–52, and correspondence files (including some minutes), 1928–64 of the Wallpaper Trades Superannuation Society. Minutes, 1918–75; accounts, 1920–73; annual reports, 1920–67; rulebooks, 1938–58; journals, 1926–77; some branch records; agreements, 1922–64; and correspondence and subject files, 1917–75, of the Wallpaper Workers' Union.

SOCIETY OF LITHOGRAPHIC ARTISTS, DESIGNERS, ENGRAVERS AND PROCESS WORKERS

SLADE was formed in 1922 as the result of several successive mergers within the industry; it amalgamated with the NGA in 1982. Its papers (listed as NRA 9377) consist of Executive Council and National Council minutes, 1931–82; Delegate meeting reports, 1948–78 and 1981; annual reports, 1945–80; various post-war minutes series; trade lists, 1921–73; copies of the *Process Journal*, 1949–52 and 1964–66; most issues of the *Slade Journal*, 1969–82, and a run of the *Lithographer*, 1952–66. The records of SLADE's London District have also been deposited. They comprise District Committee minutes, 1946–49, 1956–73, and 1975–81; branch minutes, 1958–68 and 1974–77; News Panel minutes for the period 1926–60; Engraving Section minutes, 1946–53; Litho-Section minutes, 1946–61; News Section minutes, 1946–60; and wages data, 1960s.

TYPOGRAPHICAL ASSOCIATION

Printed minutes of delegate meetings, 1861–1963; correspondence and subject files up to 1966, including those concerning industrial negotiations and individual union branches, and Half-Yearly Reports, 1913–55 (incomplete for the pre-war period). A list is available (NRA 22527).

Papers of the former Belfast Typographical Society (otherwise known as the Belfast Branch of the Typographical Association and from 1977 as the Northern Ireland Graphical Society or as the Belfast Branch of the NGA) have been deposited at PRONI (ref. D.1050/18).

NATIONAL INSTITUTE OF ECONOMIC AND SOCIAL RESEARCH
The National Institute was founded in 1938, upon the initiative of the industrialist Sir Josiah Stamp, to carry out investigations into economic problems which could not be adequately attempted by individual academic researchers, to secure the coordination of economic research in the United Kingdom, and to prepare and disseminate accurate statistics for the benefit of policymakers, researchers and the public. It has subsequently continued a tradition of conducting applied research into economic problems of public concern. A brief history of the first fifty years of NIESR's operations was published in the May 1988 issue of the *National Institute Economic Review*.

NIESR's papers have been retained at its offices, in the care of the Secretary. Surviving material includes minutes of the Executive Committee and the AGM since 1938; ledger books, quarterly accounts and petty cash books, and correspondence files. Copies of the Annual Report and of NIESR's publications such as the quarterly Review, discussion papers and briefing notes, are held on the premises in the Library. In the case of the latter material permission for access should be sought in writing from the Librarian, otherwise from the Secretary.

NATIONAL INSTITUTE OF INDUSTRIAL PSYCHOLOGY
The Institute was founded in 1921 by Dr. C.S. Myers, Director of the Cambridge Psychological Laboratory, as a non-profit-making scientific organisation for the service of industry and commerce. Its aim was to promote the application of psychology and physiology to industrial questions. It operated both on a contract basis and by conducting research into problems of general interest. Operations expanded considerably in the 1960s with the support of the Ministry of Technology, but the withdrawal of this funding at the end of the decade caused acute difficulties and the Institute finally closed *c.* 1976.

Following its closure, the archives of the Institute were deposited at the LSE Library. The collection of 20 volumes and 85 boxes includes Executive Committee minutes, 1921–53; Scientific Advisory Committee minutes, 1952–72; Finance & General Purposes Committee minutes, 1949–73; annual reports, 1937–75; account books and registers, 1921–69; and correspondence with officers and members of Council, 1933–77. Staff files, which cover the period 1928–77, are closed. There are also subject files relating to Vocational Guidance and Testing (1928–74) and to the Institute's research projects (1921–73). Correspondence with clients survives for 1942–77.

NATIONAL LEAGUE OF THE BLIND AND DISABLED
A small trade union of blind and disabled persons, the National League has been affiliated to the TUC since 1902. Before it incor-

porated disabled workers as well, it was known solely as the National League of the Blind. It seeks to improve the provision by national and local government of education and training for blind and disabled persons and of sheltered workshops for their employment, and campaigns to ensure the adequacy of state allowances. It also acts as a trade union on behalf of those employed in local authority workshops.

The papers now in the Modern Records Centre, University of Warwick (ref. MSS 349) include files relating mainly to wages and conditions for blind and disabled workers and workshop disputes, mainly 1950s–70s, but with some earlier and later material.

Researchers should be aware that certain papers of the Scottish District Council of the National League have now been deposited in the National Library of Scotland (ref. Acc 9418). A list is available (NRA 31018). The material, which was deposited in 1987, comprises Council minutes for 1942–79 and copies of the Annual Report of 1968–69 and 1976–85.

NATIONAL AND LOCAL GOVERNMENT OFFICERS' ASSOCIATION NALGO was founded in 1905 as the National Association of Local Government Officers. In 1930 it amalgamated with the National Association of Poor Law Officers and in 1963 with the British Gas Staff Association. Although originally an association for local government staff, in the post-war period the union also recruited members in the nationalised industries. In 1993 it joined with NUPE and COHSE to form a new union, UNISON.

It is understood that many of NALGO's records, which had been used by Alec Spoor in writing the official history *White-Collar Union: Sixty Years of NALGO* (London, 1967), were destroyed in late 1973. The surviving archive is now in the care of the Modern Records Centre, University of Warwick (ref. MSS 20). It comprises various series of minutes (including the National Executive Council, the Finance and General Purposes Committee, and the Service Conditions and Organisations Committee) for the period 1905–65; the journal *Local Government Service/Public Service*, 1944–82 and 1984; copies of circulars, 1964–72; material on the reorganisation of the National Health Service, 1965–74; and the

West Midlands district records, 1960–74. In addition the collection includes the records of the NALGO Insurance Association Ltd., otherwise known as LOGOMIA (namely minutes, 1913–66; annual reports; balance sheets; and miscellaneous printed matter, 1891–1951) and the papers of the NALGO Provident Society (e.g. minutes, 1914–60; proceedings of meetings, 1924–48).

A further significant amount of material relating to NALGO may be found at the Modern Records Centre in the Peter Morgan papers (ref. MSS 262), Morgan was a member of the National Executive Council of NALGO, 1963–85, and President of the Union, 1981–82.

NATIONAL MARRIAGE GUIDANCE COUNCIL
The National Marriage Guidance Council (a limited company and registered charity) was established in 1947 as the successor to the Marriage Guidance Council, founded in 1938. NMGC is a federation of local Councils (now operating under the name of RELATE Centres) which covers the United Kingdom except Scotland, where there is a similar but wholly independent organisation called Marriage Counselling Scotland. The national federation is responsible for the training and supervision of local counsellors and the development of standards of service at the local level.

Minutes, annual reports, special reports (including submissions to government enquiries on various matters of law and social policy), financial records, correspondence (variously classified) and subject files of NMGC covering almost the whole period of its existence, and that of its predecessor, are held at the head office. Of these documents, only the Annual Reports and the accounts and certain of the special reports have been published. Access to other archive material may be granted by special arrangement, for which application should be made to the Director.

NMGC does not hold archives of its constituent local Marriage Guidance Councils. Enquiries about these would have to be addressed to the Managers of the RELATE Centres in the areas under consideration; addresses can be supplied by the head office.

NATIONAL PAWNBROKERS' ASSOCIATION
The National Pawnbrokers' Association was

founded in 1892 and incorporated in 1931. Its object is to provide a central organisation for pawnbrokers in Great Britain and Northern Ireland; it seeks to represent its members' interests before the appropriate national authorities and regulates the conduct of their businesses. The archives of the Association for the period 1900–72 have been deposited in the Guildhall Library (ref. MSS 22306–33). A list is available for the collection (NRA 31275).

NATIONAL PEACE COUNCIL The National Peace Council was established in 1904 to organise national conferences in Britain, and was put on a permanent footing in 1908 following the 17th Universal Peace Conference held in London. It has existed continuously since then, although from 1923 to 1930 it was known as the National Council for the Prevention of War. It is an independent umbrella organisation bringing together local, regional and national groups involved in all aspects of peace work. There is an associated educational charity, the United World Education and Research Trust (UWT), established in 1958.

The archive has been deposited at the LSE Library, with the exception of recent papers (i.e. those of the last fifteen years), which are retained at the NPC's offices. Minutes included in the archive are those of the Council from 1908 (missing 1930–33, 1960–63); Executive Committee from its establishment in 1916 (missing 1930–37); the UWT from 1958; the London Council for Prevention of War, 1924–32, and the London Peace Council, 1926–32. In addition there are annual reports from 1918 (missing 1942, 1961–62 and 1962–63); conference reports for the period since 1933; financial records, 1918–59; the *Peace Year Book*, 1910–57 (missing 1912, 1934, 1951); *Peace Aims* pamphlets nos. 1–61, dating from the 1940s and 1950s; a large collection of NPC and UWT publications; and comprehensive files on NPC's and UWT's correspondence, projects, conferences, publications etc.

Recent papers are sent to the LSE Library every ten years. They may be used by accredited researchers and may be photocopied for personal use on the understanding that copyright for all archive material is retained by NPC. Bona fide researchers may be granted access to the retained papers on application to the National Peace Council.

NATIONAL PLAYING FIELDS ASSOCIATION The National Playing Fields Association was established in 1925 as an independent charity to campaign for the provision of conveniently located recreational space for all. Today it seeks to acquire and improve land for sport, recreation and play.

The minutes, files and publications of the Association for the period 1920–79 have been deposited in the National Archives (ref. CB1–CB4). More recent papers are retained at the Association's offices. Surviving material comprises Council and Executive Committee minutes to date; the minutes of former committees (Grants & Loans, Technical, and Development), and a run of the Annual Report from the inaugural meeting in July 1925. Copies are also retained of the newsletter *Play Times*. There is a collection of legal records kept in respect of covenants or deeds of dedication for playing fields, which are not open to researchers but concerning which the NPFA is able to answer enquiries. Persons interested in examining any papers should contact the General Secretary at the head office.

NATIONAL PRIMARY EDUCATION ARCHIVE The archive is located at the Institute of Education, University of London. The Institute also holds the papers of Robin Tanner (1940–89) for the period 1940s onwards.

NATIONAL REFERENDUM CAMPAIGN Relevant material is contained in the papers of Sir Neil Marten, sometime Chairman of the Campaign, which have been deposited in the Bodleian Library (ref. MSS. Eng. hist. *c.* 1130–59, e.385; misc. a.29). These papers consist largely of material from groups opposed to UK membership of the EC, including the Safeguard Britain Campaign (q.v.)

NATIONAL SOCIETY FOR CLEAN AIR AND ENVIRONMENTAL PROTECTION The NSCA is a registered charity whose aim is to secure clean air through the reduction of air, water and land pollution and the minimisation of noise and other contaminants. It originated as the Coal Smoke Abatement Society (founded 1899), which later became the National Smoke Abatement Society. The Society adopted its present name in 1958 to indicate that it was not solely concerned with smoke pollution. NSCA is a founder member of the International Union of Air Pollution Prevention Associations. It seeks to promote public policy on environmental protection by publications and conferences, and maintains an Information Service and Library at its headquarters.

The NSCA retains its records at its headquarters. A list is available (NRA 24469). The papers include the archive of the Coal Smoke Abatement Society. NSCA Council minutes exist from 1972 and Committee minutes from 1982. Yearbooks and annual reports are retained for the period since 1920; conference papers exist from 1905 onwards and workshop papers from 1972. An extensive series of subject files covers the NSCA's activities, on such topics as smoke control, acid rain, global warming, energy and waste management, and UK and EC legislation on environmental protection. Persons wishing to use the archive should contact the Information Department.

NATIONAL SOCIETY OF CONSERVATIVE AGENTS The National Society of Conservative and Unionist Agents was established in 1891 to promote the interests of the constituency agents of the Conservative Party, and to examine problems relating to political organisation, registration and related matters.

The main collection of the Society's papers has been deposited in Westminster Central Library (ref. Acc 485). It includes minute books of the AGM, Council meetings and subcommittees for the period 1895–1949, the last volume of which incorporates a list of the Chairmen and Hon. Secretaries of the Society for 1891–1962. A list is available to the collection (NRA 16749). Researchers should also be aware that the LSE Library holds minute books of the Metropolitan Conservative Agents Association dated 1891–1947. A list is available (NRA 29731).

NATIONAL SOCIETY FOR THE PREVENTION OF CRUELTY TO CHILDREN Formed in 1844, the Society works to prevent private and public wrongs to children or corruption of their morals.

It has retained its records from foundation. The main series of papers are minute books, annual reports and branch reports, and individual case histories. The journal, *Child's Guardian*, dates from 1887.

Only the printed material is available to researchers, since case histories are classified as confidential. Applications should be addressed to the Public Relations Officer.

NATIONAL SOCIETY FOR THE PREVENTION OF VENEREAL DISEASE The Society was founded in 1919. Two boxes of correspondence, newspaper cuttings and pamphlets for the period 1937 to 1955 have been deposited in the Contemporary Medical Archives Centre of the Wellcome Institute (ref. SA/PVD). A list is available (NRA 24909).

NATIONAL SOCIETY FOR PROMOTING RELIGIOUS EDUCATION The Society was founded in 1811 to promote a religious education under the auspices of the Church of England and, until the advent of the state system from 1870 onwards, it was the pioneer in providing schools and education for the masses. During the 20th century the role of the Society was to promote religious education within the state system, while at the same time supporting Church schools and training colleges. The National Society is an integral part of the Church of England and works closely with the Education Board of the General Synod.

A substantial archive, dating back to the foundation of the Society, has been deposited at the Church of England Record Centre. Besides the minutes of the various committees, the bulk of the manuscript material consists of c. 15,000 files of correspondence, the majority of which concern individual schools and training colleges. Other files deal with matters of policy, correspondence with the Department of Education on religious education matters, submissions to government committees, etc. For the post-war era there are files concerning each Education Act, although the papers concerning the Society's work on the religious education provisions of the 1944 Act have unfortunately been lost.

Surviving printed material includes a run of Annual Reports issued since the Society's foundation, and a collection of both its own publications and those of other education societies. A history of the Society was published in 1958 by H.J. Burgess, *Enterprise in Education* (NSPRE/SPCK). Material deposited at the Record Centre is usually subject to a thirty-year rule, and further enquiries should be directed to the National Society Archivist.

NATIONAL TRUST The National Trust for Places of Historic Interest or Natural Beauty was set up in 1895. All the Trust's administrative records have been retained and are subject to a thirty-year rule of access. Estate papers of properties which have passed into the care of the Trust are not, however, kept at the head office but are either retained at each site or have been deposited in the relevant County Record Office. All enquiries should be directed to the Archivist/Records Supervisor of the National Trust. Researchers should be aware that some records of the Northern Ireland Region of the National Trust for the period c. 1945–70 have been deposited in the Public Record Office of Northern Ireland.

NATIONAL TRUST FOR SCOTLAND The National Trust for Scotland – which is separate from and not subordinate to the English organisation – was founded in 1931 on the initiative of the Association for the Preservation (now Protection) of Rural Scotland. It was established as a statutory body four years later. The objects of the Trust are the maintenance of buildings in its care and the management of lands as open spaces or places of public resort. Due to the relatively less dense population of Scotland, it has a wider role in countryside preservation than does the National Trust for England and Wales.

A substantial archive has been retained at the Trust's offices. It includes minutes of the Council since 1931; the AGM since 1932; Executive Committee since 1931; Finance Committee (renamed Investment Committee in 1969) from 1934; Business Committee, 1946–48; Administrative Subcommittee from 1949, and the Publicity Subcommittee, 1955–64. Post-war minutes also exist for other technical, advisory and local committees. More recent minute books contain material such as reports, memoranda and duplicated correspondence. The archive also contains a vast series of administrative and correspondence files dating from the 1930s, covering all aspects of the Trust's work. The Trust holds full sets of two publications: the *Year Book*, issued since 1932, and the biannual *Newsletter* since 1948.

Persons wishing to use the papers should apply in writing to the Director of the Trust.

NATIONAL UNION OF AGRICULTURAL AND ALLIED WORKERS The records of this union have been deposited in the Rural History Centre, University of Reading. They include Executive Committee minutes, 1907–45 and conference reports, 1913–47.

Branch records for Staffordshire, Warwickshire and Cheshire are held at Staffordshire Record Office, and are subject to a sixty-year closure rule. The collection comprises accident, redundancy, tied cottage and other categories of case files, 1958–83.

NATIONAL UNION OF CIVIL AND PUBLIC SERVANTS The Union was formed on 1 January 1988 by the merger of the Society of Civil and Public Servants and the Civil Service Union. The Civil Service Union was founded in 1917 as the Minor Grades Association, and amalgamated in 1960 with the Civil Service Association of Minor Grades to form the present union.

CIVIL SERVICE UNION

The records are preserved at the Union's headquarters. They are incomplete but important material has nonetheless been retained. National Executive Council minutes exist back to 1936, and membership records from the date of foundation. Reports of the NEC from 1936 onwards include the main information on wage agreements and negotiations. Copies of the *Journal* from 1943 are preserved, in addition to reports by Honorary Organisers from 1963 and papers relating to legal cases from 1964. A series of files concerning the contract cleaning dispute, c. 1960–70, has been deposited at the Modern Records Centre, University of Warwick (ref. MSS 111).

SOCIETY OF CIVIL AND PUBLIC SERVANTS

The earliest known predecessor of SCPS was the Association of Clerks of Second Division, which was in existence in 1895. It was subsequently reformed and renamed the Association of Executive Officers of the Civil Service in 1920. In 1922 it merged with the Association of Staff Clerks and Other Civil Servants (founded in 1916). The ASC founded the Society of Civil Servants in 1918, but the two groups maintained a separate existence until the SCS amalgamated with the Association of Executive Officers in 1931 to form the Society of Civil Servants (Executive, Directing and Analogous). This was itself renamed the SCPS in 1976. The deposited SCPS archive includes records of the Ministry of Health Inspectorate Associations and the Ministry of Food Section. The material held at Warwick (ref. MSS 232) has been listed (NRA 24976). The collection includes minutes, 1938–68; Society of Outdoor Staffs of the Ministry of Health minutes, 1931–47; Ministry of Food Co-ordinating Committee etc, 1948–54; annual accounts, 1951–53; investment registers, 1944–70; general and other ledgers, 1950–71; registry-organised correspondence and other papers, mainly 1945–71.

NATIONAL UNION OF DOMESTIC APPLIANCES AND GENERAL OPERATIVES

NUDAGO was established in 1890 as the National Union of Stove Grate, Fender and General Light Metal Workers, being a combination of those workers in the Rotherham district. The archive of the union, which comprises the executive Council minutes, Secretary's reports, conference papers, accounts and financial records for the period since 1894, has been placed in the Rotherham Archives and Local Studies Section, Brian O'Malley Central Library, Rotherham. A list is available (NRA 29316).

NATIONAL UNION OF DOMESTIC WORKERS

Certain records of the union covering the period 1938–53, have been included among the minutes and subject files of the Trades Union Congress (q.v.) deposited at the Modern Records Centre, University of Warwick (ref. MSS 292). Further enquiries should be directed to the Archivist.

NATIONAL UNION OF FOOTWEAR, LEATHER AND ALLIED TRADES

NUFLAT was created in 1970 by the amalgamation of the National Union of Boot and Shoe Operatives, the Amalgamated Society of Leather Workers, the National Union of Leather Workers and the National Union of Glovers and Leather Workers (q.v.). The NUBSO itself had originally been formed in 1874. It is the principal union organising manual workers in the footwear manufacturing industry.

The records have been deposited in Leicestershire Record Office (ref. DE 4093). A list is available (NRA 38937).

Certain records of other predecessor unions also survive. The records of the Amalgamated Society of Leather Workers, for the period 1892 to 1972 (and including minutes, accounts etc) have been placed in the West Yorkshire Archives Service (ref. C 140). A list is available (NRA 31983).

NATIONAL UNION OF GLOVERS AND LEATHER WORKERS

The archive has now been transferred to the Modern Records Centre, University of Warwick (ref. MSS 359). It was formerly deposited at the old National Museum of Labour History.

NATIONAL UNION OF HOSIERY AND KNITWEAR WORKERS

The union was set up in 1945 by the amalgamation of a number of small district unions in the Midlands, where the industry was primarily concentrated. In 1971 it united with the Amalgamated Society of Operative Lace Makers and Auxiliary Workers, which had itself been formed in 1874 from textile unions in the Nottingham area. N.H. Cuthbert's *The Lace Makers' Society* (1960) provides a history of trade unionism in the industry from 1760 to 1960. The official history of the NUHKW, *Hosiery Unions 1776–1976* by Richard Gurnham, was published in 1976.

A collection of records of certain predecessor unions has been placed in Leicestershire Record Office. The papers principally comprise the records of the Leicester and Leicestershire Trimmers Association, and those of the Leicester Hosiery Union. A list is available (NRA 21103).

The records of the Amalgamated Society of Operative Lace Makers have been deposited in the University of Nottingham Library (ref. LM, LM2, LM3). The available material includes accounts, 1876–1971; benefit and superannuation registers, 1909–71; membership records, 1937–71; correspondence, 1950–71, and minutes of the Trustees (from 1921), the Council (1942–71), the Quarterly Meeting (1913–71), and of individual trades' sections (e.g. Curtain Section Committee, 1906–53; Plain Net Section, 1904–51). Incorporated in the collection are papers of the British Lace Operatives Federation (minutes, 1917–72; cash book, 1919–71).

NATIONAL UNION OF INSURANCE WORKERS
The NUIW was formed in 1964 by the union of the National Amalgamated Union of Life Assurance Workers (NAULAW) and the National Federation of Insurance Workers. Until 1985 it was a federation of three independent unions but subsequently it has become a single organisation.

Certain records of the NUIW, its predecessors and related organisations are in the care of the Modern Records Centre, University of Warwick. The principal collection, MSS 144, consists of minutes of the NAULAW General Executive Council and its committees, 1918–64; subject files from the 1930s to 1970s (particularly concerning relations of the Co-operative Insurance Society and the Union of Shop, Distributive and Allied Workers), and some local records, namely the Romford and East London branch minutes, 1961–64, and Scottish Legal Section minutes, 1949–63.

In addition the collection includes papers relating to the National Union of Pearl Agents (which was formed from NAULAW in 1926 and later became the ASTMS Pearl Section), e.g. *Pearl Agents' Gazette*, 1926–59; NUPA/NUIW Pearl Section circulated minutes, 1961–68 and 1970–71; records of deputations, 1964–66; NUIW Pearl Section negotiation files, 1965–72, and minutes of the Retired Members' Society of the National Union of Insurance Workers for 1970–75.

Further relevant material is preserved in collections of personal papers at Warwick. The papers of Frank Crump (also MSS 144), Albert Best (MSS 141), Albert Vandome (MSS 158) and also S. P. Long (MSS 142) should be consulted.

Researchers should be aware that papers of the Northern Ireland section of NAULAW for the period 1930–56 have been deposited at the Public Record Office of Northern Ireland (ref. D1050/3).

NATIONAL UNION OF JOURNALISTS
The NUJ was formed in 1907 by secession from the Institute of Journalists and is now the world's largest organisation of personnel in the media industries. Attempts to amalgamate with the Institute in 1921, 1945–48 and 1967–71 proved unsuccessful. An account of the union by C.J. Bundock, *The NUJ: A Jubilee History 1907–57*, was published by Oxford University Press (1958).

An extensive collection of records for the period 1907–55 has been deposited at the Modern Records Centre, University of Warwick (ref. MSS 86), of which the post-war material includes NEC minutes and Education, Finance and various subcommittee minutes from 1914 to 1955; two boxes of the personal papers of J.S. Dean, and a file of papers relating to the NUJ's submission to the Royal Commission on the Press of 1961. A list is available (NRA 19139).

Minutes of all committees for the subsequent period (in bound form up to the late 1970s) are retained at the NUJ's offices, as are copies of the Annual Report (which gives details of membership) and of the reports of the Annual Delegate Meetings in bound form from the 1920s onwards. Annual accounts are likewise kept on file but only current correspondence is retained, except in exceptional circumstances where it is maintained for record reasons. The NUJ has at various times responded to Royal Commissions, official enquiries etc. and copies of such submissions will have been retained in the subject files, but these are not indexed at present. Applications for permission to view the papers should be addressed to the General Secretary.

NATIONAL UNION OF LABOUR ORGANISERS AND ELECTION AGENTS
The National Union of Labour Organisers was established to represent the interests of the constituency agents of the Labour Party. A collection of its records has been deposited in Birmingham Central Library, namely the minutes of the Executive Committee for the period 1959–63 and the minutes of the Midland District Committee for 1941–53. Certain papers of the East Anglia District (including minutes) for 1950–79 are reported to have been deposited in Suffolk Record Office (ref. GG/410).

NATIONAL UNION OF LOCK AND METAL WORKERS
The only union catering exclusively for workers in the lock, key and safe industries, the National Union was founded in 1889 as the National Amalgamated Lock, Latch and Keysmiths Trade Society by trade unionists in the Wolverhampton district, which has remained the traditional centre of

the British industry. It continues as a rare example of a truly industrial union, one which recruits at all grades in the industry and has exclusive negotiating rights.

The NULMW has retained its records at its headquarters. These consist almost exclusively of minutes and reports; financial records, correspondence and subject files are unavailable. The surviving minutes for the post-war era are those of the annual and general meetings and the Executive and Finance Committees, although none is a complete series; for the period 1948–59 the only available material is the minutes of the Wolverhampton and Willenhall District Committees. Annual Reports have been retained for 1949–68, 1970–79, 1981, 1983, 1985 and 1987. Persons wishing access to the archive should apply in writing to the General Secretary.

NATIONAL UNION OF MINEWORKERS The national records of the NUM have not been deposited and no detailed information on their extent is known. However, a very large amount of material has been placed in local repositories. A selection is arranged below alphabetically by area:

1. *Durham* Collections deposited at the Durham County Record Office include the Durham Miners' Association (covering the period 1872–1980s) and also the Durham County Collier, Enginemen's, Boilerminders' and Firemen's Association (ref. D/EFB 1–92). This collection covers the period *c.* 1872–1963, and includes minute books, financial records, day books, arbitration committee minutes, files of correspondence and some branch records.
2. *Kent* Records, 1915–80, of the Kent Area of the NUM are held in the Kent Archives Office.
3. *Lancashire* The Bolton Metropolitan Borough Archives hold the records of the Lancashire Miners' Union and of the Lancashire and Cheshire Colliery Tradesmen and Kindred Workers Association. The association became a constituent association of the NUM (Lancashire Tradesmen's Area) in 1945. In July 1968 it became the NUM North-Western Area. The collection consists of Executive Committee Minutes, 1921–68; periodic (including annual) reports and accounts, 1920–34; correspondence

files (1951–78) on various subjects including Wages Rates, National Insurance Acts, Branch Correspondence, Political Affiliations etc.

Certain records (up to 1960) of the Lancashire and Cheshire Miners' Federation, as well as records of the Lancashire and Cheshire Miners' Permanent Relief Society are held in Wigan Record Office. They comprise minutes, 1874–1947; valuation books, 1908–60, financial and legal papers, and pre-war ledgers.

4. *Leicestershire* Records (to 1945) of the Leicestershire Miners' Association (ref. DE 3540) are deposited in Leicestershire Record Office.
5. *Northumberland* Records of the Northumberland Colliery Mechanics' Association are in Northumberland Record Office. They include minutes of pre-war committees and delegate meetings; council, 1928–48; annual conferences, 1905–47; account books, 1876–1957; compensation case records, 1900–42; and superannuation fund accounts, 1907–51.

The records of the Northumberland and Durham Miners' Permanent Relief Fund have been deposited in Tyne and Wear Record Office (ref. ACC 919). A list is available (NRA 21125).

6. *North Wales* The surviving records are held in the NUM Area Office at Wrexham and have been listed by Clwyd Record Office. This repository also holds the records of the Denbighshire and Flintshire Miners' Federation. These comprise minutes, correspondence and other papers, 1889–1982.
7. *Scotland* The records of the NUM (Scotland) are in the National Library of Scotland. The collection (in 321 boxes) covers the period 1911–85. It includes minutes, related correspondence and papers; branch and area correspondence files, 1958–80; organisation files, 1958–66; and many subject files (including those on the election of area officials, pit safety and reports on the state of the mining industry).

The records of the former Lanarkshire Miners' Union and the NUM (Lanarkshire Area), covering the period 1887–1962, have also been deposited in the National Library of Scotland (ref. Dep 227). Also deposited in the National Library of Scotland are the NUM records for the Ayr region for the period 1938–67. The National

Library also has the records of the Scottish Colliery Enginemen, Boilermen and Tradesmen's Association for the period 1877 to 1965 (for further details, see *Sources, 1900–51*, vol. I, p. 233).

8. *Somerset* Records of the Somerset Miners' Association, and of predecessor unions, are in Bristol University Library.

9. *South Wales* Many records of the South Wales Miners' Federation and the NUM (South Wales Area) are in University College Swansea. Other material can be found in the Gwent Record Office and Glamorgan Record Office.

10. *Staffordshire Record Office* Records of the NUM (Midlands Area) for the period 1928–79, were deposited in 1986.

11. *Warwickshire* Minutes of the Warwickshire Miners' Association, 1903–35 and a list of members, 1940–54, are held in Warwickshire Record Office.

Note: Researchers may also wish to refer to the papers of prominent NUM leaders, e.g. William Ernest Jones (Hull University Library) and Lawrence Daly (Modern Records Centre, Warwick University).

NATIONAL UNION OF PUBLIC EMPLOYEES

The union was founded in 1888 as the London County Council Employees' Protection Association. The name was changed in 1894 to the Municipal Employees' Association. This split in 1907, one section retaining the title MEA (and absorbed into the National Union of General and Municipal Workers in 1924), the other creating the National Union of Corporation Workers. This changed its title to National Union of Public Employees (NUPE) in 1928. NUPE is now part of UNISON.

From 1987 onwards, NUPE began depositing its records at the Modern Records Centre, University of Warwick (ref. MSS 281). The collection includes Executive Committee minutes, 1929–93, General Purpose Committee minutes, 1940–58, 1969–71; Organisation Committee minutes, 1952–62; material on the working conditions of county council roadmen; some documentation on relations with other unions; circulars, 1939–59; annual reports, 1941–49, 1959–67; the Journal, 1931–81, and area conference minutes. Further more recent material has now been added.

In addition records of NUPE (Scottish Region) are deposited in the National Library of Scotland. They include Divisional Officer's correspondence with head office and branches, 1929–57; head office correspondence and papers, 1928–52; papers on National Joint Industrial Councils, 1937–62; on conferences, 1937–54; and Scottish Office branch records, etc.

NATIONAL UNION OF RAILWAYMEN

The union was formed in 1913 by the amalgamation of the Amalgamated Society of Railway Servants (established 1872), the United Pointsmen's and Signalmen's Society (established 1880), and the General Railway Workers' Union (established 1890).

A very extensive collection of records has been deposited in the Modern Records Centre, University of Warwick (ref. MSS 127). Virtually no records appear to have survived for two of the small constituent unions, the GRWU and the UPSS, but for the NUR and the ASRS an extensive series of records has been preserved. Pre-1945 material is described in the *Consolidated Guide to the Modern Records Centre*. For the post-war period, deposited records include: various series of minutes, reports and publications (up to 1990) including NUR printed reports, proceedings and Executive Council minutes, 1954–72; minutes of Conciliation Boards, Wage Boards and other negotiating bodies, 1909–60; extensive subject files on topics such as pay, productivity, redundancy and working hours, 1955–70, on line closures and BR development policy, 1958–65, and small companies/dock agreements; certain branch and district council records, including some for the (London and) South West District Council, 1914–67; reports and rules relating to various railway charity funds; Legal Department records; and copies of the *Railway Review* 1913–90.

The Modern Records Centre also holds material deposited by the University's Industrial Relations Research Unit. This consists of completed questionnaires, correspondence, memoranda and other papers relating to NUR reorganisation, etc.

The union is now part of the National Union of Rail, Maritime and Transport Workers.

NATIONAL UNION OF SEAMEN

The union was founded in Sunderland in 1887 as the National Amalgamated Sailors' and Firemen's Union of Great

Britain and Ireland. In 1894 it went into voluntary liquidation and was re-formed as the National Sailors' and Firemen's Union. The name was changed in 1926 to the National Union of Seamen. The Hull Seamen's Union was absorbed in 1922. The NUS joined the National Union of Railwaymen in 1990 to form the National Union of Rail, Maritime and Transport Workers.

A major collection of the union's records is held at the Modern Records Centre, University of Warwick (ref. MSS 175). The initial deposit includes Executive Council minutes, 1911–59; finance (and general purposes) minutes, 1911–53; some branch records, 1907–77, including minutes for Sunderland (various dates between 1887 and 1968) and Bristol, 1921–50; correspondence and subject files, 1909–68; seamen's journals and other publications, 1911–66; press-cuttings, 1903–76; records relating to the Isle of Man Steam Packet Company, 1917–63; agreements with Liverpool shipping companies, 1917–65; demarcation arrangements with Liverpool painters, 1947–49, and small groups of ephemera relating to more recent disputes. More recent material has now been deposited for the 1960s–80s.

The British Seafarers' Union material contained within the NUS collection covers the pre-war era.

NATIONAL UNION OF STUDENTS The NUS was formed in 1922 'to represent past and present students from a national and international point of view' and 'to promote the educational and social interests of students in entire independence of all political or religious propaganda'. It is composed of the student organisations of universities, polytechnics and institutes of further education, which it provides with information and advice and supportive services through its student Area Organisations.

A large proportion of the non-current records has been deposited at the Modern Records Centre, University of Warwick (ref. MSS 280). The papers mainly cover the period of the 1960s to 1980s. In addition the Modern Records Centre has received the papers of David Gilles, a former NUS Executive Committee member. Other records are retained by the NUS.

NATIONAL UNION OF TEACHERS Formed in 1870 as the National Union of Elementary Teachers, it changed its name in 1889 to the National Union of Teachers.

A substantial collection of records has been deposited in the Modern Records Centre, University of Warwick (ref. MSS 179). A list is available (NRA 33798). A further major deposit was received in March 1996. The material includes records of the predecessor organisation, the National Union of Elementary Teachers; various NUT committee minutes, including Finance, 1890–1966, Organisation and Membership, 1891–1963, and some Annual Reports issued between 1955 and 1983.

NUT local records are or will be deposited in local record offices, and researchers should contact the MRC and the NUT Head Office to determine the present location of a particular region's records.

NATIONAL UNION OF WOMEN TEACHERS The NUWT was founded in 1906 as a pressure group within the National Union of Teachers to campaign for equal pay for women staff; it held its first conference in 1910. Within a decade it had broken away to form an independent union due to the NUT's lack of progress on the issue. After World War II it was involved in a renewed campaign for equal pay; when this was finally achieved in 1961, it was decided to wind up the union. The NUWT had no connection with the Union of Women Teachers, which was founded in 1966 and later amalgamated with the National Association of Schoolmasters (see separate entry for the NASUWT in this Guide).

The entire archive of the NUWT has been deposited in the library of the Institute of Education, University of London. It is a substantial collection running to over 600 files. None of the material is any longer restricted. Persons wishing to use the collection should apply to the Archivist at the library.

The papers consist of a complete series of minutes of the various union committees (General Council, General Purpose and Organisation, Education, Legal and Tenure, etc.) and reports of the annual conferences from foundation until 1961. There are also the ledger books and records of the legal fund, and an incomplete series of the union's journal, *The Woman Teacher*, from 1936 until dissolution.

However, the bulk of the material is an extensive series of subject files covering the period from the early 1920s until 1961. It covers issues of women in teaching (e.g. equal pay, married women teachers, headships etc.), and general educational issues such as classroom size, corporal punishment, the school leaving age, examinations, and teacher training. In addition the subject files contain extensive material dealing with political matters, both educational (e.g. 1944 Education Act) and general (e.g. franchise for women). Each of these categories contains both papers emanating from the NUWT itself and those of other groups – political parties and professional organisations – and numerous pamphlets and press-cuttings. Surviving correspondence appears to be included in the subject files and not organised other-wise. The NUWT archive also contains a number of the records of its individual branches, but these have not yet been fully identified.

NATIONAL UNITED TEMPERANCE COUNCIL
The records, covering the period 1897–1982, have been deposited in the London Metropolitan Archives. Further details of the history of the temperance movement in Britain and its archives are given in *Sources, 1900–51*, vol. I, pp. 253–54.

NATIONAL VIEWERS' AND LISTENERS' ASSOCIATION In 1993 the papers and correspon-dence of the National Viewers' and Listeners' Association, including correspondence and various publications of Mary Whitehouse, were deposited in Essex University Library. The collection is listed.

NATIONAL WOMEN CITIZENS' ASSOCIA-TION The Association was founded in March 1918 immediately prior to the granting of female suffrage, in order to foster a more active concept of citizenship among women and to encourage them to stand for elected office. It had a substantial branch structure which was reinvigorated after World War II by the creation of its Northern and Southern Federations. In 1946 the National Council for Equal Citizenship, and in 1949 Women for Westminster (q.v.), were incorporated in the Association. It was dissolved in 1974, but local branches continued in existence and in 1975 certain former officers decided to revive the national body as a small central organisation (known as the National Association of Women Citizens) to disseminate information among these branches.

The papers of the Association have been deposited in the Women's Library. Lists of the collections are available (NRA 20625, 33700). The records include minutes of the Executive Committee, 1949–74, and of meetings with the Committee of the chairmen of local associations, 1954–72; AGM agendas and minutes, 1947–74; minutes of Council meetings, 1968–70; the AGM attendance book, 1956–72; the Executive Committee attendance book, 1954–66; annual conference reports and papers, 1961–73; and reports of the Conferences of Women Members of Local Government Authorities in England and Wales, 1947–73 (with agendas and papers from 1962). In addition there are files of correspondence with local branches, mostly for the period from the late 1960s to 1973.

The collection includes runs of the quarterly journal *The Woman Councillor*, nos. 1–15 (1945–48), and its successors, *The Woman Councillor and Citizen* (1949–51) and *Newsletter* (1952–73), and a number of assorted leaflets and pamphlets from the 1930s to the 1960s. Certain papers of the Southern and the Northern Federations and of several local branches have also been deposited.

Researchers should also be aware that the papers of the Scottish Council of Women Citizens' Asso-ciation for the period 1918–82 nave now been deposited in the Scottish Record Office (ref. GD1/1076). Further enquiries should be directed to the Keeper of Records of Scotland.

NATIONALISED INDUSTRIES CHAIRMEN'S GROUP The papers of the NICG were deposited in the LSE Library in April 1990 when the organisation ceased to function. They commence with the records of meetings between chairmen of the nationalised industries, and the General Meetings. After 1976 the structure was formalised by the establishment of a Standing Committee, the Council, an Advisory Committee and the Finance Panel. The Nationalised Industries Overseas Group and the European Panel undertook the co-ordination of the Group's work abroad. The papers contain much useful information on the policy of government towards the national-ised industries.

The main series of papers are as follows: Chairmen's meetings agenda, minutes and correspondence, 1973–75; General Meeting agenda and minutes, 1976–78; Standing Committee papers, 1976–78; agenda and minutes of and reports to the Council, 1978–89; Advisory Commmittee papers, 1978–89; organisational papers, 1973–90, being principally correspondence files organised by subject; subject files on relations with HM Government, 1977–89 (including records of ministerial meetings); agenda, minutes and briefings of the Finance Panel, 1977–86; records of the European Panel, 1972–89; the papers of the Nationalised Industries Overseas Group (including minutes of other NICG Committees, correspondence, papers on overseas visits and foreign relations, and records of various working parties of the Group), 1976–90. In addition there are copies of reports published by the NICG in the 1980s and papers relating to public inquiries on nationalised industries, 1986–88.

NEVER AGAIN ASSOCIATION No central archive for this anti-war group has been located, but reference should be made to the Alan Crosland Graham papers, deposited in the LSE Library (ref. Coll Misc 771). These contain a file of minutes and correspondence of the Never Again Association as well as correspondence with a similar group, Allies Inside Germany.

NEW STATESMAN The literary archive of this influential left-wing weekly, covering the period 1913 to 1988, was offered for sale at Sotheby's in 1991. It was subsequently acquired by Sussex University Library. Under such editors as Kingsley Martin (until 1960), John Freeman (1964) and Paul Johnson (1970) the *New Statesman* achieved its peak circulation.

The material acquired by Sussex University Library includes the archive of editorial correspondence and in-house files from 1943–88. The collection comprises over 250 files (the equivalent of eight large filing cabinet drawers) containing many thousands of letters and documents, including principally huge quantities of letters to editors, on a vast range of political, social and international issues, with carbon-copies of outgoing letters, as well as files relating to such matters as advertising,

readers' reports, review copies, foreign rights, finances, and to writings on specific subjects. Nearly all the major political and literary figures of the post-war left are represented in the collection. The papers have now been listed (NRA 38437).

Separate from the above papers are some editorial files which were acquired earlier by the City University, London.

NEWMAN ASSOCIATION The object of the Association, which was founded in 1942 as a successor to the University Catholic Federation of Great Britain, is to further the mission to the world of the Christian religion with particular reference to the Roman Catholic Church and the example of the life and work of the Venerable John Henry Newman. The Association organises conferences etc. and publishes the results of the study and research undertaken in pursuit of its object. A journal, *The Newman*, is published three times a year and an Annual Report is also issued. The archives of the Association are retained in the care of its various officers and enquiries concerning the papers should be directed to the Hon. Secretary, care of the registered office.

The material which has been retained is known to include the minutes of the AGM from 1942 onwards. Copies of the Association's Annual Report, journal and occasional publications are available at the British Library.

NEWSPAPER PUBLISHERS ASSOCIATION LTD Founded in 1906 as the Newspaper Proprietors Association, the company is a trade organisation representing the member groups which publish national daily and Sunday newspapers. The archive is effectively not available. All pre-war records apart from minutes were destroyed by enemy action during World War II. Subsequent material, including minutes of the Council and other meetings, is confidential.

Researchers may wish to refer to the entry for Sir George Pope, pp. 158–9.

NO ASSEMBLY CAMPAIGN The No Assembly Campaign was formed to urge Welsh electors to vote against the proposal of devolution for Wales in the referendum of March 1979. Its chairman Lord

Gibson-Watt subsequently donated the papers to the National Library of Wales. The material comprises general correspondence for the three months of January to March 1979; press releases; copies of speeches and lists of meetings; and miscellaneous press-cuttings. A list is available (NRA 26130).

NORTHERN ARTS ASSOCIATION The records of the Association comprising minutes, files, reports etc. for the period 1961 to 1989 have been deposited with the Tyne and Wear Archives Service.

NORTHERN FRIENDS PEACE BOARD The Board was established in 1913 as a result of a widespread wish among members of the Religious Society of Friends to provide a witness to the traditional Quaker values of peace at a time of international tension. Subsequently the Board has continued its work to promote peace, justice and reconciliation by organising conferences, seminars and exhibitions throughout the north of England on a variety of environmental, social and international issues. It co-operates closely both with Quaker Peace and Social Witness (a committee of the national Society) and with the individual northern Quaker meetings. It is independent of any central funding from the Religious Society of Friends and relies on donations and voluntary contributions from meetings.

Records of the Board for the period 1913 to 1986 have been deposited with the West Yorkshire Archives Service. A list is available (NRA 24585). Deposited papers include minutes of Board and Executive Meetings for this period; annual reports and financial records prior to 1976, and correspondence and subject files (e.g. relating to conferences and international visits) for the period 1978 to 1985. Copies of the Board's publications and its publicity posters are also available. Papers covering the subsequent period are retained at the Board's offices. Persons seeking permission to use either the deposited collection or the retained records should check access with the Archivist.

NORTHERN IRELAND COUNTY COURT OFFICERS' ASSOCIATION Certain papers of the Association for the period 1936–60 have been deposited in the Public Record Office of Northern Ireland (ref. D3778). They mainly comprise correspondence with the Ministry of Home Affairs and the Crown and Peace officers, and the subjects covered relate principally to the conditions of service and remuneration of the officers. The collection numbers *c.* 80 documents.

NORTHERN IRELAND PUBLIC SERVICE ALLIANCE The Public Service Alliance is the principal government officers' trade union for Northern Ireland. Certain of its papers for the period 1919 to 1975 have been deposited at the Public Record Office of Northern Ireland (ref. D1050/9). The collection incorporates the papers of the Ulster Public Officers' Association (UPOA), formed in 1919; the Northern Ireland Civil Service Association (NICSA), formed in 1934; the Civil Service Professional Officers' Association (CSPOA), known prior to 1951 as the Association of Professional and Technical Officers in the Civil Service of Northern Ireland, and the Northern Ireland Civil Service Alliance, which was established by NICSA and CSPOA in 1959 and which adopted its present title in 1972.

The papers of the above constituent unions comprise largely minutes, correspondence files and reports. Specifically, the collection is known to include the minutes of the Central and Executive Council of UPOA for the periods 1930–49, 1954–69 and 1971–73, and of its AGM for 1952–64, and the minutes and correspondence of NICSA for 1933–61. Later papers may have been retained by the union itself and further enquiries should be directed to the Secretary.

O

OIL AND CHEMICAL PLANT CONSTRUC-TORS' ASSOCIATION The OCPCA was founded in 1968 as the successor to the Advisory Panel for Oil Refinery and Chemical Plant Constructors, set up in 1958 and dissolved in 1969. The OCPCA was subsequently joined by the Refractory Users' Federation (founded 1947) and the Gas Refractories and Coke Oven Contractors' Association. The association amalgamated with the National Engineering Contractors Employers' Association (NECEA) to form the Engineering Construction Industry Association from 1 April 1994.

The records have been deposited in the Modern Records Centre, University of Warwick (ref. MSS 91). They include minutes; records of the Finance, General Purposes, Training and Industrial Relations committees, 1969–85, and negotiation files relating to various national agreements signed between 1967 and 1986. Records of the Coke Oven Contractors' Association comprise minutes, 1963–73; accounts, 1967–73; working files, 1970–75, and constitutions of the COCA and GRCOCA. A later deposit is classed as MSS 91/OCP.

OPEN DOOR COUNCIL Founded in 1926, the Open Door Council strove to ensure equality of legal treatment for the woman worker. It had a strongly internationalist stance from its inception and a conference in Berlin in 1929 organised by the Council's international committee led to the formation of the Open Door International. The ODC thereafter served as the British arm of the international organisation. The work of the former was truncated by World War II, but it was very active again in the 1950s with most members coming from Scandinavia, Belgium and Great Britain. However, membership shrank considerably in the following decade and although ODI was never formally dissolved it effectively ceased operations around 1974.

The papers of both the Open Door Council and the Open Door International were deposited in the Women's Library in 1976. A list is available (NRA 29383). The ODI records had previously been in the care of the incumbent Hon. Secretary and consequently were transferred from country to country as appropriate; the surviving material is partly in French and German, as well as English. It comprises the minutes of Board meetings, 1947–59 and 1968–73; reports and conference resolutions, 1929–38 and 1946–66; papers of the 7th, 8th, 9th and 10th conferences; copies of the constitution and charters; correspondence files, 1947–60 and 1966–74; circular letters, 1949–59; collected printed leaflets and public statements of ODI, mainly addressed to various agencies of the United Nations, and publications of other official and governmental organisations. The Open Door Council material itself consists of an intermittent series of annual reports, 1926–65; papers and agendas of the annual meetings, 1954–63; and resolutions, 1951–53.

OPEN SPACES SOCIETY Founded in 1865 to challenge the legality of the enclosure of common land in London, this body, which was the first national conservation organisation in the UK, adopted the name Commons, Open Spaces and Footpaths Preservation Society in 1910 (although it is now usually known by the shortened version). The aims of the Society are to preserve public open spaces and footpaths and promote public access to the countryside. Today it primarily advises local authorities on footpath preservation.

A large quantity of papers has been deposited in the House of Lords Record Office, where enquiries should be addressed, but a substantial archive remains at the Society's headquarters. Papers include minutes of the Executive Committee since 1926; the Finance and General Purposes subcommittee from 1954, and the Central Rights of Way

Committee from 1958. There are also a number of agendas and minutes of AGMs. The bulk of the archive consists of case files, most of which concern the ownership of common land, enclosures, and the infringement of footpaths, and largely cover the 1930s to 1950s. A complete run of the quarterly journal (which also contains the annual report) exists from 1927. A list is available (NRA 24471). Those wishing to study the material should write to the General Secretary.

OVERSEAS MISSIONARY FELLOWSHIP The Fellowship's predecessor, the China Inland Mission, was originally founded in 1865 with the object of spreading Christianity in inland China. When missionary work in China became impossible in 1951 the sphere of operations was transferred to East Asia, and the mission changed its name to the above in 1965.

Papers relating to the Fellowship's post-1951 activities are retained at the British National Office. The material includes the following series of minutes: British Isles Council (formerly London Council) from 1951, indexed to 1978; CIM Corporation, 1951–87; Overseas Missionary Fellowship Ltd, 1958–84; Finance Committee, from 1951; Executive Committee, from 1951 and indexed to 1970; Advisory Committee, from 1978; and Communications Unit, from 1962. Accounts and personal membership files exist for the post-1951 period. Copies of publications have also been retained, including the monthly magazine *The Million/East Asia Missions* from 1951 to date and *Young Asia* for the period 1951–62. The collection incorporates examples of internal publications such as directories of members and bulletins. Applications for permission to consult any papers should be addressed to the Home Director at the British National Office.

P

PALESTINE SOLIDARITY CAMPAIGN The Campaign was established (as the Palestinian Solidarity Liaison Committee) in April 1982 by a number of British and Middle Eastern political organisations to coordinate activities in support of the Palestinian people. It supports the Palestinian Declaration of Independence of 1988 and self-determination for that people; recognises the Palestine Liberation Organisation as their sole legitimate representative, and opposes Zionism and anti-Semitism and all forms of racism. It publishes a bi-monthly magazine, *Palestine Solidarity.* and a monthly bulletin for members.

The PSC retains its own papers to date, which comprise minutes of all committee meetings and annual conferences since April 1982; copies of the annual report (first issued in 1982), the magazine and the bulletin; financial records such as invoice and receipt books, and correspondence, which is arranged separately for individuals and the regional branches of PSC. All records, with the exception of the membership list, are open to bona fide researchers and further enquiries should be directed to the Secretary of PSC.

PARENTS AGAINST INJUSTICE PAIN is a charitable organisation established in 1985 which seeks to advise and counsel parents, relatives and professional carers in cases in which children are mistakenly reported to have been victims of child abuse. It organises training courses on the issue for child care practitioners and maintains lists of specialist doctors and solicitors.

The papers of PAIN have been retained at its head office. Extant material comprises minutes of the quarterly meetings of the Trustees since 1986; copies of the quarterly newsletters since 1987, the Annual Report since 1989, and research reports and evidence submitted to official enquiries; annual audited accounts and ledger books from 1985 onwards; and

correspondence files from that date organised by subject and by originating body. These papers may be made available to researchers with the written permission of the Chairman. PAIN also retains individual case history files, which remain closed indefinitely except with the consent of the person concerned. However, anecdotal case histories may be used anonymously in research and enquirers may be referred to families with their permission and in consultation with PAIN.

PARLIAMENT FOR WALES CAMPAIGN The records of the Merioneth County Committee of the Parliament for Wales Campaign for the period 1951–54 have been deposited at the National Library of Wales. Other material for 1953–56 is reported to be available in the papers of Elwyn Roberts (Secretary of Plaid Cymru (q.v.) from 1964 to 1971), likewise at the National Library. Researchers should check on later deposits at the National Library.

PARLIAMENTARY ASSOCIATION FOR WORLD GOVERNMENT The Parliamentary Group for World Government (subsequently the Parliamentary Association for World Government) was founded in 1945 by Henry Osborne MP, to introduce federalist ideas into national politics.

An extensive collection of records, mainly covering the period 1952–64, was deposited in Sussex University Library in April 1977. A list is available (NRA 20887). The material includes printed papers, accounts, minutes, reports and correspondence of the Parliamentary Association for World Government. The collection also contains annual reports and balance sheets of the World Association of Parliamentarians for World Government/World Parliament Association.

PATIENTS ASSOCIATION The records since 1963 have been placed in the Contemporary Medical

Archives Centre, Wellcome Institute (ref. SA/PAT). The collection includes administrative files, AGM papers and minutes together with correspondence with patients.

PEACE TAX CAMPAIGN The Peace Tax Campaign was begun in 1977 by the Cornish Quaker Stanley Keeble, who had been attempting to withhold from the Inland Revenue that portion of his taxes which might contribute to military expenditure. With the support of the Peace Pledge Union and the Quaker Peace Committee he established the Peace Tax Campaign to press for a change in the law which would permit conscientious objectors to pay taxes directly to government agencies engaged in 'peace building'. A London office was established in 1985. The majority of the Peace Tax Campaign's work consists of lobbying the British and European Parliaments. In 1991 the organisation adopted the fuller title, Conscience – the Peace Tax Campaign.

The records of the Campaign are kept at its offices. Minutes of the Executive Committee and the AGM have been retained since 1981 and those of the monthly Development Committee minutes since 1986, but none of these series is complete. Annual Reports and reports of occasional day schools also exist. Financial records prior to 1985 remain in an unsorted state but subsequent records have been sorted. Correspondence for the period c. 1979– from individual members and affiliated organisations is unsorted, but later material is arranged alphabetically for members, by constituency for MPs, and by organisation for government departments, political parties, international bodies etc. Subject files consist of legislation relating to matters of conscience (sorted by date of introduction); past campaign literature, including leaflets and advice pamphlets; copies of articles in other publications; press-cuttings; press releases; and a complete set of newsletters since 1978. These files are arranged by date. Current membership records are unavailable. Persons wishing access to the papers should apply in writing to the Executive Committee.

PEDESTRIANS' ASSOCIATION The safety campaigner Lord Cecil of Chelwood (1864–1958) founded the Pedestrians' Association for Road Safety in 1929, the same year in which he introduced the Road Vehicles Regulation Bill to reduce the growing number of accidents in the UK. The Association exists to campaign for the introduction of road safety measures and the stricter administration of traffic laws.

A small archive has been retained at the Association's offices; in principle it is open for academic research and enquiries should be addressed to the Secretary. A list is available (NRA 24474). Surviving papers include the minutes of the Committee complete since 1929, excepting 1962–69 which are missing. There is also one file containing agendas and minutes of the Executive Committee, memoranda, Secretary's reports, draft Annual Reports, and circulars. Correspondence files have been maintained since 1980. Those financial records which exist date mainly from the 1970s with only one ledger surviving for an earlier period (1950–65), although statements of accounts are included with the Annual Report. A complete series of this report exists for 1930–74 (lacking 1933, 1935, 1969 and 1971); thereafter it has been published in the journal. Copies of the *Quarterly News Letter* and the journal *Walk* (previously entitled *The Pedestrian* and *Arrive*), which replaced the newsletter in 1951, are available for 1946–63 and the period since 1970.

The Association formerly shared offices with the Open Spaces Society (q.v.) and some of its archive was stored with the records of that society. The papers of its first Secretary T.C. Foley (d. 1979) have also been kept. The papers of the international trade unionist Paul Tofahrn, deposited at the Modern Records Centre, University of Warwick (ref. MSS 238), contain one file relating to the Pedestrians' Association, of which he was an executive member.

PLAID CYRMU The party was founded at the Pwllheli Eisteddfod in 1925 as a result of the union of two smaller groups based on the University Colleges at Bangor and Aberystwyth.

Extensive records of the party have been deposited in the National Library of Wales. A detailed list (in Welsh) is now available (NRA 40395). Some of the earlier deposits, mainly of pre-1945 material, are described in *Sources, 1900–51*, vol. I, pp. 212–13. Records deposited since then include further records of the Executive Committee, 1932–50; branch records (including Bangor, Cardiff, East Glamorgan and

Montgomery); files on the 1943 University of Wales by-election, and much material on the various campaigns the party has waged. Among the most recent deposits are minutes and papers relating to the Swansea branch and to the Ceredigion constituency committee.

The Welsh Political Archive at the National Library of Wales issues a regular *Bulletin* recording new accessions. Local Record Offices throughout Wales may have other branch records.

POLICE FEDERATION OF ENGLAND AND WALES

The Police Federation is the professional association for police officers. It was established in 1919 and its papers since that date have been retained, including minutes and Annual Reports. Financial records and correspondence (organised by subject) are held on microfilm. Readers are advised to direct further enquiries in writing to the Head of Research. Material is only available on site with prior permission.

POLICY STUDIES INSTITUTE

This economic planning group has now been enlarged by a merger with a similar body, Political and Economic Planning (PEP). Some records, 1931–82, have been placed in the LSE Library. These mainly relate to the work of PEP, which was established in 1934 and aimed to contribute to more effective planning and policy-making by government and industry by studying selected problems and publishing the results. Its original purpose was to outline and advocate a National Plan, at a period when such a concept was novel and controversial. The collection is mostly open (except for a few personal or confidential files). A list is available. The material consists of administrative papers (minutes and miscellaneous papers, including correspondence, accounts, reports, trustee papers, etc); research papers; and press-cuttings.

POLISH INSTITUTE AND SIKORSKI MUSEUM

The Institute, based in London, was founded in 1945 as the General Sikorski Historical Institute. After amalgamation with the Polish Research Centre in 1966 it adopted its present name. The archives of the Institute itself consist of minutes of General Meetings (since 1966), Council Meetings (since 1978) and Executive Committee Meetings. There are also financial records and correspondence. The Institute also houses very extensive archives of Polish organisations and individuals for World War II and for the post-45 period. The best introduction to these is given in the *Guide to the Archives of the Polish Institute and Sikorski Museum*, edited by Waclaw Milewski *et al.* (1985).

POLITICAL ECONOMY CLUB

The papers, from as early as 1821, have been deposited in the LSE Library. The post-war material includes membership records, some correspondence and incomplete Secretary's files.

POLITICAL STUDIES ASSOCIATION

Many records of the association have been deposited in the LSE Library. They include minutes, correspondence and conference papers, 1950–83, as well as papers relating to its early history deposited by Professor George Jones (ref. M1628). A summary box list is available, but material continues to accrue. Special conditions of access apply.

POPULATION CONCERN

Some archives of this organisation can be found in the Contemporary Medical Archives Centre, Wellcome Institute.

POST OFFICE ENGINEERING UNION

The POEU was formed in 1887 as the Postal, Telegraph and Linemen's Movement. In 1896 a related union was formed, the Amalgamated Association of the Postal Telegraph Department, which in 1901 joined with the Postal, Telegraph and Linemen's Movement to become the Post Office Engineering and Stores Association. A further amalgamation occurred in 1915 from the National Association of Telephone Operators and the National Society of Telephone Employers. Not all members joined: the clerks from NSTE were absorbed into the Civil Service Clerical Association, which became the Civil and Public Services Association; other grades, such as the inspectors, formed their own union, the Post Office Inspectors' Association, now the Society of Post Office Inspectors. The current name of the POEU was adopted in 1919.

An extensive deposit of archives is held in the Modern Records Centre, University of Warwick (ref. MSS 135). The collection includes various series of minutes, 1920–60; accounts, 1936–52; wage claim records, 1927–59; some extensive correspondence files; various records of Whitley Councils, 1919–69; extensive runs of publications, 1883–1960, and the *Journal*, 1920–73. Extensive recent deposits include material from the 1980s concerning privatisation.

Researchers should note that the Belfast Branch of the POEU has deposited records with the Public Record Office of Northern Ireland (ref. D1050/19). These cover the years 1946 to 1984, and include minutes of the Council of Post Office Unions (which later became the British Telecommunications Unions' Committee, BTUC), 1974–84, and BTUC papers relating to the privatisation of British Telecom in 1983.

POSTAL, TELEGRAPH AND TELEPHONE INTERNATIONAL Extensive archives are in the International Institute of Social History, Amsterdam. The most recent deposit includes records for the period 1963–94.

PRESS ASSOCIATION The records for the period 1865 – *c*. 1980 have been placed in the Guildhall Library, London.

PRINTING AND KINDRED TRADES FEDERATION The Federation was founded in 1901 on a national basis to represent the interests of all printing workers in negotiations with employers. Its object was to 'secure unity of action amongst the various affiliated unions'. The Federation was officially dissolved on 30 April 1974.

Surviving records of the Federation have been deposited in the Modern Records Centre, University of Warwick (ref. MSS 43). The collection includes minutes and papers, 1910–74; financial records, 1902–60; conference minutes and papers, 1899–1973; *The Bulletin*, 1927–54; agreements, 1936–61; and extensive subject files, 1930s–70s.

PRISON REFORM TRUST The Trust is a national charity established in 1981 to campaign for a more rational and humane penal policy. It seeks to reduce the proportion of offenders who are given cusodial sentences and presses for reform of the prison system. The Trust publishes widely on the issue and offers advice to prisoners and others who wish legally to pursue grievances with the prison authorities.

The papers are in the care of the Trust's Administrator at its offices. They comprise minutes of the Executive Committee and of the Trustees from the date of foundation; miscellaneous committee papers; the Annual Report from 1981/82 onwards and miscellaneous reports of seminars and public meetings; copies of all published reports, booklets, pamphlets, etc., and all issues of the Trust's magazine *Prison Report*. There also survives correspondence with the Home Office and Prison Department and files relating to campaigns and activities (including a limited amount of correspondence prior to 1981 concerning the setting up of the Trust itself), and subject files which incorporate a large volume of press-cuttings and copies of press releases and submissions to official enquiries, etc. All applications for access should be made to the Administrator.

PRO FIDE Some relevant papers of the organisation (originally Catholics United for Faith) can be found in the papers of Sir Patrick Wall deposited in the Brynmor Jones Library, University of Hull. These papers include the original circular letters for Catholics United for Faith (1969–70) and files about its establishment as Pro Fide (1970–71). There are lists of original members of Pro Fide, the draft manifesto, newsletters and very extensive later correspondence (e.g. with Cardinal Basil Hume).

PROFESSIONAL ASSOCIATION OF TEACHERS
The Professional Association of Teachers was founded in 1970 by two Essex teachers, Ray Bryant and Colin Leicester, who disapproved of the industrial action then being undertaken by teachers. Every member of PAT undertakes to abide by the 'Cardinal Rule' of the Association, which is to eschew industrial action, and strike action in particular.

The records of the Association are held at its registered offices or where appropriate at the Scottish office. Certain papers are confidential (access being allowed only to members of the Association) and these include minutes of meetings of the National Council and its administrative committees since 1970; the Scottish Executive Committee; and the AGM. Annual reports to the AGM submitted by each of the Committees of the Council and by the Hon. Secretary are likewise confidential, as are ledger books, membership registers, correspondence and the annual members' *Handbook*, published since 1973. Material in the public domain includes policy and press statements; booklets and miscellaneous documents giving advice; the annual Conference Brochure (i.e. the agenda) published since 1976, and copies of PAT's publications, including the *Professional Teacher*, which has been published in broadsheet form from 1970 to 1984 and subsequently as a termly journal. Researchers wishing access to the confidential material should apply in writing to the National Council of the Association.

PROGRESSIVE LEAGUE There are some papers in the LSE Library, to where enquiries should be addressed.

PROTESTANT ALLIANCE The Alliance was founded in 1845 by the 7th Earl of Shaftesbury, the social reformer. It has as its aim the 'maintenance of Protestantism', which is interpreted as being the defence of evangelical Christianity and fundamentalist biblical interpretation and the maintenance of the established constitution of the Church. The Alliance has retained its own papers, including a run of its official organ *The Reformer*, which are in the care of the General Secretary.

PROTESTANT AND CATHOLIC ENCOUNTER (PACE) Some records, including minutes, reports and pamphlets, 1968–95, have been deposited in the Public Record Office of Northern Ireland (ref. D 4098).

PUBLIC AND COMMERCIAL SERVICES UNION A large deposit of records, including those of predecessor bodies, including the Society of Civil and Public Servants, *c.* 1885–1998, can be found in the Modern Records Centre, University of Warwick (ref. MSS 415).

PUBLIC MORALITY COUNCIL The Council (originally known as the London Council for the Promotion of Public Morality) was founded in 1899 to combat vice and indecency in London, and to stimulate their repression by the legal means which were already available, but neglected. It continued until 1969, concentrating later on opposition to sex and pornography in general, as well as in the theatre, cinema and media.

The records of the Council, 1899–1965, have been deposited in London Metropolitan Archives. Few relate to the early period of its activity. The material includes annual reports (to 1953 with some gaps) and the minutes of the Council and various special committees (*c.* 1940–65). There are also some subject files.

PUBLISHERS ASSOCIATION A trade association founded in 1896. All but the most recent of its papers have now been deposited in the library of the University of Reading. The material held consists largely of the minutes of the meetings of the Council (the main policy-making body) and of the divisional Board (i.e. the educational, international and home affairs departments of the Association). Copies of circulars to members, and of the Association's reports or submissions to various authorities on major issues of the day are also included in the collection. The papers are available for consultation within certain limitations and with the written consent of the Association. Researchers should apply to the Chief Executive for permission to examine the collection.

PUGWASH MOVEMENT (THE) The Pugwash Movement was a humanistic movement within the international scientific community, which was provoked by the publication in July 1955 of the Einstein-Russell Manifesto opposing war. Its first conference was held two years later in the Canadian town of Pugwash. Its aims were to consider – in a series of conferences and without the direct influence of public authorities – the role of the scientist in modern life and how science might be harnessed to productive rather than destructive ends; this was to be achieved by informing governments of the consequences of scientific developments and by seeking to educate public opinion. The British philosopher and radical humanist Bertrand Russell was its first elected President and a substantial archive of correspondence and printed material relating to Pugwash may be found in the Bertrand Russell Archive at McMaster University, Hamilton, Ontario, Canada (ref. X 2/1 and X 2/2). Six boxes of papers, 1960–86, concerning Pugwash Conference Proceedings are in the LSE Library (ref. M 1912).

R

RADICAL ACTION There are papers of this Liberal pressure group with the papers of Honor Balfour, now in the Bodleian Library, Oxford.

RADICAL SOCIETY The Society was co-founded by the former Labour and SDP MP Neville Sandelson, who was its chairman in 1988. His papers are in the LSE Library.

RAILWAY DEVELOPMENT SOCIETY The RDS has campaigned for an improvement to rail services since its formation as the Railway Development Association in 1978. At present the papers are in the care of the Secretary and the Archivist. They are known to include minute books of both the specialist committees of the Society (covering freight rail, passenger rail, parliamentary liaison and international affairs) and of the National Conferences, since the date of foundation. Financial records and correspondence are closed to non-members, but a *Factfile* booklet has been compiled listing all reports and documents held by RDS. The Society also produces a quarterly newsletter *Railwatch*; and a history of the Society, *Fighting for Rail*, was published in 1988. Persons wishing to examine the papers should in the first instance contact the Administrative Officer.

RAINER FOUNDATION The Rainer Foundation had its origins in the Police Court Missions of 1876, which were taken over by the judicial authorities in the 1930s to form the modern Probation Service. Today it continues to campaign for the reform of laws and legal practices which discriminate against young people.

The Rainer Foundation has retained its papers. These consist of minutes of committee and council meetings from 1934 onwards; annual reports from 1882; correspondence files, and copies of reports published since 1876. There is also a substantial photographic archive. Appointments for access to the papers should be made through the Appeals Office.

RAMBLERS' ASSOCIATION A voluntary association and registered charity composed of several hundred individual walking clubs, the Ramblers' Association was established in 1934–35 in succession to the National Council of Ramblers Federation. Its aims include the preservation of the countryside, but this is always recognised as being subordinate to encouraging public access to open spaces.

A large archive has been retained at the Association's offices. Papers consist of a general minute book series from 1934 (containing the minutes of the National Council and the Executive Committee as well as of other committees such as Finance and General Purposes and Membership and Publicity), and the records of the predecessor organisation. There are separate minute books for the Countryside Fund committee (1964–); Footpaths Subcommittee (1974–); Welsh Council (1974–); and Finance and Administrative Subcommittee (1975–). Files of committee papers such as agendas, reports, balance sheets, budgets and membership figures have been kept since 1949. A file exists of the correspondence of the former Secretary Tom Stephenson (1958–68). No financial records are available for the period prior to 1965. Correspondence and administrative files are arranged by area, individuals, and other organisations. The publications series is particularly large and includes Area circulars (1948–72), Area newsletters (1969–71), press releases, and journals, handbooks and guides. Complete sets of the official journal, *Ramblers' News* (1949–60) and *Rucksack* (1960–) have been retained. Annual Reports exist for 1946, 1948–49 and 1952–57.

The Association is not normally able to make its papers available for academic research. However, applications from research workers known to the

Association, or introduced by persons so known, will be given sympathetic consideration.

REFUGEE ACTION An independent agency to assist refugees to Great Britain from Vietnam, Refugee Action was established in 1981 to help their resettlement in the United Kingdom. The records which have been retained comprise all committee minutes and copies of the Annual Report (entitled Director's Report prior to 1989–90) from 1981 onwards. Financial records, correspondence for the period 1981–91 and files of various project papers are also available. All of the material is confidential with the exception of published reports (which include the Annual Report), and permission to consult these may be sought from the Administrator.

REFUGEE COUNCIL The Refugee Council was established in 1981 by the merger of the British Council for Aid to Refugees (BCAR) and the Standing Conference on Refugees (SCOR). The Council exists to campaign for refugees' rights in Great Britain and abroad, and to advise individuals of their legal position as refugees. The archives of the BCAR and SCOR have been retained by the Council. The papers of the Refugee Council itself may be classified as comprising the minutes of the Executive Council; official correspondence with government and United Nations officials, and individual refugee case files. Further details may be obtained from the Head of Information, but it should be understood that owing to the Council's limited resources access to the papers is likely to be restricted.

RELEASE The Release Collective was founded in 1967 to provide legal advice to young people who claimed harassment by the police. It has subsequently developed as a national alternative legal and welfare organisation, with a deep involvement in drug counselling.

Its records have been placed in the Modern Records Centre, University of Warwick (ref. MSS 171). The initial deposit consisted of 11 boxes of correspondence files, c. 1968–75; minutes, 1972–74; case papers; publications; and material relating to similar alternative organisations. A second deposit, largely comprising administrative records, 1968–76, and a series of social psychiatric day books, 1973–76,

has also been made. Researchers should note that access to unpublished material is severely limited.

RELIGIOUS SOCIETY OF FRIENDS A Christian body also known simply as the Society of Friends, or more usually as the Quakers, the Society was founded in the 17th century by the English divine George Fox. It represents the extreme wing of the historical Puritan movement in Great Britain. Both in its worship and its work of service in the fields of peace and relief from distress, the Society displays its belief in a priesthood of all believers and in the importance of personal religious experience.

The records of the Society are retained by its Library at Friends House, which is open to members of the Society and other researchers by appointment. A fifty-year rule operates with respect to the papers but this may be waived by the Library Committee of the Society at its discretion.

The supreme governing body of the Society in Great Britain is the London Yearly Meeting. Its minutes are extant from 1672; and the series of printed *Proceedings* from 1857 onwards contains certain documents presented to or issued by the meeting, reports of the committees, and from 1876 a summary of proceedings of the Meeting for Sufferings, the standing executive committee of the Yearly Meeting. Indexes are available for the period 1668–1974.

The Yearly Meetings and the Meetings for Sufferings have under them a number of standing committees whose records have been retained. Among the more important of these are committees on Peace (1888–1965); its successor on Peace and International Relations (records to 1978); East-West Relations (1950–51, 1955–65); Race Relations (1928–72); Social and Economic Affairs (1945–74); Penal Affairs (1920–72); Education (1902 to date); Allotments (1926–51); Palestine (1944–51), and the refugee relief committee, the Friends Service Council (1927–78), which was itself succeeded by Quaker Peace & Service (now Quaker Peace and Social Witness). For a number of these committees reports to the Yearly Meeting may be found in the *Proceedings* of the latter.

The Library acts as a repository for the private papers of individual Quakers; there is also available a typescript Dictionary of Quaker Biography and other compilations such as the Index of Quaker Members of Parliament.

RESEARCH DEFENCE SOCIETY RDS was founded in 1908 to defend the use of responsible animal experimentation for the benefit of medical science. The complete archive of the Society from the date of its foundation has been deposited at the Contemporary Medical Archives Centre of the Wellcome Institute (ref. SA/RDS). The material includes minutes; correspondence; financial and membership records; publications (including the journal *Conquest* and the *Newsletter*); subject files concerned with legislation on animal experimentation; scrapbooks and newspaper cuttings files; and photographs and tape-recordings. The files, which were kept by J.D. Spink during his period as Treasurer of the Society from 1976 to 1983, are incorporated with the archive. Enquiries should be addressed to the Archivist of the CMAC.

RETURNED VOLUNTEER ACTION Returned Volunteer Action, founded in 1960 as the Voluntary Overseas Service Association, is an independent organisation of overseas volunteers and development workers. Its membership is composed of returned and serving volunteers who seek to raise public awareness about the realities of global development; RVA supports a public education programme and training course for volunteers. Papers which have been retained include Executive Committee minutes from 1966; copies of the quarterly magazine *Comeback* (which includes conference and administrative reports) from 1970 to date; financial records for the statutory period, and correspondence files for the preceding two years. Correspondence related to fundraising is kept for five years. Applications for access to the material should be addressed to the registered office of RVA.

REVOLUTIONARY COMMUNIST PARTY Some records of this left-wing group are deposited in the Modern Records Centre, University of Warwick. They include discussion bulletins and leaflets, 1944–49; the *Party Organiser*, 1946–48; left faction papers; photographs; and press-cuttings (ref. MSS 75). A separate deposit includes a subject file, re redundancy, 1944–49 (ref. MSS 151).

Reference should be made to the records of the International Marxist Group, also held in the MRC.

RIGHTS OF WOMEN There are papers in the Women's Library, London Metropolitan University. The collection includes policy papers, correspondence, source material etc., 1975–90.

ROAD HAULAGE ASSOCIATION Some sixteen local road hauliers' organisations amalgamated in December 1944 to form this association. These groups were previously joined in the National Road Transport Federation, which also embraced those interested in passenger and freight transport. In 1944 the Federation divided into the Road Haulage Association, the Passenger Vehicle Operators' Association and the Traders' Road Transport Association (now the Freight Transport Association). The Road Haulage Association aims to protect the interests of individuals and firms engaged in the transport of goods by road for hire or reward.

Some records have been placed in the Modern Records Centre, University of Warwick (ref. MSS 234). The material falls into two categories:

Records of the Secretary's Department These include selected subject files, mainly 1950s and 1960s, including the Channel Tunnel; docks delays; denationalisation and disposals; road and rail relations; Transport Amendment Bill (1950–51); Transport Act (1953); and the Transport Freedom Rallies (1968).

Records of the Industrial Relations Officer's Department These include Road Haulage Wages Council minutes, 1944–72; subject files, mainly 1960s and 1970s, including the National Negotiating Committee; dock labour disputes over the handling of containers; West Midlands dispute (1968); and companies' agreements and procedures. Access is restricted.

ROLLS ROYCE JOINT SHOP STEWARDS COMBINE There are papers in the Modern Records Centre, University of Warwick (ref. MSS 390). A list is available (NRA 42672).

ROTARY INTERNATIONAL IN GREAT BRITAIN AND IRELAND Rotary International, founded in 1905, is a worldwide association of service clubs for business and professional persons whose objectives are to serve their communities locally, nationally, and internationally and to encourage high ethical standards in all vocations.

The papers of Rotary International in Great Britain and Ireland are retained at the offices of its Secretariat. The material includes the minutes of the General Council (the association's governing body) since its inception in 1911; copies of annual reports; a number of committee reports; financial records for the statutory period of seven years; and correspondence files. Non-routine correspondence is periodically disposed of, although material of a legal or constitutional nature may be retained. Access to the archive is normally available to Rotarians or to persons engaged in academic research; owing to the limited facilities available, a fee may be required for those wishing to use a substantial amount of material. Interested persons should apply in the first instance to the Manager of the Communications Department.

ROWETT RESEARCH INSTITUTE The papers are held by the Institute (based in Aberdeen). There is much material on nutrition, Boyd-Orr himself, as well as the work of the International Union of Nutrition Societies. A list is available (NRA 40831).

ROYAL ASSOCIATION FOR DISABILITY AND REHABILITATION RADAR has retained its own papers since its establishment in 1977, but these are reported closed as the Association does not have sufficient resources to be able to assist researchers with their enquiries.

ROYAL BRITISH LEGION The Royal British Legion grew out of several ex-servicemen's organisations founded during World War I: the National Association of Discharged Sailors and Soldiers; the National Federation of Discharged and Demobilised Sailors and Soldiers; the Comrades of the Great War, and the Officers' Association. These bodies amalgamated in 1921 to form the Legion, whose objective is to promote the welfare of ex-servicemen and their dependents. The prefix 'Royal' was granted to the Legion on its fiftieth anniversary in 1971. *The Official History of the British Legion* by Graham Wootton was published in London in 1956.

A very full archive of papers is retained at the Legion's headquarters and dates back to the amalgamation in 1921, with a very limited selection of material of the predecessor organisations. The Legion's own papers comprise minutes and verbatim records of the annual conference; annual conference reports; minutes of the Executive, Finance and Standing Committees; volumes of monthly and special circulars; and a complete set of the *British Legion Journal* from July 1921 onwards. Only a very limited amount of correspondence and financial records is available, because these are not ordinarily retained for more than four years. Applications for permission to consult the papers should be directed to the General Secretary.

ROYAL BRITISH NURSES ASSOCIATION The archives, now much more available for access by researchers, remain at the Association's Chelsea headquarters. An extensive list is available (NRA 41542).

ROYAL COLLEGE OF MIDWIVES The college has retained its archives. Enquiries concerning scope and access should be directed to the archivist.

ROYAL COMMONWEALTH SOCIETY Founded as the Colonial Society in 1868 to provide a focal point for persons interested in the Empire and its promotion, the Society offers members a study centre and social facilities, and disseminates information about the Commonwealth. During its lifetime, the Society has been known as the Royal Colonial Institute, the Royal Empire Society and, since 1957, by the present name.

The records of the RCS include minutes, correspondence, reports and research papers (published annually in the Society's *Proceedings*) and its journal, formerly *United Empire* and now *Commonwealth*. Apart from internal records, the RCS holds the archives of other groups such as the British Association of Malaysia and the Royal African Society.

The papers have now been placed in Cambridge University Library, to where enquiries should be addressed.

ROYAL ECONOMIC SOCIETY The organisation was founded in 1890 as the British Economic Society and incorporated as the Royal Economic Society in

1902. The archives, 1890–1961, were given on indefinite loan to the LSE Library in December 1979 (ref. Acc No M1445), through the good offices of Professor Aubrey Silberston. They consist of minute books (7 vols, 1890–1970), cash books (7 vols, 1890–1961), ledgers (8 vols, 1890–1956), registers of members (4 vols, 1891, 1901–10, 1921–30, 1949–66) and a journal of income and expenditure (1937–74). The archive is still accruing (e.g. minutes for 1975–90), but the collection is open.

ROYAL GEOGRAPHICAL SOCIETY The Royal Geographical Society was founded in 1830. Its objectives are the advancement of geographical science and the improvement and diffusion of geographical knowledge. A substantial collection of material is maintained in the Library at the Society's offices. The papers comprise the unpublished minutes of the Council and its various Committees (e.g. Expeditions, Research, Education, etc) since 1830; Annual Reports from 1945 onwards; copies of the Pamphlet Series nos. 1–4 (1945–47) and Research Papers nos. 1–5 (1948–70) on miscellaneous topics published by the Society; Finance Committee minutes and some ledgers and cash books, from 1945 to date; administrative correspondence files and papers relating to the Ordnance Survey Review 1979–83 and the RGS Consultative Committee on the Ordnance Survey 1983–84; the minute book and correspondence of the Organising Committee for the International Geographic Congress held in London in 1964, and expedition reports and administrative papers from expeditions sponsored by or approved and aided by the Society from 1948 to the present (including the Mount Everest expedition of 1953). The Library of the Society holds complete sets of the journal, *Proceedings*, and supplementary papers.

The Library and Archives are open to Fellows and Members only, but other persons may be admitted by permission of the Director and Secretary. Maps, photographs, and those expedition reports which have been duplicated and circulated are open to the public at the Society's offices. In all cases enquiries should in the first instance be directed to the Archivist. It should also be noted that the Society holds the archives of the Mount Everest Foundation (established 1955) and the International Geographic Union.

ROYAL HUMANE SOCIETY Founded in 1774 and incorporated by Royal Charter in 1959, the Society exists to commend and reward those who risk their lives saving others. Its Committee holds monthly adjudication meetings and annually awards a gold medal for the most meritorious case of bravery in the Commonwealth. The Society has retained all its papers since inception at its offices.

ROYAL INSTITUTE OF BRITISH ARCHITECTS RIBA is the principal professional association and learned society for architects in the UK. Its origins lie with the Architectural Society, which was established in 1831 to raise the low professional standards of the period. Its initial aim was to establish a British School of Architecture and the Institute, which was incorporated by royal charter in 1837, has always been an important educator in the field.

RIBA's archive is deposited in the British Architectural Library at its own headquarters. A list is available (NRA 13990) and persons wishing for access should write to the Chief Executive. The papers include minutes of the Council and Ordinary General Meetings from 1834; the Annual and Special Meetings from 1885; and the Executive Committee from 1925. In addition, there are available the minute books of numerous subcommittees such as those concerned with membership, professional conduct, student probations and architectural competitions. The administrative files of these committees have also been retained.

The following series of publications is available within the collection: the *Journal*, complete from 1834; the *Kalendar of RIBA* from 1886–87 to 1965–66 (when it was succeeded by the *Directory* until 1970 and then by the *Directory of Practice* and the *Directory of Members*), and the *Quarterly Bulletin* from 1967. Separate Annual Reports exist for 1947 to 1971; before and after this date they are included in the *Journal*. In addition to the RIBA archive, the British Architectural Library contains the papers of the Architects' Benevolent Society, the Architecture Club, the Circle Group, the Design and Industries Association, and the Ecclesiological Society.

ROYAL INSTITUTE OF INTERNATIONAL AFFAIRS The Royal Institute of International

Affairs is an independent organisation dedicated to promoting the study and understanding of all aspects of international affairs, through lectures, discussions, research and publications. It was founded in 1920 and granted a royal charter six years later.

The RIIA maintains the UK's leading specialist library on international affairs at its headquarters at Chatham House. The Press Library holds a large collection of British and foreign newspaper cuttings for the period after 1972 (the collection for 1940–71 is now available at the British Library Newspaper Library at Colindale in London). Copies of the RIIA's annual report, its journals (the quarterly *International Affairs* and the monthly *The World Today*), and all its published research reports are also available in the Library, which is open to members and to bona fide researchers on payment of a fee. The archives of Chatham House are separately maintained and incorporate the papers of the Council and its Committees; records of the general administration, of the branches of Chatham House and related groups, and of the organisation of the RIIA's meetings, study groups and conferences; selected correspondence files; subject files relating to individual research projects, the journals (including the *British Yearbook of International Law*), and other publications; and papers of the Institute of Pacific Relations and the British Commonwealth Relations Committee.

The Council of the RIIA has ruled that all archives will, in principle, remain closed for thirty years; that those sections relating solely to the affairs of Chatham House itself (such as the files of the Council and its Committees) will be permanently closed, and that other sections may be opened after thirty years to bona fide researchers. Further enquiries should therefore be directed to the Archivist or to the Librarian of the RIIA at Chatham House.

Researchers should be aware that a file of papers from the Far Eastern Department of the RIIA is available in the Library of the School of Oriental and African Studies, University of London (ref. MS 186361 ff). It comprises a set of miscellaneous material such as handouts from British Embassies and conference papers for the period *c.* 1927–62.

ROYAL INSTITUTE OF PUBLIC ADMINIS-TRATION The archives of the Institute, founded in 1922, are in the University of Birmingham Library.

ROYAL INSTITUTE OF PUBLIC HEALTH The archives of the Institute (formerly the Society of Medical Officers of Health) are in the Wellcome Contemporary Medical Archives Centre. See p. 390.

ROYAL NATIONAL INSTITUTE FOR THE BLIND The organisation was originally established in 1862 as the National Institute for the Blind; in 1914 it combined with the British and Foreign Blind Association. A Royal Charter was granted in 1953. It is a voluntary organisation which aims to complement existing statutory provision for the visually handicapped by providing services which may be too specialised or extensive for any single local authority to supply. Its objects are to promote the better education, training and welfare of the blind and to support work aimed at preventing blindness. The RNIB archive includes minutes of its committees and Boards of Governors from 1890 to the present; a full set of Annual Reports; copies of all papers published as a result of research commissioned by the RNIB; and correspondence files, organised by subject and largely dating from the 1930s. Material is kept either at the RNIB's Archives or at its Reference Library; interested persons should apply to the Reference Librarian.

ROYAL NATIONAL INSTITUTE FOR THE DEAF RNID was founded in 1911 to promote the interests of hearing-impaired persons in the United Kingdom. It provides residential and sheltered accommodation and employment training programmes for the deaf, and has substantial technical and research departments based in London and in Glasgow.

At its headquarters the RNID provides a comprehensive information service and maintains a substantial library, which is one of the foremost in the world on the subject of speech and hearing disorders. The Library holds complete files of the annual reports (including balance sheets) and conference reports issued since 1911, and copies of all published research papers. These may be made available to researchers on application to the Librarian. Committee minutes, correspondence and subject files, and financial records are in the care of the Administration and Finance Departments and remain confidential. Enquiries concerning this material should be addressed to the Chief Executive.

ROYAL NATIONAL LIFEBOAT INSTITUTION

RNLI was founded in 1824 as the National Institution for the Preservation of Life from Shipwreck and adopted its present name in 1854. The archives of the Institution have been preserved at its headquarters. Surviving papers include minutes of the Committee of Management and copies of the annual report from 1824; minutes of the principal Subcommittes (e.g. Finance) from 1851; the *Lifeboat Journal* from the date of its first publication in 1852, and records of the individual lifeboat services from 1850. A library of related reference material is also maintained. The archives are available to serious researchers on written application.

ROYAL SCOTTISH SOCIETY FOR THE PREVENTION OF CRUELTY TO CHILDREN

The Scottish National Society for the Prevention of Cruelty to Children was formed in 1889. Early on in its history the passage of the Prevention of Cruelty to Children Acts in 1889 and 1894 gave the Society the legal justification to intervene if necessary between the parent and the child, but it has always seen its primary duty as being to teach parents to care. The Society affiliated with its English equivalent in 1895 to form a National Society for the UK, but it resumed its independence in 1907 and subsequently in 1922 it was granted a royal charter. It has now adopted the name Children 1st. The Scottish Children's League of Pity was established in 1893 as a junior and fund-raising branch. A centenary history of the Society, *A Stone on the Mantlepiece* by B. Ashley, has been published.

An archive of the Society's papers has now been deposited in the Scottish Record Office (ref. GD409). These include the minutes of Council, Executive Committee and other committees, 1897–1982 (which are subject to a thirty-year rule); Annual Reports of the Executive Committee, 1934–76 and 1980; various files of the Society's reports and correspondence on subjects affecting children; case history files for the period 1963 to 1980 (closed until 2081); miscellaneous publications; and collections of press-

cuttings, 1913–68. Other papers are reported in Glasgow Caledonian University.

ROYAL SOCIETY FOR INDIA, PAKISTAN AND CEYLON

The Royal Society incorporates three earlier organisations: the East India Association, the National Indian Association, and the India Society. The former had been established in 1866 to promote the welfare of the inhabitants of India; it was active in making public representations in the 19th century and during the 1930s, but did not adopt a specifically party political position on any issue.

Papers for the period 1870–1984 have been deposited at the India Office Library (ref. MSS Eur F 147) on permanent loan from the Council. They comprise 21 volumes and 15 boxes and include minute books for the period 1873 to 1963; financial papers, *c.* 1865–1963; and correspondence and general papers, 1876–1958. An official history, *Four Score* (ed. Sir John Cumming) was published in 1947. Also within the collection are the papers of the India Society (founded in 1910 for the appreciation of Indian art and literature) and the National Indian Association (established in 1870 to promote the educational and social development of India).

ROYAL SOCIETY FOR MENTALLY HANDICAPPED CHILDREN AND ADULTS

The Society, which is usually known by the acronym MENCAP, was founded in 1946 to increase public awareness and understanding of the problems of people with a mental handicap. It was unable to provide any information about its papers, but enquiries may be directed to the Chief Executive.

ROYAL SOCIETY FOR NATURE CONSERVATION

With a total membership of over 250,000, RSNC is a major voluntary organisation concerned with wildlife protection in the UK. It was founded in 1912 as the Society for the Promotion of Nature Reserves in order to preserve sites in perpetuity which were to be granted to the National Trust. Its aims were subsequently altered by royal charter in 1916 to allow it to manage the reserves itself. The name was changed to the Society for the Promotion of Nature Conservation by a second royal charter in 1976 and the present title adopted in 1981. In the post-war period the Society has been much more influential in national conservation policy, being active in the establishment of the Nature Conservancy in 1949 and the Council for Nature in 1958.

The RSNC archive has been retained at its headquarters. Formal administrative records consist of the Council and Executive Committee minutes since 1920; other committee minutes (e.g. Reserves, 1959–63, and Conservation Liaison, 1968–70); Council and committee signature books, 1912–73; and a register of correspondence, 1962–73. In addition there are over 150 boxes of correspondence, reports, press-cuttings etc. from 1912 onwards on all aspects of the Society's work. Publications which have been kept include the *Handbook* (1923–69) and its successor *Conservation Review* (which contains the Annual Report). Published accounts are available since 1912; other financial records (e.g. ledgers) are incomplete.

In principle the papers are available for academic research and applications for access should be made to the Chief Executive.

ROYAL SOCIETY FOR THE PREVENTION OF ACCIDENTS

The Royal Society was formed in May 1940, but its antecedents included the London Safety First Council (1917) and the British Safety First Association (1918). These amalgamated in 1924 to form the National Safety First Association. The records have been deposited in Liverpool University Archives (ref. D 226). A list is available (NRA 25023).

ROYAL SOCIETY FOR THE PREVENTION OF CRUELTY TO ANIMALS

The RSPCA originated in a society founded in London in 1824 to promote the humane treatment of animals, following the passage of a private Bill to Prevent Cruel and Improper Treatment of Cattle two years earlier. In 1840 Queen Victoria granted it a royal charter. The Society seeks to encourage humane attitudes towards animals and to prosecute instances of cruelty. It remains the only animal charity to have a corps of Inspectors throughout England and Wales to observe infringements of the law.

The records of the RSPCA are retained at its headquarters. The minutes of the Council Meetings exist from 1824 onwards (missing 1914–18), subject to a fifty-year closure rule. Retained correspondence is arranged in subject order, e.g. dogs, horses,

performing animals, oil pollution, etc. Persons wishing to use either of these collections should contact the Archivist. Other material is available in the Library. Annual Reports have been produced from 1835, and statements of income and expenditure are issued annually to members along with the Report. Latest copies of both may be sent to research students upon request; otherwise researchers should contact the Librarian for an appointment to view older material. The Society also retains copies of its magazines.

ROYAL STATISTICAL SOCIETY

The Society was established in 1834 and has retained its complete archive from this date. The papers comprise minutes of the Council and the Committee, and Annual Reports and the *Journal*. Correspondence and financial records have only been kept on an *ad hoc* basis. A list is available (NRA 14718). Further enquiries should be directed to the Executive Secretary of the Society.

ROYAL TELEVISION SOCIETY

The society has retained its archive of official and working papers since 1927. There are also personal papers of some pioneers of television.

ROYAL TOWN PLANNING INSTITUTE

The Royal Town Planning Institute has its origins in the introduction of the first UK planning legislation in 1909 and was set up in 1913 to provide a forum for the discussion of planning issues outside existing professional bodies. It only really emerged as a modern professional organisation with the development of planning in World War II and following the enactment of the 1947 Town and Country Planning Act. A royal charter was granted in 1956 and the word 'Royal' adopted into the title in 1976. Today the Institute acts as an information agency on planning matters and lobbies government on behalf of the profession.

An archive has been retained at the Institute's headquarters and there is a list (NRA 24455). The listed papers include minute books of the Council for the period 1913–60, and of various committees from 1943 to 1960 including *inter alia* the Education, Finance, Parliamentary, Membership, and Research Committees. Minutes are also available for the

AGMs from 1914 to 1967, and for the Town Planning Joint Examination Boards of the period 1956–59. The Institute retains complete sets of its publications, including the *Journal* from 1914 (renamed *The Planner* in 1973), which incorporates statements of accounts and reports of Annual Meetings, Annual Conferences and Summer Schools, and the *Year Book* from 1934. There is a file of press-cuttings for 1970–79. In principle the Institute is willing to make its papers available for academic research and interested persons should write to the Librarian.

Researchers should also be aware that a large collection of the papers of Sir George Pepler (1882–1959), sometime President of the International Federation for Housing and Town Planning, has been deposited at the Strathclyde Regional Archives. A list is available (NRA 12634).

ROYAL WELSH AGRICULTURAL SOCIETY (CYMDEITHAS AMAETHYDDOL FRENHINOL CYMRU CYF) The Society was founded in 1904. Certain of its papers for the period 1904–55 have been deposited at the National Library of Wales. A list is available (NRA 26130). The material largely concerns the organisation of agricultural shows.

RUNNYMEDE TRUST The Runnymede Trust was set up in 1968 to research into issues concerning race equality and to provide policy recommendations and advice. Minutes of Trustees' meetings have been maintained since 1968 and copies of correspondence relating to the establishment of the Trust in the period 1965–68 have also been kept. For many of the research projects carried out since 1968 there are also files of correspondence still in existence and there are day files for all correspondence, arranged in sequence, since *c.* 1984. All ledger books have been kept. It is understood the Trust's records have now been placed in Middlesex University Library.

RUSSIAN REFUGEES AID SOCIETY Founded as the British branch of the Russian Red Cross, the Society was formerly the Russian Benevolent Society; it adopted its present name in 1978. It is dedicated to promoting within the United Kingdom the well-being and relief of refugees from those places which were formerly parts of the Russian Empire, and it maintains residential homes for those who are elderly.

The Society has an extensive archive of papers concerning refugees in the United Kingdom for the post-1921 period, retained at its offices. These records do not, however, include any Red Cross documents. The Society is not able to allow scholars to consult material in person, but the General Secretary may be able to assist with particular enquiries. As the Society is a charity, researchers would be expected to make a donation proportionate to the extent of their enquiry. Enquiries should be addressed to the General Secretary.

Researchers should note that the LSE Library has papers of the Russian Refugees Relief Association (ref. M 1771).

S

SABBATH OBSERVANCE EMPLOYMENT BUREAU This bureau was set up in 1909 with the aim of obtaining employment for those who wished to observe the Sabbath and other holy days. The papers for the period 1909–75 have been deposited in the Hartley Library, University of Southampton (ref. MS 178). Further material is available in the papers of the bureau's president, Harris M. Lazurus, which are also deposited in the Hartley Library (ref. MS 130).

SAFEGUARD BRITAIN CAMPAIGN Relevant material may be found in the papers of Sir Neil Marten, sometime Chairman of the National Referendum Campaign, now deposited in the Bodleian Library (ref. MSS. Eng. hist. *c.* 1130–59, e.385; misc. a.29). The collection consists largely of the papers of groups opposed to UK membership of the European Community.

SAFERWORLD Saferworld is an independent, non-partisan group whose objective is to persuade public opinion that the security of nations is as much dependent upon preservation from economic and environmental threats as from military ones. It was established in April 1989 and operates by publishing research papers on politico-military issues. The papers of Saferworld comprise copies of published material and its correspondence and subject files. Minutes are not kept, but an annual reports series is to be produced. Enquiries should be directed to the organisation.

ST DAVID'S FORUM This non-political body was established in 1987 to hold biennial meetings at which topics of relevance to Welsh society (such as education and the future of the Welsh economy) are discussed.

The Welsh Political Archive at the National Library of Wales has received the Steering Committee Minutes, 1988–91, some correspondence (relating mainly to administrative matters) and the reports generated by each forum.

ST JOAN'S SOCIAL AND POLITICAL ALLIANCE Founded as the Catholic Women's Suffrage Society in 1911 to answer Catholic-based attacks on the suffrage movement, the Alliance was a strictly non-party political and constitutional organisation, and one which was open to men. It joined the Council of Federated Suffrage Societies in 1912 and adopted St Joan as its patron; its name was changed in 1923. After the achievement of female suffrage in 1918 the Alliance sought to establish the social and economic equality of women in other spheres. It was effectively superseded during the 1950s by its international arm, the St Joan's International Alliance.

Collections of papers of both organisations have been deposited in the Women's Library (q.v.). Lists are available (NRA 20625, 29387). The papers of the St Joan's Social and Political Alliance comprise committee minutes, 1911–44; annual reports, 1943–67; the journal *Catholic Citizen* from 1915 onwards; and 23 volumes of newspaper cuttings (mainly biennial) covering 1911–52. The papers of the International Alliance include Committee minutes, 1946–52, 1970s and 1981–82; UK Section committee minutes, 1971–76; minute books of annual meetings, 1958–65; AGM resolutions of the 1960s and 1970s; collected bulletins and pamphlets for the 1950s to the 1980s; subject files on women in the Roman Catholic Church and Christian feminism; and files of newspaper cuttings for the 1970s.

The Women's Library also holds the records of the Alliance's German section for 1952–81, which include correspondence files. A number of the German activists were members of the Bundestag, and the section campaigned in the political forum as well as within the Church. Its relations with the UK organisation were particularly close.

SALVATION ARMY Founded among the destitute poor of London in 1865 by the Revd William Booth, the organisation was first styled the Christian Mission but became the Salvation Army in 1878. It is engaged in evangelical, medical, educational and social work throughout the world.

Many original records were destroyed by enemy action during World War II. However, a useful collection of published and unpublished material has been assembled in the archives of its Heritage Centre. A list is available (NRA 43166).

THE SAMARITANS The Samaritans is the registered charity founded in 1953 by Chad Varah to offer advice and confidential counselling, in particular to those who may be experiencing suicidal tendencies. It provides a telephone service nationwide. Its records are retained at the General Office. In view of the confidential nature of the work, committee minutes and correspondence are not available for research. However, the published Annual Reports and accounts, newsletters, conference and special reports, and subject files (which consist of press-cuttings, published articles and historical publicity material, and training aids) may be released with permission of the Samaritans. Interested persons should seek the advice of the Information Officer at its headquarters.

SAVE EUROPE NOW This campaign was launched at the end of World War II to help alleviate the distress and disruption caused in Central Europe by the war. Relief schemes were launched, food and clothing collected and appeals made for funds. Victor Gollancz was Chairman. One particular feature of the campaign was its petition to the Government in 1947 seeking the repatriation of Italian prisoners of war in Britain. The campaign was wound up in 1948.

No central archive has been located, but four files relating to the organisation are available within the Gollancz papers at the Modern Records Centre, University of Warwick (ref. MSS 157/3/SEN).

SAVE THE CHILDREN FUND The Save the Children Fund (SCF) was founded in 1919 by two sisters, Eglantyne Jebb and Dorothy Buxton, in response to reports of starvation in Central Europe

after World War I, to aid children irrespective of race, religion or nationality. Since that time it has provided aid, both emergency and long-term, in countries around the world.

All those papers of the SCF which are still in existence are stored in its headquarters. Many papers relating to the period 1930–65 were destroyed towards the end of the 1960s. Those that remain are currently being sorted and a catalogue is in preparation. The papers are in principle available for research, although until they are fully listed enquiries will normally be conducted through the Archivist. Apart from Annual Reports and similar material, none of the material has been published.

There exists an almost complete set of minutes of the SCF Council from 1922 to the present day. There are also minutes of the Executive Committee (1938–), the Finance Committee (1926–) and, more recently, the Overseas and Welfare Committee. A complete set of the Annual Report of the United Kingdom SCF is available, as well as more recent reports from the Scottish and Northern Ireland Branches. In addition there are ledgers (1921–80s) and correspondence and subject files, particularly the files of the Hon. Secretary (c. 1921–28), the Director-General (1968–85), and files of the Overseas Department (1947 to the present); only the Secretary's files would normally be available for research although queries about the others may be answerable by the Archivist. A complete set of the publication *The World's Children* from its inception in 1920 has been retained. The SCF has also deposited a number of films at the National Film Archive, but a photographic collection is maintained at the headquarters.

The SCF does not have any plans to deposit its papers elsewhere; access to them is normally via the SCF Archivist.

SCOPE SCOPE, formerly, the Spastics Society, was founded in 1952 by a group of parents of children with cerebral palsy and is the largest national charity working with adults and children who have the condition.

An archive is retained at SCOPE's headquarters which incorporates the records of the operational divisions of the central organisation. The papers include a complete series of the minutes of the

Executive Council and its seven subcommittees since its foundation (available to members of SCOPE upon application); copies of the Annual Review and the Annual Report and Accounts (available to any enquirer), and correspondence files organised in day files and by subject. Persons wishing to consult the material should write to the Company Secretary at the headquarters. The records of the six Regional Offices and of individual schools and centres are separately maintained and any enquiries concerning these should be directed to the relevant office in each local area.

SCOTLAND-USSR SOCIETY The Society was founded to further Scottish-Soviet understanding and friendship by promoting cultural, educational and other exchanges. Relevant material is available at the National Library of Scotland in the papers of Thomas Murray (ref. Acc 9083), who was general secretary of the Society from 1936 to 1950. The material includes journals and notes of Murray's visits to the USSR and Eastern Europe in 1945–49. A list is available (NRA 29279). Later records, namely minutes, correspondence, annual reports etc. for 1942–88, have been deposited at Strathclyde Regional Archives. A list is available (NRA 32973).

SCOTTISH AGRICULTURAL ORGANISATION SOCIETY This society has retained its records. A list is available (NRA 24340).

SCOTTISH ASSOCIATION FOR MENTAL HEALTH Certain papers of the Association, including the records of the Scottish Child Guidance Council, were presented to the National Library of Scotland in 1978. There is a list to the collection (NRA 29180). The Association was established at a meeting in Glasgow in 1923 on the initiative of several Special School teachers from Paisley, but at the first AGM the title of the organisation was changed to that of the Scottish Association of Mental Welfare, in order to reflect an extension of the Association's concerns from the care of mentally handicapped children alone to a fostering of mental wellbeing in general. In 1938 the Association amalgamated with the Scottish Child Guidance Council (which had been established in 1934) to form the Scottish Association for Mental Hygiene, a body which subsequently adopted the present title.

The collection at the National Library of Scotland includes the papers of the predecessor organisations. Among the post-war material there are the minutes of the AGM and the Executive Committee, 1951–63; minutes, correspondence and papers concerning the adoption of the new constitution, 1968–76; and the minutes of local Voluntary Associations Committees, 1961–75. Correspondence files include the Secretary's and Treasurer's communications with various affiliated local Voluntary Associations, 1949–75, and correspondence for the period 1970–75 with other voluntary organisations. Association conference papers included in the deposit consist of correspondence, invitations, programmes and organisation papers for the period 1971–76. Administrative papers include general office files for 1953–75, and financial records, e.g. correspondence on subscriptions and donations, 1972–75, general income and expenditure books, 1921–76, signed accounts, 1957–67 etc.

SCOTTISH CAMPAIGN FOR NUCLEAR DISARMAMENT The Scottish branch of the Campaign for Nuclear Disarmament was established in 1958. Its stated aim – in addition to the national objective of achieving unilateral nuclear disarmament by the United Kingdom – is to demand a 'nuclear-free' Scotland without nuclear weapons or nuclear dumping as 'the conscientious right of a nation within a nuclear state'. The papers of Scottish CND for the first decade of its existence have been deposited at the Mitchell Library, Glasgow. The organisation was in abeyance during the period 1969–72, but retains all its subsequent records at its headquarters and applications for access to the papers should be made by researchers to the Secretary.

SCOTTISH CAMPAIGN TO RESIST THE ATOMIC MENACE (SCRAM) SCRAM was formed in November 1975 to unite opposition from a variety of organisations, including the Friends of the Earth, to plans for a nuclear power station at Torness in East Lothian. Although its initial objective was not successful, SCRAM has continued as a research and campaigning organisation on nuclear issues, publishing the bi-monthly *Safe Energy Journal* and providing information to all interested parties.

The archives of the Campaign for the period 1970–94 have been placed in the National Library of Scotland (ref. Acc 11607).

SCOTTISH CONVENTION OF WOMEN The origins of the Scottish Convention of Women lie in a meeting in Edinburgh in 1974 organised by Ms Maidie Hart, the Scottish representative on a government-appointed Coordinating Committee for organising celebrations for the United Nations International Women's Year (1975). The Convention, formally established in February 1977, grew from the need to organise Scottish activities for the International Women's Year and the subsequent Decade for Women, and to coordinate the many Scottish women's organisations. Its activities included the preparation of a 'Scottish Plan of Action for Women'; organisation of biennial conventions and short conferences on health, equal opportunities and other economic and legal issues; and preparation of submissions to the government and other official inquiries.

The records of the Convention for the period 1974–86 have been deposited in the National Library of Scotland (ref. Acc 9395), for which a list is available (NRA 30999). The deposit includes Executive Committee minutes and agendas, 1978–86; papers and letters for the Executive Committee's consideration, 1980–84; AGM papers, 1976–86; Chairwoman's reports, 1977–84; correspondence concerning meetings and conferences of the Convention, 1977–85; examples of nos. 1 to 12 of the publication *Convention Notes*, 1977–83; correspondence files and associated papers on the organisation of the Convention, 1976–85; correspondence with the Equal Opportunities Commission and other bodies, 1974–86 etc.

SCOTTISH CO-OPERATIVE WOMEN'S GUILD The first branch of the Guild was formed in 1890 under the auspices of Kinning Park Co-operative Society in Glasgow, and the national organisation itself was established two years later. The papers for the period 1893–1988 are reported to be in Strathclyde Regional Archives (ref. CWS1/39), where they comprise part of the collection of the Scottish Co-operative Wholesale Society.

SCOTTISH COVENANT ASSOCIATION The Scottish Covenant Association was formed in 1951 by the merger of the National Covenant Committee and the Scottish Convention. Reference should also be made to the entries in this Guide for the Scottish National Party and the Scottish Secretariat.

Papers have been deposited at the National Library of Scotland. They include (ref. Acc 6649 and Acc 7295/4–8) three minute books of Executive and National Committees of the Scottish Convention for the period 1942–49, which also contain minutes and related papers of the AGM of 1948 and agendas of the Scottish National Assembly for 1948–51. The deposited records of the successor Association (ref. Acc 7295/9–12) cover the decade 1951–61 and comprise the agenda of the inaugural meeting, correspondence, minutes, constitutional papers, circulars and press-cuttings; a membership register, 1954–55; copies of the *Newsletter*, 1953–56; an incomplete run of *The Highlands and Islands Covenanter* for 1952–58; and *The Covenanter* of April 1960. A list is available (NRA 29195).

SCOTTISH FOOTBALL ASSOCIATION A very full collection of the papers of the Association for the period from its foundation in 1873 until 1985 has now been deposited in the National Library of Scotland (ref. Acc 9017). There are available minute books, 1879–1983/84; agendas, 1936–85; Annual Reports, 1882/83–1980; copies of the articles of association and special resolutions, 1903–53; players' registers, 1893–1970; cash books, 1875/76–1970/71; and press-cuttings, 1902–86. Handbooks of the Association for 1892–1985 and of the Scottish Football League for 1892–1977 are likewise available. The collection also includes the minutes and correspondence of the Scottish Standing Conference of Sport for the period 1973–77.

SCOTTISH LAND-OWNERS' FEDERATION The Scottish Land and Property Federation was established in 1906. It amalgamated with the Scottish Mineral Owners' Committee and the Argyll Lands Association in 1947, and adopted its present title in 1950. The Association seeks to encourage legislation conducive to the protection of land-ownership and to promote co-operation between owners and tenant farmers.

Full records of the Federation exist from the date of its foundation. A complete set of general minute books has been retained at its offices along with letter books from 1906; files of memoranda from 1951, and copies of its publications, including the journal which was known as the *Scottish Landowner* from 1950 and as *Landowning in Scotland* from 1968. Correspondence files prior to 1960 are understood to have been deposited at the Scottish Record Office; these contain some administrative records, e.g. Chairman's papers and AGM and committee files. Enquiries concerning the later papers should be made to the Director.

SCOTTISH LICENSED TRADE VETO DEFENCE FUND A collection of papers has been deposited at the Mitchell Library, Glasgow. The collection of 12 boxes contains a large number of files on a wide range of topics relating to the licensing trade and the affairs of the Fund (covering the period 1920 to 1977). There is considerable material on veto polls held in various Scottish wards and on parliamentary lobbying and legislation on licensing.

SCOTTISH MOTHERS' UNION The Scottish Mothers' Union was an organisation separate from the Mothers' Union (q.v.) in England, although it had its origins in meetings addressed by the latter's founder Mrs Mary Sumner. The first branch was established in Dunblane in 1890. The Scottish Mothers' Union existed until its dissolution in 1983, at which time most of its active branches affiliated to the English organisation.

A very full collection of papers of the Scottish Mothers' Union has now been deposited in the National Library of Scotland (ref. Acc 9008). A list is available (NRA 29084). It incorporates the minutes of the General Council, 1897–1930 and 1938–83, the Executive Committee, 1899–1982, and the AGM, 1930–83 (including those of the Special General Meetings for 1958–70); a register of members, councillors and directors, 1932–82; a cash book, 1939–49; and correspondence files on the history of the Union, negotiations for reunion with the Scottish League of Wives and Mothers, 1957–58, and on the formation of the Mothers' Union in various dioceses, 1957–58.

SCOTTISH MOTOR TRADE ASSOCIATION The association, which was formed in 1903, has retained its records. These include minute books since 1919. The archive has been listed (NRA 24920).

SCOTTISH NATIONAL PARTY The party was founded in 1928 as the National Party of Scotland. It merged in 1933 with the Scottish Party (founded in 1930) and then adopted its present title. The aim of the SNP is to abrogate the union of Scotland with England and to secure full independence within the European Community.

The SNP deposits papers at regular intervals at the National Library of Scotland, which also has a considerable amount of other material relating to the nationalist movement in Scotland. Reference should be made to list NRA 29195. One early collection (ref. Acc 7295) comprises minutes of the National Executive Committee, 1944–48; reports of policy committees to the National Council and National Executive Committee, 1946–66; examples of the first and second issues of *The Scottish Newsletter*, 1954–55; files of local and Parliamentary election leaflets, 1945–75; copies of the leaflets of other nationalist organisations and examples of anti-nationalist political literature; a file of SNP election and EEC referendum posters; the financial records of the *Newsletter* for 1953–57; and a receipts and payments ledger of 1956–59. The collection also contains letters and press-cuttings of the predecessor National Party of Scotland. A later deposit (Acc 10754) comprises correspondence, papers and files of news releases, 1965–89, Relevant material (especially minutes of meetings) may be found in the correspondence of Arthur Donaldson (ref. Acc 6038), which is arranged in ten boxes and covers the period 1924–72.

SCOTTISH RAILWAY DEVELOPMENT ASSOCIATION This organisation shares the aims of the Railway Development Society (q.v.). The papers of the Glasgow Group for the period 1966–74, comprising correspondence, reports and press-cuttings, have been deposited in the Strathclyde Regional Archives (ref. TD 1216). A list is available (NRA 34960). The organisation is now the Scottish Association for Public Transport.

SCOTTISH RIGHTS OF WAY SOCIETY LTD. The successor to the Scottish Rights of Way and Recreation Society (whose own predecessor was established in 1845), the Scottish Rights of Way Society was reconstituted in 1946 and now advises local authorities on the preservation of rights of way throughout the country.

A substantial archive exists, the larger part of which has now been deposited at the Scottish Record Office (ref. GD335). These papers include the Director's minute books from 1844; files of correspondence with local authorities, organised by county, and miscellaneous subject files concerning relevant legislation. Available publications include Annual Reports for 1948–49, 1957 and 1960–89 (in addition to those included in the minute books), and collections of press-cuttings for 1952–55 and 1969 to date. A list is available (NRA 24451; NRA[S] 2281). Academic researchers wishing to use the papers may apply to the Hon. Secretary.

SCOTTISH SCHOOL MEDICAL OFFICERS ASSOCIATION The records of this body have been listed (NRA 27039).

SCOTTISH SECRETARIAT The Secretariat was founded in 1929 to promulgate information about the Scottish nationalist movement. A substantial collection of papers covering the period 1929 to 1963 was purchased by the National Library of Scotland in 1964 (ref. Acc 3721). A list is available (NRA 29272). The records consist of general correspondence files (boxes 1–40); the personal correspondence of a former director R.E. Muirhead (boxes 41–77); papers relating to the Scottish Home Rule Association, although this material is pre-war in date (boxes 78–85); files emanating from the Scottish National Party (boxes 86–105), which comprise largely the records of individual branches prior to 1939, except for finance records (1928–55), policy papers (1928–43), records of the National Council (1928–48) and SNP Youth Section papers (1940–46); subject files of the Scottish National Congress, 1950–63 (boxes 106–121); one box of papers of the Scottish Federation of the Union of Democratic Control (q.v.) for 1919–27; and a series of press-cuttings, 1918–33 (boxes 123–145).

SCOTTISH STEEL CAMPAIGN The campaign sought to save the Scottish steel industry. A collection of unsorted papers has been deposited in Strathclyde Regional Archives.

SCOTTISH STUDY GROUP ON THE FEDERATION OF RHODESIA AND NYASALAND The Group was established in Edinburgh in 1960 by Scots businessman William Thyne, with the approval of the Government of the Federation. Its aims were to propagandise on behalf of the colonial government.

The records of the Scottish Study Group form the main part of Thyne's personal papers, which have been deposited at the Centre for Southern African Studies, University of York. They comprise steering committee minutes, membership records, letters to the press, circulars and memoranda, and Thyne's personal correspondence. His correspondents included the Federation Prime Minister Sir Roy Welensky (1960–65), Garfield Todd, etc.

SCOTTISH TRADES UNION CONGRESS The STUC is a separate body which is organisationally and financially independent of the Trades Union Congress (q.v.) in England and Wales, from which it split in 1897 over the issue of the affiliation of trades councils.

A large quantity of the STUC's papers has been deposited at the National Library of Scotland (ref. Acc 5513). A list is available (NRA 16445). The collection consists of microfilms of the minutes and related papers of the Congress and the General Council for the years 1945–60 (Mf. MSS. 200–207); 1960–66 (Mf. MSS. 217–219), and 1966–70 (Mf. MSS. 232–236). Two further collections at the NLS contain the correspondence of the General Council with the National Union of Journalists and the National Union of Bank Employees for 1927–57 (ref. Acc 4333), the General Council's correspondence concerning trades councils, 1948–66, and trades councils' minutes files, 1959–72 (ref. Acc 4683).

Other Scottish TUC papers are reported in Glasgow Caledonian University.

SCOUT ASSOCIATION The aim of the Scout Association, which was founded in 1907 by Lord Baden-Powell, is to promote the development of young people in achieving their full physical, intellectual, social and spiritual potential as individuals and as responsible citizens by providing progressive training under adult leadership.

The records of the Association are housed in the Archive Department at its headquarters at Baden-Powell House (NRA 41172). They may be seen by researchers who make a prior appointment with the Archivist. Retained papers include a large collection of correspondence and other documents relating to the Founder, most of which has been microfilmed; Committee minute books from 1908 (some of whose contents are, however, confidential and not open to inspection); copies of the annual report and of published special reports, including the Post War Commission papers of 1944 and the Chief Scout's Advance Party Report of 1966; financial records and ledgers not yet in the care of the Archives Department; and correspondence files ordinarily organised by subject but including several distinct collections, such as the papers of the late Deputy Chief Scout Percy Everett. The Archives Department also maintains a reference library, photographic collection, and a considerable quantity of memorabilia.

SECONDARY HEADS' ASSOCIATION The Association was formed in 1978 by the amalgamation of the Headmasters' Association and the Association of Head Mistresses. The latter had been founded in 1874 by Frances Mary Buss and, until the amalgamation, represented headmistresses in both the independent and state sectors. The Headmasters' Association was a later creation, dating from 1891, which served head teachers in England, Wales and Northern Ireland (a separate body existed for Scotland). Both constituent organisations participated in the 'Joint Four' (q.v.).

The records of both predecessor organisations have been deposited on indefinite loan at the Modern Records Centre, University of Warwick. The earliest papers of the Headmasters' Association were not preserved systematically but the post-war collection (ref. MSS 58) is complete. The archive includes various series of minutes for the period 1938–77; conference and council meeting papers for 1956–74; ledgers for 1895–1948; financial records for 1939–73; reports of 1907–70; the *Bulletin* for 1960–69; the triennial *Review* for 1908–73; pamphlets on professional matters; and some correspondence files. There is a list available (NRA 24512).

The collection of the Association of Head Mistresses (ref. MSS 188) incorporates various series of minutes from 1879 to 1977 (including those of the Executive Council from 1928); annual reports,

1895–1977; registers, 1896–1977; accounts, 1934–73; the *International Bulletin* for 1965–72; some correspondence and subject files, 1914–77, and some branch records from 1908. There is a list (NRA 24513).

The correspondence of the London branch of the Secondary Heads' Association for the year 1978 has also been deposited at the Modern Records Centre in collection MSS 218. The National Library of Wales has a collection of papers accumulated by Dr John Herbert during his membership of both the Welsh Secondary Schools Association and of the Secondary Heads' Association. A list is available for this collection (NRA 26130).

SHELTER (NATIONAL CAMPAIGN FOR THE HOMELESS) This pressure group was launched in 1966. One of its first directors was the Liberal politician Des Wilson. Shelter has played a prominent part in formulating new strategies to solve the housing crisis in Britain.

The earlier archives of Shelter are readily available on a microfiche published by Harvester Press. This contains unpublished minute books of the Board of Management, all Shelter's pamphlets, research reports, press releases, bulletins and Annual Reports.

SHIPBUILDERS' AND REPAIRERS' NATIONAL ASSOCIATION The Association was formed in 1967 by the amalgamation of the Shipbuilding Employers' Federation (est. 1899), the Dry Dock Owners' and Repairers' Central Council (1910) and the Shipbuilding Conference (1928). It served to negotiate centrally with trade unions in the industry and to reach agreement between employers concerning cartelisation arrangements. The SRNA was wound up in 1977 when the shipbuilding industry was nationalised. Researchers should also be aware that certain papers of the Ship and Boat Builders' National Federation have been deposited at the Modern Records Centre, University of Warwick (see British Marine Industries Federation).

The archive has been deposited in the National Maritime Museum (ref. SRNA/1–11). The SRNA's own 'current' file series survives for 1967–77 (SRNA/8). The papers of the Shipbuilding Employers' Federation comprise minute books and a complete set of circulars, 1899–1965, and a very large number of subject files which include correspondence, memoranda, statistical returns and agreements. The SEF prepared labour statistics on a weekly and monthly basis and these are retained for 1936–60. The Dry Dock Owners' and Repairers' Central Council records consist of minutes, 1910–59; circulars, 1910–56; and a subject file series. Surviving papers of the Shipbuilding Conference include circulars, 1928–69, and subject files on every aspect of the commercial and trading activities of the industry. Certain papers of the National Association of Marine Enginebuilders for the period 1938 to 1977 are also included in the archive.

In addition to these records, the following regional and sectoral associations have also deposited their papers:

1. *Clyde Shipbuilders' Association* Minute books and other records, 1865–1976, are with Strathclyde Regional Archives (ref. TD241). There is a list (NRA 18718).
2. *Fishing Boat Builders Association* Minutes, 1938–77, are in Aberdeen University Library. There is a list (NRA 25421).
3. *Institution of Engineers and Shipbuilders in Scotland* Minutes and papers, 1857–1959, are at the Glasgow University Archives and Business Record Centre (ref. UGD168/1–10). A list is available (NRA 25306).
4. *Liverpool Shipowners' Association* Records, 1895–1960, are in the Archives Department of the National Museums and Galleries on Merseyside. A list is available (NRA 25222).
5. *Mersey Ship Repairers' Association* Minutes, 1911–79, are in Liverpool City Record Office.
6. *North of England Shipowners' Association* Minutes, 1871–1965, and other records are with the Tyne and Wear Archives Service. There is a list (NRA 22517).
7. *North East Coast Ship Repairers' Association* Records, 1889–1977, are deposited with the Tyne and Wear Archives Service. A list is available (NRA 21708).
8. *South Coast Engineering and Shipbuilding Employers' Association* Records, 1902–78, have been deposited at Southampton City Record Office (ref. D/SES). There is a list (NRA 23201).

9. *Tyne Shipbuilders' Association* Minutes, 1891–1965, and other records are with the Tyne and Wear Archives Service. There is a list (NRA 21710).
10. *Wear Shipbuilders' Association* Records, 1853–1970, are with the Tyne and Wear Archives Service. There is a list (NRA 22558).

SHOTTON STEEL WORKERS' ACTION COMMITTEE In 1992 a very large deposit of papers of the Action Committee was received by the Modern Records Centre, University of Warwick (ref. MSS 316), through the good offices of M.G. Hughes, who was chairman of the Committee from 1972 to 1989. The material, which includes minutes, relates to the Committee during the period 1972–89, and to the Shotton TUC Steel Industry Consultative Committee and the Iron and Steel Trades Confederation Unemployed Members branches at Hawarden Central and Bidston Central. The papers detail alternative proposals for the Shotton Steel Works, including, for example, the possibility of a non-British Steel Corporation plant on the site or the attempt to persuade the Japanese vehicle manufacturing company Nissan to locate its UK plant there. It is also reported that other papers of the Committee for the period up to 1977 have been deposited at Clwyd Record Office.

SIMON COMMUNITY The Simon Community was founded in 1963 to care for the rootless and socially isolated homeless.

Material relating to its work which had been deposited in the Modern Records Centre, University of Warwick by Martin Wright, a former member of the National Executive and chairman of the Cambridge Cyrenians Ltd, has now been placed in Liverpool University Archives. The collection consists of Wright's correspondence with and concerning the Simon national organisation, and with other local Cyrenian groups, 1964–74; minutes; financial reports; and Simon publications, including incomplete runs of *Simon Star*, 1964–74 and *Social Action*, 1969–72. In a second deposit, the MRC received additional minutes, reports, draft publicity material and correspondence, 1972–74.

Researchers should note that the papers of Anton Wallich-Clifford (*d.* 1978), the founder of the Simon

Community, have also been placed in Liverpool University Archives.

SIX POINT GROUP The Six Point Group was a non-party organisation founded in 1921 by Viscountess Rhondda to achieve six goals: satisfactory legislation on child assault and for the protection of the widowed mother and unmarried mother and child; equal rights of guardianship for married women; equal pay for teachers; and equal opportunities for men and women in the civil service. Later these evolved into six more general aims of equality – political, occupational, moral, social, economic and legal. The Group was both feminist and non-partisan, although many of its activists were prominent on the political left (e.g. Dora Russell and Vera Brittain). The Six Point Group was dissolved in 1983.

The archive of the Group was then deposited in the Women's Library by the sometime Hon. Secretary, chairman and president, Hazel Hunkins-Hallinan. A list is available (NRA 29380). The papers consist of Executive Committee minutes and occasional agendas, 1935–80; AGM signed minutes and agendas and annual reports and newsletters, 1931–78; officers' administrative papers and correspondence to 1976; Hampshire Branch circulars, minutes, reports, and monthly publications, 1964–67; and North-West Branch papers, 1973–77. In addition there are miscellaneous publications from the 1920s to 1970s; membership lists, 1930s–79; files on individual campaigns (e.g. married women's status, taxation and social security, women in the professions); nine files of papers on public and social meetings, 1943–79; and newsletters and circulars, 1941–79.

SOCIAL CARE ASSOCIATION SCA was founded in 1949 as a professional body for those working in the social care field. The papers, retained at the Association's head office, comprise committee minutes and annual reports from the early 1950s onwards, and financial records, subject files, and published reports for the last six years. General correspondence is retained for a year only. There is no restriction on access to these papers if permission is obtained in advance.

SOCIAL CREDIT PARTY OF GREAT BRITAIN The party was formed in September 1935 to continue the work of earlier allied groups (such as the Kibbo Kift and the Greenshirt Movement for Social Credit) in advocating the adoption of social credit policies. The party was dissolved in May 1951 but an attempt to revive it was made in 1976. The records of the Social Credit Party, together with its predecessor groups, and some records of similar organisations such as the Social Credit League, have been deposited in the LSE Library. A list is available (NRA 35366). The collection is open. The material includes National Assembly minutes, 1948–50; SCP Consultative Council papers, 1946–47; lists of members at dissolution; correspondence files generated during and after the party's lifetime; and SCP publications. In addition, the LSE Library has the General Assembly minutes, financial papers, and publications of the second Social Credit Party, and correspondence of C.J. Hunt, treasurer of the Social Credit Political League, 1962–81. The Modern Records Centre University of Warwick has the Social Credit Library of Eric de Maré (ref. MSS 376).

SOCIAL DEMOCRATIC PARTY The SDP originated on 25 January 1981 as the Council for Social Democracy, an organisation led by four disaffected Labour politicians (Shirley Williams, David Owen, William Rodgers and Roy Jenkins). The SDP was formally set up as an independent party on 26 March 1981. Most of the SDP joined with the Liberal Party in 1988 to form the Social and Liberal Democrats, but a small group continued an independent existence under David Owen.

An extensive collection of SDP archives has been deposited in the Albert Sloman Library, University of Essex. The collection comprises extensive committee papers and correspondence (59 boxes), including minutes etc of the Steering Committee, 1981–82, National Committee, 1982–87, Finance and General Purposes Committee, 1981–88, Organisation Committee, 1981–87, Policy Committee, 1981–87 etc. Included in this collection are papers on by-elections, records of the Parliamentary Advisory Committee, and extensive series of working group papers. There are also policy files; 'Partnership for Progress' files; Chief Executive/National Secretary files; SDP election files; the Organisation archive;

Area Party files; and a Press Archive and a collection of 'Gang of Four' speeches and press releases. A parallel collection of speeches and press-cuttings excluding the 'Gang of Four' is also maintained. A handlist to the collection is available (NRA 34700, this list may also be consulted at the LSE Library). Access to almost all material is available to serious scholars. At present the only exceptions are the SDP audio-visual material and the SDP Area Party files. New material continues to be added to the Essex deposit.

In 1991, the University of Essex Library also received the archive of the Tawney Society, the 'think-tank' of the SDP. It also houses the papers of SDP activists. These include Lord MacLennan, Lord Wrigglesworth and Lord McGivan.

In addition to the SDP archive at Essex, reference should also be made to relevant material at the LSE Library. This houses the extensive post-war records of the Liberal Party. Within this deposit there is much material on SDP-Liberal relations, the Alliance, by-election campaigns and the politics of the 1988 merger. The LSE Library also houses relevant papers of the Union of Liberal Students.

Records of the SDP in Scotland are reported in Glasgow Caledonian University.

SOCIALIST ACTION Socialist Action was formerly known as the International Marxist Group. A substantial number of internal records was deposited in January 1985 at the Modern Records Centre, University of Warwick (ref. MSS 128). These consist of the minutes of the National Committee, Political Committee and other committees, 1975–81 and 1983; discussion bulletins, 1976–79; internal information bulletins, 1978–80; pre-conference discussion bulletins, 1968; international internal information bulletins, 1969–73, 1977 and 1979–80; international internal discussion bulletins, 1973–80; weekly *Notes to Organisers* (later *National Briefing*), 1974–81; *London Notes*, 1979–80; and some subject files. There are also internationally circulated papers of International Socialism, 1968–77; the Fourth International United Secretariat, 1979, and People's Democracy (the Irish Section of the Fourth International), 1978–81. Latterly the Modern Records Centre has received further committee and conference minutes, accounts, membership returns and

correspondence files covering the late 1970s to early 1980s.

There are also available certain personal collections which contain material relevant to the International Marxist Group, namely the papers of E.A. Whelan (ref. MSS 95), which include minutes, internal bulletins, office files and pamphlets for the period 1967–74, and the collection of Bob Purdie (ref. MSS 149), containing IMG correspondence relating to Ireland. There is a list available (NRA 20864) for these papers.

SOCIALIST COMMENTARY Some records of this left-wing journal have been deposited with the Modern Records Centre, University of Warwick (ref. MSS 173). The collection includes minutes of business meetings, 1954–59, some workbooks of Dr Rita Hinden as editor, some *Socialist Commentary* files concerning policy decisions and contacts with MPs and prominent authors. There are files of the journal and others such as *Socialist Vanguard* and *Contact*. See also the entries for Socialist Vanguard Group and Socialist Union.

SOCIALIST HEALTH ASSOCIATION This body was originally founded by Dr Somerville Hastings in 1930 as the Socialist Medical Association. Its aim is to work for a socialised and comprehensive national health service under democratic control.

The papers for the period 1912–76 have been deposited in the Brynmor Jones Library, University of Hull (ref. DSM) and a list is available (NRA 17257). This first deposit included the minute books of the Central Council and Executive Committee, 1946–70; proceedings of the Annual Conference, 1963–70; Policy Committee minutes, 1946–56, 1959–60; Social Committee minutes, 1947–53; General Practitioner Subcommittee minutes and papers, 1948–51; Campaign (Propaganda) Committee minutes and papers, 1950–51; Mental Health Subcommittee records, 1950–54; Trade Union Liaison Committee minutes, 1966–68; and files of press-cuttings, 1925–76. In addition there are subject files on the Association's work, 1941–66; membership and finance records, 1953–61; and copies of SMA circulars, 1930–60, and the *Branch Bulletin*, 1946–50. More recent records, including branch, membership and financial records, 1970–89, have now also been deposited.

SOCIALIST PARTY OF GREAT BRITAIN The Socialist Party of Great Britain (also known as the Socialist Party and as the SPGB) is a political party set up in 1904 to campaign, solely and exclusively, for the establishment of a socialist society, defined as a social system based on the common ownership and democratic control of the means of production, by and in the interests of the whole community. Its founders had broken away from the Social Democratic Federation 'to establish a genuine Socialist organisation' (Declaration of Principles, 1904).

The papers, retained at the Party's headquarters, are complete since 1904 and include minutes, annual reports, financial records and correspondence (which is organised by subject, although neither consistently nor systematically). Some records were destroyed by enemy action during World War II. Material may be consulted on request to the General Secretary.

SOCIALIST REGISTER Annual files of correspondence relating to the publication *Socialist Register* are included among the papers of one of its former editors, John Saville, who served in that capacity from 1964 onwards. The papers have been deposited in the Brynmor Jones Library, University of Hull (ref. DX/70).

SOCIALIST REVIEW GROUP Relevant material can be found in the Ken Tarbuck papers deposited in the Modern Records Centre, University of Warwick (ref. MSS 75). A list is available (NRA 21336). The material comprises a National Committee minute book, 1950–53, a Birmingham branch minute book, 1950–53, some correspondence and an incomplete run of *Socialist Review*, 1950–61. Reference should also be made to the Kuper papers, also at the Modern Records Centre, which contain photocopied minutes and issues of the *Socialist Review*, 1956–58 (MSS 250).

SOCIALIST SOCIETY The Socialist Society was established in 1982. It is the sponsor of the Socialist Movement, which was founded in 1989 to propagate the work of the Chesterfield and Sheffield Socialist Conferences and to establish a co-operative organisation for all socialists of the Broad Left. A quarterly

journal, *Catalyst*, is published. The Socialist Society retains its own papers, which principally comprise minutes of the AGM and of meetings of the Steering Committee, financial records, and copies of its publications. A large proportion of correspondence was discarded in 1990 during a move of offices. Any person wishing to view the material should apply to the Steering Committee.

SOCIALIST SUNDAY SCHOOLS Minutes and correspondence of this organisation and copies of its publication *Young Socialists* for the period 1907–71, have been deposited at the Labour History Archive and Study Centre, University of Manchester.

SOCIALIST UNION Some records of this group, which replaced the Socialist Vanguard Group (SVG) in 1950, can be found in the Modern Records Centre, University of Warwick, among the SVG archive (ref. MSS 173). The material comprises minutes and Management Committee minutes, 1951–59; AGM minutes, 1952–59; membership files; finance files, 1953–59; principles, rules and information sheets; and papers relating to the Democracy Study Group, schools and meetings.

SOCIALIST VANGUARD GROUP The SVG was established in 1929 as the British Section of the Militant Socialist International (*Internationaler Sozialisten Kampf-Bund, ISK*) in Germany. The ISK had evolved in 1926 from the *Internationaler Jugendbund*, a small educational group of members of the main German Left parties, led by the philosopher Leonard Nelson. The English Group was never large, but had an influence disproportionate to its size. In 1950 the SVG was replaced by the Socialist Union (q.v.), whose journal, *Socialist Commentary* (q.v.) continued to be published after the Socialist Union was formally dissolved.

Some records have been deposited in the Modern Records Centre, University of Warwick (ref. MSS 173) by Dr Rene Saran, the daughter of Mary Saran, editor/joint editor of *Socialist Commentary*, 1941–55. A list is available (NRA 25816).

SOCIALIST WORKERS' PARTY This group was formerly known as the International Socialism Group. A number of relevant collections are deposited in the Modern Records Centre, University of Warwick. Those for the International Socialism Group include various series of minutes, 1968–70; conference documents, 1969–72; bulletins and circulars, 1969–71; leaflets and publications, 1963–68; and some correspondence, 1969–70 (ref. MSS 84).

The papers of Colin Barker (ref. MSS 152) include further records of the International Socialism Group, including minutes, circulars, bulletins and reports, 1964–73; some correspondence and subject files; papers concerning the Revolutionary Socialist League, and issues of various radical newspapers, 1967–75.

The papers of five prominent radicals, Colin Barker (ref. MSS 152), Richard Hyman (ref. MSS 84), Steve Jeffreys (ref. MSS 244), Richard Kuper (ref. MSS 250) and Stirling Smith (ref. MSS 205), include further material relating to the SWP and ISG.
The Pugh papers (ref. MSS 329) consist of papers relating to the International Socialists and Socialist Workers Party. They also include *The Militant* 1970–89 and other leftwing publications, as well as internal documents.

Additional material on these groups can also be found in the papers of Paul Mackney, which are deposited in Birmingham Central Library. This collection is uncatalogued and closed at present. Other papers may be in Glasgow Caledonian University.

SOCIETY OF BRITISH GAS INDUSTRIES The surviving records (up to 1960) of this trade association have been placed in the Modern Records Centre, University of Warwick (ref. MSS 231). The records include minutes, 1906–65, records of General Meetings and sections, and some financial records. Founded in 1905, this society was based in Leamington. A list is available (NRA 24977).

Researchers should note that the Society has retained copies of its annual reports and annual accounts.

SOCIETY OF CERTIFIED AND ASSOCIATED LIBERAL AGENTS The chief functions of the Society were the promotion of knowledge of electoral law, particularly among Liberal agents, and the promotion of the interests and welfare of Liberal agents. Records of the Society, 1895–1951, have been

deposited in the Sheepscar Library, Leeds. The Manchester Central Library holds the records of the North West District of the Society. These include an Executive Council minute book, 1903–51. A list is available (NRA 24631).

SOCIETY OF CHIEF TRADING STANDARDS OFFICERS The Society was formally disbanded in December 1985 and its functions assumed by the Trading Standards section of the Federation of Managerial and Professional Officers (FEMPO). The surviving papers were given to Leicestershire Record Office in 1990 (ref. DE3609). The material consists of the minutes of the AGM, 1971–85, and the Executive Council, 1968–85; accounts and balance sheets, 1973–86, and bank statements, 1981–86; a file of correspondence with FEMPO, 1984–86, and papers concerning the transfer of responsibilities to that organisation (August-November 1985).

SOCIETY FOR COOPERATION IN RUSSIAN AND SOVIET STUDIES Prior to 1992 this organisation was known as the Society for Cultural Relations with the USSR. It was founded in 1924 to promote mutual understanding between the British and Soviet people through cultural and educational contacts.

At present the papers of the Society are retained at its head office. They include selected minutes of the Council and its sections since 1924; a complete run of the Annual Report since that date and selected reports of conferences and exhibitions; a set of the *Anglo-Soviet Journal* from 1946 onwards; an incomplete series of ledger books for the post-war period, and selected correspondence with members. The records of the Society are available to researchers on payment of a fee.

SOCIETY FOR INDIVIDUAL FREEDOM The Society was founded in 1942 as the Society of Individualists by the publisher Sir Ernest Benn. His papers, which contain printed reports on three of its meetings and a copy of the aims of the Society, have been deposited at the Modern Records Centre, University of Warwick (ref. MSS 257).

SOCIETY OF LABOUR LAWYERS The Society was founded in 1949 by those who seceded from the existing Haldane Society (q.v.) when that body was taken over by Communist sympathisers. Certain papers of the Society, including Executive Committee minutes, AGM records and correspondence, have been deposited at the LSE Library and are currently being listed. Further enquiries should be directed to the Archivist of the LSE Library.

SOCIETY OF MEDICAL OFFICERS OF HEALTH
The records of this organisation, including correspondence and minute books, 1902–74, have been deposited in the Wellcome Contemporary Medical Archives Centre, where the records of the Association of County Medical Officers of Health for England and Wales (q.v.) are also held. A list is available (NRA 25580).

SOCIETY FOR PROMOTING CHRISTIAN KNOWLEDGE
The records of the SPCK (dating back to the 17th century) have now been deposited in Cambridge University Library (which has the parallel archives of the Bible Society). They document the work of the Society in Britain and throughout the worldwide Anglican community. The bulk of the material relates to SPCK activities in the 19th and early 20th centuries, but there are some post-war minutes of the General Board and other committees. Reference should also be made to the entry for Missionary Societies (q.v.) in this Guide.

SOCIETY FOR THE PROMOTION OF VOCATIONAL TRAINING AND EDUCATION
The Society was a voluntary organisation founded in 1972 to manage British entries in successive International Vocational Training Competitions. Such papers as may survive are presently in the care of its successor body, UK Skills, and enquiries should be directed to this organisation.

SOCIETY FOR THE PROTECTION OF SCIENCE AND LEARNING
The Society was founded as the Academic Assistance Council in 1933 and adopted its present title in January 1937. It was responsible for facilitating the settlement of academic refugees from Nazi Germany in the UK; in the post-war period it has continued to assist persecuted scholars from countries around the world.

Records from 1933–58 have been deposited in the Bodleian Library. There are over 5,000 files in the archive, the bulk of which are case files of individuals assisted by the Society. Administrative records and files of correspondence with refugee organisations have also been retained, as have certain papers of a later date, including records of the Committee/AGM which extend up to 1986. A list is available for the whole archive (NRA 31126) and further details may also be found in Adrian Allan, *University Bodies: A Survey of Inter-and Supra-University Bodies and their Records* (University of Liverpool Archives Unit, 1990).

Records over thirty years old are available to researchers. Anyone wishing to consult more recent papers or the case file of any living person must seek the permission of the Secretary of the Society. The Society also retains in its own care its original minute books and the majority of case files of refugees whom it has assisted since 1960. Enquiries should be directed to the Hon. Secretary.

SOCIETY FOR RESEARCH INTO HIGHER EDUCATION
The records of the Society, which was founded in the mid-1960s with the aim of linking academics by means of conferences and publications, have been placed in the Modern Records Centre, University of Warwick (ref. MSS 323).

SOCIETY OF SOCIALIST CLERGY AND MINISTERS
Certain minute books and papers of the Society, which later became the Council of Clergy and Ministers for Common Ownership, have been deposited in Bethnal Green Record Office (ref. P72/303). The material covers the period 1942–59 and a list is available (NRA 29479). Additional material for a similar period may be found among the papers of the Christian socialist Revd Stanley George Evans, which are held in the Brynmor Jones Library, University of Hull (ref. DEV).

SOCIETY OF TEACHERS OPPOSED TO PHYSICAL PUNISHMENT
The records are reported in the Library of the Institute of Education, University of London.

SOCIETY OF TELECOMMUNICATIONS EXECUTIVES
The society was formerly known as

the Society of Post Office Executives. Many records have been placed in the Modern Records Centre, University of Warwick (ref. MSS 124). The Modern Records Centre also has the papers of Arthur Willitt, former SPOE President (ref. MSS 116). For further details, the *Consolidated Guide to the Modern Records Centre* should be consulted.

SOCIETY OF WOMEN JOURNALISTS The records have been placed in the Bodleian Library, Oxford, to where enquiries concerning scope and access should be addressed.

SOLIDARITY (SOCIALISM REAFFIRMED GROUP) Some records of the group, established in 1960, are in the International Institute of Social History, Amsterdam. The archive spans the period 1960–83 and, besides periodicals published by Solidarity, contains correspondence from Ken Weller, Heather Russell and other members of the London group with sympathisers in the United Kingdom and elsewhere.

SOROPTIMIST INTERNATIONAL OF GREAT BRITAIN AND IRELAND A women's international service organisation seeking to maintain high ethical standards in business and the professions, and to advance the status and rights of women, the Soroptimists developed from women's clubs formed in North America and Europe in the 1920s. The object of the movement is to co-operate with inter-governmental and other organisations for the advancement of international understanding and peace; individual clubs and federations support humanitarian projects in their local communities and abroad.

The Federation of Great Britain and Ireland retains all records in both its active and archive files at its offices. Surviving papers include the minutes of the Executive Council, Programme Action Committee and the General Meetings; annual reports and various special reports on topics of concern to the Soroptimists (e.g. charitable funding, the environment, human rights and the status of women, etc.); annual audited accounts, and ledgers for the previous ten years only, and correspondence and subject files. Persons wishing to have access to the papers should apply to the Secretary.

SOUTH PLACE ETHICAL SOCIETY Founded as a dissenting congregation in 1793, the Society discarded Christian dogma during its first hundred years and since then has adopted a secular humanist position. It moved from South Place in Finsbury, London in 1929 to Red Lion Square, London WC1.

The Society retains its own papers. Although General Committee minutes are available since 1877 and are complete for the past several decades, the best guide to the Society's activities is found in its monthly journal (1897-date), now called *Ethical Record*, copies of which are available for most of the twentieth century. An Annual Report has been issued since 1901 and bound copies are held. There is an incomplete series of ledgers and cash books from 1893 onwards. Since 1910 the annual Conway Memorial Lecture has also been published.

SPANISH DEMOCRATS DEFENCE COMMITTEE The papers of this pro-Spanish Republican organisation are contained within the Will Poynter collection in the South Wales Coalfield Archive at the Library of the University College of Swansea. There is a list available to the Archive (NRA 14694).

STANDING COMMISSION ON THE SCOTTISH ECONOMY There are papers for the period 1972–76 in Strathclyde Regional Archives.

STANDING COMMITTEE ON SEXUALLY ABUSED CHILDREN The Standing Committee on Sexually Abused Children was formed in 1983 to promote good practice in the care of children who have been subject to sexual abuse; membership is open to all childcare workers without regard to practising discipline. Its papers consist of minutes of the Executive Committee and the AGM; Annual Reports; financial records, and correspondence. All material dates from 1983. Requests to consult the records should be made to the Information Officer of SCOSAC Training and Consultancy Ltd. SCOSAC also maintains an Information Centre with an extensive library on child sexual abuse and related subjects.

STANDING CONFERENCE OF WOMEN'S ORGANISATIONS In 1942 the Federation of

Soroptimist Clubs sponsored the formation of local Group Action Councils to provide for the exchange of information on issues of interest between existing local women's and family organisations and the individual branches of national voluntary service bodies. These Group Action Councils later became the Standing Conference of Women's Organisations. Communication between individual Standing Conferences was effected by means of the Women's Group on Public Welfare (see Women's Forum). The SCWO operated until 1980 under the auspices of the National Council for Voluntary Organisations but is now organised on the basis of six regional conferences with their own National Council. It cooperates in promoting the interests of women's and family organisations and in a variety of social work research projects.

The records of the Conference are maintained by the National Secretary. Existing material includes the minutes of the National Council (which meets quarterly), and correspondence files. Biennial conference and AGM reports and research publications are also available. Individual branches retain their own papers. The papers are open to anyone who would undertake to use them responsibly.

Certain papers relating to the SCWO may be found in the archive of the Women's Forum now deposited in the Women's Library (q.v.). These include records of the biennial joint conferences of the SCWO and the Women's Group on Public Welfare, 1944–76; papers of individual local Standing Conferences, covering mainly the 1940s–60s; and minutes, correspondence and reports of the SCWO Advisory Committee, 1942–75.

STATUS OF WOMEN COMMITTEE Founded in 1935 with a membership composed of both individuals and representatives of women's organisations, the Committee advocated equality of status and rights for women in the social, political, economic and cultural spheres of life. Principally it sought to achieve legislative change and, because its aims were largely realised in the 1970s by the Sex Discrimination Act and other related measures, the Committee was dissolved in 1982.

The archive has been deposited in the Women's Library (q.v.). Lists are available (NRA 33573, 34688). The papers comprise minutes of the AGM, 1970–82,

and of the main committee, 1969–79; conference programmes and reports, 1969–80; general correspondence, 1976–79 and 1981–85, and publications.

Considerably more material is available in the papers of the Committee's leading member A. Muriel Pierotti (sometime General Secretary of the National Union of Women Teachers), likewise deposited in the Women's Library. These include many of the Committee's records for the 1940s to 1970s, namely minutes of the main committee, 1945–78; financial reports, 1947–71; correspondence and minutes of the liaison subcommittee, 1970–74; minutes and agendas of the AGM, 1955–78; annual reports, 1949–74; election material, 1950–74; subject files, and general correspondence, 1948–78.

STUDENT CHRISTIAN MOVEMENT The organisation developed from the Student Voluntary Missionary Union, founded in 1892. Its original membership was of students who intended to become foreign missionaries; later its work developed to encouraging Christian Unions within universities and advancing the Christian life among students on an ecumenical basis. The SCM is a member of the World Student Christian Fellowship, which unites nearly 100 such Movements throughout the world.

The papers have been placed in the Orchard Learning Resource Centre, Selly Oak Campus, University of Birmingham. A list is now available (NRA 43314).

SWORD OF THE SPIRIT Sword of the Spirit was inaugurated by Cardinal Hinsley in 1940 to assist greater international cooperation among Catholics who wished to promote justice in war and peace. In 1941 full membership was restricted to Roman Catholics, although this retarded ecumenical collaboration. The papers of Cardinal Hinsley, which are deposited in the Westminster Roman Catholic Diocesan Archives, include extensive material on this movement (ref. AAW/Hi/2). Lambeth Palace Library holds a number of collections documenting Anglican participation in the Sword of the Spirit. These include some wartime files, 1940–41 (ref. MS 3418) and the correspondence of Bishop Bell, 1940–45.

SYNDICALIST WORKERS' FEDERATION
Some records of this group, founded in Manchester in 1950, are in the International Institute of Social History, Amsterdam. The deposit comprises publications (e.g. *Direct Action*) as well as some minutes, correspondence and material concerning National Conferences, 1960–73.

T

TASS The white-collar union of the manufacturing industry, TASS takes its name from its earlier existence as the Technical, Administrative and Supervisory Section of the Amalgamated Union of Engineering Workers (Amalgamated Engineering Union, q.v.). In January 1988 TASS amalgamated with the scientific and technical union, the Association of Scientific, Technical and Managerial Staffs (q.v.), to form the Manufacturing, Science, Finance Union.

TASS had been formed in 1970–71 when the white-collar engineering union DATA (the Draughtsmen and Allied Technicians' Association) and the Construction Engineering Union joined the Amalgamated Engineering and Foundry Workers' Union to form the Amalgamated Union of Engineering Workers (AUEW). DATA itself had previously been the Association of Engineering and Shipbuilding Draughtsmen (est. 1913) but had changed its name in 1961 to reflect the growth of its membership in the newer, technical sectors of the engineering industry.

After 1971 the AUEW consisted of four federated sections representing the different industrial sectors covered by its members, and the white-collar workers had formed the Technical, Administrative and Supervisory Section. However the federation was not a success and there were significant disputes between the Sections over the issue of proceeding to a full amalgamation. In 1984 the AUEW was re-formed to become a two-section federation, the engineers, construction and foundry workers forming one group (which subsequently took the name of the Amalgamated Engineering Union), and TASS the other. However, in 1988 TASS severed all connections with the AEU and united instead with ASTMS to form MSF.

In the intervening period a number of previously independent trade unions amalgamated with TASS, namely the National Union of Gold, Silver and Allied Trades (in 1981), the National Union of Sheetmetal Workers, Coppersmiths, Heating and Domestic Engineers (1983), the Association of Patternmakers and Allied Craftsmen (1984), the National Society of Metal Mechanics (1985) and the Tobacco Workers' Union in 1986.

The papers of TASS have been deposited along with the records of the Amalgamated Engineering Union at the Modern Records Centre, University of Warwick. The TASS material forms collection MSS 101, and it is expected that material will continue to be deposited on a regular basis. The collection is extensive and includes papers of a number of the predecessors of TASS, as well as of the current union. They may best be described under separate headings for each constituent organisation.

ASSOCIATION OF PATTERNMAKERS AND ALLIED CRAFTSMEN

Previously known as the United Patternmakers Association, the union was founded in 1872 and based in the North East of England. A *History of the United Patternmakers Association, 1872–1922* by W. Mosses was published in 1922. The papers at the Modern Records Centre comprise Executive Council minutes, 1884–1966 (indexed for 1920–66); Appeal Court minutes, 1939–65; Annual Reports, 1872–1972, and Monthly Reports, 1939–81.

DRAUGHTSMEN AND ALLIED TECHNICIANS' ASSOCIATION

Local and central conference proceedings, mainly post-war, and a run of the journal for 1918–76.

NATIONAL SOCIETY OF METAL MECHANICS

Formerly the National Society of Brassworkers and Metal Mechanics, the union was founded in 1872 as the Amalagamated Society of Brass Workers. Its headquarters was located in Birmingham and it was always particularly strong in the Midlands. A centenary history, *Founded In Brass* by M. Totten, was published in 1972.

The Modern Records Centre collection comprises National Executive Council minutes, 1928–59 and draft minutes, 1961–67; trustees' minutes, 1928–76; the minutes of the following District Councils: Midlands (1956–79), Northern (1949–79), London (1949–60, 1965, 1970–79) and Western (1941–79); minutes of the Joint Industrial Council for the Metal Bedstead Industry, 1952–60; various subject files, 1920s–80s; circulars to branches, 1952–66 and 1970–80; Birmingham Central branch minutes, 1941–73, and death benefit books, 1920–71; Bristol Branch minutes, 1952–54; Birmingham Shop Stewards' minutes, 1941–69, and title deeds to land and property in Birmingham, Derby, Dublin, Gloucestershire and Worcestershire, 1633–1961. A list is available (NRA 31438).

NATIONAL UNION OF GOLD, SILVER AND ALLIED TRADES

In 1969 the union incorporated the Society of Goldsmiths, Jewellers and Kindred Trades (originally established in 1893). A collection of records has been placed in the Sheffield City Library.

NATIONAL UNION OF SHEET METAL WORKERS, COPPERSMITHS, HEATING AND DOMESTIC ENGINEERS

In 1989 TASS presented the records and banners of the union to the former National Museum of Labour History, which deposited the papers at the Modern Records Centre. Certain items, such as rulebooks, price lists and tramping items, were retained at the Museum. Further details of the union's history may be found in *Men Of Good Character* by Ted Brake (London, 1985). The collection includes the following post-war records:

1. *Birmingham and Midland Sheet Metal Workers' Society* Minutes, 1943–49.
2. *Birmingham (Operative) Tin-Plate Workers' Society* An incomplete series of balance sheets and reports, 1892–1972.

3. *London Society of Sheet Metal Workers, Braziers and Gas Meter Makers* Minutes, 1880–1958, and records of the general meetings, 1954–66. From 1921 these minutes are those of NUSMW London District.
4. *National Society of Coppersmiths, Braziers & Metal Workers* Minutes, 1929–53; annual reports, 1950–59; monthly reports, 1913–58, and Swindon branch accounts, 1932–58.
5. *National Union of Heating and Domestic Engineers* Minutes, 1935–67, and an incomplete series of reports, 1937–45.
6. *National Union of Sheet Metal Workers, Coppersmiths, Heating and Domestic Engineers* An incomplete set of printed NEC minutes, 1960–83; final National Conference tapes, 1984; an incomplete set of biennial and other conference reports, 1947–83; a file of business reports, 1943–50; annual reports, 1961–77, 1982–83; minutes of District No. 4, 1945–52, and an incomplete set of the London District journal *Fusion*, 1947–69.
7. *Sheet Iron and Light Platers' Union* Minutes, 1930–61.

TOBACCO WORKERS' UNION

A history, *The Tobacco Workers' Union, 1834–1984*, was published in 1984. The union was founded in 1834. It was originally an all-male combination of skilled craftsmen, but in 1924–25 was transformed into an industrial union of all tobacco workers without regard to occupational status or gender.

The Modern Records Centre holds the following: Executive Committee minutes, 1904–86; annual delegate meeting reports, 1948–56; biennial delegate meeting reports, 1958–76, 1980–84; an incomplete set of annual and quarterly accounts, 1933–71; files on wage claims, amalgamations, etc; examples of circulars to branches, officers and officials; annual reports, 1881–1970; rulebooks, 1877–1980; registers of legal cases, 1958–72, and copies of industrial agreements, 1919–77.

There is also a significant series of committee and branch minutes, viz: BAT International Exports Division Industrial Negotiating Committee, 1972–80; Imperial Tobacco Industrial Committee, 1974–79; National Joint Negotiating Committee for the Tobacco Industry, 1945–49 and 1953–60; North West

England District Committee, 1950–62; Glasgow No. 1 Branch, 1945–54; Liverpool No. 2 Branch, 1956–59; London Branch, 1956–64, and Manchester No. 1 Branch, 1924–50.

This collection is listed (NRA 33299).

TAVISTOCK INSTITUTE OF HUMAN RELATIONS The Tavistock Institute is one of the few bodies in Europe which combines research in social and psychological science with professional practice. It was founded in 1946 and incorporated as a non-profit-making company with charitable status in the following year. It is governed by a Council elected at the AGM by its constitutional body, the Tavistock Association.

The surviving records have now been deposited in the LSE Library, to where enquiries should be addressed.

TELECOMMUNICATIONS STAFF ASSOCIATION The TSA was founded in 1970 following the resignation of the Executive Committee of the National Guild of Telephonists. A small deposit (one box) can be found in the Modern Records Centre, University of Warwick (ref. MSS 190). The material relates to applications and appeals, 1972–74, by TSA members and officials for recognition under the 1971 Industrial Relations Act as a sole bargaining agent and in respect of its activities as a registered trade union.

TERRENCE HIGGINS TRUST The Trust, named in memory of the first person to die of AIDS in the UK, was founded in 1982 and was the first national voluntary organisation concerned with AIDS. It originally aimed to provide gay men with information about AIDS, but now provides a wider range of services, publishes a variety of educational literature and pursues an active public education role.

The Trust has retained its archives (though these are sparse for the early 1980s). Extensive committee minutes survive. Access to material other than publications and press-cuttings would have to be agreed by the Board of Directors. Enquiries should be directed to the External Liaison Officer. See also Hall-Carpenter Archive.

THOMAS CORAM FOUNDATION FOR CHILDREN The Thomas Coram Foundation for Children (known until 1954 as the Foundling Hospital) was established by Royal Charter in 1739 and is reputed to be the first incorporated charity in the world. The Foundation has extensive records covering the development of child care and of the voluntary sector in the UK. The bulk of the records (about nine tons) has been deposited at London Metropolitan Archives, but the post-war material is largely retained at the Foundation's offices.

The papers include the original minutes of the Court of Governors of the Foundling Hospital and of the General Committee from 1739 to date; a comprehensive collection of miscellaneous reports; financial records; and a large archive of correspondence, which in most cases has not been indexed. Access to the personal records of children and their mothers is subject to a 100-year rule. Permission to view material retained at the Foundation's offices can only be granted on a case-by-case basis. Researchers are therefore advised in the first instance to contact the Director and Secretary of the Foundation.

TIDY BRITAIN GROUP The Tidy Britain Group, known until 1988 as Keep Britain Tidy Group, was established in 1954 under the auspices of the National Federation of Women's Institutes. It exists to preserve and enhance urban and rural amenities by the promotion of litter control and the fostering of both national and local environmental improvement schemes.

The Group has retained its own archive, which consists of the minutes of the Council and Finance Committee, and annual reports and accounts since 1962; correspondence and subject files for a preceding four-year period; and published special reports and information leaflets on specific issues (e.g. litter legislation). Copies of the published material are available on request, subject to availability; the remainder of the archive, which is retained at the head or regional offices as appropriate, is presently closed. Enquiries should be referred to the Deputy Director General.

THE TIMES The records of *The Times* form part of the archives of its parent company, News

International. Their contents and access conditions are described in 'The archives of News International' in *Business Archives* (1992). An earlier listing of the material is available (NRA 19359). Researchers should note that daily fees are charged for access to the collection.

TOWN AND COUNTRY PLANNING ASSOCIATION

An all-party voluntary body and registered educational charity to promote the understanding of national and regional planning policies, the TCPA evolved from the Garden Cities Association of 1899 and adopted the above name in 1941. The influence of the Association was increased substantially by the greater status attached to the profession following the 1946 New Towns Act and the 1947 Town and Country Planning Act. Today TCPA acts as a forum for the discussion and dissemination of planning policies and seeks to act as a link between professional planners, business, government and the public; it supports a Planning Aid Service which acts as an information agency and an Environmental Education Unit.

The Association has retained its records, although a quantity of material has been lost through wartime destruction and office moves. A list is available (NRA 24472). Surviving papers include Council and Executive Committee minute books for the period since 1944, which incorporate minutes of a wide variety of other conference committees (such as Finance and General Purposes, and the Management Committee), and AGM minutes from 1901.

Papers and proceedings of the Annual Conferences, 1953–66, and of Regional and Special Conferences, 1945–70, are also available. Files exist of Executive Committee papers and Director's Reports from 1964; there is a limited series of administrative files, including ones on Letchworth and Welwyn Garden Cities and the correspondence of F.J. Osborn, Hon. Secretary, 1955–70. Ledger books are retained only for the seven year period required by law. Publications include Annual Reports from 1941 to date; the weekly newsheet *Planning Bulletin* since 1947; the *Bulletin of Environmental Education*, monthly since May 1971; the journal *Town and Country Planning* since 1911 (known as *Garden Cities and Town Planning* until 1932), and other pamphlets and books.

Enquiries should be addressed to the Planning and Information Officer. Generally, files may be made accessible for research on the premises, with the exception of a limited number of current (and all personnel) files which remain confidential.

TOWNSWOMEN'S GUILDS

The Townswomen's Guilds have their origins in the Kensington Ladies Discussion Group, formed by suffragettes in 1865 to promote higher education for women. Following the achievement of universal suffrage in 1928 it was decided to create a new organisation of progressive associations in order to offer a forum in which women might cooperate to exploit their new political freedom. The name of the body was changed in 1933 from the original National Union of Societies for Equal Citizenship to the National Union of Townswomen's Guilds.

The papers remain in the care of the National Secretary. At national level all committee and sub-committee minutes exist for the period from 1929 onwards. In addition there are preserved annual reports from the first issue in 1928–29 of NUSEC's report, with some gaps during the war years; an incomplete run of the magazine *Townswoman* from 1934; financial records such as ledger books for a preceding five year period, and correspondence for approximately the last three to five years. Internal correspondence is arranged by Guild and Federation, and external correspondence by subject, organisation and individual. Chronological copies are retained by each department. Also retained are most conference programmes and some reports, copies of occasional published reports and a photographic archive. Persons wishing to consult the papers should apply to the National Secretary including a full statement of their reasons for seeking access.

TRADES UNION CONGRESS

The massive archive of the Trades Union Congress (up to 1960) was deposited in the Modern Records Centre, Warwick University, in 1988 (ref. MSS 292). A list is available (NRA 35037). The best introduction to the papers can be found in Sarah Duffield and Richard Storey (compilers), *The Trades Union Congress Archive 1920–60* (University of Warwick Library, Occasional Publications No. 19, June 1992). Researchers should note that more recent deposits continue to be made. See Alan Crookham, *The Trades Union Congress Archive 1960–70* (University of Warwick Library Occasional Publications No. 30, 1998). The booklet describes the papers in deposits MSS.292B and MSS.292C.

The most coherent body of records are the minutes and papers of the various committees through which the work of the Congress is carried out. Minutes of the Parliamentary Committee (after 1921 the General Council) date back to 1888. In addition to minutes, there are also agendas, notices and correspondence. There are minutes and papers of other committees from the 1920s, for example; Finance and General Purposes Committee, 1923 to date; Economic Committee, 1929 to date; International Committee, 1923 to date; Workmen's Compensation Committee, 1924–47; Standing Advisory Committee on Social Insurance, 1928–47, and Social Insurance and Industrial Welfare Committee, 1947 to date; and Education Committee, 1922 to date.

The very extensive subject files detailed in the booklets cover the entire spectrum of routine trade union and industrial relations' issues. They also document other aspects of TUC policy ranging from colonial and commonweath labour issues to armed forces and disarmament, civil defence and sport.

A further deposit in the Modern Records Centre has brought in additional records for 1962–91.

Records relating to TUC activities in Northern Ireland can be found within the Belfast and District Trades Union Congress collection in the Public Record Office of Northern Ireland (ref. MIC 193, formerly D1050/6). This includes minutes, agendas, annual reports and correspondence. Some sections are subject to a thirty-year closure rule. Forty-six trade unions active in Northern Ireland are affiliated to the Irish Congress of Trade Unions, which is the central authority for trade unions in the Republic of Ireland. Some ICTU records are deposited in the Irish Labour History Museum in Dublin, and further material is available in the Public Record Office of Northern Ireland (ref. D 1050/12). The papers of Jack Macgougan, a leading TUC and ICTU official, are also in the Public Record Office of Northern Ireland (ref. D3699).

TRANSPORT AND GENERAL WORKERS' UNION The TGWU, once the largest trade union in the UK, is a general union to which all types of workers may belong; its members are drawn from among production workers in nearly all manufacturing industries and it embraces clerical and administrative employees in those occupations as well. It was formed in 1922 as a result of the amalgamation of fourteen unions on the initiative of the Dock, Wharf, Riverside and General Workers' Union, in association with the National Union of Dock Labourers. Sectoral decline in membership was partially compensated during the 1970s and 1980s by a series of amalgamations with smaller unions joining the TGWU. Of particular significance were the mergers with the National Union of Vehicle Builders (in 1972) which established a new automotive trade group within the TGWU; the National Union of Agricultural and Allied Workers in 1982, and the National Union of Dyers, Bleachers and Textile Workers in the same year.

Records have been placed in the Modern Records Centre, University of Warwick (ref. MSS 126). This complex and important deposit contains a wealth of material. It is best accessed initially via the MRC website.

Records emanating from the regional offices of the TGWU have been deposited at appropriate repositories. The records of TGWU Region 8 for the period 1882–1969 and the committee minutes and correspondence up to 1985 of the Newcastle District are with the Tyne and Wear Archives Service (a list is available, NRA 20933); the Halifax District contribution books for 1948–64 have been deposited with the West Yorkshire Archive Service (ref. TU74/3–32; there is a list, NRA 22940); correspondence and minutes of the Manchester District are available at the Local Studies Unit of Manchester Central Library; the records of the North Wales Regional Committee for 1951–72 (including minutes) are at Clywd Record Office, and the minutes of the Sussex District Committee for 1961–70 have been deposited at Brighton Public Library (for which there is a list, NRA 21834).

The papers of other trade unions which have amalgamated with the TGWU in the post-war period, where these have been traced, may best be described separately below.

ASSOCIATION OF CLERICAL, TECHNICAL AND SUPERVISORY STAFFS

The papers have been deposited at the Modern Records Centre (ref. MSS 208). They comprise Coventry District Committee minutes, 1957–78; papers from conferences and arbitrations with employers, 1967–82; correspondence with employers, 1975–84, and trade agreements, 1960–69 and 1975–77.

GRIMSBY STEAM AND DIESEL FISHING VESSELS ENGINEERS' AND FIREMEN'S UNION

This union transferred engagements to the TGWU in 1976. The papers are at the Modern Records Centre in collection MSS 126 and consist of General and Committee minutes, 1937–87; six files of administrative papers, including negotiations on pay conditions and on the 'Cod War', 1960–76, and press-cuttings, 1950s–80s. A list is available (NRA 30721).

NATIONAL AMALGAMATED STEVEDORES AND DOCKERS

This union, historically a rival of the TGWU in the principal English ports, transferred engagements in 1982. The minutes and correspondence for the period from 1883 onwards have now been deposited in the Labour History Archive and Study Centre.

NATIONAL ASSOCIATION OF OPERATIVE PLASTERERS

The Plasterers' Union was established in 1860 and merged with the TGWU in 1968. Monthly and quarterly reports for 1886–1967 and the annual reports of 1891–1967 have now been deposited at the Modern Records Centre. There exists a list (NRA 8976), compiled at a time when the union was independent of the TGWU.

NATIONAL UNION OF AGRICULTURAL AND ALLIED WORKERS

The union was founded in 1906 and became the National Union of Agricultural Workers in 1920. It adopted the above name in 1966 and merged with the TGWU in 1982. The bulk of its records have been deposited at the Rural History Centre, University of Reading, and a list is available (NRA 20989). The most recent material is still in the process of being sorted but papers up to 1972 are available. Specifically these include Executive Committee minutes, 1907–45; Organising Sub-committee minutes, 1946–50; various branch minutes, 1906–49; General Council meeting and conference reports, 1913–47; annual reports and balance sheets, 1962–71; miscellaneous administrative material, 1930–72; press-cuttings, and personal ephemera. The records of the Staffordshire, Warwickshire, and Cheshire branches for 1956–83 are in Staffordshire Record Office. They include case files relating to industrial accidents, redundancy, and accommodation (i.e. tied cottages), but are subject to a sixty-year closure rule. The papers of the Oxford District of the National Agricultural Labourers Union are reported to be available in Nuffield College Library.

NATIONAL UNION OF DYERS, BLEACHERS AND TEXTILE WORKERS

The NUDBTW joined the TGWU in 1982 to form the Textile Trade Group. It had been established in 1936 by the amalgamation of the three largest unions in the dyeing, finishing, calico printing and woollen manufacturing industry, namely the Operative Bleachers', Dyers' and Finishers' Association, the National Union of Textile Workers, and the Amalgamated Society of Dyers, Bleachers, Finishers and Kindred Trades.

The papers of the NUDBTW and the TGWU Textile Trade Group remain with the union and comprise minutes of the Executive Committee monthly meetings, 1936–82, and minutes of the quarterly TGWU Textile Trade Group National Committee Meetings; Annual Conference Reports of the NUDBTW, 1976–82, and TGWU Textile Conference Reports from 1983; cash books, petty cash books and bank statements from 1970 onwards; correspondence files of the National Secretary and Finance Officer, and a small library for internal use. Persons wishing to consult the papers should apply to the Finance Officer of the TGWU Textile Trade Group.

The minutes of the predecessor unions of the NUDBTW for the period 1873–1966 have been deposited at Bradford Central Library. Kirklees District Library also holds (ref. S/NUDBTW) certain papers of the Huddersfield District of the union, namely minutes of the Executive, Accounts and other committees.

NATIONAL UNION OF VEHICLE BUILDERS

Founded as the United Kingdom Society of Coachmakers in 1834, the union became the National Union of Vehicle Builders in 1919 and amalgamated with the TGWU in 1972. The papers are now held at the Modern Records Centre (ref. MSS 126), to where they were transferred from the TGWU Vehicle Building and Automotive Museum in Coventry. They comprise National Executive Committee minutes, 1947–72; proceedings of national negotiating conferences, 1941–61; proceedings of local negotiating conferences, 1915–56; Vehicle Building and Automotive Museum files, 1973–80; copies of the union rules, 1859–1967; a run of the journal and financial reports, 1919–72; circulars, 1956–72, and newsletters, 1957–72. There is also within the collection an extensive series of regional and district records for the Birmingham, Leeds and London offices.

SCOTTISH COMMERCIAL MOTORMEN'S ASSOCIATION

The union was founded in 1898 as the Scottish Carters' Association and adopted the above name in 1964. In 1974 it became part of the TGWU. The papers have been placed in the National Library of Scotland (ref. Dep 175). They include minutes of the Executive Committee for 1928–66, accounts, letter books and the records of several branches.

SCOTTISH SLATERS, TILERS, ROOFERS AND CEMENT WORKERS SOCIETY

Merged with the TGWU in 1968. The papers are deposited at the National Library of Scotland (ref. Acc 4707) and include the minutes of the Executive Committee for 1927–61 and accounts and contribution books. A list is available (NRA 19290). The deposit incorporates the papers of the earlier Amalgamated Slaters' Society of Scotland, e.g. the Central Board minute book, 1919–50.

TRANSPORT SALARIED STAFFS ASSOCIATION

The Association was founded at Sheffield in 1897, as the National Association of General Railway Clerks. The name was changed in 1898 to the Railway Clerks' Association, and in 1951 to its present form. An extensive collection of papers has been deposited at the Modern Records Centre, University of Warwick (ref. MSS 55). The original collection includes various series of minutes, 1900–71; conference proceedings, 1899–1963; annual reports, 1899–1951; circulars, 1922–80; some branch records; some subject files, and copies of the *Railway Service Journal* and the *Transport Salaried Staff Journal*, 1965–66. A more recent deposit includes additional Finance Committee minutes, etc. (ref. MSS 55B).

TRANSPORT 2000

A federation of environmental and consumer groups, trade unions, industrial bodies and local authorities, Transport 2000 was founded in 1972 to conduct research on public transport policy, and to lobby Parliament and the responsible authorities to ensure adequate and properly co-ordinated investment in public transport.

Transport 2000 presently retains its own archive. Papers include committee minutes from 1977 to date; annual reports for the 1980s, and copies of publications, including the newsletter *Transport Report*. Financial records are unavailable. Correspondence is retained at the office for only the preceding year, but a series of subject files exists for the 1980s on all aspects of Transport 2000's work (e.g. bus deregulation, metropolitan transport policy, pedestrian access, road building etc.). Persons wishing access to the papers should apply to the Executive Director.

TY CENEDL

A group of papers of this Welsh body, 1977–95, was purchased by the National Library of Wales in 1988. A list is available (NRA 37319). The deposit comprises correspondence, minutes, promotional material etc. collected by the group relating to radical, republican and nationalist groups in Wales. There is material on, for example, the 1969 Anti-Investiture Campaign, the Free Wales Army, the Welsh Political Prisoners Defence Committee etc.

U

UK STEEL ASSOCIATION The Association, which was formed in 1997, derives from the British Independent Steel Producers Association (BISPA), which was formed in 1967, following the National-isation (Iron and Steel) Act. BISPA changed its name to the UK Steel Association in 1997. Various records have been deposited in the Modern Records Centre, University of Warwick (ref. MSS 383). For BISPA itself there are Executive Committee minutes, 1967–93, AGM papers, 1968–93, and circular letters to members, 1980–91. The files deposited include those of the Independent Steel Employers' Association, covering various aspects of industrial relations going back to the 1940s. Access to the archive is only by written application to the UK Steel Association.

ULSTER ENTERPRISE VOLUNTARY COMMITTEE The Committee was formed upon the initiative of Lord Dunleath and others in order to promote investment, particularly from abroad, in Northern Ireland. One of its leading members, Miss M.K. Lyle of Portrush, County Antrim, has deposited a collection of some 1500 documents in the Public Record Office of Northern Ireland (ref. D3601). The papers cover the period 1963–77 and include correspondence with prospective investors and business entrepreneurs on whose behalf the Committee acted.

ULSTER FARMERS' UNION The Union was established in 1917. Papers for the period 1920–66 have been deposited in the Public Record Office of Northern Ireland (ref. D1050/13). The material consists of minutes, correspondence, branch records, subscription records, yearbooks, journals etc.

ULSTER HEADMASTERS' ASSOCIATION The papers for the period 1917–86 have been deposited in the Public Record Office of Northern Ireland (ref.

D3915). They include minutes and Secretary's correspondence.

ULSTER HEADMISTRESSES' ASSOCIATION A collection of papers, consisting of correspondence, minutes and reports of the Association for 1939 to 1976, has been deposited in the Public Record Office of Northern Ireland.

ULSTER TEACHERS UNION The records, for the period 1919–67, have been placed in the Public Record Office of Northern Ireland (ref. D 3944).

UNDEB CYMRU FYDD (NEW WALES UNION) The society grew out of the Council for the Preservation of Welsh Culture, and was formally established in 1941 under the inspiration of the late T.I. Ellis. It sought to safeguard the position of the Welsh language and to advance Welsh cultural life. From 1967, when it became a charitable foundation, it worked briefly to promote the study of the Welsh language.

An extensive collection of records has been deposited in the National Library of Wales, where there is a list (in Welsh) available. The records include minute books of the Council, 1939–60; numerous files and volumes from 1939 onwards incorporating memoranda and evidence submitted to committees on matters of Welsh cultural and educational interest; correspondence and accounts of subcommittees and joint committees, and account books.

UNDEB Y CYMRU AR WASGAR (SOCIETY OF WELSH PEOPLE IN DISPERSION) The records of the society *c.* 1947–78 have been placed in the National Library of Wales. Reference should also be made to the papers of the sometime Hon. Secretary, T. Elwyn Griffiths, likewise at the National Library.

UNION OF COMMUNICATION WORKERS

The Union was formerly known as the Union of Post Office Workers (UPW). The early amalgamations which formed the UPW are described in *Sources, 1900–51*, vol. I, p. 270. Many records of the Union have now been deposited in the Modern Records Centre, University of Warwick (ref. MSS 148). The deposit includes minutes, 1919–70; conference proceedings, 1933–75 (incomplete); some circulars; pamphlets; and issues of various journals, 1883–1966. Subject files and research papers are held on various topics, including the cost of living (1935–64) and equal pay.

Reference may also be made to Michael J. Moran, *Union of Post Office Workers: A Study in Political Sociology* (London, 1974); Alan Clinton, *Post Office Workers: A Trade Union and Social History* (London, 1984), and M.J. Daunton, *Royal Mail: The Post Office Since 1840* (London, 1985).

UNION OF CONSTRUCTION, ALLIED TRADES AND TECHNICIANS

UCATT members are drawn from a wide spectrum of occupations but the largest number work within the private sector building industry, within which UCATT seeks to recruit all types of workers without distinction of craft. The present-day union was formed in July 1971 following the merger of the Amalgamated Society of Painters and Decorators, the Association of Building Technicians and the Amalgamated Union of Building Trade Workers, all of which joined the Amalgamated Society of Woodworkers. A history of UCATT by the past General Secretary Leslie Wood, *A Union To Build*, was published by Lawrence and Wishart in 1979.

The records of UCATT and its several predecessors have largely been deposited at the Modern Records Centre, University of Warwick, although there are significant holdings at other repositories. The principal collection at the Modern Records Centre is MSS 78. The UCATT material itself consists of the minutes of the national negotiating committees for Ford Motor Co., 1974–78, and oil refinery craftsmen, 1959–73; subject files, 1959–77, and union agreements, 1948–84. In addition there are minutes of the advisory panel of the UCATT Supervisory, Technical, Administrative, Managerial and Professional Section for 1979–80 and ephemera from the

1930s to 1976. The papers of the Bradford District of UCATT for the period 1933–79 are reported to have been deposited with the West Yorkshire Archives Service.

The other material held at the Modern Records Centre, and at other repositories, is best described as follows by constituent organisations.

AMALGAMATED SOCIETY OF PAINTERS AND DECORATORS

The union incorporated the National Amalgamated Society of Operative House and Ship Painters and Decorators. The Modern Records Centre holds Executive Committee minutes, 1904–70; General Council minutes, 1961–69; an investment register for 1902–64; a run of the *Monthly Journal*, 1921–70; reports, 1916–69; and rulebooks for 1960 and 1966. A list is available for these papers (NRA 23428).

AMALGAMATED SOCIETY OF WOODWORKERS

The Modern Records Centre holds General Council appeals files, 1963–67; Executive Committee minutes, 1915–68; cash books, 1949–64; printed annual reports, 1921–65; rulebooks, 1921–65; a large series of copy out-letters, other correspondence and subject files, 1916–67. A list is available for these papers (NRA 23650). Within this collection are also miscellaneous papers of the London District Management Committee for 1860–1957. Researchers should also be aware that the Management Committee minutes of the Manchester District for 1941–70 have been deposited with the Local Studies Unit of Manchester Central Library (ref. M 525; see list NRA 30884); that certain records of the Nottingham District for 1920–53 are at the University of Nottingham Library (see list NRA 7835), and that papers from the South Devon Area for the period 1931–57 are at Devon Record Office, for which there is a list (NRA 18858).

AMALGAMATED UNION OF BUILDING TRADE WORKERS

The union came into being in 1921 through the amalgamation of the Operative Bricklayers' Society of London and the Manchester Unity of Operative Bricklayers. It merged with the Building and Monumental Association of Scotland in 1942; with the National Builders', Labourers' and Constructional Workers' Society in 1952, and finally in 1969 with the Amalgamated Slaters, Tilers and Roofing Operatives Society.

Deposited at the Modern Records Centre in collection MSS 78 are various series of minutes (including those of the Executive Committee and the Rules Revision Committee), 1919–71; balance sheets, 1921–38; accounting volumes, 1938–71; union benefit payment books, 1965–72; head office circulars to branches, 1921–67; printed annual, monthly and quarterly reports, 1921–70; printed reports of the National Delegate Conference proceedings, 1922–63; rulebooks, 1921–53; some correspondence files; publications; and copies of union agreements. In addition the collection includes the minutes of the Eastern Counties Division Council for 1919–51. There is a list for these papers (NRA 8970). Miscellaneous records of the Lincoln District of the union for the period 1941–67 have now been deposited at Lincolnshire Archives (ref. Misc Dep 409/1) and a list is likewise available (NRA 25471).

The Modern Records Centre also holds Annual Reports and balance sheets for the period 1927–50 from the National Builders' Labourers' and Constructional Workers' Society, and certain papers of the Amalgamated Slaters, Tilers and Roofing Operatives Society. The latter originated with the Amalgamated Slaters' and Tilers' Provident Society of 1882; it adopted the above name in 1946, and transferred engagements to the AUBTW in 1969. The papers deposited at the Modern Records Centre were transferred there from the Brynmor Jones Library, University of Hull. There is a list for these papers (NRA 23738).

ASSOCIATION OF BUILDING TECHNICIANS

The union was established in 1919 as the Architects' and Surveyors' Assistants Professional Union. The Modern Records Centre has an incomplete series of Executive and General Council minutes, 1919–69; AGM minutes, 1919–69; accounts from the 1940s to the 1960s; a run of the journal *Keystone*, 1921–68, and other publications. There is a list (NRA 22557).

UNION OF DEMOCRATIC CONTROL The UDC was founded in September 1914 with the aim of securing a new course in diplomatic policy; its principles were the ending of the War by negotiation, no annexations, open diplomacy and general disarmament.

The UDC continued until 1967 when it was wound up and its papers deposited in the Brynmor Jones Library, University of Hull (ref. DDC). A list is available to the collection (NRA 13535). The postwar series of minutes among the surviving papers comprise those of the Executive Committee, 1915–54; Management Subcommittee, 1954–56; Branches and Affiliated Organisations Subcommittee, 1954–66, and the Publications Subcommittee, 1955. Minute books of the General Council survive for the period 1914–38 only. Financial records include ledgers, cash books, and income and expenditure accounts for 1927–66. There are a considerable number of subject files, chiefly covering the 1950s and 1960s. Only a limited amount of correspondence survives.

In addition to the subject files there are files of papers relating to the AGMs, 1960–63, general circulars to the Executive Committee, 1962–63; and a collection of the correspondence of the last Secretary of the UDC, C.R. Sweetingham, relating to the winding up of the Union and the transfer of its records to Hull (1967–74). The surviving printed material in the collection comprises a large number of books, periodicals and pamphlets published by the UDC from 1915 onwards; the only post-war material – with the exception of a very small number of books and examples of publications assembled for an exhibition on the UDC – consists of pamphlets nos. 197–286 (up to 1963). Among the miscellaneous material in the collection there are several numbered parcels (ref. DDC/4) comprising files of the 1940s and 1950s on different regions, and an original bundle of papers relating to a conference on 'The Crisis in Africa' of 22–23 October 1950.

It may be of interest to researchers that the archive contains some papers of E.D. Morel, the founding Secretary of the UDC, although these records are exclusively pre-war in date; other material relevant to the origins of the UDC may be found in the E.D. Morel Collection at the LSE Library.

UNION OF JEWISH WOMEN The Union of Jewish Women was established in 1902 as the representative body for Jewish women concerned with the welfare of educated women and girls. An archive of its papers in *c.* 28 boxes and eight volumes has now been transferred to the Hartley Library, University of Southampton (ref. MS 129). The material includes minute books for the Executive Committee, 1902–72; AGM, 1960–71; Council, 1963–70; General Welfare Subcommittee, 1946–59; the Case Subcommittee, 1943–62, and the Loan Funds Subcommittee, 1943–59. In addition there is a run of the Annual Report for 1903–61 and a number of attendance registers for the various committees, 1958–71. There is considerable material on the administration of the Helen Lucas bequest fund and Helen Lucas House (including the minutes of its committee, 1968–78; financial papers; and applications for admission, etc.).

UNION OF LIBERAL STUDENTS Some records for the period 1980–88 were deposited in the LSE Library in 1988 (ref. M1639). The collection is uncatalogued and enquiries concerning access should be directed to the archivist. In 1990, three additional boxes of papers were received from the Social and Liberal Democrats' Student Office (ref. M1687). These consist of ULS and SDP student newsletters, papers, policy files, publications and leaflets.

UNION OF SHOP, DISTRIBUTIVE AND ALLIED WORKERS The union was formed in 1947 by the amalgamation of the National Union of Distributive and Allied Workers, formed 1921, and the National Amalgamated Union of Shop Assistants, Warehousemen and Clerks, formed 1898. These incorporated smaller unions of an earlier period.

The union still retains its records. These are described in *Sources, 1900–51*, vol. I, pp. 270–71. In addition, reference should be made to the Hallsworth papers, deposited in the Modern Records Centre, University of Warwick (ref. MSS 70).

UNISON This new union was created in 1993 by the amalgamation of COHSE, NALGO and NUPE. The archives of these constituent members of UNISON have all been deposited in the Modern Records Centre, University of Warwick. In this volume, they are listed separately under their respective names. The Modern Records Centre already has extensive deposits of UNISON's own papers, including some of Rodney Bickerstaffe, the former General Secretary (ref. MSS 389).

UNITED COMMERCIAL TRAVELLERS' ASSOCIATION Some records of this association, now the UCTA section of the Manufacturing, Science and Finance Union (q.v.), have been deposited in the Modern Records Centre, University of Warwick (ref. MSS 79). The records include various series of minutes, 1888–1966; the journal (incomplete), 1883–1974; minutes and financial records of various branches.

UNITED EUROPE MOVEMENT Material concerning this organisation may be found in the papers of the publisher Victor Gollancz at the Modern Records Centre, University of Warwick (ref. MSS 157). Papers relating to a committee of this organisation known as the 'Churchill Committee', which was active in London during the 1940s, may be found in both the Churchill papers and the Duncan-Sandys papers at Churchill College, Cambridge.

UNITED KINGDOM COUNCIL FOR OVERSEAS STUDENT AFFAIRS UKCOSA is a registered charity established in 1968 to promote the interests and meet the needs of overseas students in the UK and those working with them as teachers and advisers or in other capacities.

UKCOSA retains its own archive. Available papers consist of minutes of the Executive Committee from 1968 to the present; Annual Reports since 1968, and discussion papers and special reports on topics of concern to UKCOSA (e.g. financial support for overseas students, and voluntary sector provision). Financial records, correspondence and subject files are unavailable. Persons wishing to use the archive should contact the Publications Officer.

UNITED KINGDOM TEMPERANCE ALLIANCE The United Kingdom Temperance Alliance, a limited company, was formed in 1942 to pursue the educational work of the United Kingdom Alliance, which had itself been founded in 1853 with the aim of suppressing the liquor traffic. The two organisations de-merged in the early 1980s. UKTA is now the parent body of a research organisation, the Institute of Alcohol Studies, in whose archives is deposited the historic collection of temperance materials assembled by the United Kingdom Alliance. These papers mostly cover the period from the mid-19th century to the 1930s and can be made available to researchers by appointment. The material relates to the UK in general and is indexed by author and title. Included within the collection are the records of the United Kingdom Temperance Alliance, the Band of Hope (q.v.), the Rechabites, the National Commercial Temperance Union, the British Women's Total Abstinence Union and the International Order of Good Templars. There are also temperance histories, biographies, anecdotal writings and journals.

A portion of the archive is post-war in date and comprises a continuous series of the minutes of the United Kingdom Alliance from 1871 to 1969 and of the National Temperance Federation from 1940 to 1956; bound yearbooks dated 1940–79 for the UKA and bound reports covering 1950–71 for the Christian Economic and Social Research Foundation; volumes of published CESRF study reports dated 1961–74, and certain series of correspondence, including papers of the National Temperance Foundation, the Parliamentary Temperance Group and three boxes of miscellaneous material relating to the foundation of the National Council on Alcohol. Enquiries concerning the archive should be directed to the Librarian.

UNITED NATIONS ASSOCIATION OF GREAT BRITAIN AND NORTHERN IRELAND This association was founded in 1945 to support the work of the United Nations Organisation and is the direct descendant of the League of Nations Union. The early records (together with those of the League of Nations Union) have been deposited in the LSE Library (ref. Coll Misc 509). The collection is open and a handlist available. The deposit includes various committee minutes (to 1955); records of the Women's Advisory Council, 1957–70; membership committee records, 1968–70; UNA Information Notes, 1947–52, and *UN News*, 1947–53. A later deposit has also been made (ref. M 1761) of further minute books and files *c.* 1950–92. These are open.

In addition, the records of the South East Region of the UN Association were deposited in the LSE Library in 1989 through the good offices of Frank Field, MP (ref. M1676).

UNITED REFORMED CHURCH The United Reformed Church was formed in 1972 by the union of the Congregational churches and the Presbyterian Church in England. The archives are in the care of Westminster College, Cambridge.

The official URC papers, namely the minutes and correspondence files of the individual departments of the Church, continue to be maintained by those departments for the period since 1972 and are unlikely to be made available for researchers for a number of years. The material deposited in the Library includes the published *Annual Report* and *Assembly Record* of the URC General Assembly since 1972. Among the records of the predecessor churches, the papers of the individual committees of the Presbyterian Church have been deposited and are open, but material relating to the Congregational churches has tended to be collected instead by Dr Williams' Library. The Library of the URC History Society does, however, maintain a run of the *Congregational Year Book* for the period to 1972.

Complete sets of the Society's biannual *Journal* and those of its predecessors are also available. Files relating to the service of every Presbyterian minister have likewise been deposited and are open to researchers; for the period prior to 1972, the records of certain individual Presbyterian churches (e.g. session minutes) have been deposited. For the post-1972 period the practice of the Church has been to send this latter class of material to the appropriate county record office.

UNITED SOCIETY FOR CHRISTIAN LITERA-TURE The Society was formed in 1935 by the merger of the Religious Tract Society (founded in 1799) and the Christian Literature Society for India and Africa (established 1858). Its function was to produce religious literature for the UK and the colonies, and indeed any country in which British missionaries were active. The papers of the USCL have now been deposited in the Library of the School of Oriental and African Studies, University of London. They include the minutes of the

Executive Committee, 1799–1972; the Annual Report, 1816–1962 (and that of the Scottish Committee of the Society up to 1971), and copies of published tracts c. 1920–50. A copy of *A Short History of the USCL* by J.H. Mair (1969) is also contained within the collection.

UNITED SOCIETY FOR THE PROPAGATION OF THE GOSPEL The Society for the Propagation of the Gospel in Foreign Places was founded in 1701. In 1965 it merged with the Universities' Mission to Central Africa (founded 1857) to form the USPG.

The records have now been transferred to BLCAS (Rhodes House Library), Oxford. A description of the papers (when they were still at the USPG headquarters) is given in *Sources, 1900–51*, vol. I, pp. 273–74. Enquiries concerning more recent listings should be directed to Rhodes House Library. It is understood there is a forty-year rule of access.

UNITED WOOL, SHAWL, FALL AND ANTI-MACASSAR TRADES UNION The records for the period 1907 to 1963, including a bundle of notices, circulars and accounts for 1946–58, have been deposited in Nottinghamshire Archives Office (ref. DD 129/1).

UNIVERSITIES FEDERATION FOR ANIMAL WELFARE The UFAW was founded in 1938 as a federation of university welfare societies. It seeks to promote humane behaviour towards both wild and domestic animals and, with regard to animals used in scientific research, promotes the development of techniques of investigation which might minimise the discomfort suffered. The Federation does not however 'engage on either side in public controversies relating to the legitimacy of making scientific experiments on animals'. In 1987 it assumed responsibility for the management of the Humane Slaughter Association (founded 1911). It is reported in Adrian Allan, *University Bodies: A Survey of Inter- and Supra-University Bodies and their Records* (University of Liverpool Archives Unit, 1990) that full records of the Federation have been retained at its offices.

URDD GOBAITH CYMRU (WELSH LEAGUE OF YOUTH) The papers for the period 1931–81 have been placed in the National Library of Wales, where there is a list (in Welsh) available (NRA 40456).

URDD Y DEYRNAS (LEAGUE OF THE KINGDOM) Papers for period 1918–57 are reported to have been deposited in the National Library of Wales. Further enquiries should be directed to the Keeper of Manuscripts.

V

VEGETARIAN SOCIETY There are records in Greater Manchester County Record Office. A list is available (NRA 43732).

VICTIM SUPPORT Established in 1979 to assist and represent those who have been the victims of criminal acts, and their dependents and relatives, the National Association of Victim Support Schemes retains a comprehensive archive at its offices. The material includes minutes of the Council since 1980 and of the AGM since 1981; the papers of various committees (e.g. Compensation Working Party, 1981–85, and Policy Advisory Committee, 1982–87); a run of Annual Reports from 1979–80 onwards, and copies of the national newsletter, *Victim Support*, from its first issue in February 1980. All such records are available to researchers with the written permission of the Information Manager, but public access is not at present permitted to either financial records or correspondence files.

VICTORY FOR SOCIALISM CAMPAIGN Relevant material exists in the papers of Sir Frederick Messer, photocopies of which are available in Hull University Library, and also in the papers of Lord Hugh Jenkins of Putney, which have been deposited in the LSE Library. Further papers are believed to have remained with the former secretary, Walter Wolfgang. Enquiries should be directed to the LSE Library.

VOLUNTARY EUTHANASIA SOCIETY Formerly known as the Voluntary Euthanasia Legalisation Society and then as EXIT, the Society was founded in 1935. A collection of 12 boxes of papers covering the period from 1935 to 1977 has been deposited in the Contemporary Medical Archives Centre of the Wellcome Institute (ref. SA/VES). The records include minutes, correspondence, publications and press-cuttings, and the papers of C. Killick Millard, the first Hon. Secretary of the Society (1931–*c*.1950). A list is available (NRA 25587).

VOLUNTEER CENTRE UK
The Volunteer Centre was founded in 1973 as a national resource centre to promote volunteering and to encourage good practice, whether in the statutory or private sectors. The Centre provides information, training, publications and development advice. It has retained its archive, including copies of all its publications and the papers of the Board since the Centre's foundation, but the collection is at present closed to researchers.

W

WALES FOR THE ASSEMBLY CAMPAIGN (YMGYRCH CYMRU DROS Y CYNULLIAD) The papers of this organisation, which was formed to persuade Welsh electors to vote in favour of devolution at the referendum of March 1979, have been deposited in the National Library of Wales. They cover the years 1975 to 1979, and there is a list available (NRA 26130).

The papers were deposited at the National Library in two groups. The first, consisting of pamphlets, leaflets and circular letters from the head office and press statements, was deposited in October 1985 through the good offices of Mr Dafydd Williams, General Secretary of Plaid Cymru (q.v.), along with the Plaid Cymru papers relating to the referendum campaign. Wales for the Assembly Campaign, an independent all-party campaign, was organised from an office in Neville Street, Cardiff but much of the administrative work was undertaken by staff at Plaid Cymru's office in Cathedral Road.

The second group was donated by Mr. Barry Jones, Secretary of the Campaign, in November 1985. These papers comprise minutes and correspondence of the Action Committee, 1976–77; minutes of the Campaign Committee meetings, January 1978 – February 1979; correspondence, 1977–79; publicity, speeches etc, 1978–79, and press-cuttings of the 1970s. Further enquiries concerning access should be directed to the Keeper of Manuscripts at the National Library.

WELSH AGRICULTURAL ORGANISATION SOCIETY Founded in 1922, the Society is the central organisation for agricultural cooperation in Wales, representing constituent agricultural societies nationally and providing professional guidance. Prior to 1924 there was an Agricultural Organisation Society in England also but it was dissolved in that year and its duties were assumed by the Co-operation Committee of the National Farmers' Union. The National Library of Wales holds the records of the central administration of the WAOS and of its constituent national or regional agricultural co-operative societies. Most of the pre-1945 records were destroyed when the Society moved to new premises in 1958. The existing material was donated in 1984 and the written consent of the Society's officers is needed to examine papers less than thirty years old. A list is available (NRA 27634).

WELSH COMMUNIST PARTY An initial group of papers has been placed in the National Library of Wales by Bert Pearce of Cardiff. The collection comprises files of papers deriving from the convention of the party's annual Welsh Congress, 1960–82, and from its campaigns in general elections and by-elections, 1963–83. The collection is reported to be closed.

WELSH LANGUAGE SOCIETY Since its formation in 1962, various deposits of papers have been made at intervals in the National Library of Wales. Enquiries concerning scope and access should be directed to the National Library.

WELSH SECONDARY SCHOOLS ASSOCIATION Papers accumulated by Dr. John Herbert during his membership of the Association have been deposited at the National Library of Wales. A list is available (NRA 26130). The material consists of the minutes of the General Meetings, 1964–84; minutes of the Council, 1969–84; correspondence, 1969–84; financial papers, 1965–77; papers of subcommittees and working parties, 1968–82; and miscellaneous reports and discussion papers, 1972–84.

WESSEX REGIONALISTS Some records of this group have been deposited in Bristol University Library (ref. DM 1739). A list is available (NRA 40324). The collection comprises one box file of general correspondence, 1981–96, agendas and minutes of meetings, pamphlets, policy papers etc.

WEST MIDLAND GROUP ON POST-WAR RECONSTRUCTION AND PLANNING

The archives of this group, formerly in the office of the Bournville Village Trust, were placed in Birmingham University Library in February 1967. The Group was formed in 1941 and, over the next decade, was to exercise a considerable influence on local and regional affairs. The collection (which includes minutes and correspondence) has been listed.

WIDER SHARE OWNERSHIP COUNCIL

There are papers, c. 1958–c. 2003, in the LSE Library (ref. M 3214). The collection, 65 boxes in all, includes correspondence, minutes, conference papers, reports and publications, including material relating to the merger with Proshare. There are also personal papers of George Copeman, mainly relating to employee share ownership and business management.

WIRE WORKERS' UNION

Until 1986 the union was known as the Amalgamated Society of Wire Drawers and Kindred Workers. It is the oldest trade union operating in the wire industry and was founded as a friendly society in 1840. The headquarters have always been located in Sheffield. Papers for the period 1906–64 have been deposited in Sheffield City Library (ref. 520/G) and a list is available (NRA 26196).

WOMEN AGAINST PIT CLOSURES

Some records of this group (and the South Wales Women's Support Group) can be found in Glamorgan Archives Service (ref. Acc 1999/70). The collection includes minutes and accounts, 1984–94.

WOMEN AGAINST RAPE (LONDON)

Women Against Rape (London) offers counselling, legal advice and support for women and girls who have been raped or sexually assaulted. It liaises with the police and arranges court testimony, health referrals, rehousing, claiming benefits and compensation and other practical assistance. It also seeks legislative change.

WAR has retained its archives. Whilst minutes and much correspondence are confidential, the non-confidential files are organised by subject and are available for use by the public, subject to arrangement.

WOMEN AGAINST THE COMMON MARKET

Reference should be made to the papers of Anne Kerr, former MP for Rochester and Chatham, in the Brynmor Jones Library, University of Hull (ref. DMK). The Kerr papers contain committee minutes, correspondence with other anti-Common Market organisations, such as the Common Market Safeguards Campaign (CMSC) and the Keep Britain Out Campaign, etc., and subject files relating to the national anti-Common Market campaign. A list is available (NRA 38979).

WOMEN FOR WESTMINSTER

WFW, founded in 1942, continued the work of the pre-war Central Women's Electoral Committee which had sought to increase the number of women elected to Parliament. In 1949 it was absorbed by the National Women Citizens' Association (q.v.). Its surviving records are incorporated in the Teresa Billington-Greig papers deposited in the Women's Library (q.v.). The files include newsletters for the period 1945 to 1949; educational broadsheets; pamphlets dating from the late 1940s, and the records of the Bournemouth branch for 1943–46.

WOMEN'S CAMPAIGN FOR SOVIET JEWRY

There are papers of the Campaign, 1970–93, in the Hartley Library, University of Southampton (ref. MS 254).

WOMEN'S CARAVAN OF PEACE

The Women's Caravan of Peace was a movement led by the radical feminist writer, Dora Russell, which in 1958 travelled across Europe to Moscow and back to support the cause of nuclear disarmament. Its complete papers are to be found among Dora Russell's own papers at the International Institute of Social History in Amsterdam, but researchers should note that there is relevant material among the records of the Co-operative Women's Guild deposited in the Brynmor Jones Library, University of Hull (ref. DCW). A list is available to this latter collection (NRA 20163).

WOMEN'S ENGINEERING SOCIETY The objects of the Society, which was founded in 1919, are: to promote the study and practice of engineering among women; to encourage their education in universities, and to act as a professional society for practising women engineers.

The Society retains its own archive, which consists of unpublished Council and Executive Committee minutes from 1944 to the present; Annual Reports from 1926 onwards; copies of its quarterly journal, *The Woman Engineer*, since the commencement of publication in 1919, and recent correspondence. Some of the records have been deposited with the Institution of Electrical Engineers but researchers should in all cases apply to the Secretary of the Society at the Department of Civil Engineering, Imperial College of Science and Technology, London.

Additional material is available in the papers of Ira Rischowski, which were deposited in the Women's Library (q.v.) in 1987. The records in six boxes include copies of Council minutes, 1943–77; AGM/conference papers, 1970–83; London branch committee minutes, 1959–82; and files of publications and correspondence, 1945–83. The Women's Library itself also holds copies of *The Woman Engineer* since 1938.

WOMEN'S FORUM In 1939 the Women's Group on Problems Arising from Evacuation was established under the auspices of the National Council of Social Service (NCSS) to assist the process of civilian evacuation in wartime. In the post-war era this organisation, renamed the Women's Group on Public Welfare, acted as the link between national organisations and the local branches of the Standing Conference of Women's Organisations or SCWO (q.v.). When the NCSS was restructured in 1975 to become the National Council for Voluntary Organisations (NCVO), the WGPW assumed the title of Women's Forum. However the NCVO decided to end its secretarial and financial support, and as a result the Women's Forum was dissolved in 1980.

The papers were deposited in the Women's Library (q.v.) in 1981. Files closed during or before the 1960s were weeded by the NCSS at least once and heavily in certain cases; later files were weeded

much more erratically. The material comprises Executive Committee minute books (1939–80), agendas and reports (1963–74), and correspondence (1943–73); minute books of meetings (1942–80); AGM minutes and agendas (1945 and 1948–73) and correspondence (1959–63); annual reports (1946–79); documents relating to the dissolution of the Women's Forum; publicity files (1961–70); records relating to the circulation and finance of publications (1959–69), and assorted subject files (e.g. of various committees and working parties on hygiene, housing, social security, food education, women's education, loneliness, and the organisation of women's groups).

In addition the collection contains the papers of the Council of Scientific Management in the Home (COSMITH), covering the period 1931 to 1977; the files (to 1975) of the WGPW International Advisory Group/Committee on topics of post-war reconstruction; papers of the joint WGPW/SCWO conferences (1944–76) and of individual local Standing Conferences, mostly dating from the 1940s to the 1960s, and SCWO Advisory Committee minutes, correspondence, reports and papers for 1942 to 1975.

WOMEN'S FREEDOM LEAGUE The League was established in 1907 by a number of activists who seceded from the Women's Social and Political Union on the issue of constitutional democracy. Following the achievement of partial female suffrage in 1918 the League concentrated on the aim of equal citizenship for both sexes. The League maintained close links with the International Alliance of Women. The papers have been deposited in the Women's Library (q.v.) and the post-war material in the collection consists of National Executive Committee minutes to 1961 and a pamphlet collection. A list is available (NRA 20625). A small amount of related material appears in the papers of Teresa Billington-Greig, also in the Women's Library.

WOMEN'S HEALTH CONCERN Records for the period *c.* 1970–2000 have been placed in the Contemporary Medical Archives Centre, Wellcome Institute (ref. SA/WHC).

WOMEN'S INTERNATIONAL LEAGUE FOR PEACE AND FREEDOM Founded in 1915 by Jane

Addams and Emily Greene Balch, among others, the League aimed to bring together women of different political and philosophical tendencies united in the determination to study, make known and abolish the political, social, economic and psychological causes of war, and to work for a constructive peace.

A large assortment of the League's records and other material relating to the peace movement has been deposited in the LSE Library. The collection is open and a draft handlist available. Post-1945 material includes Executive Committee minutes (to 1954); annual reports of the British Section (to 1961); copies of the *Monthly Newsheet* (to 1951), and many papers of the International Executive and of International Congresses.

The LSE Library has also received the papers acquired by Mary Nuthall, President of the WILPF, which have relevant material on the British section of the movement.

Further records of the League, 1919–99, including minutes, financial records, correspondence and campaign files, are in the Women's Library, London Metropolitan University (q.v.).

WOMEN'S INTERNATIONAL ZIONIST ORGANISATION (WIZO) Records for the period 1919–86 can be found in London Metropolitan Archives.

WOMEN'S LIBRARY The Women's Library, based in London Metropolitan University, is the essential starting point for research into women's history. The successor to the Fawcett Library, it holds the archives of innumerable women's organisations and pressure groups, as well as the papers of several hundred individuals. Some of these collections are cited in this Guide, but researchers should visit the Women's Library website.

ACTION OPPORTUNITIES

Minutes and accounts, 1976–85.

CENTRAL BERKSHIRE EQUAL OPPORTUNITIES GROUP

A non-partisan group established in January 1976 to publicise recent legislation on equal opportunities

and to monitor its implementation. The papers (largely minutes of meetings) cover the period 1976–79.

INTERNATIONAL ALLIANCE OF WOMEN

Minutes, policy and subject files, together with biographical material, publications etc., dated *c.* 1904–91 have been deposited.

NATIONAL WOMEN'S REGISTER

Launched in 1960 by Wirral housewife Maureen Nicol as an organisation of 'liberal-minded housebound wives', the body, which aimed to organise discussion groups for women, was known as the National Housewives' Register until 1987. The first twenty years are described in Betty Jarman's history, *The Lively-Minded Woman* (1981). The records comprise publicity papers for conferences (local, national and international), 1979–80; a scrapbook of the Silver Jubilee, 1985; circulars; copies of the *National Newsletter*, 1965–89, and the international bulletin *The Register*, 1977–88; publicity leaflets and press-cuttings, and the papers of a number of local groups in Bradford, Cheshire, Merton and Morden and High Wycombe East. A list is available (NRA 33570).

NATIONALITY OF MARRIED WOMEN COMMITTEE

The Committee was formed in the pre-war period to campaign for an alteration of legislation to allow a British woman to retain her citizenship upon marriage to a foreigner. The group was wound up having achieved its aim with the Nationality Act of 1948. The records, which cover the 1920s to 1940s, comprise minutes, correspondence and printed papers.

WOMEN FOR PEACE

The papers of the Woodford and Wanstead Branch are available for the period 1984–89. The Branch was influenced by the Greenham Common women's movement and also drew on a local tradition of political activism which had begun with Sylvia Pankhurst.

WOMEN IN ENTERTAINMENT

A GLC-funded body, it coordinated and represented women's theatre groups nationally. Established in 1980, it ceased operating following the termination of its GLC grant in 1987. The papers include correspondence, newsletters and published papers for 1980–85. Most of the material consists of press-cuttings and publicity material of various groups across the country.

WOMEN IN MEDIA

Active in the 1970s. The records comprise one box of correspondence and programmes, c. 1973–80.

WOMEN'S PRESS CLUB

Founded in 1943 under the presidency of Lady Rhondda the Club continued until 1972, one year after women were admitted into the Press Club itself. Possibly the most significant women's press club in the world, during World War II it succeeded in gaining for women proper recognition as war correspondents. The archives at the Women's Library are the gift of Phyllis Deakin, a founder member and journalist at *The Times*. The papers, which cover c. 1944–72, are minutes, financial records, correspondence, newsletters, photographs and membership cards.

WOMEN'S PROVISIONAL CLUB

A businesswomen's philanthropic organisation (a female equivalent of Rotary), the Club was later associated with the British Federation of Business and Professional Women (q.v.). Minutes, membership records and printed papers for 1924–79 have been deposited.

WOMEN'S MIGRATION AND OVERSEAS APPOINTMENT SOCIETY Founded in 1919 as

the Society for the Overseas Settlement of British Women, the Society was financially aided by the British government and acted in a semi-official capacity under legislation to promote female emigration. After World War II the Society became more involved in finding posts for trained women overseas, which ultimately led it to adopt the above

name in 1962 to reflect the change in its function. However, termination of the government grant led to the winding up of the Society two years later and its records were deposited in the Women's Library (q.v.), although material considered confidential was destroyed.

The papers comprise Executive Committee minute books, 1920–67; Finance Committee minute books, 1919–64; annual reports, 1920–60 and 1961–63; documents of the Society's legal incorporation under the Companies Act; records of Treasury Grants, 1919–64; correspondence files etc.

WOMEN'S PUBLICITY PLANNING ASSOCIATION The WPPA was formed in 1939 to

increase the exchange of information between existing women's organisations, both in Great Britain and abroad. It was involved in the Equal Compensation for War Injuries campaign in 1941 (which developed into the Equal Pay Campaign), and with the organisation Women For Westminster (q.v.), which originated as a committee of the WPPA in 1942. The Association was not active in any campaigns after World War II but was never formally wound up. The surviving papers have been deposited in the Women's Library (q.v.); they include minute books for the period 1939 to 1956 and the Secretary's correspondence for 1948–56. A list is available for the collection (NRA 33569).

WOMEN'S ROYAL VOLUNTARY SERVICE The

Women's Voluntary Service was founded at the invitation of the Home Secretary in 1938, during the national emergency prior to World War II, to help local authorities recruit women for the Air Raid Precautions Services. During the war it played a major role in providing humanitarian and emergency services to the civilian and military population. In the post-war era it has continued to provide volunteers for welfare work, maintain residential homes, and assist the emergency services. The name was changed to WRVS in 1966.

WRVS maintains its own records in the Archives Department at the head offices. Papers include comprehensive confidential records of the Chairman's Consultative Council; annual and regional reports since the foundation; correspondence arranged by subject, and subject files, containing miscellaneous papers arranged by topic and covering all aspects of WRVS work (e.g. hospital services, clothing stores, emergency services, family welfare, etc.). Current confidential financial records are maintained by the Finance Department. Access to these archives by non-members is allowed only with the permission of the Chairman, to whom application should be made.

WOODLAND TRUST, THE The Trust was founded in 1972 with the purpose of conserving native and broadleaved woodland by acquisition and management and replacing the woodland losses of the past by appropriate planting. The papers of the Trust remain in its care at the head office. They comprise the minutes of the Council of Management, annual reports and financial records, copies of the quarterly newsletter, and assorted correspondence files. Correspondence and minutes remain closed, but permission to consult the archival copies of the annual report and the newsletter may be sought from the Research and Information Officer.

WORKERS' EDUCATIONAL ASSOCIATION The Association was formed in 1903 with the specific aim of promoting education for the working class. Its stated object is 'to interest men and women in their own continued education and in the better education of their children.' Today it has over 800 branches arranged in 19 Districts, each governed by its own Council. A history of the WEA by Roger Fieldhouse entitled *The Workers' Educational Association: Aims and Achievements 1903–1977* was published by Syracuse University, New York, in 1977.

The archive of the WEA was transferred in 1998 from its Bethnal Green headquarters to join the TUC Library Collection at London Metropolitan University. A list is available (NRA 41853). The archive also contains records of the International Federation of WEAs (see NRA 41854). The records, 1925–93, of the Scottish WEA are in the National Library of Scotland (ref. Acc 11551).

The papers of Albert Mansbridge (1876–1952), founder of the Association, are in the British Library (ref Add MSS 65195–65368).

WORKERS' INTERNATIONAL LEAGUE Some records of this left-wing group are available at the Modern Records Centre, University of Warwick (ref. MSS 75). They include issues of *Socialist Appeal*, 1941–49, and *Workers' International News*, 1943–49. Researchers should also consult the records of the International Marxist Group, the predecessor of the Socialist Workers Party (q.v.).

WORKERS TRAVEL ASSOCIATION The records of the WTA for the period 1921–82 have been deposited in Kent Archives Office (ref. U 2543). They include copies of the Annual Report, 1925–54; Management Committee minutes, 1928–47; Finance and General Purposes Committee minutes, 1927–44; general correspondence, 1921–56; correspondence and claims concerning war damage, 1940–49; and newspaper cuttings, programmes, publicity literature, travel logs and examples of holiday brochures. There is a list available (NRA 28563).

WORKING MEN'S CLUB AND INSTITUTE UNION The Union, which is more commonly known as the Club and Institute Union (CIU), was established in London in 1862 on the initiative of the Revd Henry Solly as a non-political federation of clubs. An archive of records is maintained at the Union's headquarters and access will generally be granted to academic researchers. The surviving material includes committee minutes from 1862 onwards and copies of the Annual Report, which has been published continuously since that date and which incorporates annual accounts. Ledger books are retained only for the statutory period and are not available for inspection. Minutes of the Union's conference have been published in the monthly *Journal* since 1873, but as a result of extensive clearances in 1962 and again in 1973 no correspondence, except for current material, has survived.

WORLD ASSEMBLY OF YOUTH Relevant material, largely covering the early 1950s, is available among the papers of the Liberal Party activist Derek Mirfin, which have been deposited at the University of Bristol Library (ref. DM 668).

WORLD CONGRESS OF FAITHS The papers, deposited in the Hartley Library, University of Southampton, include minutes, correspondence, financial records, various branch records etc., 1924–92 (ref. MS 222).

WORLD DEVELOPMENT MOVEMENT The World Development Movement originated in the growing organisation of groups concerned with development education during the 1960s. In 1969 the leading development agencies founded Action for World Development to act as a co-ordinating body for local groups, and to circumvent the legal restrictions on the political activity of charitable groups. The World Development Movement, established the following year, extended its work; its constitution permits individuals as well as organisations to be members. WDM is a founder member of the International Coalition for Development Action (ICDA); since 1978 its Churches' Committee has promoted an annual programme of study and action for world development known as 'One World Week'. In particular, since the 1980s WDM has lobbied the government to increase the amount of foreign aid granted by the UK and to improve the status of the Overseas Development Agency.

WDM presently retains its archive. The papers include committee minutes since the mid-1970s for the Council and various subcommittees such as Finance, Campaigns, Churches etc, and Annual Reports for a similar period. Correspondence files are incomplete but do include some correspondence with UK government departments such as the Foreign Office and the Overseas Development Agency. There is an extensive series of newspaper cuttings on development issues on which WDM has campaigned, such as international debt, overseas aid, international trade, environment and development and the policies of the British political parties as they relate to overseas development. Financial records have also been kept, as have copies of some of WDM's publications from the mid-1970s onwards relating mainly to trade issues.

Persons who wish to use the files of newspaper cuttings or the copies of published reports retained by WDM should apply in writing to the Information Officer. Permission for access to internal documents should be sought from the Director.

WORLD DISARMAMENT CAMPAIGN UK The Campaign was founded in 1980 to promote disarmament and encourage the reallocation of military expenditure to world development. Its papers, at present retained at its offices, comprise minutes since the date of foundation; copies of its pamphlets (including a report on the June 1990 convention on disarmament, development and the environment), and the bi-monthly journal *World Disarm!* The papers would in principle be open to researchers by appointment.

WORLD EDUCATION FELLOWSHIP The Society was founded in 1921 as the New Education Fellowship. It adopted its present title in 1966 to emphasise its international scope. The Fellowship seeks improvement and reforms in world education.

The extensive records of the Fellowship have been deposited in the Library of the Institute of Education, University of London. Enquiries concerning access etc should be directed to the Librarian at the Institute.

WORLD FEDERATION OF RIGHT TO DIE SOCIETIES Records can be found in the Contemporary Medical Archives Centre, Wellcome Institute (ref. SA/OMG). The most recent deposit includes papers, 1958–2000.

WORLD FEDERATION OF SCIENTIFIC WORKERS A major series of records dating from the foundation of the Federation in 1946 has been deposited at the Modern Records Centre, University of Warwick (ref. MSS 270). The material comprises various series of minutes, 1946–92; General Assembly reports and papers, 1948–76; Treasurer's records, 1946–78; correspondence, subject files (including some generated by the Federation's Paris office) and circulars, 1947–79; *Scientific World*, 1957–92, and photographs, 1940s–70s. The collection also includes the papers of Dr. W.A. Wooster (Treasurer of the Federation), 1946–78. The Modern Records Centre continues to receive additional deposits.

WORLD JEWISH CONGRESS (BRITISH SECTION) Enquiries should be directed to the Hartley Library, University of Southampton, which has relevant papers.

WORLD SECURITY TRUST Six boxes of records relating to this organisation may be found among the papers of Lord Duncan-Sandys deposited at Churchill College, Cambridge.

WRITERS AND SCHOLARS EDUCATIONAL TRUST WSET originated in a 1971 campaign conducted by Western writers and intellectuals on behalf of the persecuted Soviet writers Ginzburg and Galanskov. At the suggestion of Russian authors, a committee was formed to assist writers who were subject to political censorship. This led to the creation of the charity Writers and Scholars Educational Trust and the associated Writers and Scholars International Ltd, which publishes the magazine *Index on Censorship*. *Index* exists to publicise cases of the restriction of free speech and the name is used loosely to describe both WSI and WSET. Both organisations seek to protect the freedom of expression and the right of access to information and do so by monitoring cases of censorship.

The archive of WSI/WSET is retained at its office. It includes the post-1971 minutes of the Council, editorial committee and finance committee, and of the trustees' annual and other meetings. Annual Reports are available for each financial year beginning with 1975–76. The accounts of WSI and WSET are separately maintained and are available for the period since 1971; other financial records are retained for the statutory period only. Copies are kept of WSI/WSET's own publications, including *Index on Censorship* since 1972, and some examples of underground publications from Europe. Substantial subject files have also been maintained, for example on individual Soviet dissidents and topics relevant to free speech. Press-cuttings files, organised by country, form a substantial portion of the archive. Those wishing to use the papers should apply to the Director.

Y

YOUNG ENTERPRISE In 1962 Sir Walter Salomon established Young Enterprise as a charitable organisation to provide young people (whilst in education or prior to full-time employment) with practical experience of business management by allowing them to run their own companies. The organisation has subsequently retained its own papers, to which access may be obtained by writing to the Chief Executive. Surviving material comprises minutes of council meetings since 1962; financial records since 1981 and financial reports from 1987, and correspondence, organised by subject and organisation, from 1980 onwards.

YOUNG MEN'S CHRISTIAN ASSOCIATION The YMCA was founded in London in 1844 and quickly expanded throughout Great Britain and abroad, embracing earlier organisations of a similar nature. The YMCA remains an inter-denominational, active missionary organisation, which promotes the physical, intellectual and spiritual fitness, training and well-being of youth. The association's activities extend to the provision of social, cultural and educational services, and close relations are maintained with the YWCA.

The papers, previously in private possession, have now been placed in the University of Birmingham (ref. Acc 2000/79). Records of YMCA Scotland are in the National Library of Scotland for the period 1910–90.

Researchers should note that the Public Record Office of Northern Ireland holds a series of records covering YMCA work in Ireland during the years 1862–67, 1887–1951 and 1951–83 (ref. D 3788). The material includes administrative and working papers and membership records. Certain items are closed.

YOUNG WOMEN'S CHRISTIAN ASSOCIATION The YWCA was formed in 1877 as a result of the merger of the Prayer Union and Lady Kinnaird's Homes. It aims to promote world-wide fellowship and understanding of the Christian faith, and to advance education and welfare, especially among young people. A separate YWCA of Scotland was set up in 1924.

A large collection of records has been deposited in the Modern Records Centre, University of Warwick (ref. MSS 243). They include minutes and papers of numerous committees; annual reports; records of YWCA work in both World Wars; correspondence and subject files, 1890s–1950s (topics include industrial legislation, female emigrant welfare and refugee assistance); YWCA testimonies and related papers of Royal Commissions and other enquiries, 1919–53; Annual Review, 1913–51; *Blue Triangle Gazette*, 1929–55; and other publications, 1870s–1970s.

YOUTH DEVELOPMENT ASSOCIATION LTD YDA (also known as the Community and Youth Development Association) is the national professional body for youth and community workers. It was founded in 1980 and incorporated the following year. Throughout its history YDA has been closely associated with the Oldham Youth Development Office, a co-ordinating and support body for voluntary and innovative youth care, which since 1991 has been replaced by the Oldham Council for Voluntary Youth Services (OCVYS).

The records of YDA are retained at its national office. These include committee minutes, copies of special reports and subject files, and correspondence (much of which refers to youth work in other countries). The Association previously held the records of the former Oldham Youth Development Office for 1979–90, but these have been transferred to the newly created OCVYS. The papers of certain related bodies are also in the care of the YDA, such as the records of the British Guild of Drugless Practitioners. Applications for access to the papers should be addressed to the Hon. General Secretary at the national office.

YOUTH HOSTELS ASSOCIATION Prompted by the growth of continental hostel movements, in 1930 the National Council of Social Services held a conference to form a national association to promote youth hostels in Britain. In the post-war era the YHA has continued to be active in international hostelling and, via its Countryside Committee, in promoting public access to open spaces and the preservation of rights of way in cooperation with other groups.

The records of the YHA are retained at its National Office. They include general minute books since 1930 (for the National Council, Executive Com-mittee, and subsidiary committees); a National Council and Executive Committee attendance book, 1956–75; a register of directors and managers, 1936–48; files of committee memoranda since 1940; correspondence and administrative files of sub-sidiary committees; and files on individual hostels. Annual Reports and balance sheets are available from 1931 to date, and there is available a complete set of the journal, known as *The Rucksack* from 1936 to 1956 (with a supplementary *Bulletin*, 1947–56); the *Youth Hosteller*, 1957–72, and *Hostelling News* since 1972. Financial records, including cash books, date from 1933. Applications for access to the papers should be made to the National Secretary. A list is available (NRA 24465).

Z

THE ZIONIST FEDERATION OF GREAT BRITAIN AND NORTHERN IRELAND The Zionist Federation of Great Britain was formed in 1898, following the Clerkenwell Conference. It took its inspiration from the World Zionist Federation founded by Dr Theodore Herzl. Until 1931 the Federation was known as the English Zionist Federation, when its name was changed to the Zionist Federation of Great Britain and Ireland. In 1966, the present title was adopted. The Zionist Federation of Great Britain and Northern Ireland is affiliated to the World Confederation of General Zionists (which was situated in Britain until 1948).

Although recent records are retained in London, most of the archival material is sent periodically to the Central Zionist Archives, PO Box 92, Jerusalem, Israel. Students of Zionism in Britain should note that the CZA has a massive amount of relevant material. A separate repository of important Jewish holdings (as distinct from solely Zionist material) is the Anglo-Jewish Archive, now at the Hartley Library, University of Southampton.

Appendix 1
Britain and the World

ABBREVIATIONS and SYMBOLS

*	papers to be deposited; bequeathed to
**	small collection (not particularly significant for post-war period)
Admin	Administration/Administrator
AM	Air Marshal
AVM	Air Vice-Marshal
BL	British Library
Bodleian	Bodleian Library, Oxford
CAC	Churchill Archives Centre
C of E	Church of England
CCG	Control Commission Germany
CMAC	Wellcome Contemporary Medical Archives Centre
Comn	Commission
CSAC	Cambridge South Asian Centre
CUL	Cambridge University Library
E	East
FBI	Federation of British Industry
Gov	Governor
ICS	Indian Civil Service
Inst	Institute
Intl	International
IOL	India Office Library
IPS	Indian Political Service
IWM	Imperial War Museum
JRL	John Rylands University Library of Manchester
LHASC	Labour History Archive and Study Centre
LHCMA	Liddell Hart Centre for Military Archives
Lib	Library
LSE	London School of Economics
MEC	Middle East Centre, St Antony's College, Oxford
MoD	Ministry of Defence
N	Northern
NAM	National Army Museum
NLS	National Library of Scotland
NLW	National Library of Wales
NMM	National Maritime Museum
PM	Prime Minister
PRO	Public Record Office
PRONI	Public Record Office of Northern Ireland
RAF	Royal Air Force
RAFM	Royal Air Force Museum, Hendon
RAI	Royal Artillery Institution, Woolwich
RAMC	Royal Army Medical Corps
RCS	Royal Commonwealth Society
RHL	Rhodes House Library, Oxford
RMM	Royal Marines Museum, Eastney
RN	Royal Navy
RO	Record Office
S	South
SOAS	School of Oriental and African Studies, London University
tspt	transcript of interview
U	University
UN	United Nations
W	West
WHO	World Health Organisation
WWI	World War I
WWII	World War II

Names followed by location of papers:

ABRAHAMS, Abraham *(British Zionist)*
Jabotinsky Inst, Israel

AIREY, Sir Terence *(Army General)*
IWM (Trieste, 1947)

Alexander-Sinclair, John (UN official)
Bodleian (UN project)

ALLISON, Oliver *(Anglican Bishop, Sudan)*
Sudan Archive, Durham

ANDERTON, Geoffrey *(RAMC officer)*
LHCMA (Anzio, Hong Kong and Korea, 1944–52)

ANSTRUTHER-GOUGH-CALTHORPE, Sir Richard
(Army Brigadier)
LHCMA

APPLETON, George *(Anglican Archbishop, Jerusalem)*
IOL (Burma, WWII)

ARNOT, John *(Army Major)*
NAM (UN ops, Congo, 1961)

ARTHUR, Allan *(ICS and Sudan)*
Durham U Lib; CSAC

Atkinson, J.B. (on World Council of Churches)
Bodleian

BADER, SIR DOUGLAS (RAF officer; aviation industry)
RAFM

BAILLIE-GROHMAN, Harold Tom *(RN Admiral)*
NMM (WWII and post-war Germany)

BAKSTANSKY, Lavy *(British Zionist)*
Weizmann Archives, Israel; Board of Deputies HQ, London

BARBOUR, Neville *(Arab propagandist)*
MEC

BARLOW, Henry *(ICS to 1947; Rhodesia)*
CSAC

BARNETT, DAME HENRIETTA (WRAF Director, 1950s)
LHCMA

BAZALGETTE, Major John *(IPS to 1947)*
IOL

BEAUMONT, Christopher *(Legal career)*
All Souls, Oxford (Indian-Pakistan Border Comn, 1947)

BELCHEM, Ronald *(Army General)*
IWM and RAI (WWII)

BELGRAVE, Sir Charles *(Financial adviser)*
Cambridge Middle East Centre (Bahrein, 1936–57)

BELL, Frank *(ICS to 1947)*
IOL

BENTHALL, Sir Edward *(Banker and politician)*
CSAC (India, 1929–56)

BILLING, Melvin *(Colonial Service)*
RHL (Rhodesia, 1930–62)

BIRD, Sir Cyril *(Ugandan politician)*
RHL

BIRD, P.B. *(RN officer)*
IWM (Monte Bello atomic tests, 1952)

BISCOE, Major Dudley *(IPS to 1946)*
IOL

BLACKALL, Sir Henry *(Colonial Legal Service)*
RHL (W Indies, W Africa, Cyprus)

BLAKE, C.H.F. *(Malayan Civil Service)*
RHL (Malayan Emergency, 1945–57)

BLAKE, Sir Geoffrey *(RN Admiral)*
NMM

BLYTHE, Wilfred *(Colonial Service)*
RHL (SE Asia, 1940s and 1950s)

BONHAM-CARTER, David *(RAF officer)*
RAFM (WWII and Hong Kong 1951–53)

BOURDILLON, Henry *(Civil servant)*
RHL (Colonial policy statements, 1950s)

BOVELL, Sir Conrad Kerr *(Colonial police officer)*
RHL (tspt re: Malaya and Nigeria)

BOWEN-BUSCARLET, Sir Willett *(RAF AVM to 1946)*
RAFM

BOWRING, John *(Army General)*
LHCMA (Brunei Rebellion, 1963)

BOYD, Sir John *(RAMC Brigadier)*
Wellcome CMAC (tropical diseases)

BOYD, Lachlan MacPherson *(Colonial Service)*
RHL (Buganda, 1949)

BRIDGEMAN, Reginald *(Anti-imperialist)*
Brynmor Jones Lib, Hull U (China, Persia and Meerut)

BROMHEAD, Sir Benjamin *(IPS to 1947)*
IOL

BROOKE, Sir Charles Vyner *(Rajah of Sarawak, 1917–46)*
RHL (Sarawak, 1945–77)

BROWN, Lt Col. ARTHUR BRIAN (Army officer, Sudan)
LHCMA (WWII and Malaya, 1947–51)

BROWN, Dr A.E. *(WHO official)*
Bodleian (UN project) (SE Asia and Africa)

BROWN, Sir Frank *(The Times journalist, India)*
IOL

BROWN, William *(Army Major)*
NAM (Gilgit territorial dispute, India-Pakistan 1947)

BROWNING, Robert *(Indian Army Ordnance)*
NAM

BRUNSKILL, George *(Army Brigadier)*
IWM (WWII and Palestine)

BRYANT, H.C.A. *(Colonial Service, 1930s–50s)*
RHL (W Africa and W Pacific)

BUCHAN, Alistair *(Journalist)*
in family possession

BUCKNALL, Gerald *(Army General to 1947)*
IWM (WWII)

BURNETT, Sir Robert *(RN Admiral)*
IWM (mostly WWI and WWII)

BURNS, Sir Alan *(Colonial Service to 1947; UN)*
RHL (WWI); IWM (tspt re: W Africa)

BUTT, Walter *(Army Major)*
NAM (Korean War)

CALVERT, James Michael *(Counter-insurgency expert)*
IWM (tspt re: Vietnam and Portuguese Africa)

CALVERT-JONES, Percy *(Army General)*
IWM

CAMPBELL, Archibald *(Colonial Office and MoD)*
RHL (1980 election, Rhodesia)

CAMINADA, Jerome *(The Times journalist, Middle East and S Africa)*
News International Archives

CAMMAERTS, Emile *(Belgian scholar)*
U London Lib (abdication of King Leopold, 1950)

CANTLIE, Sir Neil *(RAMC General)*
CMAC (mostly WWII)

CAREW-HUNT, Geoffrey *(RN Admiral)*
IWM

CARPENTER, F.W. *(Colonial Service)*
RHL (Cameroons, 1928–55)

CARR, Edward Hallett *(Historian)*
Birmingham U Lib

CARR, Sir Frederick *(Colonial Service)*
RHL (Nigeria, 1919–49)

CARSON, J.B. *(Colonial Service)*
RHL (Kenya, 1960–62)

CARY, Joyce *(Novelist and Africanist)*
Bodleian

CHENEY, John Norman *(Army officer)*
IWM (war crimes trials, Germany, 1945–46)

CHILTON, Sir Maurice *(Army General)*
IWM (WWII)

CHRISTIE-MILLER, D.G. *(Colonial Service, Kenya)*
RHL (Mau Mau campaign, 1953–62)

CLARK, Sir George *(Historian)*
Bodleian and BL

CLAYTON, Brigadier Sir Iltyd *(Diplomat)*
MEC (Cairo, 1940s)

CLIVE, Nigel (*Diplomat*)
MEC (Palestine, 1948)

CLOW, Sir Andrew (*ICS; Gov of Assam to 1947*)
CSAC

COAD, Basil (*Army General*)
IWM (WWII and Korean War)

COHEN, Israel (*Zionist author*)
Central Zionist Archives, Jerusalem

COHN, Ernest (*Legal academic*)
Reading U Lib (Allied Administration of
Germany, 1944–45 and later papers)

COLE, Robert (*Medical doctor*)
SOAS (Africans in Britain)

COLEBROOK, Edward (*Indian Police Service
to 1949*)
IOL

COLLIER, Sir Alfred (*RAF AVM; post-war Civil
Aviation*)
LHCMA

COLLINGS, Alan (*Colonial Service*)
RHL (Tanganyika, 1940s–60s; New Hebrides,
W Indies and Gibraltar, 1970s)

COODE, E. James (*Colonial Service*)
RHL (Fiji and Tonga)

CORFIELD, F.D. (*Anthropologist*)
RHL (Mau Mau research papers)

CORRY, Wilfred (*Malayan Civil Service*)
RHL (tspt)

COUTTS, Sir Walter (*Colonial Gov*)
RHL (tspt re: Kenya and Uganda, 1955–61)

COWELL, Sir Ernest (*RAMC General*)
Wellcome CMAC

COX, Arthur (*Colonial Service*)
RHL (diary of African tour with Lord Hailey,
1947)

CRAWFORD, John Scott (*Army General*)
CAC (post-war armaments production and
NATO)

CRAWFORD, M.A.A. (*Colonial Police, Malaya*)
PRONI

CREASY, Sir George (*RN Admiral of the Fleet*)
NMM**

CREASY, Sir Gerald (*Colonial Gov*)
RHL (Gold Coast and Malta)

CREE, P.B. (*RN officer*)
IWM (WWII and Dutch East Indies, 1946)

CRESWELL, John (*RN officer*)
CAC

CRICK, Wilfred (*Economist and Middle East expert*)
PRO (Anglo-American Committee on
Palestine, 1946)

CROFT, Sir William (*Diplomat and civil servant*)
IOL (WWII and Pakistan; Balanpur 1946)

CROMWELL, Tom (*Malayan Civil Service*)
SOAS

CUNNINGHAM of Hyndhope, Lord (*RN Admiral
of the Fleet*)
BL; CAC; NMM

CURREY, Harry (*RN Admiral*)
IWM

CURTIS, Gerald (*ICS to 1946*)
IOL

CUSACK, Henry (*Colonial Service*)
RHL (W Africa)

DALTON, John Cecil (*Army General*)
IWM (WWII)

DASH, Sir Arthur (*ICS to 1942*)
IOL; CSAC (Bengal and E Pakistan Comns)

DAVEY, Peter (*Colonial Service*)
RHL (Aden, 1940s)

DAVIDSON, Francis (*Army General*)
LHCMA (WWII and post-war official histories)

DAVIES, Reginald (*Colonial Service*)
Edinburgh U Lib

DAVIES, Vincent (*ICS to 1947*)
IOL

DAVY, Anthony (*IPS to 1947*)
IOL (Indian-Pakistan relations during 1947–49
period)

DE WINTON, F.S.W. *(RN officer)*
IWM (WWII memoirs, W Africa 1945–46 and
Germany, 1946–47)

DE WINTON, M.G. *(Colonial Legal Service)*
RHL (Nigeria, 1940–60)

DEMPSEY, Sir Miles *(Army General)*
LHCMA and PRO (WWII)

DENNIS, A.H. *(Army Major)*
IWM (Japanese war criminals, 1947)

DICKSON, Murray *(Director of Education,
Sarawak)*
RHL (Sarawak, 1940s–60s)

DORMAN-SMITH, Sir Reginald *(Con MP, 1935–41;
Colonial Gov)*
IOL (Gov of Burma, 1941–46)

DOUGLAS, Arthur John *(Colonial Service)*
RHL (Bechuanaland, 1961–65)

DOUGLAS, John Albert *(Anglican clergyman)*
Lambeth Palace Lib (C of E Foreign Relations
Council)

DREW, Sir Robert *(RAMC General)*
CMAC**

DRING, Sir John *(IPS; PM Bahawalpur, 1948–52)*
IOL

DUCKWORTH, Ralph *(RN officer)*
LHCMA** (mostly pre-war)

DUNLOP, Sir John Kinninmont *(Army Brigadier and
historian)*
IWM (including post-war Italy and CCG)

DURNFORD, John *(RN Admiral)*
IWM

EARLE, Peter *(Army officer)*
IWM (1944–47 diaries as liaison officer to
Montgomery)

ELLIOTT, Geoffrey *(Army officer)*
LHCMA (WWII and Malaya, 1952)

ELSTON, David *(Journalist) (The Times; Palestine Post)*
News Intl Archives

ELWIN, Verrier *(Anthropologist, India)*
IOL

EMERSON, Gerald *(IPS to 1947)*
IOL

ENGLEDOW, Sir Frank *(Agriculturalist)*
CSAC; RHL

EVANS, David *(Sudan Political Service)*
Sudan Archive, Durham U Lib

EVANS, Sir Geoffrey *(Army General)*
IWM (WWII)

EVERETT, Edward *(Colonial policeman,
W Africa)*
IWM (tspt)

EVILL, Sir Douglas *(RAF ACM)*
RAFM

EYRE-WILSON, L.D. *(Colonial Service)*
RHL (labour and race relations, Rhodesia,
1940s–60s)

FAIRBURN, Harold *(Colonial policeman, pre-war)*
RHL (1950 Comn on Malaya)

FAVIELL, John *(Army Brigadier)*
IWM (Demobilisation admin 1945–46)

FEETHAM, Richard *(South African judge)*
RHL (South Africa; Kenya 1926; Irish Boundary
Comn 1925)

FELL, Douglas *(ICS; PM, Kalat, 1947–48)*
IOL

FELL, Sir Matthew *(RAMC General)*
CMAC

FERRIS, J.W. *(Colonial Service)*
RHL (WWII and Hong Kong, 1947–67)

FIELD, Sir John *(Colonial Gov)*
RHL

FINNEY, Philip *(Indian Police Service)*
CSAC

FIRTH, Sir Raymond *(Anthropologist)*
LSE (papers re African Natl U)

FLACK, Alan *(ICS)*
IOL (Bihar, 1936–47)

FLETCHER, P.D. *(Colonial Service)*
RHL (E Aden, 1940–50)

FORDE, Daryll *(Anthropologist, Africanist)*
RHL (SE Nigeria)

FRAMPTON, Henry *(ICS to 1947)*
IOL

FRANKLIN, Henry *(Colonial Service)*
RHL (Rhodesia, 1958–61)

FRASER, James George *(Anthropologist, Africanist)*
BL

FRENCH, Godfrey *(RN officer)*
CAC (Indian Navy, 1943–54)

FURLONGE, Sir Geoffrey *(Levant Consular Service)*
LHCMA

GAFFIKIN, T.Q. *(Colonial policeman)*
RHL (Malaya 1873–1957, including Emergency, 1950s)

GALE, Sir Humfrey *(Army General)*
LHCMA (WWII)

GARDNER, J.A. *(Colonial Service)*
RHL (Kenya, 1961–62)

GARSIDE, Kenneth *(Military intelligence, WWII)*
LHCMA (Enemy Publications Committee, 1946–48)

GIBB, I.S. *(Army officer)*
IWM (memoirs including Indonesia, Singapore and Malaya, 1945–50)

GILPIN, A.C. *(UN official)*
Bodleian (UN project) (Zambia and the Congo)

GIMSON, Sir Franklin *(Colonial Gov)*
RHL (WWII internee, Hong Kong)

GLENNIE, Alan *(Colonial Service)*
RHL (Rhodesia, 1950s–60s)

GODBER, Sir George *(WHO official)*
Bodleian (UN project)

GODDARD, Sir Robert *(RAF AM)*
LHCMA

GOEPEL, John *(Political officer)*
RCS Lib (Aden)

GOLDIE, Desmond *(Army officer)*
MEC (Arab Legion)

GOMME, S. *(Army officer)*
IWM (WWII and Indonesia, 1945)

GOODLIFE, Frederick *(Colonial Service)*
RHL (Nigeria, 1950s)

GORDON, John Mackillip *(Army officer)*
NAM (military prisons, 1940s)

GORDON-FINLAYSON, James *(RAF AVM)*
IWM (logbook, mostly WWII)

GOUT, W. *(Railway official)*
IWM (Iran, 1935–55)

GRAHAM, Alan *(Con MP, 1935–45)*
LSE Library (European issues, 1930s–60s, including Poland)

GRANTHAM, Sir Alexander *(Colonial Gov)*
RHL (tspt; Fiji and W Pacific)

GRAVES, Richard *(Colonial Service)*
MEC (Palestine)

GREGORY, Sir Theodore *(Economist)*
IOL (mostly pre-war)

GRIFFITHS, John Calvert *(Colonial Legal Service)*
RHL (Hong Kong, 1974–82)

HADOW, Sir Michael *(ICS to 1947)*
IOL (India, 1930s–40s; Moscow 1942)

HAINES, William *(Colonial police officer)*
LHCMA (Malaya, 1920–50)

HALL, Daniel *(Historian)*
SOAS (South Asian history)

HALL, Sir John Hathorn *(Colonial Gov)*
Leeds U (WWI); no other papers

HALLETT, Sir Maurice *(ICS)*
IOL (Governor, United Provinces, 1939–45)

HANBURY, Harold Greville *(Legal professor and arbitrator)*
RHL (Nigeria-Biafra)

HANCOCK, Sir Cyril *(IPS and Indian Army officer)*
IOL

HANDLEY PAGE, Sir Frederick *(Aircraft manufacturer)*
RAF Museum

HARCOURT, Sir Cecil *(RN Admiral)*
IWM (WWII and Hong Kong, 1945–46)

HARRISON, Agatha *(Quaker pacifist)*
Friends' Library (India and Commonwealth)

HASKARD, Sir Cosmo *(Colonial Service)*
RHL (Nyasaland, 1951–63)

HASTED, William *(Army General and Kuwaiti official)*
CAC (WWII and Kuwait, 1950s)

HAWKINS, Sir Geoffrey *(RN Admiral)*
IWM (Malta, 1950–52)

HEANEY, George *(RE Brigadier)*
CSAC (India)

HEATHCOTE, G.C.M. *(Colonial Service)*
RHL (race relations, C Africa, 1959–60)

HECHLER, Kenneth *(Army officer)*
LHCMA (war criminals)

HEMINGFORD, 2nd Baron *(Teacher, Administrator)*
RHL (African education and Africa Bureau, 1920s–60s)

HEMMING, Francis *(Civil servant)*
Bodleian (formerly at Corpus Christi; inter-war Ireland and Spain)

HENDERSON, Kenneth *(Sudan Political Service)*
Sudan Archive, Durham U

HETT, Keir Stewart *(RN officer)*
IWM (tspt re: Yangtse incident, 1949)

HEUSSLER, R.W. *(Academic)*
RHL (Tanganyika research papers)

HIBBERD, G.F.A. *(Colonial Service)*
RHL (Africa and Singapore)

HICKENBOTHAM, Sir Tom *(IPS to 1947)*
IOL (India and Middle East)

HICKLING, Harold *(RN Admiral)*
IWM (both wars and *Voyageur* sinking, 1964)

HILKEN, Thomas *(RN officer)*
IWM (WWII)

HODGKIN, Thomas *(Academic)*
MEC (Palestine, Islam and Africa)*

HODSON, Robert *(IPS to 1947)*
IOL

HOPE-JONES, Sir Arthur *(Colonial Service and politics)*
RHL (Kenya, 1960s–80s)

HORNIMAN, William *(Army officer)*
IWM (Palestine)

HORSFALL, Geoffrey *(Colonial Legal Service)*
RHL

HOSKYNS-ABRAHALL, Sir Chandos *(Colonial Service)*
RHL

HOUNSELL, Harold *(Army General)*
IWM (WWII and post-war politics)

HOURANI, Albert *(Arab academic)*
MEC

HOW-MARTYN, Edith *(Family planning expert)*
IOL

HOWARD, Sir Douglas *(Diplomat)*
Bedfordshire RO

HOWARD, John *(Colonial Service)*
RHL

HOWARD, Philip *(Banker and businessman)*
RHL (post-war Nyasaland and Malawi)

HOWARD-DRAKE, Jack *(Civil servant)*
RHL (Africa and W Indies)

HOWELL, Paul *(Colonial Service; Foreign Office)*
RHL (Congo, 1960)

HUGHES-HALLETT, John *(RN Admiral)*
IWM (WWII)

HULLS, L.R. *(Army officer)*
IWM (post-war Italy and CCG)

HUME, Andrew *(ICS to 1947)*
IOL (India and Kenya)

HUNT, B. *(Army officer)*
IWM (India and Indonesia, 1945–46)

HYNE, Sir Ragnar *(Colonial Legal Service)*
RHL (Tonga and Fiji)

INGLIS, Alexander (*The Times correspondent*)
News International Archives (India and Canada, 1934–51)

IRWIN, Noel (*Army General*)
IWM (WWII)

IVELAW-CHAPMAN, Sir Ronald (*RAF ACM*)
IWM (WWI and WWII)

IZARD, Henry (*Colonial Service*)
RHL (Kenya and Tanganyika, 1940s–60s)

JACKSON, Sir Robert (*UN Assistant Secretary-General*)
Bodleian (UN project tspts)

JACOBS-LARKCOM, Eric (*Diplomat; army officer*)
LHCMA (China, WWII)

JAMES, U.H.R. (*RN officer*)
IWM (papers, 1916–55, including Korean War)

JASPAN, Mervyn (*Sociologist*)
Brynmor Jones Lib, Hull U (SE Asia)

JEFFREYS, P.J. (*Army Brigadier*)
IWM (Korean War)

JEVONS, Herbert (*Economist*)
NLW (Anglo-Ethiopian relations)

JONES, Sir Andrew (*Colonial Service*)
RHL (W Africa)**

JONES, Sir Melvill (*Aeronautical engineer*)
RAFM

JOUBERT DE LA FERTE, Sir Philip (*RAF ACM*)
RAFM (mostly WWI)

JUKES, J.N. (*RN officer; Colonial Service*)
IWM (India, 1946–47)

KABERRY, Phyllis (*Anthropologist*)
LSE Library (New Guinea)

KEELY, H.H. (*Burmese Civil Service*)
IWM (Burma, 1939–55)

KEEN, Frank (*League of Nations founder*)
LSE Library

KEIR, Sir David (*Historian and Academic Admin*)
RHL (Royal Comn on Medical Education in Malaya, 1953)

KENNEDY, Aubrey (*The Times journalist; BBC WWII staff*)
CAC; News Intl Archives

KERR, Sir Reginald (*Army General*)
IWM (WWII)

KERR, W. (*Army officer*)
IWM (UN relief work Italy and Yugoslavia, 1945–46)

KERSHAW, Sir Louis (*ICS*)
IOL

KETTLEWELL, Richard (*Colonial Service*)
RHL (Nyasaland, 1934–61)

KINCH, E.A. (*Arabist*)
MEC (Mosul and Kurds)

KIRKMAN, John Mather (*Army General*)
RAI**

KIRKMAN, Sir Sidney (*Army General*)
LHCMA (WWII)

KITTO, F.R.K. (*Colonial Service*)
RHL (Solomon Islands, 1950s)

KNIGHT, Sir Henry (*ICS to 1947*)
CSAC

LAMPEN, Graham (*Colonial Service*)
Sudan Archive, Durham U (Sudan, 1940s–50s)

LANCASTER, Alexander (*Army officer*)
NAM (Afghanistan, 1934–54)

LANE, P.N. (*Colonial Service*)
RHL (Uganda, 1950s)

LANGDON, William (*RAF officer*)
IWM (Turkey, WWII and post-war RAF)

LARGE, R.W. (*Colonial police officer*)
RHL (Sarawak, 1948–51)

LATHBURY, Sir Gerald (*Army General and Gov, Gibraltar*)
Airborne Forces Museum and IWM (WWII)

LATIMER, Sir Courtney (*ICS to 1947; S Africa*)
RHL (tspt re. role in High Comm Territories, S Africa, 1949–64)

LAYTON, Sir Geoffrey (*RN Admiral*)
BL (inter-war and WWII)

LEEDS, 12th Duke of *(Sir Francis Osborne, diplomat)*
BL (Vatican diaries, 1936–47)

LEESE, Sir Oliver *(Army General)*
IWM (pre-war and WWII); CAC (biographer's papers – Lewin)

LENANTON, Sir Gerald *(Timber Controller)*
IWM (WWII and CCG)

LETHEM, Sir Gordon *(Colonial Gov)*
RHL (including papers on Nigeria and British Guiana)

LEWIS, Sir Richard *(Army General and UN official)*
LHCMA (WWII and UN relief admin Europe, 1945–49)

LEWIS, Sir Willmott *(The Times correspondent)*
News International Archives (Washington, 1920–48)

LIDDELL, L.A. *(Army officer)*
IWM (Von Manstein war crimes trial, 1949)

LIPSCOMB, F.M. *(RAMC officer)*
CMAC (Belsen reports, 1945 papers on medical history of WWII)

LITTON, John *(Colonial Service)*
RHL (Macao and Malacca, China, 1948–51)

LIVIE-NOBLE, Frederick *(Anti-colonialist campaigner)*
RHL (Africa)

LLOYD, Sir Hugh *(RAF ACM)*
RAFM

LLOYD, JONES, David *(Army officer)*
CSAC (Burma, WWII)

LOCKER, Berl *(Zionist)*
Board of Deputies' Archive, Histadrut Archives, Israel; LMA, HEBREW U (tspt)

LOGAN, Sir William *(Colonial Gov)*
RHL (Africa and Seychelles)

LONGMORE, Sir Arthur *(RAF ACM)*
RAFM (mostly WWI and WWII)

LORIMER, David *(IPS pre-war; Persian scholar)*
IOL

LOTHIAN, Sir Arthur *(ICS)*
IOL

LOVERIDGE, Arthur *(Colonial Service)*
RHL (Gold Coast, 1930–56)

LUDDINGTON, Sir Donald *(Colonial Service)*
RHL (Solomon Islands, 1973–76)

LUKE, Sir Harry Charles *(Colonial Gov, pre-war)*
RHL

LYDALL, Edward *(ICS to 1947)*
IOL

MACASKIE, Charles *(Colonial Legal Service)*
RHL (Borneo)

McCALL, Anthony *(ICS)*
IOL

McCALL, Sir Henry *(RN Admiral)*
IWM

McCUTCHEON, William *(RAMC officer)*
LHCMA (Maralinga atomic weapons tests, 1956)

MacDONALD, John Frederick *(Army General)*
Scottish Borderers Regimental Museum (Korean War diary)

MacDOUGALL, David *(Colonial Service)*
RHL (Hong Kong, 1941–49)

MacDWYER, P.H. *(Indian Army officer)*
NAM (WWII; French Indo-China; Indian partition plans, 1946)

McGRIGOR, Sir Roderick *(RN Admiral)*
NMM (mainly Spanish Civil War and WWII)

McLACHLAN, Donald *(Daily Telegraph and Sunday Telegraph editor, 1954–66)*
CAC (naval intelligence, WWII)

McLEAN, Sir Kenneth *(Army General)*
IWM (WWII)

MacMICHAEL, Sir Harold *(Colonial Service)*
Sudan Archive, Durham U Lib; MEC; RHL

MacNAMARA, Playford *(Indian Army Brigadier)*
NAM

MADOC, Reginald *(Royal Marines General)*
LHCMA (WWII); RMM

MADON, K.S. *(Colonial Service)*
RHL (tspt re. 1964 Zanzibar Revolution)

MAGOR, Edward *(IPS to 1947)*
IOL

MAISNER, Aleksander *(Polish Air Force and RAF AVM)*
IWM (Poland and WWII)

MAJDALANY, Fred *(Military historian and journalist)*
IWM (WWII and Kenya emergency)

MALCOLM, Donald *(Colonial Service)*
RHL (Africa and Leeward Islands)

MAN, Christopher *(Army General)*
IWM (WWII); LHCMA (WWII)

MANBY, Mervyn *(Colonial police officer)*
RHL (Malaya and Kenya)

MANCE, Sir Osborne *(Ottoman Bank adviser and UN staff)*
MEC (Anglo-Turkish trade)

MANNING, Frederick *(RAF officer)*
LHCMA

MARCHANT, P.J.C. *(Colonial Service)*
RHL (Tanganyika)

MARCHANT, William *(Colonial Service)*
RHL (E Africa and Solomon Islands)

MARCUS, Otto *(Ugandan businessman)*
RHL (E Africa)

MARQUAND, W.J. *(Colonial Service)*
RHL (Solomon Islands)

MARSDEN, Eric *(The Times correspondent)*
News International Archives (Kenya, 1950s–60s)

MARTIN, W.J. (Army officer)
IWM

MAXWELL, J.L. *(Army officer)*
NAM (WWII and Korea)

MAY, Sir William Rupert *(IPS)*
MEC (India and Persian Gulf)

MAYBURY, Maurice *(Burmese and Ugandan Civil Services)*
IOL; RHL

MAYNES, Seaghan *(Reuters correspondent)*
IWM (war crimes tspt)

MEEK, Charles *(Colonial Service)*
RHL; IWM (tspt) (Tanganyika, 1941–60)

MEREDITH, Sir Charles *(AVM and Commandant-General)*
National Archives of Zimbabwe (Southern Rhodesian Forces)

MILES, Sir Geoffrey *(RN Admiral)*
NMM (WWI, WWII and Royal Indian Navy, 1946–47)

MILLINGTON-DRAKE, Sir Eugen *(Diplomat)*
CAC (British Council in S America, WWII)

MILLS-ROBERTS, Derek *(Army Brigadier)*
LHCMA (Milch incident, 1945)

MILVERTON, 1st Baron *(Colonial Gov)*
RHL (tspt); no other papers

MITCHELL, Alfred *(ICS and IPS to 1947)*
IOL

MOCKLER-FERRYMAN, Eric *(Army Brigadier)*
LHCMA (WWII and Hungary, 1945–46)

MOFFAT, John *(Army press officer)*
IWM (CCG)

MOLE, R.F. *(Colonial Service)*
RHL (Sarawak and Kenya)

MONTGOMERY, Col J.R. *(Anti-Slavery Society)*
Bodleian (UN project)

MOODY, Sydney *(Colonial Service)*
RHL (Mauritius and pre-war Palestine)

MOORE, Sir Henry *(RN Admiral)*
IWM (mostly WWII)

MORGAN, Sir Vaughan *(RN Admiral)*
IWM (mostly WWII and pre-war)

MORGAN, Sir William *(Army General)*
IWM (WWII)

MORRIS, Sir Edwin *(Army General)*
IWM (WWII and UN, 1946–48)

MOSSE, J.P.N. *(RN officer)*
IWM

MURRAY, Duncan *(ICS to 1947)*
IOL

NAMIER, Sir Lewis *(Historian and Zionist)*
Central Zionist Archives, Jerusalem

NAPIER, K.M. *(RN officer)*
NMM (Falkland War diaries, 1982)

NELSON, Sir John Blois *(Army General)*
LHCMA

NEWMAN, Harold *(Army officer)*
NAM

NICHOLL, Angus *(RN Admiral)*
IWM

NIHILL, Sir Barclay *(Colonial Legal Service)*
RHL (E Africa, 1950s)

NOBLE, Sir Fraser *(ICS to 1947)*
IOL

NORMAN, Charles *(Army General)*
LHCMA

NORMAN, C.R.W. *(Army officer)*
IWM (Palestine, 1947–48 and Korean
War correspondence)

OLIVER, Robert *(RN Admiral)*
NMM

O'REGAN, John *(Colonial Service)*
RHL (Ceylon, Jamaica and Nigeria)

O'REGAN, Patrick *(Army officer)*
LHCMA (Italian partisans, WWII)

PACKER, Sir Herbert *(RN Admiral)*
CAC

PARGITER, Robert *(Army General)*
IWM

PARKINSON, Roger *(Military historian)*
JRL

PATTERSON, Cecil *(Anglican bishop, W Africa)*
RHL (tspt)

PAUS, Christopher *(Trade Attaché, Norway)*
IWM (Anglo-Norwegian relations,
1940–62)

PEAKE, Frederick *(Army officer)*
IWM (Arab Legion and UK Home Defence,
WWII)

PEARCE, Sir Frederick *(ICS to 1945)*
IOL (India and Burma)

PEARSON, Sir Francis *(Con MP, 1959–70)*
IOL (ICS and Indian Army career; some later
papers)

PENFOLD, H. de L. *(Indian Army officer)*
NAM (India and post-war Germany)

PERLMAN, Melvin *(Anthropologist)*
SOAS (W Uganda)

PEROWNE, Stewart *(Orientalist)*
MEC

PESTELL, Sir John *(Rhodesian official)*
Centre for S African Studies, York U

PHILBY, Harry *(Orientalist)*
MEC

PHILLIPS, Sir Edward *(Businessman)*
RHL (E Africa, Tanganyika)

PINHEY, Louis *(IPS to 1947)*
IOL

PLEAS, Sir Clement *(Colonial Gov)*
RHL

POMFRET, Arnold *(RN Admiral)*
LHCMA (naval medicine)

POPPLESTONE, W. Harold *(The Times
correspondent)*
News International Archives (Palestine,
1945–48)

PORTER, L.E. *(RN officer)*
IWM (Persian Gulf, 1947–49)

POTTER, Arthur *(ICS to 1947; UK Civil Service)*
IOL (Burma, 1928–50)

POWELL, Ifor *(Historian)*
SOAS (Philippines)

POWELL, Richard *(Indian Police Service to 1947)*
IOL

PRETTY, Sir Walter *(Air Marshal)*
RAFM

PROCTOR, Richard *(RN Admiral)*
IWM (naval medicine)

PUGH, Lewis *(Army General)*
IWM (Gurkhas, 1966–80)

QUILLIAM, Cyril *(The Times correspondent)*
News International Archives: MEC (Middle East, 1945–51)

RANCE, Hugh *(IPS to 1947)*
IOL

RANKIN, Archibald *(RAF officer)*
RAFM

RANKIN, William S. *(UNESCO official)*
RHL (Liberia and Ethiopia, 1952–58)

READING, Marchioness of *(Zionist)*
Anglo-Jewish Archives

REDDAWAY, A.F.J. *(Colonial Service)*
RHL (Cyprus, 1955–58)

REDPATH, Alexander *(IPS to 1947)*
IOL

REID, Sir John *(WHO executive)*
Bodleian (UN project tspt)

REID, Sir Robert *(ICS; pre-war Gov of Assam)*
IOL

RENTON, James *(Army officer)*
MEC (Iraq, 1935–54)

REVINGTON, Arthur *(RAF officer)*
IWM

RICHARDS, Charles *(Missionary publisher)*
SOAS (E Africa, 1939–79)

RICHARDS, Sir Edmund *(Colonial Gov)*
RHL (Nyasaland and Basutoland, 1940s)

RICHARDSON, Dr Hugh *(ICS to 1947)*
IOL (Tibet)

RICHMOND, Sir John *(Diplomat)*
MEC

ROBERTS, Brian *(Antarctic admin)*
Scott Polar Research Institute, Cambridge

ROBERTSHAW, Sir Ballin *(RN Admiral)*
IWM

ROBERTSON, Patrick *(Colonial Service)*
RHL (Zanzibar Revolution, 1964)

ROBINSON, William Alleyne *(Army officer)*
NAM (Cameroon, 1960–61)

ROBSON, Sir Geoffrey *(RN Admiral)*
IWM

ROGERS, Thomas *(IPS to 1947)*
IOL

ROTH, Cecil *(Jewish historian)*
Hartley Lib, Southampton U

ROWE, Albert *(Scientist)*
IWM

RUSHBROOKE, Edmund *(RN Admiral)*
IWM

RUSSELL, Wilfred *(Bombay businessman)*
IOL

SALOWAY, Sir Reginald *(ICS and Colonial Service)*
RHL (Gold Coast, 1953–54)

SALTER, Jocelyn *(RN Admiral)*
IWM

SANDFORD, Sir Folliott *(Civil servant)*
CAC (W Africa, WWII)

SANSOM, Sir George *(Prof of Japanese Studies)*
Far East Centre, St Antony's College, Oxford

SAXBY, David *(The Times correspondent)*
News International Archives (E Africa, 1960s)

SAYER, Sir Guy *(RN Admiral)*
IWM (Suez, 1956)

SCHAPERA, Isaac *(Anthropologist)*
LSE Library (African tribes)

SCHARENGUIVEL, Frederick *(Colonial police officer)*
CSAC (Ceylon, 1937–56)

SCHLESINGER, Rudolph *(Sovietologist)*
Glasgow U Lib

SCOBIE, Sir Ronald *(Army General)*
IWM (WWII and post-war Greece)

SCOTT, M.B. *(Army officer)*
RHL (E Africa army mutinies and coup, 1964)

SHARWOOD-SMITH, Sir Bryan *(Colonial Gov)*
RHL (tspt, Nigeria, 1927–57)

SHATTOCK, John *(ICS to 1947)*
IOL

SIMON, Viscountess *(Anti-Slavery campaigner)*
RHL

SISSONS, V.M. *(Newspaper owner, Yorkshire)*
IWM (WWII and Indo-China, 1945–46)

SMITH, H.H.L. *(Army officer)*
IWM (India, 1945–48)

SOLAK, B.J. *(RAF officer)*
IWM (WWII and Polish *émigrés* in post-war Britain)

SOMERVILLE, David *(Colonial Service)*
RHL (Malaya, 1940s)

SOMERVILLE, Sir James *(RN Admiral)*
CAC

SORLEY, Sir Ralph *(Air Marshal)*
RAFM

SPRIGGE, Cecil *(Journalist and author)*
Reading U Lib (post-war Italy)

STANTON-IFE, Douglas *(ICS and Pakistan Civil Service)*
CSAC

STEPHENSON, G.L. *(Colonial Service)*
RHL (Nigeria, 1936–72)

STEWART, John *(Colonial Service)*
NLS (The Gambia and Jamaica)

STEYNER, G.F.H. *(Army officer)*
IWM (WWII and UN relief work, Greece, 1945–47)

STOCKWELL, R.Z. *(Army officer)*
NAM (Mau Mau 1950s and Tanganyika, 1960–61)

STONE, John *(Army officer)*
LHCMA (military engineering and atomic research)

STONE, Richard *(Colonial Service)*
RHL (tspt and notes, Uganda)

STREETEN, Gilbert *(Army officer)*
IWM (post-war Germany)

SULZBACH, Herbert *(German émigré)*
IWM (Anglo-German relations, 1930s–50s)

SUTTON-PRATT, Reginald *(Military attaché)*
Brotherton Lib, Leeds U (Scandinavia, 1938–47)

SWINLEY, CASPER *(RN officer)*
IWM (formerly in CAC; WWII and Pakistan Navy, 1950s)

SYMES, GEORGE *(Army General)*
IWM (WWII and Burma, 1945–46)

TANDY, Maurice *(IPS to 1948)*
IOL

TEACHER, Anthony *(Army brigadier)*
IWM (Atomic warfare, 1950s)

TEDDER, 1st Baron *(RAF Marshal)*
RAFM (WWI and WWII)

TENNANT, Sir William *(ICS to 1947)*
IOL

THOMAS, Sir Thomas *(Colonial Gov)*
RHL (Malay States during WWII)

THOMPSON, Sir Herbert *(ICS to 1947)*
IOL

THOMPSON, W. Scott *(Academic)*
RHL (African Unity conference, 1958–64)

THORP, Sir John *(Colonial Service)*
RHL (Kenya, St Lucia and Seychelles, 1950s)

TODD, Sir Herbert *(ICS to 1947)*
IOL

TOTTENHAM, Sir Richard *(ICS to 1946)*
CSAC

TRENCH, Charles *(IPS to 1947)*
IOL

TREVOR-WILSON, Arthur *(Army officer)*
NAM (military intelligence, 1939–86, including Hanoi)

TULLOCH, Hugh *(Colonial prison officer)*
RHL (Middle East, Far East and Africa)

TURNER, R.M. *(Colonial Service)*
RHL (SE Asia and Barbados)

TWINING, Baron *(Colonial Gov)*
  with family; other papers in PRO (CO 967/67)

TWYNAM, Sir Henry *(ICS and Gov, Bengal, 1945)*
  IOL; CSAC

VASEY, Sir Ernest *(African politician)*
  RHL (Kenyan and Tanganyikan economies, 1944–62)

VAUGHAN-LEWIS, J.R.M. *(RN officer)*
  IWM (Malaya, 1945 and Korean War notebooks)

VICKERS, Dr M. *(Political scientist)*
  RHL (Nigerian politics)

WAINWRIGHT, Robert *(Colonial Service)*
  RHL

WAITE, Herbert *(Indian police officer)*
  IOL

WALKER, Eric *(Historian)*
  African Studies Centre, Cambridge

WALLACE, Theodore *(Colonial Legal Service)*
  RHL (N Borneo, 1939–51)

WARNER, Sir George *(Pre-war diplomat)*
  Hampshire RO

WAYMOUTH, G.R. *(RN officer)*
  IWM (Yugoslavia, 1944–45)

WESTON, Bertram *(Colonial Service)*
  RHL (Cyprus, 1958)

WHEARE, Sir Kenneth *(Colonial Service)*
  RHL (Rhodesian and Nyasaland Conference, 1952–53)

WHITE, O.G.W. *(Army officer)*
  IWM (post-war Germany and Austria, and Korean War)

WHITE, Percival *(Army General)*
  LHCMA (NATO strategy, 1950s)

WHITWORTH, Reginald *(Army General)*
  IWM (WWII)

WHITWORTH, Sir William *(RN Admiral)*
  IWM

WHYATT, Sir John *(Colonial Legal Service)*
  RHL (Mau Mau, 1950s)

WILKIE, Alexander *(Colonial Service)*
  RHL

WILKINSON, William *(Army officer)*
  IWM (Austria, 1945–46)

WILSON, Sir Mark *(Colonial Legal Service)*
  RHL (E and W Africa, 1930s–50s)

WINDER, J. *(Colonial Gov)*
  Sudan Archive, Durham U Lib

WINNINGTON-INGRAM, C. *(Colonial Service)*
  RHL (Tanganyika, 1940s–50s)

WOODALL, W.N. *(Colonial Service)*
  RHL (Nigerian economy and army, 1950s)

WOODS, Sir John *(Civil servant)*
  PRO (ref BT91) and with family

WOODS, Oliver *(The Times correspondent)*
  News Intl Archives (Africa, 1934–53)

WORTH, Meredith *(IPS to 1947)*
  IOL

WYN-HARRIS, Sir Percy *(Colonial Gov)*
  RHL (N Cameroons plebiscite)

YOUNG, Peter *(Military historian)*
  NAM

ZAMFIRESCU, O. *(Romanian political exile)*
  IWM (E Europe, 1930s–60s)

ZVEGINTZOV, Michael *(Civil servant)*
  CAC (CCG, 1945–46)

Appendix 2
Domestic Politics and Society

Names followed by location of papers:

ABEL SMITH, Brian *(Professor of Social Administration)*
LSE Lib

ABERCROMBIE Sir (Leslie Patrick) *(Town planner)*
Liverpool U; PRO (HLG 85)

ACHESON, J.W. *(Civil servant)*
PRONI (Stormont finances, 1960s)

ADAMS, Samuel *(Con MP to 1945)*
LSE Lib

AICKMAN, Robert *(Inland Waterways Association Founder)*
PRO (PRO 30/82)

AINSZTEIN, Ruben *(Journalist)*
Southampton U

ALDINGTON, Lord *(Con MP, Trade Minister, 1950s)*
family possession

ALDRED, Guy *(Socialist journalist and publisher)*
Mitchell Lib Strathclyde RAO

ALLEN of Abbeydale, Lord *(Civil servant)*
no papers; tspt of interview at LSE Lib

ALLEN, Elizabeth *(Civil liberties campaigner)*
NCCL archive at Hull U

ALLEN, George Cyril *(Economist)*
UCL

ALLEN, Sydney *(Lab MP, 1945–74)*
with family

ALPASS, Joseph *(Lab MP, 1929–31, 1945–50)*
with family

AMORY, Viscount *(Con MP and Minister, 1945–60)*
no papers; tspt of interview at LSE Lib

AMWELL, Lord *(Lab MP until 1947)*
PRO (AVIA 9)

ANDERSON, Pamela *(Chairman of the Fawcett Society)*
Women's Lib

ANGELL, Sir Norman *(Lab MP and Nobel Peace Prize winner)*
Ball State U, Indiana

ANSELL, David *(Pacifist and CND activist)*
Bodleian

APPLETON, Sir Edward *(Civil servant and University Admin)*
Edinburgh U Lib

ARBERRY, Arthur *(Orientalist, London and Cambridge U)*
CUL

ARLOW, William *(Clergyman and mediator)*
PRONI (tspt, IRA negotiations, 1976)

ARMSTRONG, Edmond *(Civil servant to 1960)*
with family

ATKINSON, Norman *(Lab MP to 1983)*
family possession

AYLESTONE, Lord *(Lab MP, 1945–67)*
family possession

BAILEY, V. Gerald *(Pacifist)*
Friends' House Lib

BAILLIEU, Lord *(Industrialist and financier)*
with family

BAKER, Richard *(Environmentalist; forestry expert)*
Southampton U Lib

BALLARD, Albert *(Lab Lord Mayor)*
Sheffield City Lib

BARBOUR, William *(Alliance Party, Northern Ireland)*
PRONI

BARRINGTON-WARD, Robert *(The Times editor, 1941–48)*
News Intl Archives

BARTLETT, Percy *(Pacifist)*
Friends' House Lib

BARTLETT, Robert *(Police officer)*
CAC

BEACHAM, Audrey *(Agricultural historian)*
Bodleian

BEAMISH, Tufton *(Con MP until 1945)*
E Sussex RO

BEER, Harry *(Civil servant; Board of Trade)*
with family

BELOFF, Lord *(Oxford U academic)*
U of Buckingham*

BENN, Sir Ernest *(Publisher)*
MRC, Warwick U

BENNETT, Gareth Vaughan *(Ecclesiastical historian)*
Pusey House Lib

BENYON, William *(Con MP to 1992)*
family possession**

BETTS, Clive *(Welsh political journalist)*
NLW

BING, Harold (British Tolstoyans) *(Pacifist and teacher)*
Nottingham U Lib

BLUNDELL, Sir Robert *(Barrister and Magistrate)*
PRO (PRO 30/74)

BOARDMAN, Lord *(Con MP to 1974)*
family possession**

BONE, James *(Journalist)*
JRL, Manchester U

BRABAZON OF TARA, Lord *(Con MP and Aviation Minister)*
RAFM

BRADLEY, William *(Civil servant, Ministry of Health)*
Wellcome CMAC

BRAIN, 1st Baron *(Physician)*
Royal College of Physicians

BRAMWELL-BOOTH, Catherine *(Salvation Army leader)*
Salvation Army HQ

BROWN, Oliver *(Scottish Nationalist)*
NLS

BROXBOURNE, Lord *(Con MP, 1945–83)*
family possession

BUTTERFIELD, Sir Herbert *(Historian)*
CUL

CABORN, Richard *(Lab MP since 1983)*
Sheffield City Lib

CAIRNS, Julia (Louisa Davidson) *(Journalist)*
Women's Lib

CALDECOTT, 1st Viscount *(Con MP and Lord Chief Justice)*
CAC

CARMICHAEL, James *(ILP and Lab MP, 1946–61)*
with family** enquiries to NRA (S)

CASEY, William *(The Times editor, 1948–52)*
News Intl Archives

CHATER, Daniel *(Lab MP, 1929–31, 1935–50)*
Hull U Lib (autobiography)

CHAVASSE, Christopher *(Anglican Bishop of Rochester, 1940–60)*
Bodleian

CHESSER, Eustace *(Psychiatrist and academic)*
U of Texas Lib, Austin

CLARKE, Sir Frederick *(Educationalist)*
Inst of Education, London U

CLAY, Sir Henry *(Economist)*
Nuffield College, Oxford

CLAYTON, Philip (Tubby) *(Anglican clergyman; Toc H founder)*
Guildhall Lib; IWM

CLITHEROE, 1st Baron *(Con MP, 1934–55)*
with family; PRO (AVIA 11)

CLUNIE, James *(Lab MP, 1950–59)*
NLS (pre-war)

COCKERAM, Eric *(Con MP, 1970–87)*
own possession**

COHEN of Birkenhead, 1st Baron *(Professor of Medicine)*
Liverpool U Archives

COHEN of Brighton, Lord *(Lab Mayor and businessman)*
enquiries to U of Brighton

COLLISON, Chave *(Feminist)*
Women's Lib

COLYTON, Lord *(Con MP, 1950–56)*
St Antony's College, Oxford (to be deposited)

COMFORT, Alexander *(Writer and sexologist)*
UCL

COPE, Sir John *(Con MP after 1974)*
own possession**

COX, Idris *(Welsh Communist and miner)*
NLW

CRAIG, Alec *(Civil liberties campaigner)*
Hampstead Public Lib

CRAIG, Alwyn *(Local government, Northern Ireland)*
PRONI (post-war elections, Derry)

CRYER, Robert *(Lab MP after 1974; MEP, 1984–89)*
own possession

DAVIES, D.J. and Noelle *(Plaid Cymru activists)*
NLW

DAVIES, Edward *(Lab MP, 1945–53)*
Hanley Public Lib

DEVONS, Ely *(Economist)*
LSE Lib

DOMVILLE, Admiral Sir Barry *(Fascist activist)*
NMM

DONALDSON of Lymington, Lord *(Master of the Rolls, 1982–92)*
PRO

DUFF, Sir James *(University administrator and BBC Governor)*
Durham U Lib

DUNCAN, Sir Andrew *(Con MP, 1940–50)*
PRO (AVIA 11)

DUNCAN, Joseph *(Scottish trade unionist)*
NLS

EASTWOOD, Granville *(Trade unionist)*
Brynmor Jones Lib, Hull U

EDWARDS, Sir Ronald *(Industrialist and economist)*
with family

EVANS, Griffith Ivor *(Welsh nationalist and doctor)*
NLW

FARREN, Sir William *(Aeronautical engineer)*
CAC

FAUL, Rev Denis *(Clergyman, Northern Ireland)*
PRONI (civil rights)

FOLLICK, Mont *(Lab MP, 1945–55)*
PRO (CO 967); no other papers

FORT, Richard *(Con MP, 1950–59)*
with family

FOX, Sir Gifford *(Con MP, 1932–50)*
with family

FRASER, John Denis *(Lab MP after 1966)*
own possession

GARDNER, Sir Edward *(Con MP, 1959–66; 1970–87)*
family possession

GARMAN, Douglas *(Communist writer)*
Nottingham U Lib

GIBSON-WATT, Lord *(Con MP, 1956–74)*
family possession

GLENDEVON, Lord *(Con MP, 1945–62)*
family possession

GODWIN, Sir Harry *(Botanist and ecologist)*
Clare College, Cambridge

GOGARTY, Frank *(Civil rights campaigner)*
PRONI (collection closed)

GOLDBERG, Philip *(Secretary of the United Synagogue)*
Southampton U Lib

GOLDINGER, David *(Communist)*
LHASC

GOODEVE, Sir Charles *(Scientist)*
CAC

GOWER, Laurence *(Academic Admin)*
Southampton U Lib (Royal Comn on the Press)

GREENDALE, Walter *(Trade unionist)*
Brynmor Jones Lib, Hull U

GRIFFITH, Edward Fyfe *(Sexologist and psychologist)*
CMAC

GRIGG, John *(Historian and journalist)*
Bodleian

GRIGG, Sir Percy *(Secretary of State for War, 1942–45)*
CAC

GROSER, St John *(Clergyman and socialist)*
Lambeth Palace Lib

GRUFFYDD, William *(Lib MP, 1943–50; academic)*
with family (Celtic Studies papers; no political papers)

HAIG, Mervyn *(Anglican Bishop)*
Lambeth Palace Lib

HAIRE, Norman *(Sexologist and gynaecologist)*
U of Sydney

HAMMOND, Jenny *(Labour Mayor, Leyton)*
Waltham Forest Archive, London

HAMMOND, John *(Historian and journalist)*
Bodleian

HAMMOND, Lucy *(Historian)*
Bodleian

HANNON, Sir Patrick *(Con MP, 1921–50)*
HLRO

HARBER, Denzil D. *(Radical socialist and communist)*
MRC, Warwick U

HARBER, Julian *(CND campaigner)*
W Yorkshire Archives

HARRIES, Edgar *(Trade unionist and Labour Party official)*
NLW

HARRIS, Hugh *(Anglo-Jewish community leader)*
Southampton U

HARVIE, Christopher *(British academic, Tubingen U)*
NLS

HAYMAN, Sir Graham *(Industrialist)*
MRC (President, FBI, 1955–57)

HEADLAM, Sir Cuthbert *(Con MP, 1924–35; 1940–52)*
Durham RO

HERBERT, Sir Alan *(Ind MP, 1935–50; author)*
enqs to NRA

HERTZ, Dr Joseph *(Chief Rabbi, 1913–46)*
Southampton U Lib

HICKS, Ernest *(Trade union leader)*
MRC (Civil Service Clerical Association)

HILL, Archibald Vivian *(Cambridge U MP and scientist)*
CAC

HILL, Howard *(Sheffield Communist)*
Brynmor Jones Lib, Hull U

HODGKINSON, George *(Labour Mayor)*
Coventry City RO

HORE-BELISHA, 1st Baron *(Secretary of State for War, 1937–40; MP)*
CAC

HUDALY, David *(Journalist and Jewish historian)*
Liverpool RO

HUGHES, Hector *(Lab MP, 1945–70)*
enqs to NRA

HUME-ROTHERY, William *(Metallurgist)*
Bodleian

HUMPHREYS, George *(Fabian and local politician)*
Birmingham C Lib

HUNKIN, Joseph *(Anglican Bishop)*
Lambeth Palace Lib

HUTT, George Allan *(Journalist and historian)*
LHASC (Communist Party archive)

HYMAN, Richard *(Academic)*
MRC (Intl socialism; British industry)

INCE, Sir Godfrey *(Civil servant)*
PRO (LAB 79)

INGLEBY, 1st Viscount *(Con MP, 1929–55; Minister)*
with family (not available)

INGLEWOOD, 1st Baron *(Con MP, 1945–64)*
Cumbria RO**

IRVINE, Sir Bryant *(Con MP, 1955–83)*
E Sussex RO*

ISAACS, George *(Lab MP until 1959; Minister)*
Southwark Public Lib (cuttings only)

JACKSON of Burnley, Lord *(Scientist)*
Imperial College, London

JACOBSSON, Per *(International financier)*
LSE Lib (photocopies); Basle U (originals)

JENKINS, John Barnard *(Welsh separatist)*
NLW

JOHNSON, Walter *(Lab MP, 1970–83)*
own possession (cuttings only)

JONES, Sir Brynmor *(Scientist and administrator)*
Brynmor Jones Lib, Hull U

JONES, John Henry *(Lab MP, 1945–62)*
Rotherham Public Lib (cuttings only)

JONES, Merfyn *(Liberal Party activist)*
NLW

JONES, Tom *(Trade Union leader)*
Clwyd RO

JONES, William *(Journalist)*
NLW

JOWITT, 1st Earl *(Lib MP and Cabinet Minister)*
PRO (CAB 127/159–193 – WWII papers)

KAHN-FREUND, Sir Otto *(Law Professor)*
LSE Lib

KELLY, Sir Arthur *(Cabinet Secretary, Northern Ireland)*
PRONI (mostly photographs)

KENDREW, Sir John *(Biologist)*
Bodleian

KENNEDY, A.J. *(Nationalist politician)*
PRONI (1960s elections, Northern Ireland)

KERR, Sir Graham *(Con MP, 1935–50 and zoologist)*
Glasgow U Archives

KNOX, Sir Malcolm *(Philosopher and U admin)*
Dundee U Lib

LANE, Sir Allen *(Publisher)*
Penguin Archives; Bristol U Lib

LAWSON, Baron *(Lab MP, 1919–49; War Secretary, 1945–49)*
with family

LAZARUS, Harris *(Chief Rabbi's deputy, 1946–48)*
Hartley Lib, Southampton U

LEITH-ROSS, Sir Frederick *(Economist and banker)*
PRO (T 188)

LEWIS, F.H.V. *(Trade Unionist and local politician)*
Brynmor Jones Lib, Hull U

LEWIS, Thomas *(Lab MP, 1929–31; 1945–50)*
Southampton Central Lib (cuttings)

LINDSAY of Birker, 1st Baron *(Political scientist and U admin)*
Keele U Lib

LIPSON, Daniel *(Ind MP, 1937–50)*
with family

LLOYD, Arnold *(Educationalist)*
CUL

LOGAN, Sir Douglas *(U admin)*
London U Lib

LOVEDAY, Alexander *(Economist)*
Nuffield College, Oxford

MACGREGOR, Alasdair *(Writer)*
NLS

MANNING, Charles *(Intl Relations Professor)*
JRL

MANNING, Dame Leah *(Lab MP, 1931; 1945–50)*
LSE Lib**

MANSFIELD, Albert *(Educationalist)*
BL

MARKHAM, Sir Frank *(Con MP, 1951–64)*
IWM

MARKHAM, Violet *(Politician and social campaigner)*
LSE Lib

MARSHALL, Dr Edmund *(Lab MP, 1971–83; SDP)*
own possession

MARTINDALE, Louisa *(Surgeon)*
CMAC (women in medicine)

MATHER, Sir Carol *(Con MP, 1970–87)*
own possession

MATTHEWS, Sir James *(Labour local politician)*
Southampton City RO

MEGAW, Sir John *(Lord Justice, 1969–80)*
PRONI (Ireland Act 1949)

MENDELSSOHN, Kurt *(Physicist)*
Bodleian

MITCHELL, Joseph *(Physicist; radiotherapeutics)*
NCUACS, Bath U

MORAN, 1st Baron *(Churchill's doctor)*
Wellcome: Royal College of Physicians

MORRIS, Sir Philip *(U admin)*
Bristol U Lib

MORRIS-JONES, Sir Henry *(Lib and Nat Lib MP, 1929–50)*
Clwyd RO

MORRISON, Baron *(Co-op and Lab MP to 1945)*
Haringey Public Lib

MURNAGHAN, Sheelagh *(Northern Irish Liberal MP)*
PRONI (campaign papers)

MURRAY, Rev Raymond *(Clergyman, Northern Ireland)*
PRONI (civil rights)

NEVE, Michael *(Historian of the NHS)*
CMAC

NEWSAM, Sir Frank *(Civil servant)*
PRO (HO 317/4)

NISBET, James *(Economist)*
St Andrews U Lib

NOEL-BUXTON, Lady *(Lab MP, 1930–31; 1945–50)*
with family

NUFFIELD, 1st Viscount *(Industrialist and philanthropist)*
Nuffield College, Oxford**

ONSLOW, Countess of *(Churchill's secretary, 1941–57)*
CAC

ORR-EWING, Baron *(Con MP, 1950–70)*
family possession (cuttings, etc.)

PALMER, Eileen *(Feminist and birth control expert)*
LSE Lib

PARKE, R.A. *(Ulster Unionist Party official)*
PRONI (Northern Ireland elections)

PAUL, Leslie *(Leading Anglican layman)*
Lambeth Palace Lib (Paul Report papers)

PEART-BINNS, John Stuart *(Christian socialist and biographer)*
Brynmor Jones Lib, Hull U

PENROSE, Lionel *(Biologist)*
UCL

PETERS, Sir Rudolph *(Scientist)*
Bodleian

PHILIP, Sir Randall *(Lawyer and public servant)*
NLS

PHILLIPS, Sir Thomas *(Civil servant)*
with family**

PICTON, Jacob *(Industrial economist)*
Birmingham U Lib

PILKINGTON, Baron *(FBI President, 1953–55)*
MRC

PITT, Terence *(Lab MEP and policy adviser)*
LHASC

PLANT, Sir Arnold *(Economist)*
LSE Lib

PREST, Allan *(Economist)*
LSE Lib

PRICHARD, Caradog *(Political journalist)*
NLW

PROSSER, David *(Anglican Archbishop)*
NLW

PUGSLEY, Sir Alfred *(Engineering professor and public servant)*
Bristol U Lib

RAISON, Sir Timothy *(Con MP, 1970–92)*
own possession**

RECKITT, Maurice *(Writer and philosopher)*
Sussex U Lib

REES, Baron *(Con MP, 1970–87)*
own possession**

REGAN, John M. *(Police inspector, Northern Ireland)*
PRONI

REID, Baron *(Con MP, 1931–35; 1939–48)*
HLRO

RICKETT, Sir Denis *(Public servant; World Bank)*
Bodleian

RITCHIE, Douglas *(Broadcaster)*
CAC

ROBB, Barbara *(Geriatric health care campaigner)*
LSE Lib

ROBERTSON, Sir David *(Con MP, 1939–64)*
with family

ROBSON, William *(Public Admin Professor, LSE)*
LSE Lib

ROWNTREE, Benjamin *(Confectioner and sociologist)*
Joseph Rowntree Memorial Trust and Borthwick Inst, York

SANDERSON, Sir Frank *(Con MP, 1931–50)*
HLRO (cuttings)

SCARBROUGH, 11th Earl *(pre-war MP; Lord Chamberlain, 1952–63)*
with family

SELBORNE, 3rd Earl *(Con MP to 1940)*
Bodleian

SHACKLE, George *(Economist)*
Liverpool U Lib

SIEPMAN, Harry *(Bank director)*
Bank of England Archives

SMITH, Sir Ben *(Lab MP until 1946)*
PRO (AVIA class)

SMITH, Norman *(Lab Co-op MP, 1945–55)*
LSE Lib** no other papers

SMITH-REID, Sir Francis *(Army officer and House of Lords official)*
NAM

SPANSWICK, Ted *(Plaid Cymru activist)*
NLW

SPENCE, Robert *(Atomic scientist)*
Leeds U Lib

SRAFFA, Piero *(Economist)*
Trinity Coll, Cambridge

STAMP, Sir Dudley *(Land geographer)*
Sussex U Lib

STRACHEY, Phillipa *(Fawcett Society Secretary)*
Women's Lib

STRATHCLYDE, 1st Baron *(Con MP, 1940–55)*
LSE Lib (tspt)

TAWNEY, Richard *(Historian and socialist)*
LSE Lib

TAYLOR, Vincent *(Methodist minister)*
Methodist Archives, Manchester U

THOMAS, Vernon *(Trade Unionist)*
Bodleian

THOMPSON, Sir Richard *(Con MP, 1950–74)*
family possession

TINBERGEN, Nikolas *(Scientist)*
Bodleian

TOMLINSON, Ruth *(Women's issues campaigner)*
Women's Lib

TOPHAM, Tony *(Trade unionist and historian)*
Brynmor Jones Lib, Hull U

TRANMIRE, Baron *(Con MP, 1929–74)*
family possession

UPCOTT, Sir Gilbert *(Civil servant)*
Devon RO

UPHAM, Martin *(Radical activist)*
Brynmor Jones Lib, Hull U

VAIZEY, Lord *(Educationalist)*
Hoover Inst, California

VERULAM, 6th Earl *(Con MP, 1943–45 and 1950–59)*
with family

VIDLER, Alexander *(Theologian)*
E Sussex RO

VINCENT, Sir Graham *(Civil servant)*
Brotherton Lib, Leeds U (pre-war)

WALLACE, Baron *(Lab MP, 1945–50 and 1964–74)*
family possession

WALLICH-CLIFFORD, Anton *(Simon Community founder)*
Liverpool U Lib

WARREN, Kenneth *(Con MP, 1970–92)*
own possession**

WAVERLEY, 1st Viscount *(Ind Nat MP to 1950)*
IOL (pre-war)

WELLS, Frederick *(Industrial economist)*
Nottingham U Lib

WHITELEY, William *(Lab MP, 1922–32 and 1935–55)*
with family

WHYTE, John *(Political scientist)*
PRONI (1970s civil liberties)

WICKENDEN, Chris *(Radical socialist)*
Ruskin College, Oxford

WILLIAMS, Alwyn *(Anglican Bishop)*
Durham U Lib

WILSON, Sir Garnet *(Local politician)*
Dundee District Archives

WILSON, R.N. *(Stormont MP)*
PRONI

WISEMAN, F.C. *(Fascist activist)*
IWM

WORMALD, Dame Ethel *(Local politician)*
Liverpool RO

WORRALL, Dr Stanley *(Clergyman and mediator)*
PRONI (tspt)

WRIGHT, Sir Norman *(Agriculturalist)*
Reading U Lib

YORKE, Peter *(Industrialist)*
PRO (PRO 30/84)

Appendix 3
Archives relating to Northern Ireland
Jane Leonard

This article summarizes the archival material which has been located relating to post-war politics in Northern Ireland. Nationalist, unionist and labour groupings have undergone many splits, amalgamations and name changes in this period, and in particular, since the start of the Troubles in the late 1960s. This entry places political parties and interest groups under four headings:

I Labour and Radical
II Nationalist and Republican
III Unionist
IV Other (groups who were established in response to the Troubles, such as the Alliance Party and the Peace People).

For researchers of this period, the two starting points in Belfast are the Public Record Office of Northern Ireland (PRONI), which holds much material relating to parliamentary unionism and nationalism, and the Northern Ireland Political Collection at the Linen Hall Library. This collection includes much periodical and ephemeral literature and is a particularly rich source for the records of loyalist and republican fringe and paramilitary groups. A detailed catalogue to the collection is available and the first section of the collection (periodical holdings) is now available on microfilm. A number of libraries, such as the LSE, have purchased this microfilm (and the LSE's own election ephemera collections also contain material from Northern Irish constituencies). The Linen Hall Library additionally holds the archives of several prominent individuals and lobbying groups, such as the Northern Ireland Civil Rights Association (NICRA).

Elsewhere in Northern Ireland, the Centre for Contemporary Conflict at the University of Ulster has steadily developed an oral history project whose participants include several leading politicians and radical campaigners.

Historians of organised labour in Northern Ireland should bear in mind that several trade unions operating in Northern Ireland have their headquarters in Dublin, and that the recently-established Irish Labour History Museum in Dublin holds much material of relevance. Similarly, the Modern Records Centre at the University of Warwick contains several collections of British trade unions active in Northern Ireland. Where records of Northern Irish branches and regions of British trade unions have been located, these are described in these unions' main entries in this guide (for example, see National Union of Insurance Workers). A number of Irish and Northern Irish trade unions, economic bodies and cultural associations have their own entries in this guide, including the Irish Association for Cultural, Economic and Social Relations, the Irish Co-operative Organisation Society, the Northern Ireland County Court Officers Association, the Northern Ireland Public Service Alliance, the Services Industrial Professional Technical Union, the Teachers Union of Ireland, the Ulster Enterprise Voluntary Committee, the Ulster Headmasters Association and the Ulster Headmistresses Association. Reference should also be made to the main guide entry for the Trades Union Congress.

In Dublin, the National Library of Ireland and the Archives Department of University College, Dublin hold collections relating to post-war republicanism, the establishment of the SDLP, and cross-border cultural and political study groups.

The museums and archives of British regiments stationed in Northern Ireland since the 1960s are a further (though largely unquarried) source of material. The Imperial War Museum in London holds a number of useful collections documenting the conflict, including some records of the 1970s 'Bring Back the Boys from Ulster' campaign.

Pre-1945 political archives in Ireland are described in an Appendix to *Sources, 1900–51*, vol. I, pp. 293–305. Details of specialist archive repositories throughout Ireland are given in Seamus Helferty and Raymond Refausse's *Directory of Irish Archives* (Dublin, 1999). The best introduction to the various political parties, politicians, campaigns, para-military bodies, acts of legislation and terminologies in contemporary Northern Ireland is W.D. Flackes and S. Elliott, *Northern Ireland. A Political Directory 1968–88* (Belfast, 1989).

I LABOUR AND RADICAL

In the post-war era, there were several different labour parties active in Northern Ireland, including the Northern Ireland Labour Party (NILP), the Commonwealth Labour Party, the Labour Party (UK), the Labour Party (Republic of Ireland) and the Workers' Party.

The principal NILP archive is deposited in PRONI and covers the period from the 1940s onwards (ref. D2704 add). It includes minutes; correspondence; conference and election papers; files on issues such as electoral and local government reform and employment and housing discrimination; pub-lications, and press releases. PRONI also holds a collection of NILP circulars, 1930–61 (ref. D2162) and the records of the NILP Central Women's section. Researchers should note that PRONI holds the private papers of several leading NILP members including Jack Beattie (ref. D2784), Jack Macgougan (ref. D1676), Samuel Napier (ref. D3702) and a former NILP Chairman, F.V. Simpson (ref. D3223). The Macgougan papers include records of the Armagh NILP branch for the 1945–47 period, while the Napier collection contains NILP conference reports, policy statements and correspondence, 1940–77. The Simpson papers include minutes of the NILP executive committee and minutes of the Women's Advisory Council, 1961–70, party con-ference papers, 1960–74, and correspondence, 1958–71. The Linen Hall Library holds extensive runs of various NILP journals.

Further NILP material is available in the Irish Labour History Museum, Dublin. This includes records of the Pottinger branch in Belfast, 1968–74; files of council and committee minutes on issues such as direct rule, relations with the UK Labour Party and education; election ephemera, and NILP journals. The papers of Barry Desmond, Andrew Boyd and John De Courcy Ireland in the Archives Department, University College, Dublin also contain relevant material.

For UK Labour Party records of relevance to Northern Ireland, the main archive at the Labour History Archive and Study Centre in Manchester should be contacted. Some pamphlets and press-cuttings on the party's Northern Irish policy are deposited in PRONI (ref. D3876 and D2784) as are the papers of Anthony Mulvey, which include material on the Labour Party's Friends of Ireland group, active in the 1950s (ref. D1862).

The papers of Harry Diamond, held in PRONI, include some records relating to the Irish Labour Party's branches in Northern Ireland, among them a minute book for the Falls branch, Belfast, 1952–53. The rest of the Diamond papers comprise a mis-cellaneous collection of items and printed matter, 1936–64, on the Irish Labour Party, Irish socialist republican groups and the anti-partition move-ment (ref. D2474). The Jack Beattie papers also have material on the Irish Labour Party. Other material on the Irish Labour Party's work in Northern Ireland can be found in the De Courcy Ireland and Desmond papers at UCD.

A collection of papers relating to the Irish Socialist Republican Party, 1973–77, has been deposited in PRONI by Mrs Bernadette McAliskey (the former MP Bernadette Devlin).

The Workers' Party, which contests elections in both the Republic and Northern Ireland, evolved from a merger of Official Sinn Fein and the Repub-lican Clubs in 1982. Following a split in 1991, a new party, Democratic Left, was established which the bulk of the Workers' Party's members and elected representatives in the Republic have joined. Both the Dublin and Belfast offices of the Workers' Party have retained their records. Election ephemera and party newsletters etc. are available in the Linen Hall Library.

Few records have been located for the smaller

labour and radical parties. A copy of the 1944 constitution and standing orders for the Commonwealth Labour Party is deposited in PRONI (ref. D1195/5/1) and the papers of the party's leader, Harry Midgley, may also be deposited in PRONI in due course. The papers of Samuel Napier include a minute book of the Commonwealth Labour Party, 1943–48 (ref. D3702).

Very few details have been obtained about the extent and nature of the Communist Party of Ireland's archives. The CPI was first formed in 1921, split in 1941 and reformed in 1970 when the CP of Northern Ireland merged with the Irish Workers' League and Irish Workers' Party. PRONI holds the papers of Sean Murray, General Secretary of the CPNI until 1967 (ref. D2162). The collection is generally closed although the CPI permitted Mike Milotte to use it for his book, *Communism in Modern Ireland* (1984). The collection contains private and political correspondence; diaries; speeches; press-cuttings; printed pamphlets and election ephemera, and material relating to other labour and radical groups. PRONI also holds some circulars relating to the CPI (ref. D2162) and some issues of *Unity*, the CPI journal (ref. D2702). Further issues and other CPI periodical literature are available in the Linen Hall Library. Reference should also be made to the Communist Party of Great Britain (q.v.).

II NATIONALIST AND REPUBLICAN

The main nationalist party in Northern Ireland is the Social Democratic and Labour Party (SDLP) which was established in 1970. The bulk of its support was drawn from members of the former Nationalist Party, the National Democratic Party and the Republican Labour Party. PRONI holds some records relating to the Nationalist Party, 1968–70 (ref. T3062/1–14) and also has a collection of minutes, correspondence and press-cuttings relating to the National Democratic Party, 1965–70 (ref. D3079). PRONI also holds the papers of two Nationalist MPs, Cahir Healy and Anthony Mulvey, which are a valuable source for the Nationalist Party's fortunes at Westminster and Stormont in those years (refs. D2991, D1862). The SDLP deposits its papers in PRONI at regular intervals. As many of its earlier records were stolen from the party's headquarters in

the early 1970s, the material now held at PRONI largely dates from 1972 onwards (ref. D3072 and D3072add). It includes files on party policy, internal organisation and conferences, liaison with other parties etc, 1972–82; election manifestos; and *c.* 650 files of correspondence and conference material, 1972–82. The SDLP has informed this Guide that local SDLP records have remained with branches. Manifestos and other election ephemera are available at the Linen Hall Library. The papers of Sean MacEntee, in University College, Dublin, include material on SDLP fundraising and support in the Republic, 1972–78 (ref. P67).

Little archival material has been located relating to Sinn Fein in the post-war period. The National Library of Ireland and the Archives Department of UCD hold much significant material for the party's role in the 1918–24 period. The Linen Hall Library holds extensive runs of SF publications and journals, including *An Phoblacht* (copies of which are also in the National Library of Ireland and the British Library). PRONI holds very little material on contemporary Sinn Fein other than election ephemera and a few miscellaneous collections. Extensive collections of election ephemera produced by Sinn Fein (and related groups such as the Republican Clubs and the H-Block campaign) can be consulted in the Linen Hall Library.

Records relating to the Anti-Partition League (Cumann Briseadh na Teorann) have been deposited in several archives. This organisation (and its sister group, the Anti-Partition Association) was active in the 1945–57 period, and was formed to mobilise nationalist opinion against the partition of Ireland. It was backed in Britain by many Irish emigrants and a section of the Labour Party. The papers of Maire Comerford, in the National Library of Ireland, Dublin, include APL correspondence, membership records, speeches, press releases and papers relating to contacts with Scottish and Breton nationalists, *c.* 1948–57 (ref. Ms 21939–21940). The same library has the minute book of the Anti-Partition Association, 1950–52, and some related items including a press-cuttings album on the anti-partition movement and the revived IRA campaign of the mid-1950s (ref. Ms 25006). Additional material on the republican movement during the 1950s and 1960s is available in the Irish Republican Publicity Bureau collection (ref. Ms 22938) and in the Sean Cullen papers (ref. Ms 22733), both of which are also in the National Library of Ireland.

Further APL material is in the Mulvey and Beattie papers in PRONI. Some records of the London Area Committee of the APL, 1947–48, are in the MacEntee papers at University College, Dublin, which also contain material relating to Saor Eire, a left-wing republican group, 1944–47 (ref. P67). The papers of Ernest Blythe and Desmond Ryan, also in UCD, contain further material on the APL. UCD also holds a minute book of the National Aid Society, detailing efforts to subsidise IRA members interned in the Curragh and other prisons in the Republic, 1944–53 (ref. P41). Further material on the anti-partition movement and on Catholic voter registration in Derry during the 1940s and 1950s is available in the papers of F.E. MacCarroll, which are in PRONI (ref. T2712add).

The papers of Bob Purdie, deposited in the Modern Records Centre, University of Warwick, include material relating to the civil rights movement, the Irish Solidarity Movement, the Anti-Internment League and the Troops Out Movement (ref. MSS 149).

III UNIONIST

The main unionist party in Northern Ireland, the Ulster Unionist Party (UUP), split in 1972 following the imposition of direct rule from Westminster. The bulk of its members formed the Official Unionist Party. Since 1989, the OUP has been renamed the UUP. As with the old UUP of 1922–72, this party is closely linked to the Ulster Unionist Council with whom it shares a headquarters. The other parties to emerge from the 1972 split were the Democratic Unionist Party (DUP) founded by the Reverend Ian Paisley; the Unionist Party of Northern Ireland, founded by the late Lord Faulkner, and the Vanguard Unionist Party. A number of moderate former UUP members joined with moderate nationalists to form the Alliance Party.

The main UUP archive is held in PRONI and covers the development of the party and the UUC from the late 19th century to the 1980s. The material in PRONI includes speeches, policy statements, press and propaganda material, 1943–74 (ref. D3441, D3816 and D1726). The records of the UUC cover the

period 1892–1981 (ref. D1327). Branch records in PRONI include a minute book of the North Down Unionist Association, 1929–73 and unbound minutes and correspondence, 1968–86 (ref. D1327) and press-cuttings concerning the North Antrim Unionist Association, 1946–70 (ref. D3121). The role of women is documented in the records of the Ulster Women's Unionist Council, 1907–61 (ref. D1098), and at a local level in the papers of the North Antrim Women's Unionist Association, 1956–67 (ref. D2706). Additional material on the wartime and post-war role of women in Ulster unionism is available in the papers of Lady Londonderry, who was President of the UWUC (ref. D3099/8/36 and D3099/8/40). The minutes of Queen's University Belfast Unionist Students Association, 1946–71, are a particularly useful source (ref. D2919). Additional records of the OUP branch in Queen's University are contained within the papers of Derek McAuley, which also include correspondence and other papers relating to the Conservative Students' Association at Queen's, 1978–86 (ref. D3794). For the wider world of unionist identity and culture, reference should be made to the minute books and correspondence files of the Irish Unionist Alliance and the Southern Irish Relief Association, 1922–55, which are also in PRONI (ref. D989). These contain much valuable material on the economic, social and cultural position of unionists living south of the border, and Southern Unionists who migrated to Northern Ireland and other parts of the UK after 1922.

The records of groups such as the Belfast-based Unionist Society and the Grand Orange Lodge of Ireland contain similar material on the cultural life of Ulster unionism. The Unionist Society has deposited minutes, correspondence and other papers, 1942–77 in PRONI (ref. D3292). Few records relating to post-war Orangeism have been deposited, but some journals, including the Grand Orange Lodge of Ireland's *The Orange Standard* and the Grand Lodge of Scotland's *The Orange Torch*, are held in the Linen Hall Library. Further material relating to the Orange Order can be found in PRONI in the private papers of unionist politicians. It is reported that the Royal Black Preceptory, the senior sister body of the Orange Order, has retained archives at its headquarters in Brownlow House, Lurgan, County Antrim.

Historians of the UPNI should note that the papers of Lord Faulkner document both his years in the UUP and (from 1974) in the UPNI (ref. D3591). The UPNI failed to poll well in the many elections held in Northern Ireland during the 1970s and was wound up in 1981. Apart from the Faulkner papers, there is a separate UPNI collection also at PRONI which consists of c. 250 files of minutes, correspondence, press-cuttings, statements and speeches 1974–81 (ref. D3061 and D3061add). This material is closed at present. There is also a further smaller collection of UPNI material in PRONI comprising press statements, speeches and cuttings (ref. D3816).

No information about the archives of the Democratic Unionist Party and the Vanguard Unionist Party has been obtained, although it may be surmised that the private papers of the Reverend Ian Paisley (still in his possession) will form a valuable source for historians of the DUP. As with all of the unionist parties, DUP and Vanguard election ephemera, journals and branch newsletters are available in the Linen Hall Library. The Linen Hall Library also holds similar material for loyalist para-military groups such as the Ulster Defence Association and the Ulster Volunteer Force.

No information has been received concerning the records of the London-based Friends of the Union group, but researchers should note that the papers of prominent members (such as Sir John Biggs-Davison whose papers, deposited in the House of Lords Record Office, are currently closed) may contain relevant material.

IV OTHER

The following groups all came into being as a direct response to the Northern Ireland Troubles or as part of the civil rights movement which predated the revival of sectarian violence in the late 1960s.

Alliance

This party was established in 1970 and draws support from both sections of the community in Northern Ireland. No details about its main archive were available before this volume went to press. Relevant collections deposited in PRONI include the papers of W. Barbour (concerning his candidacy in the 1975 Constitutional Convention elections, ref. D3793), a set of party circulars and statements (ref. D2966) and some election ephemera (ref. D230). Further ephemera and party newsletters are held in the Linen Hall Library. The Linen Hall Library also has some papers deposited by the Alliance Party politician and former Lord Mayor of Belfast, David Cook. Prior permission to consult the Cook collection is required from the librarian.

Campaign for Democracy in Ulster

This group, set up in the late 1960s, monitored civil rights in Northern Ireland and was based in London. Several leading Labour MPs were members. Some papers are deposited in PRONI (ref. D3026). Additional material is available in the papers of Kevin McNamara and Stan Orme.

Campaign for Social Justice in Ulster

This civil rights group was established in Dungannon in 1964. Some material is deposited in PRONI (ref. D2993).

International Fund for Ireland

This was established by the British and Irish governments following the signing of the Anglo-Irish Agreement in 1985. It aims to further mutual understanding between nationalists and unionists in Ireland and, in particular, by funding economic, social and cultural projects along the Irish border. The Fund is financed by contributions from the United States, Canada, Australia, New Zealand and the European Community. The records of its Belfast office for the period 1986–89 have already been deposited in PRONI. The collection is currently closed to researchers. Copies of the Fund's Annual Reports and newsletters can be obtained from its Dublin and Belfast offices.

New Ireland Group

This cross-community research group was set up in 1982 in succession to the New Ireland Movement. Both were founded by John Robb, an Ulster surgeon and peace campaigner who was a member of the

Republic of Ireland's Senate during the 1980s. Some minutes and correspondence, 1969–75, have been deposited in PRONI, but the main archive is contained within Mr Robb's papers, which span the last thirty years and are deposited in the Linen Hall Library. They include minutes, policy, research and conference papers, annual reports and extensive correspondence with political and religious leaders north and south of the border. The collection also includes policy papers, correspondence and statements relating to the New Ireland Movement and submissions made by various groups to the 1983 New Ireland Forum. Access to the collection is subject to the consent of the librarian.

New Ulster Movement

Some records relating to the work of this cross-community group which was active in the late 1960s and early 1970s have been deposited in PRONI.

Northern Ireland Civil Rights Association (NICRA)

Two large collections of NICRA material are held in the Linen Hall Library. The John McGuffin collection comprises approximately 80 boxes of papers relating to both NICRA and People's Democracy (see below). The McGuffin material largely consists of periodical literature with some NICRA circulars, reports and other papers concerning civil rights marches and internment. The second collection consists of 6 boxes of papers, formerly in the possession of the late Madge Davison, a leading civil rights campaigner. They contain very full records of NICRA's activities in the 1971–76 period and include minutes; correspondence files (particularly relating to internment); newsletters including *Civil Rights* and *Civil Rights News*; reports, questionnaires, and statements by persons interned without trial in the early 1970s; branch records including some for the Derry, Tyrone, and Newry offices; lobbying and publicity material relating to legislation such as the Emergency Prisons Act, the Official Secrets Act and the Incitement to Hatred Act; case files on republican prisoners in Long Kesh (the Maze), HMS Maidstone and prisons in the Irish Republic; leaflets, posters and other ephemera, and press-cuttings. The col-

lection also documents NICRA's contacts with international peace and human rights groups.

Further NICRA material has been deposited in PRONI by Professor Kevin Boyle.

Peace People

This peace movement was established by Catholic and Protestant women in Belfast in the aftermath of the killing of three children in 1976. The group's founders were awarded the Nobel Peace Prize later that year. The organisation was less prominent during the 1980s and 1990s but continues to research the conflict and promote better cross-community relations. The Peace People has retained its records, which include press releases and speeches. Copies of the Peace People journal are available in the Linen Hall Library.

People's Democracy

The very extensive John McGuffin collection at the Linen Hall Library includes several files relating to this group which originated as a student radical group campaigning for civil rights in the late 1960s. The McGuffin papers include minutes, agenda, policy documents, reports, membership papers, publicity material and copies of the newsletters *Unfree Citizen* and *Free Citizen*. Further material, including People's Democracy press releases and cuttings, notes of meetings and printed pamphlets, 1968–75, are held in PRONI (ref. D3219 and D3297).

Protestant and Catholic Encounter Group

Relevant material is available within the papers of this group's founder, Dr Gerald Newe, which are deposited in PRONI (ref. D3687). Reference should also be made to the main entry in the guide for the Irish Christian Fellowship.

Lastly, it should be noted that the Troubles have been responsible for the eclipse of many political traditions, among them Ulster Liberalism. Inactive in Ulster from the early 20th century, the party was re-established there in 1958 as the Ulster Liberal Association. It had a very low profile during the 1970s and 1980s and has not contested recent elections. A collection of newsletters, press releases and correspondence, 1969–71, is deposited in PRONI (ref. D3219), together with some election manifestos from the mid-1960s (ref. D2105) and newsletters and ephemera, 1960–73 (ref. D2951). The papers of the association's chairman, Revd Albert McElroy, are also in PRONI (ref. D3342), as are a few items relating to the election campaigns of Sheelagh Murnaghan, the only Ulster Liberal elected to the Stormont parliament (ref. D2931/16/1–4 and D2043/11/1–11). Issues of the party journal, *Northern Radical*, 1966–75, are available in the Linen Hall Library.

Select List of Major Websites

Balliol College, Oxford
www.balliol.ox.ac.uk/

Birmingham Central Library
www.birmingham.gov.uk/centrallibrary.bcc

Birmingham University Library
www.library.bham.ac.uk/

Bodleian Library, Oxford
www.bodley.ox.ac.uk/

Bristol University Library
www.bris.ac.uk/is/

British Library
www.bl.uk/collections/manuscripts.html

Cambridge University Library and Archives
www.lib.cam.ac.uk

Cardiff University College Library
www.cardiff.ac.uk/schoolsanddivisions/
divisions/insrv/libraryservices/index.html

Centre of South Asian Studies, University of
Cambridge
www.s-asian.cam.ac.uk/

Christ Church, Oxford
www.chch.ox.ac.uk

Churchill College, Cambridge
www.chu.cam.ac.uk/

City of Westminster Archives Centre
www.westminster.gov.uk/libraries/archives/
index.cfm

Dublin University College Library
www.ucd.ie/archives/

Duke University Library
www.library.duke.edu/

Durham County Record Office
www.durham.gov.uk/recordoffice

Edinburgh University Library
www.lib.ed.ac.uk/resources/collections/
specdivision/

Friends House Library
www.quaker.org.uk/library/

Glamorgan County Record Office
www.glamro.gov.uk/

Glasgow City Archives
www.glasgow.gov.uk/en/Residents/Leisure_Cult
ure/Libraries/Collections/ArchivesandSpecial
Collections/

Glasgow University Archives
www.archives.gla.ac.uk/

Guildhall Library
www.history.ac.uk/gh/

Hackney Archives
www.hackney.gov.uk/index/council/
departments/communityleisure/archives.htm

Hampshire Record Office
www.hants.gov.uk/record-office/index.html

Harvard University Library
www.hul.harvard.edu/

Hoover Institution on War
www-hoover.stanford.edu/hila/

House of Lords Record Office
www.parliament.uk/parliamentary_
publications_and_archives/parliamentary_
archives.cfm

Hull University Library
www.hull.ac.uk/lib/

Imperial War Museum
www.collections.iwm.org.uk/server/show/
nav.00g002

International Institute of Social History
www.iisg.nl/

Ipswich and East Suffolk Record Office
www.suffolkcc.gov.uk/sro/

John Rylands University Library
www.rylibweb.man.ac.uk/

Kent Archives Office
www.kent.gov.uk/e&l/artslib/archives/
home.html

King's College Library
www.kcl.ac.uk/depsta/iss/library/

Labour History Archive and Study Centre
www.82.71.77.169/index.html

Lambeth Palace Library
www.lambethpalacelibrary.org/

Lancashire Record Office
www.lancashire.gov.uk/education/lro/

Leeds University Brotherton Library
www.leeds.ac.uk/library/spcoll/brocoll.htm

Leicestershire Record Office
www.leics.gov.uk/index/community/
museums/record_office.htm

Liddell Hart Centre for Military Archives
www.kcl.ac.uk/lhcma/home.htm

Lincolnshire Archives Office
www.lincolnshire.gov.uk/

Liverpool Record Office
www.liverpool.gov.uk/

Liverpool University Library
www.liv.ac.uk/library/

London Metropolitan Archives
www.cityoflondon.gov.uk/lma

London University College Library
www.ucl.ac.uk/library/

London University Institute of Education Library
www.ioe.ac.uk/infoserv/ishome.htm

LSE Library
www.lse.ac.uk/library/

Manchester Central Library
www.manchester.gov.uk/libraries/central/

Marx Memorial Library
www.marxlibrary.net/

Middle East Centre, St Antony's College
www.sant.ox.ac.uk/areastudies/
middle-east.shtml

Modern Records Centre, University of Warwick
Library
www2.warwick.ac.uk/services/library/mrc/

National Archives
www.nationalarchives.gov.uk

National Archives of Ireland
www.nationalarchives.ie/

National Archives of Scotland
www.nas.gov.uk/

National Library of Ireland
www.nli.ie/

National Library of Scotland
www.nls.uk/

National Library of Wales
www.llgc.org.uk/

National Maritime Museum
www.nmm.ac.uk/

Newcastle Upon Tyne University Library
www.ncl.ac.uk/library/

Norfolk Record Office
http://archives.norfolk.gov.uk

Northamptonshire Record Office
www.northamptonshire.gov.uk/Community/
record/about_us.htm

Northern Ireland Public Record Office
www.proni.gov.uk

Northumberland Record Office
www.swinhope.myby.co.uk/NRO/index.html

Nottinghamshire Record Office
www.nottinghamshire.gov.uk/archives

Nuffield College Library, Oxford
www.nuff.ox.ac.uk/library

Oxfordshire County Record Office
www.oxfordshire.gov.uk

Parkes Library
www.library.soton.ac.uk/hl/parkes/index.shtml

Queen's University Library
www.qub.ac.uk/lib/

Reading: BBC Written Archives Centre
www.bbc.co.uk/thenandnow/

Reading University Library
www.library.rdg.ac.uk

Rhodes House Library, Oxford
www.bodley.ox.ac.uk/boris/guides/rhl/

Royal Institute of International Affairs
www.riia.org/riia/index.html

Rural History Centre
www.ruralhistory.org/

Ruskin College Library, Oxford
www.ruskin.ac.uk

School of Oriental and African Studies Library
www.soas.ac.uk/library/index.cfm

Senate House Library
www.ull.ac.uk/

Sheffield Central Library
www.sheffield.gov.uk/in-your-area/libraries/
find/central

Sheffield University Library
www.shef.ac.uk/~lib/special/special.html

Shropshire Salop Record Office
www.shropshirearchives.co.uk

Somerset Record Office
www.somerset.gov.uk/archives

Southampton University Library
www.archives.lib.soton.ac.uk/

Staffordshire County Record Office
www.staffordshire.gov.uk/archives

Sussex University Library
www.sussex.ac.uk/library

Swansea University Library
www.swan.ac.uk/lis/index.asp

Trinity College, Dublin
www.tcd.ie/Library/

Tyne & Wear Archives Service
www.thenortheast.com/archives/

Warwickshire County Record Office
www.warwickshire.gov.uk/countyrecordoffice

Wellcome Institute of the History of Medicine
Library
library.wellcome.ac.uk

West Sussex Record Office
www.westsussex.gov.uk/ccm/navigation/
libraries-and-archives/record-office/

West Yorkshire Archive Service
www.archives.wyjs.org.uk/

Wiener Library
www.wienerlibrary.co.uk/

Dr Williams Library
www.dwlib.co.uk/dwlib/

Women's Library
www.thewomenslibrary.ac.uk/

Index of Surname Changes

From:	*To:*
Jones, Sir (Frederick) Elwyn	Elwyn-Jones, Baron
Kerr, Archibald Clark	Inverchapel, Baron
Lampson, Sir Miles	Killearn, 1st Baron
Lennox-Boyd, Alan Tindal	Boyd of Merton, 1st Viscount
Lindemann, Frederick	Cherwell, 1st Viscount
Lloyd, Geoffrey William	Geoffrey-Lloyd, Baron
Lloyd George, Gwilym	Tenby, 1st Viscount
Lloyd, John Selwyn Brooke	Selwyn-Lloyd, Baron
Loder, John de Vere	Wakehurst, 2nd Baron
Lubbock, Eric Reginald	Avebury, 4th Baron
Lyttelton, Oliver	Chandos, 1st Viscount
Mackie, John	John-Mackie, Baron
Maclay, John Scott	Muirshiel, 1st Viscount
Macmillan, Harold	Stockton, Lord
Macpherson, Niall	Drumalbyn, Lord
Makins, Sir Roger	Sherfield, Viscount
Marquis, Sir Frederick	Woolton, 1st Earl of
Maud, Sir John (Redcliffe)	Redcliffe-Maud, Baron
Maxwell-Fyfe, Sir David	Kilmuir, 1st Earl of
McDiarmid, Hugh (pseudonym)	Grieve, Christopher Murray
Millar, Sir Frederick R.H.	Inchyra, 1st Baron
Neame, Mrs Humphrey	Monroe, Elizabeth
Ramsbotham, Sir Herwald	Soulbury, Viscount
Recchioni, Vero (pseudonym)	Richards, Vernon
Rees-Williams, David Rees	Ogmore, Baron
Rolph, C.H. (pseudonym)	Hewitt, Cecil Rolph
Royle, Sir Anthony	Fanshawe of Richmond, Lord
Sandwich, 10th Earl of	Montagu, Victor
Sandys, Duncan Edwin	Duncan-Sandys, Baron
Sidney, William Philip	De L'Isle, 1st Viscount
Soskice, Sir Frank	Stow Hill, Lord
Strauss, Henry George	Conesford, 1st Baron
Thomas, James Prudon	Cilcennin, 1st Viscount
Thomas, (Thomas) George	Tonypandy, Viscount
Trevor-Roper, Hugh	Dacre, Lord
Walker-Smith, Sir Derek	Broxbourne, Lord
Williams, Francis	Francis-Williams, Baron
Williams, Marcia	Falkender, Baroness
Wood, Edward	Halifax, 1st Earl of
Wood, Richard Frederick	Holderness, Baron
Woodhouse, Christopher	Terrington, Lord
Woodruff, Philip (pseudonym)	Mason, Philip

Index of Organisations and Societies

Routledge History

British Political History, 1867-2001: Democracy and Decline
3rd Edition
Malcolm Pearce and Geoffrey Stewart

'This substantial textbook is written with the explicit aim of keeping its readers awake...it will entertain students and stimulate discussion' – *Valerie Cromwell, Times Higher Education Supplement*

'The news that this excellent textbook is receiving a new edition that will bring it up to date is very welcome' – *Rohan McWilliam, Anglia Polytechnic University, Cambridge*

Bringing the coverage right up to date, and including new material, this third edition of *British Political History, 1867–2001* is an accessible summary of major political developments of British history of the last one hundred and forty years.

Analyzing the changing nature of British society and Britain's role on the world stage, Pearce and Stewart also outline the growth of democracy and the growth in the power of the state against a background of party politics.

New coverage includes:

* domestic affairs from 1992 to 2001
* John Major's Government
* the creation of 'New' Labour and the 'Third Way'
* Blair's first ministry
* developments in Northern Ireland from 1995 through the Easter Peace Deal into 2001
* the 2001 General Election results and implications.

HB 0-415-26869-9 PB 0-415-26870-2

Available at all good bookshops
For ordering and further information please visit
www.routledge.com

Routledge History

Britain since 1945: A Political History
6th Edition
David Childs

Praise for previous editions
'Every politics student's dream.' - *Simon Henig, Sunderland University*

'A readable, lucid work which many students and their teachers will find enormously helpful.' - *Kenneth Morgan, Times Literary Supplement*

'A full, well-organised, workmanlike and readable account.' - *Teaching History*

'The clear, well organized chronological approach supported by numerous statistical tables and combined with Professor Child's lucid and readable style makes this an excellent reference book for any senior pupil studying British post-war politics.' - *Jerry Teale, History Teaching Review*

This is the sixth edition of what has become the standard textbook on contemporary British political history since the end of World War II. This authoritative chronological survey discusses domestic policy and politics in particular, but also covers external and international relations. The new and improved edition of this important book brings the picture to the present by including the following additions:

* 11th September 2001
* the Iraq war and after
* the election of Iain Duncan Smith and Michael Howard as leaders of the Conservative party
* the issue of immigration
* the new royal wedding
* the 2005 election
* the importance of China on the British stage.

Britain since 1945 is essential reading for any student of contemporary British history and politics.

HB 0-415-39326-4   PB 0-415-39327-2

Routledge History

The Routledge Atlas of British History
4th Edition
Martin Gilbert

This new edition of a compelling atlas tells the changing story of England, Ireland, Scotland and Wales, as well as presenting a cartographic overview of the expansion and gradual disintegration of Britain's overseas empire.

The fourth edition now includes:

- politics: from the Saxon kingdoms and the collapse of Britain's French Empire to the Jacobites, Parliamentary Reform, the Commonwealth and Europe

- war and conflict: from Viking attacks and the Norman Invasion to the Armada, World Wars I and II and the twenty-first century war in Iraq

- trade and industry: from the post-Norman economy and Tudor trade to industrial unrest and the opening of international trade routes

- religion: from the Saxon Church to the Reformation

- society and economics: from civilian life in Roman Britain to the Industrial and Agricultural revolutions, the Great Strike and the pattern of humanitarian aid

HB 0-415-39550-X PB 0-415-39551-8

Available at all good bookshops
For ordering and further information please visit
www.routledge.com